D0222753

SYNTHESIS,

COMPOSITION,

AND PERFORMANCE

SECOND EDITION

COMPUTER MUSIC

SYNTHESIS, COMPOSITION, AND PERFORMANCE

Charles Dodge

Dartmouth College

Thomas A. Jerse

Boeing Company

Schirmer Books
An Imprint of Simon & Schuster Macmillan
New York

Prentice Hall International
London   Mexico City   New Delhi   Singapore   Sydney   Toronto

Copyright © 1985, 1997 by Charles Dodge and Thomas A. Jerse

All rights reserved. No part of this book may be reproduced or transmitted in any form or by any means, electronic or mechanical, including photocopying, recording, or by any information storage and retrieval system, without permission in writing from the Publisher.

Schirmer Books
An Imprint of Simon & Schuster Macmillan
1633 Broadway
New York, NY 10019

Library of Congress Catalog Number: 96-53478

Printed in the United States of America

Printing number

2   3   4   5   6   7   8   9   10

Library of Congress Cataloging-in-Publication Data
Dodge, Charles.
   Computer music : synthesis, composition, and performance / Charles Dodge,
Thomas A. Jerse. — [2nd ed.]
      p.   cm.
      Includes index.
      ISBN 0-02-864682-7 (alk. paper)
      1. Computer music—Instruction and study.   2. Computer composition.
   I. Jerse, Thomas A.   II. Title.
   ML1092.D54 1997   96-53478
   786.7/13—dc21   CIP
                                                                MN
This paper meets the requirements of ANSI/NISO Z39.48–1992 (Permanence of Paper).

Table of Contents

Preface to the Second Edition

More than a decade has passed since the first edition of this text was written. In that time, tremendous strides have been made in the hardware and software of computer music that have greatly increased the accessibility of the medium. Today inexpensive personal computers found on millions of desktops around the world have more computing power and memory capacity than many of the mainframe computers in use at the time of the first writing. Similarly, the ease with which graphical information can now be presented to the musician has greatly improved the usability of the computer, enhancing the productivity of practitioners of the art. Furthermore, computer music performance practice has been decidedly influenced by the establishment and widespread commercial availability of the MIDI interface that enables the digital control of diverse pieces of computer-music hardware.

Despite its relative age in this fast-moving discipline, the text has continued to enjoy widespread acceptance throughout the world. This success is due in part to the decision to describe the synthesis algorithms with flowcharts rather than in terms of any particular computer-music language or system. This second edition introduces several synthesis and sound modification techniques that have blossomed in recent years. It further incorporates many new compositional examples and describes the trends in modern performance practice.

The text is divided into five parts. Chapters 1, 2, and 3 introduce the fundamentals necessary to an understanding of the field—computers, psychoacoustics, and digital audio. In the second part, chapters 4 through 9 describe a wide range of techniques for sound synthesis. Additive, nonlinear, and subtractive synthesis remain time-honored techniques, but several methods of synthesis-from-analysis have been added, including phase vocoding. In addition, granular synthesis and synthesis using physical models have been well developed since the first edition and are each given separate chapters. In the third part, Chapter 10 details approaches to sound modification including much of the recent research on sound source localization, and discusses the techniques available to composers of *musique concrète*. Chapter 11 comprises the fourth part of the text and gives both stochastic and deterministic methods of computer-aided composition. The final part, chapter 12, presents modes and techniques of the performance of computer music.

The text demonstrates that there are many diverse approaches to enlisting the computer in the production of music, and thus the text can be used in several different ways depending on the interests and background of the reader. After mastering the fundamentals presented in the first three chapters, the reader interested in synthesis should become familiar with the flowchart method for describing an algorithm and the basic technique of signal generation presented in sections 4.1 through 4.6. At this point, the synthesis techniques of the remainder of chapter 4 and those of chapters 5 through 9 can be covered in the order of interest. Those primarily interested in sound modification techniques can skip to chapter 10, and those wishing to approach computer-aided composition can read chapter 11 as well as concentrating on the sections of chapters 4 through 9 that give compositional examples of the various synthesis techniques described. The performance practices described in chapter 12 are not specific to any synthesis technique so that this chapter may be read at any time after reading the first three chapters.

Chapter 11 includes programming examples to realize various algorithms used in the compositional process. Because there are many different approaches to computer-music programming, the choice of the language to describe these examples was, as before, a difficult, controversial decision. In the end, we decided to change from FORTRAN to C++ because of the widespread instruction currently available in that language. We believe that this choice will not present a significant challenge to those wishing to translate these algorithms into other languages because the examples are short and do not require massive data structures. All examples were compiled and tested using Turbo C++ (version 3.1) from Borland International.

Many people listed in the preface to the first edition helped make this text a reality. In the preparation of the second edition, the authors are greatly indebted to Christine Brown Jerse for her expert transcription and proofreading skills. At Dartmouth, graduate students Colby Leider, Kevin Parks, and Leslie Stone were diligent in freely helping to create specific items for inclusion in the second edition. Professors Jon Appleton and Larry Polansky were enormously supportive of the effort. In addition, we acknowledge the use of facilities at the Bregman Center for Electroacoustic Music at Dartmouth College and the Department of Electrical Engineering at The Citadel in the preparation of the text, examples, and figures for the second edition.

Charles Dodge, *Dartmouth College*
Thomas A. Jerse, *Boeing Company*
April 1997

Preface to the First Edition

Computer music activity has proliferated in recent years. It has grown from its somewhat specialized origins as an interdisciplinary subfield of electronic music, digital signal processing, and experimental music to occupy an increasingly central position in the technologies of professional recording and home audio, as well as electronic music synthesis and composition. The expanded use of digital electronics in music is likely to continue; what we are now experiencing may be only the beginning of an era in which computer technology predominates in all aspects of the reproduction and synthesis of music.

The purpose of this book is to provide the musician with an entry into the three main fields of computer music—*synthesis, composition,* and *performance.* The material is presented in such a way that a person with little background in mathematics or engineering can be brought to the point where he or she can comprehend the evolving developments in the computer music field.

The text is divided into four parts. Chapters 1 and 2 present the fundamentals of computer music: computers, digital audio, and psychoacoustics. The second part, chapters 3 through 7, details the many techniques of sound synthesis and modification. The third part, chapter 8, covers the application of the computer to composition. The final part, chapter 9, describes performance practices and compositional approaches that have been used in live performance of computer music.

Because computer music is multifaceted, we have designed the book to be used in several ways. By reading it in the normal sequence, the diligent musician with little or no previous experience in computer programming or electronic music synthesis will develop a basic level of understanding over the entire range of the field.

In a classroom situation, the instructor could begin with the first three chapters to build the fundamentals of computer music systems, psychoacoustics, and synthesis. At this point, various synthesis techniques can be selected from chapters 4 through 7 in any order. This material, of course, would be supplemented by the user's manual for the synthesis system available to the students. Both chapters 8 and 9 may be presented independently of the psychoacoustic and synthesis topics. The instructor may wish to skip certain of the more technical sections in the chapters on synthesis, such as the final sections of both chapters 4 and 6 and the final three sections of chapter 5.

The home computer user already acquainted with the principles of computer system organization and programming can start with section 1.3, *Software for Computer*

Music, and learn the fundamentals of digital audio systems. After this initial reading, the reader might focus on the psychoacoustics and synthesis chapters (chapter 2 through 7), computer-aided composition (chapter 8), or computer-music performance (chapter 9), depending on his or her particular interests and applications.

A composer of music for either acoustic instruments or electronic sounds can read this book with an eye to its implications for the composition of music. Once again, the interests of the reader will determine the particular parts of the book to be read. In addition to reading the chapter on computer-aided composition (chapter 8), a composer might concentrate on the sections in chapters 3 through 7 concerning compositional applications of particular sound-synthesis techniques. Chapter 9 also contains descriptions of a number of compositional applications of real-time performance in computer music.

When writing about computer music, it is especially difficult to strike a balance between generality and direct application to a specific system. We have chosen to present in flowchart form the designs for particular computer-generated sounds, rather than limit the book's usefulness to any single sound-synthesis language or system. With the aid of the appropriate user's manual, the reader can implement the flowchart designs into the sound-synthesis language on an available system.

In addition, the appendix contains computer programs for most standard synthesis algorithms. While this collection of algorithms does not constitute a complete sound synthesis language, it can assist the reader in gaining a more detailed technical understanding of the algorithms and also serve as a basis for developing other synthesis algorithms. The reader without access to a synthesis language can use the appendix and the examples in sections 1.3A and 3.6 as starting points in developing synthesis software.

All the computer programming examples in the book are written in the FORTRAN language. Selecting a language proved to be a difficult task, fraught with compromises. The decision to publish the routines in FORTRAN was based on various considerations, including FORTRAN's widespread use, its relative efficiency of execution on many systems, and the great familiarity of many computer programmers with FORTRAN. Some readers will want to translate the FORTRAN routines into other programming languages. This should be reasonably simple, owing to the short length and relative linearity of the programs. However, the way in which subprograms are passed data and store intermediate results is quite different in some languages. Therefore, the translator must check these procedures carefully.

A number of individuals donated considerable amounts of their time in assisting the authors to write this book. Katharine Schlefer Dodge helped the authors both in the organization of their thoughts and the expression of their ideas. Her attention to the book provided the impetus and focus for the project. Without her help on the first draft of the manuscript, the book would not have been written.

Johan Sundberg, professor in the Department of Speech Communication and Music Acoustics of the Royal Institute of Technology in Stockholm, aided tremendously in the formulation of both the chapter on psychoacoustics and the sections of chapter 6 concerning the synthesis of the singing voice. His advice was always willingly offered and invariably enriched our work.

A number of computer music professionals read the first draft of the book and made helpful suggestions for strengthening it. These included Lejaren Hiller and his student Charles Ames of the State University of New York at Buffalo; William Buxton of the University of Toronto; and Steven Haflich of the Experimental Music Studio at the Massachusetts Institute of Technology.

John Chowning of the Center for Computer Research in Music and Acoustics and Stanford University was extremely generous with his time in explaining the intricate details of his composition *Stria*. Similarly, composers Roger Reynolds, Morton Subotnick, Charles Wuorinen, Larry Austin, Jon Appleton, Paul Lansky, and John Melby were each most helpful in editing the commentary on their computer music.

Joseph DiMeo, our student at Brooklyn College and the C.U.N.Y. Graduate Center, programmed all the instrument designs of the book, first into Music 360 and later into Music 11, thereby proving that a reader could actually program the instrument designs from the flowcharts and descriptions in the text. Other students of computer music at Brooklyn College diligently and patiently provided feedback on various drafts as the book evolved.

Stephen Bown, member of the technical staff of Hewlett-Packard, Santa Rosa, graciously assisted with the section on digital noise generators.

David Warrender, president of Euphonics in Sebastopol, California, painstakingly reviewed several early versions of the manuscript, and his thoughtful comments resulted in numerous improvements.

Finally, we would like to acknowledge the full cooperation of our employers. The Hewlett-Packard Company granted a leave of absence to one of us (Jerse) to take the position of Technical Director of the Brooklyn College Center for Computer Music for the academic year 1979–1980. It was during that year that this book began to take form. The authors also gratefully acknowledge the use of Hewlett-Packard facilities for word-processing the text and generating many of the figures by computer.

Charles Dodge, *Brooklyn College of the City University of New York*
Thomas A. Jerse, *Hewlett-Packard Company*
September 1984

COMPUTER MUSIC

SYNTHESIS, COMPOSITION, AND PERFORMANCE

1

Fundamentals of Computer Music

1.1 COMPUTERS

Regardless of the specific purpose to which it is applied, a computer performs two basic functions: it rapidly executes a sequence of instructions (a *program*), and it stores and recalls large amounts of information (*data*). A computer may be characterized by its speed of operation, the type of instructions it can execute, and the capacity of its memory.

The term *hardware* refers to the electronic equipment that forms a computer system. The amount and type of electronic circuitry that constitute the hardware determine the capability of the computer. Most computer users are generally not concerned with the inner workings of the machine. The user ordinarily becomes aware of the hardware only when it limits the types of tasks the user wants to perform; that is, when the hardware does not operate rapidly enough to perform a task within the desired period of time or when the computer's memory is too small to contain the needed programs or data. The term *software* refers to the programs that a computer can execute. Computer systems have a large collection of programs that perform a variety of tasks. An essential part of the software of the computer system is a group of programs known as an *operating system*. The operating system assists the user in creating new programs and otherwise smooths the interaction of the user with the hardware. Without an operating system, the computer hardware would be so difficult to use that its utility would be severely limited.

Software is valuable only if its instructions can be executed by the hardware. In the same way, computer hardware represents only the potential capability of the computer; without software, it can do nothing meaningful. Therefore, the acquisition of computer hardware is only the beginning. Development and accumulation of software are the means for accomplishing the desired tasks. It is a long-term, ongoing process. (Software will be discussed in further detail later.)

Figure 1.1 diagrams the functional arrangement of a computer system. The *central processing unit* (CPU) is the nerve center of the computer. It controls the operation of the system by reading and interpreting the instructions of a program and then executing them. The types of instructions available include mathematical and logical operations as well as instructions for the movement of information. These instructions may also make decisions based on data that are either stored in the computer or received from external devices. The ability to make decisions greatly extends the usefulness of the computer beyond that of a calculator.

The *memory* holds both programs and data. It is divided into distinct locations in

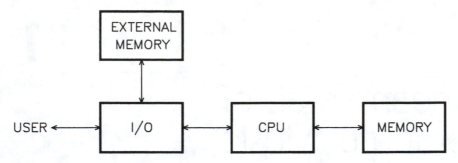

FIGURE 1.1 The functional arrangement of a computer system.

which items of information are stored. A unique numerical address distinguishes each memory location. The CPU stores information by "writing" a numerical value into a specific memory location; it retrieves information by "reading" a stored value. The numerical value represents either a program instruction (e.g., "add two numbers") or a datum such as a number, a character, an attribute of a sound, or anything else the programmer determines. However, no matter what it represents, the stored entity is in numerical form.

When the power is switched on or the "reset" button is pushed by the operator of a computer, the internal hardware gives the CPU the address of the memory location containing the first program instruction. Execution begins from that point. Subsequent instructions are taken from successive memory locations unless an instruction directs the CPU to "branch" to another instruction elsewhere in memory. For example, a computer can be configured to display a menu of available software at power-on and then wait for the user to input a choice. Upon receipt of the user's selection, the computer branches to the appropriate instruction to activate the desired program.

During the execution of any CPU instruction, references may be made to other memory locations for storage or retrieval of either data or further instructions. The example program of figure 1.2 adds the numbers found in memory locations 104 and 105 and stores the results in location 106. Figure 1.2a shows the contents of memory before the program starts. Note that the contents of the first four locations are interpreted as instructions, and the contents of the last three locations (starting with location 104) are interpreted as data. The first instruction causes the contents of location 104 (1230) to be loaded into a specific place in the CPU called a *register*. A register is a special memory location that can be used by the CPU more easily than main memory. The next instruction brings the contents of location 105 (3017) into the CPU and adds it to the data already in the register (the contents of memory location 104). The register holds only the result of the addition (4247); the two original numbers are no longer present inside the CPU. Next, instruction 102 moves the result into location 106 for storage. Finally, instruction 103 halts the program and the memory contains the values shown in figure 1.2b. In a modern computer, the end of a program never halts the operation of the machine; instead, it branches either to a point where the computer waits for user input or to the beginning of another program.

The numbers contained in locations 100 through 103 are the numerical codes for the instructions. The leftmost digit of the code determines the instruction type. "0" means stop,

Address	Contents	Meaning
100	1104	LOAD 104
101	3105	ADD 105
102	2106	STORE 106
103	0000	STOP
104	1230	DATA
105	3017	DATA
106	0000	DATA

a) Before execution

Address	Contents	Meaning
100	1104	LOAD 104
101	3105	ADD 105
102	2106	STORE 106
103	0000	STOP
104	1230	DATA
105	3017	DATA
106	4247	DATA

b) After execution

FIGURE 1.2 Contents of a computer memory before and after the execution of an example program.

"1" means load, "2" means store, and "3" means add. The right three digits of the code indicate the memory location to be used in the operation. (The stop instruction does not use the memory, so the right three digits of instruction 103 have no meaning.) This numerical method of instruction representation was invented for the purpose of the example. The format and codes used in actual computers vary widely among computer product lines.

The stored program gives the computer the flexibility to perform a large set of diverse tasks because the program can be changed rapidly by changing the contents of the memory. In the earliest computers, the program and data did not share the same memory, and so program changes were more difficult sometimes even requiring alteration of the hardware. In the late 1940s, John von Neumann first carried out the idea of utilizing the same memory for both data and instructions. This concept represented a milestone in computer design, because it permitted instructions to be treated as data. Programs could be written to generate other programs, thereby greatly facilitating the translation of the programmer's ideas into instructions for the computer. (See section 1.2.)

The smallest unit of information that a computer can recognize is the *bit*. A bit represents the position of an electronic switch inside the computer hardware. A computer switch, like a light switch, can assume only one of two states, off or on. The two possible states of a bit are numerically denoted as 0 and 1 (hence, the name "bit" is a contraction of the term "binary digit"). To enable the storage of a datum that can assume a large number of possible values, each memory location is composed of a group of bits. The pattern of the bits determines the contents of a location. For example, 2 bits can assume four unique patterns: 00, 01, 10, and 11. Thus, a memory location made up of 2 bits will contain one of four distinct values. In general, n bits can assume 2^n unique states. The number of bits per location varies among computer product lines. The most popular approaches use an even power of 2, such as 8, 16, or 32.

The *byte* is used almost universally to measure memory capacity. Nearly all manufacturers define a byte as a group of 8 bits. A byte, therefore, can assume any of 2^8 or 256 unique states. A modern computer typically contains millions of bytes in two types of memory. *Read-only memory* (ROM) stores data that cannot be altered during the normal operation of the computer. Special equipment is used to write the contents of this type of memory, generally when the computer is manufactured. The ROM memory is used, among other things, to contain special programs to direct the system during the power-on sequence. *Random-access memory* (RAM) forms the bulk of computer memory, and its contents are routinely written to and read by the CPU. The amount of RAM determines the size of programs and their data sets that can successfully run on a computer.

A CPU instruction may occupy from one to several bytes. Many machines use variable-length instructions—instructions whose length varies with their purpose. This arrangement makes for more efficient use of memory, since simpler instructions need not occupy the same amount of memory as more complex ones. The number of bytes used to store a datum also varies. For example, 1 byte is used to store a single character such as the letter G. In this case, the actual contents of the byte is a numerical code that has been agreed upon by programmers to represent the letter G. The most widely used coding standard is known as *ASCII* (American Standard Code for Information Interchange). It consists of a set of 128 numerical codes that represent alphanumeric characters, punctuation marks, and special control codes such as carriage return. The 8-bit pattern 01000111, for example, is the ASCII code for the uppercase letter G.

Numerical values generally occupy from 1 to 8 bytes, depending on their format and the precision with which they are stored. The way in which numbers are represented in a computer can have significant effects on the quality of the computer-generated sound. We will discuss these effects in section 3.2 and other places throughout the text. Here, we will introduce the two most widely used numerical data formats: integer and floating point.

We are all familiar with the decimal number system, which is so named because it is based on the number 10. It is also called a positional number system, because the value of an individual digit in a group of digits depends on its position relative to the other digits. Each position is worth 10 times as much as the position to its right. For example, the number 247 is evaluated as

$$2 \times 10^2 + 4 \times 10^1 + 7 \times 10^0 = 247$$

The same approach applies in evaluating a group of bits. Because the binary number system is based on the number 2, each bit position in the group is worth twice as much as the position to its right. Thus, the binary number 1001 is evaluated as

$$1 \times 2^3 + 0 \times 2^2 + 0 \times 2^1 + 1 \times 2^0 = 9$$

Table 1.1 shows the decimal equivalents of some binary numbers. This binary format for representing numbers in a computer is called *integer* representation, because only whole numbers can be represented. The number of bits used determines the available range of integers. Generally, 16 bits (2 bytes) are used to store integers. When both positive and negative numbers are provided for, this gives a range of −32,768 to +32,767. When a larger range of integers is needed, 4 bytes are ordinarily used.

1 =1	10000 =16
10 =2	100000 =32
11 =3	1000000 =64
100=4	10000000 =128
101=5	100000000 =256
110=6	1000000000 =512
111=7	10000000000 =1024
1000=8	100000000000 =2048
1001=9	1000000000000 =4096
1010=10	10000000000000 =8192
1011=11	100000000000000 =16384
1100=12	1000000000000000 =32768
1101=13	10000000000000000 =65536
1110=14	100000000000000000 =131072
1111=15	1000000000000000000 =262144

TABLE 1.1 Some binary-to-decimal equivalents

Many computer applications require a range of numbers greater than that made possible by even a 4-byte integer format. Furthermore, the ability to represent numbers with fractional parts is often needed. For these reasons, *floating-point* representation was developed. A number such as 824.68 can be written as

$$824.68 = 0.82468 \times 10^3$$

The exponent, 3, signifies the number of places that the decimal point had to be shifted to the left in order to be in front of the first digit. The other half of the floating-point number, 0.82468, is known as the mantissa. A number with a magnitude less than 0.1, such as 0.068514, can be represented as

$$0.068514 = 0.68514 \times 10^{-1}$$

The negative exponent indicates that the decimal point must be moved to the right in order to be in front of the first nonzero digit. A computer stores a floating-point number as a separate mantissa and exponent. A power of 2 or a power of 16 is generally used rather than a power of 10, but the principle is the same. The floating-point data format provides for the representation of a much larger range of numbers than the integer format. However, the CPU performs mathematical operations involving floating-point numbers considerably more slowly unless it contains special hardware for performing floating-point calculations.

In a typical format, 4 bytes are used to store a floating-point number, split approximately into 1 byte for the exponent and 3 bytes for the mantissa including the sign. The number of bits used for the mantissa determines the number of significant digits represented in the mantissa. The use of 3 bytes (24 bits) gives a resolution that is equivalent to nearly seven decimal digits. When greater accuracy is needed, more bytes are appended to the mantissa. A popular format known as double precision uses a total of 8 bytes and gives a little over 15 decimal digits of resolution.

In order to do something useful, a CPU must have mechanisms for accessing information from external sources and for reporting the results of its calculations. *Input/output* (I/O) devices make possible a wide range of interactions. Some types of I/O devices provide the means for communication between the computer and its users. These devices interface (connect) with the CPU and convert the electronic signals inside the CPU into a form that can be interpreted by the user. For example, a visual display on the computer enables the user to receive messages from the CPU in both text and graphical form. Today, most computers display information on the screen of a cathode ray tube (CRT) similar to the ones found in television sets. Portable computers use liquid crystal displays (LCDs) owing to their small size and weight. Other types of devices are used to change the physical actions of the user into electronic signals. For instance, most computers include a keyboard that allows the user to type instructions to the computer. Utilizing the appropriate devices, the computer can communicate with its users through a wide variety of visual, aural, and tactile means. Section 1.4 and chapter 12 detail many of the I/O devices that have been used for music.

Certain types of I/O devices enable a computer to exchange information with other computers. A modem permits data transmission over an ordinary telephone line. Local-area-network interfaces allow computers at an installation to communicate with each other. Today, systems such as the Internet and the World Wide Web enable the exchange of vast amounts of information on a global scale.

Another widely used class of I/O equipment is the mass-storage device. These devices form the external memory of a computer system. They hold programs and data that are not currently being used by the CPU. The storage medium is most commonly a magnetic one, such as a disk or a tape. External memory is usually larger than internal, running into over a billion bytes on some disks. With removable media, such as digital tapes and floppy disks, the computer's memory is limited only by the number of tapes and disks available. Removable media also enable the transportation of information between computer systems. The CD-ROM has become very popular for distributing information because it holds hundreds of millions of bytes, but unlike magnetic storage devices, once it is encoded new information cannot be written over the current contents. Section 1.3 will discuss the organization of the contents of storage devices.

We are fortunate to live in a time when the cost of computers is falling almost as fast as their performance is rising. It is common for individuals to own personal computers that have capabilities exceeding those of the computers that could only be found in advanced research laboratories two decades ago. At one time, making computer music required access to a large computer system; now, most practitioners use individual computers. The most common type used, owing to its relatively low cost, is the personal computer. Although technological advances are blurring the distinction between a workstation and a personal computer, the more expensive workstation can run programs faster and often has more memory. Larger computers, once called mainframes and mini-computers, are now seldom used for computer music because so much computing power is available in a smaller, less expensive form.

In comparing the capabilities of computers, clock frequency is a general indication of their execution speed. Owing to variations in hardware design, there is not necessarily a one-to-one relationship between clock frequency and the number of instructions the computer can perform per second.

To increase the speed at which computer music can be realized, some systems incorporate separate digital signal-processing chips. These small devices are tailored for rapid calculations on data streams such as those used to represent an audio signal. They are installed in a computer system and controlled by the CPU.

1.2 COMPUTER PROGRAMMING

In theory, a computer can be programmed to perform any task that can be defined. The programmer must determine a procedure (*algorithm*) that can be written as a sequence of instructions. Each step of the algorithm must be defined unambiguously, and there must be a clear path to the completion of the algorithm. The results of an algorithm are called outputs, and, of course, any useful algorithm must have at least one output. An algorithm may accept data (inputs) to use in determining the output(s), but inputs are not a necessity.

As an example of an algorithm, consider the procedure used by a beginning piano student to play a simple, single-voice piece.

1. Find beginning of piece.
2. Read first note.
3. Go to step 5.
4. Read next note.
5. Depress appropriate piano key on the appropriate beat.
6. Count duration in beats and release key.
7. Was this the last note?

    If yes, then go to step 8.

    If no, then go to step 4.
8. End of algorithm.

The output of this algorithm is the sound produced by the piano. The input to the algorithm is the data sequence (notes) on the sheet of music. Finite completion of the algorithm is assured if there is a finite number of notes in the piece. This particular algorithm makes a decision, but this is not the case with every algorithm.

A programmer communicates algorithms to a computer by means of a programming language. The languages used are called *artificial* languages, as opposed to the natural languages of human communication. They differ from natural languages in that their structure and syntax are rigidly defined; that is, the programmer's intentions must be explicitly declared. Many different programming languages have been developed. The language selected for expressing a particular program depends on several factors: the type and complexity of the algorithm(s) to be communicated, the languages available on the computer system being utilized, the form of the data to be used by the program, and the programmer's familiarity with the available languages.

A computer can be programmed by entering directly into memory a list of numerical values (see figure 1.2) corresponding to the actual instructions to be performed. This approach is called *machine-language* programming because it conforms directly with the internal configurations required by the machine. It is both tedious and time-consuming. Moreover, it obscures the goal of the program, because the programmer must define the operations on a more primitive level. As a result, machine-language programming normally is used only by people who design and repair the hardware.

It is possible to communicate an algorithm to the computer in a language more intelligible to the user, if there is a program available to translate the encoded algorithm into machine language for the computer. Nearly every computer system has such translating programs. When using a computer language, the programmer produces a written text of a program, enters it into the computer, and then invokes a translating program. Depending on the type of translator, the translated instructions are either executed immediately or stored in a form that can be executed on demand.

Programming languages are sometimes compared on the basis of their similarity to machine language. A *low-level* language is close to machine language. The most widely used low-level language is assembly language. Generally, one statement in assembly language will create a single machine-language instruction when translated. The set of machine instructions differs among computer product lines, and so a given assembly-language program can be executed only on the type of machine for which it was written. The most effective use of assembly language is for communication of algorithms that must be executed with optimum speed and efficiency. Usually, only computer specialists write programs in assembly language.

Most programming is done in a *high-level* language. This allows the programmer to communicate in terms that are more familiar to the programmer and suited to the task at hand. The use of high-level languages confers several benefits, one of which is shorter program texts. For example, the following program fragment, written in the high-level language FORTRAN, calculates the average of two numbers:

```
X=12.4
Y=3.6
AVG=(X+Y)/2
```

After this portion of the program is run, the variable (see glossary) AVG would be equal to 8. On most computers, the operation of division, represented in the example by the symbol "/", requires the execution of a long sequence of machine-language instructions. In addition, the variable names X, Y, and AVG used to represent the data each correspond to a specific memory location in the computer, but the programmer needs neither to know nor to specify the numerical memory address. Thus, the use of a high-level language has relieved the programmer from specifying much of the detail of the actual operation of the computer. Shorter program texts contribute to increased programming productivity and accuracy. High-level languages also make it unnecessary for the programmer to be intimately familiar with the architecture of the system hardware.

Another important advantage of most high-level languages is machine independence. Machine-independent languages allow the same program to be transported between computers that have different machine languages (assuming that each machine has the appropriate translating program).

There are many high-level languages. Among the best known are BASIC, C, C++, COBOL, FORTRAN, and LISP. Each language is optimized for solving specific classes of problems. For instance, C, FORTRAN, and BASIC are optimized for algorithms that are best expressed algebraically, whereas LISP is aimed at communicating artificial-intelligence algorithms. *Problem-oriented* languages have been invented that address a relatively narrow problem area. Such languages are closer to the actual tasks that need to be done and further from the demands of the computer. In these problem-oriented languages, the more cumbersome algorithms have already been written for the user by computer specialists. The remainder of the work can be programmed in a language that enables a more straightforward formulation of the task at hand. Numerous languages have been developed for music, and some of them will be discussed in sections 1.5 and 4.11.

Two basic methods are available for translating a program written in a high-level language into machine language: compilation and interpretation. The programs that accomplish these tasks are called *compilers* and *interpreters,* respectively. A compiler reads through high-level program text, written in a language such as FORTRAN, and generates another representation of the program in a lower-level form called an *object file.* This file is then linked with any previously stored routines used in the program and converted to an *executable file* that contains the machine-language version of the program. The computer can then be instructed to execute the compiled program at any desired time. It can be run as many times as desired without having to repeat the compilation process.

A compiler performs the tasks of program translation and execution as two distinct, sequential steps; an interpreter interweaves them. After an interpreter reads a statement from the high-level program text, it determines the exact set of machine instructions required to perform the operations indicated. Those instructions are then executed immediately, and the interpreter moves on to the next statement. Thus, instead of having a discrete compilation step, the translation process occurs throughout the execution of the program. Programs that are interpreted run much more slowly than compiled ones. Nevertheless, interpreters enjoy widespread use, in part because they make finding program errors easier. Sound synthesis programs generally perform an enormous number of calculations, and so are most commonly compiled.

To simplify their task, programmers often divide programs into a main program and one or more subprograms called *functions* or *subroutines.* A subroutine contains an encoded algorithm for accomplishing a specific task and is employed in the following way. The CPU starts execution at the beginning of the main program. When the CPU encounters an instruction that calls for the use of the subroutine, the address of the first instruction of the subroutine is loaded into the CPU. This action causes the CPU to begin executing the instructions of the subroutine. When the subroutine is completed, the control of the CPU returns to the point in the program just after the location from which it was called. Thus, the same subroutine can be called from several different places in a program, or even from other subroutines. When a subroutine is called, the calling program may supply or pass data to be used in determining the actions of the subroutine. A datum passed to a subroutine is known as an *argument* or *parameter.*

Subroutines are an important part of most computer music programs. For example, sound synthesis programs generally divide the sound-generating algorithms into separate subroutines. The parameters passed to the subroutines determine the character of the sound produced. (See section 1.5B and the chapters on sound synthesis.) In the area of computer-aided composition (see chapter 11), composers have used subroutines that perform particular tasks on musical passages such as transposing them.

A *function* is a special type of subroutine found in many computer languages. When a function is called, it is passed values that are used in calculating the value of the function. The result of the calculation is returned for use in the calling program. For example, a function can be written to calculate the square of a number. In FORTRAN, this function would take the form:

```
FUNCTION SQUARE(X)
SQUARE=X*X
RETURN
```

X is the parameter that is passed to the function. The * operator signifies multiplication. In the main program, the function could be used in a statement such as the following:

```
V=SQUARE(5.0)
```

When this statement is executed, the variable V would take on the value of 25.

1.3   OPERATING SYSTEMS AND FILE ORGANIZATION

A typical computer has access to a large number of programs and data sets. It would be very difficult for a computer user to take advantage of all this information and capability if the computer systems did not have an organized collection of software known as an *operating system* (OS) to manage and control the operation of the computer. An OS furnishes many useful services. For example, an OS contains the software for communication through the I/O devices, such as the procedure that enables users to enter commands from a keyboard. An OS also provides for the orderly transition of control of the CPU from one program to another, thus making it possible to link programs together. The OS also makes it easy for the user to handle the information stored in the mass-storage devices. This important service will be described later in the section.

Simple operating systems provide for a single process. In other words, only one program can be run at a time because the CPU is devoted exclusively to executing the current program. More advanced operating systems provide for *multitasking*. This feature allows more than one system user and also permits individual users to run more than one program simultaneously. In these cases, the OS must serve as an arbiter between the programs, allocating computing resources with the aim of achieving the most efficient system operation possible. In addition, the OS must ensure that one program does not disturb another. There are several approaches to the handling of multiple programs—the most popular is *task switching*. In this mode, the OS allocates the sequential use of the CPU to each program for a small interval of time called a *slice*. During a slice, the CPU executes the program of the designated user, and any inputs received from that user are serviced. If the slices are short enough that only a small time elapses between successive services of a given program, each user will have the impression of having uninterrupted access to the computer. However, when the overall usage of the computer is high, the users will suffer a noticeably slower response to their inputs. More sophisticated computers incorporate multiple CPUs (*multiprocessing*) to increase their ability to handle a large volume of programs. In these systems, the OS allocates the work load among the CPUs as efficiently as possible.

When computers were first developed, the amount of data that could be processed and stored was relatively limited, so that organizing data was fairly simple. Before magnetic media were available, programs and data were stored on paper, either as punched holes in a stack of cards or as holes in a paper tape. Hence, different data sets and programs were easily distinguishable as physical entities.

The development and subsequent refinement of magnetic storage technology enabled an enormous amount of information to be stored in a small volume at a very low cost. Furthermore, the invention of magnetic disks allowed nearly random access to the data. Reaping the benefits of this technology required the creation of a system to organize the contents of the magnetic media so that a large number of diverse programs and data sets could be systematically stored on the same disk. The basic storage element recognized by the operating system in a modern computer is the *file;* it may contain a program, a collection of data, or both. The length of a file is determined by its contents. To execute a program that is stored in external memory, the CPU incorporates the program into the main memory by "loading" the appropriate file and then instructing itself to begin execution at the beginning of the new program. Data files may contain any type of information. A program can instruct the CPU to transfer the contents of a particular data file into the main memory for use in its operations. For example, a program can be written to take a data file containing a description of musical sound and, utilizing the appropriate I/O devices such as those described in section 1.4, convert the data into sound.

To manage the large number of files on a computer system, the files are ordinarily grouped into *directories,* which are divided into *subdirectories.* For example, the administrator of a system used by many individuals might create a separate directory for each user. Users are then free to establish their own subdirectories to organize their projects. In fact, modern operating systems permit multiple levels of subdirectories so that the users can organize their files to best meet the requirements of their work.

There are many types of files; those relating to computer programs are generally categorized as source files, object files, and executable program files. A *source file* contains the list of program instructions in text form as typed in by the programmer. In order to create computer instructions, the source file is fed into a translation program, which creates an *object file.* The object file is not suitable for execution; it must first be linked with any special routines specified in the source file in order to create an *executable program file.* The desired program can now be run by requesting its executable file from the operating system. If a change in the program is desired, the programmer must go back and modify the source file, retranslate it into an object file, and then link it into executable form before running it again.

Data files are used as inputs and outputs to programs, and their nature and type depend on the requirements of the programs. The most widely used type of data file is the *text file*, which stores characters in ASCII format. Text files are used to store data, program listings, a list of commands to a music synthesis program, and a wide variety of other purposes. There are many other types of data files; for instance, each of the major commercial word-processing programs defines its own type of data file. Spreadsheet programs specify other types of data files, as do graphics programs, and so on. Each of these file types has a unique format that renders it incompatible with other programs unless translation software is available.

The principal types of data files found in most computer music systems are *score files*, which describe the sequence of events in a composition; *instrument files*, which describe the process to be used for sound generation or modification; and *sound object files*, which contain the record of a sound in digital form. The first two types are often specified in text form and will be described in sections 1.5 and 4.6, respectively. Several formats have been defined for sound object files; the simplest just record a sequence of numbers corresponding to the digital signal that describes the sound (see chapter 3). More sophisticated file formats include a "header" at the beginning of the file which contains information about the file format and the way in which the digital signal that follows is to be played back.[1] As described in chapter 12, *MIDI data files* contain a sequential list of commands for controlling electronic musical instruments equipped with that commercially available interface.

1.4   THE USE OF A COMPUTER IN AUDIO SYSTEMS

A computer system can generate and manipulate sound in several different modes of operation, but for it to do so the sound must be represented in a format suitable for processing by the computer. How does a digital computer, designed to manipulate numbers, work with sound? Acoustical energy in the form of pressure waves can be converted into an analogous electrical signal by an appropriate transducer such as a microphone. The transducer produces an electrical pressure, called *voltage*, that changes constantly in sympathy with the vibrations of the sound wave. To demonstrate that the voltage describes the sound received by the microphone, it can be connected to an amplifier driving a loudspeaker; in this way, the electrical signal may be converted back into sound and compared with the original. Because the change in voltage occurs analogously to the vibrations of the sound, the electrical signal is called an *analog* signal.

To change an analog signal into a form suitable for use by a digital computer, the signal must be converted into numbers. Two types of I/O devices link the digital computer with the analog world. These types are distinguished by the direction of transformation. *Analog-to-digital* (A/D) converters transform voltages into numbers, and *digital-to-analog* (D/A) converters transform numbers into voltages. The characteristics and limitations of data converters will be described in more detail in chapter 3, but for the purposes of this section they can be simply thought of as devices that enable a sound to be changed into a stream of numbers or vice versa.

The simplest use of a computer in an audio system is *digital recording* (figure 1.3a). The A/D converter transforms the incoming analog signal into digital form, and the

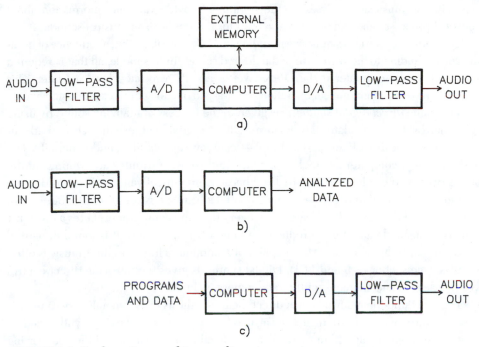

FIGURE 1.3 Configurations used in an audio system.

computer stores this digital signal on an external memory device such as a disk or tape. For playback, the computer retrieves the stored signal from memory and sends it to the D/A converter for retransformation. The low-pass filters prevent the digital signal processing from introducing unwanted components in the sound. Their necessity will be explained in chapter 3.

Digital recordings have several advantages over analog ones. Because the recording medium stores numbers rather than an analog signal, it offers superior noise performance and protects the sound more effectively against degradation during long-term storage. In addition, regardless of the number of generations removed, a copy of a digital recording maintains complete fidelity to the original.

The configuration of figure 1.3a can also be used for *signal processing*. Here, the computer modifies the digital signals before passing them to the D/A converter for reconversion. The modifications can be as simple as mixing the signal applied to the input with another digital signal previously stored in external memory. The use of a computer enables very complex operations such as removing the orchestral accompaniment from behind a singing voice. Other uses of the computer in this mode include modulation (chapter 4), filtering (chapter 6), and reverberation (chapter 10).

The computer can also be programmed to analyze signals (figure 1.3b). When operating as a *signal analyzer,* the computer takes a digital signal and mathematically determines its characteristics. For example, a computer analysis can reveal the acoustical characteristics of a speech sound. The analytical capability of the computer makes it a powerful tool for the researcher in psychoacoustics. Chapters 2 and 7 will detail some of these applications. For the musician, analyses by the computer provide valuable information about acoustical processes and can be used as a basis for the synthesis of musical sounds.

The computer can also synthesize sound (figure 1.3c) by calculating a sequence of numbers corresponding to the waveform of the desired sound. In this mode, all that is required in addition to the computer is the D/A converter and its associated low-pass filter. This arrangement is the minimum configuration necessary to obtain computer-generated audio.

The name *direct digital synthesis* is given to the process of realizing sound by using digital hardware to calculate its waveform. Direct digital synthesis has several advantages over synthesis with analog hardware—accuracy, repeatability, and generality. The signals inside a computer are highly accurate, and so the attributes and timings of the sounds produced can be precisely realized because numerical values with considerable accuracy can be used to describe them. A related advantage is repeatability. Because of the accuracy of the direct digital synthesis, every time the computer executes a given list of instructions and data, it will produce the same results. Because it is found in natural sounds, the introduction of a certain amount of randomness into computer music is often desirable (see sections 4.9 and 11.1). Digital synthesis gives the musician direct control over the degree and character of the randomness included.

The most important advantage of direct digital synthesis is its generality. Because any sound can be converted into a digital signal, it follows that any sound can be synthesized by using the appropriate algorithm to calculate its digital representation and then converting it. Thus, sounds generated digitally can, in theory, be arbitrarily complex and have any character. That is, the sound of one or a hundred symphonic instruments or of one or a hundred barnyard animals may be realized using the same general-purpose computer system.

One of the greatest challenges of digital synthesis is the determination of the algorithm to produce a desired sound. Chapters 4 through 9 will detail most of the current techniques. Many synthesis models are based on the analysis of natural sound. *Synthesis from analysis,* as this is called, can be used to reproduce the analyzed sound, but more often musicians modify the analyses to produce new extensions of the original sound.

1.5   SOFTWARE FOR COMPUTER MUSIC

1.5A   An Overview

A large body of software, some requiring specialized hardware, has been developed to simplify the task of making music with a computer. In fact, such a proliferation of systems and methods has taken place that the range of choices can seem overwhelming. Most musicians approach the computer with a set of preconditions that limits their options. For example, some of the computer music systems now available require expensive purchases of hardware that are clearly out of the price range of most individuals. Other preconditions can be less prosaic—a musician may be looking for a system that enables a certain type of computer synthesis, such as granular synthesis. In this section, we will detail many of the current approaches to music with computers, but we will concentrate on those that are available as "freeware" and require little special-purpose hardware beyond a computer with a sound system. Keep in mind that not all systems are available for every type of computer; some will only function on a computer with a certain operating system, one with a certain language compiler, or even a particular brand or model of computer.

Most computer music software falls into four broad categories: algorithms for sound synthesis, algorithms for modification of synthesized or sampled sound, programs to assist the musician in composing with sound from the computer and/or sound from acoustic instruments, and programs that enable a computer performance of a composition. This division of computer music activity is based on traditional musical activity, but it is not the only possible model. Much has been done in recent times to make the computer come as close as possible to making music in "real time." For example, there are numerous implementations, many of them in special-purpose hardware, to speed the algorithms for sound synthesis and modification and for the computer performance of a composition. Composition programs have always taken fewer computational resources than the other three divisions, and have more rarely required special-purpose hardware to make their implementation sufficiently fast.

Figure 1.4 shows the relationships among the most commonly encountered methods of realizing computer music. The musician selects the algorithms for sound synthesis, using software that aids in its specification; or, alternatively, the musician selects the sound file to be modified. The musician determines the use of these synthesized or sampled sounds by producing a score, often with the assistance of a score-editing program or composing program. Performance practice in computer music encompasses a broad

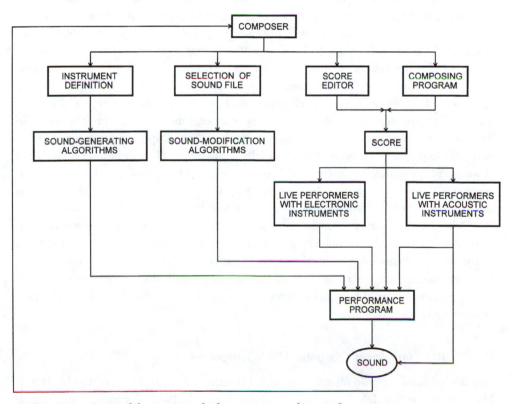

FIGURE 1.4 Some of the ways in which composers make use of a computer.

range of possibilities, from a computer-generated score played by acoustic instruments to a program that, during performance, combines a score in computer memory with the algorithms for sound synthesis to produce sound with no performance or compositional intervention. Notice that the methods shown in the figure form a loop. The feedback that the musician receives from the performance can be applied to revisions of the composition just as in traditional composition.

When using the computer as a sound synthesis medium, the musician determines the sound palette for a composition and then attempts to formulate the appropriate algorithm(s) to generate it. Each of these algorithms, called *instruments,* produces a particular type of sound. A computer instrument need not be restricted to producing single tones at a time, but can be designed to generate any number of simultaneous parts, as well as long, evolving sounds. Each algorithm has inputs, known as *parameters,* that control various aspects of the sound produced. The number and type of these inputs are determined by the instrument designer, depending on what the composition requires. Common parameters include acoustical attributes such as pitch, amplitude, location, and controls on timbral aspects of the sound. (See chapter 2.) The parametric values for a computer instrument come from data stored in the computer's memory or from a peripheral device actuated by a performer.

When using the computer to modify existing sound files, the musician chooses the modification techniques appropriate to the musical goal. A great deal of research has been done in this area, and some software packages deal specifically with sound modification. Chapters 4 through 10 will present the principles of synthesis instrument design and sound modification techniques, with illustrative examples.

Once the instruments of the computer orchestra are defined, the musician must describe how and when the instruments are to play. This ordinarily takes the form of a score—a list of musical events. Each event can be thought of as a "note," in the sense that it calls upon an instrument to perform, even though the event need not be a note in the traditional sense. For example, a single event might call upon an instrument that is designed to play several successive or simultaneous tones. The minimum specification of an event identifies the instrument that is to play and the time at which the event begins, with additional parameters required by the instrument. Examples of various sorts of score encoding in several widely used music languages will be discussed.

Once the score and the descriptions of the instruments have been entered into the computer, they can be combined by a *performance program:* a program that turns instructions and data into sound. Performance programs vary widely, depending on the hardware and the amount of manual intervention desired during performance. In chapter 12, various modes of live performance and many of the control devices used by performers will be discussed.

1.5B   Examples of Computer Music Languages

The first general-purpose program for sound synthesis was Music 3, created by Max V. Mathews at the Bell Telephone Laboratories in the early 1960s. Its successor, Music 4, was exported to a few American universities, where computer music activity began to

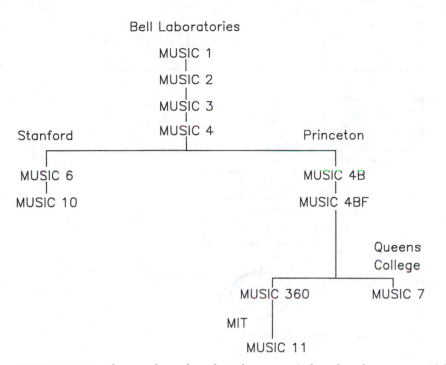

FIGURE 1.5 Family tree of sound synthesis languages. (*Adapted, with permission of the author, from the* Musician-Machine Interface in Computer Music, *by Stanley Haynes, doctoral dissertation, University of Southampton, 1979.*)

proliferate and new programs were devised to suit local circumstances. Figure 1.5 displays a "family tree" of the sound synthesis programs that evolved from Mathews's earliest experiments in the late 1950s to the situation in the early 1980s. The geographical dispersion of the languages also indicates structural differences among them. The figure is roughly chronological from top to bottom.

The center of the tree shows the programs developed by Mathews and his group at Bell Laboratories. The branch on the right shows variants of Music 4 that Godfrey Winham and Hubert S. Howe produced at Princeton University and the subsequent developments of that program: Music 360 and Music 11[2] by Barry L. Vercoe and Music 7 by Howe. The branch on the left shows the music compilers Music 6 and Music 10 produced at Stanford University. In most instances, the languages are no longer in use because the computers for which they were written, or the languages they were written in, are obsolete.

The Music 4 family of languages represents the oldest and most widely dispersed approach to computer music.[3] The "Music *N*"–derived programs still in use, for all their differences of detail and structure, include Csound,[4] Cmusic,[5] and Cmix,[6] among others. Figure 1.6 illustrates the process by which the Music *N*–type sound synthesis programs make sound. The first step (1a) is for the musician to create the orchestra by defining the instruments (following, of course, the rules of syntax for the particular language). Each instrument is designed to produce a particular type of sound and has input parameters

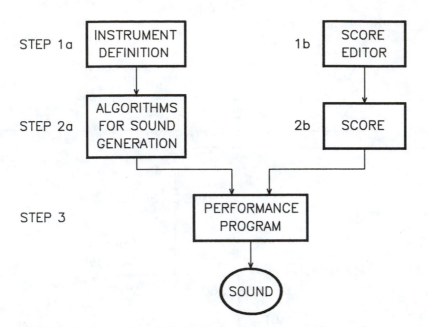

FIGURE 1.6 Process by which Music N–type languages make sound.

that control various characteristics of the sound, such as duration, loudness, and pitch. Examples of typical methods of instrument design in a variety of sound synthesis languages will be shown in section 4.6.

The second part of step 1 (1b) is to provide input to the particular score editor associated with the system. With step 1, the musician's input to the sound synthesis process is complete. Steps 2 and 3 are performed by the computer without intervention by the musician. In step 2, the instrument definitions are translated into a machine-language program, and the input from the score editor is compiled (if necessary) to put the score into the proper format for the processing of step 3. In step 3, the program actually "plays" the score on the instruments, thus creating the sound. The processing of a note of the score in step 3 consists of two stages: initialization and performance. At the initialization of a note, those values that are to remain fixed throughout the duration of the note are set, most often by obtaining parameter values for that note from the score. During the performance of a note, the computer calculates the actual output corresponding to the sound.

Figure 1.7 shows some of the most widely distributed computer music software in use in the mid-1990s. The facilities listed represent an extremely broad range of musical possibilities, from "freeware" to commercially available systems, and from deferred-time software that runs very slowly on home PCs to real-time computer music instruments. Under the direct digital synthesis heading, the first three entries are descendants from Mathews's work at Bell Laboratories. As their names imply (Csound, Cmusic, Cmix), all are written in the C programming language and run on a variety of brands and models of computers. The Chant program takes a different approach to synthesis, concentrating on the creation of sounds with resonances known as *formants* (see chapter 2) by a technique known as "FOF" (see chapter 8). The UPIC[7] system imple-

DIRECT DIGITAL SYNTHESIS	DIGITAL SOUND MODIFICATION
Csound	Sound Hack
Cmix	Protools by Digidesign
Cmusic	Dyaxis
Chant	Sonic Solutions
UPIC	RT
MIDI-controlled hardware	MIDI-controlled samplers
Granular synthesis	"Outboard" digital signal processors

SCORE PREPROCESSORS AND COMPOSING PROGRAMS	PROCESS SCHEDULERS FOR REAL-TIME CONTROL
Score 11	MAX
Common Music	Vision
HMSL	Studio Vision
	Cypher
	HMSL

FIGURE 1.7 Some of the most widely distributed music software in the 1990s.

ments another approach to synthesis—one that is intended to help realize graphically input representations of music—using computer systems with an elaborate graphical user interface.

A digital synthesizer is usually a musical instrument with a standard clavier keyboard in which there is the high-speed implementation in special-purpose hardware of standard synthesis algorithms. Yamaha made the first-low cost, portable digital synthesizer, the justly famous DX-7, in the early 1980s. Since that time a number of different companies have made digital synthesizers widely available. Another approach to sound synthesis, one that implements a non-Helmholtzian approach is known as *granular* synthesis. Its principle of viewing sound particles as acoustical quanta was first articulated by the physicist Dennis Gabor shortly after World War II and espoused by composer Iannis Xenakis in his search for non-Fourier approaches to computer sound synthesis. There are a number of systems for producing sound with granular-synthesis techniques, of which we will write in chapter 8.

The second column of figure 1.7 lists some of the software developed to take advantage of the explosive increase in the size of disk storage in the late 1980s, allowing computers to store sounds in digital form for subsequent modification and mixing. In fact, Cmix, listed above under sound synthesis, was one of the first computer music software packages to treat mixing on an equal footing with synthesis. Soundhack[8] provides two important tools to the musician working on a Macintosh[9] computer: a facility for converting the data format of sound files for use in more than a single sound synthesis, modification, or mixing system; and user-friendly routines for performing a wide range of computer techniques for modifying and analyzing the frequency content of stored sound. RT is a program that enables the real-time mixing of sound files. The application was originally made for use on the NeXT computer and now runs on other computers that use the UNIX[10] operating system. Protools,[11] Dyaxis,[12] and Sonic Solutions[13] are all commercially available hardware/software systems that implement real-time manipulation (mixing, equalizing, modifying, etc.) of sound files stored on hard disk. The power of these systems, along with the advent of multitrack digital tape recorders, has revolutionized the design and function of the commercial recording studio.

The digital sampler has taken its place alongside the digital synthesizer as an instrument for musical performance. It often comes with a clavier-style keyboard and a library of sampled sounds of acoustic music instruments and sound effects, and even electronically synthesized sounds. The digital sampler is usually controlled from the computer by a MIDI interface (see section 12.3) that enables real-time computer control. Finally, "outboard" digital sound modification hardware includes digital reverberators and sound processors that have become standard equipment in recording studios and in live computer music performance. These devices use special-purpose digital hardware to realize sound modification algorithms such as reverberation, flanging, and equalization in real time. In many of these devices, the inputs can be changed in real time using the same sort of MIDI control applied to digital synthesizers and digital samplers.

Under the heading of score preprocessors and composition programs in figure 1.7, we have listed a few of the literally thousands of programs that have been written to assist in the creation of music with computers. Score preprocessors and composition programs can be used for a variety of musical purposes. For example, the program may provide a facility to express a musical idea or motive, such as a scale, in a set of symbols that the computer can translate into a code for the computer synthesis system. Alternatively, the computer may take the user's input and perform the desired calculations and then present its output in music notation for instrumental performance.

In its original form, the Music N family of computer synthesis software had very simple facilities for expressing the relationships among musical events—scores. Score input in this form (using lists of alphanumeric characters) offers special difficulties for the musician. In a conventional musical score, time runs from left to right and musical detail is shown vertically. In a computer music score, time runs from top to bottom with the musical detail on the horizontal dimension. Example 1.1 shows score input for one of the most common current Music N languages, Csound, for the music in the example. Each line in the score input for the language consists of an alphabetic code, i, followed by numerical values. The alphabetic code denotes the type of statement (only statements that generate notes are shown), and the numbers represent parameter values that will be passed to an instrument. Each parameter resides in a "field" called a p-field. In example 1.1, the code makes use of five p-fields. In the Csound coding "1" is in the first p-field, "0" is in the second, "1" is in the third, and so on.

The coding in our example assumes a rather simple computer instrument using only the parameters of instrument number, starting time, duration, frequency, and amplitude. *Frequency* and *amplitude* are acoustical attributes of tones corresponding to pitch and loudness, respectively. (See chapter 2.) Pitch is specified in hertz (cycles per second).

```
i1 0 1 284 20000
i1 1 1 329 20000
i1 2 1 370 20000
i1 3 1 392 20000
i1 4 1 440 20000
i1 5 1 493 20000
i1 6 1 554 20000
i1 7 1 568 20000
```

EXAMPLE 1.1 Music example and its coding in Csound for a simple instrument with five parameters.

The choice of the amplitude value of 20,000 to represent the dynamic level *mf* in the score is an arbitrary decision. The actual value would vary from system to system.

The disadvantages of the score encoding shown in the example above are obvious—too many keystrokes with too little visual or conceptual similarity between the musical score and the computer score. Solutions to these problems (by more efficient and intuitive score encoding) are shown below, but for certain kinds of computer music—ones employing a few events played on complex instruments to which many parameters are passed—this sort of coding is quite efficient. It is precisely this kind of score that was used to good advantage for Variations 7–8 of J. K. Randall's *Lyric Variations for Violin and Computer*.[14] Each "note" or event consists of many parameter values which control the complex, evolving sonorities. Since each event is so complex and extended, relatively few notes are needed to create a very rich texture. In the Randall example, only 12 notes are played in the entire two-minute section of music; the notes, each 20 seconds in duration, enter singly and overlap the succeeding note by 10 seconds.

A score preprocessor provides a useful facility for entering certain types of music into the computer. It is particularly useful for music with many notes intended to be played on relatively simple computer instruments. Score preprocessors enable the musician to express the notes of a composition in a sort of shorthand. From this description, the preprocessor creates the note list in the format required for input to the particular music synthesis program. One of the score preprocessors made in the late 1970s and still in use today is Score 11. Originally made for score input to the Music 11 language (a direct predecessor of Csound), Score 11 provides input to the Music *N* family of languages. Example 1.2 shows the Score 11 text for the scale shown in example 1.1.

Common Music,[15] created by Heinrich Taube, is a truly general computer language for music composition. Common Music offers the user a broad range of compositional input options and then the choice of exactly in what form to present the output. The possibilities range from output to a computer music notation system for instrumental performance, through the score format for a number of direct digital synthesis systems, to the

```
i1 0 8;
p3 rh 4*8;
p4 no d4/e/fs/g/a/b/cs5/d;
p5 nu 20000;
end;
```

EXAMPLE 1.2 Score 11 code for the scale of Example 1.1.

MIDI code to drive external MIDI devices. The LISP-like format of the language takes some getting used to for the uninitiated, but the musical rewards can be considerable.

HMSL (Hierarchical Music Specification Language)[16] is another language that provides the facility for specifying compositional algorithms. Initiated around 1980 by Larry Polansky, David Rosenboom, and Phil Burk and continuing to evolve since then, HMSL is especially well-suited for creating computer music that involves some sort of compositional process. The language was devised to provide a facility for communicating musical information in real time, and literally hundreds of composers have used the HMSL language to create real-time, interactive compositions. See the description of the music of Polansky in chapter 12 for examples of how HMSL has been applied in his music.

Other languages designed to enable computer music in real time include MAX and Cypher. MAX, named for the inventor of direct digital synthesis (and much, much more) Max V. Mathews, was written by Miller Puckette when he was at IRCAM. It was subsequently expanded by David Zicarelli at Opcode Systems, where the software is published for use on Apple Macintosh computers. MAX is a "graphical programming environment for developing real-time musical software applications."[17]

Cypher is Robert Rowe's language for creating music in real time.[18] Typically, Cypher is used to create computer music in real time on the basis of the musical activity it senses in the live performance of another (usually human) performer. It does this by "listening" to the other player and creating its own music to fit with it on the basis of pre-established rules and data.

The computer music languages described above use lines of text to describe musical events and have been used to create a large portion of the computer-music literature. This approach propagated, in part, because the display of graphical information on a computer screen was originally so technically difficult that it was only found on sophisticated systems in major research centers. Today, text-based programs still enjoy wide usage, especially for the creation of complex musical events, but the excellent computer graphics available even on inexpensive personal computers have led to the development of a wide variety of programs for composing and editing music that display data graphically. Graphics have the advantage of being able to present significantly more information on a screen than text.

Many of the commercially available programs for processing music are called *sequencers* because they control a sequence of events. One of the earliest programs for specifying and controlling a series of musical events was developed as part of the GROOVE system which was in use at Bell Laboratories from 1968 to 1979.[19] The program ran on a minicomputer and provided the signals required to drive an analog synthesizer. A particularly useful feature was the ability to compile the actions of a performer and then make the record available for editing. In this way, Max Mathews was able to implement his Conductor Program which divided the activities into three steps: (1) score input, (2) rehearsal, and (3) performance. The score, a note list consisting of pitches and durations, was entered one note at a time from a keyboard. In rehearsal mode, the musical parts were played separately and then edited to adjust phrasing, accents, dynamics, and other aspects of the performance style. During performance, aspects such as tempo, dynamic level, and balance could be manipulated.

Modern sequencer programs make much the same division of activity. Computer graphics enable a series of events to be displayed in several different ways. Two standard methods are the traditional common music notation (CMN) and the piano-roll notation. In the latter format, events are shown as rectangles. The vertical position of the rectangle indicates the pitch of the event and the length of the rectangle designates the duration.

The time-base parameter of a sequencer program sets the temporal resolution available to the composer. It usually measured in ticks per quarter note.

Sequencer programs can allow the entry of musical information by several means. An event can be specified by typing a particular set of codes from a computer keyboard, it may be input graphically using a mouse or other pointing device, or it might come from performing an event on a traditional musical interface such a piano-style keyboard which has been connected to the computer through the appropriate interface.

Editing is an important function of a sequencer program. Modifications may be applied to a single event, groups of events, or on a continuous basis.[20] In the latter case, a particular parameter is applied across a specified range of time rather than to specific events. For example, the imposition of a decrescendo over a time frame affects the loudness during every event falling in that range.

The *scope* of an edit specifies the range to be modified. Programs differ in the types of scopes available, but they all allow a sequential groups of notes to be selected. This feature permits a designated group to be modified with operations that are usually directed toward motivic manipulation such as transposition or inversion (see section 11.2). The group of events can also be replicated to another place in the score. More sophisticated programs permit nonconsecutive events to be placed in the scope of an edit. For example, a composer could specify that all instances of F♮ be changed to F♯ over a range of measures. Or one might want to increase the amplitude of the first note of every measure to accent it.

Sequencer programs are generally installed on systems that incorporate digital synthesis hardware. In addition to creating the possibility of live performance, this feature affords the composer the valuable opportunity to hear and refine a work in progress. The playback capability can include the ability to specify a scope such as certain lines or particular groups of notes. A section of the score can be "looped" so that it plays over and over. Some programs allow manual variation of the tempo during playback and some enable immediate transposition of pitch as the score plays.

NOTES

1. Pope, S. T., and van Rossum, G. "Machine Tongues XVIII: A Child's Garden of Sound File Formats." *Computer Music Journal,* 19(1), 1995, 25–63.

2. Vercoe, B. *Reference Manual for the MUSIC 11 Sound Synthesis Language.* Cambridge: Experimental Music Studio, MIT, 1979.

3. Mathews, Max V. *The Technology of Computer Music.* Cambridge: MIT Press, 1969.

4. Gather, John-Philipp. *Amsterdam Catalogue of Csound Computer Instruments.* Self-published, 1995.

5. Moore, F. R. "The Computer Audio Research Laboratory at UCSD." *Computer Music Journal,* 6(1), 18–29.

6. Garton, Brad. "Using Cmix." *ICMA Array*, 13(2) 1993, 23–24.

7. Lohner, H. "The UPIC System: A User's Report." *Computer Music Journal*, 10(4), 1986, 42–49.

8. Erbe, Tom. "Soundhack Manual." Lebanon, N.H.: Frog Peak Music, 1994.

9. Macintosh is a trademark of Apple Computer, Inc.

10. UNIX is a registered trademark of AT&T.

11. Protools is a product of Digidesign.

12. Dyaxis is a product of Studer Editech.

13. Sonic Solutions is a trademark of Sonic Solutions, Navato, Calif.

14. Randall, J. K. "Lyric Variations for Violin and Computer." Open 5, Red Hook, N.Y., 1993.

15. Taube, H. "Common Music: A Musical Composition Language in Common Lisp and CLOS." *Computer Music Journal*, 15(2), 1991, 21–32.

16. Polansky, L., Burk, P., and Rosenboom, D. "HMSL (Hierarchical Music Specification Language): A Theoretical Overview." *Perspectives of New Music*, 28(2), 1980, 136–178.

17. Puckette, M. "Something Digital." *Computer Music Journal*, 15(4), 1991, 68.

18. Rowe, R. *Interactive Music Systems: Machine Listening and Composing.* Cambridge: MIT Press, 1993.

19. Mathews, M. V., and Moore, F. R. "GROOVE—A Program to Compose, Store, and Edit Functions of Time." *Communications of the ACM*, 13(12), 1969, 715–721.

20. Yavelow, C. "MIDI and the Apple Macintosh." *Computer Music Journal*, 10(3), 1986, 11–47.

2

The Acoustics and Psychoacoustics of Music

Acoustics is the study of the physics of the production, transmission, and reception of sound. It quantifies the energy, time variation, frequency content, and location of a sound. However, this study is not sufficient to describe the way things "sound." The workings of the ear, nervous system, and brain all affect our perception of sound. *Psychoacoustics* is the study of the way humans perceive sounds. Here, the concern is with the subjective response to the sound in terms of its pitch, loudness, duration, timbre, and apparent location. Although the categories of psychoacoustics reflect the divisions of acoustics, there is, in fact, considerable interrelationship among them. For example, our sensation of pitch is time dependent, and our perception of loudness varies considerably with pitch and timbre. This chapter will present the basic measurements of acoustics, describe the transducer mechanism of the human ear, and then discuss the psychoacoustic response of pitch, loudness, duration, and timbre. Chapter 10 explores the role of location in the perception of sound.

The study of the literature of psychoacoustics can be a great aid in making computer music, but it must be remembered that the musician's ear is the final arbiter in determining how to use the computer as a musical instrument. Thus, the principles discussed below are offered as guidelines to help the musician take full advantage of the capabilities of the medium.

2.1 SOUND AND THE EAR

Sound is produced by a vibrating source. The vibrations disturb the air molecules that are adjacent to the source by alternately pulling apart and pushing together the molecules in synchronism with the vibrations. Thus, the sound source produces small regions in the air in which the air pressure is lower than average (*rarefactions*) and small regions where it is higher (*compressions*). These regions of alternately rarefied and compressed air propagate away from the source in the form of a sound wave much in the same manner as the troughs and crests of an ocean wave. When a sound wave impinges on a surface (e.g., an eardrum or microphone), it causes that surface to vibrate in sympathy with the wave. In this way, acoustic energy is transferred from a source to a receptor (listener) while retaining the characteristic vibration patterns of the source.

The pattern of pressure variations in time produced by a sound is known as the *waveform* of the sound. Figure 2.1 illustrates the waveform of a simple tone. When the waveform is above the axis, there is compression; points below the axis indicate rarefaction.

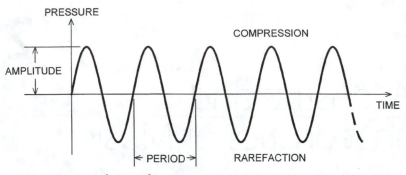

FIGURE 2.1 Periodic waveform.

Examination of the waveform in the figure reveals that it is made up of a repeating pattern. Such a waveform is called *periodic.* The smallest complete unit of the pattern is known as a *cycle,* and the amount of time occupied by a single cycle is known as a *peri-od* (see figure 2.1). For sounds in the range of human hearing, waveform periods vary between approximately 0.00005 and 0.05 second. Two units of time found useful in acoustics are the *millisecond* (ms), which is one-thousandth (0.001) of a second, and the *microsecond* (μs), which is one-millionth (0.000001) of a second. Thus, the range above (0.00005 to 0.05 second) can be alternatively expressed as 50 μs to 50 ms.

The rate at which the cycles of a periodic waveform repeat is called the *frequency* of the waveform. Frequency is measured in hertz (Hz), formerly known as cycles per second. Frequency is the mathematical inverse of period, and so a waveform with a peri-od of 1 ms has a frequency of 1000 Hz (i.e., there are 1000 repetitions of a cycle each second). A useful unit of measure for describing frequencies in the upper audio range is the *kilohertz* (kHz) which represents 1000 Hz. The range of human hearing is approxi-mately 20 Hz to 20 kHz, although this varies somewhat among listeners and listening conditions. Frequency correlates physically with the perceived tone height, or pitch, of a sound, so that tones with higher pitches have higher frequencies. (See section 2.2.)

Amplitude is the amount of change, positive or negative, in atmospheric pressure caused by the compression/rarefaction cycle of a sound. It is indicative of the amount of acoustic energy in a sound and is the most important factor in the perceived loudness of a sound. (See section 2.4.) Figure 2.1 illustrates the amplitude of the waveform shown. Amplitude is measured in Newtons per square meter (N/m^2)—that is, as a force applied over an area. The threshold of audibility represents an amplitude of approximately 0.00002 N/m^2. At the other end of the range, an amplitude of 200 N/m^2 is the threshold of feeling at which the entire body senses the vibrations.

The *intensity* of a sound characterizes the rate at which energy is delivered in the audible sensation associated with amplitude. Intensity is a measure of the power in a sound that actually contacts an area such as the eardrum. It is proportional to the square of the amplitude. That is, if the amplitude of a sound doubles, the intensity increases by a factor of 4. Intensity is expressed as power applied over an area in watts per square meter. The range of intensities that a human can perceive is bounded by 10^{-12} W/m^2 at the threshold of audibility and 1 W/m^2 at the threshold of feeling.

The intensity of a sound is perceived nearly logarithmically. This is one of the two principal modes of perception; the other is linear. A phenomenon is logarithmic if a change between two values is perceived on the basis of the *ratio* of the two values. In this case, a change from 0.1 to 0.2 (a ratio of 1:2) would be perceived as the same amount of increase as a change from 0.4 to 0.8. Therefore, in the perception of acoustic energy, a reduction in the intensity of a tone from 0.1 W/m² to 0.01 W/m² will be judged to be similar to a reduction from 0.001 W/m² to 0.0001 W/m².

In the case of linear perception, the change between two values is perceived on the basis of the *difference* between the values. Thus, a phenomenon is perceived linearly if a change from 0.1 to 0.2 is judged to be the same amount of increase as a change from 0.7 to 0.8.

The *decibel* (dB) is a logarithmic unit of relative measurement used to compare the ratio of the intensities of two signals. The decibel is proportional to the logarithm of the ratio of two intensities and, therefore, is particularly well suited for the purpose of comparing the intensities of two sounds. The ratio, R_I, of two signals with intensities I_1 and I_2, respectively, is given in decibels by:

$$R_I = 10 \log_{10} \frac{I_1}{I_2} \quad [\text{dB}]$$

By convention, a base-10 logarithm is used.

Although the decibel was defined to compare the intensity of two signals, it has commonly come to be used to compare the amplitudes of two signals as well. The ratio in decibels, R_A, of two signals with amplitudes A_1 and A_2, respectively, is given by:

$$R_A = 20 \log_{10} \frac{A_1}{A_2} \quad [\text{dB}]$$

This use of the decibel is proper only when the amplitudes are measured under the same set of conditions. For example, two signals of the same amplitude on two different computer music synthesis systems could well have different intensities, and so the above equation could not be used correctly. In most cases on a single system, however, the decibel is both a correct and a convenient means of comparing amplitudes. For example, when an amplitude doubles, the increase corresponds to 6 dB.

The decibel is sometimes used to give absolute measurement of acoustic intensity. Implicit in this kind of measurement is the existence of a reference "sound-pressure level" to which the signal is being compared. In acoustics, the reference sound-pressure level is generally taken as the threshold of audibility. A sound at that level has a value of 0 dB SPL, where SPL denotes sound-pressure level. Conversational speech has an intensity of approximately 60 dB SPL, while shouted speech is closer to 80 dB SPL. A sound at the threshold of feeling has a level of 120 dB SPL, and so the range of audibility (120 dB) represents a ratio in amplitudes of one to one million. To put the SPL scale in perspective, figure 2.2 shows the range of intensities that can be produced by several well-known sound sources.

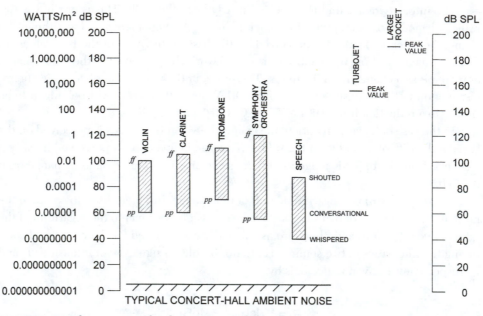

FIGURE 2.2 The intensity of audio sources on the SPL sound scale.

The shape of a cycle of a periodic waveform has a large effect on the way it sounds. We will discuss waveshapes in more detail in section 2.6. At this point, we will introduce the simplest and most fundamental pattern of vibratory motion, the *sinusoid*. The periodic waveform diagrammed earlier in the section (figure 2.1) is an example of a *sinusoidal* pattern. Its characteristically smooth shape shows no abrupt changes in pressure and there are no sharp points on the waveform. When the waveform is at a point near 0, it has a steep slope indicating that the pressure is changing quickly. At points near both the positive and negative peaks of the waveform, the pressure is changing more gradually, resulting in the rounding of the tips of the waveform as shown. Sinusoidal oscillations in sound can be approximated with a struck tuning fork when the sound has almost died away; that is, the tines of the vibrating fork move up and down in a nearly sinusoidal manner, producing sinusoidal variations in air pressure. A perfectly sinusoidal sound waveform is difficult to generate by mechanical means, but electronic systems can generate very accurate sinusoids.

To gain an understanding of sinusoidal motion, consider the motion of the spoke in the wheel shown in figure 2.3. Suppose that the radius of the wheel (and, hence, the length of the spoke) is 1. Let's measure the height of the tip of the spoke above the axle for various positions of the wheel. When the spoke is lying horizontally, it is at the same level as the axle, and so the height is 0. When the spoke points straight up, the height is 1. When it points straight down, the height is –1, where the minus sign indicates that the tip is below the axle. Thus, for any position of the wheel, the height of the spoke tip always falls between –1 and +1.

Let the wheel rotate in a counterclockwise direction with a constant speed of one revolution per second. How does the height of the tip vary with time? Figure 2.4 shows

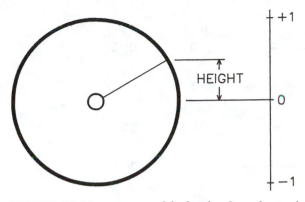

FIGURE 2.3 Measurement of the height of a spoke tip above the axle of a wheel.

the progress of the tip height, measured every 1/12 of a second, as the wheel turns. Our experiment begins as the spoke points horizontally to the right, and so the initial height is 0. After 1/12 of a second (0.083 second elapsed time), the tip height reaches a height of 0.500. By 2/12 of a second (0.167 second), the tip rises to 0.86, but the round shape of the wheel causes the tip height to increase more slowly as the tip gets closer to the vertical position. The spoke arrives at a height of 1 at 3/12 (0.25) seconds, thus completing one-quarter of a revolution. As shown in the figure, the tip height then begins to decrease, becoming 0 at an elapsed time of 6/12 (0.5) seconds when the spoke points horizontally to the left. The tip height then continues to decrease, taking on negative values. At 9/12 (0.75) seconds elapsed time, the spoke points straight down and the tip height takes on its most negative value, −1. The tip then starts to rise, crossing the original horizontal position at 1 second as the wheel finishes one revolution. If the wheel continues to rotate at the same speed, the pattern will repeat itself with a period of one second and, thus, with a constant frequency of 1 Hz.

The pattern traced by the height of the spoke tip *versus time* is known as a sinusoidal waveform. It represents the purest form of motion because it is produced only when the wheel turns smoothly with a constant rate. If the wheel turns in some other way, such as speeding up or slowing down during the course of a revolution, the spoke tip will move in a more complicated pattern. We will discuss the analysis and implications of complex waveforms in section 2.6.

We can use the spoke-in-the-wheel analogy to introduce another attribute of waveforms, *phase*. Phase provides a means to mark a specific point on a waveform or to compare the positions of two waveforms relative to each other. A circle encompasses an angle of 360° and so the spoke in the wheel rotates through an angle of 360° during the course of one revolution. In one revolution of the wheel, the sinusoidal motion of the height of the spoke tip goes through one cycle. Therefore, one cycle of a waveform is said to include 360° of phase. Instead of plotting the waveform versus time, it can also be plotted versus phase as in figure 2.5. This method of waveform representation is independent of frequency, because frequency indicates the rate at which the phase of a waveform changes. In other words, a waveform with a frequency of 1 Hz can also be

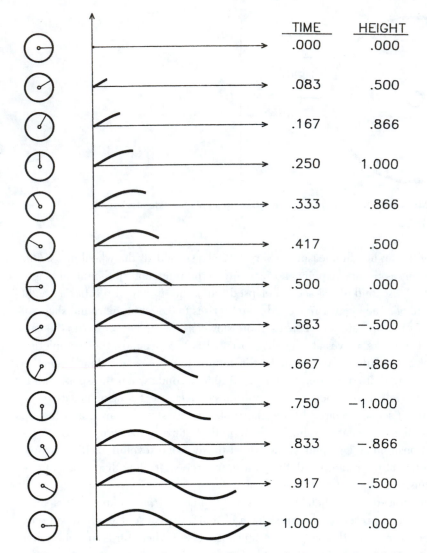

TIME	HEIGHT
.000	.000
.083	.500
.167	.866
.250	1.000
.333	.866
.417	.500
.500	.000
.583	−.500
.667	−.866
.750	−1.000
.833	−.866
.917	−.500
1.000	.000

FIGURE 2.4 Generation of a sine wave by tracing the time pattern of the height of a spoke tip on a rotating wheel.

characterized as exhibiting a phase rate of 360°/second, a 2-Hz waveform runs at 720°/second, and so on. In computer music, a particular waveform may be repeated at several different frequencies during the course of a composition in order to obtain different pitches. Hence, it is often useful in computer music to define a single cycle of a waveform only in terms of its phase. (See chapter 4.)

The phase of a particular point on a waveform is measured as an angle from some reference position, most commonly taken as the point where the waveform has a value of 0 and is increasing. On the wheel, this corresponds to the spoke pointing horizontally to the right. When the waveform is at the reference point, it has a phase of 0° degrees.

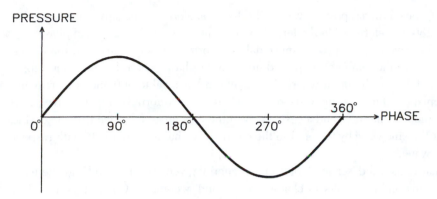

FIGURE 2.5 Representation of a waveform in terms of phase.

At its peak, the waveform has a phase of 90°, which on the wheel can be visualized as the 90° angle formed between the spoke standing vertically and the horizontal reference position. When the waveform is 0 and decreasing, the phase is 180°, indicating that the waveform is midway through a cycle of 360°. At its most negative value, the waveform has a phase of 270°, and when it returns to its original value of 0, the phase is 360°, or equivalently 0°, since the waveform is back to where it started.

Phase is also used to compare the relative position of two waveforms. One of the waveforms is chosen as a reference and the position of the other waveform is compared to it. For example, in figure 2.6, waveform A leads waveform B; that is, it reaches its peak amplitude before waveform B. (At first glance, this relationship might seem incorrect because B is shown to the right of A, but the horizontal axis represents elapsed time, so that points on the left happen earlier.) To quantify the relationship between waveforms, the distance between them is measured in terms of phase. In the figure, the difference between waveforms is 30°, and so waveform A is said to lead waveform B by 30°. Stated another way: the phase of waveform B with respect to A is –30°. A phase comparison of two waveforms is meaningful only when the waveforms have the same frequency or, in the more general case, when the ratio of the frequencies is an exact integer. A sinusoidal waveform that has a phase of 180° is exactly inverted from one with a phase of 0°. In other words,

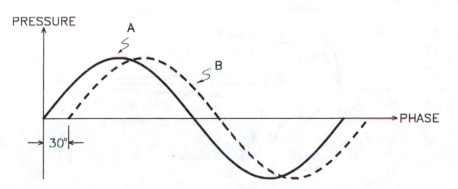

FIGURE 2.6 Phase comparison of two waveforms. Waveform A leads waveform B by 30°.

when the 0° waveform has positive values, the 180° waveform has negative ones, and vice versa. The 180° waveform is often referred to in the literature as being "out of phase."

There are two major types of sinusoidal waveforms: the *sine wave* and the *cosine wave*. They have the same shape; they differ only in phase. The reference phase for a sine wave is taken at the point where the waveform has a value of 0 and is increasing. The reference point on a cosine wave occurs when the waveform is at its positive peak. Figure 2.7 plots a sine wave and a cosine wave on the same axis. Notice that the cosine wave leads the sine wave by 90°, and so the cosine wave has a phase of 90° with respect to the sine wave.

The mathematical description of acoustic energy given above is the language used by acousticians and engineers to characterize sound accurately. Computers also deal with sound in these terms, so that such knowledge is necessary for computer musicians. However, because the results of their work are ultimately conveyed to listeners, it is also essential that they understand the mechanisms that enable humans to respond to acoustic energy.

Sound received by the ear is processed by the auditory system, which extends from

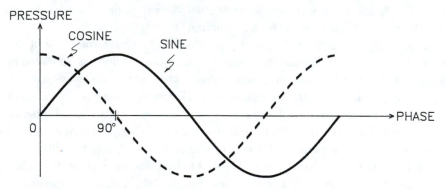

FIGURE 2.7 Cosine wave plotted relative to a sine wave.

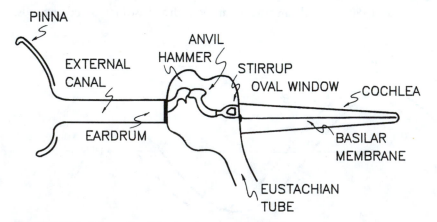

FIGURE 2.8 Schematic of the hearing apparatus of the ear.

the outer ear to the cerebral cortex. The ear acts as a transducer, converting the mechanical motion of vibration patterns to neural impulses. Figure 2.8 illustrates the important parts of this physical apparatus. When the sound reaches the ear, it travels down the external canal to the eardrum. Here, it imparts its characteristic pattern of vibratory energy to the eardrum, which transmits vibration to the ossicles, a chain of three bones, the hammer, the anvil, and the stirrup. The stirrup transmits the motion to a membrane called the oval window, causing a traveling wave to propagate in the fluid in the cochlea, which, in turn, stimulates the hairs on the basilar membrane. Nerves attached to these hairs transmit the stimulus to the brain. When periodic, sinusoidal vibrations at frequencies within the range of audibility reach the inner ear, they excite nerve endings at places on the basilar membrane, proportional to the frequency of the tone.[1] The sensation of loudness is primarily determined by the amount of acoustical energy received by the ear.

The remaining sections of this chapter will describe the ways in which listeners analyze sound received by the ear to form a percept.

2.2   PITCH

Pitch is our subjective response to frequency. It is the main sensation caused by the stimulation of nerve endings on the basilar membrane.

The approximate range of audible frequencies is between 20 and 20,000 Hz. The frequencies from 200 to 2000 Hz comprise the region of greatest perceptual acuity and sensitivity to change of frequency. This region occupies two-thirds of the basilar membrane; the remaining high frequencies contact only one third of it. Discrimination of frequency for sinusoids becomes increasingly difficult when the duration of the tones presented to the listener grows shorter but is independent of amplitude.

For the listener to detect a change in frequency of a single sinusoidal tone, the change must be greater than the "just noticeable difference" (JND) in frequency. It is postulated by some that the JND corresponds to some minimum spatial separation between points of stimulus on the basilar membrane. The exact value of the JND, like so many psychoacoustical determinations, varies from one listener to the next and according to the method of testing. For the statistically "average" individual, the JND for isolated sinusoids is 3% at 100 Hz and 0.5% at 2000 Hz.[2]

There is a nonlinear relationship between pitch perception and frequency—the stimulation on the basilar membrane occurs at points almost exactly proportional to the logarithm of the frequency. For higher frequencies, at least, when the frequency doubles, the distance between the points of stimulation on the basilar membranes changes by approximately a constant distance (approximately 3.4 mm). Thus, listeners compare tones on the basis of the musical interval separating them—that is, on the basis of the ratio of their frequencies—rather than the difference between them. For example, the pitch interval of an octave corresponds to a frequency ratio of 2:1. We perceive this interval to be "the same" wherever it occurs in the frequency continuum. Figure 2.9 shows the frequencies of the piano keyboard. The piano keys are labeled with the notation for pitch used throughout this book: a pitch-class/octave notation where C4 designates middle C. Notice that the frequency of A3 (220 Hz) is exactly one-half the frequency of the tone an octave above, A4 at

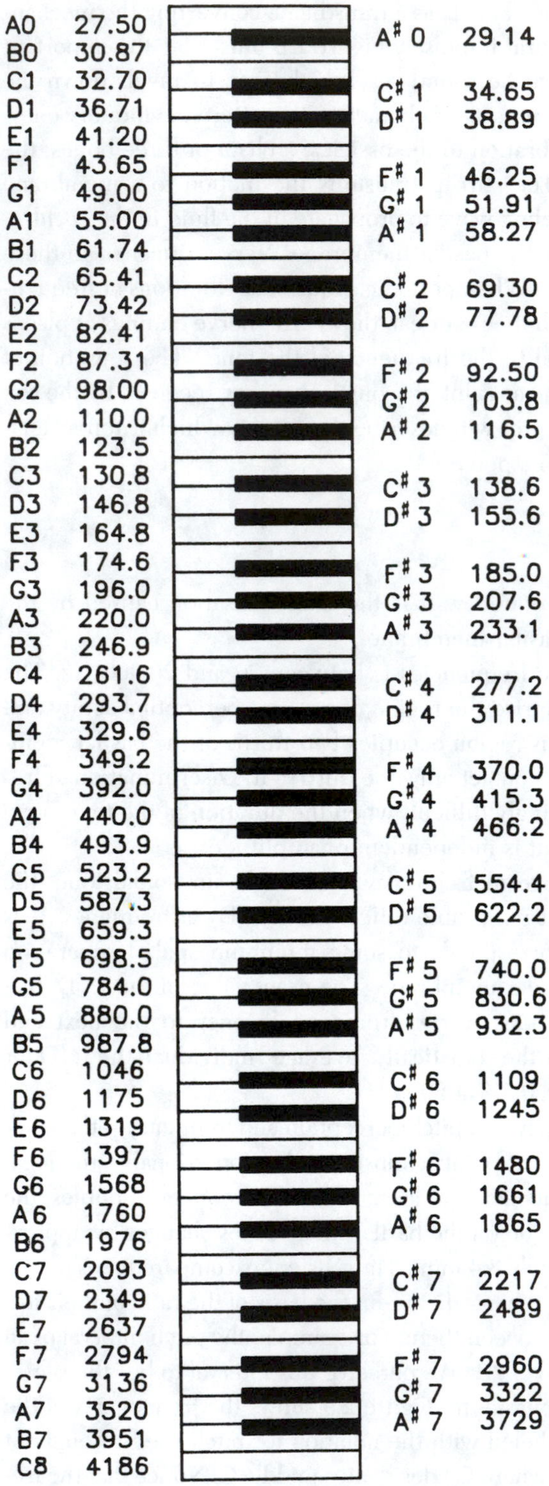

A0	27.50		A# 0	29.14
B0	30.87			
C1	32.70		C# 1	34.65
D1	36.71		D# 1	38.89
E1	41.20			
F1	43.65		F# 1	46.25
G1	49.00		G# 1	51.91
A1	55.00		A# 1	58.27
B1	61.74			
C2	65.41		C# 2	69.30
D2	73.42		D# 2	77.78
E2	82.41			
F2	87.31		F# 2	92.50
G2	98.00		G# 2	103.8
A2	110.0		A# 2	116.5
B2	123.5			
C3	130.8		C# 3	138.6
D3	146.8		D# 3	155.6
E3	164.8			
F3	174.6		F# 3	185.0
G3	196.0		G# 3	207.6
A3	220.0		A# 3	233.1
B3	246.9			
C4	261.6		C# 4	277.2
D4	293.7		D# 4	311.1
E4	329.6			
F4	349.2		F# 4	370.0
G4	392.0		G# 4	415.3
A4	440.0		A# 4	466.2
B4	493.9			
C5	523.2		C# 5	554.4
D5	587.3		D# 5	622.2
E5	659.3			
F5	698.5		F# 5	740.0
G5	784.0		G# 5	830.6
A5	880.0		A# 5	932.3
B5	987.8			
C6	1046		C# 6	1109
D6	1175		D# 6	1245
E6	1319			
F6	1397		F# 6	1480
G6	1568		G# 6	1661
A6	1760		A# 6	1865
B6	1976			
C7	2093		C# 7	2217
D7	2349		D# 7	2489
E7	2637			
F7	2794		F# 7	2960
G7	3136		G# 7	3322
A7	3520		A# 7	3729
B7	3951			
C8	4186			

FIGURE 2.9 Frequencies and pitches of the equal-tempered piano keyboard.

440 Hz, which is one-half the frequency of A5 (880 Hz). Follow a chromatic scale up the keyboard from A3 to A4. Observe that there is not a constant frequency difference between any two adjacent tones; that is, to find the frequency of a tone, one cannot simply add a constant to the frequency of the previous tone. Section 2.3 shows several systems for determining the frequency relationship among tones in music—tuning.

In actual practice, listeners generally receive sounds that are much more complex than the single sinusoid described above. When a sound comprised of multiple sinusoids reaches the ear, the cochlear fluid responds by assuming a motion that is a combination of the vibration patterns of the component frequencies. In this case, the pitch or pitches to be perceived depend(s) not only on the values of the frequencies themselves, but also on the relationship among them.

One possible relationship among frequencies is that they are related harmonically; that is, the frequencies are related as whole-number multiples. In this case, even though each harmonic tone stimulates a different spatial location on the basilar membrane, the perception will "fuse" into that of a single pitch at the *fundamental* frequency. The fundamental is the frequency that is the largest common divisor of the harmonically related frequencies. Each of the sinusoids is called a *harmonic* or *harmonic partial* of the tone and is given a number based on its ratio to the fundamental frequency. As an example, figure 2.10 shows a diagram of a complex periodic tone comprised of five harmonic partials. The fundamental frequency is 100 Hz, the second harmonic is at 200 Hz, the third harmonic is at 300 Hz, and so on, up to the fifth harmonic at 500 Hz. (For convenience, the fundamental may also be referred to as the first harmonic.) The figure shows how the harmonics add together to form the complex waveform.

Periodicity is thought to be a factor in our perception of a single pitch at the fundamental frequency when the multiple frequencies are harmonically related. As shown in

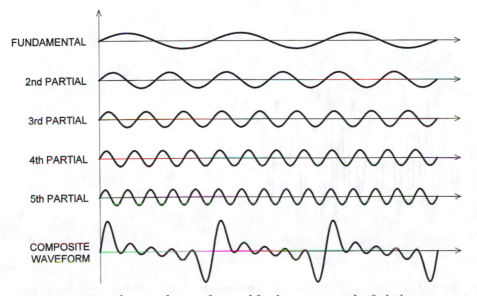

FIGURE 2.10 Complex periodic waveform and five harmonic partials of which it is comprised.

figure 2.10, when harmonic partials add together, they form a periodic waveform that repeats at the fundamental frequency. One theory postulates that our hearing mechanism traces with time the pattern of repetition of the waveform to determine the period of the waveform. The listener then accepts the frequency corresponding to the measured period as the fundamental frequency.

In the region of approximately 20 to 2000 Hz, the fusion of harmonic partials into the sensation of a single pitch operates even when the fundamental frequency is absent.[3] The remaining partials continue to form a pattern of repetition at the frequency of the difference in frequency between adjacent harmonics, that of the fundamental. Figure 2.11 shows two waveforms with the same fundamental frequency. The first (figure 2.11a) is comprised of partials 1 through 7; the second (figure 2.11b), of partials 4 through 7. Notice that the period of the two waveforms is identical, and therefore they will sound at the same pitch.

Two sinusoidal tones that are not harmonically related may reach the ear at the same time with the same amplitude. If the frequency ratio of the two tones is sufficiently

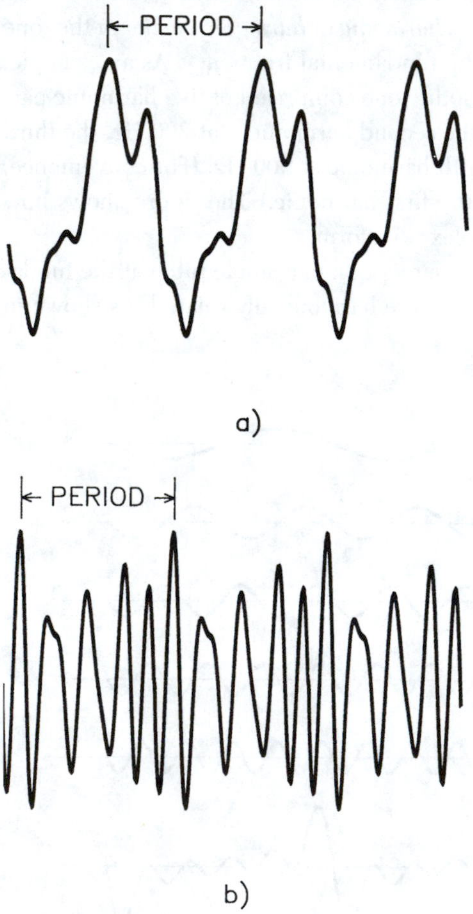

a)

b)

FIGURE 2.11 (a) Three cycles of a waveform containing harmonics 1 through 7. (b) Three cycles of a waveform containing only harmonics 4 through 7.

large, two distinct tones will be perceived. For instance, a tone at 111 Hz sounded with one at 1055 Hz (1:9.5) will create the percept of two separate tones. When the frequency ratio of the two tones is very small, the listener will perceive a single pitch at the average of the two frequencies. For example, two sine tones at 219 and 220 Hz will be perceived to have the same frequency as a single tone at 219.5 Hz.[4] In addition, closely spaced tones produce a sensation of beating at a rate that is the *difference* between the frequencies of the two tones. Thus, the two sine tones in the example cause a beating sensation of one beat per second. The beating is perceived as a periodic change of the amplitude of the resultant tone. Figure 2.12 illustrates this situation.

A phenomenon similar to the beating of two fused tones occurs when two tones are tuned close to an octave. The beating occurs at a rate corresponding to the difference between the frequency of the tone near the octave and the frequency exactly an octave above the lower tone. This "beating of mistuned consonances" disappears above around 1500 Hz.[5]

Beating between tones can also be observed, although much more weakly, when the difference between the two tones occurs at or near the interval of the pure fifth (3:2 in frequency ratio) or the pure fourth (4:3 in frequency ratio). For example, violinists tune the open strings by listening for beats between strings tuned a fifth apart.

The inclusion of nonharmonic partials in a sound ensures that, in most circumstances, beats will be heard. Beating can, in turn, help the tone to sound more lively. Section 4.12 includes a particularly good example of Jean-Claude Risset's compositional use of beats among the harmonics of complex tones that are tuned within a few hundredths of a hertz of each other.

Two closely tuned pure tones will cause a beating sensation until the difference between their frequencies exceeds about 10 to 15 Hz. Within the region of beating lies the *limit of discrimination:* a point at which the frequency separation of two tones is sufficiently large for the listener to perceive two separate tones. At separations just outside the range of beating, there is a region described by acousticians as *tonal roughness.* This percept is associated with the *critical band,* which determines the ability of the ear to discriminate adjacent tones. According to this theory, when the ear receives two tones

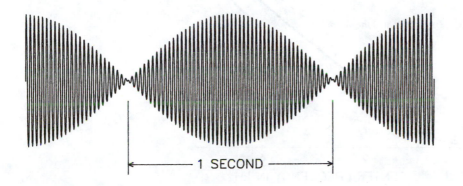

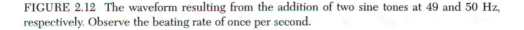

FIGURE 2.12 The waveform resulting from the addition of two sine tones at 49 and 50 Hz, respectively. Observe the beating rate of once per second.

close in frequency, there will be a certain amount of overlapping of the neurons stimulated on the basilar membrane. This phenomenon causes the sensation of two tones to be more complex than it would be for tones with greater separations. The frequency difference between tones at which the sensation abruptly changes from roughness to smoothness is known as the critical band.[6]

The width of the critical band varies with the frequency. It is a large percentage of the average frequency of two tones that are at low frequencies, and a small percentage for two tones of high frequencies. Figure 2.13 shows the change of width of the critical band with frequency. Above about 440 Hz, the width of the critical band is roughly constant at around one-fourth of an octave—that is, around the musical interval of a minor third (around 19%). The fact that the critical band is a larger interval at low frequencies helps explain the common usage of larger musical intervals in the bass register of most music. The width of the critical band plays a role in the perception of loudness and timbre, as well.

2.3 MUSICAL TUNING

Most computer-music synthesis systems offer the musician complete freedom of choice with respect to tuning. This situation differs greatly from the fixed intonation of many acoustic and some electronic instruments. Indeed, the freedom to choose a particular tuning scheme for music has encouraged experimentation in composition with intervallic relationships unavailable before computers. In the following section, we will describe the properties of four common systems for tuning: equal temperament, Pythagorean tuning, just intonation, and meantone tuning.

Equal temperament with 12 semitonal divisions of the octave is by far the most common system of musical intonation used today in Western music for keyboard instru-

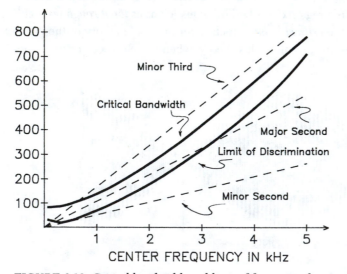

FIGURE 2.13 Critical bandwidth and limit of frequency discrimination as a function of center frequency. (*Based on* Introduction to the Physics and Psychophysics of Music, *by Juan C. Roederer. Published with the permission of Springer-Verlag, Heidelberg, Germany.*)

ments. In the general case of equal temperament, an interval I is divided into a number of intervals N all of equal size (i.e., all having equal *ratios* of frequency). The expression for calculating the basic equal-tempered division, i, in the particular tuning system is $i = I^{1/N}$ (i is the interval I raised to the $1/N$ power). For the 12-tone equal-tempered system, the basic division of the octave ($I = 2$) is the semitone, and so $i = 2^{1/12}$. Thus, two adjacent tones in this system tuned a semitone apart have a frequency ratio of $1{:}2^{1/12}$, or 1:1.05946. For instance, the pitch A4 has a frequency of 440 Hz; the next semitone, A♯4, sounds at $440 \times 1.05946 = 466.2$ Hz.

The generalized ratio for any interval in the system is $i = 2^{m/12}$, where m is the number of semitones comprised in the interval. For example, the ratio for the equal-tempered perfect fifth (7 semitones) is $1{:}2^{7/12}$, or 1:1.49828. Table 2.1 summarizes the frequency ratios for the intervals in 12-tone equal temperament. All equal-tempered intervals of the same size have the same frequency ratio and thus "sound the same." This fact enables the transposition of music in equal temperament to any pitch level without its becoming "out of tune." The generality of the equal-tempered collection comes at what for most is a minor expense: the intervals that result from the tempering are only close to, but not exactly, those with the simple ratios of the harmonic series. Thus, all the intervals of the equal-tempered collection, except the octave, will "beat".

To facilitate comparisons and measurements of tuning, the octave is divided into 1200 equal parts. The smallest division is called a cent, with a frequency ratio $1{:}2^{1/1200}$, or 1:1.0005778. Thus, the octave is accorded 1200 cents, and the equal-tempered semitone has 100 cents; that is, $1200 \div 12 = 100$. The perfect fifth of equal temperament comprises seven semitones and has 700 cents.

The *Pythagorean* and *just* tuning systems are made with very different musical goals

	EQUAL TEMPERAMENT		PYTHAGOREAN		JUST		MEAN–TONE	
	Ratio	Cents	Ratio	Cents	Ratio	Cents	Ratio	Cents
Unison	1:1	0	1:1	0	1:1	0	1:1	0
Aug unis					1:1.055	92	1:1.045	76
Mi 2nd	1:1.059	100	1:1.053	90	1:1.067	112	1:1.070	117
Maj 2nd	1:1.122	200	1:1.125	204	1:1.125	204	1:1.118	193
Mi 3rd	1:1.189	300	1:1.185	294	1:1.200	316	1:1.196	310
Maj 3rd	1:1.260	400	1:1.265	408	1:1.250	386	1:1.250	386
P 4th	1:1.335	500	1:1.333	498	1:1.333	498	1:1.337	503
Tritone	1:1.414	600						
Aug 4th			1:1.404	588	1:1.406	590	1:1.398	580
Dim 5th			1:1.424	612	1:1.422	610		
P 5th	1:1.498	700	1:1.500	702	1:1.500	702	1:1.496	697
Mi 6th	1:1.587	800	1:1.580	792	1:1.600	814	1:1.600	814
Maj 6th	1:1.682	900	1:1.687	906	1:1.667	884	1:1.672	890
Aug 6th					1:1.778	996	1:1.747	966
Mi 7th	1:1.782	1000	1:1.778	996	1:1.800	1018	1:1.789	1007
Maj 7th	1:1.888	1100	1:1.898	1109	1:1.875	1088	1:1.869	1083
Octave	1:2	1200	1:2	1200	1:2	1200	1:2	1200

TABLE 2.1 Comparison of frequency ratios for four tuning systems

from equal temperament. Here, the object is to create a collection of pitches—a scale, usually—from the simple ratios found in the harmonic series. The rationale usually given for this is that these are "beat-free" intervals. In other words, the tones form many of the same intervals found between members of a harmonic series—for example, 3:2, 5:4, 6:5, 9:5, and so on. As we see below, some of the intervals created in the just and Pythagorean systems are quite distant in size from their equal-tempered namesakes.

In Pythagorean tuning, the harmonic ratios 3:2 and 4:3 are invoked to generate all the tones of a particular scale. For example, to generate the tones of the key of C, we create an upper tone, "G," at 3:2 in frequency to "C," then down to "D," a tone at the ratio of 4:3 to "G." The upper fifth to "D" is "A." "E," the lower fourth to "A," is followed by its upper fifth, "B." The octave of "C" is based on the 2:1 ratio, and the final tone of the scale, "F," is the lower fifth to the upper "C." Figure 2.14 shows the frequency ratios of the individual tones to "C" and to their neighbors. We can replicate the scale in any octave to make a full gamut for musical use. Notice, however, that the scale has no sharps or flats. When we use the same method (3:2 frequency ratio) to generate all 12 tones, a *comma*, or disparity in intonation, results. As an example, consider the cycle C, G, D, A, E, A, E, B, F♯, C♯, G♯, D♯, A♯, E♯, B♯. The frequency ratio between any two adjacent pitches in the cycle is 3:2, and so the frequency of B♯ can be calculated by multiplying the frequency of the fundamental C by 3/2 twelve times. Therefore, the frequency ratio between the B♯ twelve-fifths above the fundamental C and the fundamental is $(3/2)^{12}:1$, or 129.74634:1. The enharmonic equivalent of that B♯, namely C, is seven octaves above the fundamental C, a frequency ratio of $2^7:1$ or 128:1. Thus, there is a considerable difference in intonation between C and B♯. This *Pythagorean comma*, which has a frequency ratio of 129.74634:128, or 1.01364:1 (a disparity of 23.5 cents), is clearly audible.

In the system of just tuning, we generate a scale with beat-free major and minor thirds (5:4 and 6:5, respectively) as well as pure fourths (4:3) and fifths (3:2). Figure 2.15 shows the frequency ratios of tones in a diatonic just scale to "C" and to their neighbors. One of the just system's great virtues is that some of its most frequently used triads (I, IV, and V) are built of the beat-free ratios 4:5:6. One of the scale's problems lies in the unequal size of its major seconds. As a result, certain intervals in the system create obvious beating. The diatonic just system can also include all 12 tones by dividing each whole step into two semitones. The problems are such that, for keyboard instruments, most compositional use of the system—in order to preserve a maximum of pure inter-

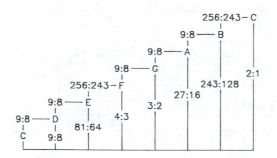

FIGURE 2.14 The frequency ratios of the tones to C and to their neighbors in Pythagorean tuning.

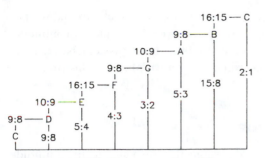

FIGURE 2.15 The frequency ratios of the tones to C and to their neighbors in just intonation.

vals—must employ diatonic pitch collections that avoid modulations to keys that are more than two sharps or flats away.

Meantone tuning represents something of a compromise between the Pythagorean and just tuning systems. It results in major thirds that are slightly smaller than those of the Pythagorean system and minor thirds that are slightly larger. The fifths and fourths deviate from pure intervals, as well.

The scale tones of meantone tuning are generated by a cycle of fifths in which each fifth is lowered from the 3:2 ratio by about 5 cents, resulting in a ratio of 1.49533:1. This method of lowered fifths is used in extending the system to include sharps and flats, as well (traditionally, C♯, F♯, G♯, B♭, and E♭). In music with wider use of accidentals, the system begins to break down. One reason for this is the so-called "wolf fifth" produced by the interval G♯–E♭. It comprises a full 739 cents and is more than a third of a semitone sharp.

Table 2.1 compares the four intonation systems discussed. The composer of computer music freely chooses the intonation system according to the design and demands of the music. Of course, the tuning for acoustic instruments will not always be in agreement with these schemes. It is well documented that the piano, usually thought of as an ideal instrument for playing in equal temperament, is actually tuned with the size of its octaves "stretched." The stretched octaves relate to the inharmonicity in the tones of the piano themselves, and suggest a relationship between timbre and tuning that some composers, most notably Wendy Carlos, have advocated.[7]

Moreover, studies have shown that nuance in performance of vocal and instrumental music includes stretching the musical intervals in ways that do not conform to any standard intonation system. This is often due to the function of the pitches in the musical context, and the stretching is expected by the listener.

Much computer music has been made using 12 equal-tempered divisions of the octave, but many different systems have been invented and employed, as well. Jon Appleton,[8] Clarence Barlow,[9] Gary Kendall,[10] and Larry Polansky,[11] to name only a few, have made computer music outside the 12-tone equal-tempered system. Polansky has used a variety of approaches to incorporating just intonation in his music. One idea he has implemented, uniquely suited to computer music, is "adaptive tuning"—that is, music in which the size of the intervals between tones is calculated to accommodate different musical contexts.[12]

Section 5.11 examines John Chowning's *Stria*, which employs a unique system for interrelating frequencies in music—by equal-tempered divisions of a pseudo-octave made by projecting the golden-mean ratio (1:1.618 . . .) over the frequency continuum. Section 10.3B will describe Gerald Bennett's use of another tuning system, based on the measurement of the salient events in a recording of a Native American instrument, in his piece *Rainstick*.

2.4   PERCEPTION OF AMPLITUDE

The *loudness* of a sound is a measure of the subjective response to its amplitude. Loudness is strongly influenced by the frequency and spectral composition of the sound. Thus, the minimum detectable change in amplitude of a tone—its JND in amplitude—depends on both the spectral content and the amplitude of the tone. Generally, in the musically relevant ranges of frequency and amplitude, the JND in amplitude for a sine tone is between 0.2 and 0.4 dB.[13] Figure 2.16 shows a comparison of the JNDs for pure tones at 70, 200, and 1000 Hz.

Figure 2.17 displays the contours of a *Fletcher-Munson curve*. The contour lines represent the amplitude levels at which single sine tones of different frequencies sound equally loud. For example, the figure shows that near the threshold of audibility, in order for pure tones of 100 and 1000 Hz to sound equally loud, the amplitude of the lower tone must be boosted by almost 40 dB. The figure also demonstrates that the ear is most sensitive to sound in the range from 250 to 3000 Hz, and that below 60 Hz and above 10 kHz the loss of sensitivity is considerable.

When the listener is presented with more than one tone, the perceived loudness varies with the frequency and amplitude relationships among the tones. This is a result of *masking*—the reduction in sensitivity to amplitude due to the fatigue of neurons on the basilar membrane. Thus, in the presence of a louder tone, a soft one may not be heard at all. The threshold of masking is defined as the amplitude level at which the soft-

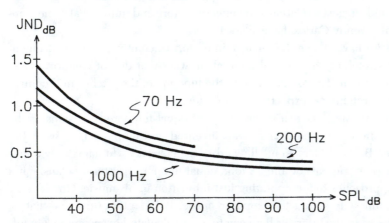

FIGURE 2.16   Just noticeable difference (JND) in sound pressure level for three frequencies. (*From* The Acoustical Foundations of Music, *by John Backus. Published with permission of W. W. Norton Co., Inc.*)

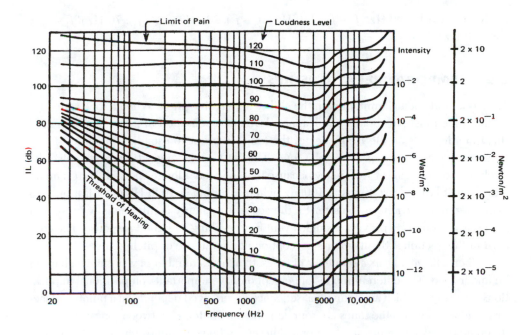

FIGURE 2.17 Fletcher-Munson diagram of equal loudness for tones of different frequencies. (*Reprinted from* Introduction to the Physics and Psychophysics of Music, *by Juan C. Roederer with the permission of Springer-Verlag, Heidleberg, Germany.*)

er tone disappears. It depends strongly on the frequency difference between the tones, on the amplitude of the louder tone, and to a lesser extent on the frequency of the louder tone. Masking is particularly effective when the tones occupy the same critical band. In many cases, a tone that has an amplitude of only 15 to 20 dB less than a stronger one will not be perceived. When the tones are close enough in frequency to cause beating, the masking threshold is slightly reduced. For two loud tones outside the same critical band, the tone with the lower frequency more easily masks the upper tone. Low-amplitude sounds outside the same critical band do not generally mask each other.[14]

Masking occurs not only for simultaneous tones, but also for tones that occur in succession. Under many circumstances, the neuron fatigue caused by a louder, previous tone can affect our perception of a softer, subsequent tone.

Whenever a pure tone sounds with sufficient loudness, the ear creates "aural harmonics" not present in the tone. For example, a loud 1-kHz tone can produce sensations at 2 kHz, 3 kHz, and so on. In addition, a pair of tones with frequencies f_1 and f_2 causes the aural system to add tonal sensations, "combination tones," that are combinations of the presented frequencies. The strongest additional sensation is a tone at the difference in frequency of the two tones $(f_2 - f_1)$. With complex tones, sensations occur at the differences in frequency between the fundamentals and all their harmonics. The most noticeable products are defined by the relationships of $2f_1 - f_2$ and $3f_1 - 2f_2$. The sensation is fainter for higher harmonic numbers. For instance, the most significant additional sensations produced by the two loud, complex tones at 150 Hz and 190 Hz, respectively, are heard at 40 Hz $(f_2 - f_1)$, 110 Hz $(2f_1 - f_2)$, 230 Hz $(2f_2 - f_1)$, 70 Hz $(3f_1 - 2f_2)$, and 270 Hz $(3f_2 - 2f_1)$.

2.5   TEMPORAL RELATIONSHIPS

Time is a fundamental limitation on the ability to perceive pitch. When a tone sounds, a certain time must pass before the listener develops a sensation of pitch. The length of this time depends on the frequency of the tone. In order to establish pitch, a listener must receive a number of cycles of a tone. Thus, it takes a longer time to perceive the pitch of a tone at a lower frequency because that tone has a longer period. For example, a tone must last at least 40 ms at 100 Hz, whereas a tone at 1000 Hz must last only 13 ms.[15] In granular synthesis (chapter 8), the acoustical energy is intentionally presented in very short bursts to prevent a single event from evoking a pitched response. The concern in this section is the listener's perception of a sequence of pitched tones.

When a listener hears a sequence of tones, there are a number of ways in which it can be understood. The different modes of perception have important compositional implications. The way in which any individual sequence is perceived depends on a number of factors: the rate at which the tones are sounded, the pitch interval between tones, amplitude differences between tones, and timbral differences between tones, among others. The foremost determinant is the compositional context in which they are presented. While the results of scientific tests such as those described below are useful for determining general perceptual principles, the results can change with the experience and expectations of the listeners. For example, a theme or motive in a work, once well established, can be presented in ways normally thought to render it melodically incomprehensible and still be understood. The electronic works of Milton Babbitt contain examples of this effect.

In the examples that follow, we will consider sequences played on a single instrument with little variation in dynamic level. This will enable us to show more clearly the effect of both the rate at which the sequence is played and the pitch interval between members. The three primary ways of perceiving a sequence are: as a single line, as divided into multiple sublines, or as fused into a single sound.[16] In the first case, where the sequence is heard as a single line, it is said to evoke temporal *coherence*. The second case, where the listener partitions the sequence into two or more separate lines, is known as *fission*. Several of the organ works of J. S. Bach include sections that demonstrate this effect. The last case, where the sequence is played so rapidly that it forms a single audible entity, is known as *fusion*.

Consider a melodic line of 11 tones where the even-numbered tones and the odd-numbered tones are separated in register. As shown in figure 2.18a, at a rate of 5 or 6 tones per second, a listener would hear the sequence as a coherent succession. At a faster tempo—10 to 12 tones per second (figure 2.18b)—the high tones group together to form a separate stream from the low tones. At an intermediate tempo, around 7 or 8 tones per second, one can direct one's attention to any one of three percepts: a succession of alternating high and low tones, a stream of higher tones by themselves, or a stream of lower tones. At a high tempo (> 20 tones per second), the listener will perceive the line as a fusion into a single complex sonority.

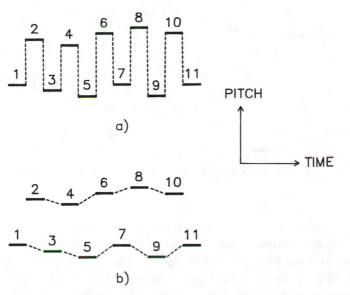

a)

b)

FIGURE 2.18 (a) Perception of a sequence of tones sounded at five or six tones per second as temporally coherent. When the same sequence is played at 10 to 12 tones per second, fission can occur as shown in (b).

The size of the interval between the adjacent tones in the sequence will affect the speed at which the sense of temporal coherence gives way to fission. In the case of a trill, when the interval separating the two alternating tones is small, around one half step, the sequence evokes temporal coherence until the alternation rate is accelerated beyond about 20 tones per second. One then hears a fusion of the two tones into a single sound. However, with a sequence of tones comprised of large intervals in the general range of a 12th, even at moderate speeds the listener can split the tones into successions by register.

Alternation of two tones at high rates can produce other effects as well. Consider the rapid alternation of two tones separated by a large interval: even when the higher tones are not equidistant in time between the lower ones, the high and low tones will sound evenly spaced. Figure 2.19 illustrates this situation. The effect would be lost at small pitch intervals.

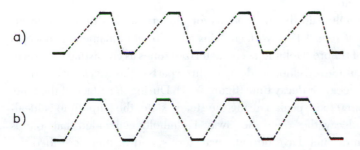

a)

b)

FIGURE 2.19 At high speeds and large melodic intervals, tone sequence (a) with uneven rhythms sounds like the tone sequence (b).

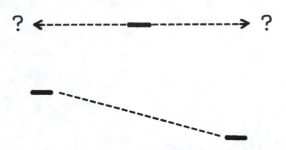

FIGURE 2.20 At large intervals and rapid speeds, it may be difficult to tell where in the sequence the high note sounds.

When a rapid two-tone sequence is played at a small interval, a whole or half step, the order of the two tones is easily perceived. However, when the intervals are greatly increased, the situation becomes more complicated. To some listeners, the tones sound simultaneous, while to others, the order of the two tones is unclear. At high speeds where the tones jump between registers over large intervals, the listener loses the effect of a constant speed. The passage will appear to consist of subphrases proceeding at different rates.

This effect can be even more ambiguous in a three-tone sequence. Figure 2.20 illustrates very rapid sequences of three tones with which a wide registral span separates one tone from the other two. Even though the listener perceives the two tones in the same register as belonging to the same group, it may not be possible to determine the temporal order of the other tone.

2.6   CLASSICAL THEORY OF TIMBRE

Musical *timbre* is the characteristic tone quality of a particular class of sounds. Musical timbre is much more difficult to characterize than either loudness or pitch because it is such a diverse phenomenon. No one-dimensional scale—such as the loud/soft of intensity or the high/low of pitch—has been postulated for timbre, because there exists no simple pair of opposites between which a scale can be made. Because timbre has so many facets, computer techniques for multidimensional scaling have constituted the first major progress in quantitative description of timbre since the work of Hermann von Helmholtz in the 19th century.

Hermann von Helmholtz laid the foundations for modern studies of timbre in his book, *On the Sensations of Tone*.[17] This work contains a wealth of fundamental concepts necessary for the study of timbre. Helmholtz characterized tones as consisting of a waveform enclosed in an amplitude envelope made up of three parts—the attack, or rise time; the steady state; and the decay, or decay time (figure 2.21). During the attack of the tone, the amplitude grows from 0 to its peak. During the steady state, the amplitude is ideally constant. During the decay, the sound dies away. Helmholtz concluded that sounds which evoke a sensation of pitch have periodic waveforms, and further described the shape of these waveforms as fixed and unchanging with time. He also established that the nature of the waveform has a great effect on the perceived timbre of a sound.

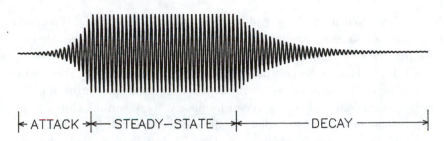

← ATTACK → ← STEADY–STATE → ← ——————— DECAY ———————— →

FIGURE 2.21 The three principal segments of a tone that takes the form of a Helmholtz model.

   To determine which characteristics of a waveform correlate best with timbre, he made use of the work of Jean Baptiste Fourier, who proved that any periodic waveform can be expressed as the sum of one or more sine waves. As an example, consider the two sine waves illustrated in figure 2.22a and b, in which the lower wave repeats with three times the frequency of the upper. If at every point in time (along the horizontal axis) we add the values of these waveforms together, the sum will be the entirely new periodic waveform drawn in figure 2.22c. Fourier showed that every periodic waveform is comprised of a unique set of sinusoids whose frequencies are harmonically related (see section 2.2). Thus, any waveform can also be described in terms of the sinusoidal components that it contains. Each sinusoid in the set is characterized by three parameters: frequency, amplitude, and phase relative to the fundamental (see section 2.1). The first two parameters have a large effect on the perceived timbre of the sound. However, the phase relationships among the

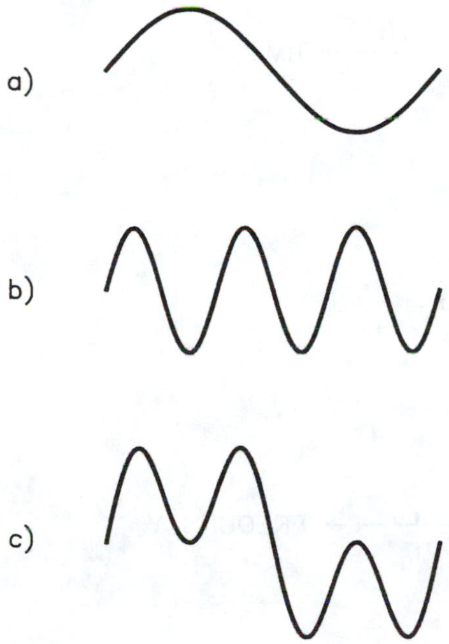

a)

b)

c)

FIGURE 2.22 The addition of two sinusoids, (a) and (b), to obtain the complex waveform (c).

sinusoids have only a minimal effect and will be discussed near the end of this section. Spectral components are sometimes called the *partials* of a waveform, and in the case of a harmonic spectrum, they can be called *harmonics* or *harmonic partials*.

In the general case, Fourier demonstrated that any signal, regardless of whether its waveform is periodic, can be described either by its pattern of amplitude versus time (its waveform) or by its distribution of energy versus frequency (its spectrum). Either form of this dual representation is sufficient to describe the signal completely. Thus, it is common to speak of the two *domains* in which a signal can be described: the time domain and the frequency domain.

The spectrum of a waveform is found mathematically by taking the Fourier transform[18] of the waveform—a complex mathematical procedure, the specifics of which are outside the scope of this text, although chapter 7 will detail the application of Fourier transforms to digital signals to extract spectral information.

It can be instructive for the musician to develop a sense of the relationship between a sound's waveform and its spectrum. Figure 2.23a illustrates the waveform of a square wave: a waveform that spends 50% of the time at its most positive sound pressure and the other half at its most negative sound pressure. The period of the waveform is denoted by T. The waveform repeats at its fundamental frequency f_0, which is related to the

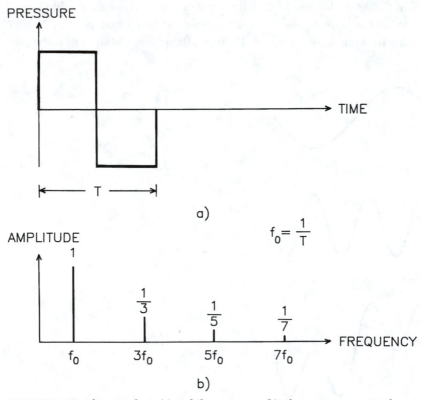

FIGURE 2.23 The waveform (a) and the spectrum (b) of a square wave. Each vertical bar in (b) corresponds to a single spectral component.

period by the equation shown in the figure. The spectrum of a square wave, shown in figure 2.23b, contains components that are odd harmonics of the fundamental. The amplitudes of the components diminish with increasing harmonic number in proportion to the harmonic number. Thus, for example, the amplitude of the seventh harmonic is one-seventh of the amplitude of the fundamental. To demonstrate that this is indeed the spectrum of a square wave, we can build a cycle of the waveform by simple addition of the sound-pressure patterns of the individual components of the spectrum. This process is called *additive* or *Fourier synthesis*. (Chapter 4 details this basic synthesis technique.) Figure 2.24 shows the results of adding the first N harmonics found in a square-wave spectrum for different values of N (i.e., the highest frequency found in the waveform is Nf_0). Observe that the higher the number of harmonics included, the more "square" the waveform becomes. Even after 15 harmonics are added together, the waveform is still not perfectly square. The reason for this is that a "perfect" square wave could exist only in a system allowing an infinite number of harmonics.

Figure 2.25 illustrates the waveforms and spectra of some other signals commonly encountered in analog electronic music studios. As might be expected, the spectrum of a sine wave is very simple. A sine wave has no harmonics, and so its spectrum contains energy only at a single frequency (figure 2.25a). Figure 2.25b shows a triangular wave and its spectrum, which contains only odd-numbered harmonics. The amplitude of the harmonics falls off with frequency in proportion to the square of the harmonic number ($1/N^2$). Thus, for example, the amplitude of the fifth harmonic is 1/25 of the amplitude of

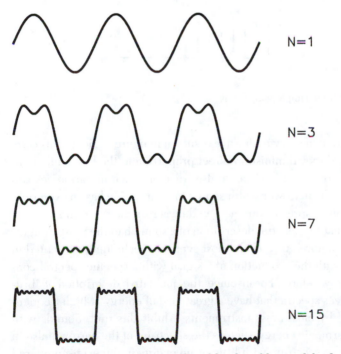

N=1

N=3

N=7

N=15

FIGURE 2.24 The waveform produced by the addition of the first N partials of a square-wave spectrum.

WAVEFORM   SPECTRUM

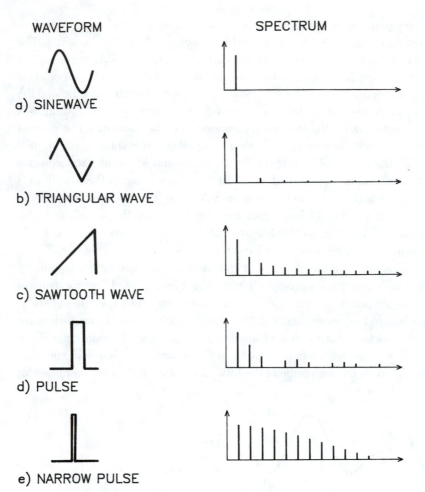

a) SINEWAVE

b) TRIANGULAR WAVE

c) SAWTOOTH WAVE

d) PULSE

e) NARROW PULSE

FIGURE 2.25 The spectra of some simple waveforms.

the fundamental. The spectrum of a sawtooth wave is shown in figure 2.25c. In this case, all harmonics are present and they diminish in direct proportion to the harmonic number. Figure 2.25d shows the relation between a pulse waveform rich in harmonics and its spectrum. The pulse with the narrower width shown in figure 2.25e has an even richer spectrum, hence its energy is spread even more widely across the spectrum.

Helmholtz concluded that the spectral description of a sound had the most straightforward correlation with its timbre. As a result, most synthesis techniques presented in this text will be concerned with the production of a signal with a specific spectral content, rather than a particular waveform. For instance, the qualitative description of "brilliant" or "bright" characterizes spectra that have a great deal of energy at high frequencies. The spectra produced by most brass instruments exhibit this trait. Sounds with extreme amounts of high-harmonic energy, such as the spectrum of the narrow pulse in figure 2.25e, sound "buzzy." A spectrum with little or no energy in the even-numbered harmonics characterizes the particular timbre that is produced by the clarinet in its low

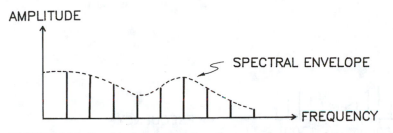

FIGURE 2.26 Graphical approximation of a spectral envelope from a spectral plot.

register. Most percussive sounds have spectra that are not even close to being harmonic. For example, the clangorous sound of a bell is the result of its highly inharmonic spectrum. In addition, research has shown that many pitched acoustical instruments exhibit spectra that are slightly inharmonic; that is, the overtones are slightly mistuned from exact harmonics. This characteristic causes the sensation of beating in the tone, contributing to its liveliness.

The *spectral envelope* of a sound is one of the most important determinants of timbre. The spectral envelope outlines the distribution pattern of frequency energy in a spectrum. The spectral envelope of a periodic waveform can be graphically approximated by connecting the tops of the bars in a plot of harmonic amplitude versus frequency. Figure 2.26 shows how a spectral envelope is approximated from a spectral plot.

Examination of the spectral envelopes of the waveforms most frequently encountered in both digital-synthesis and acoustic-instrument tones shows them to be "band-limited." That is, there is a frequency above which the tones contain no significant amount of acoustic energy. (Of course, the ear is also a band-limited receiver because it can sense energy only within a certain frequency range.) The *bandwidth* of a sound is the width of the frequency region in which significant components of a complex sound reside—one of a number of useful means of characterizing spectra. Spectra are often characterized by the swiftness at which the energy in the spectrum decreases with frequency. This measure is known as the *rolloff* of the spectrum and is the slope of the spectral envelope. For example, the amplitudes of the harmonics of a sawtooth wave (figure 2.25c) roll off in proportion to the harmonic number. Thus, the spectral envelope diminishes by a factor of 2 for each doubling in frequency. Recall from section 2.1 that halving an amplitude can be expressed as a reduction of 6 dB, and so the rolloff of a sawtooth wave is 6 dB/octave. In the triangular wave of figure 2.25b, the amplitudes of the harmonics roll off with the square of the harmonic number. In this case, doubling the frequency reduces the spectral envelope by a factor of 0.25 or 12 dB, resulting in a slope of 12 dB/octave. Max Mathews and J. R. Pierce have observed that "normal musical instruments tend to produce a spectrum which decreases faster than 6 dB per octave, but not as fast as 12 dB per octave."[19]

For the synthesis of sound, we need a more detailed understanding of the relationships among fundamental frequency, spectrum, and timbre. If two tones with the same amplitude envelope and about the same fundamental frequency have identical relationships among their spectral components, their timbres will sound the same; however, if

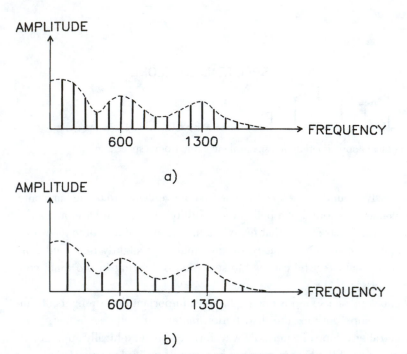

FIGURE 2.27 Spectra on tones with different fundamental frequencies—100 Hz in (a) and 150 Hz in (b)—exhibiting similar formant structures.

two tones of different fundamental frequencies have the same distribution of energy among their partials, they often will not be judged to have the same timbre. Our perception of timbral similarity is largely based on the presence of spectral energy in absolute-frequency bands. Therefore, the triangular wave in figure 2.25b will not have the same timbre in all registers. For a fundamental frequency of 50 Hz, the predominant energy of the triangular wave will be in the region 50 to 450 Hz; a triangular wave with a fundamental frequency at 250 Hz will have most of its energy in the frequency region 250 to 2250 Hz.

Two tones with different fundamental frequencies that are judged to have similar timbres will not have the same relationships among the amplitudes of the spectral components. Rather, their spectral envelopes will exhibit peaks of energy in the same frequency regions. In figure 2.27a, the spectrum of the 100-Hz tone has peaks around its sixth and thirteenth partials (i.e., around 600 and 1300 Hz). The 150-Hz tone (figure 2.27b) has peaks around its fourth and ninth harmonics, in the same frequency regions as those of the 100-Hz tone. Given other similar characteristics, these two tones will be judged to have similar timbres. The spectral peaks in absolute-frequency regions are called *formants*. Composer A. Wayne Slawson has explicitly used formants as a compositional element (see section 6.10).

Human voices and most acoustic instruments exhibit formants in their spectra. Their characteristic sound results from a system consisting of an excitation source, such as vocal cords or a vibrating reed, and a resonating system, such as the vocal tract or a length of

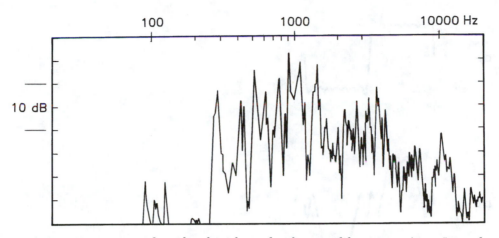

100   1000   10000 Hz

10 dB

FIGURE 2.28 Response of a violin plate obtained with sinusoidal excitation. (*From "How the Violin Works," by C. M. Hutchins, in* Sound Generation in Winds, Strings, Computers, *Publication No. 29 of the Royal Swedish Academy of Music, edited by Johan Sundberg. Reprinted with permission of the editor.*)

tubing. The resonating system causes the amplitudes of the partials occurring in certain frequency regions to be emphasized. This produces formant peaks in those regions, which are related to the size, shape, and material of the resonating body. The same peaks will be present, in greater or lesser prominence, on all tones of the instruments, regardless of the fundamental frequency of the source. This explains why, in many instruments, different tones produced on the same instrument have a similar tone quality.

Figure 2.28 shows the resonances of the plate that forms the back of a violin.[20] Notice that the resonance peaks on the violin are quite narrow. Vibrato on the violin, a quasi-periodic, relatively small change in frequency of the tone at a rate of 5 to 10 Hz, produces a very lively sound. The peaks and valleys in the curve illustrate the frequency regions at which the partials caused by the bowing action will be resonated or attenuated. This is because the resonances produce spectral changes by attenuating and emphasizing the harmonics passing through them at the vibrato rate.

Formant peaks bear a relation to the critical bands of frequency perception. Adjacent harmonics above about the fifth fall within the same critical band; therefore, the listener can judge only the relative acoustic energy present in a general region of the frequency continuum. The strengths of the individual harmonics within a critical band combine to produce the percept of a net amount of energy present in that band. Thus, when presented with a rich spectrum, a listener will usually be unable to detect the presence of a single, high-numbered harmonic other than to note its contribution to the net energy found within a particular critical band.

As stated above, each component in a harmonic spectrum is characterized not only by an amplitude and a frequency, but also by a phase measured relative to the fundamental. For example, in a spectrum made up of cosine wave components with the same phase, when the fundamental waveform reaches its maximum value, all the other harmonics are also at their peak.

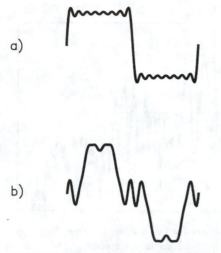

a)

b)

FIGURE 2.29 These two waveforms have the same spectral amplitudes but the phase between the partials is different. In (a) the square wave is generated with 15 partials, all of the same phase. In (b) the third and fifth partials have their phases opposite to the fundamental.

The phase of the components directly affects the shape of the periodic waveform. Figure 2.29a shows a square wave approximated by summing 15 harmonics, all of the same phase. Figure 2.29b shows the quite different waveshape that results from setting partials 3 and 5 to a phase of 180°. (When the fundamental peaks, the third and fifth harmonics are at their most negative value.) Helmholtz observed that changing the phase of partials has, as a rule, a minimal effect on the perceived quality of the sound, even though the shape of the waveform can be radically different. Therefore, when repeated with the same frequency, the two waveforms in the figure would produce essentially the same timbre. Studies using computers to generate waveforms with spectra of arbitrary phase have confirmed that a change in the phase of components produces a small change in timbre (small in comparison with the result of changing the strengths of the harmonics). The greatest difference in timbre is between complex tones containing all sine or all cosine components and those containing alternate sine and cosine components. Still, the change in timbre is small; in one study, it compared to changing the slope of the rolloff of the harmonics by between 0.2 and 2.7 dB per octave.[21]

2.7 MODERN STUDIES OF TIMBRE

The Helmholtz model of musical sound, a fixed waveform in an envelope, represents the most significant work done in research on musical acoustics in the 19th century. Since then, researchers have attempted to determine more accurate models of natural sound. Digital recording has enabled the modern researcher to show that the waveform (and hence the spectrum) can change dramatically during the course of a tone.

Almost all recent studies of timbre have been based on analysis by synthesis. With this method, the validity of any analysis can be tested by resynthesis.

As mentioned in section 2.6, the Fourier transform enables researchers to obtain the spectrum of a sound from its waveform. A computer technique that performs a Fourier transform on a digital signal is the *discrete Fourier transform* (DFT). The DFT is computationally intensive, but through a clever ordering of the computer operations involved in performing a DFT, Cooley and Tukey were able to reduce the number of computer operations significantly. Their algorithm is known as the *fast Fourier transform* (FFT);[22] additional information on its characteristics and limitations will be given in chapter 7.

In his *Computer Study of Trumpet Tones* (1966), Jean-Claude Risset[23] employed an algorithm based on the FFT to gain information about the spectral evolution in trumpet tones. (The FFT by itself does not have sufficient resolution to determine accurately the spectrum of any arbitrary sound. However, if the fundamental frequency of the sound is evaluated prior to the application of the transform, the FFT can be made to estimate the harmonic amplitudes with relative precision. Other techniques, as described by Moorer,[24] have also been used.) Where Helmholtz and other early researchers applied a Fourier transform to the steady-state portion of the tone, Risset "windowed" the samples of the trumpet tone. That is, the tone was analyzed by taking the Fourier transforms in successions of small groups of a few hundred samples. The typical window width for analysis—5 to 50 ms (i.e., 20 to 200 windows per second)—enables one to "view" the sound as a succession of short-term spectra. In this way, Risset was able to determine the time behavior of each component in the sound. He found that each partial of the tone has a different envelope. This clearly contrasts with the basic Helmholtz model in which the envelopes of all the partials have the same shape.

Risset drew the following conclusions from his analyses: the spectrum of a trumpet tone is nearly harmonic; the higher harmonics become richer as the overall intensity increases; there is a fluctuation in the frequency of the tone that is fast, small in deviation, and quasi-random; successively higher harmonics have slower rises to maximum amplitude during the attack; and there is a formant peak around 1500 Hz.[25]

Issues raised in Risset's interpretations of the trumpet analyses have been elaborated in subsequent studies. Risset observed that the evolution in time of the trumpet's spectrum plays an important part in the perception of the instrument's characteristic timbre. Other researchers following Risset made systemic use of computer analysis to classify the spectral evolution of tones on a variety of instruments. James A. Moorer and John Grey have published computer analyses showing the evolution in time of the spectra of a violin tone,[26] a clarinet tone, an oboe tone,[27] and a trumpet tone.[28] As an example, figure 2.30 displays the spectral progression of a trumpet tone. Notice that no two partials have envelopes with the same shape. As Risset found, the higher harmonics attack last and decay first. In addition to the amplitude progression, the analyses determine the frequency variation of each partial in the tone. It was found that the partials are rarely precise harmonics. The frequency of each partial fluctuates during the course of the tone, and this fluctuation can be particularly erratic during the attack of the tone. Resynthesis of the tone without the fluctuations in frequency produced a discernible change in the character of the tone.

The spectral progression shown in figure 2.30 contains a great deal of fine-grained detail—small fluctuations in the amplitude of a given harmonic. Can such data be sim-

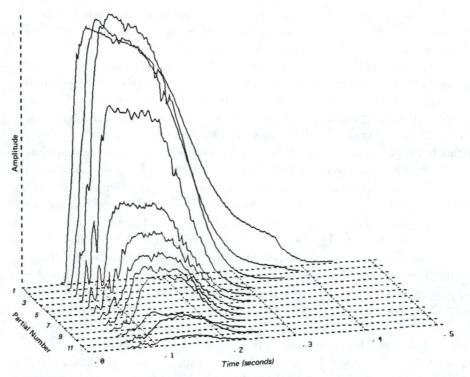

FIGURE 2.30 The amplitude progression of the partials of a trumpet tone as analyzed by Grey and Moorer. (*Reprinted with permission of* Computer Music Journal.)

plified and still retain the character of the tone that was analyzed? To find out, Grey, as Risset had done before him, approximated the amplitude variations of each partial with line segments, employing roughly eight segments per envelope. Using these simplified data, he was able to synthesize trumpet tones that were perceived to be virtually identical to the original recordings. Thus, the small, rapidly varying component of an amplitude envelope does not contribute significantly to the perception of timbre. Further, it was possible to approximate the frequency record of each partial with line segments and retain the character of the tone. In computer music, synthesis algorithms that directly recreate the partials of a tone (see section 4.7) generally use data stored as approximate line segments. This significantly reduces the amount of data required to represent a tone.

When viewing analyses such as those in the *Lexicon of Analyzed Tones,* it is important to be aware that resynthesis using the data is usually effective only within a small range of frequencies. For example, a tone based on the data but raised an octave from the original will most often not evoke the same sensation of timbre. Similarly, changing the duration often creates a different timbre. Further, patterns of spectral evolution differ markedly for differences in loudness. Risset has pointed out that, as the dynamic level increases, the higher partials of trumpet tones are raised in level relative to the other partials. For instance, the synthesis of a fortissimo tone taken from the analysis of a mezzo-piano tone will generally exhibit the "volume-control effect." That is, the increase in loudness will appear to be imposed on the tone rather than the natural result of the physics of the musical instrument. Certain of the models for synthesis discussed in later chapters include provisions for change of spectral-evolution pattern with change of loudness.

When presented with a group of spectral components, a listener may or may not fuse them into the percept of a single sound. One of the determining factors is the *onset asynchrony* of the spectrum, which refers to the difference in entrance times among the components. For example, the slower rise times of the higher partials during the attack portion of a tone have been investigated by Grey and Moorer[29] and McAdams.[30] Grey and Moorer found that the onset asynchrony was typically in the range of about 20 ms. McAdams has found, for synthesized examples, that if the onset asynchrony of components exceeds 30 to 70 ms, the spectral components form a less-strong percept of fusion into a single sound.

Rudolph Rasch[31] has noticed a related phenomenon with regard to the synchronization of tones in chords in polyphonic music. He has found that a certain amount of asynchrony in starting times of chord tones actually improves our ability to perceive the individual tones while we continue to perceive the chord as a whole. Rasch has shown that the effect obtains best when the attacks of the tones are spread over a time span of 30 to 50 ms. Beyond that limiting amount of asynchrony, however, the tones no longer seem simultaneous. They are heard as appearing in successive order.

The fluctuations in frequency of the various partials are usually necessary for the partials to fuse into the percept of a single tone. John Chowning[32] and Michael McNabb have demonstrated the importance of periodic and random vibrato in the perception of sung-vowel timbres. A demonstration tone first introduces the fundamental frequency, then adds the harmonics of the spectrum, and finally applies the vibrato to all the components. Chowning observed that it is only with the addition of the vibrato that the "tone fuses and becomes a unitary percept."

It is apparent that timbre is multidimensional. The perception of timbre involves correlating a number of factors of the tone, including the nature of the attack, the harmonic content, and the tuning of the partials. To some extent, the amplitude, pitch, and temporal aspects all contribute to our characterization of timbre. A number of researchers have sought a set of independent dimensions for timbral characterization.[33] In recent years, computer techniques for multidimensional scaling have aided in this research.

Unquestionably, the use of Fourier-based analysis techniques has greatly advanced our ability to synthesize a range of musical sounds that were previously denied to us. However, note should be made of some competing theories of musical timbre. Gerald Balzano, writing in the mid-1980s,[34] has argued the case for a physical-correlate model of musical timbre—a theory by which we designate similarity of timbre on the basis of how we believe the sound was made. Balzano, in this thought-provoking article, writes: "The kinds of things we are capable of hearing that are important for timbre perception are events like pounding, blowing, plucking, rolling, whistling, screaming, and all sorts of physical processes that words can only hint at but which are nonetheless specified in the underlying dynamics of the signal." Indeed, one line of modern acoustical research has to do with building computer-based models of the physical systems that produce sound (see chapter 9). With an accurate computer model of the physical instrument, the computer musician can "play" sounds that are related by the physical limits of the instrument. There are a number of different, often quite successful, approaches to physical modeling.[35]

Taking a very different approach, Dennis Gabor, in a seminal article,[36] proposes that Fourier analysis is not the most favorable way to approach a model of sound. He writes, "Fourier analysis is a timeless description in terms of exactly periodic waves of infinite duration. . . . [I]t is our most elementary experience that sound has a time pattern as well as a frequency pattern." Gabor argues for the creation of some mathematical technique for analyzing sound that would include the time/frequency duality of sound from the beginning. A synthesis technique known as *granular* synthesis has come into existence in an attempt to create the kind of sonic event that cannot be easily rendered using an approach based on Fourier synthesis.[37] We will detail granular synthesis in chapter 8.

Of considerable concern to composers of computer music is to find the means for creating sounds that represent systematic transformations from one recognizable timbre to another. A number of analytic tools provide facilities for creating this kind of "sound morph." The MQ analysis/Lemur synthesis package from the CERL group at the University of Illinois and the Soundhack analysis/synthesis system both provide facilities for sound "morphing." In fact, John Chowning's composition *Phonée*[38] provides a number of striking examples of sounds made by timbral interpolation between well-defined models. (See section 5.1I for a discussion of *Phonée*.) A. Wayne Slawson, too, has made systematic application of principles of timbral similarity to create compositional operations on timbre in his music analogous to those of pitch and rhythmic manipulation. We discuss his composition *Colors* in section 6.10.

In summary, the results of modern research into the nature of timbre offer valuable insights for the computer synthesist. Few "natural" sounds take the form of the classical model of an invariant waveform enclosed in an envelope. Instead, their spectral content varies substantially during the course of the tone. Listeners expect this characteristic in what they hear, and so an important key to synthesizing interesting sounds is the selection of algorithms that produce dynamic spectra.

2.8   MUSIC COGNITION

Increasingly, the use of the computer has enabled musicians to direct their attention not only to making music with the computer, but also to the study of the nature of musical understanding itself. The accuracy and flexibility inherent in the computer synthesis of sound has enabled psychoacoustical experiments to be performed to a level of detail previously unattainable. This new field has attracted the attention of some notable researchers, particularly those coming from the field of cognitive psychology.

Work in music cognition covers a range of issues from broad, culturally induced phenomena to those facets of our aural response that can be said to stem from innate processes at the level of neural impulses. However, most researchers in the field attempt to apply their efforts to articulating cognitive principles that hold for all people, regardless of their particular musical culture. While they are sensitive to cultural differences in music making and musical materials, some universal traits among the world's musical systems have been observed: "Among the universals built into the world's musics are (1) the use of discrete pitch intervals, (2) octave equivalence, and (3) the presence of four to seven focal pitches in an octave."[39]

One of the major contributions to our understanding of how the mind makes sense of sensory data from the ears is articulated in the seminal work *Auditory Scene Analysis* by psychologist Albert S. Bregman.[40] In introducing the field, Bregman takes the example of a sound spectrogram. He observes that the representation of sound in a spectrogram is not so very different from the way the basilar membrane is set up for audition: the x-axis of the spectrogram corresponds to time and the y-axis to the spread of frequencies along the membrane, from low to high. Bregman goes on to observe that with the addition of the ability to store the spectrographic information, even briefly, the mind is very much indeed like a reader of spectrograms, but with the major difference that the sounds that reach the inner ear for our consideration are rarely as clearly isolated as those shown in sound spectrograms. "The real world is a great deal messier," he observes. Thus, at the very foundations of the study of auditory scene analysis is a concern for how the mind assigns an order of groupings to the often confusing array of sounds it hears. Bregman makes the point that although the mechanisms of perceptual grouping are only now the subject of fruitful study, they are present even in small children—he gives the example of the infant who hears and tries to imitate the mother's voice while ignoring the squeaking sound of the rocking cradle.

A fundamental concept of auditory scene analysis is that of *auditory streams.* Bregman writes, "An auditory stream is our perceptual grouping of the parts of the neural spectrogram that go together." Stated another way, a stream can be thought of as a group of acoustical events that display sufficient congruity to be interpreted by the listener as an entity.[41] In the simplest case, a monophonic sound framed by silence will be perceived as a unit. In polyphonic music, composers can create auditory streams by strongly articulating a particular group of tones, or by introducing other forms of consistency such as a distinct timbre to the tonal sequence. This latter effect explains how a melody played on an oboe can slice through the sound of a symphony orchestra.

Other techniques are available to enhance the perception of streams. Registral displacement of the stream from the other voices is a common technique for highlighting a musical sequence. In a different approach, the spatial separation of the apparent source of a stream can be used to feature its sound. A sequential group of tones sounded with sufficient loudness may also be perceived as a stream, although in practice this technique is most often combined with timbral similarity. As previously described in section 2.5, the rate at which the tones are played can also affect the perception of streams, as can the listener's familiarity with the musical content of the stream.

A singular timbre is commonly used to distinguish streams, but an interesting compositional technique is to cross-fade from one timbre to another during the course of a stream. This evolution is most successful when the composer retains common elements such as a similar rhythmic pattern during the change. In other words, the percept of a stream may be lost if too many attributes are changed at the same time.

NOTES

1. Roederer, Juan C. *Introduction to the Physics and Psychophysics of Music* (2nd ed.). New York: Springer-Verlag, 1979, 21.

2. Ibid., 23.

3. Benade, Arthur H. *Fundamentals of Musical Acoustics.* New York: Oxford University Press, 1976, 66.

4. Roederer, 27.

5. Roederer, 39.

6. Scharf, Bertram. "Critical Bands." In J. V. Tobias (ed.), *Foundations of Modern Auditory Theory* (vol. 1). New York: Academic Press, 1970, 157–202.

7. Carlos, Wendy. "Tuning: At the Crossroads." *Computer Music Journal,* 11(1), 1987, 29–43.

8. Appleton, Jon. "Eros Ex Machina." On CD accompanying M. Mathews and J. R. Pierce, *Current Directions in Computer Music Research.* Cambridge: MIT Press, 1989, 74.

9. Barlow, Clarence. "Two Essays on Theory." *Computer Music Journal,* 11(1), 1987, 44–60.

10. Kendall, Gary. "Composing with a Geometric Model: Five-Leaf Rose." *Computer Music Journal,* 5(4), 1981, 66–73.

11. Polansky, Larry. "Paratactical Tuning: An Agenda for the Use of Computers in Experimental Intonation." *Computer Music Journal,* 11(1), 1987, 61–68.

12. Ibid.

13. Roederer, 81.

14. Backus, John. *The Acoustical Foundations of Music* (2nd ed.). New York: Norton, 1977, 143–146.

15. Ibid., 128.

16. Van Noorden, L. A. P. S. "Temporal Coherence in the Perception of Tone Sequences." Unpublished paper, Institute for Perception Research, Eindhoven, The Netherlands, 1975.

17. Von Helmholtz, Hermann. *On the Sensations of Tone.* London: Longmans, 1885. (The original English translation by Alexander J. Ellis was reprinted by Dover, New York, 1954.)

18. Bracewell, Ronald N. *The Fourier Transform and Its Applications* (2nd ed.). New York: McGraw-Hill, 1978.

19. Mathews, M., and Pierce, J. "Harmonic and Non-harmonic Partials." *IRCAM Rapports,* 28, 1980.

20. Hutchins, C. M. "Bowed Instruments and Music Acoustics." In Johan Sundberg (ed.), *Sound Generation in Winds, Strings, and Computers.* Stockholm: Royal Swedish Academy of Music, 1980.

21. Plomp, Reinier. *Aspects of Tone Sensation.* New York: Academic Press, 1976, 90.

22. Cooley, J. W., and Tukey, J. W. "An Algorithm for the Machine Computation of Complex Fourier Series." *Math Computation,* 19 (April), 1965, 297–301.

23. Risset, Jean-Claude. *Computer Study of Trumpet Tones.* Murray Hill, N.J.: Bell Telephone Laboratories, 1966.

24. Moorer, James A. "On the Segmentation of Continuous Musical Sound by Digital Computer." Report STAN-M-3, Center for Computer Research in Music and Acoustics, Stanford University, 1975.

25. Morrill, Dexter. "Trumpet Algorithms for Computer Composition." *Computer Music Journal*, 1(1), 1977, 46–52.

26. Moorer, J. A., and Grey, J. M. "Lexicon of Analyzed Tones (Part 1: A Violin Tone)." *Computer Music Journal*, 1(2), 1977, 39–45.

27. Moorer, J. A., and Grey, J. M. "Lexicon of Analyzed Tones (Part 2: Clarinet and Oboe Tones)." *Computer Music Journal*, 1(3), 1977, 12–29.

28. Moorer, J. A., and Grey, J. M. "Lexicon of Analyzed Tones (Part 3: The Trumpet)." *Computer Music Journal*, 2(2), 1977, 23–31.

29. Grey, John M., and Moorer, J. A., "Perceptual Evaluations of Synthesized Musical Instrument Tones." *Journal of the Acoustical Society of America*, 62, 1978, 454–462.

30. McAdams, Steven. "Spectral Fusion and the Creation of Auditory Images." In Manfred Clynes (ed.), *Music, Mind, and Brain: The Neuropsychology of Music*. New York: Plenum Press, 1982.

31. Rasch, Rudolph. "Aspects of the Perception and Performance of Polyphonic Music." Doctoral dissertation, Institute for Perception TNO, Soesterberg, the Netherlands, 1978.

32. Chowning, John. "Computer Synthesis of the Singing Voice." In Johan Sundberg (ed.), *Sound Generation in Winds, Strings, and Computers*. Stockholm: Royal Swedish Academy of Music, 1980.

33. Grey, J. M. "An Exploration of Musical Timbre." Doctoral dissertation, Stanford University, 1975.

34. Balzano, Gerald. "What Are Musical Pitch and Timbre?" *Music Perception*, 3(3), 1986, 297–314.

35. Cook, Perry. "SPASM, a Real-Time Vocal Tract Physical Model Controller." *Computer Music Journal*, 17(1), 1993, 30–44. Välimäki, V., and Karjalainen, M. "Digital Waveguide Modeling of Wind Instrument Bores Constructed with Truncated Cones." *Proceedings of the 1994 International Computer Music Conference*. San Francisco: Computer Music Association, 1994, 423–430. Smith, Julius III. "Physical Modeling Synthesis Update." *Computer Music Journal*, 20(2), 1996, 44–56.

36. Gabor, Dennis. "Acoustical Quanta and the Theory of Hearing." *Nature*, 159(4044), 591–594.

37. Roads, C. "Granular Synthesis of Sound." In C. Roads and J. Strawn (eds.), *Foundations of Computer Music*. Cambridge: MIT Press, 1985, 145–159.

38. Chowning, John. *Phonée*. Wergo (WER 2012–50), 1988.

39. Dowling, W. J., and Harwood, D. *Music Cognition*. Orlando: Academic Press, 1986, 4.

40. Bregman, Albert S. *Auditory Scene Analysis: The Perceptual Organization of Sound*. Cambridge: MIT Press, 1990.

41. Belkin, A. "Orchestration, Perception, and Musical Time: A Composer's View." *Computer Music Journal*, 12(2), 1988, 47–53.

3

Fundamentals of
Digital Audio

Section 1.4 introduced the basic configurations used in the application of computers to audio signals. This chapter will describe the process of converting analog signals to digital form and back again in some detail. The restrictions, errors, and limitations imposed by the numerical representation of an audio signal will be discussed. The final section addresses the issues raised by the speed at which digital audio can be synthesized or processed.

3.1   SAMPLING OF SIGNALS

When an acoustic wave strikes a microphone, a voltage is produced that varies in accordance with the pattern of the wave. To enable computer processing of the sound, this analog signal is converted to a sequence of numbers by applying it to an analog-to-digital (A/D) converter. The conversion process relies on the principle that, at any point in time, an analog electrical signal can be assigned an instantaneous value by measuring its voltage. For example, it is possible to state that exactly 3.01 seconds after a certain sound began, the corresponding electrical signal had a value of 0.7071 V.

The analog voltage that corresponds to an acoustic signal changes continuously, so that at each instant in time it has a different value. It is not possible for the computer to receive the value of the voltage for every instant, because of the physical limitations of both the computer and the data converter. (And, of course, there are an infinite number of instances between every two instances.) Instead, the analog voltage is measured *(sampled)* at intervals of equal duration. The output of the sampling process is a discrete or digital signal: a sequence of numbers corresponding to the voltage at each successive sample time. Figure 3.1 shows a signal in both digital and analog form. Observe that the analog signal is continuous; that is, every point on the waveform is smoothly connected to the rest of the signal. The digital signal is not continuous because it consists of a sequence of specific values sampled at discrete times. In the literature of engineering, this method of representing an analog signal by a sequence of numbers is known as *pulse code modulation* (PCM).

The amount of time between samples is known as the *sampling interval* or *sampling period.* Its inverse, the number of times the signal is sampled in each segment, is called the *sampling rate* or *sampling frequency* (f_s) and is measured in hertz (samples per second).

One might assume that the more samples taken of a phenomenon, the more accurately it could be represented—which suggests that anything less than an infinite sam-

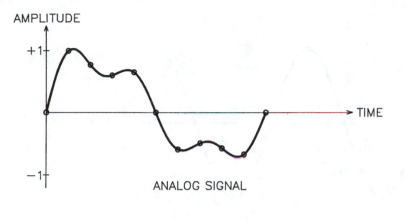

AMPLITUDE

+1

0

−1

TIME

ANALOG SIGNAL

{0,1,.77,.60,.65,0,−.59,−.49,−.57,−.67,0}

DIGITAL SIGNAL

FIGURE 3.1   Signal represented in both analog and digital form. The dots on the waveform represent the sampling points.

pling rate would cause some error in the digital signal. Fortunately, a mathematical analysis of the sampling process reveals that no error will be introduced by a finite sampling rate that is more than twice the fastest rate of change of the signal being sampled. That is, the chosen sampling rate must be faster than twice the highest frequency contained in the analog signal. Conversely, the highest frequency contained in the analog signal must be less than half the sampling rate. This maximum, $f_s/2$, is called the *Nyquist frequency* (pronounced "nye-kwist") and is the theoretical limit on the highest frequency that can be properly represented in a digital audio system.

To ensure that the frequencies in the analog signal are below the Nyquist frequency, an analog low-pass filter is placed before the A/D converter as shown in figure 3.2. Similarly, a low-pass filter is connected to the output of the D/A converter to ensure that all the frequencies in the analog output signal are in the proper range. A filter separates signals on the basis of their frequencies (see chapter 6); it passes signals of certain frequencies while significantly reducing the amplitudes of other frequencies. In this application, an ideal low-pass filter would permit frequencies below the Nyquist frequency to pass unchanged, but would completely block higher frequencies. Real low-pass filters, however, are not perfect, with the result that the usable frequency range is limited, in practice, to a little more than 40% of the sampling rate instead of the full 50%.

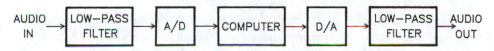

FIGURE 3.2   The use of low-pass filters to prevent aliasing in a digital audio system.

AMPLITUDE

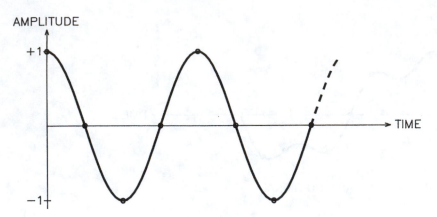

FIGURE 3.3   Sampling a 10-kHz tone at a 40-kHz rate.

The faster the sampling rate, the higher the frequency that can be represented, but the greater the demands on the speed and the power consumption of the hardware. Full-fidelity audio systems are designed to cover the upper limit of human hearing, near 20 kHz. There are many sampling rates in use for audio, chosen both for technical and for historical reasons.[1] One standard sampling rate for digital audio is 48 kHz, which puts the 20-kHz frequency range at 41.67% of the sampling frequency. Compact disks use a rate of 44.1 kHz to store the information, but use a more complicated D/A conversion scheme to obtain the full audio bandwidth.

To further understand the frequency limitations of a digital audio system, consider the system diagrammed in figure 3.2. The computer has been programmed to transfer sample values from the A/D converter to the D/A converter as fast as they are taken. Thus, if the system works perfectly, the analog signal emerging from the output will be an exact replica of the analog signal applied to the input. Suppose a 10-kHz sinusoidal tone is sampled by the A/D converter at a rate of 40 kHz as illustrated in figure 3.3. The resulting digital signal will be the sequence {1, 0, –1, 0, 1, 0, –1, 0, . . .}. When the digital signal is reconverted by the D/A converter, the low-pass filter smooths the digital signal so that a 10-kHz sinusoidal tone appears at the output. Why does the low-pass filter smooth the samples into a sinusoidal wave and not into something else, such as the triangle wave that would be made by connecting the sample values with straight lines? The low-pass filter places a restriction on the highest frequency of the analog signal that comes out of it. In the example, any waveform other than a sinusoid would contain frequencies that exceed the maximum frequency passed by the filter (see section 2.6). In the general case, there is one and only one analog waveform that will fit the sequence of numbers of a given digital signal and also contain no frequencies above the Nyquist frequency.

What would happen if there were no low-pass filter on the analog input and a signal were sampled that contained a frequency above the Nyquist frequency? Consider a 30-kHz sinusoidal tone sampled at a 40-kHz rate as in figure 3.4. The resulting digital signal of {1, 0, –1, 0, 1, 0, –1, 0, . . .} is the same as that of the 10-kHz tone shown in figure 3.3. Thus, when the digital signal is converted back to analog form, the output of the low-pass filter will

AMPLITUDE

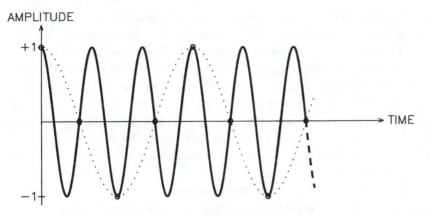

FIGURE 3.4   Sampling a 30-kHz sinusoidal tone at a 40-kHz rate. The samples also describe a 10-kHz sinusoid as shown by the dotted line.

be a 10-kHz sinusoidal tone. The 30-kHz tone has the same sample values as a 10-kHz tone, and so it is said to assume an "alias" at 10 kHz. Aliased tones are caused by *undersampling*—sampling below the Nyquist frequency for a particular tone. In this example, a sampling frequency of at least 60 kHz would be required to properly represent the 30-kHz tone.

Once a signal appears in a digital system under an alias, there is no way that it can be returned to its original frequency because there is no way that a computer can determine whether a particular frequency is the product of proper sampling or undersampling. In a digital system, the alteration caused by the sampling process of frequencies higher than the Nyquist frequency is known as *aliasing* or *foldover*.

A low-pass filter at the input to an A/D converter effectively prevents aliasing in a digital signal simply by limiting the range of frequencies going into the converter. In the digital synthesis of sound, however, aliasing can occur in a more subtle way. Suppose that, on a system with a 40-kHz sampling rate, a user writes a program with the intention of producing a 30-kHz sinusoidal tone. The digital signal that the program would generate is identical to the sequence in the examples above, {1, 0, –1, 0, 1, 0, –1, 0, . . .}, and therefore would be converted into a 10-kHz sinusoidal tone. Thus, in the computer synthesis of sound, the synthesis algorithms and their corresponding parameters are ordinarily specified in such a way that all frequencies produced by the computer instrument fall below the Nyquist frequency (see section 4.4.) Certain composers, such as James Dashow, have made use of foldover to produce chordal structures.[2] Such a system requires the accurate calculation of the values of the aliased frequencies.

To describe aliasing mathematically, let f_{in} be either a frequency applied to the input of an A/D converter or a frequency intended to be contained in a synthesized sound. Let f_{out} be the frequency emerging from the low-pass filter at the output. When f_{in} is less than the Nyquist frequency, $f_{out} = f_{in}$ as expected. For values of f_{in} between $f_s / 2$ and f_s, the relationship between f_{in} and the actual frequency output (f_{out}) is

$$f_{out} = f_s - f_{in}$$

In this region of f_{in}, observe that f_{out} and f_{in} move in opposite directions. If a system with a 40-kHz sampling rate were programmed with the objective of producing an ascending glissando from 22 to 39 kHz, the sound synthesized would actually descend from 18 to 1 kHz.

This type of aliasing more often manifests itself in another way. Suppose that a sound with a rich harmonic spectrum that exceeds the Nyquist frequency is programmed to glissando upward. The fundamental and the first few harmonics would sweep upward, while the higher harmonics (frequencies greater than $f_s/2$) would move downward during the course of the tone. This process is called *heterodyning*. The aural effect of these simultaneous upward and downward glissandi is similar to the squeal that sometimes occurs when fine tuning a short-wave radio.

Foldover occurs on every multiple of the sampling rate, and so frequencies higher than the sampling frequency will also cause unwanted responses. The general relationship is

$$f_{out} = | nf_s - f_{in} |$$

where n is a nonnegative integer chosen for a particular value of f_{in} such that f_{out} is less than the Nyquist frequency. Thus, at a 40-kHz sampling rate, an output of 10 kHz would result from inputs of 10 kHz ($n = 0$), 30 kHz ($n = 1$), 50 kHz ($n = 2$), and so on.

3.2 QUANTIZATION ERRORS

Another parameter that can affect the fidelity of a digital signal is the accuracy with which the numerical value of each sample is measured. To explain these effects, we will first introduce two closely related concepts, *dynamic range* and *signal-to-noise ratio*. A characteristic that is a good indicator of the quality of any system that processes sound is *dynamic range:* the ratio of the strongest to the weakest signal that can exist in the system. Dynamic range is expressed in decibels (see section 2.4); a large ratio makes possible clear sounds. For a symphony orchestra in a typical concert hall, the dynamic range is measured as the ratio between the hall's ambient noise and the loudest orchestral sound. The ratio of amplitudes is generally around 1:32,000, or 90 dB.

The dynamic range of an electronic sound system is limited at the lower end by the background noise contributed by the electronic components and at the higher end by the level at which the greatest signal can be represented without distortion. Manufacturers specify the performance of their equipment under optimum conditions; the actual dynamic range available to someone listening to an electronic sound system will be smaller if the loudspeakers of the system are placed in a noisy environment.

A characteristic associated with dynamic range is the *signal-to-noise ratio* (SNR), which compares the level of a given signal with that of the noise in the system. The term *noise* can take on a variety of meanings, depending on the environment and even the tastes of the listener. In this context, it refers to the residual signal that is extraneous to the desired signal. In a concert hall, this would be the "background noise" that is always present, such as that produced by the ventilation system, regardless of what is happening on stage. In electronic sound systems, noise generally takes the form of a hissing sound. The SNR is expressed in decibels, and a large ratio indicates a clear sound. The dynamic range of an electronic system predicts the maximum SNR possible; that is, under ideal conditions, the signal-to-noise ratio equals the dynamic range when a signal of the greatest possible amplitude is present. The ratio will be somewhat smaller on soft sounds. As an example, consider a digital sound system with a constant noise level and a dynamic range of 80 dB. The largest signal possible would have an amplitude 80 dB above the noise level, but a signal with a level 30 dB below the maximum would exhibit an SNR of only 50 dB.

The SNR of a good analog tape recorder can approach 70 dB, with an improvement to greater than 90 dB possible through commercially available noise-reduction techniques. The SNR of a digital audio system can be even greater. A prime determinant of system performance is the resolution with which the data converters transform digital signals into analog and vice versa. When a conversion takes place, the analog signal is said to be quantized because its digital form can be represented only to a certain resolution. For example, suppose that a D/A converter is capable of representing a signal in 0.001-V steps. If a sample were calculated as 0.01227 V, it would be converted to 0.012 V—an error of 0.00027 V. The net effect of this type of error, called a *quantization error,* is the addition of some form of unwanted component to the sound. The amount and audible effect of the quantization error depends on the resolution of the converter and the type of signal being converted.

The resolution of most data converters is measured in bits, corresponding to the binary size of the datum used to represent each sample of the digital signal. For example, on a particular sample an A/D converter with 12 bits outputs one of $2^{12} = 4096$ possible values. Suppose that the analog audio signal connected to the input of the converter could fluctuate over the range from –10 to +10 V—a total range of 20 V. The size of a quantization step, corresponding to the value of one bit, would then be 20 ÷ 4096 = 0.004883 V/bit, which also bounds the error that can be incurred.

In the case where the audio signal is constantly changing (as it is in music), the dynamic range and hence the best signal-to-quantization-noise ratio (SQNR) that can be achieved is slightly more than 6 dB/bit. For example, a system with 16-bit linear data converters has a dynamic range of around 96 dB, predicting that the noise in the system will be 96 dB below a signal that has the largest amplitude possible in the system. The noise level does not change with the signal level, so that signals with amplitudes lower than the maximum value will exhibit less than the maximum SQNR. For instance, a sound with an amplitude 40 dB below the maximum would have a SQNR of only 56 dB.

The nature of the audio signal helps to determine the audible character of the noise. When the sound constantly changes and is well above the noise level, listeners generally perceive the quantization noise as the "hissing" normally associated with noise. On the other hand, when reasonably steady tones are produced or the signal level is close to the noise level, the quantization "noise" will usually sound more like distortion. Sometimes the frequencies produced by the distortion are aliased to yield sounds that are more objectionable than the 6-dB/bit SQNR would predict.[3] The quantization noise on very low-level signals of any type adds distortion to the sound that is sometimes heard as a tone dies away at the end of a section of a digital recording of music.

In musical applications, the use of 12-bit data converters yields an audio quality roughly equivalent to that available from a good analog tape recorder without any noise-reduction devices. The SQNR of a 16-bit system is essentially equivalent to the performance of most advanced noise-reduction schemes for analog tape.

The type of data conversion process just described, in which the input voltage range is split into equal quantization steps, is known as *linear* conversion. It is the most widely used because the sample values are easiest to process. Other available types of data converters[4] improve their performance by using unequal quantization steps, but at the cost of more difficult processing.

In recent years, some high-end studios have begun to use systems with 20 bits of resolution. This approach is not motivated by an attempt to obtain a possible SQNR of over 120 dB; such a large range exceeds the capabilities of the ear in any listening environment. Instead, the extra bits are used to increase the available dynamic range for representing the largest samples of impulsive sounds such as those produced by percussive and plucked instruments as will be explained in the next section.

3.3   ARITHMETIC CONSIDERATIONS

The precision with which the computer represents sample values and performs arithmetic operations internally can also have an effect on the quality of the digital audio. Section 1.1 introduced two numerical data formats, integer and floating point. If the sample values are processed as integers, the number of bits used correlates with the SQNR as about 6 dB per bit; floating-point numbers correlate with the SQNR ratio as 20 dB per equivalent decimal digit.

The mathematical operations used to calculate samples can have a deleterious effect on the SQNR. When two numbers are combined by an arithmetic operation, a rounding or truncation error can result.[5] As an example, consider the floating-point product of 11.22×20.12, in a data format that has a resolution of two decimal places. The result, 225.7464, when truncated becomes 225.74, with an error of 0.0064. Although the effect of this one particular error would probably go unnoticed, the cumulative effect of such errors can be audible when using an algorithm that employs a number of multiplies to calculate each sample. To avoid this problem, programs working with audio generally use data formats that represent the samples with more resolution than the data converters. The number of additional bits or equivalent decimal digits necessary depends on the number and type of the mathematical operations used. The standard floating-point format found in most computer languages has enough resolution to accommodate most synthesis algorithms. On the other hand, the standard 16-bit integer format used for calculation does not have enough resolution to take full advantage of the dynamic range available from a 16-bit D/A converter. To ameliorate this problem, commercially available 16-bit digital signal-processing chips perform their internal arithmetic in at least 32 bits.

Another way that audio quality can be degraded is by generating signals that exceed the dynamic range of the system. In a D/A conversion system, the dynamic range is limited on the upper end by the maximum value that can be accepted by the data converter. For example, most 16-bit converters have a range from –32,768 to +32,767. A sample value given outside of that range will not be converted properly. When a digital signal describing a tone contains a single, out-of-range sample, a click will usually be heard during the

D/A conversion. When a significant proportion of the samples in the digital signal are out of range, severe distortion results. Therefore, in using algorithms to synthesize sound, the musician must choose parameters for the algorithm that ensure that all output samples fall within the range of the D/A converters used on the system. However, the sample values should be large enough to maintain a good SQNR.

Maximizing the SQNR while strictly avoiding out-of-range samples represents a significant challenge in the digital recording and processing of sound. In particular, sounds such as a struck drumhead or a plucked string exhibit a peak amplitude that is large compared to their average amplitude during the course of the tone. Other sounds, such as those ordinarily produced by a wind instrument, have a much smaller ratio of peak to average amplitude. As an example, figure 3.5 illustrates medium-duration waveforms characteristic of a guitar and a trombone digitized on a 16-bit system. Both are played at the same pitch (A4). The energy contained in the waveforms is equal, but the peak value of the guitar waveform is a little less than eight times larger than that of the trombone. Thus, 3 additional bits are required to represent the sound of a plucked string; yet the perceived SQNR would be approximately the same. The extra bits are called the *headroom* of the system. They are necessary to prevent distortion, but do not necessarily reduce the listener's impression of the system noise level.

The issue of headroom is much more critical in digital recording than in analog recording. A large peak value in an analog system will undergo a certain amount of amplitude compression, but this imperfection in the sound will be considerably less noticeable

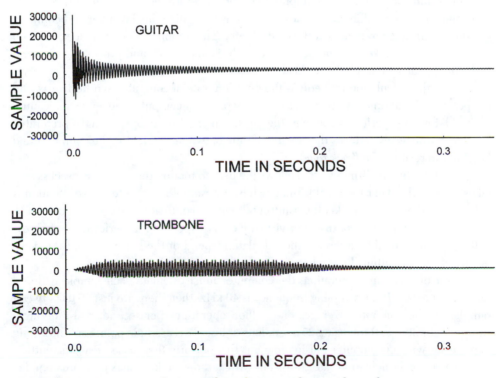

FIGURE 3.5   Comparison of guitar and trombone waveforms with equal energy.

than when a digital sample overflows. The maximum level in an analog system must still be carefully controlled, but the perceived acoustic penalty paid for a signal level over the peak range is not nearly as severe.

As mentioned in the previous section, some modern digital recording systems use 20 bits to supply additional headroom. The goal of this approach is to obtain a perceived SQNR equivalent to at least a 16-bit system while providing an additional 4 bits for faithfully capturing the peaks of impulsive waveforms.

3.4   DATA RATES

There are three rates associated with the process of sound synthesis: the sampling rate (described in section 3.1), the calculation rate, and the control rate. In direct digital synthesis, the *calculation rate* is the speed at which the hardware calculates sample values in accordance with some acoustical model of sound production. It is dependent on the type of machine and the particular algorithms used. The *control rate* is the speed at which significant changes in the sound synthesis process occur. For example, the control rate in the simplest program would be the rate at which the notes are played. In actual practice, there are usually several significant events during a sound, but the control rate is much slower than the sampling rate and typically ranges from 1 to 1000 events per second.

The idea of a control rate is possible because many parameters of a sound are "slowly varying." For example, the vibrations in the waveform of a sound oscillate at an audio frequency, but the average peak amplitude of the waveform changes much more slowly over time. The more efficient synthesis programs recognize this behavior and compute the slowly varying parameters at the control rate.[6] The notion of slow variance of certain parameters is also a key assumption in the analysis, modeling, and processing of sound and will appear several places in this text.

When the calculation rate equals the sampling rate, a computer synthesizer is said to operate in "real time." Without real-time operation, a computer music system cannot be used for live performance. For the musician, real-time operation is preferable because it drastically reduces the amount of time between instructing the computer and hearing the results (*feedback time*).

An interactive real-time system allows the user to modify the synthesis process as it takes place and to hear the results immediately. An example of an interactive situation is a digital synthesizer with a knob permitting the musician to adjust the tempo of a score in real time. Interactive control over virtually every aspect of the performance process is theoretically possible, although the calculation speed of the hardware and the complexity of the algorithms limit what can be done in practice.

To enable real-time operation, the computer must calculate each sample within a sampling interval. If the sampling frequency is 40 kHz, then there are just 25 μs between samples. If the computer averages one million operations per second, real-time algorithms are limited to those using 25 operations or less. This example points out the strong impetus for writing computer music programs that perform their tasks very efficiently.

To achieve a calculation rate consistent with audio sampling rates on more complex algorithms, special-purpose digital hardware such as a digital signal-processing (DSP) chip is attached to a host computer. This hardware executes a number of algorithms very quickly, with the host computer specifying (at the control rate) the calculations that are to be performed. The internal architecture of such a digital synthesizer usually places restrictions on the number and complexity of synthesis algorithms available. Thus, an increase in execution speed is often accompanied by a loss in potential generality in the number, type, and complexity of sounds that can be made. For a great many purposes, the advantages of real-time operation far outweigh the loss of complete flexibility.

Practical hardware for real-time, direct digital synthesis was developed after the mid-1970s. Before then, computer-synthesized sound was almost exclusively realized in a deferred mode of operation. This mode is used at installations without real-time hardware or when the desired digital processes are too complex to be implemented on currently available real-time hardware. When the calculation rate is slower than the sampling rate, the calculated sample values must be stored in the computer's external memory such as on a disk. Upon completion of the calculation of a score, the stored sequence of samples can be converted in real time using a simple program that reads the disk and sequentially sends each sample to a D/A converter. Use of the deferred mode greatly increases the feedback time to the musician.

The availability of "online" D/A conversion facilities has helped to minimize the waiting time. Digital-to-analog converters are said to be online when they are attached to the same computer that calculates the sample values. Before these were widely available, the less desirable procedure of off-line conversion required the calculated set of sample values to be physically transferred onto some medium, usually a digital tape, and then loaded onto another computer system outfitted with a conversion apparatus. Sometimes a significant geographic distance separated the two computers and the digital tape had to be mailed or otherwise transported to the conversion site.

Another undesirable characteristic of the deferred mode is the large amount of data storage necessary. For example, just one minute of stereophonic sound at a 48-kHz sampling rate is ordinarily represented by 11.52 million bytes, a large amount of data. As a result, musicians using this mode often realized their projects a small section at a time, taping the intermediate results.

NOTES

1. Pope, S. T., and van Rossum, G. "Machine Tongues XVIII: A Child's Garden of Sound File Formats." *Computer Music Journal*, 19(1), 1995, 29–30.

2. Dashow, James. "Three Methods for the Digital Synthesis of Chordal Structures with Non-harmonic Partials." *Interface*, 7, 1978, 69–94.

3. Blesser, B. A. "Digitization of Audio: A Comprehensive Examination of Theory, Implementation, and Current Practice." *Journal of the Audio Engineering Society*, 26(10), 1978, 739–771.

4. Moore, F. R. *Elements of Computer Music*. Englewood Cliffs, N.J.:Prentice-Hall, 1990, 51–53.

5. Rabiner, L. R., and Gold, B. *Theory and Application of Digital Signal Processing*. Englewood Cliffs, N.J.: Prentice-Hall, 1975.

6. Boulanger, R. "Conducting the MIDI Orchestra, Part 1: Interviews with Max Mathews, Barry Vercoe, and Roger Dannenberg." *Computer Music Journal*, 14(2), 1990, 34–46.

4

Synthesis Fundamentals

Sound synthesis is the generation of a signal that creates a desired acoustic sensation. This chapter begins with the fundamentals of signal generation and presents techniques of additive synthesis, modulation, and noise generation. Several example computer instrument designs are given along with compositional examples.

4.1 COMPUTER INSTRUMENTS, UNIT GENERATORS, AND SOUND-SYNTHESIS TECHNIQUES

In computer music, the term *instrument* refers to an algorithm that realizes (performs) a musical event. It is called upon by a computer program that is interpreting either a score stored in memory or the actions of a performer on a transducer. The instrument algorithm calculates the sample values of an audio signal using inputs, known as parameters, received from the calling program. For example, an instrument designed to play a single, simple tone might be passed parameters controlling the duration, frequency, and amplitude of the tone. Other parameters can be passed that affect other aspects of the sound. When designing an instrument, the musician determines the number and nature of the parameters to be passed. These are based on a choice of which attributes of the sound will be controlled *externally* during the generation of the sound. An instrument can also be designed to accept an audio signal in digital form as an input to be processed by the algorithm.

There are many ways to specify and provide control of computer instruments. At the lowest level, the musician writes a step-by-step program to generate sample values. It can be difficult at this level to have a sense of how to modify the algorithm to produce a particular sound, and the overall musical plan can be obscured by the necessary attention to detail.

The next level of specification improves both conceptual clarity and programming convenience by dividing a complete sound-generating algorithm into smaller, separate algorithms called *unit generators*. Each unit generator has input parameters and at least one output. Each performs a specific function of signal generation or modification, or the combination of signals. Many music languages express synthesis algorithms in terms of unit generators, using them as the building blocks with which instruments are made. The internal algorithm of each unit generator has been determined and encoded by the music systems programmer. The musician's task is to interconnect the inputs and outputs of the unit generators to achieve an overall synthesis algorithm that produces the desired result. The unit generator is a useful concept because it minimizes the amount of knowledge of the inner workings of each algorithm required on the part of the musician, while retaining considerable flexibility for the construction of synthesis algorithms.

Individual unit generators and methods of interconnecting them will be demonstrated in the next three chapters to explain the synthesis of specific sounds.

With signal-generating models, the third level of specification, the musician chooses from a set of available synthesis techniques. In this case, the computer is preprogrammed with the appropriate interconnections of unit generators. The musician selects a technique and specifies the parameters necessary to control it. Available sound synthesis techniques include additive, subtractive, distortion (nonlinear), and granular synthesis. *Additive synthesis,* described in this chapter, is the summation of several simple tones to form a complex one. In *subtractive synthesis* (chapter 6), the algorithm begins with a complex tone and diminishes the strength of selected frequencies in order to realize the desired spectrum. Many of the additive- and subtractive-synthesis instruments use data derived from the analysis of natural sound. Chapter 7 will describe various *synthesis-from-analysis* techniques. *Distortion synthesis* (chapter 5) encompasses several techniques where a controlled amount of distortion is applied to a simple tone to obtain a more complex one. A widely used member of this class of techniques is frequency modulation, which can be thought of as the distortion of the frequency of a tone. Another technique, waveshaping, is the distortion of the waveform of a tone. *Granular synthesis* (chapter 8) assembles its sounds from a multitude of bursts of energy that are too short to be perceived musically by themselves.

The last level of instrument specification is the *physical model* (chapter 9). This method requires extensive technical research on the part of the music systems programmer. The musician is given a model of a sound production process with variable parameters to achieve a particular sound. For example, the software might simulate a violin with a list of parameters given in terms of some of the physical attributes of the modeled instrument. The musician could then alter the character of the tone by changing such parameters as the volume of the body, the bowing point, the placement of the bridge, and so on. The primary benefit of a physical model is to give the musician a means to predict intuitively, to some degree, the effect of timbral modification. For instance, an increase in body volume would be expected to lower the frequency of many of the resonances in the tone.

Physical models have been created of many instruments and of speech. In addition, they have been used for describing processes that modify sounds, such as the specification of reverberation on the basis of the physical characteristics of a room. (See chapter 10.) As it continues to develop, this method is becoming a more widely available means of providing musicians with a more intuitive approach to computer instrument design than with the direct specification of the parameters of a signal-processing algorithm.

4.2 SIGNAL FLOWCHARTS

Unit generators will be used to define the fundamental synthesis techniques presented in this, the central portion of the text. A *signal flowchart,* such as the example in figure 4.1, is a graphical representation of the way in which unit generators are interconnected to form an instrument. The symbols for the various unit generators will be given as they are introduced throughout the text.

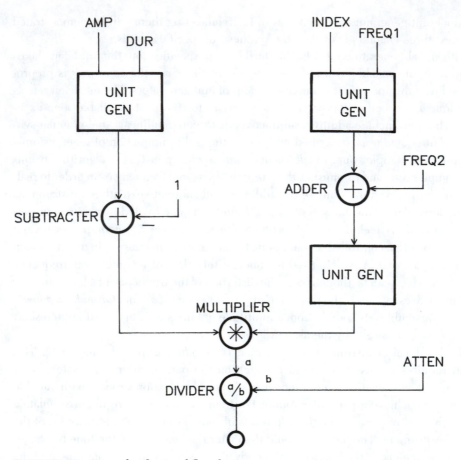

FIGURE 4.1   Example of a signal flowchart.

There are two basic rules that apply to the interconnection of unit generators: (1) An output of a unit generator may be connected to one or more input(s) of one or more other unit generator(s). Thus, an output can drive more than one input. (2) Outputs may never be connected directly together. The direct connection of outputs would result in an ambiguous situation when, as is usually the case, the unit generators provided conflicting numerical values. In the generalized unit generators of the example, the inputs go into the top of the symbol and the outputs emerge from the bottom of the symbol.

Outputs can be combined by mathematical operations. The most common combinatorial operation is addition, represented in a signal flowchart by the symbol for the adder shown in figure 4.1. An adder has two or more inputs, denoted by arrows, and one output. The principal use of an adder is to mix signals together. The operation of subtraction also uses an adder. In this case, the *sign* of the subtrahend is reversed just before it enters the adder. This is indicated by a minus sign placed near the arrow connecting the subtrahend to the adder.

The signal flowchart shown in figure 4.1 includes a multiplier and a divider, as well. Multiplying a signal by a constant with a value greater than 1 increases the amplitude of the signal; this process is called *amplification.* The reverse process, *attenuation,* is obtained through multiplying by a constant less than 1. Multiplication and division on a general-purpose computer can take substantially longer to perform than addition or subtraction; therefore, the instrument designer tries to minimize the number of these operations. However, many modern systems incorporate special hardware that performs multiplication and division very rapidly so that this consideration becomes less important. The use of division requires special care. To avoid errors, the instrument designer must make certain that the divisor can never assume a value of 0 because the resulting quotient is infinite. On some systems, such an error can cause the synthesis program to cease operation, or at least generate an unexpected sample value, producing an associated "click" in the sound.

The instrument diagrammed in the example flowchart is controlled by six parameters indicated by the mnemonics such as AMP, DUR, and so on. The value of each parameter is passed from the main program to the instrument each time the instrument is called upon to produce a sound. Parameters are best labeled with descriptive mnemonics. For example, the parameter that controls the amplitude of an instrument is often designated AMP.

Every instrument must have at least one output. The flowchart symbol for an output is a small, empty circle usually located at the bottom of the chart. There may be multiple outputs usually corresponding to a multichannel audio system.

4.3   THE OSCILLATOR

The unit generator fundamental to almost all computer sound synthesis is the *oscillator.* An oscillator generates a periodic waveform. The controls applied to an oscillator determine the amplitude, frequency, and type of waveform that it produces. The symbol for an oscillator is shown in figure 4.2. The symbol inside the oscillator (WF in this case) designates the waveform of the oscillator. The symbol can be a mnemonic of a particular waveform or a drawing of one cycle of the waveform. The numerical value that is fed into the left input sets the peak amplitude of the signal. The numerical value applied to the right input determines the frequency at which the oscillator repeats the waveform. Depending on the system, the frequency can be specified in one of two ways: (1) an actual number of hertz, or (2) a sampling increment—a number proportional to the frequency, which will be explained below. The input on the right side of the oscillator, PHASE, determines at which point on the waveform the oscillator begins. PHASE is

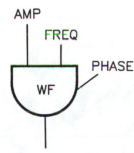

FIGURE 4.2   Flowchart symbol for an oscillator. The phase input is often not used.

usually not specified unless required for an explicit purpose. The output of the oscillator is a sequence of samples which forms a digital signal representing the waveform.

One method of implementing an oscillator algorithm specifies the waveform as a mathematical function of time. Thus, in order to generate a sine wave using this method, the algorithm would have to calculate the value of the mathematical function, sine, on every sample. This method (*direct evaluation*) is prohibitively slow for most functions.

For the sake of efficiency, most digital oscillators use a stored waveform: a waveform that is evaluated prior to the generation of any sound. The computer calculates the value of many uniformly spaced points on a cycle of the waveform, and stores them in computer memory as a block called a *wave table*. Thus, a wave table consists of a long sequence of numbers, each corresponding to the sampled value of successive points on the waveform. Once the waveform has been stored, the oscillator can generate sample values by simply retrieving values from the wave table—a much faster operation for the computer than evaluating the mathematical function of the waveform directly.

To understand the operation of a digital oscillator, consider the wave table in figure 4.3, which contains one cycle of a sine wave stored in 512 numerical entries. Each entry is marked by a numerical address, denoted in this case by integers from 0 through 511. The oscillator algorithm maintains a numerical value, called the *phase*, which indicates the address of the entry currently in use. At the beginning of its operation, the oscillator

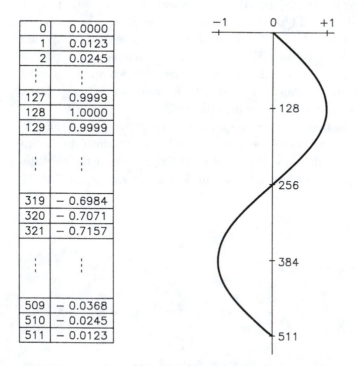

FIGURE 4.3 Wave table containing one cycle of a sine wave.

is given an initial phase value, which denotes the first entry in the wave table to be used. On every sample the oscillator algorithm obtains the current phase value (ϕ) and adds it to an amount that is proportional to the frequency of operation. The new phase value determines the entry used to calculate the next output sample. The amount added to the phase on every sample is called the *sampling increment* (SI): the distance in the wave table between successive entries selected by the oscillator. When the phase value exceeds the number of the last entry in the table, it is "wrapped around" to a point near the beginning of the table by subtracting the total number of table entries from that phase. In this example, the number of the last entry in the table is 511. If $\phi = 512$ after adding the sampling increment, then the oscillator algorithm would modify the phase so that $\phi = \phi - 512 = 0$, thereby returning the phase to the first location of the table. Hence, the oscillator algorithm can be thought of as scanning the wave table in a circular fashion.

The two varieties of digital oscillator commonly encountered in computer music are the *fixed sampling rate oscillator* and the *variable sampling rate oscillator*. The remainder of this section describes the operation of the fixed sampling rate oscillator. In modern practice, variable sampling rates are used for sound modification and will be described in section 10.3A.

Using the wave table in figure 4.3, suppose that the sampling rate is 40 kHz and the oscillator is programmed to scan through the wave table with a sampling increment of 1; that is, one entry at a time. There are 512 entries in the table and the table contains one cycle, so it would take 512 samples to produce one cycle. Therefore, the fundamental frequency of the oscillator would be $40{,}000 \div 512 = 78.13$ Hz.

If a tone one octave higher is desired, the oscillator would be programmed to retrieve values from every other entry in the wave table (SI = 2). Because the oscillator would go through the wave table twice as fast, there would be half as many samples per cycle (256), and the fundamental frequency of the oscillator would be $40{,}000 \div 256 = 156.25$ Hz. This result is twice as large as the previous example, which makes sense because the wave table is scanned at twice the speed.

To obtain a frequency f_0 using a wave table with N entries, the required sampling increment is

$$\mathrm{SI} = N \frac{f_0}{f_s}$$

For example, given $N = 512$ and a sampling rate (f_s) of 40 kHz, a 2.5-kHz signal would require a sampling increment of 32. In other words, if the oscillator starts at entry 0 in the wave table, sequential entries 0, 32, 64, . . . will be taken from the wave table.

Except for certain select frequencies, the sampling increment will not be an exact integer. For instance, with $N = 512$, generating a 440-Hz tone at a 40-kHz sampling rate requires a sampling increment of 5.632. Suppose, in this case, that the oscillator starts at a phase equal to 0. On the first sample, it retrieves the waveform value from that location. On the next sample, the phase is $0 + 5.632 = 5.632$. How does the oscillator treat a phase with a fractional part, if the entries in the wave table are marked by integers? There are three techniques: truncation, rounding, and interpolation.

In *truncation,* the fractional part of the phase is ignored in determining the wave table entry, so that in this case the value is taken from entry 5. To calculate the next phase, however, the oscillator includes in its addition the fractional part of the current phase. Thus, on the next sample, the phase is 5.632 + 5.632 = 11.264, causing the sample to be taken from entry 11. The process continues on each successive sample.

When *rounding* is used, the entry taken is the value of the phase rounded to the nearest integer. Thus, for the example above, the first three wave table values are taken from entries 0, 6, and 11, respectively. Rounding yields a slightly more accurate waveform than truncation, and takes more computation time.

Of the three techniques, *interpolation* gives the most accurate approximation of the waveform. When a phase falls between two integer values, the waveform is calculated as a weighted average of the two entries between which the phase falls. If, as above, the phase is 5.632, the oscillator algorithm interpolates the waveform value as a weighted average of entries 5 and 6. In this case, the phase is 63.2% of the distance between 5 and 6, so the waveform would be evaluated as the sum of 63.2% of entry 6 and 36.8% of entry 5. This process can be thought of as taking the waveform value on a straight line that connects the values of successive wave table entries, resulting in a smoother waveform. Interpolation adds an extra multiplication to the oscillator algorithm and thus increases the amount of computation time.

The inaccuracies introduced in the waveform by any of the three techniques discussed previously evidence themselves as some form of noise or other unwanted signal in the sound. The amount and quality of the noise created depends on the waveform, on the table size, on the value of the sampling increment, and on the technique used. The larger the table size, the better the signal-to-noise ratio. (See section 3.2.) Let k be related to the table size (N) by $k = \log_2 N$. For example, the value $N = 512 = 2^9$ gives $k = 9$. If the entries in the table are stored with sufficient precision to prevent significant quantization noise (see section 3.2), the worst SNR that can occur is given by the approximate expressions $6k - 11$ dB for truncation, $6k - 5$ dB for rounding,[1] and $12(k - 1)$ dB for interpolation.[2] Neglecting for a moment the quantization noise contributed by the data converters, an oscillator using a 512-entry table, for example, would produce tones with no worse than 43, 49, and 96 dB SNR for truncation, rounding, and interpolation, respectively.

The actual SNR of a sound would be determined by combining the quantization noise due to the data converters and the noise resulting from fractional phase. The noise level resulting from fractional sampling increments varies directly with the amplitude of the signal. Thus, unless the noise due to fractional phase is below the level of the quantization noise, the SNR due to this effect is the same on loud sounds as it is on soft sounds.

As might be expected, the expressions above show that methods requiring more computation time or larger table size perform better. The performance of any method can be improved by increasing the table size, and so the digital-oscillator designer is faced with a common compromise: computation speed versus memory size. Many computer music systems make available both truncating and interpolating oscillators to allow the musician to make the compromise between sound quality and computation speed based on the application of a particular oscillator.

4.4   DEFINITION OF THE WAVEFORM

Generally, the musician need not directly specify a numerical value for each location in the wave table. Computer music programs enable a more simple method of entry: either by entering its representation versus time or by specifying which frequency components it contains. The definition of the waveform versus time can be made by specifying the mathematical equation that relates the amplitude of the desired waveform to its phase. The waveform versus time can also be defined by a piecewise linear means. Here, the waveform is defined by specifying a number of representative points on the waveform. These points, called *breakpoints,* are the points where the waveform changes slope. When filling the wave table, the software connects the breakpoints with straight lines. In most programs, breakpoints are specified as a pair of numbers: phase and amplitude at that phase.

The specification of waveforms in terms of amplitude versus time can, however, sometimes lead to unexpected results. If, at the frequency at which it repeats, the waveform contains any harmonics above the Nyquist frequency, they will be folded over (aliased), thereby producing unexpected frequencies in the sound. Suppose in a system with a 20-kHz sampling rate, a musician specified a sawtooth waveform (figure 4.4a) and used it in an oscillator programmed to produce a tone at a frequency of 1760 Hz. The sixth harmonic of 1760 Hz would be 10,560 Hz, which is above the Nyquist frequency of 10 kHz. Therefore, the sixth harmonic would fold over to 20,000 − 10,560 = 9440 Hz. The seventh harmonic, expected at 12,320 Hz, would sound at 7680 Hz, and so on. Figure 4.4b illustrates the intended spectrum of the sawtooth wave and figure 4.4c

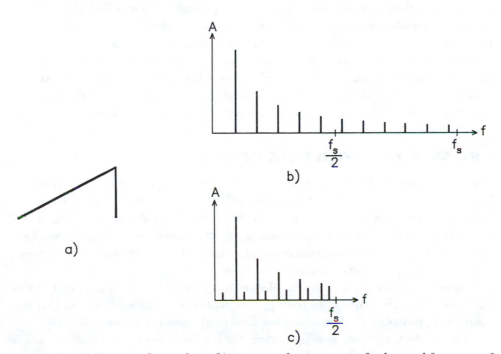

FIGURE 4.4   (a) Sawtooth waveform; (b) its expected spectrum at a fundamental frequency of 1760 Hz; and (c) its actual spectrum after conversion at a 20-kHz sampling rate.

shows how unexpected components appear in the spectrum at the output of the D/A converter. A sawtooth waveform has a significant amount of energy in its upper harmonics, and so the resulting spectrum would not sound completely harmonic. To avoid foldover when specifying waveforms in terms of amplitude versus time, one should define a waveform with little significant energy in the upper harmonics. Generally, this requires the avoidance of waveforms with steep slopes, sharp points, and other abrupt changes of slope or value (see section 2.6).

A safer way to specify a waveform is in terms of its spectrum. Here, the instrument designer specifies the amplitude, the partial number, and, if desired, the phase of each component. The software then calculates and stores a single cycle of the corresponding waveform. The amplitudes of the harmonics are typically described relative to the amplitude of the fundamental. For instance, one could specify a waveform containing a unit-amplitude fundamental with a third-harmonic amplitude 10 dB below the fundamental and a seventh harmonic 22 dB down. When the waveform is defined in terms of spectral content, the musician easily knows the exact value of the highest harmonic contained in the spectrum. Aliasing can thus be avoided by limiting the fundamental frequency of the oscillator accordingly. For example, on a system with a 40-kHz sampling rate, the fundamental frequency of an oscillator producing 10 harmonics should not exceed 2 kHz.

An oscillator that is programmed to have a fixed frequency samples the stored waveform with a constant sampling increment. This process generates a periodic waveform so that the spectrum of the signal contains nothing but exact harmonics. Thus, when describing a waveform in terms of spectral content, using noninteger partial numbers will not result in a signal with an inharmonic spectrum. Suppose an instrument designer, in hopes of obtaining an inharmonic spectrum, specified a fundamental and a partial number of 2.2. When the resulting wave table is sampled by an oscillator, the signal generated would be periodic, and therefore would have a harmonic spectrum. Instead of generating a component at 2.2 times the fundamental, the energy expected at that frequency would be spread throughout the spectrum as harmonics of the fundamental. Usually, this results in a spectrum that is not band-limited, creating the potential for noticeable foldover.

4.5 GENERATING FUNCTIONS OF TIME

Chapter 2 demonstrated that the parameters of musical sound are constantly changing. Thus, in most applications the inputs to an oscillator vary with time; that is, the amplitude and frequency of an oscillator are controlled by functions of time. An oscillator can be used to generate these control functions, but synthesis systems also include envelope generators and other function generators that, because they are tailored for this specific purpose, can synthesize control functions more directly.

Figure 4.5a shows one of the simplest computer instruments. The output of the envelope generator (figure 4.5b) controls the amplitude of the oscillator, so that the instrument produces a fixed waveform enclosed in the envelope (figure 4.5c).

The simplest amplitude envelope (figure 4.6) has three segments: the *attack*, which describes how the amplitude rises during the onset of the tone; the *sustain*, which describes the amplitude of the tone during its steady state; and the *decay*, which describes how the

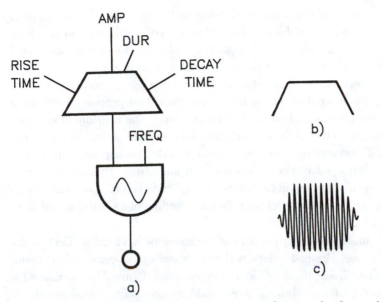

FIGURE 4.5 (a) Simple computer instrument, with its amplitude envelope (b) and its output waveform (c).

tone dies away. An envelope generator has at least four input parameters: rise time which is the duration of the attack segment, amplitude which sets the value at the peak of the attack, total duration of the envelope, and decay time. In addition, the shapes of the attack and decay segments need to be specified. Depending on the type of envelope generator, this can be done in one of two ways. Some envelope generators determine the segment

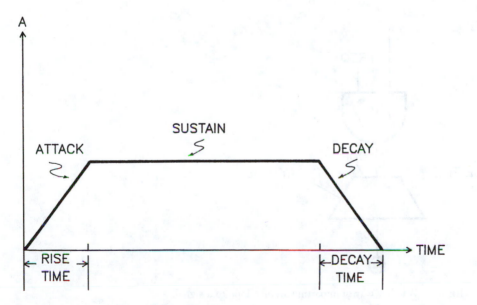

FIGURE 4.6 Simple amplitude envelope.

shape by reference to a function stored in a wave table. In this case, the entire wave table is scanned exactly once in the time of the segment. Other types of envelope generators have predetermined shapes. For example, several languages implement a unit generator called "linen," which realizes envelopes with strictly linear attack and decay segments.

On many systems, an envelope generator can be used as a signal processor. A signal is applied to the amplitude input of the envelope generator. This process results in an output signal that is the input signal encased in an envelope. The instrument of figure 4.7 is identical in function to that of the one in figure 4.5a. Instead of driving the amplitude input of the oscillator with an envelope, a constant (AMP) is applied. This causes the oscillator to produce a waveform with a constant amplitude. Passing this signal through the envelope generator imparts a pattern of amplitude variation onto the waveform. This technique is also used to enclose a digital recording of a natural sound in an envelope (see section 10.3A).

The shape of the attack and decay portions of the envelope has a great effect on the perceived timbre of a tone. Figure 4.8 depicts the two shapes most commonly encountered in computer music: linear (figure 4.8a) and exponential (figure 4.8c). Because listeners perceive amplitude on a nearly logarithmic scale, a more constant change in loudness will be obtained with an exponential shape than a linear one. Figure 4.8b and d shows how each shape progresses in terms of the logarithmic unit (decibels) which is much closer to how the ear would perceive the progression. A sound with a linear decay will appear to linger on after the beginning of the decay, and then suddenly drop off near the end of the tone. The exponential decay reflects a constant change in decibels versus time and thus will sound as a smooth diminution of amplitude. Natural vibrations almost always die away exponentially.

A true exponential shape can never reach exactly 0, and so, on many systems, the

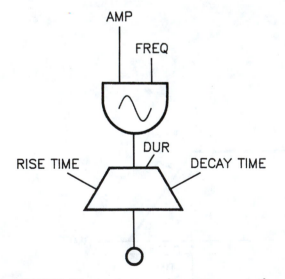

FIGURE 4.7   Another way of imparting an envelope to a signal.

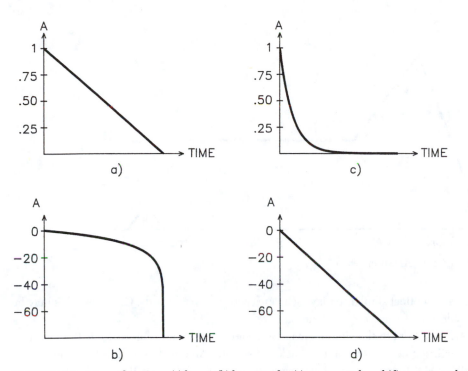

FIGURE 4.8   Decay functions: (a) linear, (b) linear in dB, (c) exponential, and (d) exponential in dB.

musician must specify the maximum and minimum values of the shape. The ratio of the two is important because it sets how quickly the amplitude changes—that is, the rate of change of the segment in dB/second. If it is desired that the minimum value result in an inaudible signal, it may not be a good strategy to make the value arbitrarily small. Suppose that an exponential attack is to last 0.1 second and the ratio is chosen as 1:1,000,000 (120 dB). This is a rate of change of $120 \div 0.1 = 1200$ dB/second. Further assume that the system has 16-bit D/A converters for a dynamic range of about 96 dB. Depending on the amplitude of the tone, the envelope will have to rise at least 24 dB before the converter begins to produce a time-varying signal. Because the envelope rises at 1200 dB/second, there will be at least a 24 dB $\div$ 1200 dB/second = 0.020 second additional delay in the onset of the tone. Therefore, the ratio chosen should be no greater than the maximum amplitude value of the system—in the case of 16 bits, 32,768:1; in the general case of N bits, $2^{N-1}{:}1$.

The duration of the attack and decay segments also has a great influence on timbre. In acoustic instruments, the attack is normally somewhat shorter than the decay. A very short attack is characteristic of percussive sounds, whereas longer attacks are found in acoustic instruments, such as the pipe organ, which produce sound by splitting a stream of air across the edge of a surface. Many acoustic instruments have longer attacks on lower pitches. Instruments that must build up a long column of air such as the tuba tend to have longer attacks. Synthesizing tones with short decays and relatively long attacks

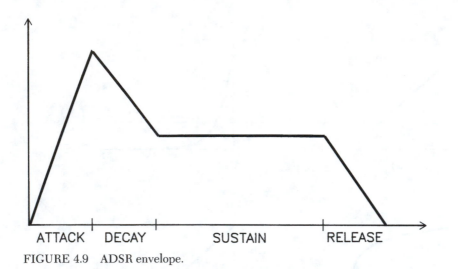

ATTACK   DECAY   SUSTAIN   RELEASE

FIGURE 4.9   ADSR envelope.

produces an effect similar to playing a tape recording backwards. Of course, this may be desirable under some circumstances.

A refinement to the simple envelope generator shown in figure 4.6 is the insertion of a fourth segment between the attack and sustain. An envelope of this type (figure 4.9) is called ADSR, representing its segments—attack, decay, sustain, and release. The ADSR shape is an attempt to imitate the envelopes found in acoustic instruments and is commonly used in inexpensive electronic keyboard synthesizers. Here, the tone remains in the sustained state until the key is released.

Envelope generators on computer music systems vary in the complexity of the types of envelopes they can realize. In many systems, the available envelope generators permit envelopes with only two or three breakpoints. When the complexity of a desired envelope exceeds the capabilities of the available envelope generators, an oscillator can be used. Figure 4.10 illustrates the realization of an amplitude envelope in this way. The waveform referenced by the envelope-generating oscillator is the desired envelope shape; the frequency of the oscillator is chosen to be the inverse of the duration of the tone so that the envelope will be generated once. To obtain a smoother envelope, an oscillator that interpolates its output value between successive wave table entries (see section 4.3) is generally used.

Musicians have also used this configuration to realize musical events that are repetitions of a tone, by programming the envelope-generating oscillator to go through several cycles during the duration of the event. For example, setting the frequency of the oscillator to 3 ÷ duration produces three repetitions.

A serious disadvantage of using an oscillator instead of an envelope generator is that the attack and decay times will be altered when the duration is changed. Unless the shape of the waveform is compensated, this will cause quite noticeable differences in timbre over a range of durations.

The first use of envelope generators was to synthesize functions of time that controlled the amplitude of an oscillator. In computer music, other functions are needed to

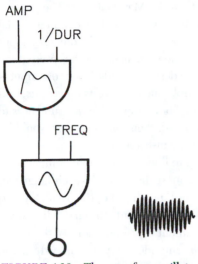

FIGURE 4.10   The use of an oscillator as an envelope generator.

control other parameters of a sound such as the frequency variation of an oscillator. As a result, many systems implement interpolating function generators to provide greater flexibility in realizing functions of time. These are often represented on a flowchart by a rectangle with a mnemonic or picture of the function inside. In using these, the musician specifies the functions of time by listing representative points on the function. For each point a pair of numbers is given: functional value and time elapsed since the previous point. (Some systems use the convention: functional value and time elapsed since the start of the function.) During synthesis, the function generator calculates values by interpolating between the breakpoints. The interpolation can be either linear or exponential, depending on the particular function generator used. For example, one could obtain a smooth glissando by specifying exponential interpolation for a function driving the frequency input of an oscillator. In this case, the function values would be given as the frequencies at the end points of the glissando.

4.6   INSTRUMENT DEFINITION IN TWO
TYPICAL SOUND-SYNTHESIS LANGUAGES

There are distinct approaches to instrument definition taken by the sound synthesis languages demonstrated below. We have chosen two rather widely circulated languages, both freely available. Despite the sometimes great differences in appearance and syntax of the languages, however, experience in the use of one of them is often sufficient preparation for the use of another with comparative ease. The programs in our examples share certain common features. For example, they use functions stored in computer memory for waveforms and other functions of time, and they include various subroutines for generating the stored functions and wave tables. They logically separate the score and the orchestra.

Csound and Cmusic can be considered descendants, however remote, of the early sound synthesis languages made at Bell Laboratories in the 1960s by Max Mathews. They have a structure that calls for the musician to supply an orchestra of instruments coded in a special language (which varies between them) and to provide a score, or note list. The orchestra input for these programs is in the form of statements coded in a new language which represent the configuration of unit generators necessary to produce the desired sounds. The score input is in the form of wave table generation statements, control statements of various sorts, and "notes" of data to be "played" by the orchestra program. For example, if an instrument is to include the option of creating tones of different frequencies, then the frequency would be supplied as a "parameter" value on a note statement for the instrument.

The flowchart diagrams in figure 4.11a and b help to illustrate a simple point: a basic instrument design in the two different languages is almost the same. In each language, the output of the envelope control unit is fed to the amplitude input of the oscillator, and the result of the oscillator is sent to the output of the instrument. In what follows, we will show the actual text that describes the two instrument representations of the figure in Csound and Cmusic, respectively. The examples are intended only to demonstrate the major differences in syntax between the languages.

Coding of instruments in the Csound language resembles assembly-language programming. The first and last statements of the instrument definition, instr 1 and endin, respectively, mark the beginning and end of instrument number 1. The unit generators are linen (linear envelope) and oscil (oscillator). The first argument of linen, p5, indicates that the amplitude of a note played on the instrument is specified as the fifth p-field (p5) of the note statement. The subsequent arguments of the linen—rise time, duration, and decay time—are specified on the note statements as p6, p3, and p8, respectively. Csound distinguishes between control rate and sampling rate operations. The result of the linen operation is placed into the storage location designated by the variable k1, which is calculated at the control rate. The position of k1 as the first argument of the oscil unit generator causes the amplitude of the oscil to be con-

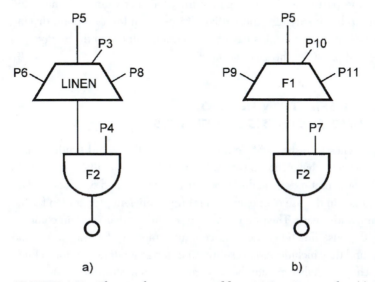

a)   b)

FIGURE 4.11   The simple instrument of figure 4.5 programmed in (a) Csound and (b) Cmusic.

trolled by the output of linen. The frequency of the oscil is taken from p4 of the note state-ment. The third argument, the number of the wave table used for the waveform of the oscil, indicates that the stored wave table number 2 will be used. The out statement's audio rate argument, a2, causes the result of the oscil operation to be sent to the output of the orchestra.

```
instr    1
k1   linen          p5,p6,p3,p8
a2   oscil          k1,p4,2
out a2
endin
```

EXAMPLE 4.1   Csound code for the instrument shown in figure 4.11a.

F. Richard Moore worked on the creation of Music 5 at Bell Laboratories with Max Mathews in the late 1960s. He created Cmusic around 1980 in the C programming lan-guage in order to make computer music in a UNIX operating system environment. Cmusic resembles Music 5 in the way the score and orchestra are encoded. In Cmusic, as in Music 5, the structure of the execution stage calls for each unit generator to contribute a number of successive outputs to a block of output samples (b1 and b2 in our example). The output block provides the means for interconnecting the unit generators.

```
ins 0 SIMPLE;
osc b2 p5 p10 f3 d;
osc b1 b2 p6 f1 d;
out b1;
end;
```

EXAMPLE 4.2   Cmusic code for the instrument shown in figure 4.11b.

The ins and end statements serve essentially the same purpose in Cmusic as in Csound—to delimit the definition of the instrument. In our Cmusic example, we call for instrument SIMPLE to be defined at time 0. We use an osc unit generator to perform the function of an envelope control unit. Its arguments are b2, the number of the loca-tion for its output; p5, its amplitude; p10, the duration of the envelope; f3, the number of the table storing the envelope shape; and d, the phase of the oscillator. The second osc statement in the example refers to another oscillator, this one used to generate the sig-nal. The first argument is b1, the number of the block for its output; b2, the input ampli-tude taken from the output of the previous unit generator; p6, the frequency; f1, the stored waveform for the oscillator; and again, d. The out statement calls for the output of the second oscillator, b1, to be sent to the output of the orchestra.

4.7   ADDITIVE SYNTHESIS

The simple instrument that was shown in figures 4.5 and 4.11 is the first configuration used to synthesize musical sound. It is based on a simplified Helmholtz model of musical sound, which consists of a waveform at a constant frequency enclosed in an envelope. The choice of waveform may be made in many ways. Early attempts at using this instrument to approximate natural sounds analyzed the steady-state spectrum of the tone to be matched.

The sound produced by this instrument differs from natural sound in two important respects. First, the amplitudes of all the spectral components are varied equally by the envelope, so that amplitudes of the components relative to each other do not change during the course of the tone. Thus, the sound lacks independent temporal evolution of the harmonics, an important characteristic of natural sound. Second, all the spectral components are exact-integer harmonics of the fundamental frequency, not the slightly mistuned partials that often occur in acoustically generated sounds.

As explained in chapter 2, each spectral component of a sound can be represented by its own independent amplitude and frequency functions. The synthesis of a tone based on this model (figure 4.12) requires a separate sinusoidal oscillator for each partial, with the appropriate amplitude and frequency functions applied to it. The output from each of the oscillators is added together to obtain the complete sound. Hence, the name additive synthesis is used to designate this technique.

Additive synthesis provides the musician with maximum flexibility in the types of sound that can be synthesized. Given enough oscillators, any set of independent spectral components can be synthesized, and so virtually any sound can be generated.

The amplitude and frequency functions can be obtained from the analysis of real sounds as described in chapter 2. The name *Fourier recomposition* is sometimes used to describe the synthesis from analysis, because it can be thought of as the reconstitution

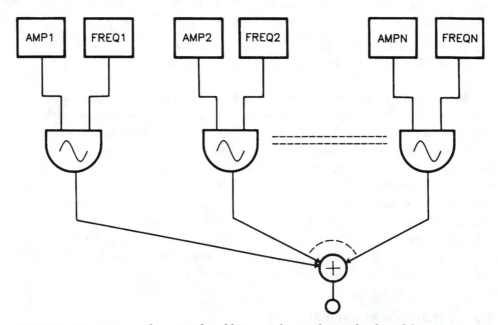

FIGURE 4.12   Basic configuration for additive synthesis. The amplitude and frequency inputs of each oscillator derive from independent function generators, which usually take the form of envelope generators or oscillators.

of the time-varying Fourier components of a sound. Additive synthesis has proven capable of realizing tones that are "indistinguishable from real tones by skilled musicians."[3]

Of course, the instrument designer is not restricted to using functions obtained from analyses. When choosing functions, however, it is helpful to have a knowledge of the behavior of functions that describe natural sounds. For example, in many acoustic instruments, the higher harmonics attack last and decay first. Knowing this, a musician might choose to synthesize an unusual sound using a set of functions with the opposite characteristic.

New, natural-sounding functions can be generated by interpolating between sets of functions that have been derived by analysis.[4] Musicians can use this technique to transform gradually the sound of one instrument into that of another. The normal way to interpolate between two functions is to take a weighted average between comparable points on each function. For example, to generate a function of time that is 30% of the way between function 1 (F1) and function 2 (F2), the new function is formed as the sum of 70% of F1 and 30% of F2. However, applying this technique to two amplitude functions that peak at different times creates a new function, which lacks a single, sharp maximum. Instead, the peak of the function broadens, spread between times of the peaks of the original functions. Upon synthesis, this discrepancy introduces an additional timbral element that is unrelated to either of the original sounds. To preserve a clear, single maximum, and hence more timbral similarity with the original sounds, the time at which the maximum of the new function occurs is interpolated between the times of the original functions. For example, suppose F1 peaks at 0.1 second and F2 peaks at 0.15 second. The function that is 30% of the way between F1 and F2 would peak at $0.7 \times 0.1 + 0.3 \times 0.15 = 0.115$ second. Having established the time of the maximum, the attack portion of the new function is interpolated between the attack portions of the original functions. Similarly, the decay portion is interpolated using the decay portions of the originals.

Additive synthesis produces high-quality sound but requires a comparatively large amount of data to describe a sound because each of the many oscillators requires two functions. A further complication arises because a given set of functions is normally useful only for limited ranges of pitch and loudness. If a set is determined by analysis for a specific pitch, then it will produce the timbral quality of the original source in only a small pitch interval around that point. Any formants present in the spectrum will move directly with the fundamental frequency. Thus, much of the timbral similarity between the tones of different pitches will be lost. In addition, the functions are highly sensitive to dynamic level, so that a set determined for a *mezzo forte* will produce an unrealistic *pianissimo*. To fully realize the benefits of additive synthesis, it is necessary to have either a large library of function sets or a complex scheme for altering a function set on the basis of pitch and amplitude during performance. (The spectral interpolation technique described in section 4.10 reduces the data storage requirements without a perceptible loss in quality.)

An advantage of additive synthesis is that it provides complete, independent control over the behavior of each spectral component. However, such a large number of controls on the timbre can make it difficult for the musician to know how to achieve a particular sound. A practical disadvantage of additive synthesis is that it requires a large number of unit generators. When synthesizing complex sounds, it is not unusual to employ 10 or more oscillators with their associated function generators in the synthesis of a single voice. This characteristic differs from and motivates the synthesis techniques presented in subsequent chapters, which use fewer unit generators.

4.8   MODULATION

Modulation is the alteration of the amplitude, phase, or frequency of an oscillator in accordance with another signal. Modulation has been used for many years in radio communications to transmit information efficiently. Musicians have exploited various modulation techniques in electronic music to create distinctive sounds efficiently.

The oscillator that is being modulated is called the *carrier oscillator.* If it were run without modulation, it would generate a continuous waveform called the *carrier wave.* When modulation is applied, the carrier wave is changed in some way. The changes are in sympathy with the modulating signal, so that the output of the carrier oscillator may be thought of as a combination of the two signals. The nature of this combination depends on the modulation technique used and will be examined below.

The spectral components of a modulated signal are classified into two types: *carrier components* and *sidebands.* The frequency of a carrier component is determined only by the frequency of the carrier oscillator. The frequency of a sideband is determined by both the carrier frequency and the frequency of the modulation.

4.8A   Amplitude Modulation

There are three main techniques of amplitude modulation: "classical" amplitude modulation, ring modulation, and single-sideband modulation. The letters AM are most often used to denote the first type. Ring modulation finds use in several techniques of computer music and will be presented in section 4.8B; the application of single-sideband (SSB) modulation to computer music is rare and will not be discussed here.

Figure 4.13 diagrams an instrument that implements classical amplitude modulation (AM). The carrier oscillator has a constant frequency of f_c and the modulating oscillator a frequency of f_m. For this example, the waveform of each oscillator is a sinusoid. The output from the modulating oscillator is added to a value that expresses the amplitude the carrier oscillator would have if there were no modulation. The amplitude of the modulating oscillator is expressed as a proportion of the unmodulated amplitude of the carrier oscillator. This proportion is denoted by the variable m, which is called the *modulation index*. When $m = 0$, there is no modulation and the carrier oscillator generates a sinusoid with a constant amplitude of AMP. When m is larger than 0, the carrier wave will take an envelope with a sinusoidal variation (figure 4.13b). When $m = 1$, the amplitude of the modulating oscillator equals the unmodulated amplitude of the carrier oscillator and 100% modulation is said to take place.

When both the carrier and the modulating waveforms are sinusoids, the spectrum of an AM signal (figure 4.14) contains energy at three frequencies: the carrier frequency (f_c) and two sidebands $(f_c + f_m$ and $f_c - f_m)$. The amplitude of the component at the carrier frequency does not vary with the modulation index. The amplitude of each sideband is a factor of $m/2$ less than the amplitude of the carrier, showing that this modulation process splits the energy between equally upper and lower sidebands. For example,

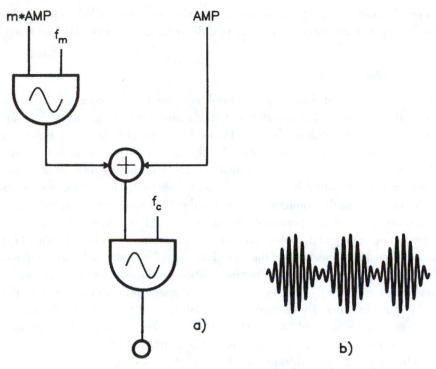

a)

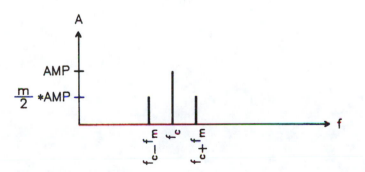

b)

FIGURE 4.13 Simple instrument (a) that implements amplitude modulation and its output waveform (b).

when $m = 1$, the sidebands will have one-half the amplitude of the carrier, and therefore will be 6 dB below the level of the carrier.

The frequency of the modulation determines how a listener perceives the AM sound. If f_m is less than about 10 Hz, the ear will track the individual amplitude variations. When f_m is greater than 10 Hz, but small enough that the carrier and both sidebands fall within the same critical band, the tone will sound with a loudness proportional to the average amplitude of the modulating waveform. A value of f_m that exceeds one-half the critical band causes the sidebands to be perceived individually, creating the sensation of additional loudness. Musicians have used amplitude modulation to create electronic "tremolo"

FIGURE 4.14   Spectrum of the AM signal produced by the instrument of figure 4.13.

by using a small modulation index and subaudio modulating frequency. When the modulation index is close to unity and f_m is small, a markedly pulsating sound will be produced.

4.8B   Ring Modulation

When modulation is applied directly to the amplitude input of a carrier oscillator, the process created is known as *ring modulation*. Other names for it are *balanced modulation* and *double-sideband (DSB) modulation*. Figure 4.15 illustrates the signal flowchart for an instrument where one oscillator ring modulates another. The amplitude of the carrier oscillator is determined only by the modulating signal, so that an absence of modulation ($A = 0$) causes the output from the instrument to go to 0. This characteristic is a noticeable departure from the configuration used in the AM technique described above.

Although ring modulation operates on the amplitude of the carrier, it is most often used to alter the frequency of a sound. When both the carrier (f_c) and modulating (f_m) signals are sinusoidal, the spectrum of the modulated signal contains only two frequencies: $f_c + f_m$ and $f_c - f_m$. In other words, ring modulation produces sidebands but no carrier. Because neither f_c nor f_m appears directly in the spectrum, the frequency of the sound can be quite different. For example, if $f_m = 440$ Hz and $f_c = 261$ Hz, the resulting spectrum contains energy only at 179 Hz and 701 Hz, frequencies that are not harmonically related to the originals or to each other. Given the amplitude of the modulating signal in figure 4.15 as A, both sidebands have amplitudes of $A/2$.

Ring modulation is often used for sound modification. All frequencies in a sound that is applied directly to the amplitude input of an oscillator (figure 4.16) are changed by ring modulation. Suppose a speech sound with a fundamental frequency of 100 Hz ring-modulates a sinusoidal oscillator with a frequency of 1123 Hz. The sound that emerges contains the sum

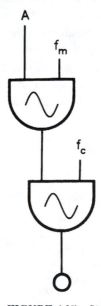

FIGURE 4.15   Simple instrument that implements ring modulation of one oscillator by another.

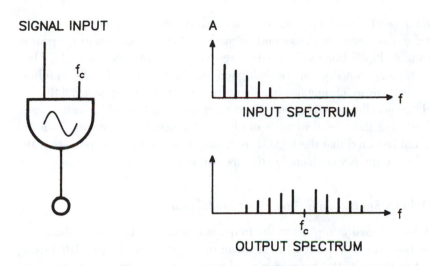

SIGNAL INPUT

f_c

A

INPUT SPECTRUM

f

f_c

OUTPUT SPECTRUM

f

FIGURE 4.16   Alteration of the spectrum of a signal by ring modulation.

and difference between each harmonic of the speech and 1123 Hz. Thus, the spectral component that was the fundamental of the speech sound is output at both 1023 Hz and 1223 Hz, the former second harmonic (originally at 200 Hz) appears at 923 Hz and 1323 Hz, and so on. The formerly harmonic speech now sounds inharmonic and may not be intelligible.

Ring modulation may be realized without oscillators just by multiplying two signals together. Thus, the multiplier shown in figure 4.17 is a general-purpose ring modulator. Two signals are often combined in this way for the purpose of frequency alteration. Suppose that two sine waves, with amplitudes A_1 and A_2 and frequencies f_1 and f_2, respectively, are multiplied together. The resulting spectrum will contain frequencies of $f_1 - f_2$ and $f_1 + f_2$, and the amplitude of each component will be $A_1A_2/2$. Observe that if either signal has an amplitude of 0, there will be no output from the modulator. Composers such as Jean-Claude Risset (see section 4.12) and James Dashow[5] have used this form of ring modulation for the creation of chordal structures.

The multiplication of two complex sounds produces a spectrum containing frequencies that are the sum and difference between the frequencies of each component in the

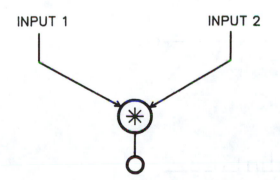

INPUT 1   INPUT 2

✳

FIGURE 4.17   A multiplier is a general-purpose ring modulator.

first sound and those of each component in the second. If there are p components in the first sound and q components in the second, as many as $2pq$ components can appear in the output. Thus, multiplication can be used to create dense spectra. For example, if two signals, each with four components, are multiplied together (figure 4.18), the resulting sound will have as many as 32 components. There would be fewer components if the two signals were harmonically related because some of the sidebands would have the same frequencies, reducing the overall number of observed spectral components. To avoid aliasing, it should be noted that the highest frequency produced by this process is the sum of the highest frequency contained in the first sound and the highest in the second.

4.8C   Vibrato Simulation by Frequency Modulation

When a modulating signal is applied to the frequency input of a carrier oscillator, *frequency modulation* occurs. *Vibrato*, a slight wavering of pitch, can be simulated using the instrument in figure 4.19. The carrier oscillator generates a tone at the specified amplitude and frequency (f_c), and the vibrato oscillator varies that frequency, at the vibrato rate, by a maximum amount equal to the vibrato width. Thus, the instantaneous frequency of the carrier oscillator changes on every sample, varying between f_c plus the vibrato width and f_c minus the vibrato width. Its average frequency is f_c.

  The vibrato width is usually specified as a proportion of the fundamental frequency

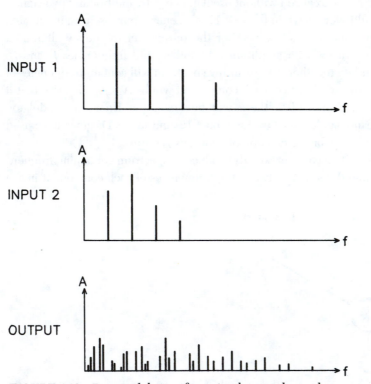

FIGURE 4.18   Ring modulation of two signals to produce a dense spectrum.

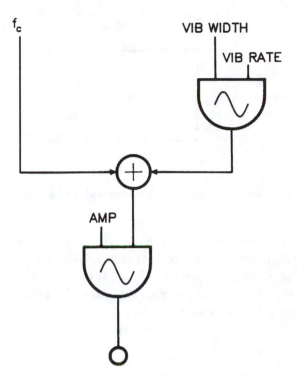

FIGURE 4.19   Simulation of a simple, periodic vibrato.

of the tone and is ordinarily no more than a few percent of f_c. In order for the frequency modulation to be perceived as vibrato, the vibrato rate must be restricted to frequencies below the audio range. The vibrato found in natural sounds can be quite complex. Its rate and width often changes during the course of a tone and frequently contains a certain amount of randomness. Chapter 7 will discuss one of the more complicated forms of natural vibrato, that of the singing voice.

When a large vibrato width at an audio rate is used, the aural effect is no longer that of a simple vibrato. Under these conditions, frequency modulation becomes a powerful synthesis technique capable of producing a wide variety of timbres. Chapter 5 will cover the theory and applications of frequency modulation synthesis in detail.

4.9   NOISE GENERATORS

An oscillator is designed to produce a periodic waveform with well-defined spectral components. The spectrum is a *discrete spectrum;* that is, the energy is found at specific, harmonically related frequencies. The opposite of a discrete spectrum is a *distributed spectrum,* in which energy exists everywhere within a range of frequencies. Most of the noise sounds found in nature have distributed spectra, and thus algorithms designed to generate distributed spectra are called *noise generators.*

Certain phenomena have the characteristic that their repeated occurrence, even under the same set of conditions, will not always lead to the same result. Members of

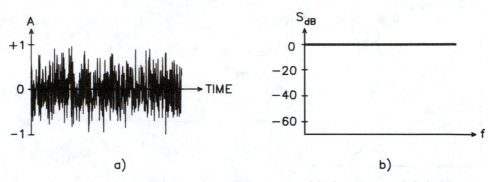

FIGURE 4.20   (a) Segment of the waveform of white noise and (b) the spectrum of ideal white noise.

this class are called *random phenomena*. Even though the exact outcome cannot be predicted, they exhibit a certain amount of statistical regularity that can be used to describe them and to predict the probability of any given occurrence. The statistical characterization of a random signal is used to determine its frequency. (Additional explanation of random processes can be found in chapter 11 as they are applied to composition.)

In sound synthesis, randomness is used to generate distributed spectra. The waveform pictured in figure 4.20a is a segment of the waveform of white noise. If it were digitized, there would be no recognizable pattern of sample values; in fact they would appear to be randomly distributed. The amplitude of the digitized white noise is characterized by a range—the interval within which the maximum and minimum sample values occur. In the figure, the range is –1 to +1. Because, unlike a periodic waveform, a repeating pattern of samples cannot be identified, signals of this type are referred to as *aperiodic*. White noise has a uniformly distributed spectrum as shown in figure 4.20b. Between any two frequencies a fixed distance apart, there is a constant amount of noise power. For instance, there is the same amount of noise power in the band between 100 and 200 Hz, as there is between 7900 and 8000 Hz. White noise makes the "hissing" sound often associated with white noise generated by electronic means.

The unit generator that produces nearly white noise is often called RAND and has an amplitude input. Its symbol is shown in figure 4.21a. The amplitude input sets the range of the permissible output sample values, and hence the amplitude of the noise. If a value AMP is applied to the input, the sampled noise will range between –AMP and +AMP.

The basic algorithm used to generate white noise simply draws a random number on each sample. This makes a good, but not perfect, white-noise source. The spectral distribution of such a generator is shown in figure 4.21b. It deviates slightly from a uniform distribution because of a frequency bias inherent in the process of sample generation. The actual spectral distribution $S(f)$ at frequency f is given by

$$S(f) = \frac{\sin\left(\pi \dfrac{f}{f_s}\right)}{\pi \dfrac{f}{f_s}}$$

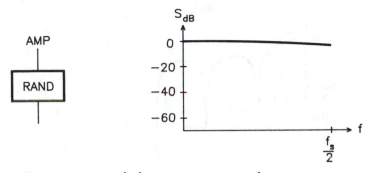

FIGURE 4.21   Digital white-noise generator and its spectrum.

True white noise would have $S(f) = 1$. Over most of the spectrum, the generated noise power is very close to this ideal. At the Nyquist frequency, $S(f_s / 2) = 0.6366$, showing that the power is down less than 4 dB from a true uniform distribution at the top of the frequency range.

White noise has a very large bandwidth. Sometimes it is desirable to narrow the bandwidth by reducing the amount of high-frequency energy in the noise. A noise source with most of its power at low frequencies will make a rumbling sound. An algorithm that synthesizes this kind of spectrum draws random numbers at a rate less than the sampling rate. The unit generator that accomplishes this is often called RANDH (figure 4.22a) and has two inputs: amplitude and the frequency (f_R) at which random numbers are drawn. (On some systems, the frequency is not specified directly, but by a number proportional to f_R, in the same way that the sampling increment is proportional to the frequency of an oscillator.) Choosing random numbers at a rate lower than f_s implies that a random number is held for a few samples, until the next one is to be drawn. For example, if $f_s = 40$ kHz and $f_R = 4$ kHz, the algorithm chooses a random value, outputs it for the next 10 samples, and then chooses another.

When noise is generated by this process, many of the samples are related to each other because their value is the same as the previous sample. This relatedness reduces the noise power in the higher frequencies. The lower the frequency f_R, the smaller the amount of high-frequency energy that will be contained in the noise. Thus, f_R can be thought of as a control on the "bandwidth" of the noise. Figure 4.22b illustrates the spectrum when $f_R = f_s / 6$. The shape of the spectrum in the general case is given by the product of two functions as

$$S(f) = \frac{\sin\left(\pi\dfrac{f}{f_R}\right)}{\pi\dfrac{f}{f_R}} \frac{\sin\left(\pi\dfrac{f}{f_s}\right)}{\pi\dfrac{f}{f_s}}$$

A variation on this technique, one that provides noise spectra with even greater attenuation of the high frequencies, involves interpolation. As before, random numbers are drawn at a rate (f_R) that is lower than the sampling rate. Instead of holding the value

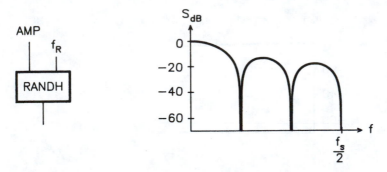

FIGURE 4.22   Digital noise generator (a) in which noise samples are generated at a rate lower than the sampling rate and its spectrum (b).

of the last random number until the next one is drawn, the samples in between draws are interpolated linearly between successive random numbers. This can be visualized as connecting successive random numbers with straight lines. The unit generator that performs this algorithm is often called RANDI (figure 4.23a).

Figure 4.23b illustrates the spectrum of such a noise generator when $f_R = f_s / 6$. Observe the diminished amount of high-frequency energy. The general shape of the spectrum is given by

$$S(f) = \frac{f_R^2 \left[1 - \cos\left(2\pi \dfrac{f}{f_R} \right) \right]}{2\pi f f_s \sin\left(\pi \dfrac{f}{f_s} \right)}$$

It is possible to realize noises with other types of spectral distributions such as $1/f$ (see section 11.1G), in which the spectrum is distributed in inverse proportion to the frequency. Other techniques, such as the one proposed by Siegel, Steiglitz, and Zuckerman,[6] are available for generating random signals with specifiable spectral densities.

How does the computer, which is designed to store and process numbers accurately and reproducibly, obtain seemingly unpredictable random numbers? One way is to sample

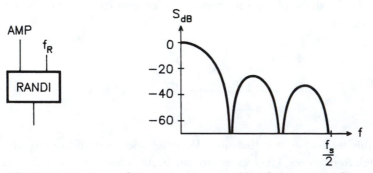

FIGURE 4.23   Interpolating noise generator (a) and its spectrum (b).

an external random physical process such as thermal noise, but this requires additional hardware. A less expensive and more commonly used approach is to employ an algorithm called a *pseudo-random number generator*,[7] which produces a sequence of numbers that satisfy most of the criteria for randomness, with the notable exception that the sequence repeats itself. Fortunately, it is possible to make the period of the sequence so long that for most purposes it can be considered random. A pseudo-random number generator actually creates a discrete harmonic spectrum, but the spectrum is so extraordinarily dense that, for most musical applications, it is indistinguishable from a truly distributed one.

Pseudo-random number generators generally use the most recently generated random number as a basis for calculating the next. As a result, most algorithms give the user the option of specifying a "seed" value. When a seed is specified, the first random number will be calculated on the basis of the seed value. Therefore, starting from the same seed will always yield the same sequence of random numbers. This facility allows two different computer runs involving the generation of pseudo-random numbers to have exactly the same results.

4.10   SYNTHESIS BY MEANS OF SPECTRAL INTERPOLATION

The additive synthesis of tones using the data from prior spectral analyses can re-create tones that are very close to the original. As stated above, the principal drawback to this technique is the large data sets required to represent each timbre. When given the need for a single instrument to have separate data sets for tones in different pitch regions and at different dynamic levels, the impetus for data reduction is strong indeed. One approach, previously described in section 2.7, is to approximate the records of the dynamic spectra with a small number of straight-line segments. In this way, each partial of the tone would be described by simple linear amplitude and frequency envelopes. Beginning with the work of Risset, this method has proven effective in synthesizing realistic tones, but further data reduction can be achieved by the method of spectral interpolation.[8]

As diagrammed in figure 4.24, spectral-interpolation synthesis requires two oscillators, each with a different waveform stored in its wave table. The mix between the two oscillators is controlled by the interpolation parameter x. When x is set to 0, the output consists of only the waveform (WF0) produced by the left oscillator. By contrast, setting x to unity results in the output waveform (WF1) from the right oscillator because the signal contributed by the left oscillator is both added to and subtracted from the output resulting cancellation. The intermediate value of $x = 0.4$, for example, would produce an output that combined 60% of WF0 with 40% of WF1. Figure 4.25 shows an example of the constantly changing waveform produced when x is linearly advanced between 0 and 1.

The method takes advantage of the relatively slow changes exhibited in the waveform during most of the course of a tone. A succession of short-term spectra of the tone to be synthesized is derived. From this analysis, a few representative breakpoints are designated between which the spectra will be interpolated. The density of these breakpoints depends on how quickly the tone is changing. During the attack portion, many individual spectra are required, but during the sustain portion, the harmonic content is changing so slowly that only a few breakpoints can be used.

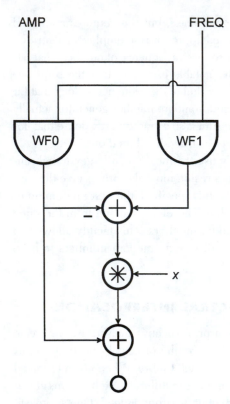

FIGURE 4.24   An instrument that interpolates between the outputs of two oscillators with parameter x controlling the mix.

The data used for spectral-interpolation synthesis are most frequently obtained by the analysis of acoustic sounds. The input is broken down into a series of short-term spectra (see section 7.2), and an analysis algorithm is applied to determine the number and temporal position of the breakpoints required. The algorithm positions the breakpoints by applying a routine that minimizes the spectral error over the course of the tone between the original signal and the one produced by spectral interpolation. To simplify the analysis and storage requirements, it is assumed that the phase of the partials relative to each other has a negligible aural effect. When the spectral-interpolation technique is used to create instruments that simulate natural ones, data must be taken at many different pitch and dynamic levels; but the considerable data compression inherent in this technique at each level makes such an approach practical.

4.11   INSTRUMENT DESIGNS

Each of the chapters of this book in which sound synthesis techniques are discussed includes a number of instrument designs. Because it is anticipated that the readers will be using a variety of musical programming languages, we have used flowcharts to express the instrument designs. The instrument designs are offered as a guide to what

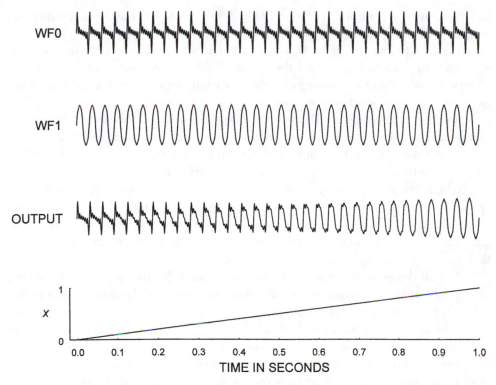

FIGURE 4.25   Waveform produced by interpolating between waveforms WF0 and WF1 as parameter *x* linearly increases as shown.

has been done with a particular sound synthesis technique. The instrument designs are neither exhaustive nor definitive; they are simply offered here as a starting point for the reader to develop a personal vocabulary of designs for computer synthesis.

Some instrument designs are likened to traditional instruments to give the reader a sense of their sound. The timbral impression evoked by these instruments on isolated notes is similar to the stated instrument. In a composition, their identification and their ability to hold the listeners' interest may also depend on the phrasing used and whether or not their musical part is idiomatic to that instrument.

4.11A   Translating Flowchart Diagrams into Music Synthesis Code

Translating flowchart diagrams into written instrument definitions is a task that many musicians find initially difficult. Following is a general guide to the process. It is divided into two stages: analysis of the flowchart and coding of the instrument.

There are three steps involved in analyzing a flowchart. The first step is to find the output or outputs from the instrument. This helps show the basic structure of the instrument. Step 2 consists of designating the separate branches and subbranches of the instrument. By doing this, the musician divides the instrument into its component parts in order to know how to direct the flow of the signal from one unit generator to the next.

In step 3, the musician finds the sources for all the inputs and the destinations of the outputs of all the branches of the instrument.

When starting to encode the instrument design into the sound synthesis language, it is essential to make certain that the use of all the unit generators in the design is understood as well as the meaning of their inputs and outputs. Consult the manual for the particular sound synthesis language to be sure. Start the encoding with the uppermost unit generator either in the flowchart or in a branch of the flowchart. Write out the unit generator name, label its output (if appropriate in the language used), and fill its inputs from the initialization values. It is good practice for most sound synthesis languages to list the initialization values in a separate section at the head of the instrument.

Next, follow the same procedure for the subsequent unit generators of the branch or subbranch until the instrument is coded completely. Keep in mind that the inputs of unit generators to which the outputs of other unit generators are connected ordinarily get their values at performance time. Inputs not fed from other unit generators obtain their values at initialization time.

After all the branches of the instrument are coded, interconnect them by means appropriate to the language used. Finally, direct the results of the instrument into the output(s) by means of an output statement.

Following are some hints for proofreading the code that describes an instrument: (1) check that no unit generators have been omitted; (2) make certain that all unit generators input are of the correct form (e.g., that an input expecting a frequency in hertz is not given a frequency in some other notation); (3) make sure that all unit generators are given the required number of inputs; and (4) check to be certain that all stored functions referred to by the unit generator have the right contents.

Common mistakes in instrument coding include sending the output of one unit generator to the wrong input of the next, or sending it to the wrong unit generator entirely. Be meticulous in checking every input of every unit generator and in carefully labeling the branches of the instrument. Ample comments should appear at the head of the instrument to identify its function and characteristics.

After encoding the instrument design, check the code for correct syntax by invoking the orchestra translation program. The translator will make a trial translation of the code into machine language and give error messages if the syntax is faulty. Next, the musician should try out the instrument on a few typical notes in order to hear whether the instrument does what is wanted. It is possible, and indeed common, for a design to be syntactically correct but not to give the desired results. The trial tones will also be helpful in establishing the limits of the instrument's usefulness. Most instruments show great differences in sound, depending on such factors as note length, register, and amplitude.

Finally, the instrument must be tested in a musical context to find out whether it is appropriate for the musical articulation desired. At this point, such issues as the balance of the instrument with copies of itself in different registers, the balance of the instrument with other instruments in the same and other registers, and masking become important. It is often necessary at this point to recast parts of the instrument to fit the demands of the context in which it will be used.

4.11B   Instrument Design Examples

Our first instrument design uses ring modulation to produce a band of noise. Controls on both the center frequency and the width of the band are provided. While more focused noise spectra can be synthesized by filtering white noise (see section 6.8), this method is both efficient and useful for many musical purposes.

As shown in figure 4.26, a noise generator ring-modulates a sinusoidal oscillator. This process translates the noise generator's low-frequency noise to a higher-frequency region, centering the noise band at the frequency (FREQ) of the oscillator. The amplitude input to the noise generator (AMP) directly controls the amplitude of the noise band. The frequency at which the random noise is generated, f_R, determines the bandwidth of the noise (see section 4.9). If the bandwidth is sufficiently small, the noise will be perceived as pitched. A noise band with a width of 20% of the center frequency will produce a good sensation of pitch. A noise band with a bandwidth of 5% of the center frequency will sound less "noisy" and have a highly focused pitch. A glissando of a noise band can be synthesized by programming the oscillator to a glissando. James Tenney realized the glissandoing noise bands of his *Noise Study* in this way.[9]

Figure 4.27 shows another use of a noise band created with random ring modulation. Jean-Claude Risset used this technique to simulate the sound of the snares in a drum instrument.[10] The three oscillators each contribute different components at different amplitudes. The decay of F2 is steeper than that of F1, so that the two oscillators on the left side (labeled NOISE and INHARM), which contain the higher-frequency components of the sound, die away sooner than the oscillator on the right (FUND). The latter oscillator samples a stored sine tone producing a tone at the fundamental frequency. The INHARM oscillator samples a stored waveform (F3) consisting of partials 10, 16, 22, and 23 with relative amplitudes 1, 1.5, 2, and 1.5, respectively. When the frequency of the INHARM oscillator is set to 1/10 that of

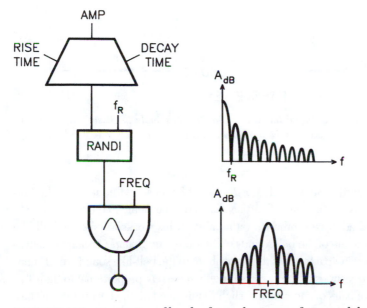

FIGURE 4.26   Generation of bands of noise by means of ring modulation.

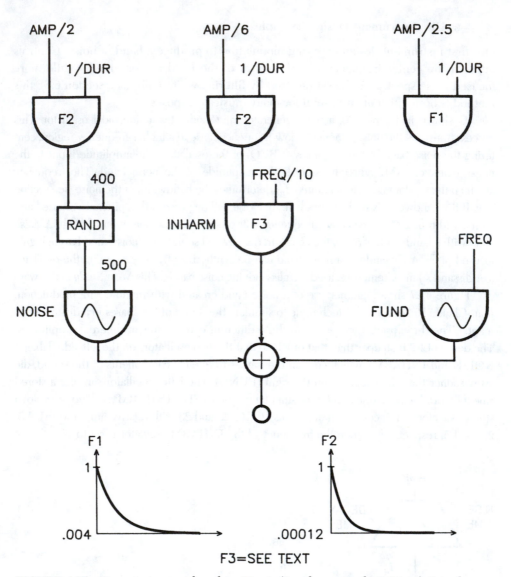

FIGURE 4.27   Drum instrument based on Risset. *(Based on example in Risset's* Introductory Catalogue of Computer-Synthesized Sounds. *Reprinted with permission of Jean-Claude Risset.)*

the FUND oscillator, its partials sound at 1, 1.6, 2.2, and 2.3 times the frequency of the fundamental, producing in this way a group of partials that is nonharmonic to the fundamental.

Risset has employed additive synthesis in a number of his works to produce bell-like sounds. A design based on one of the bell sounds of the *Computer Sound Catalog*[11] is shown in figure 4.28. The three principal features that contribute to the bell-like sound are: (1) nonharmonic partials; (2) decay times of the partials roughly inversely proportional to their frequency; and (3) beating of pairs of components, slightly mistuned on the lowest two partials.

Risset points out that while the partials are inharmonic, they are not tuned arbitrar-

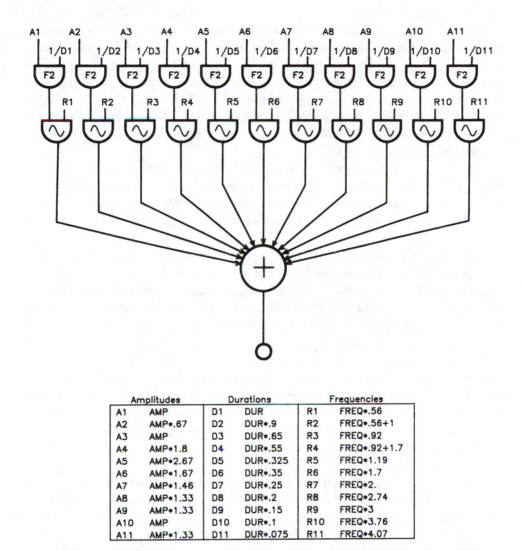

Amplitudes		Durations		Frequencies	
A1	AMP	D1	DUR	R1	FREQ*.56
A2	AMP*.67	D2	DUR*.9	R2	FREQ*.56+1
A3	AMP	D3	DUR*.65	R3	FREQ*.92
A4	AMP*1.8	D4	DUR*.55	R4	FREQ*.92+1.7
A5	AMP*2.67	D5	DUR*.325	R5	FREQ*1.19
A6	AMP*1.67	D6	DUR*.35	R6	FREQ*1.7
A7	AMP*1.46	D7	DUR*.25	R7	FREQ*2.
A8	AMP*1.33	D8	DUR*.2	R8	FREQ*2.74
A9	AMP*1.33	D9	DUR*.15	R9	FREQ*3
A10	AMP	D10	DUR*.1	R10	FREQ*3.76
A11	AMP*1.33	D11	DUR*.075	R11	FREQ*4.07

FIGURE 4.28   Bell instrument based on Risset. *(Based on example in Risset's* Introductory Catalogue of Computer-Synthesized Sounds. *Reprinted with permission of Jean-Claude Risset.)*

ily. The first five partials of bell tones approximate the following: a fundamental, a minor third, a perfect fifth, a "hum tone" at an octave below the fundamental, and the "nominal" at an octave above the fundamental. The ratios in frequency for this grouping of partials are 1:1.2:1.5:0.5:2. In his design, Risset extends the series to include higher partials, and tunes the partials to the following ratios—0.56:0.92:1.19:1.70:2:2.74:3:3.76:4.07.

The waveform of each component is a sinusoid and the envelope (F2) is an exponential decay from 1 to 2^{-10}. The duration used in the *Sound Catalog* is 20 seconds. When implementing the design suggested in the figure, it is advisable to use a method of "turning off" the oscillator pairs after their playing time has elapsed, in order to save computation time.

Another of Risset's designs from the *Computer Sound Catalog* is shown in figure 4.29. It represents a computer instrument that produces an "endless glissando" or *Shepard tone*. Psychologist Roger Shepard discovered that the apparent register of tones in musical scales could be made ambiguous by carefully controlling the amplitude of the partials of the tones. Shepard produced scales that were perceived as "circular" in pitch—while appearing to move continuously in one direction along the scale, they actually never left the register in which they began. Risset extended this principle to achieve the same effect with glissandoing tones as well.

The design is a highly controlled glissando configuration in which 10 interpolating oscillators track the same amplitude and frequency functions. Each sinusoidal oscillator is controlled by two interpolating oscillators sampling amplitude and frequency functions, respectively. The function F3, which controls the frequency, is exponential. This produces a constant change of musical interval per unit time. F3 decays from 1 to 2^{-10}, producing a frequency change of 10 octaves over its duration. Each pair of controlling oscillators has the same initial phase. However, their phase is offset by 1/10 of a cycle from the phase of a neighboring pair. This corresponds to a phase offset of 51.2 when using a wave table of 512 locations. Because F3 exponentially decays from 1 to 2^{-10}, the phase offset of 1/10 cycle results in the 10 oscillators glissandoing downward in parallel octaves. When an oscillator reaches the end of F3, it "wraps around" to the beginning of the function and continues. Ordinarily, such a large discontinuity in frequency (a 10-octave jump) would cause a click and destroy the effect of smooth glissandoing. However, during the transition, the amplitude function (F2) is at its minimum value, preventing our hearing the click. On the other hand, when a tone passes through the midrange, F2 greatly emphasizes it. The effect of summing the 10 sinusoidal oscillators together is that of a continually glissandoing tone in which no change of register occurs.

Risset has observed that the computer must have sufficient word length to accurately represent the phase in order to prevent noticeable roundoff error. For the acoustical illusion to be effective, a sufficient duration must be used. Risset chose 120 seconds for the completion of the entire cycle of 10 glissandos. He used the design and other closely related ones in his composition, *Mutations I* (see section 4.12).

A useful class of sounds for certain kinds of musical textures is *choral tone*, which is analogous to the effect in acoustic music of more than one instrument or voice playing a line in unison. A spectral analysis of a group of instruments playing in unison reveals a significant amount of *spreading* in components of the spectrum; that is, the energy of each component will be more widely distributed about its average frequency than when a single instrument is playing. This is the result of slight mistunings of the instruments and the lack of correlation among their vibratos.

The effect can be approximated by adding another copy of the computer instrument design at 1 or 2 Hz away from the original and then applying a small (approximately 1%) amount of random frequency deviation to both instruments. The randomness is best implemented with a noise generator that has most of its energy below 20 Hz. Also, because voices do not enter and exit at exactly the same times, a small amount of random deviation in their starting times and durations, as well as in the breakpoints of their envelopes, is desirable. Another method that uses delay lines is described in chapter 10.

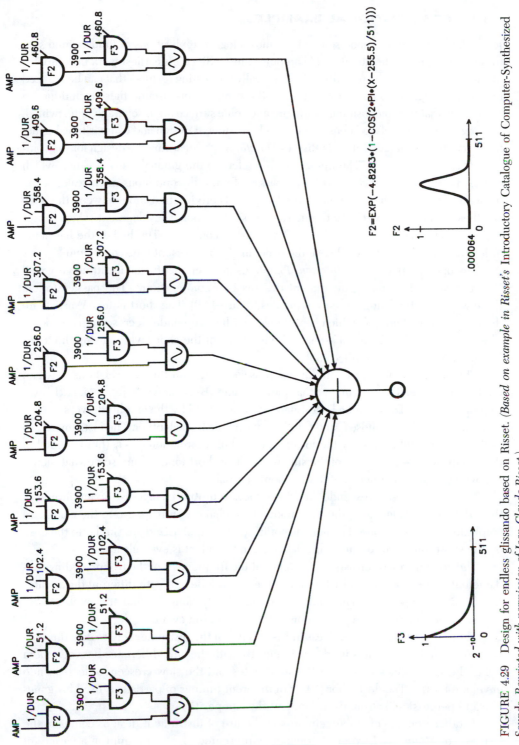

$F2 = EXP(-4.8283*(1-COS(2*PI*(X-255.5)/511)))$

FIGURE 4.29 Design for endless glissando based on Risset. *(Based on example in Risset's* Introductory Catalogue of Computer-Synthesized Sounds. *Reprinted with permission of Jean-Claude Risset.)*

4.12   COMPOSITIONAL EXAMPLES

Jean-Claude Risset has made some of the most elegant applications of fundamental synthesis techniques in the literature of computer music. Since his earliest work in computer music, Risset has shown an ability to find sonically interesting textures that can be realized uniquely by digital synthesis. Risset then builds compositions around these techniques in such a way that the compositional structure and sonic surface are inseparably intertwined.

A good example of a composition in which instrument design and compositional structure serve to support each other is Risset's *Mutations I*.[12] Regarding the design for the composition, Risset has said, "The title *Mutations* refers to the gradual transformation which occurs throughout the piece, and to the passage from a discontinuous pitch scale, at the beginning, to the pitch continuum in the last part. There is a transition between the scale and the continuum, in particular through a process of harmonic development, which causes the successive harmonics of the notes of a chord to come out. The higher the harmonic order, the finer the pitch step, hence the scale finally dissolves into the continuum."[13]

The opening passage of *Mutations I* contains three elements that illustrate very well Risset's way of integrating instrument designs into composition.[14] The passage offers three ways of articulating a group of pitches (figure 4.30). The short notes (A) articulate the tones of the chord (B), which is prolonged with a crescendo-decrescendo envelope. The gonglike sound (C) at 4.0″ echoes the harmony of the chord while fusing the tones into the perception of a unified timbre.

The design of the instrument for this passage brings out the interrelations between pitch and timbre. The instrument that plays (A) and (B) is shown in figure 4.31. It uses ring modulation of a sine tone by a square wave specified by the amplitude-versus-time approximation. Risset chose f_0 and f_1 to be inharmonic to each other. The instrument has as its predominant frequency the lower sideband of the relation $f_1 - f_0$ (fundamental of the square wave – frequency of the sine wave). The short tones sound somewhat metallic, owing to the prominence of nonharmonic partials.

The crescendo-decrescendo chord produces a timbre change as the amplitude of the sidebands, produced by the ring modulation, changes in response to the change in amplitude of the sine tone. The nonharmonic partials emphasized are similar to the ones on the short tones, but because they last longer, the effect is even clearer.

The gonglike tone consists of sine tones at the frequencies of the five preceding fundamentals, all encompassed by the same attack envelope and with different decay rates for the five components. The timbre is unmistakably gonglike and the pitch quality unmistakably echoes the same harmony as the preceding events.

There is a great resourcefulness in Risset's use of the instruments to realize this passage. A single instrument is used for (A) and (B), with the only difference between them being the sharp attack (0.01″) for the short notes and the slow crescendo-decrescendo envelope for (B). The design for (C), with different tunings of partials, is used for gonglike and percussionlike sounds throughout the composition.

Another example of resourcefulness in the use of instrument designs comes in the last part of *Mutations I*, where frequency is presented as a continuum in a variety of ways. The most striking representation is in the "endless glissando," the design for

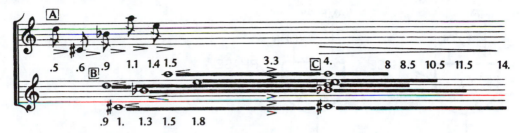

FIGURE 4.30   Three ways of articulating pitches from Risset's *Mutations. (Based on example in Risset's* Introductory Catalogue of Computer-Synthesized Sounds. *Reprinted with permission of Jean-Claude Risset.)*

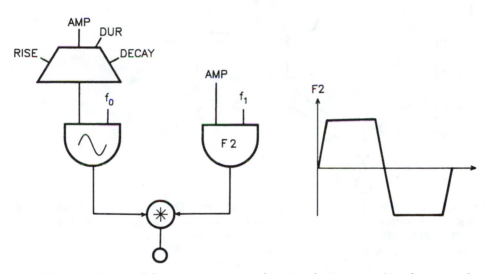

FIGURE 4.31   Ring-modulation instrument used in Risset's *Mutations. (Based on example in Risset's* Introductory Catalogue of Computer-Synthesized Sounds. *Reprinted with permission of Jean-Claude Risset.)*

which was described in section 4.11. A variation on that design is used in the last part of *Mutations I.* Here the glissando is eliminated, so that one perceives only the gradual change of emphasis in pitch among the 10 octaves (figure 4.32).

Risset's *Inharmonique*[15] for soprano and tape is also based on an acoustic scenario. The composer writes, "In *Inharmonique*, sounds emerge from noise, then the voice emerges from the tape sounds, flourishes, and is eventually sent far away and buried under the tape sounds."[16] He continues, "The title *Inharmonique* refers to the systemic use of synthetic tones made up of precisely controlled inharmonic partials. Such tones are composed like chords, and they can either fuse into pitched clangs or be diffracted into fluid textures."

Much of the precompositional effort for *Inharmonique* was in creating groups of chords. The chords served as the pitch material for the piece. They are heard in the earlier parts of the work as fused, pitched clangs and later in the work as "fluid textures." The transformation from one to the other is effected with remarkable simplicity and ele-

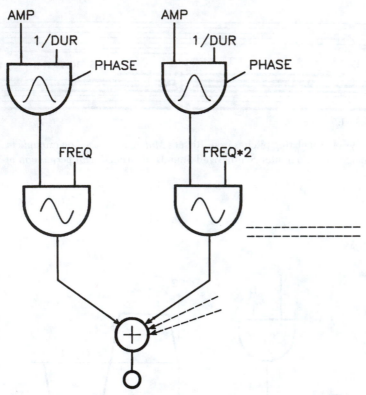

FIGURE 4.32 Design to produce gradual change of octave. The phase of each controlling oscillator is offset from that of the oscillator on its left by an amount equal to the wave-table length divided by the number of branches. (*Based on example in Risset's* Introductory Catalogue of Computer-Synthesized Sounds. *Reprinted with permission of Jean-Claude Risset.*)

gance: simply by changing the amplitude envelope of each component from that of an exponential decay to a gradual rise and decay.

The first stage in the precomposition was to specify the pitched clangs and to enter them into the Music 5 score of the work. Risset has described this as "composing the sound itself."[17] The data shown on the next page were used to produce two of the "bell structures" for *Inharmonique*. All the bell structures were specified as data to be turned into Music 5 notes by a PLF subroutine.

The PLF subroutine that processes the SV1 statements makes any transposition of the structure specified in the score and creates the many individual notes needed to realize the bell structures. All partials are given the same starting time. Risset's usual practice is to assign greater durations to the lower tones of the chord. To use the same score to produce a diffracted texture, the only change needed is to assign an envelope to each component that, instead of having an exponential decay, has a slow rise and a gradual decay. In some places in *Inharmonique,* the tempo is doubled when creating a diffracted texture in order for the transformation to take shape more rapidly. The effect will

	No. of Components	Global Ampl.	Subjective Frequency	Instr. No.	Component		
					Fr.	Dur.	Ampl.
SV1 0 1210	11	1400	226	3	224	20	150
					225	18	100
					368	13	150
					369.7	11	270
					476	6.5	400
					680	7	250
					800	5	220
					1094	4	200
					1200	3	200
					1504	2	150
					1628	1.5	200
SV1 0 1700	13	740	86.2	4	35	15	60
					82	20	200
					82.4	17	150
					165	20	200
					200	15	300
					342	6	200
					425	5	150
					500	7	200
					895	4	50
					1303	2	40
					1501	1	50
					1700	4	60
					2200	1.5	40

be for the tones not to fuse into the percept of a clang, but rather to be heard as a fluid succession of tones from high to low.

For the noise sounds at the beginning of *Inharmonique*, Risset uses a design for creating bands of noise by ring-modulating a sine wave with noise (figure 4.33). The bands of noise change in amplitude, bandwidth, and center frequency throughout each note.[18]

In the instrument design, PEAK AMP sets the maximum for each note. The envelope of each note, multiplied by the peak amplitude throughout the note, causes the amplitude to change in the pattern of F5 or F6. For *Inharmonique*, Risset actually has each note played by a pair of "twin" instruments—one of the designs shown in the figure using F5 for its envelope, the other identical to it except that its envelope is controlled by the shape of F6. The outputs of the twin instruments are sent to separate channels, and so the effect is an exchange of sound back and forth between the loudspeakers in the course of the note.

The average width of the noise band is determined by the value of the constant

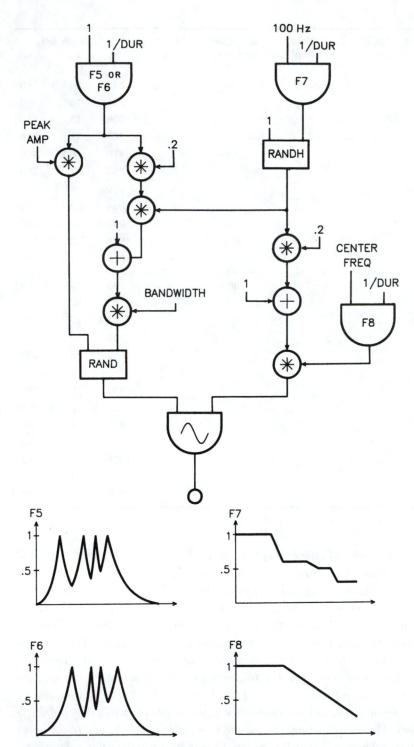

FIGURE 4.33 Instrument from Risset's *Inharmonique*. *(Based on design published in* Inharmonique, Analyse de la Bande Magnetique de l'Oeuvre de Jean-Claude Risset, *by Denis Lorrain. Published with permission of Jean-Claude Risset.)*

BANDWIDTH. The bandwidth changes, however, in response both to the shape of the amplitude envelope and to the output of the RANDH unit generator in the right branch of the instrument. The rate at which the RANDH puts out a new value is 100 Hz at the beginning of each note and decreases through two intermediate rates to 30 Hz for the final sixth of the note. Thus, the envelope is first scaled to the range between 0 and 0.2 by the first multiplication of the left branch and then to a value between ±0.2 by a new random value at the rate of 100 to 30 Hz. The value 1.0 is then added to make the value in the range 0.8 to 1.2. The final multiplication in the left branch then results in a bandwidth that fluctuates at random within ±20% of the BANDWIDTH constant.

There is an overall direction to the change of center frequency for each note: the note begins around its initial value and, after 200/512 of its duration, begins to fall linearly to one-quarter of its value. The actual value of the center frequency fluctuates at random within ±20% of its value.

While several examples of nonharmonic partials, such as those discussed above, are evident in the "metallic" quality of many of the sounds in *Inharmonique*, there are also passages in which the harmonic series itself is prominent. A tone can be "thickened" by placing next to it identical tones of slightly different frequencies. A good example of this effect can be heard in the section of the work which begins at $T = 3$ minutes. There, the texture is dominated by long dronelike tones of various durations on $A = 55$, 110, and 220 Hz. Clearly heard above the fundamentals are cascades of tones that are arpeggiating downward through the harmonic series. The effect is caused by the very slow beating of components that are very close in frequency. The spectrum of all the tones is one rich in higher partials that are only slightly less emphasized than the fundamental (figure 4.34).

A single dronelike tone is made by placing nine oscillators with identical waveforms and envelopes very close together in frequency. For example, the nine oscillators of the first tone are tuned to 110, 110.03, 110.06, 110.09, 110.12, 109.97, 109.94, 109.91, and 109.88 Hz. A highly complex pattern of beating is set into motion by the small differences in frequency between not only the nine fundamentals but also all the harmonics of all the tones. The harmonics will beat with each other at different rates; whether they are in phase at a given moment will cause them to be either emphasized or attenuated.

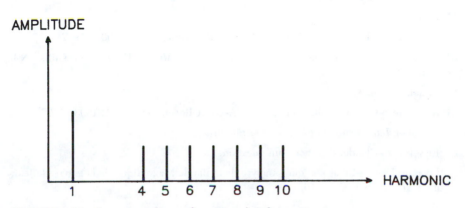

FIGURE 4.34   Spectrum of tones from Risset's *Inharmonique*.

This effect is possible only when using accurate, stable oscillators that interpolate between successive output samples.

The cascade effect takes place when the harmonics come into phase successively from the highest harmonic on down to the fundamental. There are many other breathtaking effects in *Inharmonique,* and the reader is directed to a text, in French, by Denis Lorrain for explanation and details of design of both the instruments and the score.[19]

NOTES

1. Hartmann, W. M. "Digital Waveform Generation by Fractional Addressing." *Journal of the Acoustical Society of America,* 82, 1987. 1883–1891.

2. Moore, F. R. "Table Lookup Noise for Sinusoidal Digital Oscillators." *Computer Music Journal,* 1(2), 1977, 26–29. Reprinted in C. Roads (ed.), *Fundamentals of Computer Music,* Cambridge: MIT Press, 1985.

3. Risset, Jean-Claude. *Computer Study of Trumpet Tones.* Murray Hill, N.J.: Bell Telephone Laboratories, 1966.

4. Grey, John. "An Exploration of Musical Timbre." Doctoral dissertation, Stanford University, 1975.

5. Dashow, James. "Three Methods for the Digital Synthesis of Chordal Structures with Non-harmonic Partials." *Interface,* 7, 1978, 69–94.

6. Siegel, L., Steiglitz, K., and Zuckerman, M. "The Design of Markov Chains for Waveform Generation." *Proceedings of the Institute of Electrical and Electronics Engineers (EASCON),* October, 1975.

7. Knuth, Donald. *The Art of Computer Programming (vol. 2): Seminumerical Algorithms.* Reading, Mass.: Addison-Wesley, 1969, 1–160.

8. Serra, M.-H., Rubine, D., and Dannenberg, R. "Analysis and Synthesis of Tones by Spectral Interpolation." *Journal of the Audio Engineering Society,* 38(3), 1990, 111–128.

9. Tenney, James. "Noise Study." *James Tenney Selected Works 1961–1969,* Frog Peak and Artifact Recordings (FP001/ART 1007), 1992.

10. Risset, Jean-Claude. *Introductory Catalogue of Computer-Synthesized Sounds.* Murray Hill, N.J.: Bell Telephone Laboratories, 1969. Reprinted with CD recording. *Computer Music Currents 13,* Wergo (WER 2033–2), 1994.

11. Ibid.

12. Risset, Jean-Claude. "Mutations." INA-GRM Recording (INA C 1003), 1987.

13. Schrader, Barry. *Introduction to Electro-Acoustic Music.* Englewood Cliffs, N.J.: Prentice-Hall, 1982, 197.

14. Risset, *Introductory Catalogue.*

15. Risset, Jean-Claude. "Inharmonique." INA-GRM Recording (INA C 1003), 1987.

16. Schrader, *Introduction to Electro-Acoustic Music.*

17. Risset, Jean-Claude. Private communication.

18. Lorrain, Denis. "Inharmonique, Analyse de la Bande Magnetique de l'Oeuvre de Jean-Claude Risset." *Rapports IRCAM,* 16, 1980.

19. Ibid.

5

Synthesis Using Distortion Techniques

In their efforts to synthesize natural-sounding spectra, musicians have sought means that are more efficient than additive synthesis. Several of the techniques developed have been conveniently grouped into a class called *distortion synthesis* (or *nonlinear synthesis*). The class includes frequency modulation, nonlinear waveshaping, and the explicit use of discrete summation formulas. This chapter will concentrate on the first two techniques, both of which have found extensive application in the digital synthesis of musical sounds. The chapter concludes with three examples of synthesis methods that explicitly use discrete summation formulas.

Whereas additive synthesis uses a separate oscillator for each spectral component, a distortion-synthesis technique uses a small number of oscillators to create spectra with many more components than the number of oscillators. Each distortion-synthesis technique affords the musician single-parameter control over the spectral richness of the sound. Thus, time-evolving spectra can be produced with relative ease.

5.1   FM SYNTHESIS

Audio synthesis by means of *frequency modulation* (FM), pioneered by John Chowning,[1] is perhaps the single greatest advancement in improving the accessibility of high-quality, computer-synthesized sound. Frequency modulation can be thought of as the alteration or distortion of the frequency of an oscillator in accordance with the amplitude of a modulating signal. The vibrato instrument described in section 4.8C is an example of an instrument that implements frequency modulation. It uses a subaudio vibrato rate and a vibrato width of less than a semitone, so that the resulting sound has a perceptibly slow variation in its fundamental frequency. However, when the vibrato frequency is in the audio range and the vibrato width is allowed to become much larger, FM can be used to generate a broad range of distinctive timbres that can be easily controlled.

5.1A   Basic Technique

The most basic FM instrument, diagrammed in figure 5.1, consists of two sinusoidal oscillators. A constant carrier frequency, f_c, is added to the output of the modulating oscillator and the result is applied to the frequency input of the carrier oscillator. If the amplitude of the modulating signal is 0, there is no modulation and the output from the carrier oscil-

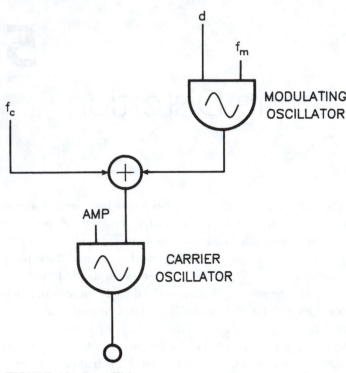

FIGURE 5.1   Basic FM instrument.

lator is simply a sine wave with frequency f_c. When modulation occurs, the signal from the modulating oscillator, a sine wave with frequency f_m, drives the frequency of the carrier oscillator both above and below the carrier frequency. The change in the frequency of the carrier oscillator is proportional to the amplitude of the signal from the modulating oscillator. When, on a given sample, the output of the modulating oscillator is positive, the frequency of the carrier oscillator is larger than f_c. Conversely, a negative output sample from the modulating oscillator drives the frequency of the carrier oscillator below f_c.

The peak frequency deviation (or simply, *deviation*) is defined as the maximum amount of change from f_c that the frequency of a carrier oscillator undergoes. The deviation, referred to as d, is set by the value applied to the amplitude input of the modulating oscillator. This value is expressed in terms of hertz or sampling increment. It is not inappropriate for a "frequency" to be applied to an amplitude input: in FM, the digital signal coming out of the modulating oscillator represents a frequency that is to be combined with the carrier frequency.

The maximum instantaneous frequency that the carrier oscillator will assume is $f_c + d$, and the minimum is $f_c - d$. If the deviation is large, it is possible for the carrier oscillator to have a negative number applied to its frequency input. In a digital oscillator, this corresponds to a negative sampling increment, forcing the oscillator's phase to move backward. Most, but not all, digital oscillators are capable of doing this. Those that cannot are of limited usefulness for FM synthesis because the maximum deviation cannot exceed the carrier frequency.

5.1B   The Spectrum of Simple FM

In simple FM, both oscillators have sinusoidal waveforms. The frequency-modulation technique can produce such rich spectra that it is seldom necessary to use more complicated waveforms. In fact, when one waveform with a large number of spectral components frequency-modulates another, the resulting spectrum can be so dense that it sounds harsh and undefined.

Because frequency modulation is a well-known technique of radio communication, its spectrum has been well characterized. Figure 5.2 illustrates the spectrum of an FM sound. There are spectral components at the carrier frequency and on either side of it, spaced at a distance equal to the modulating frequency. These upper and lower sidebands are grouped in pairs according to the harmonic number of f_m. Mathematically stated, the frequencies present in a simple FM spectrum are $f_c \pm k f_m$, where k is an integer that can assume any value greater than or equal to 0. The carrier component is indicated by $k = 0$.

The distribution of power among the spectral components depends in part on the amount of frequency deviation, d, produced by the modulating oscillator. When $d = 0$, no modulation occurs and therefore all of the signal power resides in the component at the carrier frequency. Increasing the deviation causes the sidebands to acquire more power at the expense of the power in the carrier frequency. The wider the deviation, the more widely distributed is the power among the sidebands and the greater the number of sidebands that have significant amplitudes. Thus, the deviation can act as a control on the bandwidth of the spectrum of an FM signal.

The amplitude of each spectral component is determined by both the deviation and the frequency of modulation. To describe these amplitudes mathematically, it is useful to define an *index of modulation, I,* as

$$I = \frac{d}{f_m}$$

The amplitude of each sideband depends on the index of modulation as shown in table 5.1. The amplitude of the carrier (the "zeroth sideband") is equal to $J_0(I)$. Thus, the absolute value of the amplitude of the kth sideband is given by $J_k(I)$, where J is a Bessel function of the first kind, k is the order of the function, and the argument is the index of modulation.

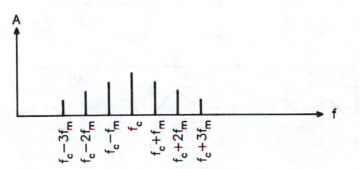

FIGURE 5.2   Spectrum of simple FM exhibiting sidebands through $k = 3$.

	Lower		Upper	
k	Freq	Amp	Freq	Amp
1	$f_c - f_m$	$-J_1(I)$	$f_c + f_m$	$J_1(I)$
2	$f_c - 2f_m$	$J_2(I)$	$f_c + 2f_m$	$J_2(I)$
3	$f_c - 3f_m$	$-J_3(I)$	$f_c + 3f_m$	$J_3(I)$
4	$f_c - 4f_m$	$J_4(I)$	$f_c + 4f_m$	$J_4(I)$
5	$f_c - 5f_m$	$-J_5(I)$	$f_c + 5f_m$	$J_5(I)$
⋮	⋮	⋮	⋮	⋮

TABLE 5.1   Sidebands of simple FM

Bessel functions are mathematical functions that can be used to solve several equations, one of which is the FM equation. Their values can be computed by means of an infinite sum, which is easily approximated by preprogrammed functions found in modern numerical analysis programs. Another method of evaluation is to refer to the tables of Bessel functions commonly found in handbooks of mathematical functions.[2] The table shows that the amplitude of the odd-numbered lower sidebands is the appropriate Bessel function multiplied by −1. This pattern is a direct consequence of the relationship $J_{-k}(I) = -J_k(I)$ when k is odd.

Figure 5.3 displays Bessel functions plotted for orders 0 through 5. When there is

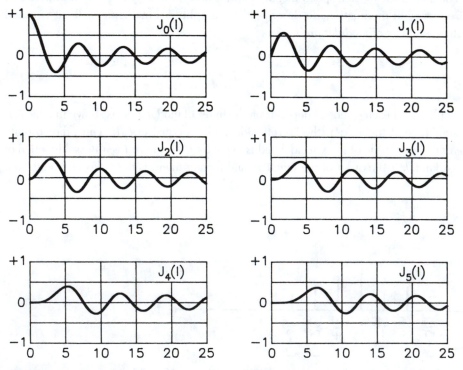

FIGURE 5.3   Bessel functions of orders 0 through 5.

no modulation, the index of modulation I is 0 and the Bessel functions of every order except the zeroth order are zero-valued. Because $J_0(0) = 1$, all the signal power resides in the carrier frequency as expected.

The graphs illustrate that the amplitudes in the higher-order sidebands do not become significant until the value of I is large. In general, the highest-ordered sideband that has significant amplitude is given by the approximate expression $k = I + 1$, where I is rounded to the nearest integer. Knowing the carrier and modulating frequencies, this relationship is useful for estimating the index of modulation at which foldover of the highest significant spectral component will occur.

Notice that the plot of Bessel functions shown in figure 5.3 indicates that a sideband can have either a positive or a negative amplitude, depending on the value of I. When the amplitude is positive, the component is said to be "in phase," meaning it has a phase of 0°. Conversely, a negative amplitude indicates that the component is "out of phase," and its phase equals 180°. Out-of-phase components are graphically represented by plotting their amplitudes downward as in figure 5.4.

The phase of a spectral component does not have an audible effect unless other spectral components of the same frequency are present. In this case, the amplitudes of all these components will either add or subtract from each other, depending on their respective phases.

As shown in figure 5.4, frequency modulation produces components both above and below the carrier frequency. Because they are the difference between two frequencies, it is quite common for some of the lower sidebands to have negative frequencies. To predict their effect on the resultant sound, it is convenient to form a net spectrum by folding the negative frequencies around 0 Hz to their corresponding positions as positive frequencies. The act of folding the component reverses its phase, and so a sideband with a negative frequency is equivalent to a component with the corresponding positive frequency with the opposite phase. In other words, folding a negative-frequency component with a negative amplitude results in a component at the corresponding positive frequency with a positive amplitude. Similarly, a negative-frequency component with a positive amplitude subtracts from its corresponding positive-frequency component when folded over.

In computing the spectrum of an FM waveform, if a component with amplitude x is present at the frequency of a folded component with amplitude y, then x and y must be

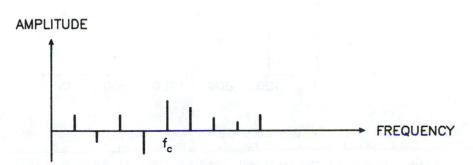

FIGURE 5.4   FM spectrum in which some of the components have negative amplitudes.

combined. In this case, the phases of the components are important; if they have the same phase, they are added; if they have different ones, they are subtracted.

As an example, consider the spectrum produced when $f_c = 400$ Hz, $f_m = 400$ Hz, and $I = 3$. Figure 5.5a shows the computed spectrum with the relative phases of the components indicated. Figure 5.5b shows how the phases of the negative-frequency components reverse as they are folded into positive frequencies. For instance, the positive component at -1200 Hz is subtracted from the component at 1200 Hz. Figure 5.5c shows the magnitude of the net spectrum, which corresponds to its audible properties.

Several useful properties can be inferred by examining the ratio of the carrier frequency to the modulating frequency. Defining

$$\frac{f_c}{f_m} = \frac{N_1}{N_2}$$

where N_1 and N_2 are integers with no common factors, the fundamental frequency (f_0) of the resulting sound will be

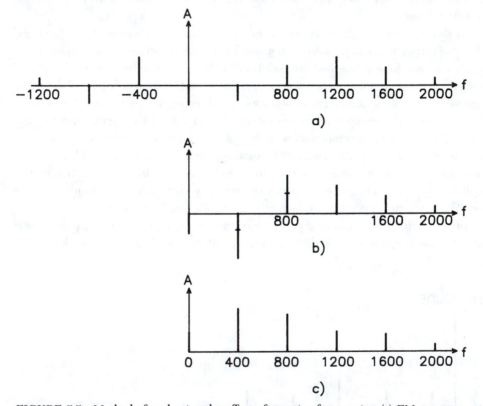

FIGURE 5.5   Method of evaluating the effect of negative frequencies. (a) FM spectrum with negative frequencies; (b) folding the negative-frequency components around 0 Hz and adding them to the existing positive-frequency components; (c) net spectrum displaying just the magnitude of the components.

$$f_0 = \frac{f_c}{N_1} = \frac{f_m}{N_2}$$

This fundamental equation applies to some of the other types of distortion synthesis. If $N_2 =$ 1, then the spectrum contains all the harmonics of f_0. If $N_2 = M$, where M is an integer greater than 1, then every Mth harmonic of f_0 is missing. For example, if $N_2 = 2$, the spectrum will lack even harmonics. When $N_2 = 1$ or $N_2 = 2$, the folded negative-frequency components will coincide with the positive components and must be combined. For any other value of N_2, none of the folded negative-frequency components coincides with a positive one. This suggests that spectra produced in the first case will not be as dense as the spectra produced when N_2 is greater than 2 (assuming the same index of modulation in each case).

If either f_c or f_m is an irrational number, then N_1 and N_2 cannot be defined. In this case, an inharmonic spectrum results, such as the one illustrated in figure 5.6a, where $f_c{:}f_m = 1{:}\sqrt{2}$. When N_1 and N_2 have large integer values, the listener will tend to perceive the tone as inharmonic, because N_1 and N_2 will imply relationships among high harmonics with a low fundamental where no "tonal fusion" takes place. For example, sound produced with a ratio of 5:7 (1:1.4), as in figure 5.6b, is close to that produced when the ratio is $1{:}\sqrt{2}$ (1:1.4142 . . .).

The basic FM instrument shown in figure 5.1 uses a sine wave in both the modulating and the carrier oscillators. At the beginning of the FM sound synthesis process, both are

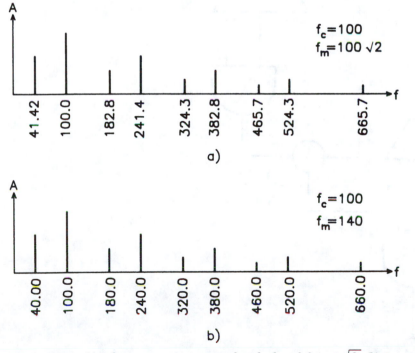

FIGURE 5.6   (a) Inharmonic spectrum produced when $f_c{:}f_m = 1{:}\sqrt{2}$. (b) Spectrum produced when $f_c{:}f_m = 5{:}7$.

assumed to have an initial value of 0 because they start at the left side of the sine wave shown. This configuration, based on the pioneering work of Chowning, produces the particular spectrum described in this section. When other phase relationships exist between the oscillator waveforms, such as when one oscillator uses a sine wave and the other a cosine wave, the spectral components generated have different phases than the ones described here.[3] The difference in the resulting spectrum of the sound will be particularly audible when the $N_1:N_2$ ratio is such that the negative-frequency components combine with positive ones. The FM instrument designs appearing in this text produce the results described when the specific waveforms shown are used. Synthesis with other phase relationships between the carrier and modulating waveforms will not, in many cases, produce the same sound.

5.1C Obtaining Dynamic Spectra

Because FM has a single index for controlling the spectral richness of a sound, its use simplifies the synthesis of time-varying, dynamic spectra. The index of modulation controls the spectral content of an FM signal, and so an envelope applied to the index will cause the spectrum to change with time. Figure 5.7 illustrates a simple instrument that produces dynamic

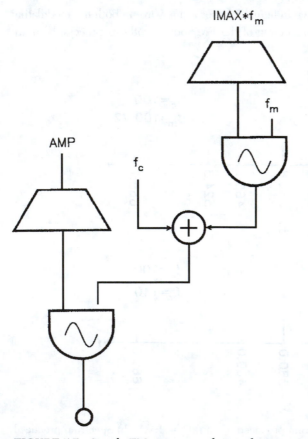

FIGURE 5.7   Simple FM instrument that produces time-varying spectra.

spectra. Notice that there are two separate envelopes, one for the spectrum and one for the amplitude. IMAX is the maximum value that the index will assume. To drive the modulating oscillator, IMAX is converted to a deviation by multiplying it by the modulating frequency.

The progression of the spectral components with index can be complicated when the effects of the folded negative sidebands are taken into account. By examining the shape of the Bessel functions in figure 5.3, it is not hard to see that the evolution of an FM signal generally has a certain amount of "ripple" in it. That is, as the index increases, the amplitude of any particular component will not increase smoothly, but instead will alternately increase and decrease, sometimes passing through 0. The amount of ripple is somewhat proportional to the maximum value of the modulation index. To demonstrate, figure 5.8 plots the time-varying spectrum produced by the instrument of figure 5.7 with the parameter values indicated. Observe the ripple in the evolution of the spectrum.

Unlike additive synthesis, frequency modulation allows only certain types of spectral evolutions. Ordinarily, it will not be possible for a musician to match on a point-by-point basis the component amplitudes of a spectrum obtained from an acoustic analysis. However, an effective strategy can be to select the spectral envelope that will realize the desired evolution of the overall richness, the bandwidth, of the spectrum. Because time evolution of the richness of the spectrum is an important element in the perception of timbre, a wide variety of tones can be synthesized by this technique.

5.1D   Simple FM Instrument Designs

Figures 5.9 and 5.10 illustrate John Chowning's designs[4] for producing a variety of instrument-like tones with simple FM. On many systems, the functions F1 and F2 could be realized by using envelope generators instead of oscillators. The tone quality produced by the design can be varied by altering any of three factors: the ratio $f_c : f_m$, the maximum value of the modulation index (IMAX), and the function shapes for the

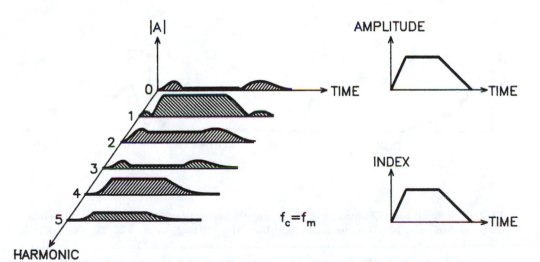

FIGURE 5.8   Dynamic spectrum produced by the instrument of figure 5.7.

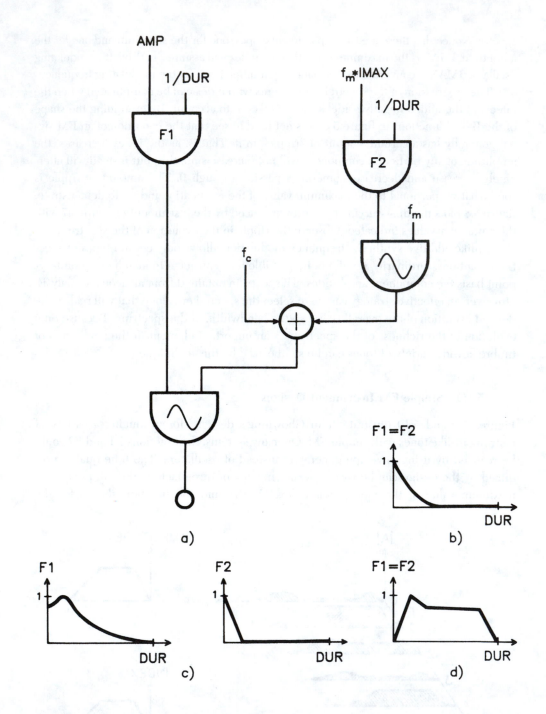

FIGURE 5.9   (a) Basic Chowning FM instrument; (b) function for bell-like timbre; (c) function for wood-drum sound; and (d) function for brasslike timbre. *(Based on design in "The Synthesis of Complex Audio Spectra by Means of Frequency Modulation," by John Chowning. Published in* Journal of the Audio Engineering Society, *21(7), 1973. Reprinted with permission of the author.)*

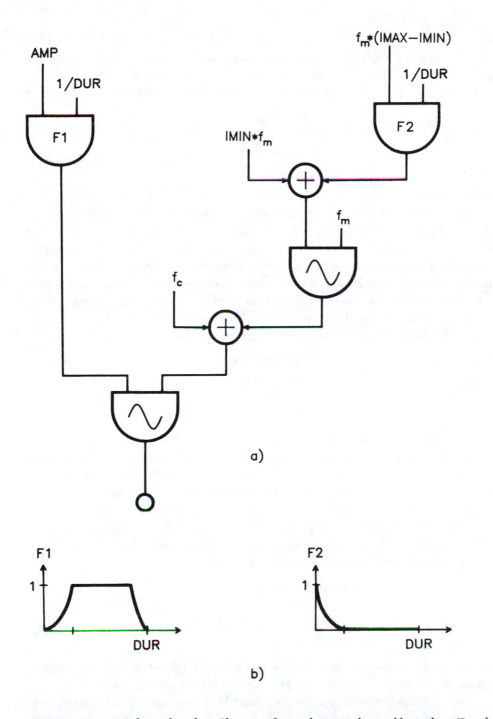

FIGURE 5.10 FM design based on Chowning for producing a clarinet-like timbre. *(Based on design in "The Synthesis of Complex Audio Spectra by Means of Frequency Modulation," by John Chowning. Published in Journal of the Audio Engineering Society, 21(7), 1973. Reprinted with permission of the author.)*

amplitude and for the index of modulation. The amplitude parameter (AMP) should be scaled for all the examples to a value appropriate to the particular system used. The topology of figure 5.9 is used for the first three FM instrument designs that follow.

For bell-like tones, Chowning suggests the following parametric values:

DUR = 15 seconds
f_c = 200 Hz
f_m = 280 Hz (i.e., an f_c:f_m ratio of 5:7)
IMAX = 10

The function shown in figure 5.9b is used for both the amplitude envelope and the envelope applied to the index of modulation. The exponential decay of the amplitude is characteristic of bell sounds. The shape of the function applied to the index of modulation creates a rich, inharmonic spectrum at the beginning of the tone. During the decay, the bandwidth of the spectrum continually diminishes until, near the end of the tone, the sound is essentially a sine wave at the carrier frequency. To obtain a bell-like sound, the duration must not be made too short. If the "bell" is not allowed to ring out for at least 2 seconds, listeners will perceive this tone as more of a "clank."

For FM wood-drum like tones, Chowning recommends:

DUR = 0.2 second
f_c = 80 Hz
f_m = 55 Hz
IMAX = 25

The functions for wood-drum tones are shown in figure 5.9c. The function to control the index of modulation causes an inharmonic spectrum with wide bandwidth during the attack. After a short time, the index drops to 0 and the drum tone becomes simply a decaying sine wave at the carrier frequency, so that a clear pitch will be perceived at that frequency. The duration is a critical cue for these drum tones and cannot be longer than about 0.25 second without destroying the percussive effect. Raising the carrier frequency in the range of 200 Hz with the same f_c:f_m ratio produces a sound closer to that of a wood block.

FM brass-like tones can be produced with:

DUR = 0.6 second
f_c = 440 Hz
f_m = 440 Hz (an f_c:f_m ratio of 1:1)
IMAX = 5

The same envelope function (figure 5.9d) is applied to both the amplitude and the index of modulation. Lowering the value of IMAX to 3 yields a more muted brass tone.

Figure 5.10a shows the design for obtaining FM clarinet-like tones. Chowning suggests using the following values:

DUR = 0.5 second
f_c = 900 Hz
f_m = 600 Hz (an f_c:f_m ratio of 3:2)

$$\text{IMIN} = 2$$
$$\text{IMAX} = 4$$

The shapes of the functions are shown in figure 5.10b. The fundamental frequency produced by this instrument will be $f_c / 3$ (300 Hz when using the values above). Notice that because the denominator of the $f_c{:}f_m$ ratio is 2, the resulting tone will contain no even harmonics. The use of two modulation indices ensures that the resulting modulation index will never drop below the value of IMIN. Increasing IMAX to 6 produces a more strident attack. A small, constant value may be added to the modulating frequency, causing the folded sidebands to beat with the upper sidebands. This technique can result in a more realistic tone.

5.1E   Use of Two Carrier Oscillators

An important characteristic of many natural sounds is the presence of fixed formants. Without provision for them, several classes of sounds cannot be satisfactorily synthesized. Even when great care is exercised in choosing the parameters of an FM instrument so that a peak is placed at some desired point in the spectrum, the peak will be valid only for a small range of the values of the index of modulation. Also, the peak in the spectrum is not fixed; it will move with the fundamental frequency of the sound. Passing the signal from any instrument through a band-pass filter (see chapter 6) will yield an accurate, immobile formant, but a more economical and, in many systems, a more practical approach is described below. This method can only approximate fixed formants, but the results are often satisfactory.

The use of two carrier oscillators driven by a single modulating oscillator (figure 5.11) provides a means for formant simulation. The index of modulation of the first carrier oscillator is I1. The modulating signal delivered to the second carrier oscillator is multiplied by a constant (I2/I1) in order to provide a second index of modulation with the same time variation as the first. The second carrier oscillator produces a spectrum that is centered around the second carrier frequency. Because its index of modulation (I2) is typically small, the spectrum has its strongest component at the second carrier frequency. When the two FM signals are added together, the overall spectrum has a peak at the second carrier frequency. The audible effect is to add a formant to the sound. The amplitude of the second carrier oscillator is proportional to (and usually less than) the amplitude of the first by the factor A2. The relative strength of the formant can be adjusted by changing this parameter.

The second carrier frequency (f_{c2}) is chosen to be the harmonic of the fundamental frequency (f_0) that is closest to the desired formant frequency (f_f). Mathematically stated,

$$f_{c2} = nf_0 = \text{int}\left(\frac{f_f}{f_0} + 0.5\right)f_0$$

That is, n is the ratio, rounded to the nearest integer, of the desired formant frequency to the fundamental frequency. The second carrier frequency remains harmonically related to f_0; the value of n changes with f_0 in order to keep the second carrier frequency as

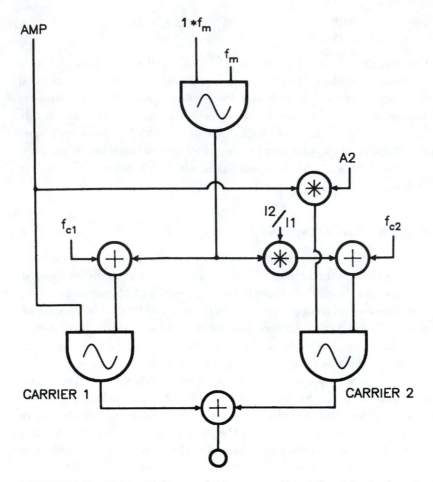

FIGURE 5.11   FM instrument employing two carrier oscillators for formant simulation.

close as possible to the desired formant frequency. For example, if the desired frequen-cy is 2000 Hz, then for f_0 = 400 Hz, the fifth harmonic will be used. As f_0 is increased, f_{c2} will remain the fifth harmonic until f_0 becomes greater than 444.4 Hz, when the fourth harmonic will be closer to 2000 Hz.

5.1F   Double-Carrier FM Instruments

Dexter Morrill has made extensive use of *double-carrier* FM in his computer synthesis of trumpet tones.[5] The design shown in figure 5.12 is based on one of his algorithms. For convenience, it is divided into a main instrument and a vibrato generator.

In the main instrument, the two carrier oscillators have frequencies at the funda-mental frequency and the first formant frequency, respectively. The maximum value of the index of modulation for the first carrier oscillator is IMAX. The peak index of mod-ulation for the second carrier oscillator is obtained by scaling the output of the modu-lating oscillator by the ratio of the second index to the first, IRATIO. The amplitude of

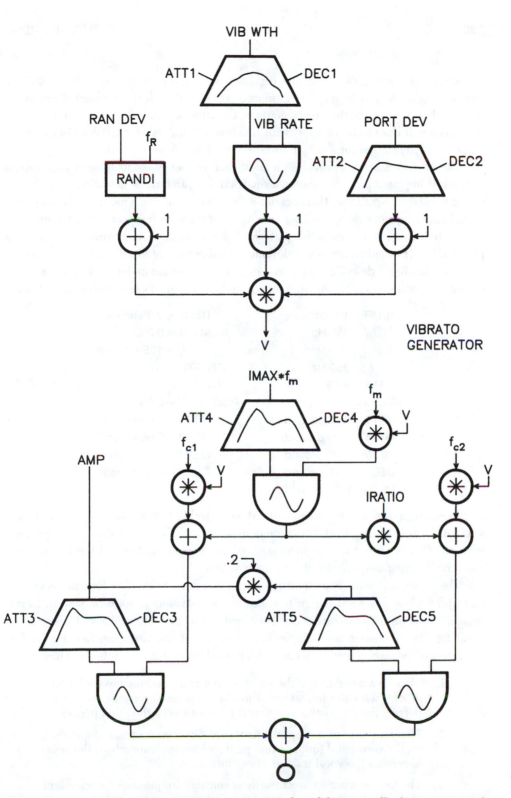

FIGURE 5.12 Double-carrier trumpet instrument. (*Adapted from Morrill's design. Reprinted with permission of* Computer Music Journal.)

the second carrier is 20% that of the first, thus setting the amplitude of the simulated formant at the desired level. The harmonics associated with the formant decay more quickly than the rest of the components of the trumpet tone. On many systems, the envelopes will have to be realized with function generators or oscillators because the shapes are too complex for a simple three-segment envelope generator.

The vibrato generator provides an additional frequency modulation of both carrier systems. It imparts a periodic vibrato, a small, random, frequency deviation, and a portamento to each trumpet tone. This part of the instrument ensures a more lifelike tone. The portamento frequency deviation keeps the pitch of the note from sounding too uniform. Its function shape determines the pattern of deviation, and its maximum deviation is PORT DEV. The random frequency deviation simulates one of the characteristics of trumpet tones that Risset describes.[6] Vibrato is especially important on longer tones. Some values for the parameters of the instrument adapted from Morrill's example are as follows:

DUR = 1 second	DEC5 = 0.3 second
f_{c1} = 250 Hz	RANDEV = 0.007
f_{c2} = 1500 Hz	f_R = 125 Hz
f_m = 250 Hz	VIB WTH = 0.007
IMAX = 2.66	VIB RATE = 7 Hz
IRATIO = 1.8 / 2.66	PORT DEV = 0.03
ATT3 = 0.03 second	ATT1 = 0.6 second
ATT4 = 0.03 s econd	ATT2 = 0.06 second
ATT5 = 0.03 second	DEC1 = 0.2 second
DEC3 = 0.15 second	DEC2 = 0.01 second
DEC4 = 0.01 second	

In coding a score for this instrument, Morrill used Leland Smith's SCORE program[7] to obtain, from one note to the next, random deviation of certain values of his parameter lists. This ensured that the succession of notes would not sound mechanical as a result of too great a uniformity of parameter values.

The principle of using more than one carrier frequency to simulate formants is extended in John Chowning's FM design to realize the female singing voice on vowels. In this design, Chowning uses two carrier oscillators and one modulating oscillator. The oscillators are all tuned in whole-number multiples of the same frequency. Chowning has discerned six characters of the singing soprano voice which guided his design for synthesis.[8] They are:

1. There is a weighting of the spectral energy around the low-order harmonics with the fundamental as the strongest harmonic, thus supporting the theory that the lowest formant tracks the pitch period.

2. There are one or more secondary peaks in the spectrum, depending on the vowel and fundamental pitch, which corresponds to the resonances on the vocal tract or upper formants.

3. The formants are not necessarily at constant frequencies independent of the fundamental pitch, but rather follow formant trajectories which may either ascend or descend, depending on the vowel, as a function of the fundamental frequency.[9]

4. The upper formants decrease in energy more rapidly than does the lowest formant when a tone is sung at a decreasing loudness.

5. Only the lowest formant is prominent at the amplitude thresholds of the attack and decay portions, while the upper formants only become pronounced as the overall amplitude of the signal approaches the quasi-steady state.

6. There is a small but discernible fluctuation of the pitch period even in the singing condition without vibrato.

Using these principles as a guide, Chowning designed the instrument shown in figure 5.13. The design resembles the trumpet of the previous example in that it uses two carrier oscillators and makes provision for vibrato with random deviation. The singing-soprano design also includes a slight portamento, but only during the attack portion of the note. The design includes a set of arrays that use the pitch of the note to determine values for the second formant frequency, the amplitude of the second carrier (A2), and the modulation indices for both carriers. A different set of arrays is used for each vowel. Following is an example of the sorts of values used for the design:

AMP = in the range of 0 < AMP < 1

PITCH = in the range of G3 < PITCH < G6

f_m = PITCH

A2 = the relative amplitude of the second carrier, between 0 and 1 in value—
see figure 5.14

A1 = the relative amplitude of the first carrier = 1 − A2

f_{c1} = first carrier frequency = PITCH

f_{c2} = second carrier frequency = INT (f_2 / PITCH + 0.5), where f_2 is the
frequency of the upper formant, obtained from figure 5.14

I1 = modulation index for the first carrier, computed from the data in figure 5.14

I2 = modulation index for the second carrier, computed from the data in
figure 5.14

VIB WTH = 0.2 $\log_2$PITCH

VIB RATE = between 5 and 6.5 Hz, depending on PITCH

One of the striking features of Chowning's tapes produced with this instrument can be heard in the examples where the two carriers enter one at a time, 10 seconds apart. Ten seconds after the entrance of the second carrier, the vibrato with its random deviation is applied equally to the two carriers. Until the application of the vibrato, the two carriers do not fuse into a single aural image of a "voice." Chowning observes that by itself, "the spectral envelope does not make a voice."

5.1G   Complex Modulating Waves

Up to this point, the only FM instruments that have been considered are those in which the waveform of each oscillator is a sine wave. While many interesting timbres can be synthesized this way, certain others require a more complicated modulating waveform. Because

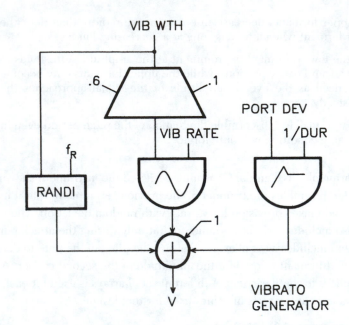

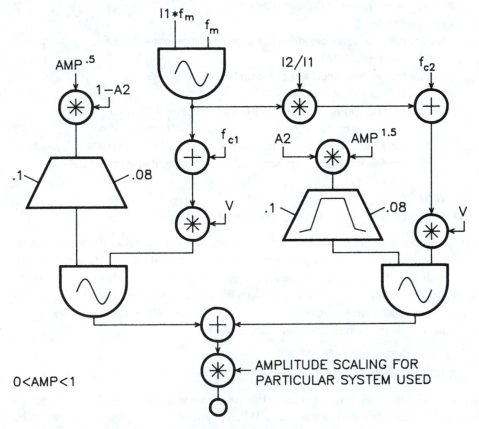

FIGURE 5.13   FM soprano instrument based on Chowning.

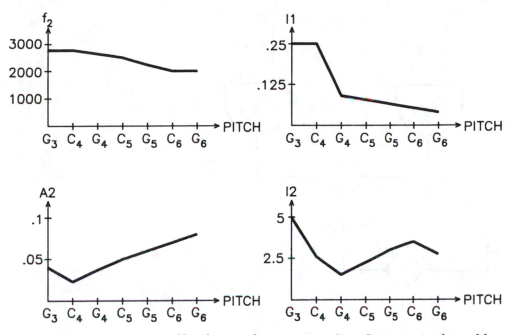

FIGURE 5.14 Parameters used by Chowning for FM soprano. *(From "Computer Synthesis of the Singing Voice," by John Chowning, in* Sound Generation in Winds, Strings, Computers, *Publication No. 29 of the Royal Swedish Academy of Music, edited by Johan Sundberg. Reprinted with permission of the editor.)*

the process of frequency modulation produces such rich spectra, a complex modulating wave generally needs to consist of no more than two or three spectral components. Figure 5.15 illustrates an instrument in which the frequency of the carrier oscillator is modulated by a complex wave that is the sum of two sine waves. In principle, this instrument could have been realized with a single modulating oscillator whose waveform was the appropriate combination of components, but employing independent oscillators permits variation of the relative amplitudes and frequencies of the modulation components.

The spectrum of this instrument will contain a large number of frequencies. If the carrier frequency is f_c and the modulating frequencies are f_{m1} and f_{m2}, then the resulting spectrum will contain components at the frequencies given by $f_c \pm i f_{m1} \pm k f_{m2}$, where i and k are integers greater than or equal to 0. To indicate when a minus sign is used, the value of i or k will be superscripted with a minus sign. For instance, the sideband with a frequency of $f_c + 2f_{m1} - 3f_{m2}$ will be denoted by the pair: $i = 2, k = 3^-$.

Independent indices of modulation can be defined for each component. I_1 is the index that characterizes the modulation that would be produced if only the first modulating oscillator were present; I_2 is that of the second. The amplitude of the ith, kth sideband $(A_{i,k})$ is given by the product of Bessel functions[10] as

$$A_{i,k} = J_i(I_1) J_k(I_2)$$

When i or k is odd and the minus sign is taken, the corresponding Bessel function assumes

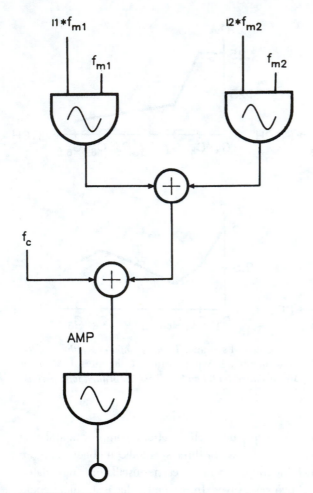

FIGURE 5.15   FM instrument with a complex modulating wave.

the opposite sign. For example, if $i = 2$ and $k = 3^-$, the amplitude is $A_{2,3} = -J_2(I_1)J_3(I_2)$. For $i = 3^-$, $k = 1^-$, the amplitude is $[-J_3(I_1)][-J_1(I_2)]$, and the two negative signs cancel when the two factors are multiplied.

In a harmonic spectrum, the net amplitude of a component at any frequency is the combination of many sidebands. As before, when a sideband has a negative frequency, it is folded around 0 Hz with a change of sign in its amplitude. For example, when $f_c = 100$ Hz, $f_{m1} = 100$ Hz, and $f_{m2} = 300$ Hz, the spectral component present in the sound at 400 Hz is the combination of sidebands given by the pairs: $i = 3$, $k = 0$; $i = 0$, $k = 1$; $i = 3^-$, $k = 2$; and so on. The components at -400 Hz come from $i = 2^-$, $k = 1^-$; $i = 1$, $k = 2^-$; $i = 5^-$, $k = 0$; and so on. The overall amplitude at 400 Hz, $A(400)$, is the sum of the amplitudes of all contributing components.

$$A(400) = J_3(I_1)J_0(I_2) + J_0(I_1)J_1(I_2) - J_3(I_1)J_2(I_2)$$
$$+ J_2(I_1)J_1(I_2) - J_1(I_1)J_2(I_2) + J_5(I_1)J_0(I_2) \cdots$$

The above expression shows only the three lowest-order terms for both the positive- and negative-frequency components. In fact, there are an infinite number of i, k dyads that produce a sideband at ± 400 Hz. The actual number that contributes significantly to the overall amplitude is determined by the modulation indices. For given values of I_1 and I_2, one can calculate the maximum values of i and k for which the Bessel functions of that order have significant values. This information predicts the frequency of the highest significant component in the resulting spectrum, and so can be used to avoid aliasing.

Because so many sidebands are produced by this technique, lower indices of modulation can be used to obtain the same amount of spectral richness. This approach can be advantageous because the time evolution of the harmonics is smoother at lower indices.

5.1H   FM Instrument with Complex Modulation

Figure 5.16 shows the flowchart for an instrument based on Bill Schottstaedt's simulation of stringlike tones with an FM design.[11] The design entails a single-carrier oscillator and three modulating oscillators. It sounds best in the range of a cello when using the following parametric values.

$$f_c = \text{pitch of the note} \qquad I1 = 7.5 / \log_e f_c$$
$$f_{m1} = f_c \qquad I2 = 15 / \sqrt{f_c}$$
$$f_{m2} = 3f_c \qquad I3 = 1.25 / \sqrt{f_c}$$
$$f_{m3} = 4f_c$$

Notice that the indices of modulation vary with the fundamental frequency of the tone. Multiplying the modulation indices by 2 or 3 produces more strident tones, according to the designer.

A vibrato is implemented, similar to the one used in the trumpet design, except that here it is without the undershoot of the pitch of the tone. The *chiff,* or attack noise of the bow, is simulated with a noise band centered at 2000 Hz using a bandwidth of 20% of the carrier frequency. The function applied to the noise causes it to cease 0.2 second after the attack of the note.

The increase in spectral richness of the tone during the attack is simulated by adding the envelope F1 to each index of modulation. In his article, Schottstaedt also includes some advice for making other string instrument effects, such as *sul ponticello, pizzicato,* and the choral effect.

5.1I   Compositional Examples

The compositions by John Chowning[12] represent distillations of extensive research into computer techniques for the synthesis of sound. His expertise in acoustics and psychoacoustics plays a major role in formulating his pieces, as does his interest in expressing physical phenomena mathematically. Yet, artistically, each of his compositions is highly unified—usually around a particular technique or relationship. For example, *Turenas* (1972) demonstrates the travel of sound in a quadraphonic space (see section 10.3B); *Stria* (1976) illustrates the use of computer synthesis of sound to interrelate the small-scale sound design of

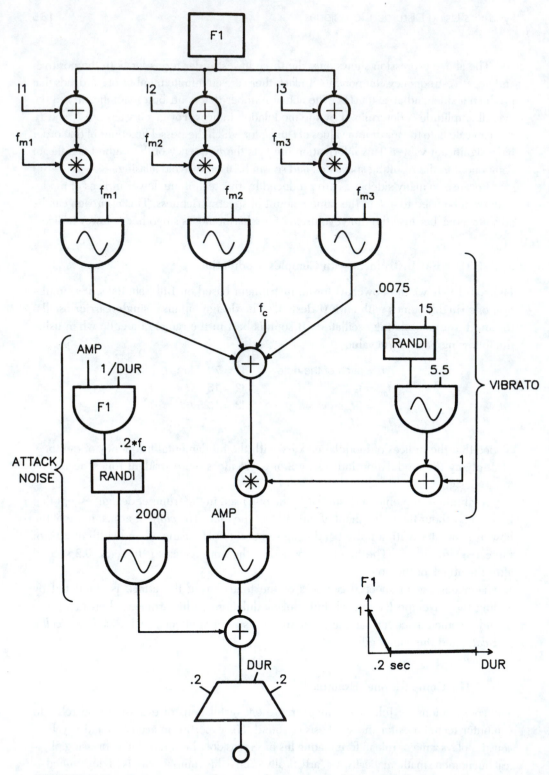

FIGURE 5.16 String-tone simulation utilizing a complex modulating wave based on Schottstaedt.

the composition to its overall formal structure; and *Phonée* (1981) implements the psychoacoustic principle of spectral fusion as a guide to whether its sounds at any given moment seem "electronic" in origin or originating with the human voice.

Several aspects of *Stria* are based on the numerical "golden mean" ratio (1:1.618 . . .), which has been put to various artistic uses throughout the ages. The Greeks thought the golden-mean ratio to embody the most pleasing spatial proportion and used it in architecture to relate the length and width of structures. Béla Bartók used the same ratio in certain of his compositions to relate the durations of movements. Relationships of both time and frequency in *Stria* stem from the projection of the golden-mean ratio. In addition, the climax of the work occurs at the point in time that divides the piece into two sections according to the same ratio. The sounds in *Stria* are predominantly long with an almost complete absence of percussiveness. Although there is some change in location of the sound during the course of the 18-minute work, the movement is very gradual.

Chowning devised a unique system of frequencies for *Stria*. The pitch space of the piece is defined as occupying eight pseudo-octaves—an interval of pitch that has the ratio of 1:1.618 instead of the usual 1:2. Each pseudo-octave is divided into nine equal-interval frequency divisions. The eight pseudo-octaves for *Stria* are arranged three above and five below the reference frequency of 1000 Hz.

Figure 5.17 is a sketch of the shape of the 18-minute piece, with the pseudo-octave frequency scale at the vertical axis and time indicated on the horizontal axis. The overall shape of the composition represents a mirror image of conventional musical structure, in that the climax occurs at a low point in frequency instead of the more usual high point. Similarly, the conventional relationships between the durations of high and low sounds is reversed. In *Stria*, the longest events are those of the highest pitch. They all enter and leave with long rise and decay times. The lower the tone, the faster the rise and decay, and the shorter the tone itself. At the climax of the piece, the lowest tones are also the shortest in the composition.

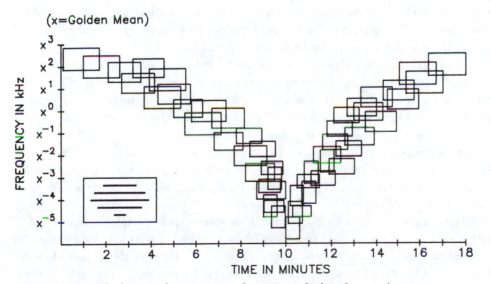

FIGURE 5.17   The large-scale compositional structure of John Chowning's *Stria*.

Each block, one of which is shown in the insert to figure 5.17, comprises a number of tones that enter in temporal golden-mean proportions. For instance, in the case of five tones, the center tone enters first and exists last. Each of the five tones of each package is at a frequency represented by one of the nine equal-interval divisions of a pseudo-octave.

The FM instrument design for a single tone reflects the golden-mean ratio as well. One carrier and two modulating oscillators are used. (See section 5.1G.) The carrier and modulating frequencies are related in golden-mean proportions, with the second modulating frequency detuned slightly from the first to produce beating, and thus liveliness, in the sound of each tone.

In *Phonée*, Chowning works with both short, impulsive sounds and long, slowly changing sonorities. *Phonée* posits two extremes of perception as a polarity—bell-like percussion sounds and the timbres of sung vowels. The composition then explores the perceptual gradations between the two extremes. The concern for "timbral interpolation" has occupied the Stanford group for some time, and *Phonée* is, at one level, a compositional application of that fascinating phenomenon. There are other perceptual dilemmas to be heard in *Phonée*, as well. For example, there are a number of instances of the effect of vibrato on our perception of spectral fusion. Electronic-sounding timbres turn immediately into the timbres of sung vowels simply by the equal application of properly randomized vibrato to all the spectral components (the design for implementing this effect is shown in figure 5.13). To produce this effect, Chowning modified the vibrato generator by applying envelopes to the vibrato width and rate so that they are 0 at the beginning of the event and increase in value after a time delay of sufficient length for the timbre to be perceived initially as "electronic."

The timbral polarities—bell-like sounds and sung vowels—are realized in different ways. The bell-like sounds are produced by an FM design using an $f_c{:}f_m$ ratio which is an irrational number, producing a sound containing nonharmonic partials. The vowel timbres are made with a double-carrier design with no inharmonicity of spectral components. The two classes of sounds have other characteristics that differ as well. Bells have a sharp attack with maximal spectral richness in the attack and simplification of the spectrum with time after the attack. Vowel timbres have much more gradual rise and decay shapes and require vibrato for their characteristic quality.

Many of the sounds in *Phonée* fall in the "cracks" between the two polarities. Chowning creates these new sounds by combining salient features of one type of sound with those of the other. Figure 5.18 shows the evolution of such a tone. The tone begins with a characteristic bell clang. During the initial decay of the bell tone, the highest components decay most rapidly. During the next segment, the vibrato is gradually applied individually to each of the remaining components. This causes each component to separate from the percept of a unified bell timbre into an individual "singing voice" on that component. The result is a group of singing voices in the place of the bell tone. Finally, the gradual reduction of the vibrato along with the bell-like decay complete the tone.

The computer instrument for creating these notes is quite complex. It consists of an FM design with as many as six carrier oscillators, tuned inharmonically to each other. To produce the bell-like timbre at the beginnings and ends of tones, the indices of modulation for all but the first oscillator are set to 0, and an inharmonic $f_c{:}f_m$ ratio is used. Then, in order to create the transformation of each of the bell partials into a singing

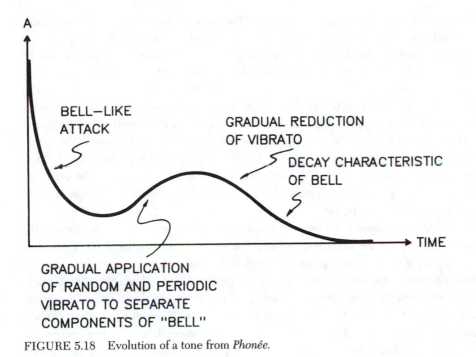

FIGURE 5.18   Evolution of a tone from *Phonée*.

voice at the same frequency, the indices of modulation are increased. As they increase, random and periodic vibrato are applied to evoke the percept of a singing voice.

In fact, the overall shape of the composition reflects the structure of one of the characteristic "bell-changing-to-vowel" tones. As the work progresses, there is more and more prominence of the singing voice capped by a great profusion of tones sung by a "basso profundissimo." From there to the end, the singing voice plays a less central role.

5.2   SYNTHESIS BY WAVESHAPING

In addition to the technique of frequency modulation synthesis presented in the first portion of this chapter, there are other methods of sound synthesis that operate by changing the shape of a sine wave in order to achieve a desired spectrum. This section will describe the use of waveshaping to change a waveform based on its amplitude, and then a few other useful discrete summation formulas will be presented in section 5.3 for the synthesis of spectra with a controlled bandwidth.

5.2A   Basic Technique

Waveshaping is a second technique of distortion synthesis that realizes spectra that have dynamic evolution of their components. Like FM, it is more computationally efficient than additive synthesis for the realization of complex timbres. Unlike FM, waveshaping provides the capability of generating a band-limited spectrum with a specifiable maximum harmonic number.

The spectrum produced by a waveshaping instrument changes with the amplitude of the sound. Because this change corresponds to the characteristics of the spectra of acoustic instruments, waveshaping synthesis has proven effective in the production of tones that resemble those of traditional instruments. The synthesis of brass tones has been particularly successful.[13]

Waveshaping is the distortion of the amplitude of a sound—a process that produces an alteration in the waveform. A simple example of this type of distortion can be heard in the clipping that occurs when an audio amplifier is overdriven. However, the introduction of carefully controlled distortion to a signal can be used to yield a broad range of musically useful timbres. Like FM synthesis, waveshaping provides for the continuous control of the spectrum by means of an index, making possible dynamic spectra through time variation of the index.

The signal-flow diagram of a basic waveshaping instrument is shown in figure 5.19. The central element of any such instrument is a *waveshaper*, or nonlinear processor that alters the shape of the waveform passing through it. In a linear processor, such as an ideal amplifier, a change in the amplitude of the input signal produces a like change in the output signal. For example, doubling the amplitude of the input signal will cause the amplitude of the output to double also. The shape of the waveform is not changed, so that while the amplitude of each spectral component doubles, their strength relative to each other is preserved. In a nonlinear processor, the relationship between input and output depends on the amplitude of the input signal and the nature of the nonlinearity. Therefore, increasing the amplitude of the input will cause the output waveform to change shape. When the shape of the waveform is modified, its spectrum changes, which generally results in an increase in the number and intensity of the harmonics. Our discussion will concentrate on the use of waveshaping to enrich the spectrum of a simple sound, such as a sine wave.

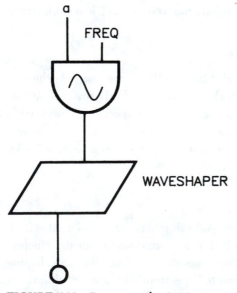

FIGURE 5.19   Basic waveshaping instrument.

5.2B   Transfer Functions

A waveshaper is characterized by its *transfer function,* which relates the amplitude of the signal at the output to the input. This function can be represented graphically, as in figure 5.20, with the amplitude of the input signal plotted on the horizontal axis and the amplitude of the output signal on the vertical axis. Thus, for a given input value, the output of the waveshaper can be determined by finding the corresponding output value on the graph of the transfer function. By repeating this process for each sample of an input waveform, a graphic description of the output waveform can be constructed, as in the figure.

The shape of the output waveform, and hence its spectrum, changes with the amplitude of the input signal. For the indicated transfer function, figure 5.21 shows the output waveforms and their spectra produced by sine waves of different amplitudes. Notice that the amount of distortion introduced is strongly dependent on the level of the input signal: the spectrum becomes richer as the input level is increased.

The musician can gain some sense of a transfer function's audible effect from its graphic representation. A processor with a straight-line (linear) transfer function (figure 5.22a) will not produce distortion, but any deviation from a straight line introduces some form of

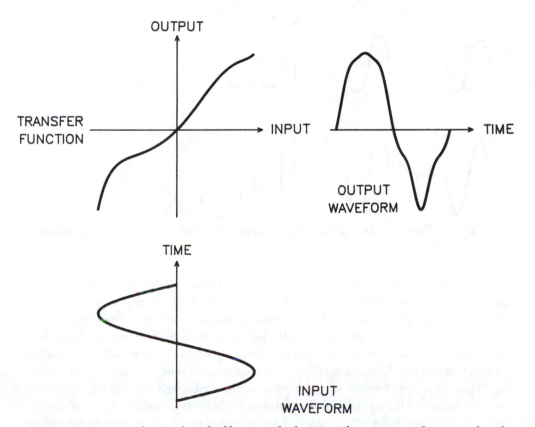

FIGURE 5.20   Waveshaping described by a transfer function. The output waveform is produced by finding the value of the transfer function corresponding to the input waveform.

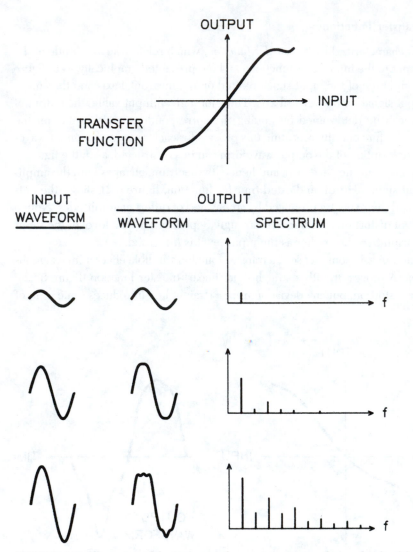

FIGURE 5.21 Illustration of the increase in harmonic content as the amplitude of the input increases.

distortion. The transfer function illustrated in figure 5.22b is linear close to the center of the axes but diverges increasingly from its initial slope. Small signals are thus passed with little alteration of their spectrum, while large ones are substantially distorted. The more extreme the change in slope, the larger is the number and intensity of the harmonics added. When the transfer function is symmetric about the center of the graph (figure 5.22b), it is called an odd function and the spectrum of the distortion contains only odd-numbered harmonics. When the transfer function is symmetric about the vertical axis (figure 5.22c), the transfer function is said to be even, and thus produces only even harmonics. An even transfer function, therefore, doubles the fundamental frequency of the input signal, and hence raises the pitch of the sound by an octave. A transfer function with an abrupt jump (figure 5.22d), sharp points (figure 5.22e), or wiggles (figure 5.22f) will produce more harmonics than a

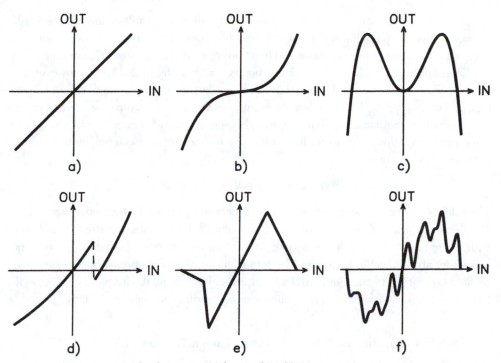

FIGURE 5.22   Six transfer functions: (a) linear, (b) odd, (c) even, (d) with an abrupt jump, (e) with sharp points, and (f) with ripple.

smoother function. In fact, a transfer function with a sharp point or an abrupt jump always produces an infinite number of harmonics, and thus aliasing.

To enable its behavior to be analyzed in the frequency domain, the most useful way to describe a transfer function is algebraically. The amplitude of the signal input to the waveshaper is represented by the variable x. The output is then denoted by $F(x)$, where F is the transfer function. This notation indicates that the value of F depends on the value of x. An example of a linear transfer function is $F(x) = 0.5x$ (figure 5.23a). In this case, any signal

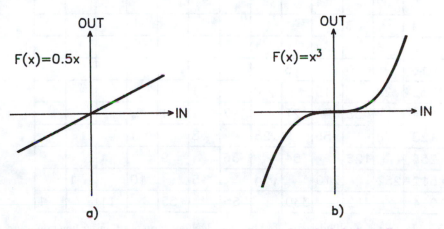

FIGURE 5.23   Examples of transfer functions that are described algebraically.

applied to the input will be transmitted to the output with its amplitude reduced by one-half. A transfer function is nonlinear when it has terms that contain x raised to a power other than 1, or when it contains other mathematical functions of x, such as the logarithm or tangent. A simple example of a nonlinear transfer function is $F(x) = x^3$ (figure 5.23b). In this case, the output will be a distortion of the input because the value of each input sample is cubed as it is passed to the output. Thus, doubling the input causes the output to increase by eight times.

To control the maximum harmonic in the spectrum and, hence, avoid aliasing in waveshaping synthesis, a transfer function is normally expressed as a polynomial, which has the following form:

$$F(x) = d_0 + d_1x + d_2x^2 + \cdots + d_Nx^N$$

The value of each coefficient d_i $(d_0, d_1, d_2, \ldots)$ is chosen by one of the methods given below. The degree or order of the polynomial is N, the value of the largest exponent. When driven with a sine or cosine wave, a waveshaper with a transfer function of order N produces no harmonics above the Nth harmonic. The musician can, therefore, predict the highest harmonic frequency generated and avoid aliasing either by limiting the frequency of the oscillator that drives the waveshaper or by tailoring the transfer function accordingly.

5.2C   Calculating an Output Spectrum from a Transfer Function

When the nonlinear processor is driven by a sinusoidal waveform, the amplitudes of the various harmonics of the output can be calculated from the transfer polynomial using table 5.2.[14] The table shows the amplitudes of the harmonics produced by a term in the polynomial when the amplitude of the driving sinusoid is 1. The symbols along the top

	DIV	h_0	h_1	h_2	h_3	h_4	h_5	h_6	h_7	h_8	h_9	h_{10}	h_{11}
x^0	0.5	1											
x^1	1		1										
x^2	2	2		1									
x^3	4		3		1								
x^4	8	6		4		1							
x^5	16		10		5		1						
x^6	32	20		15		6		1					
x^7	64		35		21		7		1				
x^8	128	70		56		28		8		1			
x^9	256		126		84		36		9		1		
x^{10}	512	252		210		120		45		10		1	
x^{11}	1024		462		330		165		55		11		1

TABLE 5.2   Harmonic amplitudes produced by each algebraic term of a transfer function

of the table, denoted in the form h_j, represent the amplitude of the jth harmonic. Each line in the table has an associated divisor (DIV); the true value of any entry is the listed value divided by the divisor for that line.

As an example, suppose the transfer function $F(x) = x^5$ is driven by a cosine wave with an amplitude of 1. That is, the variable x signifies the cosine wave. The table shows that the output will contain the first, third, and fifth harmonics with the following amplitudes:

$$h_1 = \tfrac{1}{16}(10) = 0.625$$

$$h_3 = \tfrac{1}{16}(5) = 0.3125$$

$$h_5 = \tfrac{1}{16}(1) = 0.0625$$

For mathematical convenience, the amplitude of the zeroth harmonic is equal to $h_0 / 2$. Thus, the value in the table is two times larger than the actual amplitude of this particular harmonic. This term has a frequency of 0 Hz, and therefore serves to offset the output signal by a fixed amount. That is, it is a constant value added to each sample of the signal. Since a constant does not fluctuate, it contributes nothing to the perceived sound. This phenomenon needs to be taken into account, however, since a large offset can cause the sample values to exceed the range of the system without causing the signal to sound louder.

When a polynomial has multiple terms, the output is the sum of the contributions of each term. For instance, if $F(x) = x + x^2 + x^3 + x^4 + x^5$ is driven with a unit-amplitude sinusoid, the amplitudes of the components in the output spectrum are

$$\frac{h_0}{2} = \tfrac{1}{2}\left[\tfrac{1}{2}(2) + \tfrac{1}{8}(6)\right] = 0.875$$

$$h_1 = 1 + \tfrac{1}{4}(3) + \tfrac{1}{16}(10) = 2.375$$

$$h_2 = \tfrac{1}{2}(1) + \tfrac{1}{8}(4) = 1.0$$

$$h_3 = \tfrac{1}{4}(1) + \tfrac{1}{16}(5) = 0.5625$$

$$h_4 = \tfrac{1}{8}(1) = 0.125$$

$$h_5 = \tfrac{1}{16}(1) = 0.0625$$

The reader might recognize table 5.2 as the right side of Pascal's triangle and the entries to be the binomial coefficients. The table can be extended by adding two adjacent numbers on the same line and writing the sum below the space between them. The value of h_0 is twice the value of h_1 from the previous line, and the divisor is increased by a factor of two each time. For example, for x^{12}, the divisor would be 2048, $h_0 = 2 \times 462 = 924$, $h_2 = 462 + 330 = 792$, and so on.

As expected, the table shows that a particular term of the polynomial does not produce harmonics with numbers greater than its exponent. It further indicates that an even power of x will produce only even harmonics and that an odd power generates only odd harmonics. This characteristic is another advantage of polynomial representation because it affords the instrument designer independent control of the odd and even harmonics of a sound.

Thus far, the analysis has been applied for a sinusoidal input whose amplitude is 1. What, then, is the general relationship between the amplitude of the input sinusoidal waveform and the amplitude of a given harmonic? Let the input to a waveshaper be a cosine wave with an amplitude of a. The output in polynomial form becomes

$$F(ax) = d_0 + d_1 ax + d_2 a^2 x^2 + \ldots d_N a^N x^N$$

where x, as above, symbolizes a cosine wave with an amplitude of 1. The harmonic amplitudes can still be determined using table 5.2, but the contribution of each term is multiplied by a, raised to the appropriate power. The dependence of the amplitude of any harmonic on the value a is usually indicated by writing the amplitude of the jth harmonic as a function, $h_j(a)$. Using the example of $F(x) = x + x^3 + x^5$ and substituting ax for x, the harmonics at the output will be calculated as:

$$h_1(a) = a + \tfrac{1}{4}a^3(3) + \tfrac{1}{16}a^5(10)$$

$$h_3(a) = \tfrac{1}{4}a^3 + \tfrac{1}{16}a^5(5)$$

$$h_5(a) = \tfrac{1}{16}a^5$$

These harmonic amplitudes are plotted against the value of a in figure 5.24. Notice that the spectrum becomes richer as the value of a increases. Because it exercises so much control over the richness of the spectrum, a is called a *distortion index*. It is analogous to the index of modulation of FM synthesis, in that it is a single parameter that determines the spectral content. For simplicity, the index is often limited to values between 0 and 1.

When the waveform applied to the waveshaper is nonsinusoidal, the resulting spectrum is more difficult to predict and is often not band-limited. The spectrum of a waveform produced by passing a complex waveform through a nonlinear processor cannot be calculated simply as the sum of the distortion applied to the individual spectral components of the input waveform. Instead, a Fourier transform is performed on the output waveform to determine its spectrum. Thus, for reasons of conceptual simplicity and to obtain band-limited spectra, the majority of waveshaping instruments use a sinusoidal oscillator to drive the nonlinear processor.

5.2D   Selecting a Transfer Function

The success of an instrument that uses waveshaping synthesis is largely dependent on the choice of transfer function. There are three principal approaches to the choice: spectral matching, graphical, and heuristic.

In *spectral matching*, a transfer function is determined that will make the output of the waveshaper match a desired steady-state spectrum for a particular value of the distortion index. This can be accomplished through the use of *Chebyshev polynomials*, usually denoted as $T_k(x)$, where k is the order of the polynomial. (T signifies that it is a Chebyshev polynomial of the first kind.) These polynomials have the useful property that when the

$h_j(a)$

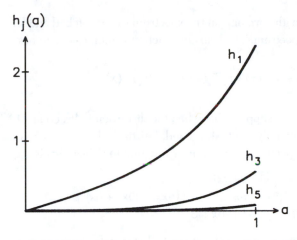

FIGURE 5.24   Harmonics amplitude versus distortion index for $F(x) = x^5 + x^3 + x$.

transfer function of a waveshaper is $T_k(x)$ and a cosine wave with an amplitude of 1 is applied to the input, the output signal contains only the kth harmonic.[15] For example, a transfer function given by the seventh-order Chebyshev polynomial results in an output of a sinusoid at seven times the frequency of the input. (This relationship exists only when the amplitude of the input is 1.) Table 5.3 lists the Chebyshev polynomials through the 11th order. Higher-order polynomials can be generated from the relationship:

$$T_{k+1}(x) = 2xT_k(x) - T_{k-1}(x)$$

A spectrum containing many harmonics can be matched by combining the appropriate Chebyshev polynomial for each desired harmonic into a single transfer function.

$T_0(x) = 1$
$T_1(x) = x$
$T_2(x) = 2x^2 - 1$
$T_3(x) = 4x^3 - 3x$
$T_4(x) = 8x^4 - 8x^2 + 1$
$T_5(x) = 16x^5 - 20x^3 + 5x$
$T_6(x) = 32x^6 - 48x^4 + 18x^2 - 1$
$T_7(x) = 64x^7 - 112x^5 + 56x^3 - 7x$
$T_8(x) = 128x^8 - 256x^6 + 160x^4 - 32x^2 + 1$
$T_9(x) = 256x^9 - 576x^7 + 432x^5 - 120x^3 + 9x$
$T_{10}(x) = 512x^{10} - 1280x^8 + 1120x^6 - 400x^4 + 50x^2 - 1$
$T_{11}(x) = 1024x^{11} - 2816x^9 + 2816x^7 - 1232x^5 + 220x^3 - 11x$

TABLE 5.3   Chebyshev polynomials through the 11th order

Let h_j represent the amplitude of the jth harmonic in the spectrum to be matched and let N be the highest harmonic in that spectrum. The transfer function is then calculated as

$$F(x) = \frac{h_0}{2}T_0(x) + h_1 T_1(x) + h_2 T_2(x) + \cdots + h_N T_N(x)$$

As an example of spectral matching, suppose that when the distortion index equals 1, it is desired that the spectrum contain only the first, second, fourth, and fifth harmonics with amplitudes of 5, 1, 4, and 3, respectively. The transfer function to realize this is:

$$F(x) = 5T_1(x) + 1T_2(x) + 4T_4(x) + 3T_5(x)$$
$$= 5x + 1(2x^2 - 1) + 4(8x^4 - 8x^2 + 1) + 3(16x^5 - 20x^3 + 5x)$$
$$= 48x^5 + 32x^4 - 60x^3 - 30x^2 + 20x + 3$$

When the distortion index assumes a value other than 1, this transfer function generates different spectra. The relationships between the various harmonic amplitudes and the distortion index, a, can be calculated from the transfer function using table 5.2, as before. These amplitudes are plotted three-dimensionally versus index and harmonic number in figure 5.25. Observe that the third and zeroth harmonics are not present when $a = 1$, but at other values of the distortion index, they are no longer balanced out. At small values of the distortion index, the spectrum is dominated by the fundamental and zero-frequency term.

Another more intuitive means of selecting the transfer function is based on the choice of its *graphical shape*. Some general principles relating the shape of the transfer function to the harmonics produced were given above. To avoid aliasing, the selected graphical shape should be approximated by a polynomial, with the order of the approx-

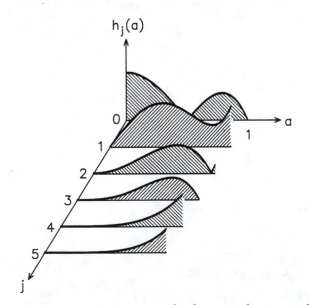

FIGURE 5.25   Harmonic amplitudes versus distortion index for $F(x) = 48x^5 + 32x^4 - 60x^3 - 30x^2 + 20x + 3$.

imation set to the highest harmonic number desired. The computer can be programmed to perform this task.

A *heuristic* selection of the coefficients of the transfer polynomial can sometimes be effective. For best results, the instrument designer should choose the signs of the terms of the polynomial carefully. If the signs of all the terms are the same, the function will become increasingly steep with the distortion index, resulting in exceptionally bright timbres. More subdued timbres can be obtained by following the pattern found in the Chebyshev polynomials where the signs of the even-and-odd-order terms alternate independently. This will yield a flatter transfer function that produces a less brilliant sound. With experience, the musician can develop an intuitive understanding of the relationship between the coefficients and the sound produced. Interactively altering a set of coefficients originally produced by the combination of Chebyshev polynomials is a good way to begin to develop this skill.

5.2E   Considerations for Dynamic Spectra

As in FM synthesis, waveshaping facilitates the production of dynamic spectra because the distortion index can be varied with time. Of course, the transfer function used determines the amount and type of spectral controls possible. It would be simplest and probably the most musically useful if the index increased the amplitudes of all the harmonics smoothly. Polynomials that do this without producing extraordinarily brassy sounds are uncommon. If the polynomial is chosen for a less brilliant spectrum, there is often considerable ripple in the evolution of the harmonics with distortion index (unless the spectrum has an unusually small amount of harmonic energy). The higher the order of the transfer function, the harder it will be to obtain smooth spectral evolutions. Also, polynomials that are obtained by matching a spectrum in which the highest harmonics have relatively large amplitudes tend to produce much more spectral ripple than those where the harmonic amplitudes diminish with harmonic number.

If spectral matching is used to determine the transfer function, the smoothness of the spectral evolution can be improved by selecting the signs of the harmonic of the desired spectrum such that the signs of the even and odd harmonics are alternated independently.[16] Thus, the even harmonics would have the following pattern, starting with the zeroth: $+, -, +, -, \ldots$. The odd harmonics, starting with the first, would take the same form. When the even and odd harmonics are combined to make a complete spectrum, the overall pattern becomes: $+, +, -, -, +, +, -, -, \ldots$. Applying this method to the example of spectral matching given above yields a spectrum to be matched that contains only the first, second, fourth, and fifth harmonics with amplitudes of 5, −1, 4, and 3, respectively. The resulting transfer function is

$$F(x) = 48x^5 + 32x^4 - 60x^3 - 34x^2 + 20x + 5$$

While the spectrum at the value of the distortion index where the matching takes place is not audibly affected, this method results in a smoother spectral evolution.

As another example, the evolution of the harmonics with distortion index is plotted for two different cases in figure 5.26. Figure 5.26a shows the result when the spectral

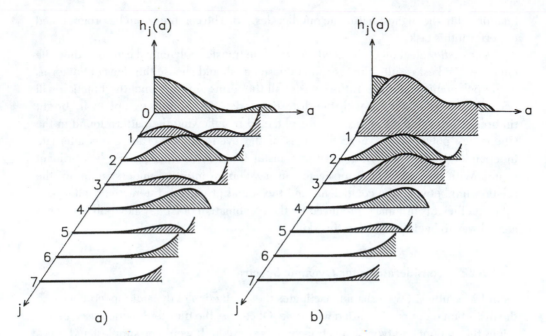

FIGURE 5.26   Harmonic evolution when a spectrum is matched with the amplitudes (a) 4, 2, 3, 0, 2, 3, 2 and (b) 4, –2, –3, 0, 2, –3, –2.

amplitudes, starting with the first harmonic, 4, 2, 3, 0, 2, 3, 2, are matched. Figure 5.26b illustrates the evolution when 4, –2, –3, 0, 2, –3, –2 are matched. Observe the vastly different behavior of the first and third harmonics with distortion index.

5.2F   Implementation of a Nonlinear Processor

It is not practical to have the computer calculate the value of the output of the wave-shaper by directly evaluating the transfer function for each sample. It is more efficient to calculate values of the transfer function for a number of input amplitudes and to store them in a table prior to performance. (This approach is quite similar to storing a wave-form in a wave table that is referenced by a digital oscillator.) In the waveshaper, location in the table of the output value is obtained from the amplitude of the input signal. The instrument designer must ensure that the samples entering a waveshaper fall within the range of locations of the table. For example, if a 512-entry table has its locations marked by the integers 0 to 511, then the output of the oscillator driving the waveshaper must be scaled accordingly. Examples of this appear in section 5.2H.

As demonstrated for the digital oscillator (section 4.3), the use of a finite table size causes small inaccuracies in the output value when the input amplitude falls between entries in the table. In a waveshaper, these inaccuracies are heard as slight increases in the amount of harmonic distortion, and therefore are seldom objectionable.

5.2G Amplitude Scaling

The distortion index also controls the amplitude of the sound, so that changes in spectrum will be accompanied by changes in loudness. This relationship corresponds to the behavior of acoustic instruments, where louder playing ordinarily produces more overtones. Although this general relationship between amplitude and spectrum is correct, it is rare that the desired spectral and amplitude envelopes can both be obtained from a single envelope, particularly when the transfer function provides large amounts of distortion. Excessive loudness variation with spectral content often results, producing excessively bright tones. The amplitude variation with spectral content can be so extreme that the effective dynamic range of the tone of the sound exceeds the limitations of the system. When a secondary amplitude envelope is placed on the output of the waveshaper, the overall envelope of the sound becomes the product of the distortion index and the amplitude envelopes. When the interdependence between amplitude and spectrum is tempered, the amplitude envelope can be more easily chosen.

One method of compensation is to multiply the output of the waveshaper by a *scaling factor* which is a function of the distortion index.[17] If $S(a)$ is the scaling function, then the output is $OUT(ax) = F(ax)S(a)$. Because the scaling function is almost always complicated, it is impractical to calculate its value every time the distortion index is changed. Instead, it is stored as the transfer function of a second nonlinear processor, which is driven directly by the distortion index, a. Thus, in a waveshaping instrument like the one shown in figure 5.27, the distortion index is applied to both the sinusoidal oscillator and the processor containing the scaling function.

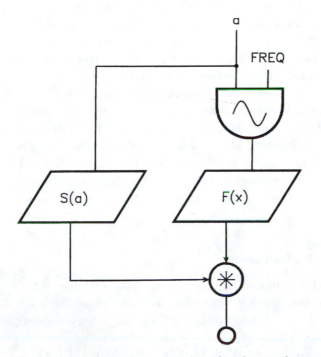

FIGURE 5.27 Implementation of a scaling function by means of second nonlinear processor.

The scaling is applied to the output signal according to some criterion. A practical method is to equalize the power in the signal to a constant value. For true power scaling, the scaling function is chosen as

$$S(a) = \frac{1}{\sqrt{\frac{1}{4}h_0^2(a) + h_1^2(a) + \cdots + h_N^2(a)}}$$

The relative strengths of the harmonics still vary with the distortion index just as they would without scaling, but the amplitude of the entire spectrum is raised or lowered by the appropriate scaling factor to keep the output power constant. However, this method does not work when the distortion index equals 0 because the scaling function becomes infinite. The instrument designer may choose to work around this by setting $S(0)$ to a large, but noninfinite, value.

Peak scaling defines a scaling function where the peak amplitude of the output waveform is always the same. With a distortion index of a, the input to the waveshaper assumes values between $-a$ and $+a$. To peak-scale the output, it is divided by the maximum magnitude of the transfer function for that range of inputs. Thus, the scaling function is

$$S(a) = \frac{1}{\max|F(\alpha)|_{-a \leq \alpha \leq a}}$$

The audible effect of this kind of scaling varies tremendously with the shape of the transfer function. When the transfer function is either continuously increasing or decreasing (i.e., has no peaks or valleys), this scaling method tends to equalize the power to some extent, although not with the accuracy of true power scaling. When the transfer function has ripples, an unusual relationship between amplitude and spectrum results because the scaling function has several plateaus yielding a limited amount of power equalization for some regions of distortion index and considerable power variation in others.

The use and type of a scaling function depends on the choice of transfer function and the type of sound to be synthesized. As in FM synthesis, waveshaping with true power scaling allows the amplitude and spectral envelopes to be independent, but at the same time eliminates one of the musical advantages of waveshaping synthesis—the change in spectral content with amplitude. A strategy that is often more effective is to choose a scaling function providing a more restrictive variation of loudness with distortion index. For some transfer functions, this can be done with peak scaling; in other cases, a modified power scaling function is more effective.

5.2H   Example Waveshaping Instruments

Jean-Claude Risset designed and used in composition a nonlinear waveshaping instrument in the late 1960s.[18] The design, shown in figure 5.28, creates clarinet-like tones through nonlinear distortion of sine tones into tones with harmonic series containing only the odd-numbered partials.

The transfer function of the waveshaper is stored in a table with a length of 512 loca-

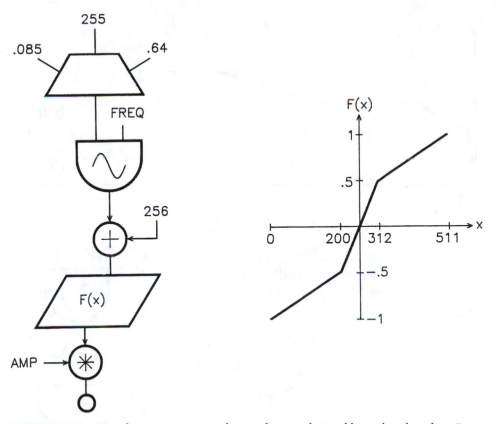

FIGURE 5.28 Waveshaping instrument that produces a clarinet-like timbre, based on Risset. *(Based on example in Risset's* Introductory Catalogue of Computer-Synthesized Sounds. *Reprinted with permission of Jean-Claude Risset.)*

tions. The transfer function is specified graphically in a piecewise linear manner. The samples from the output of the oscillator fall in the range ±255, which is one-half the table length minus 1. To this value is added the constant value of 256. Thus, the values used to reference the waveshaper oscillate in the range from 1 to 511. The entries in the waveshaper table are scaled to the range ±1 and subsequently multiplied by the desired amplitude. As Risset points out, because the transfer function is not band-limited, this design, when used at a sampling rate of 20 kHz, will generate objectionable aliasing on tones with fundamental frequencies above about 1500 Hz.

Figure 5.29a shows the design for a nonlinear waveshaping instrument that produces simple, "brassy" tones. The design includes a scaling function (F1) to temper the variation of amplitude with spectrum. The linear rise in the distortion index causes distortion in the tone to increase rapidly during the attack. During the steady state, the distortion index has a value of 0.7, so that the harmonic content is less brilliant. During the decay, the harmonic content at the high frequencies falls off first. The transfer function was obtained by matching the spectrum shown in figure 5.29b.

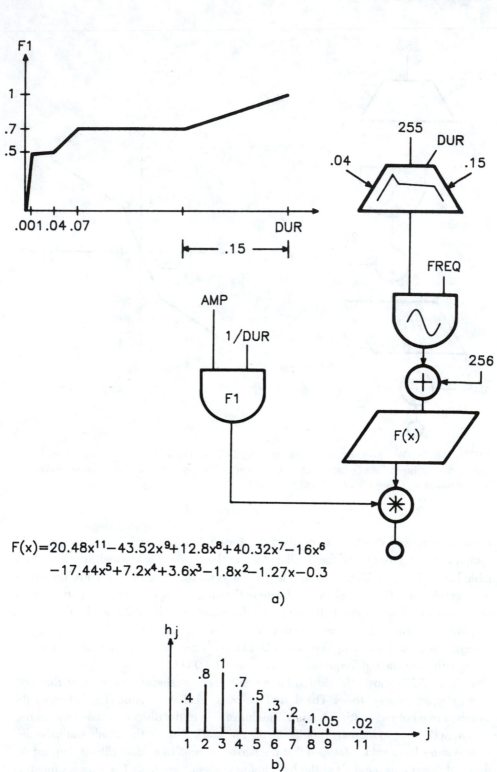

$$F(x)=20.48x^{11}-43.52x^9+12.8x^8+40.32x^7-16x^6$$
$$-17.44x^5+7.2x^4+3.6x^3-1.8x^2-1.27x-0.3$$

a)

b)

FIGURE 5.29 (a) Waveshaping instrument with a "brassy" timbre and (b) spectrum that was matched.

5.2I   Use of Ring Modulation with Waveshapers

The technique of waveshaping described above provides strictly harmonic spectra that, in general, become richer with increasing distortion index. This makes it easy to synthesize tones in which the lower harmonics attack first and decay last. However, the basic technique does not readily provide for the synthesis of certain other harmonic evolutions. A simple variation on the basic technique increases the types of sounds that can be synthesized, makes possible inharmonic spectra, and facilitates formant simulation.[19] In this approach, the output of a waveshaper is multiplied by a sinusoidal tone as shown in figure 5.30a. This results in ring modulation, which produces a spectrum containing a replicated image of the spectrum of the shaped tone both above and below the modulating frequency. The lower image is reversed (figure 5.30b). If the shaped and modulating frequency tones have fundamental frequencies of f_1 and f_2, respectively, the frequencies produced are the sum and difference of f_2 with each harmonic of f_1—that is, with an Nth-order transfer function, $f_2 \pm jf_1$, where $j = 0, 1, 2, \ldots, N$. The corresponding amplitude of each component is $0.5(A2)h_j$, where A2 is the amplitude of the modulating wave and h_j is the amplitude of the jth harmonic of the shaped wave.

The result bears some similarities to simple FM synthesis. If the ratio of the frequencies is given as

$$\frac{f_1}{f_2} = \frac{N_1}{N_2}$$

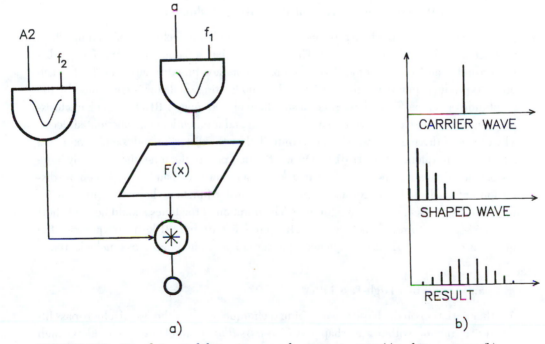

a)   b)

FIGURE 5.30   Use of ring modulation in a waveshaping instrument (a) and its spectrum (b).

where N_1 and N_2 are integers with no common factors, then the fundamental frequency (f_0) of the resulting waveform is

$$f_0 = \frac{f_1}{N_1} = \frac{f_2}{N_2}$$

When N_1 is even, only odd harmonics are produced. If f_1 or f_2 is an irrational number, then N_1 and N_2 cannot be defined as integers and an inharmonic spectrum results.

If f_2 is less than f_1 times the order of the transfer function (i.e., $f_2 < Nf_1$), negative frequencies result. These are transformed into positive frequencies by folding them around 0 Hz (see section 5.1B). If there is a component at the corresponding positive frequency, the folded component is added to it to form the net spectrum. The phase of the components must be considered when they are combined. Unlike FM, the folding process does not necessarily reverse the phase of a component. If the modulating waveform and the input to the waveshaper are both cosine waves, the folded components are added in phase. If the modulating wave is a sine wave, the components are out of phase and must be subtracted.

Placing an envelope on the distortion index realizes a dynamic spectrum. In addition, it is usually necessary to place an amplitude envelope on the modulating oscillator to obtain the desired overall envelope of the sound. If the transfer function has a constant term, the modulating tone is heard even when the distortion index drops to 0. This can be useful in realizing certain timbres.

5.2J   A Waveshaping Instrument Using Ring Modulation

Figure 5.31 shows a waveshaper that uses the ring modulation technique of section 5.2I to produce a pitched-percussion sound. The instrument has separate envelopes for the distortion index and the amplitude. The two oscillators are tuned inharmonically to each other to produce an inharmonic spectrum. The modulating oscillator is controlled by the amplitude envelope F2, and generates a sine tone of frequency FREQ. As is characteristic of most percussive sounds, F2 has a rapid rise and a much longer, exponential decay. The oscillator driving the waveshaper is controlled by the distortion index and produces a sine tone of frequency 0.7071FREQ. During the first part of the tone, the relatively large distortion index causes the shaped wave to occupy a rather wide bandwidth. When the distortion index falls to 0, the constant term in the transfer function allows the pure tone of the modulating oscillator to come through. The duration of the tones should be kept short (< 0.25 second), to retain the characteristic percussive timbre. At lower frequencies the timbre is drumlike; at higher frequencies the sensation of pitch becomes much clearer.

5.2K   Use of a High-Pass Filter

Another variation on the basic waveshaping technique involves the use of a high-pass filter in conjunction with a waveshaper. A *high-pass filter* is an element that allows high frequencies to pass through and attenuates low ones (see chapter 6). This method has

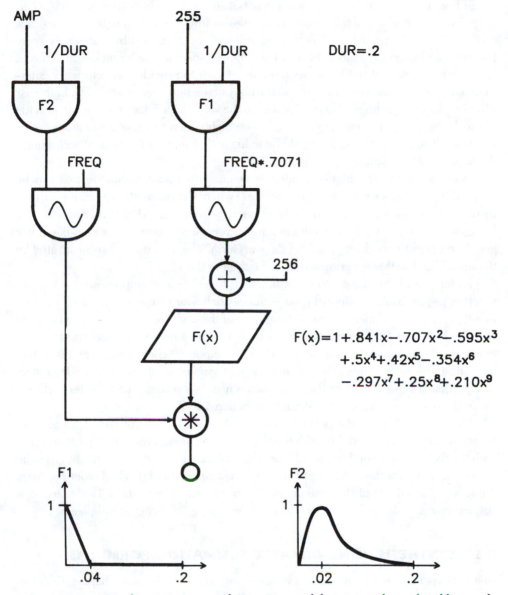

FIGURE 5.31 Waveshaping instrument that uses ring modulation to produce a drumlike sound.

been demonstrated by James Beauchamp[20] and has been successful in the synthesis of realistic brass tones. The method is based on a mathematical model of the acoustical processes used to produce a tone on a brass instrument. The parameters of the model are determined from the analysis of actual instrument characteristics.

The spectrum of the sound produced by blowing into an unattached mouthpiece is a nonlinear function of its loudness—the harder the player blows, the richer the spectrum of the sound. The body of the natural brass instrument serves not only to resonate the sound from the mouthpiece into a clear pitch, but also acts as a high-pass filter. The computer instrument of figure 5.32 approximates the mouthpiece action with the sine-wave oscillator and the waveshaper. The transfer function is determined by matching a spectrum that is obtained by analysis of actual mouthpiece spectra at different dynamic levels.

The parameters of the high-pass filter are chosen to provide characteristics determined from acoustical measurements on the body of the brass instrument. The high-pass filter emphasizes the higher harmonics, and so the waveshaper does not need to provide as much high-frequency energy. Thus, the transfer function will give a smoother evolution with distortion index, and it would be unlikely that such an instrument will require dynamic amplitude scaling.

Waveshaping with a high-pass filter is generally a useful technique that can be adapted to the synthesis of other types of sound where the parameters are not necessarily determined from analysis. It does, however, require that the digital hardware have a large dynamic range in the numbers that it can represent, because the high-pass filter greatly reduces the peak amplitude of the waveform. The amplitude is reconstituted by the multiplication that is performed on the output of the filter.

In his use of this design to make brasslike tones, Beauchamp chose the transfer function (figure 5.32a) to simulate the nonlinear behavior of the spectrum of a cornet mouthpiece played alone. The cutoff frequency of the high-pass filter was fixed at 1800 Hz. The high-pass filter, with a constant setting of its parameters irrespective of the frequency of the instrument, contributes to the most important characteristic of this instrument design—the instrument maintains the appropriate timbre over its entire range. The particular filter algorithm that Beauchamp uses is a second-order Butterworth filter realized with the bilinear transform (see section 6.13C).

One of the primary features of this instrument design is that it produces richer spectra at higher dynamic levels. In addition, Beauchamp changes the envelope shape (F1) with the dynamic level of the desired tone. Figure 5.32b, c, and d, respectively, gives the envelope shapes for three different dynamic levels: *pp*, *mf*, and *ff*. The louder the tone, the less the amplitude of the tone diminishes during the steady state. These envelope shapes were also derived from the analysis of recordings of cornet mouthpieces.

5.3   SYNTHESIS USING DISCRETE SUMMATION FORMULAS

In addition to frequency modulation synthesis and synthesis by waveshaping, the class of techniques known as distortion synthesis includes synthesis by the explicit use of *discrete summation formulas*. This category encompasses a wide variety of algorithms.[21] Both harmonic and inharmonic spectra in either band-limited or unlimited form can be synthesized by means of various formulas.

What is a discrete summation formula? The sum of the first N integers can be written as

$$1 + 2 + 3 + \cdots + N = \sum_{k=1}^{N} k$$

where k is an arbitrary index, ranging from 1 to N. To evaluate this expression, one could

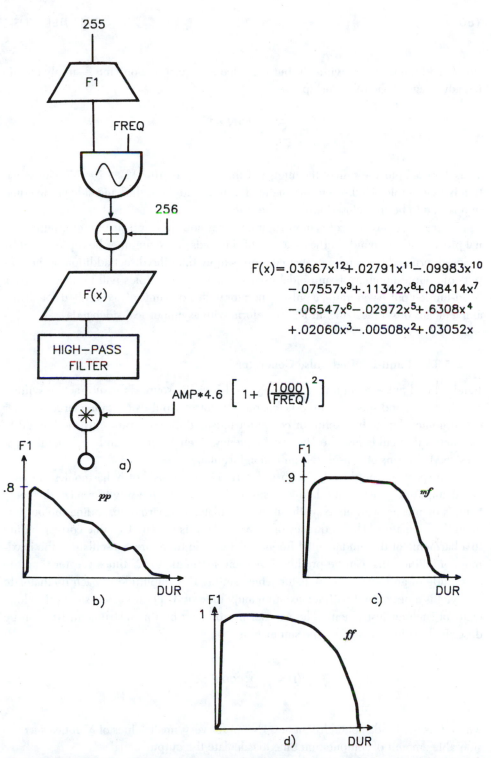

$$F(x) = .03667x^{12} + .02791x^{11} - .09983x^{10}$$
$$- .07557x^{9} + .11342x^{8} + .08414x^{7}$$
$$- .06547x^{6} - .02972x^{5} + .6308x^{4}$$
$$+ .02060x^{3} - .00508x^{2} + .03052x$$

$$AMP*4.6 \left[1 + \left(\frac{1000}{FREQ}\right)^{2} \right]$$

FIGURE 5.32 (a) Waveshaping instrument based on Beauchamp and the envelopes (b), (c), and (d) for different dynamic levels. Beauchamp evaluated $F(x)$ over the range of $x = \pm 1.4$ to fill the wave table in the nonlinear processor. (*Reprinted with permission of* Computer Music Journal.)

simply add the terms individually, but the calculation can be done more simply by taking advantage of the relationship

$$\sum_{k=1}^{N} k = \frac{N(N+1)}{2}$$

Thus, for example, the sum of the integers 1 through 10 is $(10 \times 11) \div 2 = 55$. This equation is an example of a discrete summation formula, and the right-hand side of the equation is said to be the "closed form" of the sum.

There are many discrete summation formulas and they appear often in digital signal processing. In sound synthesis, a sum of sinusoids can sometimes be represented by
a closed form, which can be evaluated more simply than the direct addition of the outputs of a large number of sinusoidal oscillators. Three examples will be given here: a
band-limited pulse generator, a pulse generator with a dynamically controlled spectrum,
and a means of synthesizing an FM waveform with asymmetrical sidebands.

5.3A   Band-Limited Pulse Generator

Band-limited pulse generators are widely used periodic sources for subtractive synthesis (chapter 6) and speech synthesis (chapter 7). Narrow pulses contain a large number
of harmonics, but to be useful for computer music, their spectrum must be limited to
harmonics that fall below the Nyquist frequency. Such a source can be efficiently synthesized by means of a discrete summation formula.

The spectrum produced, shown in figure 5.33a, consists of N harmonics, all with
equal amplitude; each of the harmonics is a cosine wave. One way to realize the spectrum is by means of additive synthesis: one oscillator per harmonic, adding the outputs
of all the oscillators. The frequency of each oscillator is assigned a value corresponding
to a harmonic of the fundamental frequency. Because there are N oscillators, the maximum amplitude that can be produced by their summation is N times greater than the
amplitude of an individual oscillator. Thus, setting the amplitude of each oscillator to
A/N yields a net output with a maximum amplitude of A. Figure 5.33b shows the flowchart of such an instrument. The waveform produced by this instrument, $f(t)$, can be
described mathematically by the summation

$$f(t) = \frac{A}{N} \sum_{k=1}^{N} \cos(2\pi k f_0 t)$$

where f_0 is the fundamental frequency. Except for very small values of N, it takes a considerable amount of computation time to calculate the output signal.

Fortunately, the sum of harmonic cosine waves has a closed form,[22] which is given by

$$\frac{A}{N} \sum_{k=1}^{N} \cos(2\pi k f_0 t) = \frac{A}{2N} \left\{ \frac{\sin[(2N+1)\pi f_0 t]}{\sin(\pi f_0 t)} - 1 \right\}$$

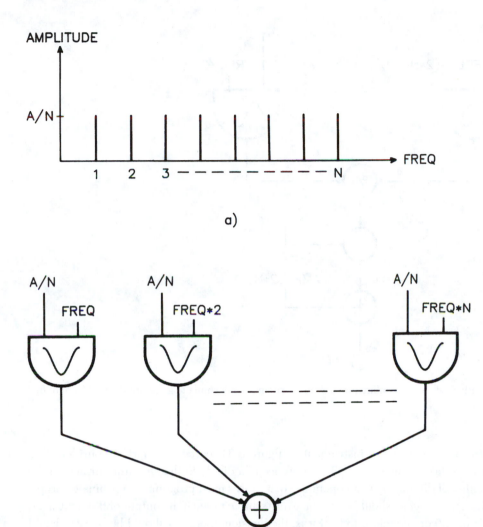

FIGURE 5.33   (a) Pulse spectrum with equal amplitude components. (b) Additive-synthesis instrument to realize it.

The right-hand side of the equation can be calculated using the configuration shown in figure 5.34. Regardless of the number of harmonics synthesized, this instrument employs just two oscillators, one for each sine function in the equation, yet realizes the same spectrum as the additive instrument of figure 5.33b. On many computer music systems, this algorithm forms the heart of a unit generator (often called BUZZ), which synthesizes band-limited pulse waveforms. Section 6.1 includes a more detailed description of this signal in the time domain.

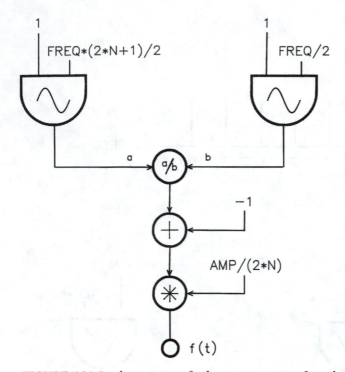

FIGURE 5.34 Implementation of a discrete summation formula to generate the spectrum of figure 5.33a.

In programming the instrument of figure 5.34, certain numerical considerations need to be taken into account. The presence of a divide in the algorithm brings up the possibility of division by 0, an operation that causes most programs to terminate abruptly. Thus, the program should check on every sample to see if the output of the right-hand oscillator is 0 or very close to 0. If it is, the division operation should be bypassed, and the value of the overall output of the algorithm set directly to the maximum amplitude, A. This method works satisfactorily for many purposes, but in some cases it might be necessary to use the following, more accurate technique. When the divisor is very near 0, instead of implementing the previous equation, the algorithm would calculate the output, $f(t)$, from

$$f(t) = \frac{A}{2N}\left\{\frac{(2N+1)\cos[(2N+1)\pi f_0 t]}{\cos(\pi f_0 t)} - 1\right\}$$

Combining the oscillator outputs by division can cause numerical roundoff errors (see section 3.3), which can degrade the signal-to-noise ratio of the output signal. In order to reduce this effect to a level consistent with other unit generators, many implementations of this algorithm use a wave table that is twice the size of the usual wave table for storing the sine wave used by the oscillators.

5.3B Pulse Generator with a Dynamically Controlled Spectrum

Figure 5.35a shows another example of another spectrum that lends itself to realization by means of a discrete summation formula. The waveform corresponding to this spectrum can be written mathematically as

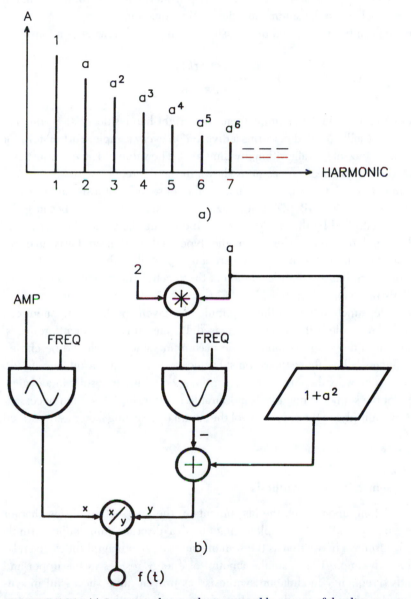

a)

b)

FIGURE 5.35 (a) Spectrum that can be generated by means of the discrete summation formula implemented by (b).

$$f(t) = \sum_{k=0}^{\infty} a^k \sin[2\pi(k+1)f_0 t]$$

Practicality requires $a < 1$, so that the amplitudes of the spectral components decrease exponentially with harmonic number. For example, when $a = 0.9$, the amplitudes of successive harmonics, starting with the fundamental, will be given by the sequence 1, 0.9, 0.81, 0.729, ... Unlike the previous example, this spectrum is not band-limited as noted by the infinity symbol above the summation sign in the equation.

This spectrum can be synthesized most easily by using the following relationship:[23]

$$\sum_{k=0}^{\infty} a^k \sin[2\pi(k+1)f_0 t] = \frac{\sin(2\pi f_0 t)}{1 + a^2 - 2a\cos(2\pi f_0 t)} \qquad a < 1$$

The instrument (figure 5.35b) that implements the right-hand side of the equation employs two digital oscillators and performs a division on every sample. Fortunately, for $a < 1$, there is no chance of this algorithm dividing by 0. The value of $1 + a^2$ is most efficiently evaluated by a nonlinear processor as shown in the figure.

This instrument, which forms the basis in a number of sound synthesis languages for a unit generator often called GBUZZ, synthesizes dynamic spectra easily because the spectrum can be controlled by the single index, a. Increasing the value of a causes the spectrum of the sound to become richer. As in other types of distortion synthesis, an envelope can be placed on the index to obtain a particular spectral evolution. This discrete summation formula exhibits a smooth evolution of the spectral components as the index is increased. This behavior contrasts with an FM or a waveshaping instrument with a complicated transfer function, where the amplitude of a given spectral component can display a great deal of ripple as the index is increased. Because this instrument produces, in theory, an infinite number of harmonics, the maximum value of a should be chosen such that components falling above the Nyquist frequency have insignificant amplitudes.

As in synthesis by waveshaping, a change in the spectral index results in a change in the loudness of the sound. While this is a desirable relationship, it is often necessary to moderate it by multiplying the amplitude of the sound by a scaling factor as described in section 5.2G.

5.3C   Asymmetrical FM Synthesis

Frequency modulation, upon which the instruments in the first section of this chapter are based, can be viewed as the implementation of a discrete summation formula because its waveform can be written as the sum of sine waves with amplitudes given by Bessel functions. In simple FM, a similar amount of energy resides in the upper and lower sidebands. Frequency modulation synthesis has proven quite successful in synthesizing a broad variety of sounds, but the symmetry limits the dynamic spectral envelopes that can be synthesized by simple FM.

Palamin, et al.[24] have advanced an FM synthesis algorithm that generates waveforms with an asymmetric spectral envelope controlled by a symmetry index r and the index of modulation I. The waveform produced by asymmetrical FM (AFM) is described by the equation with amplitude argument A as

$$f(t) = A \sum_{k=-\infty}^{\infty} r^k J_k(I) \sin[2\pi(f_c + kf_m)t]$$

This equation has a closed form that can be used to realize the spectrum most efficiently.

$$f(t) = A \exp\left[\frac{I}{2}\left(r - \frac{1}{r}\right)\cos(2\pi f_m t)\right] \sin\left[2\pi f_c t + \frac{I}{2}\left(r + \frac{1}{r}\right)\sin(2\pi f_m t)\right]$$

where exp is the exponential function.

The amplitude, A_k, of the sideband located at the frequency $f_c + kf_m$ is

$$A_k = Ar^k J_k(I) \qquad -\infty < k < \infty \qquad r \neq 0$$

In this definition, negative values of k denote lower sidebands, while the upper sidebands are marked by positive values. When $r = 1$, the spectrum is symmetric and the technique reduces to simple FM. For values of $0 < r < 1$, the lower sidebands have larger amplitudes than the corresponding upper ones. Conversely, values of $r > 1$ emphasize the upper sidebands at the expense of the lower ones. For instance, setting $r = 1.25$ produces a lower sideband at $f_c - f_m$ with an amplitude of $0.8J_{-1}(I)$ and an upper one at $f_c + f_m$ with an amplitude of $1.25J_1(I)$. The difference between upper and lower sidebands becomes more pronounced as k increases. The amplitude of the sidebands does not grow without bound for increasing k because the factor r^k rises more slowly than the Bessel function $J_k(I)$ decreases for any finite value of r.

To demonstrate the control exerted by the symmetry index on the shape of the spectrum of the generated waveform, the spectral envelope of the signal is plotted for three different values of r in figure 5.36. Observe that a value of $r < 1$ tilts the spectrum to place more power in the lower sidebands, $r = 1$ generates a symmetric spectrum, while a larger value of r pushes the majority of the energy into the upper sidebands. To uncouple the effects of negative-frequency sidebands in this pedagogical example, the carrier frequency was set to half the Nyquist frequency, the $f_c{:}f_m$ ratio to 16:1, and the index of modulation to $I = 3$. In the figure, the relative amplitude scale in decibels is referenced to the peak amplitude of a simple FM spectrum ($r = 1$). As illustrated in the figure, specifying $r \neq 1$ boosts the peak of the spectrum; values more extreme than the ones used in the example are generally not used in the synthesis of natural sounding tones to avoid excessive brightness.[25]

Simple FM ($r = 1$) has the advantageous property of automatically scaling the peak amplitude of the waveform to A, regardless of the index of modulation. In AFM, a value of $r \neq 1$ boosts the peak amplitude, and hence the power, in the waveform over that of simple FM by a significant factor that also depends on I. For example, with $I = 2$, choosing $r = 2$ or its reciprocal $r = 0.5$ gives a peak value of $4.316A$; setting $r = 4$ or $r = 0.25$ amplifies the peak amplitude by 38.189. With these latter values of r, increasing I to 4 boosts the peak amplitude of the AFM waveform over A by the large factor of 1559.4.

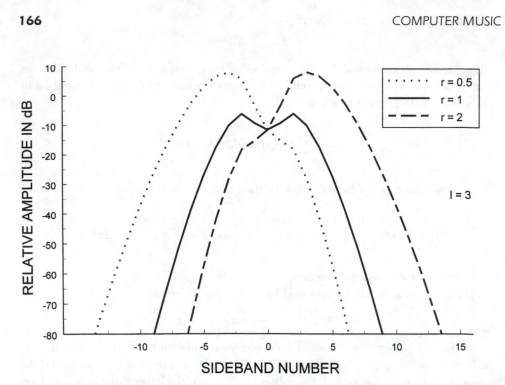

FIGURE 5.36   Spectral envelope of AFM for various values of r with $I = 3$. The amplitude is given relative to the amplitude argument A.

To prevent overflow in the system and make the spectral evolutions produced by an AFM instrument usable, the power can be normalized by multiplying the output by the scaling factor S, which depends on I and r as

$$S = \frac{1}{\sqrt{J_0'\left[I\left(r - \frac{1}{r}\right)\right]}}$$

where J_0' represents a zeroth-order modified Bessel function of the first kind.[26] In the literature of mathematics, this function is ordinarily symbolized by I_0, but that notation is not used here to avoid confusion with the index of modulation.

Figure 5.37 depicts a block diagram of an instrument to realize amplitude-scaled AFM. Instead of implementing frequency modulation directly, the *phase* of the carrier oscillator is modulated by one of the modulating oscillators. Look-up tables are used to evaluate the exponential function and the power scaling function. The argument AMP controls the peak amplitude of the waveform produced by the instrument. Although not shown in the block diagram, envelope generators on the amplitude and on the modulation index would be included in the synthesis of musical tones in the same way as these parameters are varied with time in simple FM. Shifting the spectral energy to the upper sidebands ($r > 1$) can result in an excessively bright timbre. This behavior is sometimes moderated by adding an oscillator producing a single sine wave at the fundamental frequency to the output.

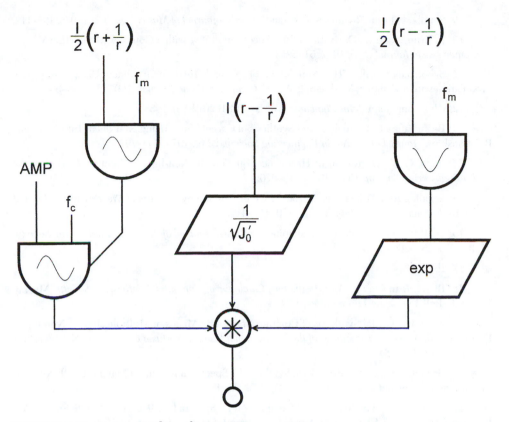

FIGURE 5.37 Instrument for realizing AFM.

NOTES

1. Chowning, John. "The Synthesis of Complex Audio Spectra by Means of Frequency Modulation." *Journal of the Audio Engineering Society*, 21(7), 1973, 526–534. (Reprinted in *Computer Music Journal*, 1(2), 1977, 46–54.)

2. Abramowitz, M., and Stegun, I. A. (eds.) *Handbook of Mathematical Functions*. Washington, D.C.: U.S. Government Printing Office, 1964.

3. Holm, F. "Understanding FM Implementations: A Call for Common Standards." *Computer Music Journal*, 16(1), 1992, 34–42.

4. Chowning. "The Synthesis of Complex Audio Spectra."

5. Morrill, Dexter. "Trumpet Algorithms for Computer Composition." *Computer Music Journal*, 1(1), 1977, 46–52.

6. Risset, Jean-Claude. *Computer Study of Trumpet Tones*. Murray Hill, N.J.: Bell Telephone Laboratories, 1966.

7. Smith, Leland. "Score: A Musician's Approach to Computer Music." *Journal of the Audio Engineering Society*, 20(1), 1972, 7–14.

8. Chowning, John. "Computer Synthesis of the Singing Voice." In Johan Sundberg (ed.), *Sound Generation in Winds, Strings, and Computers* (Publication No. 29). Stockholm: Royal Swedish Academy of Music, 1980, 4–13.

9. Sundberg, Johan. "Synthesis of Singing." *Swedish Journal of Musicology*, 60(1), 1978, 107–112.

10. LeBrun, Marc. "A Derivation of the Spectrum of FM with a Complex Modulating Wave." *Computer Music Journal*, 1(4), 1977, 51–52.

11. Schottstaedt, Bill. "The Simulation of Natural Instrument Tones Using Frequency Modulation with a Complex Modulating Wave." *Computer Music Journal*, 1(4), 1977, 46–50.

12. Chowning, John. *John Chowning*. Wergo (WER 2012-50), 1988.

13. Beauchamp, J. W. "Analysis and Synthesis of Cornet Tones Using Non-linear Interharmonic Relationships." *Journal of the Audio Engineering Society*, 23(6), 1975, 793–794.

14. Suen, C. Y. "Derivation of Harmonic Equations in Non-linear Circuits." *Journal of the Audio Engineering Society*, 18(6), 1970, 675–676.

15. Schaffer, R. A. "Electronic Musical Tone Production by Non-linear Waveshaping." *Journal of the Audio Engineering Society*, 18(2), 1970, 413–417.

16. LeBrun, Marc. "Digital Waveshaping Synthesis." *Journal of the Audio Engineering Society*, 27(4), 1979, 250–266.

17. Ibid.

18. Risset, Jean-Claude. *An Introductory Catalogue of Computer-Synthesized Sounds*. Murray Hill, N.J.: Bell Telephone Laboratories, 1969.

19. Arfib, D. "Digital Synthesis of Complex Spectra by Means of Multiplication of Non-linear Distorted Sine Waves." *Proceedings of the International Computer Music Conference*, Northwestern University, 1978, 70–84.

20. Beauchamp, James. "Brass Tone Synthesis by Spectrum Evolution Matching with Non-linear Functions." *Computer Music Journal*, 3(2), 1979, 35–43.

21. Moorer, J. A. "The Synthesis of Complex Audio Spectra by Means of Discrete Summation Formulae" (Report No. STAN-M-5). Music Department, Stanford University, 1975.

22. Winham, Godfrey, and Steiglitz, Kenneth. "Input Generators for Digital Sound Synthesis." *Journal of the Acoustical Society of America*, 47(2), 1970, 665–666.

23. Moorer, "The Synthesis of Complex Audio Spectra."

24. Palamin, J.-P., Palamin, P., and Ronveaux, A. "A Method of Generating and Controlling Musical Asymmetrical Spectra." *Journal of the Audio Engineering Society*, 36(9), 1988, 671–685.

25. Tan, B. T. G., and Gan, S. L. "Real-Time Implementation of Asymmetrical Frequency-Modulation Synthesis." *Journal of the Audio Engineering Society*, 41(5), 1993, 357–363.

26. Abramowitz and Stegun (eds.). *Handbook of Mathematical Functions*.

6

SUBTRACTIVE SYNTHESIS

Subtractive synthesis creates musical tones out of complex sources by sculpting away selected portions of the spectrum of the source. In subtractive synthesis (figure 6.1), a source with a broad spectrum, such as white noise or a narrow pulse, serves as the raw material out of which a musical tone is formed by filtering.

This chapter considers some useful sources and discusses filtering at length. Musical examples are provided to show the design considerations for computer instruments with noise and periodic sources. Several examples from the musical literature are given. The chapter concludes with a more technical description of the principles of digital filtering, along with a few filter recipes.

6.1   SOURCES

Any sound can be used as a source for subtractive synthesis. Because the subtractive process alters the spectral balance of a sound, the technique has the greatest effect when applied to sources with rich spectra. Instruments employing synthesis techniques presented in earlier chapters (e.g., FM synthesis) or external signals (such as sound sensed by a microphone) can be used as sources. However, there are two kinds of spectrally rich signal generators that are commonly used as sources: noise and pulse generators. Noise generators produce wide-band distributed spectra and are described in section 4.9. A pulse generator produces a periodic waveform at a specific frequency with a great deal of energy in the harmonics.

A *pulse* waveform (figure 6.2) has significant amplitude only during a relatively brief interval of time. The duration of that interval is called the *pulse width*. When a pulse waveform is repeated periodically, the resulting signal has a rich spectrum. The charac-

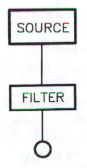

FIGURE 6.1   The basic configuration for subtractive synthesis.

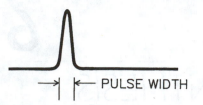

— PULSE WIDTH

FIGURE 6.2   Generalized waveform of a pulse.

ter of the spectrum is determined by the shape of the pulse and by the ratio of the pulse width to the period of the overall waveform. A small ratio (i.e., a narrow pulse) connotes a large proportion of the spectral energy at high frequencies.

Pulses can assume a myriad of shapes—rectangular, triangular, etc.—but very few shapes have band-limited spectra. To avoid aliasing when using a pulse generator in digital synthesis, the musician must select shapes with band-limited spectra. A pulse generator that is commonly used in subtractive synthesis produces a waveform with a shape that depends on the ratio of the frequency at which the pulse repeats (f_0) to the sampling frequency of the system. This type of pulse is best described in terms of its spectrum. To avoid aliasing, it contains all possible harmonics of the fundamental only up to the Nyquist frequency; each harmonic has the same amplitude. The number of harmonics in the spectrum, N, is determined by

$$N = \text{int}\left(\frac{f_s}{2f_0}\right)$$

where the function int returns the integer portion on its argument. Figure 6.3 shows the waveform for four different values of N. Notice how the pulse gets narrower as N gets larger. To avoid foldover at higher fundamental frequencies, the pulse must contain fewer harmonics, and so the pulse is wider. For example, if f_s = 40 kHz and f_0 = 440 Hz, then N = 45; but for f_0 = 1046 Hz, the signal would contain only 19 harmonics.

Using an oscillator that scans a wave table to generate this type of pulse waveform is impractical because N, and hence the shape of the waveform, varies with the fundamental frequency. Thus, many computer music systems include a unit generator (often called BUZZ), which contains an algorithm for efficiently generating this type of signal. The inputs to this unit generator, shown in figure 6.4, include the pulse amplitude, the fundamental frequency, and the number of harmonics in the pulse spectrum. Section 5.3A explains the mathematical technique used to generate the pulse waveform.

Pulse generators can be combined to produce other types of spectra. For example, suppose that a wide-band source that contained only odd harmonics was needed for a composition. It could be realized by subtracting the output of a pulse generator running at $2f_0$ from a pulse generator with a frequency of f_0. In this way, the even harmonics are removed from the spectrum. To avoid aliasing, the pulse generator at $2f_0$ would be programmed to produce fewer harmonics (N_2) than the N_1 contained in the pulse at f_0. To

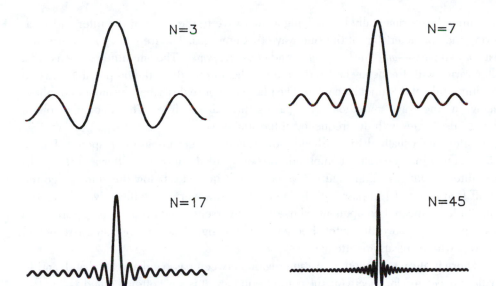

FIGURE 6.3 The waveform of band-limited pulses containing N harmonics.

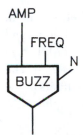

FIGURE 6.4 Flowchart symbol for the band-limited pulse generator known as BUZZ.

achieve full cancellation of the even components, the output of the generator at $2f_0$ would be multiplied by N_2/N_1 before the subtraction operation. Spectral subtraction techniques such as this require that both pulse generators have the same phase; that is, they produce their peak amplitudes at the same time.

6.2 INTRODUCTION TO FILTERING

Filters change the characteristics of sounds by rejecting unwanted components in a signal or by otherwise shaping the spectrum. A filter modifies the amplitude and phase of each spectral component of a signal passing through it, but it does not alter the frequency of any signal or any component. This section includes descriptions of low-pass, high-pass, band-pass, and band-reject filters and their effect on the spectrum of signals passing through them.

The characteristics of a filter can be described by its *frequency response*, which is determined experimentally by applying a sine wave to the input of the filter and measuring the characteristics of the sine wave that emerges. The frequency response consists of two parts—*amplitude response* and *phase response*. The amplitude response of a filter varies with frequency and is the ratio of the amplitude of the output sine wave to the amplitude of the input sine wave. The phase response describes the amount of phase change a sine wave undergoes as it passes through the filter. The amount of phase change also varies with the frequency of the sine wave.

Filters are usually distinguished by the shape of their amplitude response. Figure 6.5 diagrams the generalized amplitude responses of the low-pass filter and the high-pass filter. A *low-pass* filter (figure 6.5a) permits frequencies below the point called the cutoff frequency (f_c) to pass with little change. However, it significantly reduces the amplitude of spectral components above f_c. Conversely, a *high-pass* filter (figure 6.5b) has a passband above the cutoff frequency where signals are passed and a stopband below f_c where signals are attenuated.

There is always a smooth transition region between passband and stopband, and so a rule is necessary for specifying the cutoff frequency: it is most often defined as that frequency at which the power transmitted by the filter drops to one-half (−3 dB) of the maximum power transmitted in the passband. This convention is used in this text; it is equivalent to a reduction in the amplitude response by a factor of 0.707.

A filter that rejects both low and high frequencies with a passband in between them is called a *band-pass* filter. It is characterized either by a *center frequency* (CF or f_0) and a *bandwidth* (BW) or by two cutoff frequencies—an upper (f_u) and a lower (f_l). Figure 6.6 illustrates the generalized shape of the amplitude response of a band-pass filter. The center frequency marks the location of the center of the passband. In digital filters of the type implemented in most computer music programs, the center frequency is the arithmetic mean (average) of the upper and lower cutoff frequencies.

The bandwidth is a measure of the selectivity of the filter and is equal to the difference between the upper and lower cutoff frequencies. The response of a band-pass fil-

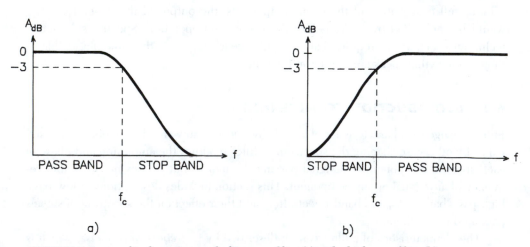

FIGURE 6.5   Amplitude response of a low-pass filter (a) and a high-pass filter (b).

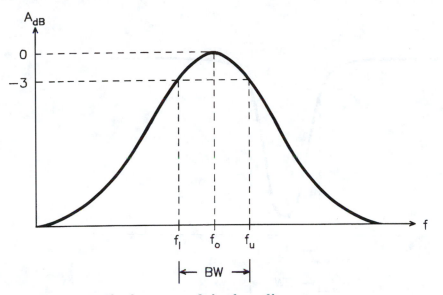

FIGURE 6.6   Amplitude response of a band-pass filter.

ter is often described by terms such as sharp (narrow) or broad (wide), depending on the actual width. The passband sharpness is often quantified by means of a quality factor (*Q*). When the cutoff frequencies are defined at the –3-dB points, *Q* is given by

$$Q = \frac{f_0}{\text{BW}}$$

Therefore, a high *Q* denotes a narrow bandwidth. Bandwidth may also be described as a percentage of the center frequency. The sharpness of a filter is chosen according to the application for which it is used. For example, a band-pass filter with a very narrow bandwidth can be used to extract a specific frequency component from a signal.

The fourth basic filter type is the *band-reject* filter. As its name implies, its amplitude response (figure 6.7) is the inverse of that exhibited by a band-pass filter. A band-reject filter attenuates a band of frequencies and passes all the others. Like a band-pass filter, it is characterized by a center frequency and a bandwidth or by lower and upper cutoff frequencies.

Engineers often describe filters in terms of poles and zeros. These terms originate in the mathematical analysis of the filter response. A *pole* places a peak in the amplitude response and a *zero* causes a valley. When a pole or zero is taken alone, its location can be described by the center frequency (f_0) and bandwidth of the peak or valley that is created in the amplitude response. The height of a peak or the depth of a valley is primarily dependent on the bandwidth. The narrower the bandwidth is, the higher the peak or the deeper the valley. The term "zero" can be misleading. At the center frequency of a zero, the amplitude response of the filter exhibits a minimum, but does not necessarily reach all the way to 0.

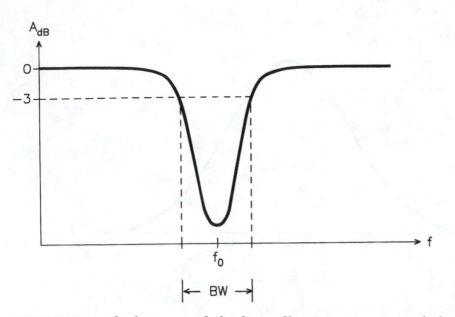

FIGURE 6.7 Amplitude response of a band-reject filter. In certain instances, the bandwidth (BW) is measured between the points at which the amplitude response is 3 dB above the minimum instead of as shown.

In a digital filter, individual poles and zeros can exist at 0 Hz and the Nyquist frequency, but at frequencies in between, poles and zeros must come in pairs, at $\pm f_0$. For example, a band-pass filter with a center frequency of 1 kHz can be made by placing two poles—one at 1 kHz and the other at –1 kHz. As described in chapter 5, negative frequencies represent a mathematical convenience. Similarly, a band-reject filter with a center frequency of 1 kHz is fashioned with a pair of zeros at ± 1 kHz. Fortunately for musicians, available computer music software contains algorithms that compute the proper locations of poles and zeros from a specification of the desired frequency response of the filter.

6.3 A GENERAL-PURPOSE FILTER

Most computer music programs include a unit generator (often called RESON) that serves as a general-purpose filter. It is usually a second-order all-pole filter and exhibits a single peak in its response. The discussion in this section applies to digital filters of that type.

A generalized symbol for a filter element is shown in figure 6.8. This element is a band-pass filter with controlling inputs of center frequency (CF) and bandwidth (BW). Under special conditions, it can be used as a low-pass or a high-pass filter. For example, a low-pass filter can be made from a band-pass filter by setting its center frequency to 0. Intuitively, one might think that the resulting cutoff frequency would be one-half the bandwidth specified, because the passband centers at 0 Hz. Hence, the upper cutoff frequency of the passband should also be the cutoff frequency of the low-pass filter. However, because of an aliasing in the frequency response inherent in the implementa-

INPUT

CF → FILTER ← BW

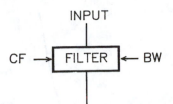

FIGURE 6.8   Flowchart symbol for a filter.

tion of digital filters found in most computer music programs, the cutoff frequency, f_c, of the resulting low pass is equal to 0.707 times the specified bandwidth, not 0.5. For example, to obtain a low pass with a cutoff frequency of 500 Hz, specify CF = 0 and BW = 707 Hz. This behavior will also affect the response of band-pass filters with low center frequencies. As the center frequency of the band-pass filter is brought closer to 0, the passband begins to widen beyond the specified bandwidth.

A high-pass filter can be made from a band-pass filter by setting its center frequency equal to the Nyquist frequency. High-pass digital filters made from the band-pass filters found in most computer music programs suffer from the same aliasing problems that affect low-pass filters. To obtain a high-pass filter with a cutoff frequency f_c, specify the bandwidth according to:

$$BW = \sqrt{2}\left(\frac{f_s}{2} - f_c\right)$$

For example, a high-pass filter with a cutoff frequency of 15 kHz in a system with a 40-kHz sampling rate is realized by the parameters of CF = 20 kHz and BW = 7071 Hz. When the center frequency of the band-pass filter is near the Nyquist frequency, the passband widens in the same way described above for filters with low center frequencies.

The other parameter normally associated with filters is *midband gain:* the ratio of output signal amplitude to input signal amplitude in the center of the passband. The natural, unscaled ratio in a digital filter has a complicated dependence on both center frequency and bandwidth. Thus, the amplitude of a signal at the center frequency may be radically changed, causing the filter element to serve also as an amplifier. To demonstrate the tremendous variation in midband gain possible, figure 6.9 illustrates the amplitude response of a filter with a 500-Hz bandwidth as the center frequency varies from 0 Hz to the Nyquist frequency. Observe that at the extremes of center frequency, the amplitude can be boosted by as much as nearly 60 dB (a factor of 1000). Such a large amplification would cause an applied signal at the center frequency of the filter to have an output amplitude that would overflow the range of the system, producing severe distortion of the sound. Similarly, the bandwidth of the filter also has a large influence on the midband gain as shown in the example of figure 6.10.

The purpose of a filter scale factor is to prevent amplification in the passband by multiplying the filter input by the number that brings the midband gain to 1. Many synthesis programs offer the choice of three types of scale factors: one for periodic signals, one for noise signals, and one to leave the filter output unscaled. The filter output is left

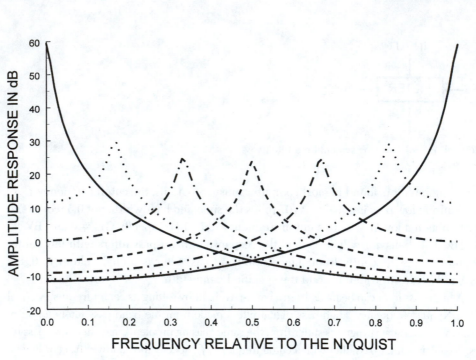

FIGURE 6.9   Variation with center frequency of the amplitude response of an unscaled filter.

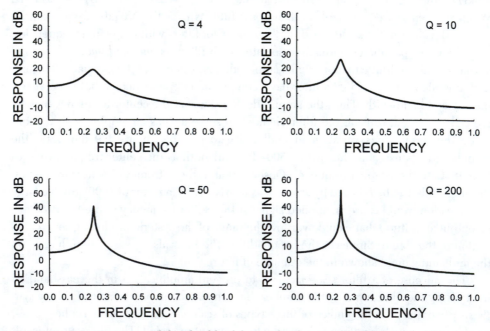

FIGURE 6.10   Variation with bandwidth of the amplitude response of an unscaled filter.

unscaled when the musician has carefully determined a succession of filter elements to be used in realizing a desired frequency response and has knowledge of the maximum possible amplitude at the output of each filter.

6.4   STOPBAND BEHAVIOR

For simple filters such as those described in sections 6.2 and 6.3, the amount of attenuation in the stopband is smallest near the cutoff frequency and continues to increase away from cutoff. A frequency not found in the passband has usually not been completely removed from the signal; it has been attenuated more than if it had been found in the passband.

The rate at which attenuation increases is known as the slope of the filter. The slope, or *rolloff*, is usually expressed as attenuation per unit interval, such as 30 dB per octave. In the stopband of a low-pass filter with a 30-dB/octave slope, every time the frequency doubles, the amount of attenuation increases by 30 dB. At four times the cutoff frequency, the attenuation is 30 dB greater than at twice the cutoff frequency; at eight times, the attenuation is 60 dB greater, and so on. A filter used for rejecting unwanted signals must have a steep rolloff. A good example is a low-pass filter used on the input of an analog-to-digital converter to prevent aliasing. Here, a steep rolloff enables a wide passband to be used for desired signals. By contrast, a filter used in an instrument design for changing the harmonic content of a source may need a gentler rolloff to allow a more natural relationship between the harmonics.

The slope of attenuation is determined by the *order* of the filter. Order is a mathematical measure of the complexity of a filter. In an analog filter, it is proportional to the number of electrical components used. In a digital filter, it is proportional to the number of calculations performed on each sample. (A more detailed explanation of order in a digital filter is given in section 6.11.) In a simple analog low-pass or high-pass filter, the rolloff is 6 dB/octave times the order of the filter. A band-pass filter generally has an even order and the slope both above and below the passband is ordinarily 6 dB/octave times half the order. Thus, the rolloff will be half as steep as that of a low-pass or a high-pass filter of the same order. This may be interpreted to mean that half the filter contributes to the rolloff below the passband and the other half to the rolloff above.

When digital filters are designed as approximations to analog filters, the rolloff of the digital filter will be similar but not identical to the analog filter being imitated. Owing to the nature of digital filters, it is not possible to maintain a constant slope throughout the stopband, and therefore it is not possible to give a precise relationship between order and rolloff. However, the general character of the relationship still holds—the higher the order, the steeper the slope.

The filter unit generators found in most computer music programs are either first- or second-order filters. The filter used to simulate the effect of adjusting the tone control of an amplifier is a first-order filter (often called TONE). Depending on the ratio of cutoff frequency to sampling frequency, it exhibits a 6-dB/octave rolloff over much of its stopband. The resonator unit generator provided (often called RESON or FLT) is a second-order filter. It tends toward a 6-dB/octave slope both above and below the passband.

6.5 FILTER COMBINATIONS

Filter designers need not be restricted to the four basic filter response shapes described previously. It is possible to tailor a filter's amplitude response to a complex contour, providing the musician with a great deal of flexibility in designing interesting spectra for instruments. One useful and conceptually simple method of obtaining complicated amplitude responses is to use the four basic filter types as building blocks (or elements) that can be combined to form a filter with a desired response.

Filter elements can be combined in *parallel connection,* as shown in figure 6.11a. When two or more elements are connected in parallel, the signal to be filtered is applied simultaneously to the inputs of all the filter elements. The outputs of all elements are added together to form a total output. Parallel connection adds together the frequency responses of all the elements; a frequency found in the passband of any of the filter elements will be passed. Only those frequencies that are not found within the passband of any element will be attenuated. For instance, a band-reject filter can be made by connecting a low-pass and a high-pass filter in parallel. The stopband of the complete filter falls in between the cutoff frequencies of the individual elements. Figure 6.11b shows the amplitude response of a filter with two passbands made by parallel connection of two band-pass filters with different center frequencies.

The other fundamental method of element combination is *cascade connection* shown in figure 6.12. (This type of connection is called "series" in some places in the literature of computer music.) In a cascade-connected filter, the elements are connected together as links in a chain. The output of the first element feeds the input of the next element, and so forth until the last element, whose output is the output of the entire filter. The amplitude response of the complete filter is calculated by multiplying all the individual

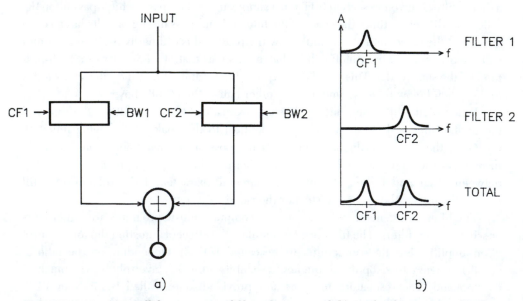

FIGURE 6.11   (a) Parallel connection of filter elements and (b) amplitude response of a filter with two passbands made by parallel connection of band-pass filters.

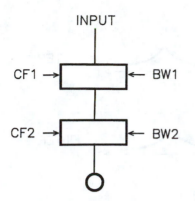

FIGURE 6.12   Cascade connection of filter elements.

responses together. If expressed in decibels, the overall amplitude response at a given frequency is the sum of the responses of the individual elements in dB at that frequency.

The order of a filter made up of cascade-connected elements is equal to the sum of the orders of all the individual elements; the complete filter will therefore have a steeper rolloff. For example, consider the cascade connection of the two band-pass filter elements with identical parameters shown in figure 6.13a. The resulting filter will be a band-pass filter with the same center frequency and a steeper slope (figure 6.13b). At the frequency at which a single element has an attenuation of 3 dB, the cascade combination has an overall attenuation of 6 dB. Thus, the 3-dB bandwidth of an individual element becomes the 6-dB bandwidth of the complete filter. The 3-dB bandwidth of the overall filter is equal to the bandwidth at which each individual element contributes 1.5 dB of attenuation. Thus, in this case, cascade con-

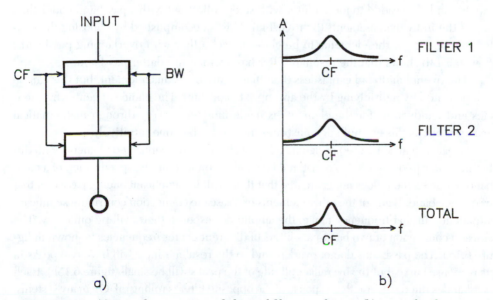

FIGURE 6.13   (a) Cascade connection of identical filters resulting in (b) an amplitude response with a narrower passband and a faster rolloff.

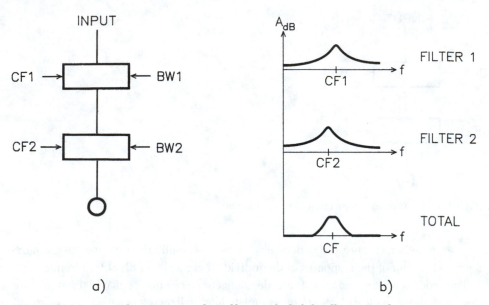

FIGURE 6.14   Cascade connection of two filters with slightly offset center frequencies to obtain a wider, flatter passband with a steeper rolloff.

nection not only increases the rolloff of the filter, it also decreases the bandwidth. Suppose two filters, each with a center frequency of 1 kHz and a 3-dB bandwidth of 100 Hz, have been connected in cascade. The resultant filter has a center frequency of 1 kHz and a 3-dB bandwidth of 65 Hz because that is the 1.5-dB bandwidth of each individual filter.

Through careful choice of center frequencies and bandwidths, band-pass filter elements can be cascaded to form a filter with steep rolloff but with a passband wider than any of the individual elements (figure 6.14a). This is accomplished by choosing the center frequencies of the elements to be close to each other with overlapping passbands. Figure 6.14b shows that the resultant filter has a wider and flatter passband.

The overall midband gain is less than that of any individual element, but this can be compensated by multiplying by the appropriate constant. The choice of center frequencies and bandwidths for the elements is made most effectively through mathematical analysis, but as this example demonstrates, much can be done intuitively.

Great care must be used designing a filter using cascade-connected elements with different center frequencies. Note that, unlike parallel connection, the specification of a passband of one element does not guarantee that there will be significant energy passed in that frequency band. If any of the other elements of a cascade connection contribute significant attenuation in that frequency range, the amplitude response there will be quite low. The cascade connection of two band-pass filters of different center frequencies is shown in figure 6.15a. The passbands do not overlap, and so the resultant filter will have two peaks in its response curve, but the overall amplitude of the peaks will be small (figure 6.15b). Each passband is tilted because the response of the opposite filter is rolling off. On many systems, a filter of this type can be made useful for subtractive synthesis by multiplying its output by a constant to reconstitute its amplitude. If the samples are represented in floating-point for-

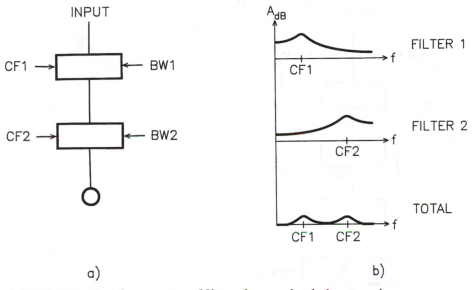

FIGURE 6.15   Cascade connection of filters whose passbands do not overlap.

mat, as is the case in most of the synthesis programs run on general-purpose computers, boosting the filtered signal will generally not increase the noise to a detectable level. In systems that use integer format, such as often used in specialized signal-processing hardware, the available range might not be large enough for this method to work without severely degrading the signal-to-noise ratio.

To permit a musician to use cascade connection freely, without the necessity of calculating the overall midband gain of the filter, some computer music programs implement a unit generator that performs a balance function. The user must specify a reference point in the signal flow, as shown in figure 6.16. This unit generator modifies the amplitude of the signal entering the balance unit, so that the average power in the signal coming out of the balance unit equals the average power of the signal at the reference point. This function is useful when implementing filters made up of several cascaded elements. The reference point is the input to the first element of the filter; the balance unit is placed at the output of the filter. Thus, the signal has the same average power coming out as going in. However, this technique is only effective when a substantial amount of the signal power falls in the passband. Obviously, if the input to the filter consists of a single frequency that is outside the passband, the balance function will boost the signal amplitude to compensate for the attenuation introduced by the filter, thus negating the effect of the filter. However, if the signal applied to the filter has many spectral components over a wide range, as is the case with noise or a pulse, the balance function can be quite useful. It allows the musician to modify the spectrum of the signal at will without dramatically altering its power.

To determine the average power of a signal, the balance function rectifies the signal and passes it through a low-pass filter. The process of *rectification* consists of taking the absolute value of the samples, which changes the negative sample values into positive ones, as shown in figure 6.17. This is a form of nonlinear waveshaping (see section 5.2)

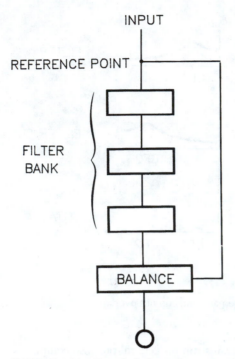

FIGURE 6.16   Use of a balance function to maintain approximately the amplitude at the output at the level of the input.

and has the effect of greatly emphasizing the even-harmonic components of the signal, including the zero-frequency (dc) term. The higher the amplitude of the signal fed into the rectifier, the larger is the amplitude of the even harmonics. The output of the rectifier is then passed through a low-pass filter with a very low cutoff frequency, which attenuates all components except for the zero-frequency term. Thus, the output of the balance

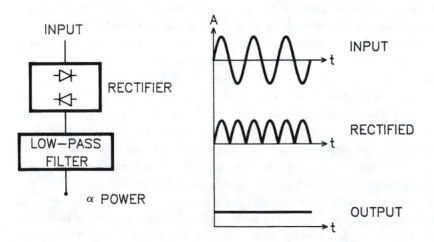

FIGURE 6.17   Method used by balance function to approximate signal power.

function is proportional to the signal amplitude, which provides a measure of average signal power. The user may specify the cutoff frequency of the filter, but normally it is sub-audio (usually 10 Hz) if the purpose is to obtain the average power of a signal.

6.6   ADJUSTABLE DIGITAL FILTERS

A digital filter algorithm works by multiplying signals and delayed images of signals by numbers called *coefficients*. Specifying a set of coefficients to a filter algorithm uniquely determines the characteristics of the digital filter. (See section 6.11.) Most computer music programs contain the algorithms to convert filter frequency characteristics to coefficients, and so users need only specify parameters such as center frequency and bandwidth. However, it takes considerable computer time to calculate filter coefficients from a given frequency response. Thus, if the frequency response of the filter is not going to change during the synthesis process, the coefficients are calculated only once, prior to the beginning of the synthesis. However, the musician is afforded a great deal of flexibility if the frequency response of the filter can be altered during the course of a sound. Therefore, the programs from the Music 4 family often implement two kinds of filter functions. The first type (often called RESON) has coefficients calculated only once, prior to the beginning of the actual synthesis process. The second type (often called VRESON) is basically the same filter, but its coefficients are calculated on every sample. The coefficients of the variable filter are calculated with equations that only approximate the desired passband, because the exact calculation takes too much computer time. The approximation used is most accurate for narrow bandwidths. When the bandwidth exceeds 10% of the sampling frequency, the characteristics of the filter actually obtained begin to deviate noticeably. To maximize computational efficiency, the musician uses variable filters only where needed.

When the filter coefficients are calculated on every sample, the need for a reasonable computation time makes impractical the calculation of a scaling factor for midband gain (see section 6.3). As a result, this kind of filter is normally used unscaled. Some computer music programs allow the musician to enter an estimate of the peak amplitude of the output signal. The program uses this guess to scale the gain for an expected midband gain of 1. However, the success of this technique is completely dependent on the accuracy of the musician's estimation. However, as a further complication, because the unscaled midband gain changes with the center frequency of the filter (see figure 6.9), the estimate will not be accurate when the filter is tuned over a broad frequency range.

Some programs, such as Csound, use another method that precisely determines the coefficients, including midband gain, of the adjustable filter without taking an excessive amount of computation time. In this method, the computer calculates coefficients at a rate lower than the sampling rate. For example, the new coefficients could be determined on every 40th sample. The reduced rate at which the filter characteristics can change is not a musical limitation unless the calculation rate falls below about 200 times per second.

A third approach to realizing a variable filter, which has been used in systems with special-purpose real-time hardware, entails calculating many sets of coefficients in advance. Each set corresponds to a different filter setting and is stored away in memory. During performance, the characteristics of a filter are changed by calling in the appropriate set. If two filter settings differ only slightly, intermediate settings can sometimes be realized by interpolating the coefficients between them. However, interpolation runs the risk of creating an unstable filter, which could add unwanted noise to the sound.

6.7   EFFECT OF FILTERING IN THE TIME DOMAIN

Every filter, in addition to having a frequency response, has an impulse response. The *impulse response* is a time-domain description of the filter's response to a very short pulse; it can also be used to determine the filter's response to any type of change in the input signal. Sometimes a filter is designed to achieve a specific impulse response (see section 10.1B), but here we will examine the time-domain behavior of filters that were designed to have a particular amplitude response.

The preceding discussion of filters focused on their frequency-dependent properties, which are determined by assuming that the signal applied to the input of the filter had been present long enough for the output of the filter to stabilize. The properties of a filter after it has stabilized constitute its *steady-state* response. However, in order to use a filter most effectively, the musician should understand not only its steady-state properties, but also its effect on signals that are changing.

The way in which a filter reacts at the beginning and at the end of a steady tone is called its *transient response*. At the beginning, the duration of the transient response is the length of time it takes for the filter's output to settle into the steady state; at the end, the duration is the length of time that it takes for the output to decay. The transient response depends on the impulse response of the filter and on the envelope of the tone that is applied. The duration of the transient response is inversely proportional to the filter bandwidth. The narrower the bandwidth, the longer it takes for the filter to respond to transients.

For example, when a sinusoidal tone is applied to the input of a filter with a center frequency equal to the frequency of the input signal, the full signal does not appear immediately at the output in most cases. Similarly, once the input tone has ended, the signal at the output of the filter ordinarily does not drop immediately to 0: it takes time for the output to build up to a steady-state value and time for it to die away after the input has ended. Figure 6.18 illustrates the waveforms of both the input and the output signals of a filter with a narrow bandwidth. Notice how the filter elongates both the attack and the decay.

Thus, it can be seen that a filter can also modify the envelope of a sound. When using subtractive synthesis, the specification of the envelope of the tone applied to the filter may have to be tempered to allow for the transient response of the filter. This is especially important when a large bank of cascade-connected filters is employed, since each filter can affect the envelope of the tone in succession.

The transient response of a filter can also become noticeable when the parameters of the filter are changed during the course of a sound. Unexpected clicks, ringing, or other disagreeable distortions may be added to the sound.[1]

As an example, figure 6.19 displays the waveforms in a system containing a low-pass filter with a variable cutoff frequency. About midway through the time interval represented in the figure, the cutoff frequency of the filter is changed to a value that is four times larger than its initial value. The lower two traces document the filter output for two meth-

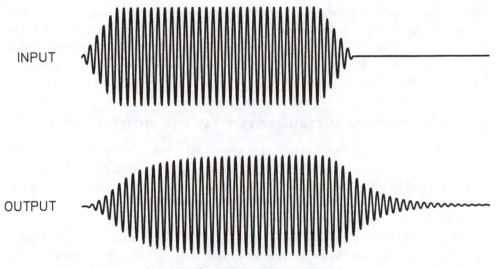

FIGURE 6.18   Alteration of the envelope of a tone by a narrow filter.

ods of changing the cutoff frequency: abruptly changing the filter parameters in a single sample and interpolating the filter parameters between the two states over a number of samples. The input to the filter is a sine wave with a frequency near the initial cutoff frequency of the filter so that the beginning of both output waveforms is a slightly attenuated version of the input. During the later portion of the waveforms, the output of the filter has nearly the same amplitude as the input, owing to the larger bandwidth provided by the increased cutoff frequency. The transient response produced by changing the filter can be seen in the central region of the output waveforms. The middle trace shows the large transient generated when the cutoff frequency is suddenly changed from one sample to the next. The audible click that would result can be avoided by interpolating the parameters of the filter between the two states. To generate the smoother transition exhibited by the

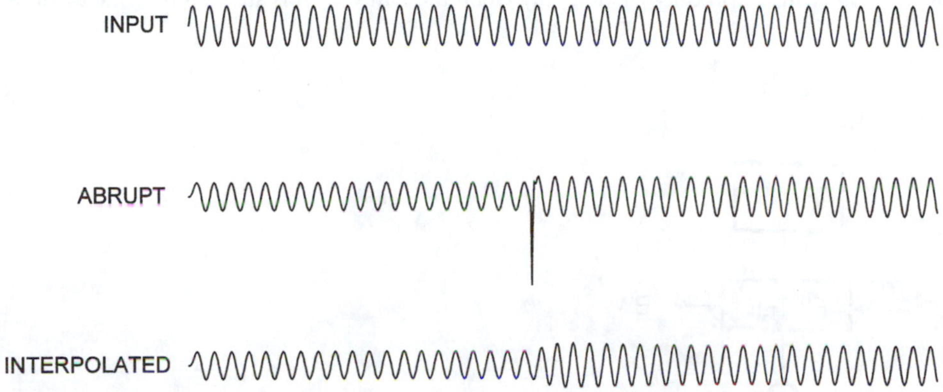

INPUT

ABRUPT

INTERPOLATED

FIGURE 6.19   The waveforms in a variable low-pass filter for two methods of changing its cut-off frequency.

lower output waveform in the figure, the cutoff frequency of the filter was allowed to vary in a continuous fashion over the course of 96 samples. The number of samples needed in a particular situation will depend on the sampling frequency, the frequencies contained in the input to the filter, the size of the change in the filter parameters, and the amount and type of transition distortion deemed acceptable.

6.8　SUBTRACTIVE INSTRUMENTS THAT USE NOISE SOURCES

Section 4.11 contains an illustration of an instrument that uses random ring modulation to create a band of noise. A similar effect can be achieved by using a digital filter on a noise source. The result will be a more concentrated band of noise at the cost of slightly more computer time. Figure 6.20 shows the flowchart for the subtractive-synthesis instrument that produces bands of noise.

With a single filter on a noise source, it is possible to obtain a variety of sound qualities. Differences in center frequency and bandwidth have striking effects. Specifying the bandwidth as a fixed percentage of the center frequency provides for the same intervallic width of noise on every filter note, regardless of register. All other factors being equal, the noise bands at various center frequencies will be perceived as belonging to the same class of sounds. A useful general rule for choosing the bandwidth is that a bandwidth of around 5% of the center frequency produces a clear pitch at the center frequency and can be used as a melodic, pitched noise instrument. Narrower bands of filtered noise produce even greater pitch focus and sound less "noisy." In the high registers, they sound more like whistles. As the bandwidth becomes a larger percentage of the center frequency, the listener has less and less sensation of pitch until the sound becomes noise, without pitch, in the register of the center frequency. A musician, working within the constraints and patterns of a composition, must find the boundaries that work best within the compositional context.

It is common for a musician to vary either the center frequency or the bandwidth or both, when using filtered noise. Figure 6.21 displays the flowchart for the computer instrument that makes the noise sounds in Charles Dodge's electronic realization of Samuel Beckett's radio play, *Cascando*.[2] The center frequency of the filter is set to 0, thus converting the filter to a low pass. The instrument produces sound only when the bandwidth is sufficiently wide to allow

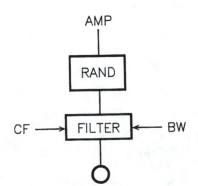

FIGURE 6.20　Instrument that produces bands of noise.

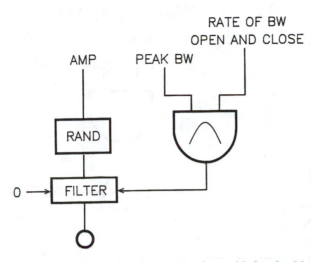

FIGURE 6.21   Noise instrument with variable bandwidth.

noise in the audio range. The cutoff frequency is changed continuously by the controlling oscillator. The amplitude of the oscillator sets the maximum cutoff frequency, and the frequency of the oscillator determines the rate of interruption of the noise. The results fall within a range of sounds described as "rustling," "thumping," and "scurrying."

It is common to apply continuous changes of both bandwidth and center frequency to noise inputs. Figure 6.22 shows an instrument for producing these effects. It uses oscillators to produce a range of time variations in center frequency and bandwidth. The amplitude argument for the left oscillator is fed a ratio of the highest to lowest center frequency and that of the right oscillator the range of bandwidth change. The frequency inputs for the oscillators determine the duration over which the variations are to take place. The waveforms of the oscillators represent the shape of the modulation. A constant is added to the output of each oscillator to ensure that CF and BW maintain minimum values. Consider a case in which the following is desired:

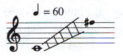

This glissando over an octave and a tritone is in the time span of 4 seconds and has a continuous change in bandwidth from 5% of center frequency at the beginning to 50% of center frequency at the end. The following parameters will be used:

DUR	= 4 s
MIN CF	= 261.6 Hz
RATIO	= 739.9 ÷ 261.6 = 2.828
MIN % BW	= 0.05
RANGE OF BW	= 0.45

The function F1 is a decaying exponential curve with a ratio of 1:1/RATIO, in this case 1:0.354.

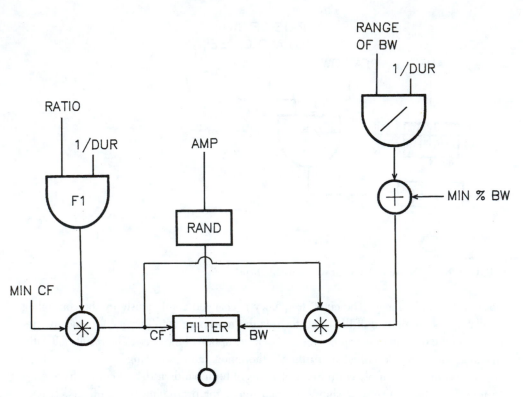

FIGURE 6.22   Instrument for producing glissandoing noise bands.

6.9   SUBTRACTIVE INSTRUMENTS THAT USE PERIODIC SOURCES

The effect of filtering a periodic source is very different from that of filtering a noise source. Because periodic sources are pitched, the center frequency and bandwidth settings have no significant effect on pitch perception. Instead, these frequency settings affect only the timbre. Figure 6.23 shows a simple filter instrument connected to a periodic source. The center frequency and bandwidth are usually set greater than the frequency of the highest pitch to be played by the instrument. The settings are not changed with pitch. This arrangement places a fixed resonance, called a *formant*, in the spectrum

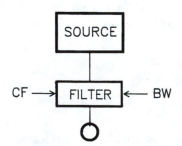

FIGURE 6.23   Filtering a periodic source.

of the sound at the center frequency of the filter. A spectral component that falls near the resonance will be emphasized because it will be attenuated less than those farther away from the resonance. The presence of fixed resonances in the spectrum is thought to contribute to our perception of timbral homogeneity. (See section 2.6.) Figure 6.24 shows a formant imparted to the spectra of tones at 250 and 450 Hz by a resonance peak at 1000 Hz. The resonance peak will emphasize the fourth harmonic of the 250-Hz tone, but will emphasize the second harmonic of the 450-Hz tone. The tones will share a timbral similarity because of the common resonance structure.

A subtractive-synthesis technique frequently used in electronic music synthesis to create musical tones from periodic sources is called *harmonic enveloping*. In this tech-

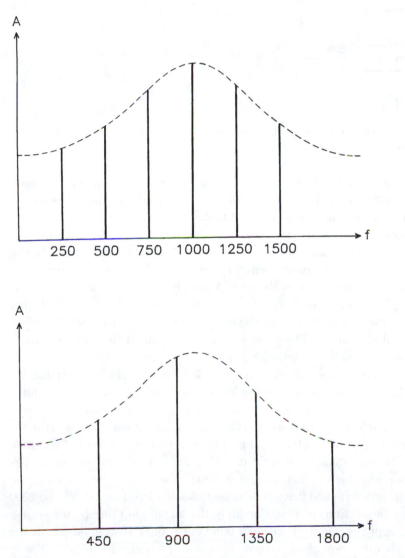

FIGURE 6.24   Two spectra with different fundamental frequencies that display the same formant.

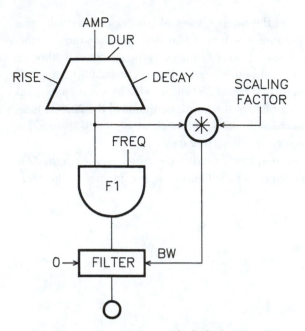

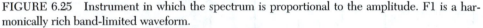

FIGURE 6.25   Instrument in which the spectrum is proportional to the amplitude. F1 is a harmonically rich band-limited waveform.

nique, a control signal, such as that from an envelope generator, is applied to the bandwidth input of a filter. This causes the relative strength of the harmonic partials to change with time, affecting both waveform and timbre.

Figure 6.25 shows a design in which the center frequency of the filter is set to 0 and the bandwidth is made to change in proportion to the amplitude of the tone. In this instrument, as in many acoustic instruments, the strength of the higher harmonics is in direct proportion to the amplitude of the tone. A tone begins with a nearly pure sine wave. As the amplitude increases during the attack, so do the amplitudes of the higher harmonics. When the tone dies away, the higher harmonics drop out first. This effect may also be useful in simulating the change in spectral content that often occurs in acoustic instruments when the dynamic level changes.

When using a design such as this, the musician must carefully determine the numerical relationship between the amplitude and the cutoff frequency of the filter. One way this can be done is to find the ratio between the highest cutoff frequency and the maximum amplitude (the exact numerical value for the amplitude will depend on the system used). The value used for the cutoff frequency is then the product of that ratio and the value of the amplitude input of the oscillator. For example, suppose the amplitude of a note were to rise to a maximum of 20,000 at the peak of the attack and the instrument designer determined that at this value the cutoff frequency should be 2000 Hz. In this case, the instrument would multiply the amplitude value by the scaling factor 0.1 before applying it to the bandwidth input of the filter. If, as in the figure, the low-pass filter takes the form of a band-pass filter with its center frequency set to 0, the actual cutoff frequency will be 0.707 times the number applied to the bandwidth input of the filter. This should be taken into account in calculating the relationship between the amplitude and the cutoff frequency.

With a single filter element, only one resonance peak can be imparted. It is often desirable or even necessary (e.g., for speech synthesis) to impart more than one resonance peak to a signal. Special expertise is required to know how to calculate center frequencies and bandwidths for a group of filters used to realize a desired response curve. Although true engineering solutions depend on mathematical analyses, it is often possible, for musical applications, to estimate filter settings that fit a given response curve adequately. The response curve shown in figure 6.26a calls for an amplitude response of a generally low-pass character with five resonance peaks. One way an engineer could synthesize the filter design is by expressing the response curve as a polynomial and factoring out each second-

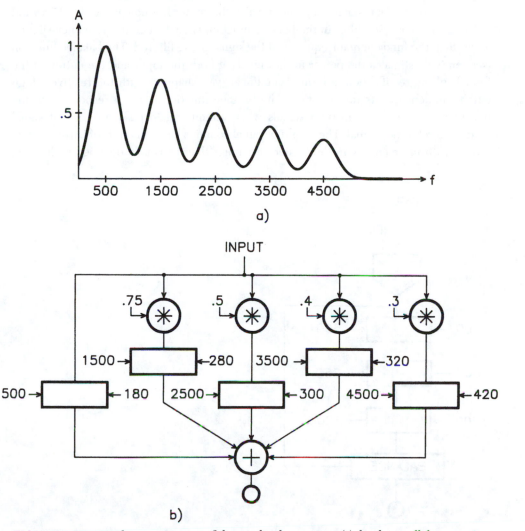

FIGURE 6.26   Rough approximation of the amplitude response, (a), by the parallel connection of five filters as shown in (b).

order filter element. This relatively difficult procedure usually results in a realization using five second-order band-pass filters connected in cascade. However, under certain circumstances, the less mathematical method of parallel-connected filters can be used to approximate roughly the desired response. In the case of the figure, five filters would ordinarily be used because the response exhibits five resonance peaks. The center frequency of each filter would be set to the frequency of one of the resonances. The input to each filter is attenuated by the amount necessary to bring the overall response to the desired shape. In the example, the attenuation multipliers are, from low to high center frequency, 1, 0.75, 0.5, 0.4, and 0.3. The resulting filter configuration is shown in figure 6.26b. It does not realize the exact amplitude response but represents a fair approximation.

Figure 6.27 contains an example of the use of the balance function in a nonstandard way. The three band-pass filters are connected in cascade in the usual way and serve the purpose of imparting resonances to the signal at the center frequencies of 500, 1500, and 3000 Hz. The low-pass filter in the balance function is given a cutoff frequency slightly lower than the fundamental frequency of the signal being filtered. The balance function (section 6.5) estimates the power in the signals at both the input and the output of the filter bank by rectification, a form of nonlinear waveshaping. With the relatively high cutoff frequency of its internal filter, the balance function is more responsive to the instantaneous variations in both signals when attempting to make the output signal match the reference signal. The resulting signal contains large amounts of harmonic distortion with more energy in the higher harmonics than is usually obtained with other,

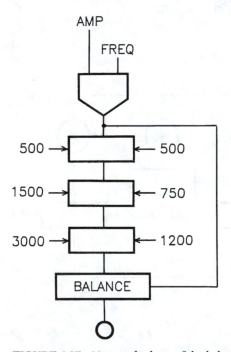

FIGURE 6.27   Nonstandard use of the balance function. The cutoff frequency of the low-pass filter inside the balance function is set close to FREQ to produce an unusual ringing in the high harmonics.

more direct forms of waveshaping. The sonic texture produced by this filtering method, particularly when reverberated, can be extremely delicate. The sound of this instrument is found in *Earth's Magnetic Field*[3] by Charles Dodge. (See section 10.3B.)

Figure 6.28 shows a method for implementing timbre change with subtractive synthesis, using banks of filters with fixed center frequencies and bandwidths. Here, the

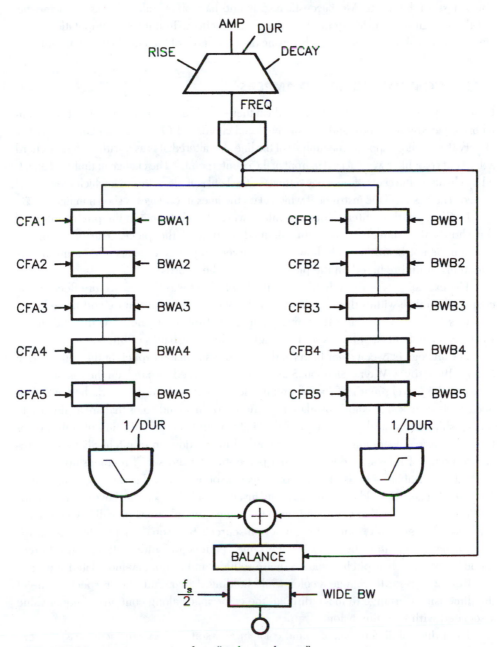

FIGURE 6.28 Instrument to produce "timbre exchange."

output of each of the two banks of filters, each with its own set of center frequencies and bandwidths, is multiplied by an envelope. The first bank sounds alone for the first third of the note; the two banks exchange amplitude levels during the second third of the note, and the second bank sounds alone for the final third. This design was used for the "lines" in Dodge's *Changes*.[4] (See section 6.10.)

The high-pass filter was included at the end of the instrument design to emphasize the "buzziness" of the source. Most acoustic instruments have an overall low-pass characteristic, but this design was created to produce the opposite effect. To improve computational efficiency, each bank was computed only during the two-thirds of the note in which it sounded.

6.10   COMPOSITIONAL EXAMPLES

Changes[5] by Charles Dodge is a work in which there are three textural elements—contrapuntal lines, percussive sounds, and irregularly placed chords. Of *Changes,* Paul Griffiths writes, "Every time a chord appears the timbres of the lines are altered: it is as if with each new chord a different color filter were placed in front of the counterpoint."[6] The change in timbre is effected by changing the center-frequency settings of the banks of filters through which the pulse is passed. The design of the instrument which plays the lines in *Changes* is shown in figure 6.28.

In *Changes,* the center-frequency values were chosen to match the pitch content of the chords that initiate each timbre-defined section of the piece. The effect of the matching is not heard in pitch, however. It serves simply as a means of creating differentiations of timbre based on the pitch content of the chords.

The exchange of amplitude between banks of filters was the means for effecting the change of timbre within the note. As *Changes* evolves, there are more and more banks of filters for each note—and thus, more change of timbre per note. At the end of the work, every note of each line is sent through six different banks of filters.

The analogy between color filters and audio filters is made explicit in the composition *Colors* (1981), by A. Wayne Slawson. Slawson has performed research on the relationships between the vowel sounds of speech and musical timbre.[7] From this work, he has developed a theory of sound color, postulating relationships in sound color that are analogous to relationships in musical pitch. His purpose is to permit the organization of sound color through musical operations ordinarily employed in the domain of pitch. Slawson postulates a group of rules in order to make a perceptually valid set of relationships in tone color.[8] They establish a basis for the explicit use of sound color relationships in his music.

Rule 1 states, "To hold the color of a sound invariant, hold its spectrum envelope invariant."

This rule implies that two sounds with the same spectral envelope will have the same color even if they result from filtering different sources. Slawson demonstrates this invariance in his composition by imposing the same sequence of filter settings on different sound sources, such as pitched sounds, noise sounds, and frequency-modulated sounds.

Rule 2 states, "To change a color while holding it invariant with respect to one of the dimensions, arrange to move through the color space along contours of equal value associated with that dimension."

The principal dimensions of sound color in Slawson's theory are "acuteness," "openness," "smallness," and "laxness." (The terms for these dimensions are freely borrowed from the literature of acoustic phonetics.) Each dimension characterizes the relation in frequency between the poles of a pair of band-pass filters. For example, acuteness relates the change in the second resonance frequency of the pair to the frequency of the first. Given a fixed frequency for the first resonance, acuteness increases with an increase in the frequency of the second resonance. Openness works in just the opposite way—for a given fixed frequency of the second resonance, openness is increased with a rise in the frequency of the first resonance. The smallness of a sound is increased by raising both resonances together, and laxness increases as both resonances move toward median values. Figure 6.29 shows the two-dimensional space for each of the four dimensions described. The vowels are inserted into the figure as references to some familiar sound colors. The contour lines denoting points of equal value in tone color are drawn onto the four diagrams.

To complete the analogy between pitch and tone color, Slawson includes two more rules that introduce *transposition* and *inversion* of sound color into his system.

Rule 3 states, "To transpose a color with respect to a dimension, shift the color in the direction of the dimension (perpendicular to its equal-value contours). When the

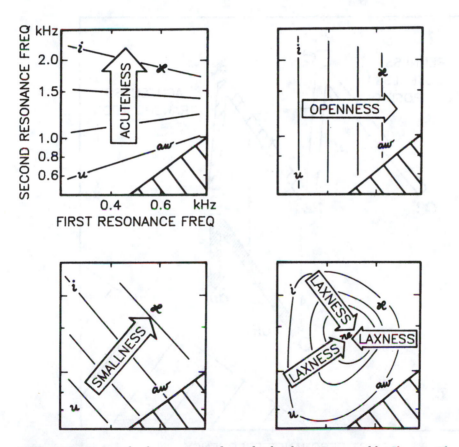

FIGURE 6.29   Equal-value contours of sound color dimensions used by Slawson. The arrows indicate the direction of increasing value for each dimension. *(Reprinted with permission of A. Wayne Slawson.)*

boundary of the space is reached, 'wrap-around' to the opposite boundary and continue shifting in the same direction." Figure 6.30 shows an example of the transposition of a sequence of colors represented by the vowel sounds nearest in the figure.

For inversion, Slawson complements the values of a particular dimension around the point of maximal laxness. His rule 3b states, "To invert a sound color with respect to a dimension, complement its value on that dimension." Slawson uses the following as an example of the inversion operation in his system. Given the sequence of colors corresponding to the set of vowel sounds /U/, /I/, /AW/, /AE/, the inversion with respect to acuteness (holding openness constant) would be /I/, /U/, /AE/, /AW/. The original inverted with respect to smallness would be /AE/, /I/, /AW/, /U/.

In *Colors,* the most prominent feature of the sonic surface is in the rapid changes of the sound color. Slawson uses a series of nine sound colors that roughly correspond to the vowel sounds: /OH/, /EE/, /UU/, /AW/, /II/, /AE/, /OE/, /AA/, and /NE/ (schwa). Slawson chose this set so that the operations of transposition and inversion with respect to acuteness, openness, and smallness would result in reorderings of the set, introducing no new colors and

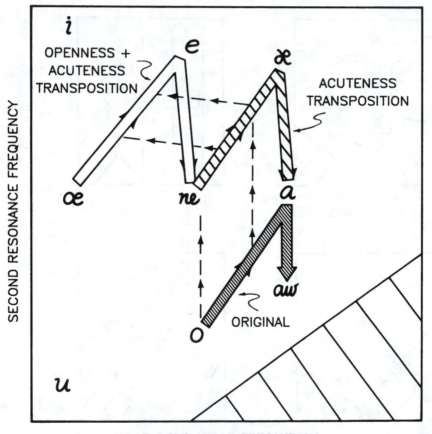

FIGURE 6.30   An example, from Slawson, of the transposition of a sequence of colors. *(Reprinted with permission of A. Wayne Slawson.)*

repeating none. The composition deals extensively with the serial property of combinatoriality. The sets used in the piece are chosen to form "color aggregates," a technique based on the model of Milton Babbitt's pitch aggregates.[9] The work is in the form of 11 variations. Throughout the piece, the color series is kept more or less the same, while the sources to the filters are changed considerably. Certain variations involve not only fixed (discrete) sound colors, but also situations in which the sound color changes continuously, as in the diphthongs of speech. Slawson's book, *Sound Color*,[10] contains an extensive discussion of the composition of *Colors* and includes a phono disk with recorded examples.

Richard Karpen's widely performed *Exchange*, for flute and tape,[11] is one of the most extensive examples of a computer work made largely with subtractive-synthesis techniques. The work was realized in 1987 at Stanford University's CCRMA using the filtering features of the real-time Systems Concept Digital Synthesizer.

The concept for the tape part of the work depends organically on the use of subtractive synthesis. Karpen writes:

> The idea [of the instrument design] was to tune the center frequencies, bandwidths, and gains of the filters so that in each note (especially the longer ones), the added outputs of all filters would create at once a distinctive timbre with a fundamental frequency, but would also create within each note, harmonic and melodic structures. The result of this is sound where there is harmony and sound color in the more traditional sense, but also harmony created within each note between the fundamental and the resonating partials. The idea in this piece, for the tape part, was to blur the distinction between sound color, harmony, melody, and counterpoint.

The basic instrument design used throughout the work is diagrammed in figure 6.31. It consists of a source signal and five band-pass filters in parallel. Figure 6.32 shows the spectra of the source signals applied to the filter bank. The source is either a band-limited pulse or simple FM with an index great enough to create significant partials nearly to the Nyquist frequency. Frequency modulation was used when nonharmonic partials were required. A very large index of modulation, based on a ratio of the sampling frequency to the fundamental frequency ($I = 0.4 f_s / f_0$), spreads the spectrum over a wide range (see section 5.1B). Such a large index created considerable "ripple" in the FM sidebands. When this behavior is coupled with the effect of the high band-pass filters with moving center frequencies (see below), one is often presented with highly articulated single-frequency components in the higher registers.

Each of the five filters has independent gain and envelope controls. The first filter acts as a low pass with its center frequency set to the fundamental frequency of the source. The second filter has its center frequency set to the partial closest in frequency to 730 Hz. That is, $CF2 = f_0 \times \text{int}(730 / f_0)$. The third filter is identical to the second except that its target center frequency is the partial closest to 1090 Hz. The bandwidths for the second and third filters are narrower than that for the first filter, but not narrow enough to cause the filter to ring at its center frequency. The vowel "ah" has prominent resonances (formants) at around 730 and 1090 Hz. Filters 1, 2, and 3 serve to fix a particular, "ah"-related but nonvocal timbre throughout the work.

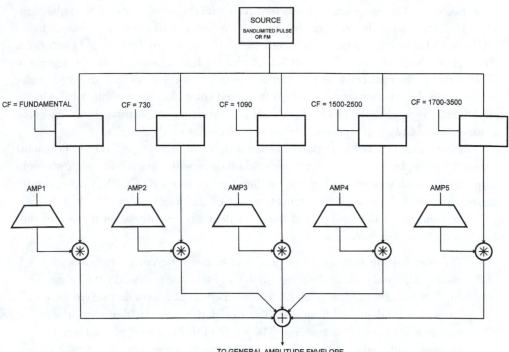

FIGURE 6.31 Basic instrument design used throughout Richard Karpen's *Exchange*. *(Reprinted with permission of Richard Karpen.)*

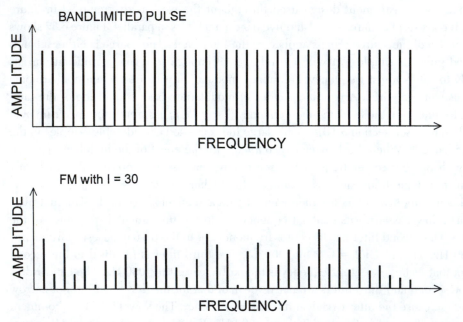

FIGURE 6.32 Spectra of signals applied to the filter bank. *(Reprinted with permission of Richard Karpen.)*

Filters 4 and 5 change their center frequencies during the course of each note. The fourth filter traverses the range 1500 to 2500 Hz and the fifth, 1700 to 3500 Hz. The rate of change for both filters is proportional to the length of the note—faster on shorter notes, slower on longer ones—but because they have independent gain and envelope, the two are not synchronized. These filters have bandwidths narrow enough to delineate clearly particular components, but not narrow enough to cause them to ring or whistle at their center frequencies.

Of the overall effect of the instrument in the piece, Karpen writes, "In the slower passages of the tape part you can sometimes hear the partials (harmonics when the source is the band-limited pulse, inharmonic components when the source is from FM) in melodic sequence." We do indeed hear the melodic activity in the harmonics (or nonharmonic partials for the FM source) several octaves above the fundamental frequencies. The effect is not unlike that of the digeridoo, in which the fundamental frequency is prominent, but the most immediately striking activity is in the high arpeggiating harmonics.

The opening of the piece consists of four pitches (G3, C4, E♭4, and F4) and their rich, largely harmonic spectra. Listening to this passage, one is struck by the richness of the activity, both harmonically and melodically. The harmonic, middle-register tones are heard behind the much higher and faster melodic activity made by the filters with the moving center frequencies. Although there are only four specified fundamental frequencies at the opening, there are eight simultaneous moving filters. Figure 6.33 shows (in the boxes) the harmonics that are highlighted by the movement of the fourth filter above each of the four fundamentals in the opening chord of the work.

6.11   DIGITAL FILTERS

A *digital filter* is a computational algorithm that converts one sequence of numbers (the input signal) into another (the output signal), with the result that the character of the signal so processed is altered in some prescribed manner. Most often, digital filters are designed to obtain a specific alteration that is characterized in terms of the filter's steady-state amplitude response. However, chapter 10 discusses digital filters that are designed to realize a particular impulse response. Filter design is an advanced art, and a complete treatment of the subject is well beyond the scope of this text. The purposes of this section are to acquaint the musician with general principles of filter algorithms and to present recipes for certain digital filters. For derivations of the recipes, the reader is referred to the extensive literature on digital filtering.[12]

The two principal types of digital filter algorithms are *nonrecursive* and *recursive*. In both cases, the output signal is calculated on every sample as a combination of the current input with previous filter inputs and outputs. A nonrecursive filter calculates the present value of the output by combining the present value of the input with past values of the input. In a recursive filter, on the other hand, the present value of the output is a combination of both the past values of the output and the present and sometimes past values of the input.

Because the filter uses past input and/or output samples in calculating its output, filter algorithms must have some means of delaying digital signals. The delay is achieved by storing previous values in memory. The number of storage locations necessary is determined by the amount of delay required. For example, an algorithm that determines its

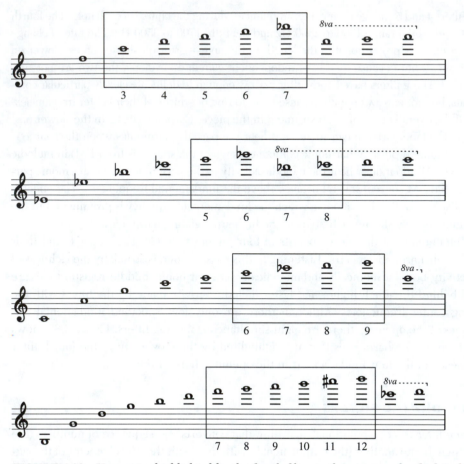

FIGURE 6.33   Harmonics highlighted by the fourth filter in the opening chord of *Exchange*. *(Reprinted with permission of Richard Karpen.)*

output from the present input sample and the previous two output samples would need two storage locations—one for the last output sample value and one for the next to last. After computing the current output sample value, the algorithm moves what had been the previous output value into the location for the next-to-last sample value. The current output sample is then stored as the last sample so that the filter is ready to compute a new output on the next sample. The length of the maximum delay (measured as a number of samples) determines the order of the filter. A high-order filter enables greater complexity or sharpness in its amplitude response but requires more computation.

In a digital filter, zeros are obtained by using algorithms that calculate the output by combining the input with past input samples. Poles are realized by combining the present input sample with past values of the output. Therefore, a nonrecursive filter can realize only zeros and, as a result, is sometimes called an *all-zero filter*. A recursive filter always realizes poles, and when it delays only output samples it is called an *all-pole filter*. The next two sections will demonstrate how to design filters that achieve poles and zeros specified by their center frequency and bandwidth.

A comparison of some properties of nonrecursive filters versus recursive filters is given below:

1. A higher-order, nonrecursive filter is generally required to obtain the same amount of selectivity in its amplitude response as that of a comparable recursive filter.

2. Errors caused by quantization, computational round-off, and coefficient inaccuracies are usually less significant in nonrecursive filters.

3. A nonrecursive filter is always stable, whereas recursive filters must be specifically designed to be stable.

There are standard notational conventions for describing filter algorithms mathematically. The current input to the filter is designated by $x(n)$ and the current output by $y(n)$. Previous input values are denoted by $x(n - m)$ and previous outputs by $y(n - m)$, where m is the number of samples that the value has been delayed. For example, $x(n - 1)$ represents the input sample just prior to the current one.

6.12   NONRECURSIVE FILTERS

6.12A   Introduction and Design Examples

The output from a nonrecursive filter is formed by combining the input to the filter with past inputs. Consider a signal-processing algorithm that forms its output by taking the average of the current input sample and the previous one. Mathematically, this can be stated as

$$y(n) = \frac{1}{2} x(n) + \frac{1}{2} x(n - 1)$$

This first-order filter is an example of a *moving-average filter*. Averaging has the effect of smoothing the waveform, which suggests that this process reduces the amount of high-frequency energy in the signal. To give a general impression of the nature of the amplitude response of this filter, we will apply a digital test signal at a specific frequency to the input and then examine the output for a repeating steady-state pattern. It will be assumed for the purposes of this analysis that all input samples prior to the application of the test signal are 0. When a unit-amplitude, digital signal at 0 Hz given by {1, 1, 1, 1, 1, ...} is applied to the filter, the output is {0.5, 1, 1, 1, 1, ...}. The first sample (0.5) is part of the transient response as the output of the filter builds up to its final value. Beginning with the second sample, the output achieves a steady-state condition, which indicates that the filter allows 0-Hz signals to pass without attenuation. At the other frequency extreme, when a unit-amplitude, cosine wave at the Nyquist frequency denoted by {1, –1, 1, –1, 1, –1, ...} is applied, the output is {0.5, 0, 0, 0, 0, 0, ...}. In the steady state, the filter completely attenuates components at the Nyquist frequency. The overall amplitude response, $A(f)$, is low-pass in nature (figure 6.34a), with a cutoff frequency at $f_s/4$, and is given by

$$A(f) = \cos\left(\pi \frac{f}{f_s} \right)$$

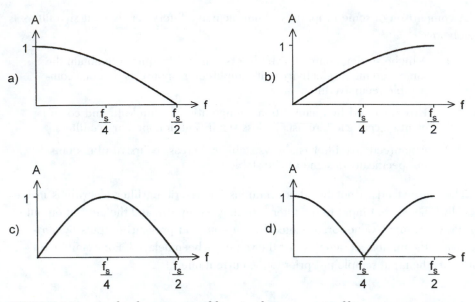

FIGURE 6.34   Amplitude responses of four simple nonrecursive filters.

There are many variations on the simple moving-average filter described above. One is to increase the number of samples that are averaged. Because the waveform receives additional smoothing, the cutoff frequency is lowered.

Instead of taking the average, one-half the difference between successive input samples can be taken. This can be stated as

$$y(n) = \frac{1}{2}x(n) - \frac{1}{2}x(n-1)$$

Using the test signal method above, the reader can verify that in the steady state at 0 Hz, the filter passes no signal, and at the Nyquist frequency, it passes the signal unchanged. Such a filter is high-pass in nature, and its amplitude response (figure 6.34b) is given by

$$A(f) = \sin\left(\pi \frac{f}{f_s}\right)$$

The cutoff frequency is $f_s/4$.

Consider a filter whose output is the average of the current input and the next-to-last input sample:

$$y(n) = \frac{1}{2}x(n) + \frac{1}{2}x(n-2)$$

Since the input is delayed by two samples, this is a second-order filter. The filter passes both 0 Hz and the Nyquist frequency unchanged. Halfway in between, at $f_s/4$, a cosine-wave input signal given by {1, 0, –1, 0, 1, 0, –1, 0, . . .} produces an output signal of {0.5,

0, 0, 0, 0, 0, 0, 0, . . .}. Therefore, this filter is a band-reject filter that blocks signals at $f_s/4$. The overall amplitude response (figure 6.34c) is the absolute value of

$$A(f) = \cos\left(2\pi \frac{f}{f_s}\right)$$

Similarly, it can be shown that

$$y(n) = \frac{1}{2}x(n) - \frac{1}{2}x(n-2)$$

is a band-pass filter with a center frequency of $f_s/4$ and an overall amplitude response (figure 6.34d) of

$$A(f) = \sin\left(2\pi \frac{f}{f_s}\right)$$

The filters above are nonrecursive and, in the general case, take the form

$$y(n) = a_0 x(n) + a_1 x(n-1) + a_2 x(n-2) + \ldots + a_N x(n-N)$$

The maximum delay used, N, is also the order of the filter. The values of the coefficients, a_k, control the frequency response of the filter. The impulse response of the filter is the digital signal $\{a_0, a_1, \ldots, a_N, 0, 0, \ldots\}$: a sequence made up of the values of the filter coefficients followed by zeros. Because the impulse response has a finite duration where it is nonzero, such a filter is called a *finite impulse response* (FIR) filter.

In order to realize a desired frequency response, one must calculate the coefficient values, a_k, for a filter. These calculations are based on the use of an inverse Fourier transform that changes the desired frequency response into an impulse response. Subsequently, the coefficients of the filter are matched to the sample values of the impulse response.

A problem arises because the filters with the best stopband behavior have impulse responses of infinite duration. To realize their behavior perfectly, a nonrecursive filter would require an infinite number of delays ($N\to\infty$) and coefficients, so that the actual implementation of a nonrecursive filter only approximates the desired response. In practice, N is chosen as a compromise between the accuracy of the approximation and the amount of memory and computation time available for the algorithm. The effect of this foreshortening of the impulse response is to introduce inaccuracies in the frequency response of the filter. These inaccuracies are most noticeable in the amplitude response as a lower-than-expected attenuation in the stopband.

DESIGN EXAMPLE: Nonrecursive approximation of an ideal low-pass filter with a cutoff frequency of f_c can be approximated by choosing the coefficients, a_k, according to

$$a_k = \frac{\sin\left[2\pi\left(k - \frac{N}{2}\right)\frac{f_c}{f_s}\right]}{\pi\left(k - \frac{N}{2}\right)}\left\{0.54 + 0.46\cos\left[\frac{2\pi\left(k - \frac{N}{2}\right)}{N}\right]\right\} \qquad 0 \le k \le N$$

with N an even number. (It can be shown that when $k = N/2$, $a_k = 2f_c/f_s$.) The impulse response of an ideal low-pass filter has an infinite duration. The factor enclosed in the braces is a *Hamming window* and is used to reduce the imperfections in the filter's frequency response caused by its finite impulse response.

As an example, figure 6.35 gives the coefficients and amplitude response when $N = 26$ and $f_s = 40$ kHz for a low-pass filter with $f_c = 2$ kHz.

DESIGN EXAMPLE: Second-order all-zero filter. Sometimes it is desirable (e.g., in speech synthesis) to realize a "zero" at a specified center frequency and bandwidth. As explained above, a zero is a region of attenuation, but the amplitude response does not necessarily go all the way to 0 at the center frequency. The bandwidth of a 0 is measured between the points that have 3 dB less than the maximum value of attenuation. The second-order all-zero filter implemented by the following equation realizes a 0:

$$y(n) = a_0x(n) + a_1x(n-1) + a_2x(n-2)$$

To obtain a center frequency f_0 with bandwidth BW, the intermediate coefficients c_1 and c_2 are calculated according to:

$$c_2 = \exp\left(-2\pi\frac{BW}{f_s}\right)$$

$$c_1 = \frac{-4c_2}{1+c_2}\cos\left(2\pi\frac{f_0}{f_s}\right)$$

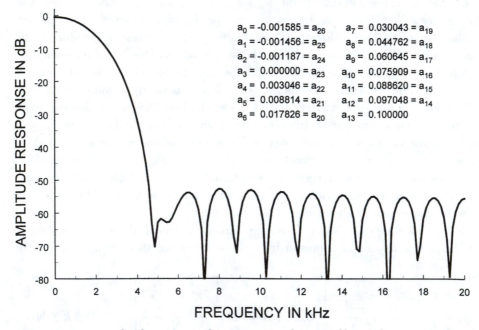

$a_0 = -0.001585 = a_{26}$ $a_7 = 0.030043 = a_{19}$
$a_1 = -0.001456 = a_{25}$ $a_8 = 0.044762 = a_{18}$
$a_2 = -0.001187 = a_{24}$ $a_9 = 0.060645 = a_{17}$
$a_3 = 0.000000 = a_{23}$ $a_{10} = 0.075909 = a_{16}$
$a_4 = 0.003046 = a_{22}$ $a_{11} = 0.088620 = a_{15}$
$a_5 = 0.008814 = a_{21}$ $a_{12} = 0.097048 = a_{14}$
$a_6 = 0.017826 = a_{20}$ $a_{13} = 0.100000$

FIGURE 6.35 Amplitude response of a nonrecursive low-pass filter with $N = 26$ and a cutoff frequency of 2 kHz.

The next step is to determine a scaling constant, D, which sets the amplitude response in frequency regions removed from the zero. For an unscaled filter, D is set equal to 1. In this case, the response varies with bandwidth and center frequency. When the bandwidth is narrow, the response at frequencies away from the zero can be quite large, even greater than 40 dB. Thus, the filter also serves as an amplifier. In certain applications, this is desirable, but caution is required because such large amplification can easily generate samples that exceed the maximum range of the system.

A scaling method that makes a filter simpler to use selects D as a combination of the other coefficients, c_1 and c_2, to achieve a certain value of amplitude response at some frequency. Often, D is chosen so that the amplitude response is 1 at 0 Hz and low-frequency signals will be passed with little change in amplitude. In this case, D is calculated as

$$D = 1 + c_1 + c_2$$

The final step is to calculate the actual filter coefficients from the intermediate coefficients and scaling constant:

$$a_0 = \frac{1}{D}$$

$$a_1 = \frac{c_1}{D}$$

$$a_2 = \frac{c_2}{D}$$

Figure 6.36 shows the amplitude response and coefficients for a second-order, all-zero band-reject filter with an amplitude response of 1 at 0 Hz, when $f_s = 40$ kHz, with $f_0 = 12$ kHz and BW = 700 Hz.

6.12B Frequency Sampling Method

The frequency sampling method enables the design of a nonrecursive filter that approximates an arbitrary amplitude response. The particular method described here results in a filter with a linear phase response—a desirable characteristic because each spectral component of a signal passing through the filter is delayed by the same amount, preventing dispersion of the contents of the signal.

The method begins by specifying the number of coefficients in the filter N, which is most conveniently chosen as an odd number. Next, a plot of the desired amplitude response is made between 0 Hz and the Nyquist frequency. As shown in the example of figure 6.37, this response is then "sampled" at $(N + 1)/2$ equally spaced points beginning at 0 Hz. The spacing Δf between the points depends on the order of the filter and the sampling frequency as

$$\Delta f = \frac{t_s}{N}$$

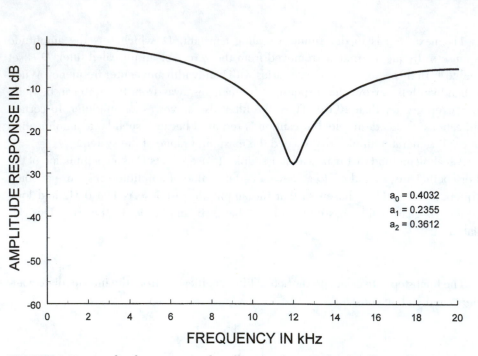

FIGURE 6.36   Amplitude response and coefficients of a second-order all-zero filter with a center frequency of 12 kHz and a bandwidth of 700 Hz.

With N odd, the last sample will fall just short of the Nyquist frequency. The individual sample values are denoted as $H(i)$ where $H(0)$ designates the sample at 0 Hz and the last sample value resides in $H[(N-1)/2]$.

A total of N filter coefficients must be determined; the first $(N+1)/2$ are calculated from

$$a_k = \frac{1}{N}\left\{ H(0) + 2 \sum_{i=1}^{(N-1)/2} |H(i)| \cos\left[\frac{2\pi i}{N}\left(k - \frac{N-1}{2}\right)\right] \right\} \qquad 0 \le k \le \frac{N-1}{2}$$

and the remaining coefficients are obtained from the symmetry relationship characteristic of a linear phase filter

$$a_{N-k-1} = a_k \qquad 0 \le k < \frac{N-1}{2}$$

To illustrate the frequency sampling technique, the design details of a low-pass filter with a cutoff frequency of 5 kHz in a system with a 30-kHz sampling rate will be presented. The desired amplitude response, shown by the solid locus in figure 6.37, will be taken to be that of an ideal low-pass filter. In the passband, the amplitude response is unity; the stopband has a constant response of 0. A realizable filter can never be this selective, but it serves as a good design goal. Choosing $N = 15$ mandates that eight samples of the response be taken as shown with a sample spacing $\Delta f \doteq 2$ kHz, giving the

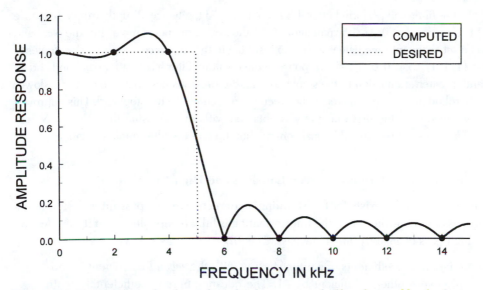

FIGURE 6.37 The desired and actual amplitude response of a filter designed by the frequency sampling method with $N = 15$.

sequence of frequency sample values as the set $H = \{1, 1, 1, 0, 0, 0, 0, 0\}$. The summation equation is then used to compute filter coefficients a_0 through a_7. The next coefficient a_8 is determined by symmetry as $a_8 = a_6$, coefficient a_9 is equal to a_5, and so on, up to $a_{14} = a_0$. (Observe that the subscripts of each coefficient pair add up to 14, which is $N - 1$.) The resulting coefficients are

$$
\begin{aligned}
a\,0 &= 0.05805305 = a14 \\
a\,1 &= 0.00000000 = a13 \\
a\,2 &= -0.06666667 = a12 \\
a\,3 &= -0.07769014 = a11 \\
a\,4 &= 0.00000000 = a10 \\
a\,5 &= 0.14194695 = a\,9 \\
a\,6 &= 0.27769014 = a\,8 \\
a\,7 &= 0.33333333
\end{aligned}
$$

As shown by the dots in the figure, the computed amplitude response of a nonrecursive filter designed with the frequency sampling method matches the desired amplitude response *exactly* at the sampling points. At frequencies in between, the computed response deviates from the desired response by an amount that depends primarily on the number of match points. The computed filter response may be thought of as a "rubber band" that is fixed at the match points. Increasing the number of match points by raising the value of N restricts the distance that the rubber band can stretch, so that the filter better approximates the desired amplitude response.

An alternative method of improving the match between the desired and actual response of the filter is to specify a transition sample between the passband and the stopband. In other words, the filter will perform better if it is not required to change abruptly from a response of 1 to a response of 0. As shown in figure 6.38, the first frequency sample after the passband can be set to the intermediate value of 0.5 resulting in the sequence of frequency samples of $H = \{1, 1, 1, 0.5, 0, 0, 0, 0\}$. The response of the resulting filter has a flatter passband and an overall greater attenuation in the stopband than the previous design at the cost of a slower rate of rolloff in the transition region between the passband and the stopband. This improved performance over the first example was obtained without increasing the value of N, and therefore does not require additional computation time in the filter implementation.

6.12C   Transforming between Low-Pass and High-Pass Filters

A simple procedure exists for transforming a nonrecursive low-pass filter design into a high-pass filter. Furthermore, the transformation is fully reversible so that its application to a high pass changes it into a low pass. The procedure is as follows:

> Given the coefficients of a filter, starting with the *second* coefficient, multiply every other coefficient by –1. The odd-numbered coefficients remain unchanged.

The resulting set of coefficients realizes a filter of the opposite type.

As an example, in a system with a 40-kHz sampling rate, the coefficients of a ninth-order low-pass filter with a cutoff frequency of 7.5 kHz have been calculated and are shown below. Applying the procedure above results in the second column of coefficients that effect a high-pass filter with a cutoff frequency of 12.5 kHz—that is, 7.5 kHz less than the Nyquist frequency.

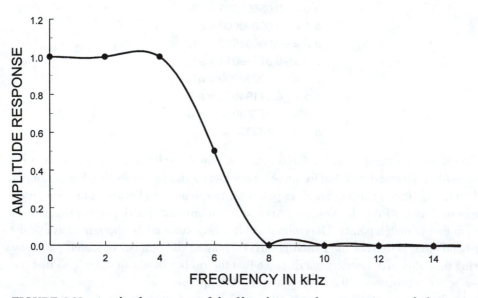

FIGURE 6.38   Amplitude response of the filter design with a transition sample between the passband and stopband.

Low-pass	High-pass
−0.012593	−0.012593
−0.055556	0.055556
0.045289	0.045289
0.300637	−0.300637
0.444444	0.444444
0.300637	−0.300637
0.045289	0.045289
−0.055556	0.055556
−0.012593	−0.012593

The amplitude responses of the two filters are plotted in figure 6.39. Reapplying the procedure to the high-pass coefficients would result in the original low-pass filter.

6.13 RECURSIVE FILTERS

A recursive filter algorithm determines its output by combining past output samples with the current and sometimes past input samples. Consider the simple, first-order recursive filter given by

$$y(n) = ax(n) - by(n-1)$$

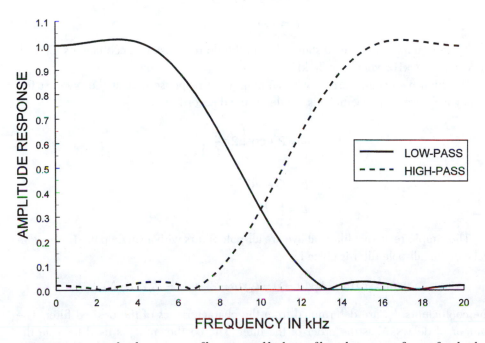

FIGURE 6.39   Amplitude responses of low-pass and high-pass filters that are transforms of each other.

where the output depends on the current input and the value of the last output. The amplitude response of this filter can assume either a low-pass or a high-pass characteristic, depending on the coefficient values. The coefficient b sets the cutoff frequency and the coefficient a is chosen for a specific value of the amplitude response in the passband.

The impulse response of this filter, determined by applying the signal $\{1, 0, 0, 0, 0, \ldots\}$ to the input, is $\{a, -ab, ab^2, -ab^3, \ldots\}$ and decays exponentially. Because its impulse response never, at least in theory, completely goes to 0, this type of filter is also called an *infinite impulse response* (IIR) filter. Depending on the coefficient values, such a filter may not be stable; in this example, specifying $b > 1$ would result in an impulse response that would grow on each successive sample until it eventually exceeded the limits of the system.

6.13A   Basic Recursive Filter Designs

To obtain a low-pass filter with a cutoff frequency of f_c and an amplitude of one at 0 Hz, the coefficients, a and b, are calculated as follows.

1.   Calculate the intermediate variable C from

$$C = 2 - \cos\left(2\pi \frac{f_c}{f_s}\right)$$

2.   The coefficients are

$$b = \sqrt{C^2 - 1} - C$$

$$a = 1 + b$$

As an example, figure 6.40 shows the amplitude response and coefficients for a filter with $f_c = 1$ kHz when $f_s = 40$ kHz.

If a high-pass characteristic with an amplitude response of 1 at the Nyquist frequency is desired, the coefficients are determined according to

$$C = 2 + \cos\left(2\pi \frac{f_c}{f_s}\right)$$

$$b = C - \sqrt{C^2 - 1}$$

$$a = 1 - b$$

The simple recursive filters above are all-pole filters with a single pole. In the general case, an all-pole filter is given by

$$y(n) = a_0 x(n) - b_1 y(n-1) - b_2 y(n-2) - \cdots - b_N y(n-N)$$

The coefficients, b_k, are determined from the characteristics of the desired filter. The number of delays, N, is the order of the filter. The coefficient a_0 is used to scale the amplitude response of the filter according to some criterion.

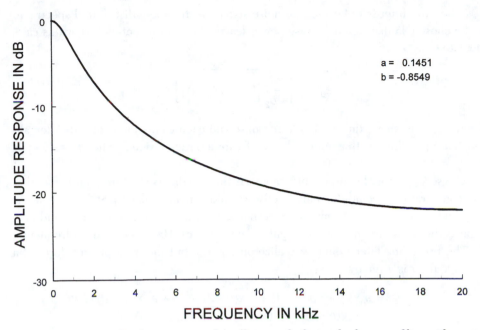

a = 0.1451
b = -0.8549

FIGURE 6.40   Amplitude response and coefficients of a first-order low-pass filter with a cutoff frequency of 1 kHz.

A commonly used filter (section 6.3) is the band-pass filter realized by the second-order all-pole filter given by

$$y(n) = a_0 x(n) - b_1 y(n-1) - b_2 y(n-2)$$

To realize a center frequency f_0 with bandwidth BW, calculate the coefficients b_1 and b_2 according to

$$b_2 = \exp\left(-2\pi \frac{BW}{f_s}\right)$$

$$b_1 = \frac{-4b_2}{1+b_2}\cos\left(2\pi\frac{f_0}{f_s}\right)$$

The coefficient a_0 is a scaling constant. It controls the ratio of output to input signal amplitude at the center frequency (midband gain). When the choice is $a_0 = 1$, the filter is said to be unscaled, and the midband gain varies with the bandwidth and center frequency as illustrated in section 6.3.

A scaling method that makes a filter simpler to use calculates a_0 from the values of the other coefficients, b_1 and b_2, for a midband gain of 1; that is, the amplitude of a signal at the center frequency will be the same coming out as going in. In this case, a_0 is calculated from:

$$a_0 = (1-b_2)\sqrt{1-\frac{b_1^2}{4b_2}}$$

When the filter is to be used on noise signals with widely distributed spectra, a_0 can be chosen so that as much noise power leaves the filter as enters it. For this case, calculate a_0 as

$$a_0 = \sqrt{\frac{1-b_2}{1+b_2}\left[(1+b_2)^2 - b_1^2\right]}$$

Figure 6.41 shows the amplitude response and coefficients for a second-order, all-pole, band-pass filter with a midband gain of 1 for a periodic signal, when f_s = 40 kHz, with f_c = 2 kHz and BW = 700 Hz.

The second-order band-pass filter above is the one that is most frequently found as a unit generator in computer music software under names like RESON or FLT. As described in section 6.3, its amplitude response deforms from a symmetric band-pass shape as the center frequency is brought close to either 0 Hz or the Nyquist frequency.

The preceding filter examples realize only poles, but the most general form of a recursive filter is given by

$$y(n) = a_0x(n) + a_1x(n-1) + a_2x(n-2) + \cdots + a_Mx(n-M)$$
$$- b_1y(n-1) - b_2y(n-2) - \cdots - b_Ny(n-N)$$

The filter has both poles (determined by the coefficients b_k) and zeros (determined by the coefficients a_k) and is capable of realizing arbitrarily complex frequency responses. The coefficients are nearly always determined by evaluating formulas that have been derived from mathematical analyses of filter responses. Heuristic selection of coefficients seldom results in a usable filter because it is easy to make a recursive filter unstable. An unstable filter can oscillate, adding unwanted components to the sound. It may even continue to generate spurious signals after the input signal has decayed to 0.

6.13B   Pole–Zero Filter

The two-pole band-pass filter discussed above must be scaled by a constant because its amplitude response at the center of the passband is considerably greater than 1, so that the signal may be unduly amplified. Further complicating the matter is the strong dependence of the scale factor on the center frequency and bandwidth. The addition of two zeros to the filter, one at 0 Hz and the other at the Nyquist frequency, creates a band-pass filter whose peak amplitude response exhibits only a small variation as the center frequency of the filter is tuned across a frequency range.[13]

The recursion equation for this second-order pole–zero filter is

$$y(n) = ax(n) - ax(n-2) - b_1y(n-1) - b_2y(n-2)$$

where

$$b_2 = \exp\left(-2\pi\frac{BW}{f_s}\right)$$

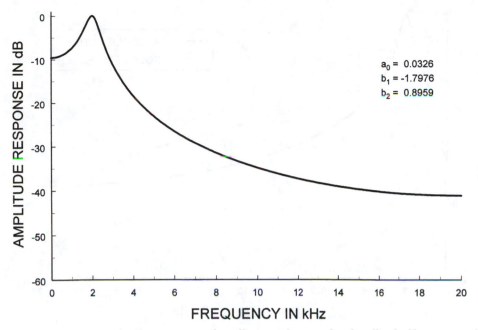

FIGURE 6.41   Amplitude response and coefficients of a second-order all-pole filter centered at 2 kHz with a bandwidth of 700 Hz.

$$b_1 = \frac{-4b_2}{1+b_2}\cos\left(2\pi\frac{f_0}{f_s}\right)$$

$$a = 1 - \sqrt{b_2}$$

This relatively efficient implementation does not give perfect scaling, but it considerably reduces the amplitude variation. When the bandwidth is less than $f_s/20$ the maximum gain of the filter is less than 1 dB.

   A comparison of the amplitude response of the second-order all-pole filter and the pole–zero filter is displayed in figure 6.42. Each filter was designed to have a center frequency of 2 kHz and a bandwidth of 400 Hz, and each is scaled for an amplitude response near 1 (0 dB) at the center of the passband. The effect of the two zeros is readily evident at 0 Hz and the Nyquist frequency of 20 kHz. The 0-Hz zero greatly increases the stopband attenuation at low frequencies compared to the all-pole filter. This attribute is desirable when the purpose of the filter is to isolate the spectral energy in the passband of the filter. On the other hand, a large amount of attenuation at low frequencies may excessively attenuate the fundamental frequency when the filter is intended to emphasize a particular region of the spectrum of a tone passing through it. The upper zero increases the rejection at frequencies near the Nyquist, but also results in the loss of a certain amount of attenuation in much of the upper stopband.

   The zero at 0 Hz makes it impossible for the filter to be used as a low-pass filter by

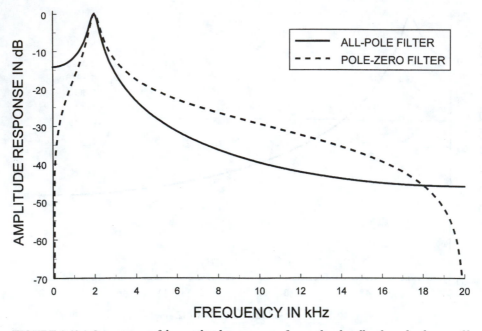

FIGURE 6.42   Comparison of the amplitude responses of second-order all-pole and pole–zero filters.

programming the center frequency to 0. Similarly, setting the center frequency to the Nyquist does not realize a high-pass filter.

6.13C   Imitating Analog Filter Designs Using the Bilinear Transform

Analog filter design has a long history and a well-developed literature. As a result, many procedures for digital filter design begin with the construction of the mathematical description of the analog filter that has the desired response. The coefficients of the digital filter are then determined by transforming the analog filter description, using the appropriate mathematical relationships. There are several methods of transformation. Each is tailored to make the digital filter's response match a certain aspect of the analog response. No transformation will result in identical filter characteristics in both the analog and the digital domains. Thus, the filter designer must choose the type of transform that matches the aspects of performance that are most important in the application.

The *bilinear transform*[14] has been found useful for many audio signal-processing applications. When applied to a second-order analog filter, it produces a recursive digital filter implemented with the following equation:

$$y(n) = a_0 x(n) + a_1 x(n-1) + a_2 x(n-2) - b_1 y(n-1) - b_2 y(n-2)$$

There are many types of analog filter responses, each of which is optimized for certain characteristics. We will apply the bilinear transform to a common one—the *Butterworth response,* which has a maximally flat passband. Several design examples follow to illustrate methods for the calculation of the coefficients of this filter for the four basic filter elements.

At the cost of increased computation, a filter of this type gives precision and stopband attenuation that are superior to those of the general-purpose filter in section 6.3.

DESIGN EXAMPLE: Butterworth low-pass filter. The application of the bilinear transform to a second-order, Butterworth low-pass filter results in a digital filter that uses the above equation. For a desired cutoff frequency (f_c) at a sampling rate (f_s), the filter coefficients are calculated as follows:

1. Calculate the intermediate variable, C, from

$$C = \frac{1}{\tan\left(\pi\dfrac{f_c}{f_s}\right)}$$

2. The coefficients are then calculated from

$$a_0 = \frac{1}{1+\sqrt{2}C+C^2}$$

$$a_1 = 2a_0$$

$$a_2 = a_0$$

$$b_1 = 2a_0\left(1-C^2\right)$$

$$b_2 = a_0\left(1-\sqrt{2}C+C^2\right)$$

As an example, for $f_s = 40$ kHz, figure 6.43 shows the coefficient values and amplitude response of a 2-kHz Butterworth low-pass filter.

DESIGN EXAMPLE: Butterworth high-pass filter. A Butterworth high-pass filter with cutoff frequency f_c can be digitally approximated by calculating the coefficients according to

$$C = \tan\left(\pi\dfrac{f_c}{f_s}\right)$$

$$a_0 = \frac{1}{1+\sqrt{2}C+C^2}$$

$$a_1 = -2a_0$$

$$a_2 = a_0$$

$$b_1 = 2a_0\left(C^2-1\right)$$

$$b_2 = a_0\left(1-\sqrt{2}C+C^2\right)$$

As an example, for $f_s = 40$ kHz, figure 6.44 shows the coefficient values and amplitude response of a 6-kHz Butterworth high-pass filter.

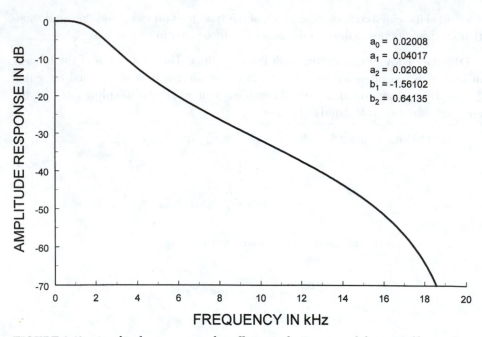

FIGURE 6.43   Amplitude response and coefficients of a Butterworth low-pass filter with a cut-off frequency of 2 kHz.

DESIGN EXAMPLE: Butterworth band-pass filter. A Butterworth band-pass filter with center frequency f_0 and bandwidth BW can be digitally approximated by calculating the coefficients according to

$$C = \frac{1}{\tan\left(\pi\dfrac{BW}{f_s}\right)}$$

$$D = 2\cos\left(2\pi\frac{f_0}{f_s}\right)$$

$$a_0 = \frac{1}{1+C}$$

$$a_1 = 0$$

$$a_2 = -a_0$$

$$b_1 = -a_0 CD$$

$$b_2 = a_0(C-1)$$

Owing to the nature of the bilinear transform, this band-pass filter cannot be converted into a low pass by choosing $f_0 = 0$ Hz or into a high pass by choosing $f_0 = f_s/2$. The amplitude response of this filter is always 0 at both 0 Hz and the Nyquist frequency.

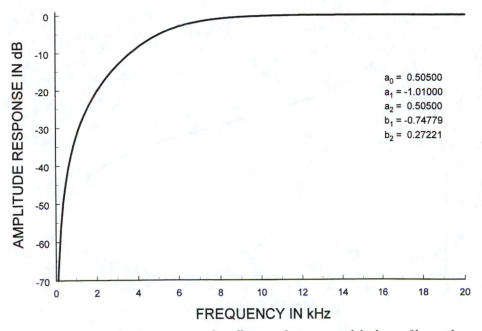

FIGURE 6.44   Amplitude response and coefficients of a Butterworth high-pass filter with a cut-off frequency of 6 kHz.

As an example, for f_s = 40 kHz, figure 6.45 shows the coefficient values and amplitude response of a Butterworth band-pass filter with f_0 = 2.5 kHz and BW = 500 Hz.

DESIGN EXAMPLE: Butterworth band-reject filter. A Butterworth band-reject filter with center frequency f_0 and bandwidth BW can be digitally approximated by calculating the coefficients according to

$$C = \tan\left(\pi \frac{BW}{f_s}\right)$$

$$D = 2\cos\left(2\pi \frac{f_0}{f_s}\right)$$

$$a_0 = \frac{1}{1+C}$$

$$a_1 = -a_0 D$$

$$a_2 = a_0$$

$$b_1 = -a_0 D$$

$$b_2 = a_0(1-C)$$

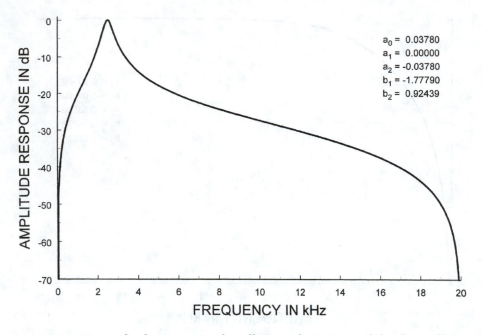

FIGURE 6.45   Amplitude response and coefficients of a Butterworth band-pass filter with a center frequency of 2.5 kHz and a bandwidth of 500 Hz.

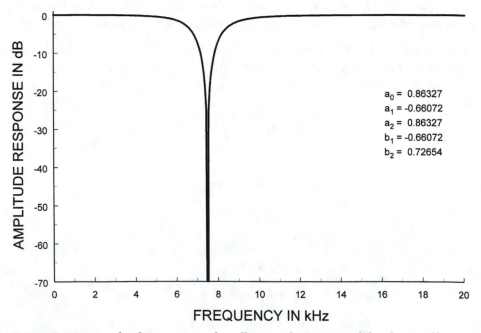

FIGURE 6.46   Amplitude response and coefficients of a Butterworth band-reject filter with a center frequency of 7.5 kHz and a bandwidth of 2 kHz.

As an example, for f_s = 40 kHz, figure 6.46 shows the coefficient values and amplitude response of a Butterworth band-reject filter with f_0 = 7.5 kHz and BW = 2 kHz.

NOTES

1. Mourjopoulos, J., Kyriakis-Bitzaros, E., and Goutis, C. E. "Theory and Real-Time Implementation of Time-Varying Audio Filters." *Journal of the Audio Engineering Society,* 38(7/8), 1990, 523–535.

2. Dodge, Charles. "Cascando." Composer's Recordings, Inc. (CRI SD454), 1983.

3. Dodge, Charles. "Earth's Magnetic Field." Nonesuch Records (H71250), 1970.

4. Dodge, Charles. "Changes." Nonesuch Records (H71245), 1970.

5. Ibid.

6. Griffiths, Paul. *A Guide to Electronic Music.* London: Thames and Hudson, 1979, 49.

7. Slawson, A. Wayne. "The Color of Sound: A Theoretical Study in Musical Timbre." *Music Theory Spectrum,* 3, 1981, 123–141.

8. Slawson, A. Wayne. "The Musical Control of Sound Color." *Canadian University Music Review,* 3, 1982, 67–79.

9. Babbitt, Milton. "Some Aspects of Twelve-Tone Composition." *The Score and I.M.A. Magazine,* 1955, 53–61. (Reprinted in *Twentieth Century View of Music History.* New York: Scribner's, 1972, 364–371.)

10. Slawson, A. Wayne. *Sound Color.* Berkeley: University of California Press, 1985.

11. Karpen, Richard. "Exchange." *Cultures Electroacoustiques 2,* Le Chant du Monde (LDC 278044/45), 1987.

12. Oppenheim, A. V., and Schafer, R. W. *Digital Signal Processing.* Englewood Cliffs, N.J.: Prentice-Hall, 1975. Rabiner, L. R., and Gold, B. *Theory and Application of Digital Signal Processing.* Englewood Cliffs, N.J.: Prentice-Hall, 1975. Steiglitz, K. *A Digital Signal Processing Primer with Applications to Digital Audio and Computer Music.* Menlo Park, Calif.: Addison-Wesley, 1996.

13. Smith, J. O., and Angell, J. B. "A Constant-Gain Digital Resonator Tuned by a Single Coefficient." *Computer Music Journal,* 6(4), 1982, 36–40.

14. Stanley, William. *Digital Signal Processing.* Reston, Va.: Reston Publishing, 1975.

7

ANALYSIS-BASED SYNTHESIS TECHNIQUES

Most of the synthesis techniques of computer music are based on the analysis of natural sound. The early synthesizers began with the simple Helmholtz model of a steady-state waveform encased in an envelope. As described in chapters 2 and 4, advances in the hardware and algorithms used for acoustic analysis made possible the more effective model of time-varying spectra on which additive synthesis is based. This chapter will detail other techniques of synthesis that use the results of an analysis. It begins with one of the areas that pioneered synthesis from analysis: the synthesis of human speech. Analysis techniques such as the short-term discrete Fourier transform and the use of wavelet functions will be described along with their limitations. The operation and application of the phase vocoder will be also be presented.

Synthesis-from-analysis systems were originally inspired by the desire to reduce the amount of data needed to represent a sound. Most of the initial work was done under the auspices of telecommunications companies with the aim of improving the efficiency of transmission. The result of an analysis is a set of parameters, often relating to the spectrum of the sound, that can, if the model is accurate, be used to resynthesize the sound. The parameters vary much more slowly than the original acoustic waveform, allowing them be sampled at a lower rate. The sets of amplitude and frequency functions that can be used by an additive-synthesis instrument given in chapter 4 are examples of such parametric data.

For the musician, synthesis by analysis offers much more than just the facility to re-create analyzed sounds. The ability to dissect, modify, and then reassemble sounds opens a wide range of musical possibilities. The parameters can be manipulated to create different sounds that retain many of the natural characteristics of the original.

7.1 SPEECH SYNTHESIS

The history of computer-synthesized speech begins in the 1950s at Bell Telephone Laboratories, where scientists and engineers were working to replicate the human voice for use in telephone systems. Musicians soon became interested in the possibility of using the synthetic voice as a musical instrument that could surpass the human voice in plasticity and range of capabilities. The element of intelligible language was thus introduced to computer music, bringing with it a broad range of theatrical, intellectual, and poetic possibilities. Even before the synthesis of intelligible speech became feasible with computers, the synthesis of certain speechlike sounds was used to create musical tones with dynamic spectra.

   In the last few years, many new types of voice synthesis systems have been developed, which offer great facility of use and accessibility. Adaptations to musical composition and performance have thus proliferated.[1] A musician who wishes to use these new technologies in a sophisticated and imaginative manner must have an understanding of not only the computer implementation, but also the linguistic, physical, and acoustical mechanisms of speech.

   This section describes the physical structure of the human vocal tract and the ways that vocal sounds are produced. It outlines the acoustics of phonetics and presents several models for the synthesis of speech on a computer. Methods of realizing music with computer-synthesized speech based on analysis are also discussed. Other methods of producing vocal sounds can be found elsewhere in this text. A singing soprano tone created by FM synthesis was described in section 5.1F, two granular synthesis approaches will be detailed in section 8.2, and a physical model of the vocal tract is presented in section 9.4.

7.1A   Speech Physiology

Figure 7.1 illustrates the major features of the vocal tract. The speech process begins in the lungs as air is forced up through the trachea, past the glottis (vocal cords), and through the cavity of the pharynx to the mouth (oral cavity). Although vibration of the glottis and the size and shape of the pharynx affect the acoustic characteristics of the voice, it is the tongue, more than any other element of the vocal tract, that creates the articulation of speech. The lips radiate the sound of the voice to the surrounding space, and at the same time their position determines certain speech sounds. When the velum (soft palate) is lowered, the nostrils contribute to this radiation, creating "nasalized" speech. Each of these articulators—the tongue (tip, middle, and back), the lips, the

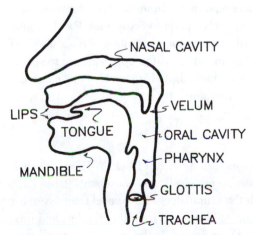

FIGURE 7.1   The principal parts of the human vocal tract.

mandible, the velum, and also the larynx—is controlled separately. Together they are used to produce *phonemes*, which are the various sounds of speech.[2]

There are three classes of excitation sources for the voice. *Voiced* sounds are caused by the quasi-periodic vibration of the glottis; *fricative* sounds, by turbulence created by constriction at some point along the vocal tract; and *plosive* sounds, by the sudden release of pressure built up behind a closure in the vocal tract. Fricatives and plosives constitute the class of sounds called *unvoiced* because the sound is produced by noise in the vocal tract, rather than by vibrations of the glottis.

The length and shape of the particular vocal tract determine the resonances in the spectrum of a voiced signal. An average vocal tract is about 17 cm in length. When at rest (in the neutral vowel position), it imparts resonances called *formants* that are approximately equally spaced in hertz: the first formant at about 500 Hz, the second at about 1500, the third at about 2500, the fourth at about 3500, the fifth at 4500, and so on. Repositioning of the articulators alters the shape of the vocal tract, thus changing the frequencies of the formants, particularly the lower ones. The frequencies of the lowest two or three formants constitute the cues necessary for phonemic differentiation of vowels.[3] The following interactions give an indication of the relationship between the articulator position and frequencies of the lower formants:[4]

1. The wider the jaw opening, the higher the frequency of the first formant.

2. The closer a point of constriction between the tongue and the roof of the mouth is to the front of the vocal tract, the higher the frequency of the second formant.

3. The greater the degree of backward curving of the tongue tip, the lower the third formant frequency.

4. Rounding the lips and lowering of the larynx causes all formant frequencies to be lowered.

Much modern research on the formant structure of speech has its roots in the examination of pictures made by the *sound spectrograph,* a machine that transforms a voice recording into a graphic representation of its spectral content versus time. For the musician, spectrograms can serve as a good starting point for illustrating the acoustics of speech. *Visible Speech,*[5] originally published as an aid to deaf people learning to speak, is not only an excellent source for these spectrograms, but also provides clear instructions for the inference of phonemes from spectrograms.

7.1B   Acoustic Phonetics

There are roughly 41 distinct sounds, or phonemes, in American English. They are usually grouped into four classes: vowels, diphthongs, semivowels, and consonants (table 7.1).

The *vowels* are voiced sounds for which the articulators of the vocal tract assume a fixed position. For example, the /OO/ in "boot" is formed by rounding the lips and raising the back of the tongue. By contrast, the /IY/ in "meet" is the result of a more open position of the lips, with the tip of the tongue placed near the front of the mouth.

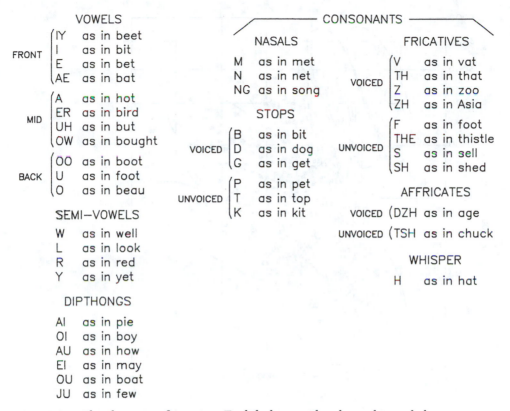

	VOWELS		**CONSONANTS**		
FRONT	IY as in beet / I as in bit / E as in bet / AE as in bat		**NASALS** M as in met / N as in net / NG as in song		**FRICATIVES**
MID	A as in hot / ER as in bird / UH as in but / OW as in bought		**STOPS** VOICED: B as in bit / D as in dog / G as in get	VOICED	V as in vat / TH as in that / Z as in zoo / ZH as in Asia
BACK	OO as in boot / U as in foot / O as in beau		UNVOICED: P as in pet / T as in top / K as in kit	UNVOICED	F as in foot / THE as in thistle / S as in sell / SH as in shed

SEMI–VOWELS

W as in well
L as in look
R as in red
Y as in yet

AFFRICATES

VOICED (DZH as in age

UNVOICED (TSH as in chuck

WHISPER

H as in hat

DIPTHONGS

AI as in pie
OI as in boy
AU as in how
EI as in may
OU as in boat
JU as in few

TABLE 7.1　The phonemes of American English shown with orthographic symbols.

Acoustically, the vowels are characterized by their formant frequencies. Peterson and Barney[6] produced the chart in figure 7.2 by plotting the formant frequencies of 10 vowels that had each been perceived to be a distinct sound when spoken by a large number of men and children. The figure gives the second formant frequency as a function of the first formant frequency. The encircled areas indicate the broad range of variation within each vowel. Figure 7.3 shows an average of the data for the first three formant frequencies of all American English vowels spoken by males in this study.

A *diphthong* is a succession of two vowel sounds and has a continuous transition from one vowel sound toward the other. The articulation of a diphthong begins at or near the position for one of the vowels and proceeds smoothly to the other. There are six diphthongs in American English: /EI/, /OU/, /AI/, /AU/, /OI/, and /JU/.

Semivowels are transitional, voiced sounds that lack a fixed characterization of resonance structure. Instead, the semivowel appropriates the characteristic resonances of the vowel to or from which it is moving. The semivowels are /L/, /R/, /W/, and /Y/.

There are five different classes of *consonants:* nasal, fricatives, stops, affricates, and the whispered /H/. Each of these is the result of a distinctive arrangement and use of the articulators, but they all include a partial or complete constriction of the vocal tract.

The *nasals*—/M/, /N/, and /NG/—are made by lowering the velum in such a way

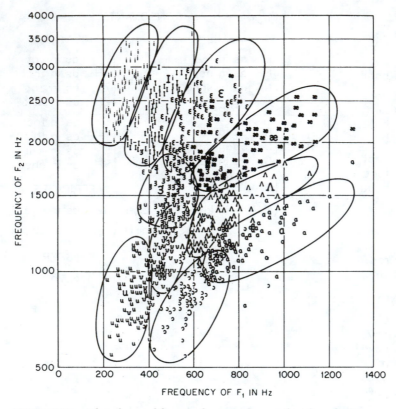

FIGURE 7.2   Plot of second formant frequency versus first formant frequency for the vowels. The data were taken for a wide range of speakers. *(From Lawrence Rabiner and Ronald W. Schafer, Digital Processing of Speech Signals, © 1978, p. 43 (after Peterson and Barney). Reprinted with permission of Prentice-Hall, Englewood Cliffs, N.J., and Journal of the Acoustical Society of America.)*

FORMANT FREQUENCIES OF VOWELS				
Symbol	Example Word	F_1	F_2	F_3
IY	beet	270	2290	3010
I	bit	390	1990	2550
E	bet	530	1840	2480
AE	bat	660	1720	2410
UH	but	520	1190	2390
A	hot	730	1090	2440
OW	bought	570	840	2410
U	foot	440	1020	2240
OO	boot	300	870	2240
ER	bird	490	1350	1690

FIGURE 7.3   Averaged formant frequencies of 10 vowels. *(From Rabiner and Schafer (after Peterson and Barney), with permission of Prentice-Hall and Journal of the Acoustical Society of America.)*

that the glottal wave is resonated through the nasal tract as well as through the vocal tract, and is radiated primarily at the nostrils. Nasalization greatly increases the length of the resonance system and introduces zeros (or antiresonances) into the spectrum of nasalized speech.

The *fricatives* can be either voiced or unvoiced. Unvoiced fricatives are made by passing a steady stream of air through the vocal tract and then constricting it at some point, causing turbulence. The placement of the constriction determines the particular unvoiced fricative. /F/ is created by a constriction near the lips; for /THE/, the constriction is near the teeth. The constriction for /S/ is near the middle of the vocal tract, and it is near the back of the mouth for /SH/.

The points of constriction for the voiced fricatives—/V/, /TH/, /Z/, and /ZH/—are the same as for their unvoiced counterparts (/F/, /THE/, /S/, and /SH/, respectively). There are two simultaneous excitation sources for each of the voiced fricatives: the glottis and the turbulence created at the point of constriction.

The *stop consonants* can also be either voiced or unvoiced. They are plosive sounds, produced by the sudden release of pressure built up behind a full constriction of the vocal tract. Again, the location of the constriction determines the characteristics of the particular stop consonant. Both the unvoiced stops—/P/, /T/, and /K/—and the voiced stops—/B/, /D/, and /G/—are distinguished by the placement of the constriction toward the front, middle, and rear of the mouth. To produce voiced stops, the glottis vibrates throughout the buildup and release of the constriction.

The *affricates* /TSH/ and /DZH/ are formed by connecting a stop and a fricative. In forming the unvoiced /TSH/, the /T/ stop is followed by the fricative /SH/, whereas the voiced /DZH/ includes a /D/ stop and a /ZH/ fricative.

The resonances of the *whispered consonant* /H/ assume the positions of the vowel that follows it, since there is no change in articulator position between the two phonemes.

7.1C   Computer Analysis of Speech

Successful speech synthesis by computer depends on an accurate analysis of speech. Research in the computer analysis of speech stems from a desire to reduce the amount of data needed to represent a speech signal. In an analysis, the speech wave is broken into segments called *windows* (see sections 2.7 and 7.2) or *frames*. For each of these segments, the analysis algorithm determines the attributes of the speech. These characteristics represent the speech sound and can be used later to re-create the analyzed sound. One of the primary functions of speech analysis is to determine the resonant characteristics of the vocal tract during the segment. Two widely used methods of doing this are *formant tracking* and *linear predictive coding*.

In formant tracking, the analysis transforms the speech signal into a series of short-term spectral descriptions, one for each segment.[7] Each spectrum is then examined in sequence for its principal peaks, or formants, creating a record of the formant frequencies and their levels versus time. The record of change in formant positions with time can then be used to reconstitute the speech signal. Formant tracking works best on a spoken male voice. It is much less accurate on female and children's voices because the relatively high fundamental frequency makes the formants harder to track. In addition, the presence of reverberation on the digital recording of the voice will seriously degrade the accuracy of this technique.

Linear predictive coding (LPC) is a statistical method for predicting future values of the speech waveform on the basis of its past values.[8] The method, which does not involve direct transformation from the time domain to the frequency domain, determines the characteristics of a filter that simulates the response of the vocal tract. Just as the vocal tract changes characteristics during the course of speech, the filter response varies from segment to segment. When driven with the proper excitation source, the filter reconstitutes the speech waveform originally analyzed. In LPC analysis, many more descriptors of the speech are derived (typically, 12 to 20) than in formant tracking (6 to 8). LPC analysis is not restricted to spoken male voices but has been successfully applied to a wide range of sounds. Section 7.1J explains the concept basic to linear prediction.

In addition to the information about the vocal tract, the analysis usually also determines whether the segment of speech is voiced or unvoiced. One analysis technique uses the ratio of high-frequency energy of the segment to its low-frequency energy as the criterion for making the determination. The ratio is significantly higher during unvoiced speech. Dividing speech into the strict categories of voiced and unvoiced is an imperfect model because a few sounds are members of both. (See below.)

Estimating the fundamental frequency of the voiced segments of speech is often part of the analysis. This can be accomplished either by examining the digitized speech wave directly as a waveform or by transforming it into the frequency domain and examining its spectrum. (However, a simple, discrete Fourier transform does not have sufficient resolution for an accurate determination. More complex techniques must be used.) Creating a pitch detection algorithm that is accurate for all types of speakers is a difficult problem. Many schemes have been developed, each of which has its own limitations and each of which provides optimum performance on a particular type of waveform. At present, there is no single method that is universally successful across a broad range of sounds.[9]

Amplitude is another attribute of speech that is often extracted by an analysis system. The average amplitude of each segment can be found by performing a power averaging of the samples contained in the segment.

7.1D   Computer Synthesis of Speech

A flowchart of a general plan for synthesizing speech with a digital computer is shown in figure 7.4. This model has been used by researchers and musicians working with a wide range of computers in natural languages. It is based on the models for analysis given above where the speech waveform has been broken down into segments.

If, at a given moment, the speech is to be voiced, then the excitation source for this model is a variable-frequency pulse generator with a fundamental frequency f_0; if the speech segment is to be unvoiced, a noise generator is used. In either case, the output of the selective source is multiplied by the gain factor (AMP) to obtain the appropriate amplitude. It is then introduced to the resonation system, which simulates the response

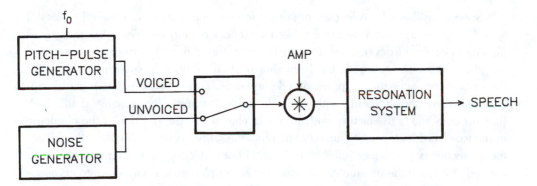

FIGURE 7.4   General plan for synthesizing speech with a digital computer.

of the vocal tract. The actual form of the resonation system depends on the method of representation: formant tracking or LPC. A resonation system can impart two different kinds of resonances into the spectrum of the speech: poles and zeros (see section 6.2). A pole is a resonance that emphasizes a frequency region. A zero is an antiresonance that attenuates energy in a frequency region. Not all speech synthesis systems make use of zeros. Zeros are necessary for synthesizing realistic nasal sounds and certain unvoiced fricatives.

For most musical purposes, it is desirable to have a variable-frequency pulse generator with a wide range and fine pitch quantization of the kind described in section 6.1. The pulse generator described there can be used in a frequency range from subaudio to half the sampling rate with very fine tuning. It generates no frequencies above the Nyquist, thus preventing aliasing. One problem inherent in this pulse generator, however, is that its harmonics are all of equal amplitude. For speech, analysis shows that the glottal excitation source has a rolloff of 12 dB/octave.[10] Thus, the pulse generator is usually followed by a low-pass filter to simulate the glottal function without inappropriate emphasis of the high-frequency region. However, this realization is also imperfect. For instance, the waveform of the pulse generator is a static one that cannot emulate the wide-band frequency modulation that accompanies the "start-up" of the vocal cords. Many of the future improvements to the quality of synthesized speech will be brought about through the use of more sophisticated excitation sources.

The general model shown in figure 7.4 has certain shortcomings as a synthesis model.[11] For example, for a given segment of speech, the synthesis must be either voiced or unvoiced, but not both. Clearly, certain phonemes such as /TH/, /V/, and /Z/ are combinations of both. This flaw is not serious enough to impair the intelligibility of the speech, but it is noticeable. Ways of circumventing the problem have been devised, but they require a far more complicated synthesis model.[12] Unfortunately, simply mixing the noise source with the pulse generator does not produce the desired effect. A more sophisticated source model that drives a physical model of the vocal tract is described in section 9.4.

There are two basic methods of performing speech synthesis on a computer: speech synthesis by rule and speech synthesis by analysis. Both methods are based on a prior analysis of speech. The difference lies in the way that the data are fed to the synthesizer.

Speech synthesis by rule grew out of recorded-voice systems in which the parts of speech were concatenated to make spoken sentences or phrases. The synthesizer uses phonemes derived from research in acoustic phonetics and applies rules for connecting the phonemes into speech. It has been shown[13] that intelligible speech cannot result from simple concatenation of prerecorded phonemes. This is because the acoustic properties of many phonemes of English are altered significantly by the context in which they occur. Some of the factors contributing to change are the position of the phoneme in the word and sentence, its surrounding phonemes, and its stress. To make the adjustments necessary to produce intelligible speech from text, computer programs have been created[14] in which the parameters of prosodics are implemented. These programs apply complex sets of rules for transforming printed English text into the sound of the spoken language. The sound of the speech produced by such systems, although intelligible, is clearly distinguishable from natural speech.

Speech synthesis by analysis sounds more realistic and personal. In speech synthesis by analysis, the synthetic speech is modeled on a recording of a voice speaking the passage to be synthesized. Thus, the speech synthesized from an analysis of a recording contains, from the outset, all of the transitions and timings of the speech. In addition, the resulting synthetic speech has the individual characteristics of the person who recorded the passage.

In making music with analyzed speech data, composers edit the analysis prior to resynthesis. Synthesis by analysis enables the independent alteration of the speed, pitch, amplitude, and resonance structure of the analyzed voice. This method of speech synthesis circumvents the major disadvantage of tape manipulation of the recorded voice—the changes in timbre and intelligibility that accompany changes in tape speed. Editing the analysis also makes it possible to rearrange the order of the elements of the speech, to repeat them, and to form choruses by creating multiple copies of the voice, with different alterations applied to each copy. Section 7.1H describes many of the ways in which an analysis can be edited for musical purposes.

7.1E   Formant Synthesis by Rule

Figure 7.5 shows the implementation of a digital formant speech synthesizer.[15] The synthesizer has two signal paths: one for voiced speech sounds, which includes the provision for whispered speech; and one for unvoiced fricative and plosive sounds. The left branch includes three variable resonances for simulation of the three lower formants, a variable pole and zero to shape the spectrum of nasalized speech, and fixed resonances for the upper formants. The unvoiced signal path consists of one zero and two poles for simulating the noise spectrum of fricatives and plosives. The user specifies a succession of phonemes giving information such as the following: a code for the particular phoneme, the duration of the phoneme, the frequency of the pulse generator if the phoneme is voiced, and the amplitude. To make intelligible, connected speech, it is necessary to implement the rules for speech transitions. Strategies for accomplishing this difficult task are suggested in several important articles.[16]

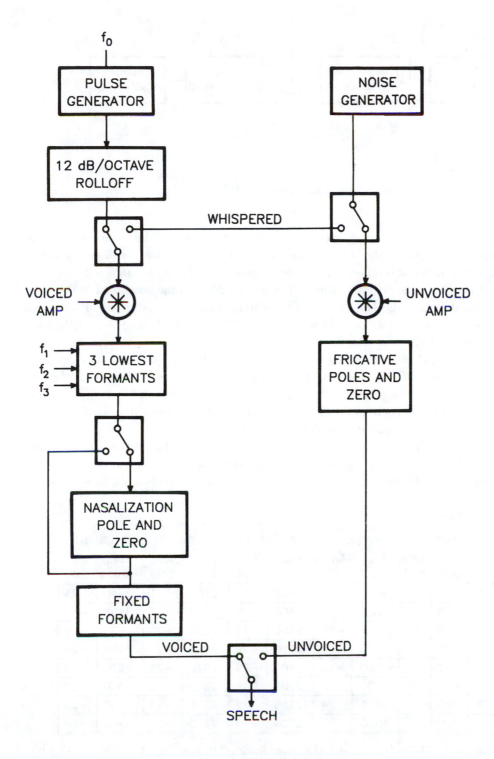

FIGURE 7.5 Speech synthesizer that directly realizes formants.

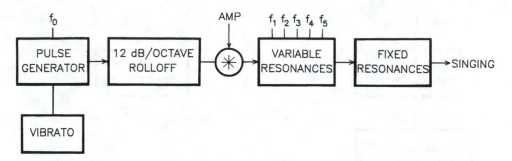

FIGURE 7.6   Formant synthesizer for singing vowels.

To synthesize a singing voice, a more elaborate model for the vocal tract must be implemented. The configuration of the vocal tract and articulators for singing results in a voice quality that is different from that of speech. Sundberg[17] has shown that operatic singers enlarge the pharynx cavity and lower the glottis in the vocal tract as they sing. The resulting acoustical effect is to lower the frequencies of the fourth and fifth formants and to place them closer together in the range of 2500 to 3500 Hz. The bulge in the spectrum so created is known as the *singing formant*.

The model for synthesizing vowel sounds in a rich vocal timbre is shown in figure 7.6. In this model, the lowest five formants are individually controlled to simulate the resonances of the singing voice. The higher resonances are included as fixed resonances in the spectrum. There is no provision for nasalization because the nasal tract contributes little to the quality of most sung vowels.

Table 7.2 shows the relative frequencies and amplitudes for the lower five formants on eight vowels sung by a male.[18] (These data were obtained from one singer and thus represent a configuration of resonances unique to a single individual.) In the formant pat-

	FIRST FORMANT		SECOND FORMANT		THIRD FORMANT		FOURTH FORMANT		FIFTH FORMANT	
Vowel	Freq [Hz]	Amp [dB]	Freq [Hz]	Amp [dB]	Freq [Hz]	Amp [dB]	Freq [Hz]	Amp [dB]	Freq [Hz]	Amp [dB]
A	609	0	1000	−6	2450	−12	2700	−11	3240	−24
E	400	0	1700	−9	2300	−8	2900	−11	3400	−19
IY	238	0	1741	−20	2450	−16	2900	−20	4000	−32
O	325	0	700	−12	2550	−26	2850	−22	3100	−28
OO	360	0	750	−12	2400	−29	2675	−26	2950	−35
U	415	0	1400	−12	2200	−16	2800	−18	3300	−27
ER	300	0	1600	−14	2150	−12	2700	−15	3100	−23
UH	400	0	1050	−12	2200	−19	2650	−20	3100	−29

TABLE 7.2   The frequencies and relative amplitudes of the formants of eight vowels sung by a male. *(Reprinted by permission of Xavier Rodet.)*

Vowel	FIRST FORMANT		SECOND FORMANT		THIRD FORMANT		FOURTH FORMANT		FIFTH FORMANT	
	Freq [Hz]	Amp [dB]	Freq [Hz]	Amp [dB]	Freq [Hz]	Amp [dB]	Freq [Hz]	Amp [dB]	Freq [Hz]	Amp [dB]
A	650	0	1100	−8	2860	−13	3300	−12	4500	−19
E	500	0	1750	−9	2450	−10	3350	−14	5000	−23
IY	330	0	2000	−14	2800	−11	3650	−10	5000	−19
O	400	0	840	−12	2800	−26	3250	−24	4500	−31
OO	280	0	650	−18	2200	−48	3450	−50	4500	−52

TABLE 7.3   The frequencies and relative amplitudes of the formants of five vowels sung by a female. *Reprinted by permission of Xavier Rodet.)*

tern for singing, the first, second, fourth, and fifth formants are lower than in speech, while the third is generally higher. These differences result from the change in size and shape of the vocal tract when the pharyngeal cavity is widened and the larynx is lowered.

Table 7.3 shows the formants of a single soprano singing five different vowel sounds.[19] The center frequencies and relative amplitudes of these vowels are summarized in the table. In all cases except /OO/, the first formant frequency is higher for the female singing voice than for the male singing voice (table 7.2). A potential source of inaccuracy in the synthesis with the data of the female singing voice is apparent: the fundamental frequency will exceed the frequency of the first formant before reaching even the middle of the soprano vocal range. A fundamental higher than the first formant will cause the voice quality to become muffled and indistinct if left uncorrected. However, Sundberg has observed that female operatic singers have a technique to circumvent this problem. They widen the jaw opening as the fundamental frequency rises. This raises the frequency of the first formant so that it "tracks" the fundamental, and it also shifts the frequencies of the other formants.

Figure 7.7 shows the movement of the first four formants in response to increasing fundamental frequencies.[20] The frequency of the fifth formant is not vowel-dependent, and so it remains fixed at 4.5 kHz in this model.

Synthesis from the five-formant model does not in itself give sufficient audible cues for the listener to designate the synthesized vocal sounds as "singing." To capture the quality of a singing voice more completely, the synthesized sound must incorporate a vibrato of a specific character. The envelope and the onset time of the vibrato are among the cues a listener uses to identify singing. Xavier Rodet and Gerald Bennett emphasize the importance of "aleatoric variations in the fundamental frequency."

For a typical male singing voice, the vibrato rate is around 5 to 7 Hz. The width of the vibrato is about ±3% to ±6% of the fundamental frequency. Rodet and Bennett have observed the aleatoric variations in the fundamental frequency of tones sung deliberately without vibrato. To synthesize these subtle changes in pitch, the amount of frequency change was allowed to vary at random in a $1/f$ manner (see section 11.1G) between 0.5 and 1.5 seconds. The amount of this change was between ±1.1% and

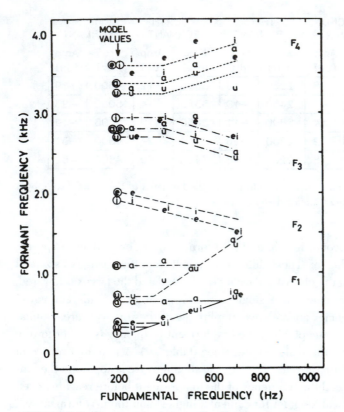

FIGURE 7.7   Formant frequencies for four female sung vowels versus fundamental frequency. *(Reprinted with permission of Johan Sundberg.)*

±3.7% for the female and between ±2% and ±5.7% for the male. The values for the periodic and aperiodic fluctuations were added together and interpolated on a sample-to-sample basis, resulting in changes that were always smooth.

A temporal cue that designates vocal sounds as singing can be heard whenever a vocal tone is preceded by a rest. The onset of vibrato in a tone following the rest is typically delayed by about 300 to 600 ms.[21]

Another important characteristic of the singing voice is the transition that occurs when the voice changes frequency. Sundberg[22] states that 75% of the frequency change observed in the voices of trained singers occurs in the first 70 ms. The change is a rapid glissando from one frequency to the next. Sundberg further observes that in a two-note *marcato*-like sequence, the fundamental of a following lower note is approached by descending past it and then coming back up to the correct pitch.

The relationship between amplitude and spectrum must be carefully considered when synthesizing singing voices. Amplitude increases, to a certain extent, with fundamental frequency. The relative amplitude levels of formants 2 through 5 vary in a non-linear way with the amplitude of the fundamental frequency.[23] Failure to provide for this in the synthesis algorithm results in the *volume-control effect* (i.e., a change in amplitude without a concomitant change in the spectrum).

7.1F   Synthesis by Analysis of Speech

In all speech synthesis-by-analysis systems, the speech is digitized and analyzed as described in section 7.1C. The output from the analysis is in the form of *frames:* blocks of data that represent the attributes of the speech for a short period of time. The term *frame* is analogous to the same term in motion picture technology, where the film is projected at a frame rate great enough to ensure the continuity of the visual image. The rate of frames in speech varies, according to the system and application, from about 20 to 200 frames per second.

A frame is defined by its amplitude, its duration, and whether it is voiced or unvoiced. If the frame is voiced, it also includes the fundamental frequency of the source. In addition, all frames include information about the resonances of the vocal tract. The particular method of specification differs from one kind of synthesis model to another. For a formant synthesizer, the resonances are specified as characteristics of band-pass filters. For an LPC synthesizer, the resonances are described by the coefficients for an all-pole filter.

A typical formant-tracking synthesizer is the same as the one that was shown in figure 7.5. Notice that although the analysis system tracks only three formants, the synthesizer generates five. The top two have fixed frequencies at 3.5 and 4.5 kHz, respectively.

Synthesis from formant tracking, while in many ways outdated in comparison to linear predictive coding, retains certain functional advantages. The principal advantage is the resonance patterns in the voice can be altered without causing the system to become unstable. However, because formant tracking is ordinarily restricted to the spoken male voice, its usefulness is limited.

In linear predictive coding (LPC), speech is analyzed to find the values of coefficients for an all-pole filter that will reconstitute its waveform. Figure 7.8 shows a diagram of an LPC synthesizer. There is more than one variety of LPC analysis and synthesis: the methods known as *covariance*[24] and *lattice*[25] are the two most widely used.

In resynthesis of the voice, the excitation source (periodic pulse or noise) is fed through the all-pole filter to reconstitute the waveform of the speech. A synthesis from an LPC analysis can sound much more realistic than one from formant tracking.

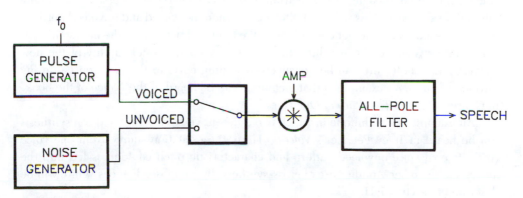

FIGURE 7.8   Digital speech synthesizer using linear predictive coding.

Covariance synthesis/analysis preserves even the most subtle individual traits of pronunciation and accent. However, unlike formant tracking, altering the vocal resonances predicted by a covariance LPC analysis is very difficult. In this case, the coefficients of the all-pole filter bear little obvious relationship to the speech spectrum. Therefore, it is extremely hard to know what changes to make to the coefficients in order to change the resonance structure of the speech. Editing the coefficients usually results in an unstable filter, rather than causing useful changes in the speech spectrum. A technique that has been used successfully to alter the spectrum of an LPC-synthesized voice depends on a transformation of all the covariance coefficients as a group, instead of editing only certain ones. It shifts the frequencies of the response of the all-pole filter.[26]

The lattice method produces speech of somewhat lower quality than covariance, but it still sounds better than speech made from formant-tracking analyses. The lattice coefficients are more stable than those of covariance, and so a certain amount of editing can be applied to them directly. The lattice coefficients act in a way like vocal tract area-function descriptors. That is, a given coefficient roughly corresponds to a cross-section of the vocal tract at a certain point. Editing certain of the coefficients can cause changes in the speech spectrum that resemble the effect of moving the lips.

LPC synthesis by analysis does not restrict the vocal model to the spoken voice, but can also be used with good results for the singing voice, including those of women and children. The LPC synthesis-by-analysis technique works well for the voice because the synthesis system assumes a pulselike vocal source that, like the glottis, is rich in harmonics. The realistic resynthesis of many other types of tones may require different excitation sources or even alternate analysis/synthesis models to be implemented.

7.1G   Cross-Synthesis

The LPC-synthesis system can be modified to permit the use of a source other than noise or periodic pulse for the excitation of the all-pole filter. The new source may be any recorded (and digitized) or synthesized sound. The only factor that influences the choice of source is the necessity for a relatively broad spectrum in order that the speech be easily understood. However, with this technique, the resonances of the analyzed voice can be used to change the spectrum of the source without necessarily becoming intelligible as speech. This will most often occur when the voiced and unvoiced portions of the analyzed speech do not coincide with the temporal patterns of the new source, or when the new source contains little high-frequency energy. Intelligibility of the new "talking" musical texture can be enhanced by adding noise to the new source during unvoiced frames. An example of that technique can be heard in the "voice of the book" in Charles Dodge's *The Story of Our Lives*.[27]

An example of a technique in which two different voices are "crossed" on synthesis can be heard in Tracy Petersen's *Voices*.[28] Here, the excitation source from one voice (with its own voice/unvoiced pattern and characteristic pitch contour) is fed into the analysis of the other. Another use of cross-synthesis by composer Frances White will be described in section 7.1I.

7.1H   Editing Analyses of Speech

The musician using analyzed speech ordinarily edits the analysis before synthesis. Editing enables the musician to alter certain characteristics of the speech and makes possible a wide range of musical effects. Editor programs for this purpose commonly provide the possibility of selectively modifying the pitch, timing, amplitude, and resonance structure of the analyzed speech. In addition, speech editors often implement operations associated with tape manipulation such as reordering the succession of phonemes and repeating parts of the speech.

Figure 7.9 illustrates the storage of analyzed speech frames in computer memory. The speech is stored in a two-dimensional array where each line represents the parameters of one speech frame with the frames ordered in time. Each column, then, contains the values of a single speech parameter, one frame after the other. The parameter *errn* is a result of linear prediction and is indicative of the voicing of the frame. A large value denotes an unvoiced frame. The threshold between voiced and unvoiced varies somewhat, but is roughly 0.07 in the system shown here. Other methods of analyzing and storing the voicing information are also in use. It is possible, with practice, to read a printout of the frame values of analyzed speech and deduce much of the same information as from a "voice print", or sound spectrogram: that is, if the phrase is known in advance, to find the word and syllable boundaries. Graphical presentation of the parameters of amplitude, frequency, and errn yields an even more readable result.

In order to edit the speech analysis, an editing program is devised where a command will change the contents of the array containing the speech frames. Typically, an editing command causes a particular kind of edit to be applied to a certain parameter

	PARAMETERS				
	1	2	3	4	5 to N
FRAME	Amplitude	Frequency	Errn	Duration	Resonances
1	90.1	0.0	0.081	0.010	( ) ( ) ( )
2	1345.4	96.0	0.061	0.010	( ) ( ) ( )
3	1984.3	96.0	0.062	0.010	( ) ( ) ( )
4	1918.9	94.2	0.051	0.010	( ) ( ) ( )
5	2583.7	88.3	0.059	0.010	( ) ( ) ( )
6	3143.0	77.1	0.067	0.010	( ) ( ) ( )
7	1587.4	77.3	0.024	0.010	( ) ( ) ( )
8	1091.6	76.4	0.013	0.010	( ) ( ) ( )
⋮	⋮	⋮	⋮	⋮	⋮

FIGURE 7.9   A method of storing analyzed speech data in computer memory. The numerical way in which the resonances are represented depends on the analysis algorithm used.

over a specified range of frames. For example, in order to set the frequency of the voice for a phoneme to 440 Hz, one needs a command that will change the appropriate parameter to the desired frequency for all the frames of the phoneme.

Following is a list of some of the most common alterations found in synthetic speech-editing systems:

MOVE: Copy some or all of the parameters of a range of frames into another range of frames. This command is often used to create repetitions of phonemes or words.

INTERPOLATE: Interpolate the values of a specified parameter for a range of frames. When applied to the duration parameter, for example, this command can cause the speech to accelerate or decelerate.

TIME: Cause the range of frames to occupy a specified time span. The musician can use this command to impose new rhythms onto the speech without necessarily altering the analyzed pitch contour.

GLISSANDO: Cause the frequencies of a range of frames to change continuously between specified limits with an exponential progression.

CHANGE: Change the contents of a specified parameter in a range of frames to a given numerical value. For example, this command can be used to fix the pitch of the speech for the duration of the phoneme without necessarily altering the natural, spoken rhythm of the speech.

RAISE: Transpose the frequency parameter of a range of frames to another pitch level. This command can be used to change the frequency of the synthetic speech without destroying the natural pitch contour of the analyzed voice.

BOOST: Raise or lower the amplitude parameter of a range of frames by a fixed number of decibels. This command also preserves the amplitude contour of the speech on which the analysis is based.

It is practical, even with a limited set of commands, to make music based on editing the analyses of recorded voices. A facility for mixing separately computed voices is most helpful.[29] This can be used, for example, to create polyphony. It can also help in creating a chorus of synthetic voices on the same text by mixing together voices that have been repeatedly synthesized with slight differences in the pitch and timing of the phonemes.

Sometimes, it is important to preserve as many of the characteristics of the original voice as possible. For example, when working with an analysis of a singing voice, it is much more effective to raise or lower the analyzed pitch contour than to change the frequency of a range of frames to the same value. Figure 7.10 shows the original pitch contour of three syllables sung by Enrico Caruso (figure 7.10a) and the effects of two different editings (figure 7.10b and c). In the first editing (figure 7.10b), the frequency of each of the frames for the syllable is the same. In the second (figure 7.10c), the characteristic vibrato and frequency jitter are, while transposed, still preserved. The result of the second case sounds much more realistic.

In the situation where one wishes to make into a pitched line syllables that were originally spoken, it is necessary to change the frequency of the frame to a single value just in order to create the sensation. One way of making the voice sound less "mechanical" is to provide a transition in the pitch of the voice for about 100 ms between the syl-

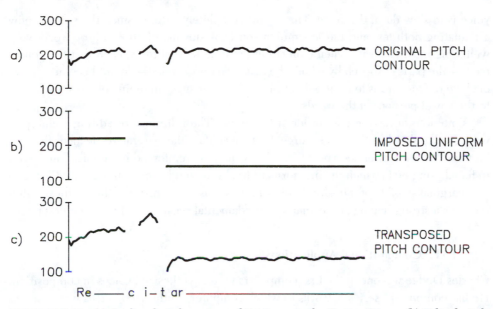

FIGURE 7.10 (a) Analyzed pitch contour of *Recitar* sung by Enrico Caruso. (b) Edited pitch contour with all frames of a syllable set to the same frequency. (c) Edited pitch contour with all frames of a syllable transposed by the same amount, thus preserving the small fluctuations of frequency characteristic of the original voice.

lables. Figure 7.11 illustrates this technique. Another technique for making the pitched synthetic voice sound more natural is by introducing a small amount of random deviation around the frequency of the voice. A deviation of about ±1.5% to ±3% changing values every 10 ms has been found suitable for this purpose.

Another means of aiding the intelligibility of pitched speech based on a recorded

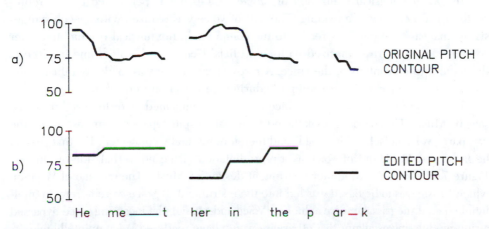

FIGURE 7.11 (a) Analyzed pitch contour of a phrase spoken by a male voice. (b) Edited pitch contour with all frames of a syllable set to insert the same frequency, except for small glissandos inserted between consecutive voiced syllables. The irregular frequency jitter of human speech is retained on synthesis through random fluctuation of the voice around the frequency of the frame.

voice is to slow down the voice. This seems completely natural, since the voice is now articulating both text and music simultaneously. A slowing of 10% to 50% works very well. One must take care when elongating the time base of the speech that the consonants—the parts of speech by which the text is comprehended—do not become "fuzzy" or slurred. One means to ensure this is to apply the changes in timing of the speech only to the vowel portions of the words.

One note of caution is in order at this point. The full range of editing techniques works well only when the vocal source does not contain the extreme resonances that can be found in some extended vocal techniques such as "reinforced harmonics," and even in female singing in which the first formant tracks the fundamental frequency. Owing to the marginal stability of the all-pole filter in these cases, the result of the synthesis often includes a strong ringing at the analyzed fundamental regardless of the specified pitch.

7.1I Compositional Applications

Charles Dodge was one of the first composers to use synthesized voices in composition. He has composed a series of works in which computer-synthesized voices were used to form the whole fabric of the compositions.[30]

His musical version of Samuel Beckett's radio play, *Cascando*,[31] shows a use of the computer-synthesized voice to articulate text directly and to control the electronic sound of the nonverbal parts of the composition.

In the play of *Cascando*, there are three parts: Opener, Voice, and Music. Opener is the central character; he controls the other two and relates directly to the audience. He continually asserts and attempts to demonstrate that Voice and Music are real and not just "in his head." Voice persistently tries to tell a story that will satisfy Opener, that will be the "right one" so that he may rest, remain silent. Music represents the nonverbal response to the same situation.

In Dodge's musical realization of *Cascando*, Opener is performed live or represented by a recording of a reading. The part of Voice was realized with speech synthesis by analysis. The part was read into the computer in the musical rhythm and, after computer analysis, resynthesized with an artificial ("composed") pitch line in place of the natural pitch contour of the voice. A raspy vocal timbre was made by infusing the voice with equal parts of noise and pitch during the vowel portions of the speech.

In *Cascando*, every speech by Voice is either accompanied by or followed by a passage by Music. The composer took the position that, despite Opener's remonstrances, the two parts were, in fact, "in his head" and therefore integrally connected. For that reason, he fashioned Music out of Voice as a representation of the nonverbal side of Opener. Figure 7.12 shows the computer instrument design for Music. The passage of Voice on which Music was to be based was fed into the instrument. If Voice were to remain intelligible (i.e., if the passage were a duet for Voice and Music), the incoming voice bypassed a ring-modulating oscillator that otherwise would have rendered Voice unintelligible.

The signal of Voice was then passed to both branches of the instrument: to a bank of comb filters (see section 10.1B) and an amplitude inverter followed by a noise generator and gating mechanism. The amplitude inversion was accomplished by subtracting the

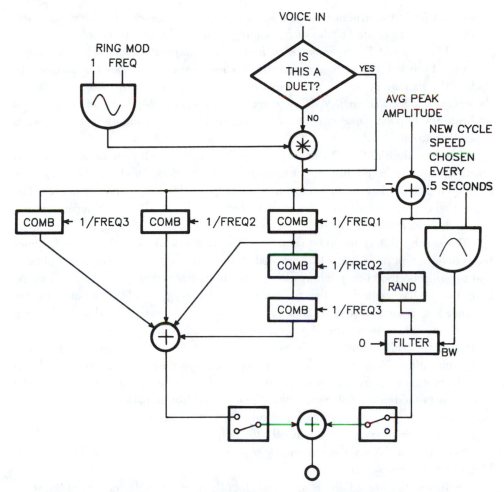

FIGURE 7.12   Computer instrument design for "Music" in Dodge's *Cascando*.

voice signal from a constant corresponding to the average peak amplitude. When the incoming voice was "on," its signal was comb-filtered at three different frequencies, both in parallel and in series, and fed on to the "nonverbal syntax" section of the instrument.

When the incoming voice was "off," its absence caused the amplitude inverter to build up and, as it did so, to drive the noise generator that was then gated repeatedly to produce "rustling," "thumping," and "scurrying" sounds. The output of the low-pass filter that acts as the gate was fed to the previously mentioned "nonverbal syntax" section of the instrument.

The final output of the instrument consists of pitch sound alone, noise sound alone, or a mixture of the two, depending on the parameters set in the score. These parameters, which control the nonverbal syntax, cause Music for the whole composition to follow, very slowly, the phonemic succession of Voice for its first solo. The preponderance of pitch or noise at a given moment in Music is a reflection of the phonemic sound (voiced or unvoiced) at the corresponding place in the first Voice solo. The pitches of

Music partake in the structure as well, in that the pitch succession for the whole composition is directly related to the succession of pitches in the first Voice solo.

Paul Lansky's *Six Fantasies on a Poem by Thomas Campion*[32] contains elegant demonstrations of musical uses of linear predictive coding in speech synthesis by analysis. In each of the six movements, Lansky emphasizes a different aspect of a single reading of the poem by actress Hannah MacCay. The composer writes, "My main intention was to explicate the implicit music in a poetry reading so that the reading itself, at the end, is explicitly musical."[33]

The procedure in the first fantasy was to "warp" the pitch contour of the recited poem. Generally, the pitch range of the original was widened and the contours were exaggerated. Then, Lansky mixed together the outputs of three separate syntheses. The pitches all change continuously in parallel intervals, while the intervals separating the voices change at different places in the poem.

The second fantasy uses two versions of the synthetic voice with different, sometimes inverted, pitch contours that proceed at different speeds. The voices and phrases end together on the same pitch (usually a vowel), which is then prolonged as a single note. Lansky has pointed out that the coda of this fantasy puts all the prolonged notes together into a paraphrase of a Campion song, "Tune thy music to thy hart." The long tones were made by elongating the desired vowel sound in the way discussed in section 7.1H. The particular sound was achieved by applying more than one impulse generator to the voice filter. The generators are tuned very close together, and each has a small random fluctuation of its frequency so that it beats with the other generators. Because the frequency of the beating falls well within the limits of discrimination, the result sounds somewhat smoother than a single randomly fluctuating generator. The reverberation applied to the final result further smooths the output.

Fantasies 3 and 5 make extensive use of reverberation techniques, and so they will be discussed in chapter 10.

In the fourth fantasy, there is no sound other than the multiple versions of the voice that articulates the poem largely in rhythmic unison and in chords that change from one section to another. The sound is created in a manner similar to that of Fantasy 2, but with the difference that here there is no pitch tracking of the original voice.

The final fantasy displays a pitched background of sustained tones made from vowel timbres that "capture and fix" certain pitches through which the reciting voice passes. This procedure is analogous to the way in which a comb filter "rings" inputs of certain frequencies. (See section 10.1B). Here, the prolonged tone is of the same vowel timbre as the syllable of the text that it prolongs.

In his *Six Fantasies on a Poem by Thomas Campion,* Lansky not only elaborates on the uses of linear predictive coding for speech synthesis by analysis, but also demonstrates the signal-processing possibilities of certain computer music techniques, such as comb filtering. The combination of techniques creates a depth of sound quality rarely achieved before in computer music synthesis. Another example of Lansky's use of LPC which also extensively incorporates granular synthesis will be presented in section 8.5.

At an early stage of her career, composer Frances White used a variety of cross-synthesis techniques to create a body of substantial works. The music, for tape alone, for live computer music realization, and for computer music with live instruments, has been performed widely and several works have been awarded international prizes.

One of her favorite musical devices is to create works that are based on recorded speech where the music is still understood as nonverbal. Her *Ogni Pensiero Vola* uses cross-synthesis of greatly time-distended speech analysis with highly filtered pitched and noise-based sonorities. In the course of that work, the speech comes closer and closer to the surface, until at the very end the title phrase of the work is heard with a minimum of modification.

Valdrada[34] is a work that uses speech analysis/synthesis techniques to produce intriguing textures that, while reminiscent of speech, are understood as "pure," nonverbal music. That said, the work is nonetheless based on a recorded reading of the Valdrada section of Italo Calvino's prose poem, "Invisible Cities." The work strives to depict the image of Valdrada, a city situated on a lake where the observer is presented with a double image of the city—the "real" one above, and the reflection in the lake below. White's work plays with the notions of doubleness and mirror image in a number of ways. Her work divides neatly into three parts.

Part 1 is based on the analysis and resynthesis of only the unvoiced parts of the recording of the text. Here, the excitation source for the resynthesis filter is itself a sharply filtered burst of noise that sounds a chordal texture. The first part has the sharp rhythmic articulation of the percussive qualities of speech. Part 2 is much less rhythmically articulated. It is based on the vowel portions of the analyzed speech. Part 3 brings the work to a close by combining the characteristics of the previous two parts into a texture that is almost speechlike.

Still Life with Piano[35] is a work for live piano and tape. In this work, the live piano plays passages—very sparse for the most part—that were previously recorded. The recording was analyzed and resynthesized with cross synthesis in such a way as to change the timing, the pitch content, and the piano timbre to a great extent. The overall effect is to create the illusion of two separate, seemingly unrelated characters wandering through the same landscape who meet up occasionally to exchange something that is not altogether clear. This intentional ambiguity is one of the most attractive features of the work.

In Judy Klein's *From the Journals of Felix Bosonnet*,[36] diverse sonic material gathered for the piece is skillfully marshaled in the creation of a powerful aesthetic statement. It is one of those rare works that can always be cited as certain proof that electronic technology can be used in the service of truly moving art.

The work is a hybrid of techniques and genres owing something to *hörspiel* (radio drama) as well as to *musique concrète* and computer music. Central to the effect of the work is the recorded spoken three-part text (in German) taken from the final entries in the Swiss writer's diaries before his suicide. In the first part, he describes his observations of the Central Train Station of his city, Basel, in the middle of the night when the only people to be seen are the homeless and the disaffected of the population. The second part is more fragmentary and the third was left unfinished.

The parts of the work that are not recorded speech were made with a variety of techniques for altering recorded sound. Perhaps the most striking effect in the work was the use of LPC analysis/synthesis on recorded cowbell sounds. The source is a recording of an entire group of cowbells (on cows—recorded live on a Swiss mountainside). The recording was then analyzed and resynthesized in much the same manner as would be the sound of the human voice, but with some differences.

The playback of the synthesis was slowed (in some places as slow as 1/100 of the original speed), allowing the microstructure of the gamelan-like group of bells to be heard. In the first part, a GBUZZ generator (see section 5.3B) is used to excite the LPC filter instead of the standard BUZZ generator, allowing the composer to designate the lowest and highest of a group of contiguous harmonics. Limiting the spectrum to harmonics 8 through 16 of a very low fundamental frequency, for example, produces both a drone and, depending on the relationship at a given moment between the sharp resonances introduced by the cowbell harmonics and the frequencies of the source sounds, melissma-like tones playing in a sort of eight-tone scale with quasi-just intonation. When the group of harmonics of the source is changed, the effect can be quite different. For instance, using harmonics 4 through 12 produces sequences that include harmonic arpeggios.

The LPC synthesis in the second section uses a noise generator to excite the all-pole filter. The partials of the bells are only hinted at, and one hears prominently the unfolding of the bells' amplitude envelopes. This section features a long cross-fade with a group of comb filters tuned to the same "scales" of harmonics described above. Gradually, the high sine-like tones of the comb filters come to replace the opening noise-like sounds of the section.

The final part of the work is made from the manipulation of the sound of a crystal glass struck by a fingernail. The duration of the sound is extended by looping (see section 10.3), and its pitch is altered by changing the sampling rate. This section was made using a Fairlight II Computer Music Instrument.

7.1J Concept of Linear Prediction

The technique of linear prediction has been available for many years and has been used in several fields. In recent years, the application of linear prediction to the analysis of speech has proven to be an excellent method for estimating the parameters of speech. The purpose of this section is to acquaint the reader with the basic concept of linear prediction. The reader wishing to approach the formidable mathematics involved is encouraged to begin by examining J. Makhoul's tutorial[37] on the subject.

The following problem is of interest in sampled data systems. Given a digital system, can the value of any sample be predicted by taking a linear combination of the previous N samples? *Linear combination* here means that each of the N previous samples is multiplied by its own coefficient and the products are added together. Stating the question mathematically, can a set of coefficients, b_k, be determined such that:

$$y(n) = b_1 y(n-1) + b_2 y(n-2) + \cdots + b_N y(n-N)$$

(The notation used in this equation was introduced in section 6.11 to describe digital filters.) If the answer is yes, then the coefficients and the first N samples of a signal would completely determine the remainder of the signal, because the rest of the samples can be calculated by the equation above.

With a finite N, the predictor coefficients generally cannot be precisely determined. What is normally done is to take a group of samples (one frame) and determine the coefficients that give the best prediction throughout the frame. The relative merit of a set of predictors can be evaluated by taking the difference between the actual sample values of the input waveform and the waveform re-created using the derived predictors. The error, $e(n)$, between the actual value, value, $y(n)$, and the predicted value, $\tilde{y}(n)$, is

$$e(n) = \tilde{y}(n) - y(n)$$

Thus, for each sample of the speech waveform, a corresponding error value can be calculated. The digital signal, $e(n)$, represents the errors and is called the *residual*. The smaller its average value, the better is the set of predictors. Schemes for determining predictors work either explicitly or implicitly on the principle of minimizing the residual.

The residual has another use. The original signal $y(n)$ can be exactly regenerated by calculating it according to

$$y(n) = a_0 e(n) + b_1 y(n-1) + b_2 y(n-2) + \cdots + b_N y(n-N)$$

where a_0 is a scaling factor that gives the correct amplitude. The reader may recognize this equation from section 6.13 as an all-pole, recursive filter with the residual applied to its input. Figure 7.13 shows this configuration schematically.

Examination of the character of the residual of a speech wave suggests a further simplification. When the speech is voiced, the residual is essentially a periodic pulse waveform with the same fundamental frequency as the speech. When the speech is unvoiced, the residual is similar to white noise. Thus, the LPC synthesis model that was presented in figure 7.8 is based on this simplification of the character of the residual. When the nonvocal sounds (e.g., tones of musical instruments) are analyzed, the residual sometimes has a different character. In this case, resynthesis using the excitation sources of the speech synthesizer will produce sounds that are dissimilar to the original.

The order of the predictor, N, determines the accuracy of the representation. The accuracy of this method improves as N gets larger, but so does the amount of computation required. What is the smallest value of N that will maintain sufficient quality in the speech representation? The answer is directly related to the highest frequency in the

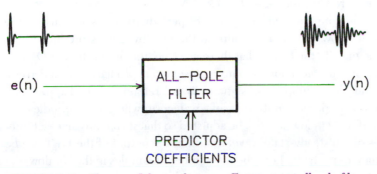

FIGURE 7.13   The use of the predictor coefficients in an all-pole filter to reconstitute the analyzed speech waveform from the residual.

speech, the number of formant peaks expected, and the sampling rate. There is no exact relationship, but in general N is between 10 and 20. A rule of thumb that has been used by some researchers is to take N as 4 plus the sampling rate in kilohertz. Thus, a system with a 15-kHz sampling rate might use $N = 19$.

The prediction of the filter coefficients for a frame makes the assumption that the process of speech production is stationary during the frame; that is, the excitation and response of the vocal tract do not change during the frame. This is usually a reasonable assumption, although audible distortion can sometimes result. This distortion can be minimized by interpolating filter coefficients between frames during the resynthesis process.

7.2   SHORT-TERM FOURIER TRANSFORM

Under the right conditions, the discrete Fourier transform (DFT) can be used to determine the spectrum of a digital signal. Its most common implementation, the fast Fourier transform (FFT), was first developed by Cooley and Tukey[38] and has made spectral analysis available for solving a broad variety of problems in many fields. The analyses produced by the DFT and FFT algorithms are identical; the only difference between them is the greatly increased computation speed afforded by the FFT as a result of a clever reordering of the operations in the DFT. Fast Fourier transform algorithms are now widely available on computer systems that process sound. The assumptions and concomitant limitations behind the algorithm are generally not apparent to the users of these systems; this section will discuss them.

To know truly the spectrum of a time-varying signal, its waveform must be known for all time; a mathematician would say that the signal $f(t)$ must be known for all t from $-\infty$ to $+\infty$. This is an unrealistic requirement for a real signal. As a result, a series of short-term Fourier transforms (STFTs)[39] is taken; that is, a succession of FFTs is performed on small portions of the waveform. The input to a particular FFT is said to be a *windowed* portion of the signal because it represents only a snapshot of the sound.

The digital signal $x(n)$ input to the FFT is a sequence of N samples windowed from the signal to be analyzed. The output, often denoted by $X(k)$, is a set of N values that describe the spectrum of the input waveform. To take full advantage of the speed inherent in the FFT algorithm, N must be chosen as an integer power of 2. The N entries in $X(k)$ are generally numbered between $k = 0$ and $k = N - 1$.

Implicit in this technique are the assumptions of periodicity and stationarity—the waveform inside the window repeats itself outside the window and is produced by a process that is unchanging. To the extent that these are true, the output from a DFT or FFT algorithm can be interpreted as an accurate representation of a harmonic spectrum. In the analysis of sound, the assumption of stationarity is a reasonably good approximation during the steady-state portion, if it exists, of a waveform where it is periodic or at least nearly periodic. If the window size can be adjusted so that it contains an exact integer number of cycles of the steady-state waveform, then the output of the DFT can be interpreted as a harmonic spectrum. Let N be the number of samples in the window; the assumed fundamental frequency of the signal being analyzed, f_0, is given by

$$f_0 = \frac{f_s}{N}.$$

The output $X(k)$ is called the kth "channel" of the FFT and contains both the amplitude and the phase of the corresponding spectral component. The component denoted by $X(k)$ is assumed to appear at the frequency kf_0 for values of k between 0 and $N/2$. Hence, the output value in channel 0, $X(0)$, corresponds to the 0-Hz (dc) component of the waveform, $X(1)$ represents the amplitude centered at f_0, and so on up to $X(N/2)$, which falls at the Nyquist frequency. Greater frequency resolution in the form of closer channel spacing can be obtained by increasing the number of samples in the window. However, a larger N increases the computation requirements and usually reduces the amount of stationarity of the process enclosed in the window.

The higher-numbered channels with values of k between $N/2 + 1$ and $N - 1$ correspond to the negative frequencies given by $(k - N)f_0$. Thus, for example, with $N = 32$ the output $X(30)$ would be centered at $-2f_0$. The negative frequencies are an artifact of the mathematics used to define the Fourier transform and do not have direct physical significance. The magnitude of the outputs found in the channels centered at frequencies kf_0 and $-kf_0$ will always have the same value because the FFT formulation represents half of the amplitude of a particular component in the positive-frequency channel and the other half in the corresponding negative one. The phase of an output channel centered at frequency $-kf_0$ will be the negative of the phase of the channel output at kf_0. Thus, to display the spectrum of a sound, all one needs to know is $X(k)$ from $k = 0$ to $k = N/2$ and double the amplitudes of each of these channels. Because channel 0 (dc) and channel $N/2$ (the Nyquist frequency) have no corresponding negative-frequency channels, the amplitudes in these two special channels should not be doubled.

Even after doubling the appropriate channel values, the outputs are a factor of N larger than the actual amplitudes of the spectral components in the waveform. The inverse DFT and FFT algorithms incorporate this factor of $1/N$ in their algorithm so that if $X(k)$ is going to be returned to the time domain with an inverse transform no action is required. However, if $X(k)$ is going to be displayed as an analytic result or resynthesized by some other means, the value in each positive-frequency channel should be divided by N, after it is doubled.

The original waveform in the window $x(n)$ can be reconstituted by taking an inverse DFT or FFT of $X(k)$. However, the reason to take a Fourier transform is to be able to examine and modify the signal in the frequency domain. Except in the special circumstances described below, $X(k)$ does not represent an exact spectrum of $x(n)$, so that taking the inverse FFT of the modified $X(k)$ does not produce the expected result.

A discrete Fourier transform (or FFT) does not have the ability to directly measure the fundamental frequency of any arbitrary waveform. Instead, the algorithm can be thought of as a bank of band-pass filters—one for each channel. If the fundamental frequency of the waveform under analysis happens to fall *exactly* at the center frequency of one of the filters in the bank, the results will be accurate; if not, the outputs $X(k)$ will not properly represent the components of a harmonic spectrum. As shown in figure 7.14, each filter is centered on the frequency of its channel but is not perfectly selective. For instance,

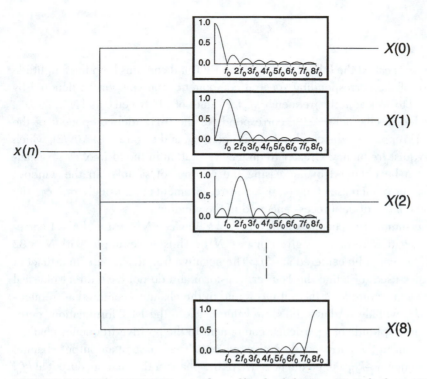

FIGURE 7.14   The DFT/FFT viewed as a filter bank for $N = 16$. Only the positive-frequency channels are shown.

the filter centered on channel 1 passes primarily information at the frequency f_0 but also can respond to energy at other frequencies as well. The filter for channel 5 is centered at the frequency $5f_0$, and so forth. Each filter in the bank has an amplitude response of 0 for all harmonics of f_0 except for the one on which it is centered. Therefore, when the signal under analysis is truly periodic with a frequency that is an integer multiple of f_0, each filter responds to energy only at its center frequency; all other harmonics are completely rejected. This situation is known as *pitch-synchronous analysis* and allows the FFT to extract the precise amplitudes of the harmonic partials in a periodic waveform.

An example will be used to illustrate the desirability of pitch synchronicity in the discrete Fourier analysis of sound. The sampling rate will be assumed to be 32 kHz and the window length will be chosen as $N = 32$ so that the channel spacing is $f_0 = 1$ kHz. The waveform to be analyzed is periodic and contains two spectral components: a fundamental with an amplitude of 1 and a third harmonic with an amplitude of 1/3. Initially, the waveform will be repeated at a frequency of 2 kHz. Because the fundamental frequency of this input signal is an integer harmonic of the channel spacing, the FFT analysis will be pitch synchronous. The magnitude of the output of the FFT, scaled by $2/N$ and shown in figure 7.15a, contains information in channels 2 and 6 at the expected amplitudes. Only channels 0 through 16 are presented in the figure because channels 17 through 31 represent negative frequencies and do not provide additional information.

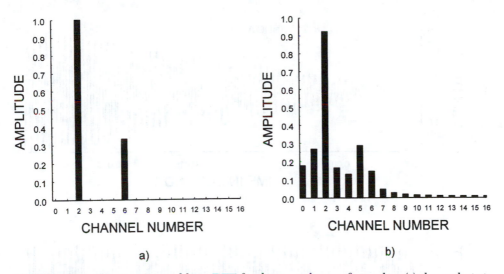

FIGURE 7.15   Spectra reported by a DFT for the example waveform when (a) the analysis is pitch synchronous, and (b) when it is not.

Now suppose that the frequency of the input waveform is changed to 1.8 kHz. Figure 7.15b displays the magnitude of the corresponding FFT output and demonstrates the effect of lack of pitch synchronicity. The principal response of the fundamental will occur in channel 2 because its 2-kHz center frequency is closest to 1.8 kHz. The response in this channel will be less than the expected amplitude of unity because the fundamental does not fall precisely at the center frequency of the channel filter. Another peak appears in channel 5 because its 5-kHz center frequency is closest to the 5.4-kHz frequency of the third harmonic. Even though the input signal contains only two spectral components, the FFT reports spectral energy in all channels, owing to leakage through the channel filters. If one were to attempt to re-create the analyzed waveform by means of additive synthesis with these data, the result would not sound like the original. Some decrease in the dispersion of the reported spectrum can be obtained by choosing a larger value of N, but the only truly accurate approach is to choose the window length such that one of the channels is centered precisely at 1.8 kHz. When this condition is satisfied, a higher channel will fall at 5.4 kHz because it is an integer multiple of the fundamental.

Even when the waveform is pitch synchronous with the analysis window, an envelope on the waveform can lead to a misinterpretation of the spectral components. For example, during the attack portion of an acoustic waveform, the condition of stationarity is violated because the amplitude of the waveform is constantly increasing. Suppose that the sinusoidal waveform enclosed in the linear attack envelope shown in figure 7.16a were being analyzed and the indicated window was defined to comprise exactly eight cycles of the waveform. The assumption of stationarity in the definition of the FFT means that it would proceed as if it were analyzing the steady-state waveform in figure 7.16b—a sine-wave amplitude modulated by a sawtooth wave. The computed spectrum shown in figure 7.17, instead of exhibiting the single spectral component characteristic

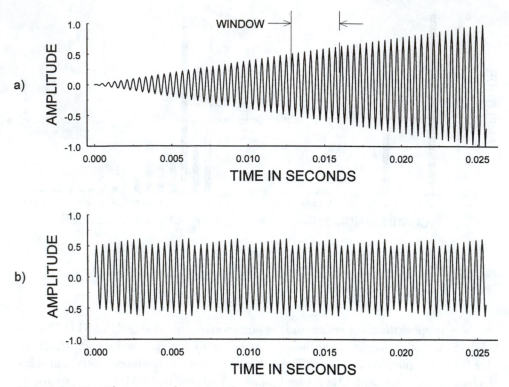

FIGURE 7.16   When an attack portion of a waveform (a) is analyzed in a window such as the one indicated, the FFT algorithm assumes that it is a periodic waveform encased in a sawtooth envelope of the form shown in (b).

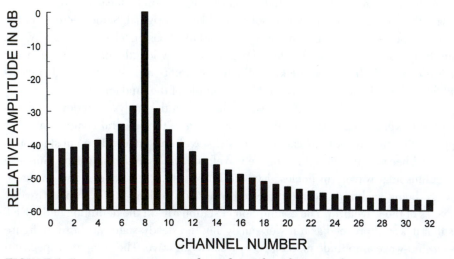

FIGURE 7.17   Discrete Fourier transform of a windowed portion of a sine wave with an increasing envelope. The amplitude (in dB) is relative to the highest spectral component.

of a sine wave only in channel 8, would spread around the fundamental frequency of the sine wave.

In summary, the DFT and its high-speed descendant, the FFT, can be viewed as a bank of band-pass filters that report the net amplitude of the spectral components that pass through each filter. They can determine the spectral distribution of the energy in a sound to the extent that the process that produced the sound satisfies the assumptions of periodicity and stationarity and also to the degree that the analysis window is pitch synchronous. As a filter bank, these algorithms are not capable of determining the precise frequency of a spectral component; they are limited by the resolution of the band-pass filters, and therefore cannot track the fine-grained frequency variations found in natural sounds without the help of additional algorithms.

Because natural sounds exhibit amplitude and frequency fluctuations during their course, true pitch-synchronous analysis is generally not a practical technique. The choice of N, the number samples in the window, is a compromise. A large value increases the frequency resolution but reduces the stationarity of the observed process. The performance of the FFT can be improved by multiplying the input waveform by an appropriate *window function*, which has its maximum value in the center of the window and tapers to a small value at each edge of the window. Each sample of the input waveform is multiplied by the corresponding sample on the window function to produce a result such as the one shown in figure 7.18.

The shape of the window function has a large influence on the frequency response of the band-pass filter bank of the FFT. The choice of a window function sets two important parameters: the bandwidth of the channel filters and the depth of the filter stopband. A fundamental relationship exists: a lower stopband is obtained at the expense of an

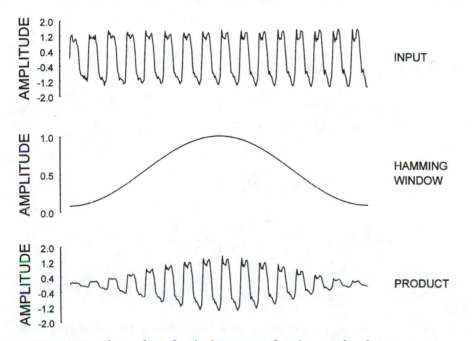

FIGURE 7.18 The product of multiplying a waveform by a window function.

increase in the bandwidth of the filter. For example, when the input signal is not multiplied by a window (sometimes this is called using a rectangular window) the filter is one channel wide and the stopband is down at least 13 dB. By contrast, the popular Hamming window is four channels wide but has a much better stopband attenuation of at least 53 dB. Numerous window functions are available to make the appropriate compromise for the purpose of the analysis.[40] The Kaiser window is notable because it is controlled by a single parameter that adjusts the bandwidth and stopband to the optimum compromise.

To characterize a sound, a succession of windows is analyzed to obtain a series of short-term spectra. Best results, especially when the frequency-domain data are to be modified prior to resynthesis, are obtained when the windows are overlapped as shown in figure 7.19. Generally, the offset between windows is chosen to be the window length divided by the window bandwidth. As an example, consider a Hamming window with a length of 1024 samples. The bandwidth of this type of window is four samples, so that the windows would be spaced 1024 ÷ 4 = 256 samples apart.

One application of the overlapping series of FFTs is the determination of amplitude and frequency parameters for additive synthesis. This information is extracted from the succession of computed spectra by tracking the significant peaks.[41] Figure 7.20 displays the positive-frequency components of a 512-point FFT; nine significant peaks would be reported for this window.

The technique of peak tracking works best on periodic or nearly periodic inputs. Upon resynthesis, the amplitude and frequency functions are linearly interpolated between analyzed points. The technique can have difficulty analyzing inharmonic sounds as well as sounds with a significant noise component. Serra and Smith have developed an extension of this method, which also identifies the random portion of the signal for inclusion in the resynthesis.[42]

FIGURE 7.19   The use of overlapping Hamming windows in the spectral analysis of a waveform.

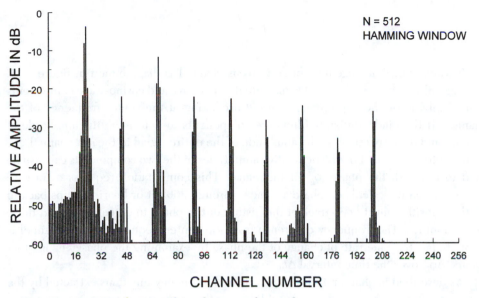

FIGURE 7.20   FFT of one window of an example signal.

7.3   PHASE VOCODER

7.3A   Basic Technique

Like the STFT, the *phase vocoder*[43] is a channelized analysis tool that measures the amplitude of the spectral components of a signal in frequency bands. The phase vocoder has the added benefit of also measuring the frequency deviation of each component from the center frequency of its channel. For instance, suppose that the window length is chosen such that the channel spacing is $f_0 = 50$ Hz. Applying a 440-Hz sinusoidal input to the algorithm would produce the largest output in channel 9 (centered at 450 Hz), but the phase vocoder would also be able to determine that the signal was –10 Hz away from the center frequency of the channel. Hence, the phase vocoder is well suited to the analysis of musical tones because it can track the fine-grained variation of the frequencies of each spectral component characteristic of natural sound.

As with the Fourier transform, the phase vocoder can be viewed as a bank of band-pass filters. The phase vocoder algorithm is most successful when the number of input samples is adjusted for pitch synchronicity within a few percent so that the harmonics align fairly well with the center frequency of the channel filters. Specifying the number of filters used (*N*) represents a compromise—there must be enough filters such that no more than one spectral component falls in any one channel, but a large *N* slows the computation of the analysis. As an additional complication, a large *N* connotes a narrow bandwidth of each channel filter, and very narrow filters may respond too slowly to extract sufficient fine-grained detail from the signal. For a periodic or nearly periodic input signal with a fundamental frequency of f_i, the optimum choice is

$$N = \frac{f_s}{f_i}$$

The functional arrangement of an analysis channel is diagrammed in figure 7.21. The algorithm separates the input signal into its sine-wave and cosine-wave components by multiplying by the appropriate sinusoid oscillating at the center frequency of the channel. It then independently filters the components to determine the amplitude of each (a_k and b_k, respectively). The amplitude of the entire signal in the kth channel, A_k, is now determined as shown. The relative amplitudes of the two components can also be used to establish the phase (ϕ_k) of the signal. This computation requires extra care because when the calculated phase advances through 360°, it ordinarily jumps back to 0°; the algorithm must keep track of the history of the phase to detect and avoid these discontinuities. The frequency difference from the center frequency of the channel is computed as the time rate of change of the phase by examining the phase change that occurs, $\Delta\phi_k$, over the time interval Δt.

As described in chapter 4, the amplitude and frequency functions extracted by the phase vocoder can be applied to an additive-synthesis instrument to reconstitute the original sound. In doing this, one should note that the frequency functions express the *deviation* from the channel filter center frequency; hence, resynthesis of the original tone requires the frequency kf_0 to be added to the kth frequency function before it is applied to the kth oscillator in the instrument. Of course, a musician may modify the sound by specifying frequencies other than kf_0.

The phase vocoder algorithm does not actually implement the N different channel filters directly. Instead, considerable computational efficiency is accrued by cleverly combining the channel operations in a manner originated by Portnoff.[44] Like the output of an STFT, half of the N channels are located at positive frequencies; the other half reside at negative frequencies. Because the data in the negative-frequency channels

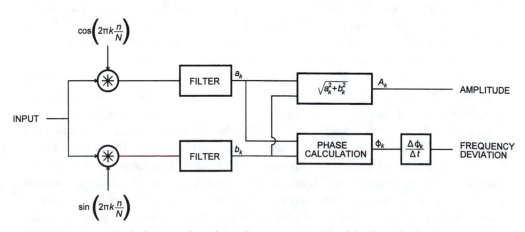

FIGURE 7.21   Block diagram describing the operation of the kth channel of a phase vocoder (n is the current sample number of the input data).

bear a direct relationship to their positive-frequency counterparts (see section 7.2), the negative-frequency outputs need not be reported.

The phase vocoder has the potential to generate a much larger data set than the input signal. Each of the $N/2$ positive-frequency channels provides an amplitude and a frequency deviation output for a total of N outputs. If these outputs are produced at the sampling rate, the data needed to represent the sound grow by a factor of N from the original waveform. Such a large expansion is generally neither practical nor necessary. When the process used to produce the sound is slowly varying, the output of the phase vocoder need only be computed every R samples. This establishes a frame rate, f_r, of

$$f_r = \frac{f_s}{R}$$

R must be small enough so that the frame rate adequately samples the time variation in the spectrum. A typical choice is $R = N/4$.[45] In this case, the data set contains twice as many samples as the original waveform. The data are often further reduced by approximating the amplitude and frequency functions with straight-line segments (see section 4.7).

Because the phase vocoder is based on a quasi-harmonic model of a monophonic tone, it is less successful when it is applied to inharmonic or polyphonic tones. The results of such analyses can be resynthesized when no modifications are made to the parameters. However, spectral components combined in the same channel lose their identity, so that the effect of changing their combination is much less predictable.

7.3B Musical Uses of the Phase Vocoder

The phase vocoder was introduced to computer music by J. A. Moorer.[46] Researchers have used it to analyze the nature of the spectrum and the perception of musical timbres. It has been particularly valuable for demonstrating the slightly inharmonic relationship that exists between the frequencies of the components in a pitched sound. The analyzed result also tracks vibrato well, even to the point of extracting the fine-grained frequency variation present on each spectral component.

For the musician, the phase vocoder offers the opportunity to make musically interesting changes to the spectrum of a natural tone before resynthesizing it. The most attractive feature and common usage of the phase vocoder for the modification of sound is the ability to independently modify the frequency and duration of a sound. The time occupied by a tone may be stretched or compressed without affecting its pitch. Multiplying the overall duration by a constant lengthens all portions of the sound. Because the majority of timbral identification occurs during the attack portion, the new tone may bear less timbral resemblance to the original than expected. This timbre change may or may not be musically desirable. To enhance the similarity with the original sound, especially when the tone is lengthened, the duration of the attack portion of the waveform can be preserved while the remainder of the tone is stretched.

The phase vocoder also enables the pitch of a tone to be modified without affecting its duration. In reconstituting a tone by means of additive synthesis, the kth channel is normally centered at the frequency kf_0, but different pitches can be obtained by centering the channels elsewhere. The simple example of transposing the pitch down an octave is realized by adding $kf_0/2$ instead of kf_0 to the kth frequency deviation function. If it is desired that the frequency deviations be the same percentage of the channel frequency as in the original, the frequency functions would be scaled by 1/2. As explained in section 2.6, the resulting sound may not exhibit timbral similarity to the original because the formant frequencies are also reduced by a factor of 2. Large transpositions of speech sounds may make them unintelligible. Smaller transpositions may have the effect of changing the perceived size of the speaker.

Other operations, such as those detailed in the speech-editing system used to modify linear predictive coding (LPC) data described in section 7.1H, can be applied prior to resynthesizing a phase-vocoded tone. The only difference is that changing the frequency in an LPC model does not shift the formants. At the cost of additional computation time, it is possible to analyze a tone with both a phase vocoder and LPC. The results are then combined in such a way that the original spectral envelope determined by LPC is applied to the modified phase vocoder data so that the pitch may be shifted without moving the formants.[47]

7.3C   Compositional Examples

One of the most effective analysis-based works of computer synthesis is Jonathan Harvey's tape work *Mortuos Plango, Vivos Voco*[48] realized at IRCAM with the aid of Stanley Haynes in 1980. The source recordings for the work were of two sorts: bell sounds and the singing voice. Harvey sets the context of the work by writing,

> It is a very personal piece in that the two sound sources are the voice of my son and that of the great tenor bell at Winchester Cathedral, England. I have written much music for the choir there, in which my son was a treble chorister, and have often listened to the choir practicing against a background of the distant tolling of this enormous black bell. The text for the voice is the text written on the bell: Horas Avolantes Numero, Mortuos Plango: Vivos ad Preces Voco (I count the fleeing hours, I lament the dead: the living I call to prayer). In the piece the dead voice of the bell is contrasted against the living voice of the boy.[49]

One of the remarkable things about the piece is how the voice and the bell are used to extend the meaning of each other. This is done through both pitch and rhythm. The work opens with a peeling of bells that gradually settles down to the prominent tolling of the tenor bell transposed to frequencies of partials contained in the original tenor tone itself. Over this is then introduced the voice sounding the most prominent partials contained in the sound of the bell, as well. One hears numerous examples throughout the work of this sort of pitch borrowing from the bell to the voice. Also, the repeated sounding of bell tones in the work is echoed in the pitch repetitions of the voice intoning the text on a single pitch near the beginning. Another prominent feature of the work is the way in which a change of envelope is used to transform the sharply articulated bell tone into a more diffuse or refracted harmonic structure. See section 4.12 for a similar practice of Jean-Claude Risset.

FIGURE 7.22   Spectral components of a bell sound used in Jonathan Harvey's *Mortuos Plango*. (*Reprinted with permission of* Computer Music Journal.)

At an early stage of work on the piece, the bell recording was analyzed. Its partials are shown in figure 7.22. In addition to the analyzed tones, a prominent F4 sounds as a result of the partials that form a harmonic series above that tone (e.g., harmonics 5, 6, 7, 9, 11, 13, 17, etc.) and are interleaved among the harmonics sounding at the same time above C3.

One of the most interesting aspects to the composition is the explicit relationship between the harmonic structure of the analyzed bell tone and the tonal centers of each of the work's eight sections. Each section is introduced by a bell tone transposed to the frequency of one of the lower harmonics of the original tone. The "bell-tonics" for the eight sections of the piece are shown in figure 7.23.

Rather than base each section simply on a transposition of all the harmonics by the same interval, Harvey uses a scheme for transforming the collection of harmonics from the original to the particular pitch center of each section. This works in the following way: figure 7.24 shows the transformation of the set of six partials starting with C4 into the set preserving the interval relationships beginning on the partial of E♭4, but transposed such that C5 remains a common tone between the two collections. This section may be heard beginning at around time 5:40 of the work. The other six transpositions are made in the same general way—by preserving a common tone in the middle of the pitch collection and transposing the other bell harmonics by the appropriate interval up or down to achieve the new pitch collection.

The work begins and ends with rather elaborate treatments of the "bell-tonics" on C4 and C3, with their attendant harmonics. By the time the C3-based section arrives, one has heard a great variety of harmony and diversity of pitch collections (listen for the B♭s and D♭s between 3:30 and 5:00). Thus, the final section of the piece displays the low-order harmonics of C3 (the first 8 or 9) in the bell along with a chord made up of transposed high-order harmonics in the voice. The effect seems to represent the final resolution of the piece in which the bell tones,

FIGURE 7.23   "Bell-tonics" for the eight sections of *Mortuous Plango*. (*Reprinted with permission of* Computer Music Journal.)

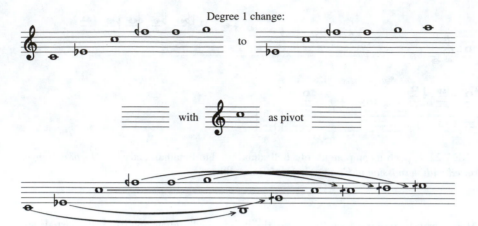

FIGURE 7.24   Transformation of the set of six partials. (*Reprinted with permission of* Computer Music Journal.)

having been thoroughly taken apart, are put back together, and multiple copies of the voice sound chords (chords, to be sure, made up of adjacent transposed harmonics).

A number of additional effects heard in the work are worth mentioning. Glissandoing plays a prominent role in the work—especially where partials of one bell chord move continuously in frequency to those of another. There are also places where the voice, through envelope change, is made more bell-like and the bell tones are made rather voice-like.

Richard Karpen's *Life Study #4* is a work based mainly on the digital signal processing of recorded sounds. Like its predecessors in Karpen's *Life Study* series, the work has been described as "aural cinema". In this work, one encounters a wide variety of sounds— galloping horses, cawing crows, human sounds (footsteps, indistinct speech), electronic sounds, and so on. Each sound is processed to place it into a new musical context created by Karpen's composition. While only one of a number of digital signal-processing techniques applied in the work, the phase vocoder is used to contribute one of the most striking sounds in the work, that of a recurring drone in the middle-high register. The drone was made by using only two of the higher channels of the phase vocoder analysis of a bagpipe drone and throwing the other channels away. The two high-frequency channels (channels 110 and 113) are then transposed down to the level at which we hear them. The transposition, in conjunction with the source, results in a very fluttery, uneven sounding drone composed of only two frequency components. While it cannot be said that the use of the phase vocoder formed the basis of the work, it is true that the phase vocoder provided just the right tool to create a striking sound for use in the composition.

Composer Joji Yuasa has a long experience in making music with speech recordings. In *Study in White,*[50] Yuasa uses phase-vocoding techniques to alter the speed of speech without changing its pitch contour, in some places, and to alter its timbre, through cross-synthesis, without changing its speed, in others. Perhaps the most strikingly phase vocoded passage of this two-movement work is the opening of the second movement, based on a poem of R. D. Laing. Here, the recorded voice is heard speaking a short phrase of the poem (a kind of imaginary dialog) and being answered by a time-distorted version of the same phrase.

As the composer indicates in his notes to the work, the phase vocoder and other processing of the recorded voice represent different layers of the personality of the poem's protagonist.

7.4 WAVELETS

In recent years, *wavelets* have become a widely used tool for the analysis of time-varying signals in a multiplicity of fields.[51] Wavelets allow the compromise between temporal and frequency resolution inherent in any analysis of sampled data to be optimized for a particular class of signals.

In Fourier analysis using the STFT (see section 7.2), the functions used as the basis for extracting the frequency-domain information are a series of harmonically related sine and cosine functions that extend over the entire length of the analysis window. For example, the functions used for computing the energy in the eighth channel (centered at $8f_0$) run through exactly eight cycles of the waveform during the window, while the functions for channel 1 (f_0) comprise only one cycle. Each channel in the resultant filter bank has the same bandwidth (Δf) and the channel center frequencies are uniformly spaced at harmonics of f_0.

Wavelet functions can take on many forms. The ones typically used for analyzing audio signals are sinusoids encased in an envelope as depicted in figure 7.25. To analyze a sound, a set of wavelets over a range of frequencies is applied. As the figure illustrates with two different wavelets shown, the duration of the envelope is adjusted with the frequency of the sinusoid, so that there is always the same number of cycles of the sinusoid in each wavelet. In other words, the higher the frequency of a wavelet, the shorter is its duration in an exact

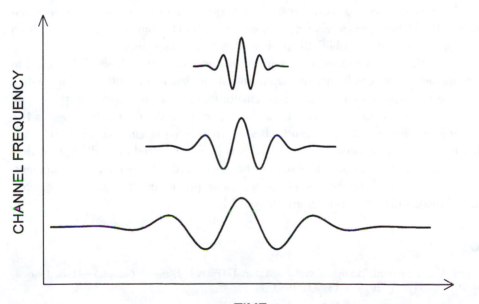

TIME

FIGURE 7.25   Two similar wavelet functions at different frequencies. Observe that each wavelet comprises the same number of cycles.

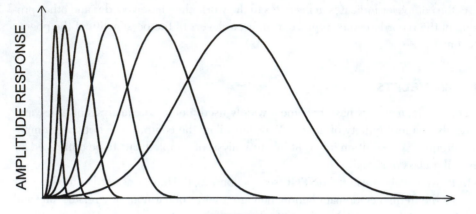

FIGURE 7.26   Frequency-domain interpretation of wavelet analysis as bank of filters.

inverse relationship. Like Fourier analysis, the result of analysis using wavelets can be viewed in the frequency domain as a bank of band-pass filters. However, in contrast to the constant bandwidth of the channel filters of the STFT, the channel filters produced using the wavelets shown have a constant ratio of $\Delta f{:}f$, where f is the center frequency of the filter. The filter bank displayed in figure 7.26 demonstrates how the bandwidth increases as the center frequency, and hence the channel number, of the filter increases. This characteristic is similar to the critical bands of human hearing where the bandwidth for discriminating frequency-domain information is approximately constant over most of the audible range. Looking at it another way, the wavelets used to obtain low-frequency information have a longer duration than the high-frequency wavelets. This corresponds to the human characteristic that a longer time is needed to establish the pitch of a low-frequency sound.

A wavelet analysis produces a record of the amplitude and phase of the signal in each channel. Sound can be resynthesized from these data in an additive fashion with a corresponding bank of oscillators.[52] The oscillator for each channel uses the appropriate wavelet function for its waveform. Transforming between domains with wavelets is a reversible process, so that the resynthesis will produce the original signal. As with the other techniques of this chapter, the musician is more interested in modifying the data prior to synthesis to create different sounds that are related to the original. The standard, previously described operations of independent pitch/time modification, spectral manipulation, and cross-synthesis are all available.

NOTES

1. Cann, Richard. "Analysis/Synthesis Tutorial" (Parts 1, 2, and 3). *Computer Music Journal,* 3(3), 1979, 6–11; 3(4), 1979, 9–13; 4(1), 1980, 36–42.

2. Rabiner, L. R., and Schafer, R. W. *Digital Processing of Speech Signals.* Englewood Cliffs, N.J.: Prentice-Hall, 1978, 38–106.

3. Fant, Gunnar. "The Acoustics of Speech." *Proceedings of the Third International Congress on Acoustics,* 1959, 188–201. (Reprinted in *Speech Synthesis,* James L. Flanagan and Lawrence R. Rabiner (eds.). Stroudsburg, Pa.: Dowden, Hutchinson, and Ross, 1973, 77–90.)

4. Mattingly, Ignatius. "Synthesis by Rule of General American English." Doctoral dissertation, Yale University, 1968, 133.

5. Potter, R. K., Koop, A. G., and Green, H. C. *Visible Speech.* New York: Van Nostrand Reinhold, 1947.

6. Peterson, G. E., and Barney, H. L. "Control Methods Used in a Study of Vowels." *Journal of the Acoustical Society of America,* 24(2), 1952, 175–184.

7. Olive, Joseph. "Automatic Formant Tracking in a Newton-Raphson Technique." *Journal of the Acoustical Society of America,* 50(2), 1971, 661–670.

8. Markel, J. D., and Gray, A. H., Jr. *Linear Prediction of Speech.* New York: Springer-Verlag, 1976.

9. Rabiner and Schafer, 135–158.

10. Fant, 188–201.

11. Rabiner and Schafer, 105.

12. Rabiner, L. R. "Digital Formant Synthesizer for Speech Synthesis Studies," *Journal of the Acoustical Society of America,* 43, 1968, 822–828. (Reprinted in *Speech Synthesis,* James L. Flanagan and Lawrence R. Rabiner (eds.). Stroudsburg, Pa.: Dowden, Hutchinson, and Ross, 1973, 255–261.)

13. Harris, Cyril M. "A Study of the Building Blocks in Speech." *Journal of the Acoustical Society of America,* 25, 1953, 962–969.

14. Rabiner, L. R. "Speech Synthesis by Rule: An Acoustic Domain Approach." *Bell System Technical Journal,* 47, 1968, 17–37.

15. Rabiner, L. R. "Digital Formant Synthesizer," 823.

16. Rabiner, L. R. "Speech Synthesis by Rule"; Coker, C. H., Umeda, N., and Browman, C. P. "Automatic Synthesis from Ordinary English Text." In James Flanagan and Lawrence Rabiner (eds.), *Speech Synthesis.* Stroudsburg, Pa.: Dowden, Hutchinson, and Ross, 1973, 400–411. Allen, J. "Speech Synthesis from Unrestricted Text." In James Flanagan and Lawrence Rabiner (eds.), *Speech Synthesis,* 416–428.

17. Sundberg, Johan. "The Acoustics of the Singing Voice." *Scientific American,* 236(3), 1977, 82–91.

18. Rodet, X., and Bennett, G. "Synthèse de la Voix Chantée Par Ordinateur." *Conferences des Journées d'Études, Festival International du Son,* 1980, 73–91.

19. Ibid.

20. Sundberg, Johan. "Synthesis of Singing." *Swedish Journal of Musicology,* 60(1), 1978, 107–112.

21. Ibid.

22. Sundberg, Johan. "Maximum Speed of Pitch Changes in Singers and Untrained Subjects." *Journal of Phonetics,* 7, 1979, 71–79.

23. Bennett, Gerald. "Singing Synthesis in Electronic Music" (Research Aspects on Singing) (Publication No. 33). Stockholm: Royal Swedish Academy of Music, 1981.

24. Atal, B. S., and Hanauer, S. L. "Speech Analysis and Synthesis by Linear Prediction of the Speech Wave." *Journal of the Acoustical Society of America,* 50, 1971, 637–655.

25. Makhoul, J. "Stable and Efficient Lattice Methods for Linear Prediction." *Institute of*

Electrical and Electronics Engineers Transactions on Acoustics, Speech, and Signal Processing, ASSP-25(5), 1977, 423–428.

26. Lansky, Paul, and Steiglitz, Kenneth. "Synthesis of Timbral Families by Warped Linear Prediction." *Computer Music Journal,* 5(3), 1981, 45–49.

27. Dodge, Charles. "The Story of Our Lives." CRI Records (CRI SD348), 1975.

28. Petersen, Tracy. "Voices." Tulsa, Okla.: Tulsa Studios, 1975.

29. Lansky, Paul. "MIX, a Program for Digital Signal Processing, Editing and Synthesis." Unpublished paper, Princeton University, 1983.

30. Dodge, Charles. "Speech Songs"; "In Celebration"; "The Story of Our Lives." CRI Records (CRI SD348), 1975.

31. Dodge, Charles. "Cascando." CRI Records (CRI SD454), 1983.

32. Lansky, Paul. "Six Fantasies on a Poem by Thomas Campion." CRI Records (CRI SD456), 1982 (re-released as CRI683, 1994).

33. Personal Commmunication, 1980.

34. White, Frances. "Valdrada." *Cultures Electroniques* 5, Le Chant du Monde. (LDC 278051/52), 1988.

35. White, Frances. "Still Life with Piano." *Cultures Electronique* 5, Le Chant de Monde (LDC 278051/52), 1988.

36. Klein, Judy. "From the Journals of Felix Bosonnet." On CD distributed at the 1989 International Computer Music Conference, Ohio State University.

37. Makhoul, J. "Linear Prediction, a Tutorial Review." *Proceedings of the Institute of Electrical and Electronics Engineers,* 63, 1975, 561–580.

38. Cooley, J. W., and Tukey, J. W. "An Algorithm for the Machine Computation of Complex Fourier Series." *Math Computation,* 19 (April), 1965, 297–301.

39. Allen, J. B., and Rabiner, L. R. "A Unified Approached to Short-Time Fourier Analysis and Synthesis." *Proceedings of the Institute of Electrical and Electronics Engineers,* 65(11), 1977, 1558–1564.

40. Harris, F. J. "On the Use of Windows for Harmonic Analysis with the Discrete Fourier Transform." *Proceedings of the Institute of Electrical and Electronics Engineers,* 66(1), 1978, 51–83.

41. Smith, J. O., and Serra, X. "PARSHL: An Analysis/Synthesis Program for Non-Harmonic Sounds Based on a Sinusoid Representation." *Proceedings of the 1987 International Computer Music Conference.* San Francisco: Computer Music Association, 1987.

42. Serra, X., and Smith, J. O. "Spectral Modeling Synthesis: A Sound Analysis/Synthesis System Based on Determinisitic Plus Stochastic Decomposition." *Computer Music Journal,* 14(4), 1990, 12–24.

43. Moorer, J. A. "The Use of the Phase Vocoder in Computer Music Applications." *Journal of the Audio Engineering Society,* 26 (Jan./Feb.), 1978, 42–45.

44. Portnoff, M. R. "Time-Frequency Representation of Digital Signals and Systems Based on Short-Time Fourier Analysis." *IEEE Transactions on Acoustics, Speech, and Signal Processing.* ASSP-28(1), 1980, 55–69.

45. Gordon, J. W., and Strawn, J. "An Introduction to the Phase Vocoder." In J. Strawn (ed.), *Digital Audio Signal Processing: An Anthology.* Los Altos, Calif.: Kaufmann, 1985, 238–239.

46. Moorer, J. A. "The Use of the Phase Vocoder."

47. Moore, F. R. *Elements of Computer Music.* Englewood Ciffs, N.J.: Prentice-Hall, 1991, 311–315.

48. Harvey, Jonathan. "Mortuous Plango, Vivos Voco." *Computer Music Currents 6,* Wergo (WER 2026–2), 1990.

49. Harvey, Jonathan. "Mortuos Plango, Vivos Voco: A Realization at IRCAM." *Computer Music Journal,* 5(4), 1981, 22–24.

50. Yuasa, Joji. "Study in White." *Computer Music Currents* 7, Wergo (WER 2027–2), 1990.

51. Kovačević, J., and Debanchies, I. (eds.). *Proceedings of the Institute of Electrical and Electronics Engineers: Special Issue on Wavelets,* 84(4), 1996.

52. Kronland-Martinet, R., and Grossman, A. "Application of Time-Frequency and Time-Scale Methods (Wavelet Transforms) to the Analysis, Synthesis, and Transformation of Natural Sounds." In G. DePoli, A. Piccalli, and C. Roads (eds.), *Representations of Musical Signals.* Cambridge: MIT Press, 1991, 45–86.

8

GRANULAR SYNTHESIS

There are several ways to view the anatomy of a sound. Its waveform records the progression of amplitude versus time, but offers only partial insight into what a listener might perceive. Considerable perceptual information is contained in the spectrum of a sound, but this representation is also limited because a spectral representation implies a constant (steady-state) signal. Granular synthesis is based on the idea that a steady-state waveform with its time-invariant spectrum, although mathematically convenient, is a physical impossibility because a waveform cannot exist for all time. It stems from a theory of acoustical quanta postulated by Gabor,[1] which recognizes that aural perception is performed in the time and frequency domains simultaneously. In this technique, the fundamental compositional elements that are used to weave the sound are *grains:* small bursts of sound energy encased in an envelope. This term is attributed to I. Xenakis,[2] who detailed an extensive theory of grain selection.

Organizing a large group of these fleeting events into a usable sound requires software that enables the composer to specify their structure on a higher level. Because an enormous number of grains are needed to produce a sound, the composer cannot designate the exact placement of each grain, but instead gives general rules for the generation of grains to the computer. The methods for controlling the temporal distribution of grains can be categorized into two main approaches. In the synchronous mode, the grains are triggered at fairly regular time intervals to produce a sound with a particular pitch period. Alternatively, the grains can be played asynchronously by randomizing the time between grains to produce a "cloud" of sound. This chapter will discuss the application of each method.

8.1 GRAIN PRODUCTION

The instrument diagrammed in figure 8.1 is one method for producing a grain of sound. The duration of the grain is generally set in the range of 5 to 50 ms to preclude a single grain from inducing a pitched response in the listener. The envelope generator is necessary because abruptly turning the waveform on and off without a transition region results in audible clicks. Several shapes have been used for the envelope; the attack and decay portions are usually mirror images of each other. Gabor used a Gaussian function (the classical bell-shaped curve) for his quanta, but the lack of a steady-state portion reduces the energy, and hence the aural effectiveness, of the grain. More typically, a "quasi-Gaussian" envelope is used where, as illustrated in the grain waveform shown in figure 8.2, the attack portion of the envelope is the left side of a bell curve. A constant-amplitude, steady-state segment follows, concluding with a decay conforming to the right side

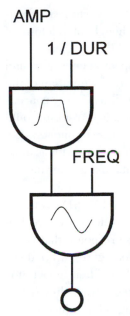

FIGURE 8.1   A method of producing a grain of sound.

of the bell curve. To conserve computing resources, the attack and decay portions are sometimes approximated with single line segments, resulting in a trapezoidal shape.

The waveform used in the oscillator of the grain generator can take a variety of shapes. The specification of a sinusoid concentrates the energy of the grain in the region of the fundamental frequency (FREQ). Using samples of natural sound for the waveform distributes the spectral energy in accord with the original source. Synthesized waveforms

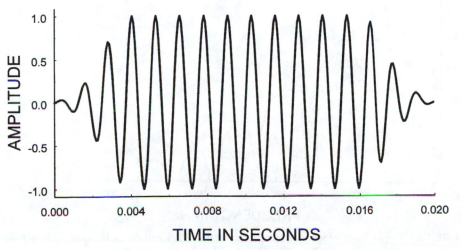

FIGURE 8.2   Example waveform of a grain of sound with a quasi-Gaussian envelope. An 800-Hz sine wave, activated for a duration of 20 ms, has identical attack and decay times of 4 ms.

such as band-limited pulses and FM signals have also been used. The resynthesis of analyzed data extracted using wavelets (see section 7.4) may also be thought of as a form of
granular synthesis where the oscillator waveforms take the shape of the wavelets.

Enclosing a periodic waveform in an envelope spreads the spectral energy around
its steady-state value by an amount that is inversely proportional to the duration of the
grain. For example, a steady-state 800-Hz sine wave would have all its energy concentrated at that frequency; the spectral envelope of a single burst of this waveform would
still be centered at 800 Hz, but would no longer comprise a single frequency. The
lengths of the attack and decay segments also influence the spectral bandwidth as illustrated in figure 8.3, which demonstrates that a faster attack results in a greater dispersion of energy across the spectrum.

There are other mechanisms for producing grains. The FOF and VOSIM systems,
to be described in section 8.2, use oscillators with customized waveforms that realize
particular spectral envelopes. Filters designed to have an impulse response that is the
desired grain waveform are another means of grain generation.[3] (See figure 8.4.) In these
designs, grains are triggered by applying impulses to the input of the filter. In fact, it is
possible to view the synthesis of vocal sounds using the linear predictive coding (LPC)
technique of section 7.1F as a form of granular synthesis. During the production of a
voiced sound, a train of impulses spaced in time by the pitch period is applied to an all-
pole filter whose characteristics are determined from a short-term analysis of a speech
waveform. The impulse response of the filter can be thought of as a grain that is successively triggered by the incoming pulses.

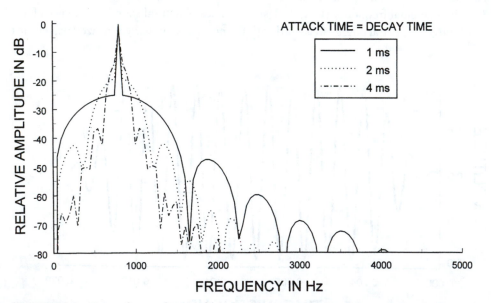

FIGURE 8.3   Dependence of spectral bandwidth on the attack and decay times of a 20-ms tone
burst with a quasi-Gaussian envelope. The enclosed waveform is an 800-Hz sine wave.

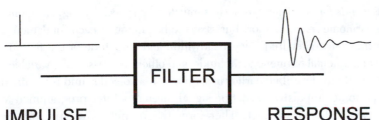

FIGURE 8.4   The use of a filter to produce a grain.

8.2   SYNCHRONOUS GRANULAR SYNTHESIS

The audible effect of a stream of grains depends not only on the waveforms in the individual grains, but also on the spacing between them. When the spacing is uniform or slowly changing (pitch synchronous mode), a sensation of pitch is perceived. Suppose that the duration of each grain in a stream is 20 ms and that as soon as one grain dies away, another begins. The repetition of grains at this constant rate results in a distinctly audible component that sounds steadily at 50 Hz (1 ÷ 20 ms). Higher pitches can be made by increasing the rate at which the grains are initiated as long as there are enough grain generators available. In other words, initiating 20-ms grains every 1 ms (a rate of 1 kHz) would require 20 instruments of the type depicted in figure 8.1 because each would have to run through its 20-ms sequence before it could begin another grain. In this regard, implementations using filters have an advantage because they can produce multiple impulse responses so that only one filter, pulsed at the rate of 1 kHz, would be required.

The spectral envelope of the waveform inside the grain determines the spectral envelope of the sound. For instance, repeating at a 220-Hz rate (A3) a grain enclosing a 3-kHz sine wave yields a spectrum containing the harmonics of 220 Hz; those nearest 3 kHz will receive the most amplitude emphasis. Increasing the rate to 261.6 Hz (C4) or any other frequency changes the spacing between the harmonics, but the peak of the spectral envelope still appears at 3 kHz. Thus, synchronous granular synthesis is a method of imparting a fixed formant into a sound, which explains the success of the FOF and VOSIM techniques described below in the synthesis of vocal sounds.

Synchronous granular synthesis is not restricted to the production of sounds with constant frequencies. Vibrato can be imparted to the sound by slowly varying the time spacing between grains. Glissandi can be realized by making the time between grain onsets a continuous function of time.

Two of the first examples of pitch-synchronous granular synthesis are the FOF and VOSIM techniques, which have been especially successful in the simulation of the singing voice. This section will discuss the principles of operation of these techniques, which generate grains with specially designed waveforms.

The synthesis model of Xavier Rodet,[4] employed in the Rodet and Gerald Bennett study, uses a scheme that creates a spectrum containing resonances without the use of filters. The computer system that implements the scheme is named Chant. Rodet's method, which he calls FOF (*fonctions d'onde formantique*) synthesis, simulates the speech by triggering multiple oscillators in a harmonic series or short bursts at the beginning of each fundamental pitch. The user specifies the center frequency, bandwidth, and amplitude of the five formants, as well as the fundamental frequency, amplitude, and other system-specific variables.

In the synthesis methods described earlier in section 7.1, a voiced sound is obtained by passing a quasi-periodic, impulsive excitation signal through a filter programmed to emulate the response of the vocal tract. Therefore, the output waveform can be described by the impulse response of the filter. Such a filter can be approximated as a group of second-order filter elements connected in parallel, one for each formant. When filters are connected in parallel, the impulse response of the complete filter is the sum of the impulse responses of the elements. In FOF synthesis, a digital oscillator is substituted for each filter element. Each oscillator is programmed, upon receipt of an impulse, to produce the waveform that is equivalent to the impulse response of the appropriate filter element. Figure 8.5 demonstrates how an impulse train excites each element so that the summation of all the responses results in a speechlike waveform. The π / β input controls the rolloff of the formant.

Rodet has analyzed both the male and the female professional singing voices to determine the parameters for a five-element FOF synthesizer and has created a catalog that contains the representation of many phonemes. This method offers the musician the conceptual simplicity of formant synthesis without computing the digital-filter algorithms.

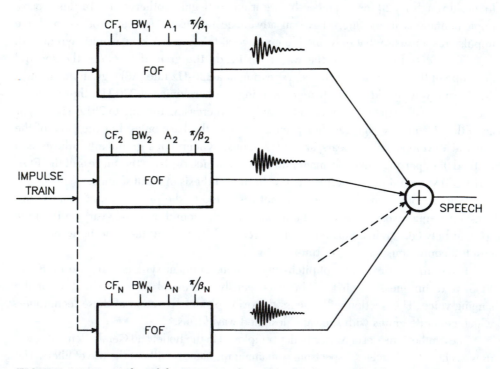

FIGURE 8.5   Basic plan of the FOF speech synthesizer. (*Reprinted with permission of Xavier Rodet.*)

Two advantages of this system are (1) the specified parameters bear a strong correlation to the acoustical attributes of the sound, and (2) the parameters must be updated only once per pitch period, making the program relatively efficient, particularly at low frequencies. Both Gerald Bennett and Conrad Cummings[5] have employed Rodet's synthesis technique to produce compositions that make extensive use of synthesis of the singing voice.

VOSIM is a technique that permits the production of rich timbres with direct control over the formant structure of the sound. The technique was developed by Werner Kaegi at the Institute of Sonology at the University of Utrecht as a result of research to determine the minimum data representation for the phonemes of speech.[6] The name is contracted from VOice SIMulation. VOSIM has also successfully simulated the sounds of certain musical instruments using relatively few parameters to describe the sound.

The basic VOSIM waveform (figure 8.6) consists of a series of pulses followed by a time interval during which the signal is zero-valued. Each pulse is a $\sin^2$ pulse; that is, the pulse is the square of a half cycle of a sine wave. The five basic parameters of a VOSIM waveform are N, the number of pulses per period; T, the duration of each pulse in seconds; M, the amount of delay between pulse groups; A, the amplitude of the first pulse; and b, the amplitude reduction factor between pulses (often specified as a percentage). The amplitude of each pulse after the first is calculated by multiplying the amplitude of the previous pulse by b. For example, if $b = 80\%$ and $N = 3$, the amplitude of the three pulses would be A, $0.8A$, and $0.64A$, respectively. The parameters are sometimes obtained by examining one pitch period of the waveform to be simulated and selecting the VOSIM parameters that best approximate the observed waveform.

The overall period of the waveform is $NT + M$; when it is repeated, the fundamental frequency (f_0) is given by:

$$f_0 = \frac{1}{NT + M}$$

The harmonic spectrum that is produced has three peaks. There are strong components at 0 Hz, at f_0, and in the vicinity of the frequency given by $1/T$. This does not mean that the spec-

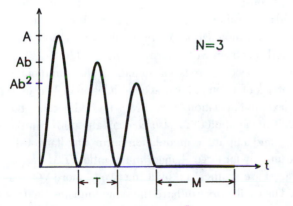

FIGURE 8.6   Basic VOSIM waveform.

trum will actually contain a component at $1/T$, but that any of the harmonics of f_0 that fall near that frequency will be emphasized. Thus, $1/T$ can be thought of as a formant frequency. This explains, in part, the success of this technique in the synthesis of natural sounds.

Certain spectral properties can be deduced from the relationships among N, T, M, and b. Assume for a moment that all the pulses have the same amplitude ($b = 100\%$). If $M = kNT$, where k is an integer, then multiples of the $k + 1$ harmonic will not be present in the spectrum. For example, when $M = NT$, the spectrum does not contain any even harmonics. Selecting M to be much smaller than NT greatly emphasizes the Nth harmonic of f_0. Double-reed instruments, such as the bassoon, have been simulated by choosing $N = 2$ and M to be small so that the second harmonic is stronger than the fundamental. Choosing the parameter b less than 100% moderates the peaks and nulls of the spectrum. For instance, when $M = NT$, decreasing the value of b below 100% increases the amplitudes of the even harmonics.

There is always a null in the spectrum at twice the formant frequency ($2/T$). The spectrum of a VOSIM signal is not band-limited, and so aliasing can be a problem for high formant frequencies. When considering aliasing, take into account that above twice the formant frequency the amplitudes of all spectral components are at least 30 dB below that of the fundamental, and above six times the formant frequency they are at least 60 dB down.

Envelopes applied to the amplitude A, the pulse width T, and the delay time M are used to obtain time-varying spectra as well as smooth transitions between sounds (particularly important in speech synthesis). Changing the value of M changes the pitch of the sound. For example, continuously increasing M causes the sound to glissando downward. As the pitch is lowered, the perceived amplitude is reduced because the waveform contains less energy. This is due to the longer delay between pulse groups. This effect can be counteracted by applying the appropriate compensating envelope to the amplitude A.

Changing the value of T changes the formant frequency. This is used to achieve time evolution of the harmonics and obtain diphthongs in speech synthesis. This evolution is different from that produced by distortion synthesis techniques such as FM, since it entails formant shifting rather than direct changes in spectral richness. If a uniform pitch is desired while the value of T is being manipulated, a compensating function must be applied to M to keep the sum $NT + M$ constant.

For the synthesis of certain sounds, the value of M is modulated with periodic and aperiodic (noise) signals, a form of frequency modulation. When a noise signal modulates M, the resulting sound has a distributed spectrum with a formant specified by $1/T$. This is used to simulate the fricative sounds of speech, percussion sounds, or the sound of the violin bow striking the string on the attack of a note. Sine-wave modulation of M is used for vibrato or wider-band FM. The maximum deviation of the FM is limited because the value of M can never be less than 0. The variation of M also changes the power in the VOSIM sound, and so both frequency and amplitude modulation occur simultaneously. The amplitude modulation is significant only for large changes in the ratio NT/M.

Sounds with more than one formant are synthesized by using two or more VOSIM oscillators and adding their outputs. The oscillators can have the same fundamental frequencies with different formant frequencies. This method, with three oscillators, has been used for formant synthesis of speech.

The algorithm to generate the VOSIM waveform is more complex than that of conventional digital oscillators. However, a real-time digital hardware oscillator that is capable of producing VOSIM waveforms complete with modulating signals can be built relatively inexpensively.[7] The inputs to the oscillator typically include the pulse width, number of pulses, amplitude, amplitude reduction factor, average delay time, deviation of M, and a choice of sine wave, random, or no modulation. The envelopes on A, T, and M can be implemented either in software or hardware.

8.3   ASYNCHRONOUS GRANULAR SYNTHESIS

In asynchronous granular synthesis, the grains are presented by randomly spacing their attack points (onsets) and randomizing their durations within a specified range. This mode of operation can be used to generate clouds of sound with specifiable temporal and spectral characteristics. The parameters are determined in accordance with the specifications of a random process (see sections 4.9 and 11.1). With this technique, no pattern can be discerned in the onset times of the grains. Similarly, the frequency of the waveform inside the grain is also a random choice. The composer controls the nature of the sound by setting boundaries on the randomly generated parameters. For example, the choice of grain duration might be constrained to the range of 10 to 20 ms. The density of grains is determined by specifying the likelihood of initiating a grain at any particular point in time. To supply direction to the music, the boundaries on the random parameters can be made functions of time so that the constraints on their selection can be loosened or tightened as the composition evolves.

A notable example of a granular-synthesis/composition system has been developed by Curtis Roads[8] which can produce sonic events called *clouds*. Some of the parameters available to control the sound cloud formation on this system are:

Start time and duration of cloud—sets the time occupied by a particular sound cloud.

Grain duration—permits the composer to set upper and lower limits on the duration of the grains.

Grain density—specifies the number of grains per second.

Grain waveform—allows the specification of single sinusoids, synthesized waveforms, and sampled waveforms. It is possible to transition from one waveform to another during the course of the cloud. A mode that randomly selects from a specified set of wave tables for a particular grain is also available.

Frequency band—defines the portion of the spectrum occupied by the cloud by setting the minimum and maximum frequencies of the waveform enclosed in the grain. The frequency used is randomly chosen within the range. In an alternate mode, a list of specific frequencies for random selection can be provided.

Amplitude envelope—determines the attack, decay, and pattern of loudness during the course of the cloud.

Spatial dispersion—allocates the sound among channels of a sound system to locate the apparent source.

Because all but the first of these parameters can vary during the formation of a cloud, it is often convenient to visualize them in graphical form. As an example, the frequency content of a particular cloud over its duration is illustrated in figure 8.7. In this instance, the spectrum is least constrained during the middle of the cloud. In general, it is best for higher-frequency grains to have shorter durations and Roads' software makes the automatic calculation of this relationship available.

Low-grain densities realize pointillistic timbres when at least twice the grain duration elapses between the initiation of grains. Silences can be heard in the cloud during times when more than 50 ms pass without a grain sounding. At higher densities, multiple grains overlap to produce complex timbres that can be made to evolve during the course of the cloud. The aural percept of the cloud varies with the width of the frequency band. A small range will give a sense of a single pitch. Increasing the bandwidth to several semitones results in a thick sound that can be similar to striking several adjacent keys on a piano at once. Wider bandwidths produce a vast cloud of sound; when the frequencies in the cloud are chosen in the continuum between the specified frequency limits, there will not be a clear sense of pitch. Choosing the frequencies from an enharmonic list (e.g., a diatonic pitch collection) can produce a chordal sound—a "harmonic" cloud—that can, for example, be programmed to evolve from one harmony to another.

Asynchronous granular synthesis provides the facility for the transition from one sound to another. For instance, the synthesis algorithm can be instructed to choose waveforms for the grains from a collection of two different sounds. At the beginning of the transition period, a high probability of choosing the first waveform is specified. As time progresses, this probability continuously lessens so that by the end of the transition it is certain that the second waveform will be chosen.

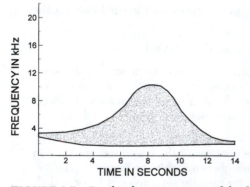

FIGURE 8.7   Graphical representation of the frequency content of a sound cloud over its duration. (*Based on C. Roads in* Representations of Musical Signals, *MIT Press, 1991. Reprinted with permission.*)

8.4   GRANULATION OF SAMPLED SOUNDS

As explained in chapter 7, sound analysis techniques such as the short-term Fourier transform (STFT) divide the sound into segments called windows and determine the parameters of the sound within this short time period. One way to view this process is as the division of the sound into a series of grains which, when played back in sequence according to the parameters of the analysis model, re-create the original sound. For the musician, a collection of grains derived from the analysis of a natural sound offers a set of building blocks from which new sounds can be assembled. To avoid clicks at the grain rate, the grains are encased in an envelope. Unless a highly pointillistic texture is desired, the grains are overlapped.

Many transmutations of the original sound are possible such as playing the grains in reverse order. The possibility of changing the duration of the sound without changing its pitch can be realized by changing the grain rate. For instance, sounding each grain twice before going on to the next one would double the temporal length of the sound. In a contrasting transformation, the pitch of a sound can be raised or lowered without changing the duration by simultaneously changing the rate at which the grains are played and the number of grain repetitions. Suppose that a sound were to be transposed up by a Pythagorean fifth (a frequency ratio of 3:2). In this case, each grain would be sounded twice, which by itself would divide the frequency by 2, but the grain rate would be increased by a factor of 3. By contrast, transposition down by the same interval (2:3) would be accomplished by successively playing each grain three times while doubling the grain rate.

Grains played in succession will exhibit audible clicks between them unless the amplitudes at the boundary between the grains are matched, or if the grains are enclosed in envelopes that taper the transitions at the beginning and end of the grains. The algorithms used for extracting grains can be programmed to include accommodations for this concern.

A set of grains derived from sampled sounds may also be performed using the techniques of asynchronous granular synthesis described in section 8.3. Random processes are used to determine the placement and relationships between grains from one or more sources.

Grains are also raw material for deterministic composition where the composer specifies the succession of grains. Grains, or more typically a particular sequence of grains, can be played as many consecutive times as desired. Sets of grains can be reordered; for example, the granular representation of a spoken text could be manipulated to change the order of the words. Potential editing operations are the same as those listed in section 7.1H to manipulate LPC analyses in speech synthesis.

8.5   COMPOSITIONAL EXAMPLES

Jean-Baptiste Barrière's *Chreode*[9] was synthesized using the FOF technique (see section 8.2) as embodied in the Chant program[10] at IRCAM. The score was prepared using the Formes software,[11] also made at IRCAM. According to the composer, the Formes software enabled the control over a wide variety of timbres through the manipulation of only "a few compositionally efficient parameters."[12]

The work is a dazzling display of the variety of musical sounds that can be made with the FOF technique. It is largely a study in a very wide range of timbre. An impressive aspect of the work is that although there is a very wide range of timbre, it is heard nonetheless as quite well unified. The work explores the spaces between poles of opposites—in timbre, texture, rhythm, and register.

The work's strong sense of cohesion is achieved in a variety of ways, including presentation of the same pitch material with differing timbres and presentation of similar timbres with contrasting pitch and register. The core timbre of the work, and the one with which the work begins, is that of the male voice singing vowel timbres in a low register. Central to the form of the work is a group of several sung male voices that recurs throughout the work, presenting characteristic motivic material. One of the audible procedures heard in the work is the interpolation of one set of material into another to achieve a smooth, often very subtle transformation from one type of sound to another. The range of sounds, as noted above, is very wide: from the singing vowel timbre in male and female voice to other nonvocal timbres, and also to such timbres as metallic and wooden sounds. At some places, notably around 6:45 of the work, the vowel timbres are rhythmically articulated and enveloped in such a way as to produce something resembling speech. There are other sounds resembling acoustic musical instruments, most notably strings. These are contrasted in places with sounds that are more obviously electronic in origin.

The work includes a number of striking contrasts and is built largely on them: contrasts between vocal and nonvocal, between sounds with seemingly acoustic origins and those that are more electronic, between passages that are rhythmically articulate and those that are more rhythmically amorphous. The strongest presentation of such a contrast occurs after the 5-minute point. Here, a passage for a small chorus of sung voices is reorchestrated (retimbred, actually) to sound like a succession of metallic chords. This contrast between the harmonic, formant-based timbres and the inharmonic, metallic timbres in presented at several crucial places in the piece, including this passage near the middle of the work and another near the end.

Curtis Roads, following the initial insights of Dennis Gabor and Iannis Xenakis, is largely responsible for the wide acceptance and interest in the use of granular synthesis techniques in computer music composition. In the midst of rapidly changing technologies for computer music, Roads managed to bring his granular synthesis methods to a state of musical maturity. The influence of his work with granular synthesis has been world-wide and has attracted many accomplished composers.

One of his first works using granular techniques is *nscor*.[13] That work was begun at University of California San Diego (UCSD) and, due to changing technologies and circumstances, was completed in more than one version over at least a decade. It has been performed widely and released on a CD.

The composition *nscor* is marked by its wide range of timbres, many of them made by combining separately produced sounds into composite "sound objects" through mixing. The component sounds in the work were created in a number computer music studios, including the UCSD Center for Music Experiments' computer music studio, the studio of the Institute for Sonology in the Netherlands, the SSSP studio in Toronto,[14] and the MIT Experimental Studio. Roads used each studio to contribute characteristic sounds for inclusion in the piece. At UCSD, for example, he used a complex, FM-based instrument to create single sounds or short phrases. The instrument admitted for a rather wide range of timbre due to its great number of parameters and multiple stored waveforms. At the Institute for Sonology, Roads used a group of fifteen VOSIM oscillators (see section 8.2) to make his textures. He used G. M. Koenig's *Project 1* composition software and the SSP (sound synthesis program) programmed by Paul Berg to control the sound. In Toronto, Roads generated a great deal of his material using the forward-looking software of William Buxton. At MIT he used Music 11 to make a number of short passages tailored to fit at particular points in *nscor*. With Music 11 Roads employed frequency modulation synthesis, waveshaping, fixed-waveform synthesis, and processing of concrete sound. The concrete sound was recorded percussion sounds which Roads treated through enveloping, reverberation and filtering.

When all of the sounds were created and catalogued, Roads made a number of mixes of the work both at MIT and at a commercial recording studio. The final result is a work with a very broad range of sound which proceeds with a great deal of contrast among its varied components.

Horatio Vaggione was one of the first composers to use granular synthesis techniques in his music. His *Octuor* (1981) is an early, effective example of his personal implementation of granular synthesis. He made the work at IRCAM on a mainframe computer using a variety of synthesis software. His goal in writing the piece was "to produce a musical work of considerable timbral complexity out of a limited set of sound source materials."[15]

The most immediately striking aspect on first hearing *Octuor* is its overall form. The work reveals three concurrent, gradually changing processes which cause the timbres of the work to evolve, over the course of its ten-minute duration, from "inharmonic to harmonic spectra, random distributions of events to periodic rhythms, and sparse textures to high-density spatial and temporal configurations."

The sound material of the work is made by taking parts (often very small parts) of five pre-existing synthesized sound files and combining the culled sounds (either as found, or altered) in ways that further the overall evolution mentioned above. The files from which the grains were taken were made using standard synthesis techniques such as FM and additive synthesis.

In his more recent compositions made using granular synthesis techniques, Vaggione often uses sampled sounds. In several of his works for live instruments and tape, the tape part is made by granulation of sounds sampled from the instrument that the tape accompanies. This often results in a homogeneous texture of live and granulated sampled sounds. Vaggione uses this relationship to excellent effect in works such as *Thema*[16] (bass saxophone and tape).

Paul Lansky's *Idle Chatter*[17] series of speech music from the 1980s is a striking use of granular synthesis as well as speech analysis/synthesis to make music. The three works in the series—*Idle Chatter, just_more_idle_chatter,* and *Notjustmoreidlechatter*—are all made with the same three basic textural elements: pitched voices "chattering" in short, often inflected tones on fragments of largely unintelligible speech (vowels and diphthongs); longer vocal tones in background harmonies that serve in some places to support the pitches of the "chatter," and which emerge prominently by themselves in other places; and a "percussion section", usually in the lower register, also made out of speech sounds.

The composer's album notes indicate that he uses three computer techniques prominently in the works: LPC, granular synthesis, and stochastic mixing techniques. The use of LPC is clear—the speech fragments were made through the familiar analysis/synthesis procedure used so effectively in Lansky's *Six Fantasies on a Poem of Thomas Campion* (see section 7.1I). The speech fragments were resynthesized at the pitch levels needed for the harmonic patterns of the works.

The rhythm of the "chattering" voices seems to have been somewhat inspired by minimalism—they chatter on at a rapid, regular pulse. The exact pattern of pulses is arrived at through stochastic mixing techniques. That is, the exact pattern of sounded pulses and rested pulses for a given voice at a given place in the piece is determined by probabilities (see section 11.1) set by the composer. The complex interaction of a number of voices all proceeding at the same pulse, but with different patterns of "on" and "off" articulations creates in places a very pleasing hocketed effect.

In register, the overall pattern of the "chattering" vocal pitches describes an arch shape. Beginning in the lower female vocal range (on the F below middle C) the pitch level gradually rises in the course of the work until a high point (G5) is reached at around time 6:50. The evolution of the vocal register then reverses itself and the pitch of the voice falls back to F3 by the end of the work.

Granular synthesis is used in the *Idle Chatter* series to create the longer vocal tones heard at most places in the works in the background. Actually, the prominence of these tones changes in the course of the series of works to the point where, at places in *Notjustmoreidlechatter* these tones assume a foreground role. The long tones, just as the chattered tones, are made from the vowel fragments of recorded speech. The long tones are made by the granular technique of repeatedly sampling a portion of a sound file while slowly changing the portion of that file to be sampled. Commonly, the portion of the file to be sampled is gradually changed from the beginning of the file to its end, and the audible result is the kind of seamless, long tone heard throughout the *Idle Chatter* series. The change of the portion of the file to be sampled results, too, in a kind of diphthong tone. A kind of choral effect also can result from taking the repetitions of the sampled sound from slightly differing parts of it.

Barry Truax has made a great number of musical works using computers since his studies at the Institute for Sonology in the early 1970s. As a composer, he has written a considerable amount of computer music software to create both the sound of his music and in its compositional design as well. A major compositional concern has been "organizing timbre at a form-determining level."[18]

His "POD" series of programs provided an interface that enabled composers to specify the broad outlines of events in a work and left the software to fill in the microscopic detail. For example, his work *Arras*[19] (1980), made using POD for compositional design and FM synthesis for sound generation, was conceived as a sort of musical tapestry. In this work, filled with thick textures, one appreciates the broad changes of its formal design within the overall context of a great surface similarity of sound. In fact, one of the features of the work is the intended ambiguity between whether a perceived fre-

AMP	INC	FREQ	FRQ.RNG	DUR'N	DUR.RNG	DELAY	RAMP	NO.VOI. W.F.#2	NO.VOI. W.F.#3	TOTAL NO.VOI.
1	100	20	20	10	1	1000	0	0		20

FIGURE 8.8   Line of control variables used by Truax. *(From B. Truax, Computer Music Journal, 6(3). Reprinted with permission.)*

quency element belongs to the background tapestry or to a foreground event. The compositional plan was to create a sensation akin to that of a large tapestry where, close up, one sees woven threads of the same or very similar repetitive patterns, but at a distance one perceives the overall shapes and designs.

Much of his work since the early 1980s has involved granular synthesis implemented with his own software. In the mid-1980s he devised a computer-based system in his studio at Simon Frasier University for making music with granular synthesis in real time. The compositional intention seems to be similar to that practiced in his earlier, FM-based works, but the implementation in real time adds a new dimension to the process.

In the granular synthesis implementation used to realize his *Riverrun*[20] (1986), Truax had a number of variables for controlling the musical output of the real-time system. First was the choice among three techniques for the generation of the grains: additive synthesis, fm synthesis, or the granulation of sampled sound. Depending on the choice of generation technique, other compositional decisions such as grain duration, offset times between grains, frequency range of the grains, etc. were required. A number of types of real-time control were implemented in the system, including the use of the computer keyboard to enter a new parameter value, changing a parameter by a specified increment, grouping parameters together in synchrony and then changing all of them together, etc.

All of the possibilities for control could be activated by single alphanumeric keystrokes during synthesis. They could also invoke sets of stored variables and presets. Figure 8.8 shows an example of a line of control variables for the system used to realize *Riverrun*. The composition itself uses the granular synthesis techniques to make a composition in which the ever-changing, stochastically generated musical texture is a metaphor for a river in which the whole is made up of an infinite number of water drops. Our perception is of the whole, but the building blocks are at the level of a drop of water.

In more recent electroacoustic works, such as *Pacific Rim*,[21] Truax uses granulation of recorded sound more extensively. Here, the granulation technique extends the range of the recorded sound and subjects it to the same sorts of transformations used in his earlier "synthetic" granular music.

NOTES

1. Gabor, D. "Acoustical Quanta and the Theory of Hearing." *Nature,* 159(4044), 1947, 591–594.

2. Xenakis, I. *Formalized Music.* Bloomington: Indiana University Press, 1971.

3. DePoli, G., and Piccalli, A. "Pitch-Synchronous Granular Synthesis." In G. DePoli, A.

Piccalli, and C. Roads (eds.), *Representations of Musical Signals*. Cambridge: MIT Press, 1991, 187–219.

4. Rodet, X. "Time-Domain Formant-Wave-Functions Synthesis." *Actes du NATO-ASI Bonas,* July 1979.

5. Cummings, Conrad. "Beast Songs." CRI Records (CRI SD487), 1983.

6. Kaegi, Werner, and Tempelaars, Stan. "VOSIM—A New Sound Synthesis System." *Journal of the Audio Engineering Society,* 26(6), 1978, 418–425.

7. Christiansen, S. "A Microprocessor-Controlled Digital Waveform Generator." *Journal of the Audio Engineering Society,* 25, 1977, 299–309.

8. Roads, Curtis. "Asynchronous Granular Synthesis." In G. DePoli, A. Piccalli, and C. Roads (eds.), *Representations of Musical Signals*. Cambridge: MIT Press, 1991, 143–186.

9. Barrière, Jean-Baptiste. "Chreode." *Computer Music Currents 4,* Wergo (WER 2024–50), 1989.

10. Rodet, X., Potard, Y., and Barriere, J.-B. "The CHANT Project: From the Synthesis of the Singing Voice to Synthesis in General." *Computer Music Journal,* 8(3), 1984, 15–31.

11. Rodet, X., and Cointe, P. "FORMES: Composition and Scheduling of Processes." *Computer Music Journal,* 8(3), 1984, 32–50.

12. Barrière, "Chreode." Album notes.

13. Roads, Curtis, "nscor." *New Computer Music,* Wergo (WER 2010–50), 1987.

14. Buxton, W., Sinderman, R., Reeves, W., Patel, S., and Baecher, R. "The Evolution of the SSSP Score Editing Tools." *Computer Music Journal,* 3(4), 1979, 14–25.

15. Vaggione, Horatio. "The Making of Octuor." *Computer Music Journal,* 8(2), 1984, 48–54

16. Vaggione, Horatio. "Thema." *Computer Music Currents 6,* Wergo (WER 2026–2), 1990.

17. Lansky, Paul. *More Than Idle Chatter,* Bridge Records (BCD 9050), 1994.

18. Truax, B. "Timbral Construction in *Arras* as a Stochastic Process." *Computer Music Journal,* 6(3), 1982, 72–77.

19. Truax, Barry. "Arras." *Pacific Rim,* Cambridge Street Records (CSR-CD 9101), 1991.

20. Truax, Barry. "Riverrun." *Digital Soundscapes,* Wergo (WER 2017–50), 1988.

21. Truax, Barry. "Pacific Rim." *Pacific Rim,* Cambridge Street Records (CSR-CD 9101), 1991.

9

PHYSICAL MODELING

In the first three decades of computer music, most of the available synthesis techniques were based on signal-generating models freely borrowed from engineering. Methods such as additive, FM, and waveshaping synthesis directly reflect the mathematical equations used to create them. The parameters available to the musician bear only an indirect correlation with the nature and quality of the sound produced. As with any instrument, a sense of the relationships can be developed by repeated usage, but the intent of physical modeling is to take advantage of the musician's experience with acoustic instruments by casting the control parameters of the computer instrument in those terms. In other words, it is considerably more intuitive to control the "bowing pressure" than the "index of modulation" when using an instrument. However, one of the difficulties in using instruments based on physical models is the determination of the specific parameter values to produce a desired sound. Here too, a considerable amount of training and practice is required for the musician to learn how to create a particular sound from the range of expression possible. Thus, the ability to compute a physical model in real time is highly desirable.

In the past decade, remarkable progress has been made in creating successful synthesis algorithms based on physical models of a wide variety of instruments and the human voice. This chapter will detail several approaches to their implementation and present examples from the literature.

9.1 APPROACHES TO PHYSICAL MODELING

A physical model concentrates on simulating the sound production process of an instrument, rather than directly trying to create its waveform by matching some spectral evolution. Physical models are generally partitioned into blocks, often corresponding to the parts of the acoustic instrument to be modeled. The most common partition is based on subtractive synthesis and divides the instrument into an *excitation*, which generates a spectrally rich signal, and a *resonator* (filter), which shapes the spectrum of the sound. Most speech synthesis algorithms are sectioned in this way (see chapter 7), for example.

The majority of algorithms are *feed-forward*, which means that the signal flows strictly in one direction: from the excitation source and through the resonator to the output as shown in figure 9.1. It also determines that changing the characteristics of the resonator does not automatically change the nature of the excitation. In other words, it suggests that the motion of the lips of a trombonist playing in a particular register, for example, does not change as the slide is adjusted. This decoupling of the source and resonator is not strictly valid for these mechanical systems; in fact, at the very least the frequency

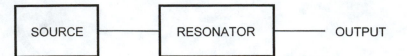

FIGURE 9.1   The basic arrangement of most physical models does not include feedback.

of the excitation must track the resonator frequency. This dependence can be realized by simultaneously programming the resonator and source frequency, but there may be additional interactive effects such as a change in the amplitude or the unfiltered spectrum of the source with resonator frequency. These interdependencies may be more complex to determine but are sometimes modeled by including *feedback:* the output waveform or its derivative is in some way injected back into the excitation source.

The resonator portion of the instrument is most often a linear element; its characteristics do not vary with the amplitude of the signal applied to it from the excitation. In other words, the frequency response of the resonator does not depend on the amplitude of the sound passing through it. The nonlinearities of the system are typically incorporated into the excitation model, which is used to reflect the change in spectral content in a sound that occurs with dynamic level.

9.2   EXCITATION

The excitation source used for a physical model is generally derived from an analysis of the instrument to be modeled. Beginning with Helmholtz, considerable effort has gone into investigating the mechanics of musical instruments, but the advent of digital audio has accelerated the research in recent years. Most research models make the division between source and resonator and are able to characterize the excitation waveform over a range of amplitude and phrasing variations. This section will discuss a few examples of the excitation produced in traditional instruments. For a complete treatment of the subject, the reader is referred to the thorough text by Fletcher and Rossing.[1]

An early example of excitation modeling was presented in section 5.2K in the trumpet synthesis algorithm of James Beauchamp. Here, the excitation waveform was produced by nonlinear waveshaping with the intent of matching spectral data derived from studies of performers playing cornet mouthpieces. The nonlinear transfer function was designed to match the spectra at various dynamic levels as the amplitude varied over its range. The analysis of the mouthpiece waveforms also showed that the amplitude envelope varies with dynamic level, and so different envelopes were stored and activated as a function of amplitude.

The excitation waveforms for the speech synthesis algorithms presented in chapter 7 are simpler: a band-limited pulse for voiced sounds and noise for unvoiced sounds. The physical model of the vocal tract to be presented in section 9.4 uses a more sophisticated model based on an analysis of glottal waveforms that also allows the noise source to be correlated with the pitch period.

As another example, figure 9.2 shows the waveforms produced by a clarinet reed[2] at

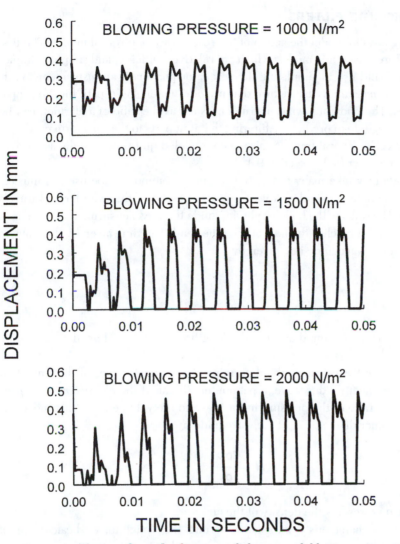

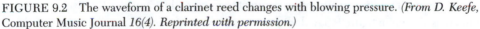

FIGURE 9.2   The waveform of a clarinet reed changes with blowing pressure. *(From D. Keefe, Computer Music Journal 16(4). Reprinted with permission.)*

different blowing pressures. Observe how a larger pressure produces not only a greater amplitude but also a larger transient pulse on the transitions of the waveform, with a concomitant increase in the bandwidth of the excitation.

The string in a bowed instrument is pulled in one direction by the bow with rosin on its surface to optimize the frictional force.[3] The string stretches until it provides enough spring force to overcome the frictional pull of the bow. At this point, the string quickly snaps back, the bow regrips the string, and the cycle begins anew. This "stick and slip" waveform is coupled into the string and propagates in both directions down the string. During the sustained portion of the tone, the waveform looks like a pulse with slightly rounded corners.

9.3   WAVEGUIDE FILTERS

There are many ways to model the action of the resonator in a physical model. The first to be discussed are waveguide models which are relatively efficient and simple to implement and have found use in simulating the resonator portion of an instrument. As its name implies, a *waveguide* is a structure that provides an enclosed path for the propagation of waves. The body of a wind instrument, such as the tube of a clarinet, can be analyzed as a waveguide to predict the filtering that it imparts to the waveform produced at the mouthpiece. The vocal tract has also been modeled quite successfully as a waveguide[4] and will be described in section 9.4.

A waveguide may take many forms, but the most common shape used in musical instruments is the hollow cylinder. A wave enters one end of the cylinder and travels down the tube. The walls of the hollow cylinder guide the wave, ensuring that it remains inside the tube until it reaches the hole at the other end. The time taken by the wave to propagate down the waveguide is τ, given by

$$\tau = \frac{\ell}{c}$$

where c is the velocity of sound and l is the length of the tube. Thus, the waveguide serves as a delay line.

The diameter of the circular tube determines the characteristics of the wave that can propagate. To quantify this wave, a parameter (R) called the *characteristic impedance* expresses the ratio of the pressure in the wave to the volume of air that moves. It is related to the inner diameter, d, of the waveguide by

$$R = \frac{2\rho c}{d}$$

The parameter ρ represents the density of the air.

The concept of characteristic impedance permits the straightforward calculation of the behavior of multiple waveguides connected in cascade. Consider the two waveguides joined as shown in figure 9.3 with different diameters (d_1 and d_2, respectively) and therefore different characteristic impedances. When a wave propagating in the first waveguide arrives at the boundary between waveguides, not all of the energy of the wave will enter

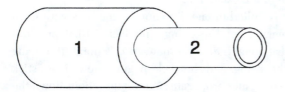

FIGURE 9.3   Cascade connection of two waveguides with different diameters.

the second one. The difference in diameters causes some of the energy of the wave to be reflected and travel back toward the input. Thus, waveguides support both a *forward* and a *backward* traveling wave simultaneously. In simulating the behavior of waveguides, the two waves are tracked independently. The forward pressure wave traveling in the first waveguide is denoted by P_1^+ while the backward wave is P_1^-. Similar designations apply to the two waves in the second waveguide.

At a boundary between dissimilar waveguides, the scattering coefficient, k, specifies the ratio of the amplitude of the reflected wave to that of the incident one. Defining the characteristic impedances of the two waveguides as R_1 and R_2 permits k to be computed from

$$k = \frac{R_2 - R_1}{R_2 + R_1}$$

For convenience, the scattering coefficient may be expressed solely in terms of the diameters of the waveguides by combining the two previous equations to obtain

$$k = \frac{d_1 - d_2}{d_1 + d_2}$$

The value of k ranges between -1 and $+1$.

The coupling between the forward and backward waves at the boundary between dissimilar waveguides is given by the set of equations:

$$P_1^- = kP_1^+ + (1 - k)P_2^-$$
$$P_2^+ = (1 + k)P_1^+ - kP_2^-$$

From these equations, the digital simulation of this two-section waveguide filter can be formulated and is shown schematically in figure 9.4. The upper delay lines conduct the forward waves, while the lower ones carry the backward waves.

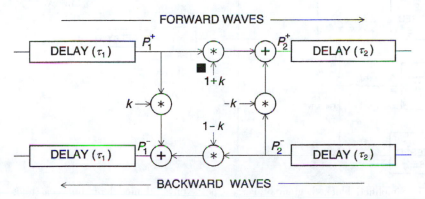

FIGURE 9.4   Schematic of a digital simulation of the interconnection of two waveguides.

9.4   PHYSICAL MODEL OF THE VOCAL TRACT

A particularly successful application of the physical modeling technique is the Singing Physical Articulatory Synthesis Model (SPASM) developed by Perry Cook.[5] It produces high-quality vocal sounds, but is efficient enough to be implemented in real time on DSP hardware. A simplified block diagram of the algorithm appears in figure 9.5.

The vocal tract is modeled by a waveguide filter with nine sections. The characteristic impedance of the sections is determined by sampling the diameter of the vocal tract at various points. The reflected wave is summed back into the filter input after multiplication by the factor g. Altering the position of the articulators such as the tongue changes the diameters, which in turn moves the frequencies of the formants provided by the waveguide filter. A display of the frequency response is presented by calculating the impulse response of the filter and then taking its Fourier transform. In this way, the user can quickly determine the effect of the position of various articulators on the formant structure. An additional waveguide filter is used to simulate the nasal tract. Corresponding with the anatomical location, its input is taken part way up the vocal tract filter using a special junction that joins three waveguide sections.

The model contains a glottal pulse generator for producing voiced speech. The unit includes separate envelope generators for the amplitude and frequency of the excitation. Two wave-table oscillators with different waveforms are used; the parameter MIX specifies the proportion of the two that appears in the output. The frequency of the glottal pulse can also be manipulated by the vibrato generator. The frequency of the vibrato and

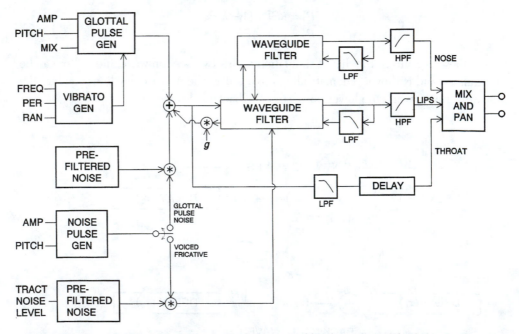

FIGURE 9.5 Simplified block diagram of Perry Cook's physical model of the vocal tract. (*Adapted from* Computer Music Journal *17(1). Reprinted with permission.*)

the amplitudes of the periodic and random components are controlled by the parameters FREQ, PER, and RAN, respectively.

A noise pulse generator relates the noise sources used for the unvoiced parts of speech to the pitch period. Each noise generator consists of a white-noise source passed through a four-pole filter to shape its spectrum. These prefiltered sources can be multiplied by the noise pulse to impress a periodic component. Most unvoiced sounds are excited by setting the switch so that these pulses are injected into the waveguide filter. Unvoiced plosive sounds are more successfully created by adding the noise directly into the forward wave in the proper proportions at the points between sections of the waveguide filter.

Three sources of radiation are implemented by the model: from the lips at the end of the vocal tract, from the nose at the end of the nasal tract, and from the throat. The latter is necessary to produce plosive consonants such as /D/ where the other paths are shut off. High-pass filters simulate the radiation characteristics of the nose and lips; a delay line is included in the throat path to account for the physical distance of the throat from the other source elements in the human body.

The outputs from three sources are mixed in the appropriate proportions. Cook's model also includes a "pan" feature that allows the signal to be allocated between two stereophonic channels.

To assist the user, the program displays a diagram of a human head sectioned vertically to show the location of the various articulators. The musician can program a particular phoneme from a library, alter the positions of the articulators, or edit the formant structure of a particular setting. The ability to interpolate sounds between several settings is also provided. Cook has further created a software synthesis system that enables SPASM to be given a preset list of commands that specify the parameters of each sound. To demonstrate the control of SPASM at a higher level, a language for the synthesis by rule of Latin text was also developed.[6]

9.5 MECHANICAL MODELS

Another approach to the physical modeling of acoustic instruments uses a technique developed for simulating the response of various physical structures to applied force. In this method, the structure to be simulated is divided into small elements and the interaction of the elements is computed using elementary equations from physical mechanics. The computational and computer memory requirements are somewhat greater than in the waveguide technique, but the model is closer to the actual physical structure of the resonator and enables nonlinearities to be included much more easily.

One of the structures analyzed in the study of basic mechanics is a mass attached to a spring as depicted in figure 9.6. When the spring is hung vertically, a point of equilibrium exists where the gravitational pull on the mass is exactly countered by the force exerted by the spring. In this position, the system is said to be *at rest*. Suppose that the mass is pulled down so that it is displaced a distance of Δx from the rest position as shown in the figure. The force exerted by the spring, F, at this point can be written as

$$F = K\Delta x$$

where K is known as the *spring constant* that governs the behavior of the spring. When the mass is released from the displaced position, it will accelerate at the rate A according to

$$F = MA$$

where M represents the numerical measure of the mass. The equation shows, as expected, that applying a stronger force to an object causes it to accelerate more quickly.

The equation for spring force characterizes a linear, *lossless* spring so that, after the weight is released, the system would theoretically oscillate forever. Naturally, every physical system loses energy as it operates; hence, the model also incorporates a damper component that applies a frictional force that depends on the velocity, V, of the element in the damper:

$$F = -ZV$$

where Z is a constant that characterizes the effectiveness of the damping process.

The CORDIS program developed by C. Cadoz and J.-L. Florens[7] uses these basic equations to model the behavior of resonators. A structure is broken up into a series of points, and a mass is assigned to each point. In this representation, the mass of an area is concentrated at a single point. This discretization introduces some error, but it can be minimal if enough points are taken. The points are connected with springs and dampers to model interactions between portions of the structure. This finite model can be realized in one dimension for a simple model of a string or thin rod, two dimensions to represent a membrane such as a drum head, and three dimensions for plates and more complex objects. Figure 9.7 illustrates a portion of a two-dimensional model where the point masses are represented by the black balls connected by lines that denote springs.

Suppose that a single point mass on the two-dimensional membrane shown is displaced downward; this action might simulate a drum stick striking at that particular point. The vertical displacement will stretch the springs attached to the point mass, which in turn will displace adjacent points by an amount proportional to the force exerted by the

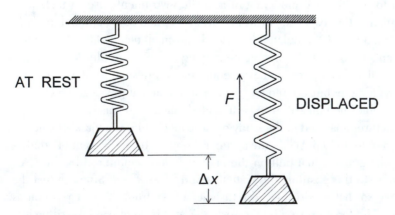

FIGURE 9.6   Schematic of a weighted spring in two positions.

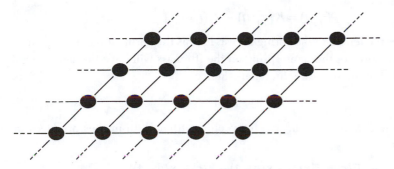

FIGURE 9.7   Two-dimensional model of a mechanical system where point masses are coupled with spring elements. Dampers (not shown) may also be connected between point masses.

connecting springs. This action propagates across the membrane as the springs carry the energy between adjacent masses. The masses placed at the edges of the membrane are fixed in order to limit the propagation of the energy to the membrane. This mechanism corresponds to the clamp that is placed around the boundaries of a drum head; it reflects the energy back toward the center of the drum.

The computational algorithm must compute and keep track of the displacement of each point mass at each sample point in time. Let $x_i(n)$ denote the displacement of the ith point mass at the nth time sample. The velocity of that mass at that time, $V_i(n)$ can then be approximated from the finite difference equation

$$V_i(n) = \frac{[x_i(n) - x_i(n-1)]}{\Delta T}$$

that is, as a change in displacement over a time interval. To simplify the computations, the system is ordinarily normalized so that ΔT has an equivalent value of 1. With this convention, the acceleration of the ith mass, $A_i(n)$, is a change in velocity, yielding

$$A_i(n) = V_i(n) - V_i(n-1)$$

Combining the two previous equations enables the acceleration to be calculated directly from the displacement values as

$$A_i(n) = x_i(n) - 2x_i(n-1) + x_i(n-2)$$

Because $F_i(n) = MA_i(n)$, the displacement on the nth sample can be computed from the previous displacements and the applied force as

$$x_i(n) = \frac{F_i(n)}{M} + 2x_i(n-1) - x_i(n-2)$$

The effect of the spring connecting the ith and jth point masses can be approximated by discretizing the spring equation to obtain

$$F_j(n) = K[x_i(n) - x_j(n) + \ell]$$

where l designates the length of the spring at rest. $F_j(n)$ is the spring force pulling on the jth point mass. The force of the same spring on the ith mass will have the same magnitude but be applied in the opposite direction—hence,

$$F_i(n) = -F_j(n)$$

In a similar fashion, a damper connected between the ith and jth masses produces the discretized forces

$$F_j(n) = Z[x_i(n) - x_i(n-1) - x_j(n) + x_j(n-1)]$$
$$F_i(n) = -F_j(n)$$

which arise because the damping depends on the velocity of displacement. When, as is often the case, both a damper and a spring are connected in parallel between point masses, the equations above are combined into single expressions for $F_j(n)$ and $F_i(n)$.

As one might imagine, a large number of points is required to model a physical structure accurately. The algorithm must systematically scan across the matrix of points to compute their displacement and associated forces on every sample. In addition, the equations show that two previous displacement values must be stored for each mass. The output from the model is taken by declaring a "listening point" where the displacement of a point or a group of points is used to determine the waveform.

A finite model such as this facilitates the incorporation of nonhomogeneous media. If the structure is made from different materials, the masses and spring constants can be specified on a local basis to reflect the characteristics of the material in each region. Nonlinearities of the mechanical system can be included by appropriately modifying the spring and damper equations at the cost of additional computational complexity.

9.6   MODAL MODELS

The modal method is derived from the coupled-mass mechanical model of the previous section. For many purposes the modal method of physical modeling represents an improvement in that it requires less computation time and also highlights the resonant frequencies of the system. Conversely, the physical identity of the intermass coupling devices is lost and the method cannot easily incorporate nonlinearities.

The formulation of a modal model begins, as in the previous method, with the discretization of the structure to modeled into an array of N point masses and their associated intermass coupling elements—springs and dampers. A large $N \times N$ matrix equation is written that relates the displacement, velocity, and acceleration of each point to the same parameters of every other point. After some mathematical manipulation,[8] the matrix equation is "diagonalized"[9]—a linear algebra process that produces N pairs of eigenvalues, which are pairs of numbers that express the resonant frequencies of the structure. The eigenvalue pairs can also be referred to as the "modes" of the structure; hence, the name modal synthesis. Each resonant mode has a center frequency and a damping factor that sets its bandwidth. Thus, one way to think about a modal model is as a filter that provides formants at the modal frequencies.

The diagonalization process combines the coupling elements in such a way as to obscure their identity. Thus, the physical parameters of a modal model cannot be varied once the eigenvalues are found. This characteristic makes it difficult to include nonlinearities in the structure, but the modal transformation still allows the structure to be excited at particular physical points. Applying an excitation stimulates the modes according to their frequency and damping factors. A periodic excitation results in a harmonic spectrum with formant frequencies and bandwidths set by the modes.

The modes are typically implemented with "elementary oscillators." These algorithms are not the wave-table oscillators used throughout most of this text—instead they are filters with an impulse response that rings at the modal frequency with the appropriate damping factor. The excitation is applied to inputs of these filters and the filtered outputs are combined according to the "pick-up" points used for coupling the output waveform. To gain computational efficency, only those modes containing significant energy are synthesized. This strategy generally results in the suppression of modes above a certain frequency without a conspicuous degradation in the sound quality.

9.7   COMPOSITIONAL EXAMPLE

The great advantage of basing synthesis on a physical model is that it can be "naturally musical." That is, the model will often supply the expected spectra and transitions by the very nature of the interaction of the different parts of the model necessary to produce the specified sound. Instead of the need to deal separately with attack transients, spectral shift with dynamic level, and other characteristics of instrumental tones, the physical model will automatically produce these as artifacts of its physical state.

One of the interesting features of physical modeling as the basis for sound synthesis is the possibility for creating "fluffed" notes. When learning to "play" a physical model, it is possible (even common) to create situations in which the model, instead of producing the desired tone, makes an unexpected, often "unmusical" sound. This is similar to the problem encountered by a beginner in attempting to make music with an instrument for the first time—the right combination and balance of forces are necessary to make musical tones. Gradually, the computer musician learns which combinations of input values to the physical model will produce the desired outputs, and which will not.

Paul Lansky's *Still Time*[10] is a four-movement work in which there are two basic textural elements throughout—environmental recorded sound and overtly musical, pitched sound. In contrast to some of Lansky's work where he consciously manipulates the recorded sound to extract what he describes as its hidden music, the recorded sound in this work acts as a kind of background or frame for the synthesized musical sound. In the course of the work one encounters striking effects where the pitch of a mourning dove or a passing motor car, for example, momentarily matches that of a tone in the musical texture.

For much of the synthesized sound in *Still Time*, Lansky used Perry Cook's physical waveguide model of a slide flute.[11] In many places in the work the sounds produced with this model seem very musical indeed. They show a kind of performance nuance that we ordinarily associate with sound produced by a live performer. For example, certain low glissando tones—tones that would be difficult to make as smoothly on a real flute—sound perfectly natural in *Still Time*.

NOTES

1. Fletcher, N. H., and Rossing, T. D. *The Physics of Musical Instruments.* New York: Springer, 1991.

2. Keefe, D. "Physical Modeling of Wind Instruments." *Computer Music Journal,* 16(4), 1992, 57–73.

3. Woodhouse, J. "Physical Modeling of Bowed Strings." *Computer Music Journal,* 16(4), 1992, 43–56.

4. Cook, P. "SPASM, a Real-Time Vocal Tract Physical Controller." *Computer Music Journal,* 17(1), 1993, 30–44.

5. Ibid.

6. Cook, P. "LECTOR: An Ecclesiastical Latin Control Language for the SPASM/Singer Instrument." *Proceedings of the 1991 International Computer Music Conference.* San Francisco: Computer Music Association, 1991, 319–321.

7. Florens, J.-L., and Cadoz, C. "The Physical Model: Modeling and Simulating the Instrumental Universe." In G. DePoli, A. Piccalli, and C. Roads (eds.), *Representations of Musical Signals.* Cambridge: MIT Press, 1991, 227–268.

8. Adrien, J.-M. "The Missing Link: Model Synthesis." In G. DePoli, et al. (eds.), *Representations of Musical Signals,* 269–297.

9. Golub, G., and van Loan, C. *Matrix Computations.* Baltimore: Johns Hopkins University Press, 1989.

10. Lansky, Paul. "Still Time." *Fantasies and Tableaux.* CRI Records (CRI683), 1994.

11. Lansky, P., and Steiglitz, K. "EIN: A Signal Processing Scratch Pad." *Computer Music Journal,* 19(3), 1995, 18–25.

10

REVERBERATION, AUDITORY LOCALIZATION, AND OTHER SOUND-PROCESSING TECHNIQUES

A computer music technique that has been widely used to enhance both electronically recorded and synthesized music is *reverberation*. The interest in this technique reflects a fascination on the part of post–World War II composers with the placement of sound sources in an acoustical environment. The development of electronics for multichannel sound has made the location of a sound source available as an element in electronic music composition. Another musical resource made possible by electronic technology is *musique concrète*—music based on the splicing, mixing, and modification of recorded sounds. The compositional examples at the end of the chapter show how these different topics support and inform each other. Together, they form a unified field of sound-processing techniques.

10.1   REVERBERATION

10.1A   Natural Reverberation

Natural reverberation is produced by the reflections of sounds off surfaces. They disperse the sound, enriching it by overlapping the sound with its reflections. This process colors the sound to some extent, imparting a change in timbre. The importance of reverberation is familiar to musicians who have played the same piece in two halls. The effect of the different reverberant characteristics of the two spaces may influence the performance in a variety of ways. For example, the tempo selected to articulate the music may have to be adjusted; the dynamics of certain instruments may have to be changed; and even the seating of the players may have to be rearranged in order to communicate the desired sound.

The amount and quality of reverberation that occurs in a natural environment are influenced by certain factors: the volume and dimensions of the space; and the type, shape, and number of surfaces that the sound encounters. Consider a hypothetical room with no furnishings and perfectly flat, solid walls (figure 10.1). Acoustical energy emanating from the source (S) travels at the speed of sound (approximately 345 m/s) in all directions. Only a small portion of the sound reaches the listener (L) directly. The listener also receives many delayed images of the sound, reflected from the walls, ceiling,

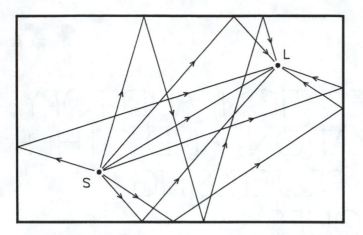

FIGURE 10.1   A few of the myriad of paths of sound travel between a source (*S*) and listener (*L*) in an ideal room.

and floor of the room. Thus, the reflections lengthen the time that the listener perceives a sound. The amplitude of any sound is reduced by an amount that is inversely proportional to the distance that it travels; therefore, the reflected sounds not only arrive later, but they also have lower amplitudes than the direct sound. This means that the reverberated sound will have a decaying envelope.

The characterization of the complex process of reverberation in a real room is particularly difficult because the quality of reverberation cannot be quantified objectively. Four of the physical measurements that have been correlated with the perceived character of reverberation are the reverberation time, the frequency dependence of the reverberation time, the time delay between the arrival of the direct sound and the first reflected sound, and the rate of buildup of the echo density.

The *reverberation time* indicates the amount of time required for a sound to die away to 1/1000 (–60 dB) of its amplitude after its source is shut off. The choice of –60 dB represents a convenience inherited from the early researchers of room acoustics. The reverberation time is not a direct measurement of how long a listener will hear a sound after its source ceases. This time is proportional to the reverberation time but depends on other factors as well, such as the amplitude of the sound and the presence of other sounds. If the reverberation time is long enough, sound will overlap extensively with its reflections and build up a dense texture. These overlappings have been traditionally used to emphasize the interval relationships between successive tones. Such environments have been used compositionally by a number of contemporary composers including Stuart Dempster[1] to build multivoice textures out of the sound of a single instrument. On the other hand, an unusually short reverberation time will minimize or even eliminate slight overlappings of musical tones. Mario Davidovsky has achieved highly pointillistic textures by using nonreverberant sounds in his electronic compositions.

In his early, pioneering studies of room acoustics, W. C. Sabine[2] concluded that the reverberation time depends on the volume of the room and the nature of its reflective surfaces. Rooms with large volumes tend to have long reverberation times. With a constant volume, an increase in either the surface area available for reflection or the absorptivity of the surfaces decreases the reverberation time.

All materials absorb acoustic energy to some extent, and so when a sound wave reflects off a surface, some of its energy is lost. Hard, solid, nonporous surfaces such as finished cement can reflect very efficiently, whereas soft ones such as curtains and porous ones such as plaster absorb a substantial amount of the acoustic energy.

The roughness of the surfaces also has an effect on the nature of the reverberation. When a sound wave strikes a surface that is not perfectly flat, part of the sound is reflected in the expected direction (figure 10.1) and part is dispersed in other directions. The rougher the surface, the greater is the proportion of energy that is dispersed. In a concert situation, there are additional surfaces for dispersion, absorption, and reflection, including furniture, carpets, people, and clothing.

The reverberation time is not uniform throughout the range of audible frequencies. Acousticians are not in complete agreement on the specific relationships that should exist between the reverberation time of the various frequency bands to produce "good" sound in a concert hall. However, it is agreed that in a well-designed concert hall the lower frequencies are the last to fade. With a few exceptions, absorptive materials reflect low-frequency sounds better than high ones. For example, a heavy carpet can reflect 10 dB less signal at 4000 Hz than at 125 Hz. However, efficient reflectors such as marble reflect sounds of all frequencies with nearly equal efficiency. With small, solid objects, the efficiency and the direction of reflection are both dependent on frequency. This causes frequency-dependent dispersion and, hence, a major alteration of the waveform of a sound.

The absorption of sound energy by water vapor in the air also contributes a frequency bias to the reverberation. The attenuation is more pronounced on high-frequency sounds and depends primarily on the humidity. The farther a sound travels through the air with any humidity at all, the greater the relative attenuation of its high-frequency components. Thus, the spectrum of the sound toward the end of the reverberation has less high-frequency energy. Surprisingly, the maximum attenuation occurs when the humidity is around 15%.[3]

Another physical quantity that has been correlated with the perceived acoustic quality of a room is the amount of time that elapses between receiving a direct sound and its first reflection. A long delay (> 50 ms) can result in distinct echoes, whereas a very short delay (< 5 ms) can contribute to a listener's perception that the space is small. A delay in the 10- to 20-ms range is found in most good halls.

After the initial reflection, the rate at which the echoes reach the listener begins to increase rapidly. A listener can distinguish differences in echo density up to a density of 1 echo/ms.[4] The amount of time required to reach this threshold influences the character of the reverberation; in a good situation, it is typically around 100 ms. This time is roughly proportional to the square root of the volume of a room, so that small spaces are characterized by a rapid buildup of echo density.

One method for measuring the acoustics of a hall involves placing a spark gap on the stage and an omnidirectional microphone in the audience. Firing the gap produces a short acoustical impulse in a nearly omnidirectional pattern. A record is kept of the sound pressure waves received by the microphone. This record, when corrected for the

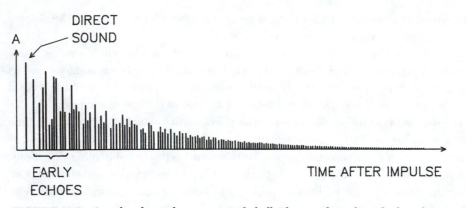

FIGURE 10.2   Simulated impulse response of a hall. The actual number of echoes been reduced for clarity.

spectrum of the spark, indicates the impulse response of the room. A simulated impulse response is shown in figure 10.2. It tends to be ragged at first, during the early echoes, but the rest of the waveform is reminiscent of noise with exponential decay. The density of the waveform is the result of the multitude of reflected waves received and the many diverse paths they travel.

An irregular amount of time between peaks is a desirable characteristic for the impulse response of a concert hall, because it indicates a relative lack of frequency bias. If there is a nearly uniform time between peaks, the reverberation in the hall will add a frequency of its own to the sound, resulting in a "metallic-sounding" decay.

The acoustics of a hall are often characterized from a listener's point of view by recording the binaural impulse response. This stereophonic record is obtained by placing a mannequin in the audience with a microphone implanted in each ear to receive the impulse. The left- and right-side signals are somewhat different primarily because of the presence of the head and the different orientation of the pinnae (external ears). (See sections 10.2A and 10.2C.)

10.1B   Digitally Produced Reverberation

In recent years, there has been extensive research into electronic techniques for simulating natural reverberation. The enormous number and great variety of reflective and dispersive surfaces found in a natural environment make creating an exact physical model of its reverberation completely impractical. However, using the techniques presented below, reverberation with a natural sound has been simulated efficiently. An electronic reverberator can be thought of as a filter that has been designed to have an impulse response emulating the impulse response of the space to be simulated.

The use of digital electronics to simulate reverberant environments permits a great deal of control over the parameters that determine the character of the reverberation. The response of a digital reverberator can be altered on a short-term basis, thus permitting reverberation to be used as a compositional element.

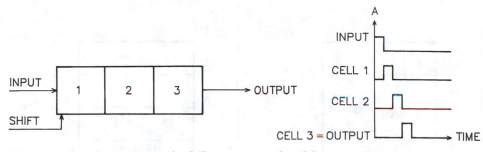

FIGURE 10.3   The operation of a shift register to realize delay.

To simulate the travel time of the indirect sound, a reverberator must have some method of delaying the signal that goes into it. There are two principal techniques for implementing delay digitally: shift registers and circular queues. A *shift register* consists of many memory cells in sequence, each of which stores one sample of a signal. Figure 10.3 shows a shift register used as a simple delay line. For simplicity in this example, the shift register is only three cells long. The figure shows how an impulse propagates from the input to the output. The shift register receives a shift signal at the sampling rate; at each sample time, the values stored in the memory cells are shifted one cell closer to the output. Concurrently, the first cell is filled with the sample that is present at the input, and the sample value stored in the last cell is taken as the output. In this example, it takes three sampling periods for the impulse to emerge from the delay line, and so the amount of delay in seconds is 3 divided by the sampling frequency. At a sampling rate of f_s = 40 kHz, the amount of delay realized by three cells is 3 ÷ 40,000 = 0.075 ms.

At audio sampling rates, a large number of cells is required for useful time delays. In the general case, a shift register of length m cells provides a delay time τ of

$$\tau = \frac{m}{f_s}$$

Shift registers are generally implemented by special-purpose hardware.

On a general-purpose computer, *circular queues* provide the most efficient means for realizing a digital delay line. The queue takes the form of a group of sequential memory cells in which samples are stored (figure 10.4). The computer keeps a pointer that marks the memory cell containing the oldest sample. At every sampling period, the computer uses the oldest value as the output from the queue and then replaces the oldest value with a new one taken from the input. Finally, the pointer is incremented so that it marks what is now the oldest sample in the queue. Figure 10.4b illustrates this action. On every sample the algorithm moves the pointer one cell down the queue, outputs the oldest value, and replaces it with the current input sample. Every time the pointer reaches the end of the memory block, it is reset to the first cell. Thus, the queue can be thought of as circular. This method for realizing delay makes efficient use of the computer, because once a sample value is placed in a memory cell, it does not move until it is replaced. As in a shift register, the amount of delay produced is directly proportional to the number of cells in the queue.

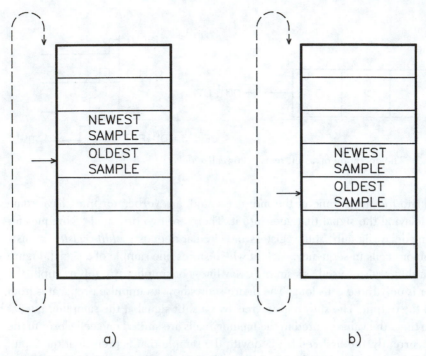

FIGURE 10.4   Circular queue both before (a) and after (b) a sampling interval elapses.

Sometimes, the scheme used for reverberation requires several different amounts of delay of the same signal. A delay line whose total length is set to the longest required delay can be "tapped" to obtain the appropriate shorter delays. Figure 10.5 illustrates the use of a tapped delay line to obtain three different values of delay. The tap points can be varied in software to dynamically change the various delays.

The process known as *convolution* uses a heavily tapped delay line to produce reverberation that bears an extremely close resemblance to that of the real hall.[5] The sound to be reverberated is fed into a delay line whose total length is the same as the reverbera-

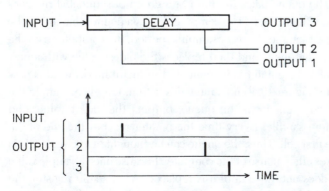

FIGURE 10.5   Tapped delay line giving several values of delay.

tion time for that hall. The delay line is tapped at every sample and the value from each tap is multiplied by the value of the hall's impulse response for that time. All the products are then added together to form the reverberated output signal.

The difficulty with convolution is that it requires an extremely lengthy computation for each sample and one memory cell for every sample period of delay. For example, if the reverberation time is 1.5 seconds and the sampling rate is 48 kHz, then 72,000 multiplications will have to be performed on every sample and the scheme will require enough memory storage to accommodate 72,000 sample values. If two channels are used to reproduce binaural reverberation, the number doubles to 144,000. Relatively expensive special-purpose hardware is now commercially available to convolve signals with long sequences, but on a general-purpose computer this method has proved far too slow to be practical.

The *recirculation* technique of M. R. Schroeder[6] uses a group of recirculating delay elements; it enables long reverberation times to be obtained using relatively few calculations and short, untapped delay lines. The elements of a Schroeder reverberator are called *unit reverberators* and consist of two types—comb filters and all-pass networks. A complete digital reverberator is built by interconnecting several unit reverberators, whose individual parameters determine the overall characteristics of the reverberator.

In a *comb filter*, the input signal enters a delay line. When it reaches the output, it is fed back to the input after being multiplied by an amplitude factor g. The time that it takes to circulate once through the delay line is termed the loop time, τ. Consider a comb filter such as the one in figure 10.6, whose loop time is 50 ms. When a unit impulse (a single sample with an amplitude of 1 preceded and succeeded by samples of 0 amplitude) is applied to its input, the impulse begins to propagate in the delay line. The output of the filter is 0 until, after 50 ms, the impulse emerges from the delay line. At this time, the output of the comb filter is the impulse with amplitude 1. Meanwhile, the impulse is multiplied by the factor g and sent back into the delay line. After 50 ms, the impulse reemerges from the delay line with an amplitude of g. Once again, the impulse is multiplied by g (yielding an amplitude of g^2) and fed back into the input. The process continues—a pulse is output every 50 ms, and each pulse has an amplitude that is a factor of g times that of the preceding pulse. The value of g must be less than 1 for the filter to be stable. Otherwise, the impulse response will continually grow until it exceeds the dynamic range of the system.

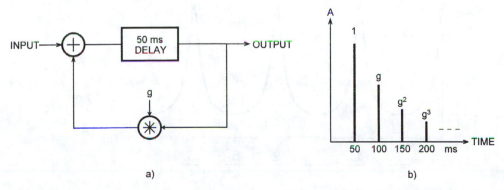

FIGURE 10.6   (a) The internal configuration of a comb filter and (b) its impulse response.

The impulse response of a comb filter (figure 10.6b), then, is a train of pulses, spaced equally in time at an interval of the loop time. It, therefore, will sound at the frequency that is the inverse of the loop time. This frequency, f_0, is sometimes called the *natural frequency* of the filter and is stated mathematically as $f_0 = 1 / \tau$. The response decays exponentially as determined by the values chosen for the loop time and g. Values of g nearest 1 yield the longest decay times. The decay time is ordinarily specified at the –60-dB point of the decay—that is, as the reverberation time (T). To obtain a desired reverberation time for the unit, g is usually approximated, given the loop time (τ), from the relationship:

$$g = 0.001^{\tau/T}$$

The loop time for a single-unit reverberator is generally chosen in relation to the characteristics of the overall reverberator, and will therefore be discussed below.

The comb filter is so named because its steady-state amplitude response (figure 10.7) is thought to resemble the teeth of a comb. The spacing between the maxima of the "teeth" of the comb is equal to the natural frequency. The depth of the minima and height of the maxima are set by the choice of g, where values closer to 1 yield more extreme maxima and minima.

In addition to its application as a component of a Schroeder reverberator, a comb filter can be used alone for the modification of sound. Thus, many systems make the comb filter available as a unit generator (figure 10.8) with two control parameters: the loop time and the reverberation time. In most implementations, the loop time is set before synthesis begins and cannot be changed during the actual calculation of sample values. However, the value of g, and hence the reverberation time, can usually be changed on every sample, if desired.

Passing a sound through a comb filter imparts certain reverberant characteristics to the sound. In addition, the incoming sound causes the filter to ring at its natural frequency, f_0, thus adding an additional pitched component to the sound at that frequency. The ringing exhibits an amplitude envelope similar to that found in most bell-like sounds—a fast attack and a longer exponential decay. Because the ringing decays expo-

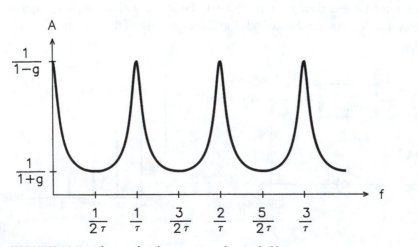

FIGURE 10.7   The amplitude response of a comb filter.

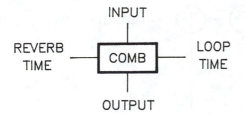

FIGURE 10.8   Flowchart symbol for a comb filter.

nentially and has an amplitude that is directly related to the amplitude of the incoming sound, the output of the filter shows many characteristics of natural sound. Section 10.3B describes the compositional usage made of comb filters in Charles Dodge's *Earth's Magnetic Field* and Paul Lansky's *Six Fantasies on a Poem by Thomas Campion.*

An *all-pass network,* in contrast to a comb filter, passes equally signals of all frequencies in the steady state. On a steady-state basis, therefore, the relative amplitudes of the spectral components of a sound will not be altered. This does not mean, however, that an all-pass network is transparent to signals. On the contrary, an all-pass network has substantial effect on the phase of individual signal components. More audibly evident is the effect of its transient response, which can impart color to the sound during a sharp attack or after a sharp decay.

An all-pass network is similar to a comb filter but more complex in its implementation. Figure 10.9a illustrates the way in which the signal recirculates through the delay line, whose length is once again called the loop time (τ). A factor g controls the decay time of the impulse response and is approximated from the reverberation and loop times as in a comb filter. As before, g must be less than 1 for stability.

The impulse response of the network (figure 10.9b), like that of a comb filter, is a pulse train with an exponential envelope. Notice that, unlike a comb filter, there is no delay between the application of the sound at the input and the appearance of sound at the output. The uniform spacing between pulses indicates that, when a short impulsive signal is applied, the network will "ring." Figure 10.10 illustrates the reaction of an all-pass network to a tone with an abrupt decay. A sinusoidal tone has been applied to the network long enough to achieve a steady-state condition. When the tone ends, the decaying output waveform has a period equal to the loop time of the network. A frequency ($1/\tau$) is thus produced that is completely unrelated to the frequency of the original input. Fortunately, most sounds have less abrupt decays, so that the effect of the transient response of the network is considerably less noticeable. However, it should be borne in mind that an all-pass filter is not totally "colorless."

Realistic reverberation can be digitally simulated through the interconnection of multiple comb and all-pass networks. When unit reverberators are connected in parallel, their impulse responses add together. When they are placed in cascade, each pulse of the impulse response of one unit triggers the impulse response of the next, producing a much denser response. The total number of pulses produced by units in parallel is the sum of the pulses produced by their individual units. The number of pulses pro-

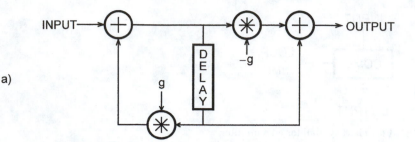

a)

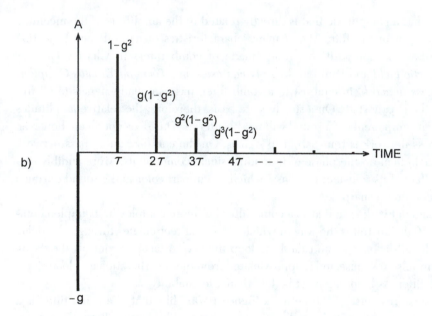

b)

FIGURE 10.9   (a) The internal configuration of an all-pass network and (b) its impulse response.

duced by units in cascade is the product of the number of pulses produced by each unit. In either case, pulses that occur at the same time add together, reducing the number of observed pulses.

When comb filters are used in a reverberator, they should be connected in parallel to minimize the spectral disturbances. A frequency that falls in a minimum of one filter might be able to pass through another. All-pass networks, on the other hand, should be connected in cascade since they are, at least in the steady state, colorless. The phase response characteristics of the individual units cause a filter made from all-pass units connected in parallel to exhibit deep notches in its amplitude response.

Schroeder proposes two methods of using comb filters (C) and all-pass networks (A) to realize artificial reverberation. An impulse applied to the reverberator of figure 10.11a initiates a decaying train of pulses from each of the comb filters. The all-pass networks in cascade serve to increase the pulse density. In the configuration of figure 10.11b, each

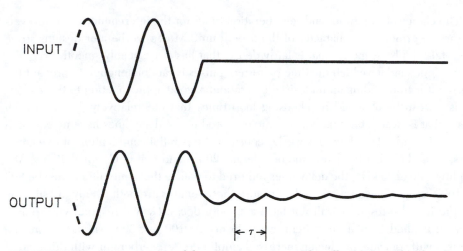

FIGURE 10.10   Demonstration of the transient response of an all-pass network. After the input tone ceases, the network "rings" with a period equal to the loop time.

pulse of the response produced by the first all-pass unit triggers the impulse response of the second, causing the impulse response to become successively denser. The topology of figure 10.11a is of the type that is implemented in programs such as Csound. Other similar configurations are possible as long as the musician follows the rule that comb filters are connected in parallel and all-pass networks are connected in cascade.

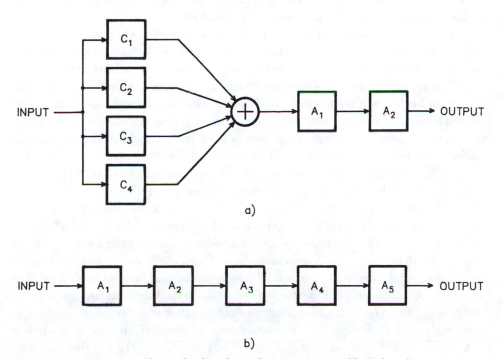

FIGURE 10.11   Two topologies for digital reverberators suggested by Schroeder.

The choice of loop times and reverberation times for the interconnected unit reverberators determines the character of the overall unit. Most reverberator designs strive for a total impulse response that is fairly dense, that has a reasonably smooth exponential envelope, and for which the time pattern of pulses is random enough to prevent the reverberator from adding an undesired coloration. A good approximation to these characteristics can be obtained by choosing loop times that are relatively prime to each other—that is, where the number of samples stored in the delay lines have no common divisors. To understand how this works, consider the parallel combination of two comb filters, C_1 and C_2. Let the loop time of C_1 equal 20 ms and that of C_2 equal 25 ms. At a sampling rate of 40 kHz, the delay lines required to realize the comb filters must be 800 and 1000 samples long, respectively. Because these lengths are both evenly divisible by 200, the impulse response will not have a smooth decay. C_1 will respond with pulses every 20 ms and C_2 will emit them every 25 ms. At 100 ms, 200 ms, and so on, the impulses will coincide, producing increased amplitude. A reverberator with this kind of impulse response will tend to produce distinct echoes and have an audible frequency bias. Setting the lengths of the delay lines to the nearest prime number of samples, respectively 799 and 997, produces a markedly better impulse response, while making only minor adjustments in the loop times to 19.98 and 24.93 ms. Now, the first coincidence of pulses does not occur until $799 \times 997 \div 40$ kHz = 19.92 seconds.

More than two unit reverberators are generally used in an actual design, and they should all have delay lengths that are relatively prime to each other. This approach realizes the densest impulse response for the number of units and distributes the time between pulses more randomly. Also, choosing prime loop times helps equalize the amplitude response of parallel combinations of comb filters.

Selection of the actual loop times depends on the type of environment to be simulated. Recall from the previous section that two of the measurements correlating with the acoustically perceived size of a space are the time delay between the direct sound and its first reflection and the amount of time that it takes for its impulse response to build up to a density of 1 echo/ms. A tiled shower may have the same reverberation time as a concert hall, but there is a definite audible difference between the two. In addition to the differences in the frequency-dependent properties of the reflective surfaces, the substantially smaller volume of the shower and the corresponding closer proximity of the walls to the listener cause not only the first reflections to arrive sooner, but also the echo density to increase more rapidly. Thus, shorter loop times are used to simulate smaller spaces.

For the reverberator of figure 10.11a, comb filter loop times chosen in the vicinity of 50 ms, with the ratio of longest to shortest of about 1.7:1, can provide concert-hall characteristics. In contrast, the tiled shower might be simulated by decreasing the loop times to values in the 10-ms range. The reverberation time of each comb filter is set to the desired time for the overall reverberator. The two all-pass networks must have relatively short loop times or there will be audible repetitions of the signal. If the loop times are too long, the echo density will not reach the 1 echo/ms threshold, resulting in an unrealistic sound (e.g., a "puffing" sound when short, impulsive sounds are reverberated). At most, the loop time for A_1 should be 5 or 6 ms, and that of A_2 should be even shorter. The reverberation time

ELEMENT	REVERB TIME	LOOP TIME	
C_1	RVT	29.7	msec
C_2	RVT	37.1	msec
C_3	RVT	41.1	msec
C_4	RVT	43.7	msec
A_1	5.0 msec	96.83	msec
A_2	1.7 msec	32.92	msec

TABLE 10.1   Parameters for a Schroeder Reverberator simulating a medium-sized concert hall (RVT indicates the reverberation time for the overall unit).

of the two all-pass networks should be fairly short (less than 100 ms), because their purpose is to thicken the density of the overall impulse response, not to lengthen its duration.

As an example, table 10.1 shows a set of parameters that has been used in the reverberator of figure 10.11a to simulate the characteristics of a medium-sized concert hall. The loop times have been chosen to be relatively prime to each other. The reverberation time (RVT) of the overall reverberator is the same as the reverberation time of each of the comb filters. For a concert-hall simulation, this value is often in the range of 1.5 to 2 seconds, but the musician can vary this parameter for other purposes.

In the configuration of figure 10.11b, the characteristics of the unit reverberators are chosen in much the same way as in figure 10.11a. Thus, the loop time of the first all-pass network is chosen in relation to the size of the room to be simulated, and the remaining loop times and reverberation times are set such that each is shorter than the previous one. The loop time of the final unit must be short enough to ensure adequate echo density.

Figure 10.12 shows the use of a reverberator to impart a sense of spaciousness to the sound of a computer instrument. Ordinarily, the single control parameter for the reverberation is the reverberation time (RVT). As previously stated, the reverberation time is defined as the time it takes for a sound at the input to the reverberator to die away at the output to 1/1000 (−60 dB) of its amplitude. It is often useful when specifying the reverberation time to specify a greater reverberation time than one imagines the sound to need. This approach can compensate for the masking of much of the reverberated signal by other tones present in the texture.

Another factor to consider when using reverberation is the amount of the signal to be reverberated. To give better definition and presence, some part of the signal is usually sent directly to the output, bypassing the reverberator. The ratio of reverberated to unreverberated output is involved in simulating the distance of the source of the sound from the listener. When the instrument is to be allocated among the channels of a multi-channel audio system, the effect of auditory spaciousness is best achieved when a separate reverberator is used for each channel. (See sections 10.2C and 10.2F.)

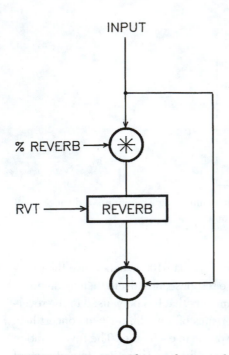

INPUT

% REVERB ⟶

RVT ⟶ REVERB

FIGURE 10.12   Use of a reverberator. The proportion of reverberated to direct sound is set by the parameter %REVERB.

10.1C   Variations of Schroeder Reverberators

Up to this point, the discussion has been restricted to methods for the production of colorless reverberation. As mentioned earlier, however, a real concert hall does in fact shade the color of the sound, because lower frequencies tend to have longer reverberation times. To simulate this, a unit reverberator may have a low-pass filter placed in its feedback path, so that the recirculating sound loses some of its high-frequency energy on every trip through the loop. This is simpler to do in a comb filter (figure 10.13) than

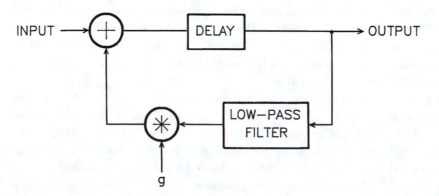

INPUT ⟶ ⊕ ⟶ DELAY ⟶ OUTPUT

LOW−PASS FILTER

g

FIGURE 10.13   Inclusion of a low-pass filter in the recirculation loop of a comb filter to shorten the reverberation time of the higher frequencies.

in an all-pass network, which requires two low-pass filters (one of which is not uncon-ditionally stable). The characteristics of the low-pass filter are chosen to simulate the dif-ference in reverberation time at different frequencies. These differences may be taken from measured concert-hall data or may be approximated. The use of this configuration has the added benefit of "smearing out" the impulse response, particularly toward the end, so that it is less likely to sound metallic.

Schroeder reverberators have been used in computer music since the mid-1960s, but one problem with them is their lack of early echoes.[7] When the loop times are cho-sen to achieve the rate of increase in echo density corresponding to a good-sized space, the first indirect sound will arrive noticeably later than it normally would in a real hall. Reducing loop times could help alleviate this problem, but would also cause the echo density to increase too quickly, creating the impression of a smaller space. To simulate early echoes, Schroeder has suggested inserting a tapped delay line in front of his stan-dard reverberator (figure 10.14).[8] The values of the delays and the multiplier coefficients $\{a_1, a_2, \ldots, a_n\}$ can be obtained by examining the impulse responses of actual halls or by calculating the arrival time and amplitude of the first few echoes from the geometry of a particular room. Normally, the first 80 ms or less of the response is realized in the delay line. The values of the coefficients tend to get smaller for taps further removed from the input. When the number of taps is large, this technique can substantially increase the amount of calculation performed in the reverberator algorithm.

10.1D   Sound Modification Techniques Using Variable Delay Lines

Certain effects can be imposed on sounds by using delay lines whose delay time can be varied on a sample-to-sample basis. Two of the most common uses of this technique are for flanging (phasing) and for producing a chorus effect.

Flanging creates a "swishing" or rapidly varying high-frequency sound by adding a signal to an image of itself that is delayed by a short, variable amount of time (figure 10.15a). A typical use of this configuration is to apply a function of time to the delay

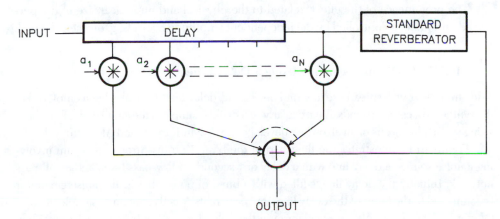

FIGURE 10.14   Method of early echo simulation based on Schroeder.

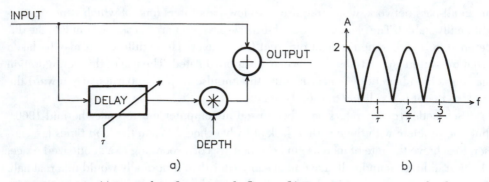

FIGURE 10.15   (a) Internal configuration of a flanger. (b) Frequency response at a fixed amount of delay and DEPTH = 1.

input that sweeps the amount of delay (τ) from a few milliseconds to 0. This produces the characteristic flanging sound. The DEPTH parameter controls the proportion of the delayed signal in the output, determining the prominence of the effect. Many implementations enable dynamic flanging, where the flanging action is proportional to the peak of the envelope passing through the flanger.

A flanger has a frequency response like that shown in figure 10.15b. At any particular value of delay, the minima appear at frequencies that are odd harmonics of the inverse of twice the delay time.[9] Thus, flangers produce their effect by dynamically changing the spectrum of the tone being processed. The amount of attenuation at the minima is set by the value of DEPTH, which has a range from 0 to 1. A value of 1 corresponds to maximum attenuation.

Another musical use of variable delay lines is to produce a *chorus effect* which changes the sound of a single instrument into that of a group of instruments playing in unison.[10] (See also section 4.11.) The technique entails the use of several variable delay lines connected in parallel (figure 10.16). The amount of delay of each line typically ranges from between 10 and 50 ms. The instantaneous value of each delay is set by a random noise generator whose spectral energy is concentrated below 20 Hz.

The prominence of the effect, related to the physical and numerical size of the perceived ensemble, is controlled by the independent amplitude controls, g, on each channel.

10.1E   Synthesis Technique Using a Delay Line

Aside from their widespread use in sound processing, delay lines have also been employed in the synthesis of certain sounds. A particularly successful example is the simulation of plucked-string sounds by means of an algorithm developed by Kevin Karplus and Alex Strong.[11]

Figure 10.17a illustrates the flowchart of the basic Karplus-Strong algorithm involving a noise source, a delay line with a delay of τ seconds, a low-pass filter, and an all-pass network. Initially, the delay line is filled with a burst of noise; that is, the noise generator is connected to the input of the delay line until each of its N cells contains a sample of noise ($N = \tau f_s$). This action places a waveform in the delay line with a broad spectrum. When

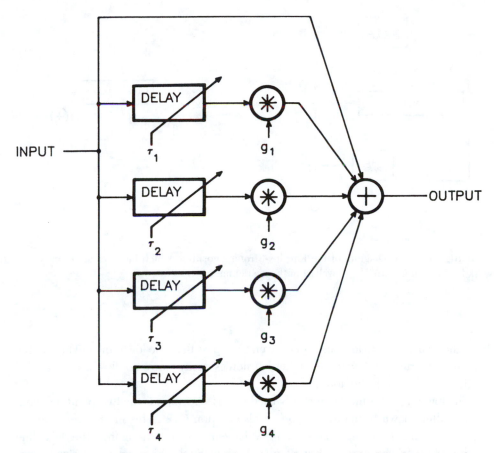

FIGURE 10.16   Method of realizing a "chorus effect" with variable delay lines. *(Based on a design in B. Blesser and J. Kates, "Digital Processing of Audio Signals," in* Applications of Digital Signal Processing, *Alan V. Oppenheim (ed.), © 1978, p. 78. Reprinted with permission of Prentice-Hall, Englewood Cliffs, N.J.)*

the delay line is full, the noise generator is disconnected and the output of the delay line is fed through a low-pass filter and then an all-pass network back into the delay line input. To understand the acoustical effect of this configuration, suppose for a moment that the cutoff frequency of the low-pass filter is well above the audio range. In this case, given that the all-pass network does not alter the amplitude of the spectrum of the sound, the waveform would continuously recirculate through the delay line. The signal observed at the output of the instrument would be a periodic waveform and, therefore, sound with a clear pitch even though a noise generator produced the original waveform.

In practice, the low-pass filter is given a cutoff frequency of one-half the Nyquist frequency, and so every time the waveform passes around the loop, it loses some of its spectral energy, imparting an exponential decay to the waveform. Because the decay time of the overall tone is inversely proportional to the fundamental frequency, tones sounded at lower pitches exhibit longer decays. The low-pass shape of the filter causes

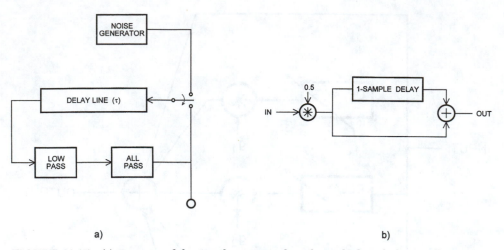

FIGURE 10.17 (a) Diagram of the Karplus-Strong algorithm, which includes an all-pass network for fine-tuning. (b) The flowchart of the averaging low-pass filter.

the higher harmonics to lose more energy on each pass than the lower ones. Thus, in the dynamic spectrum produced, the higher harmonics decay more rapidly—a salient characteristic of plucked-string tones.

The low-pass filter most commonly used in this algorithm is the two-point, moving-average filter shown in figure 10.17b (see also section 6.12). This filter determines its output by taking the average of the sample value currently emerging from the delay line and the value of the previous output of the delay line. Such a filter delays the signal passing through it by 1/2 sample. If the all-pass network were not present, the total delay around the loop would be $N + 1/2$ samples, so that the fundamental frequency (f_0) of the generated tone would be given by

$$f_0 = \frac{f_s}{N + \dfrac{1}{2}}$$

Because N is an integer, only specific values of f_0 can be obtained from this equation.

To enable accurate tunings, an all-pass network is inserted in the loop. As described in section 10.1B, an all-pass network does not change the steady-state amplitude of the spectrum, but it does change the phase of a signal by delaying it. The delay, δ, provided by the network is a fraction of a sample, giving the fundamental frequency of the instrument as

$$f_0 = \frac{f_s}{N + \dfrac{1}{2} + \delta}$$

The fractional delay is infinitely adjustable by setting the gain factor g inside the all-pass network (see figure 10.9). A good approximation for calculating g when f_0 is less than a sixth of the Nyquist frequency is

$$g = \frac{1-\delta}{1+\delta}$$

When the only available control on the all-pass-network unit generator is the reverberation time (T), it would be calculated from

$$T = -3\tau \log_{10}\left(\frac{1-\delta}{1+\delta}\right)$$

As an example, suppose that in a system with a sampling rate of 48 kHz, a plucked tone at 440 Hz is to be synthesized. In this case,

$$N + \delta = \frac{f_s}{f_0} - \frac{1}{2} = 108.5909$$

Here, N would be taken as the integer part of the result (i.e., $N = 108$), leaving δ as 0.5909 which leads to $g = 0.2571$. If the all-pass network had not been included, the closest value of N would have been 109, which would have produced a tone at $f_0 = 438.4$ Hz— a tuning error of -6.5 cents. Such errors become more objectionable and the need for the all-pass filter more urgent when f_0 is a larger proportion of the sampling frequency.

The amplitude of this instrument can be scaled by adjusting the amplitude of the noise generator. However, if this instrument is to be used at different dynamic levels in the same piece, this scaling method will produce the "volume-control" effect. In acoustic instruments, plucking a string more forcefully not only produces a louder sound, but also a richer spectrum. To simulate this effect, the noise generator can be coupled through a separate low-pass filter during the filling of the delay line. The cutoff frequency would be made proportional to the desired amplitude, so that softer sounds would have less initial spectral bandwidth.

The low-pass filter in the Karplus-Strong algorithm makes high notes shorter in duration than low ones, just as they are in physical string instruments. David Jaffe and Julius Smith[12] found that the algorithm made too great a difference in duration between the high and the low notes. They therefore introduced greater equality of duration throughout the gamut of the instrument by introducing a loss factor in the feedback loop to shorten the decay time when necessary. To stretch the decay time, the feedback filter can be changed to a two-point weighted average instead of the single-point moving average. The details of this alteration can be found in their article.

Because of its computational efficiency and natural-sounding tones, the Karplus-Strong algorithm has been implemented successfully on a variety of real-time systems. A number of extensions of the basic technique is possible, including the simulation of sympathetic strings[13] and the inclusion of nonlinear waveshaping to generate the distortion characteristic of an electric guitar,[14] among others.

David Jaffe's composition *Silicon Valley Breakdown,* for computer-generated plucked strings, is one of the best known works to use the Karplus-Strong synthesis technique. Jaffe, together with Julius Smith, found that subjective tuning discrepancies inherent in the basic technique were solved by stretching the octaves as when tuning a piano[15]— making the tones in the higher octaves slightly sharp and those in the lower registers slightly flat.

A host of additional modifications to the basic algorithm, which greatly enhance the realism of string simulation and also the musical usefulness of the technique, are described in the Jaffe/Smith article. Included are techniques for the treatment of rests and the ends of notes, glissandi and slurs, simulation of sympathetic strings and of a moving pick, and varying the character and number of attacks, among others.

The composition itself, in addition to constituting an encyclopedia of plucked-string varieties, demonstrates another of the composer's concerns—that of the subtleties of coordinating multiple voices in a polyphonic texture in such a way that a certain feeling of natural "performed-ness" comes across to the listener. Jaffe used what he calls "time maps" for enabling the relationship among simultaneous voices to be controlled and yet to have specified local freedoms of time paths for the individual voices.[16] For example at one point in *Silicon Valley Breakdown,* four voices begin a canon together, diverge greatly for a time, then come precisely together at the end of the passage.

10.2   AUDITORY LOCALIZATION

Auditory localization is the human perception of the placement of a sound source. In listening to music in a concert hall, a listener receives cues for sound location from the placement of the actual sound sources in the hall. By using at least one microphone per channel and placing them at different locations in the hall, a great deal of the localization information is preserved in a multichannel recording. In electroacoustic music, the sound may be perceived as static and one-dimensional unless the illusion of source locality is included in the synthesis. With an understanding of the perception of sound-source location, the placement of the apparent source of sound can also be used as a compositional element.

10.2A   Localization Cues from Real Sources

To perceive location accurately, the listener seeks clear cues that define the direction and distance (D) of the sound source. As depicted in figure 10.18, the direction is commonly expressed in terms of two angles: the *azimuthal* angle (ϕ), which is measured in the horizontal plane passing through the center of the listener's head; and the *elevation* angle (θ), which is measured in a vertical plane bisecting the listener. The azimuthal angle determines the position of the apparent source in the four quadrants surrounding the listener: front right, front left, rear left, and rear right. An angle of 0° is situated in front of the listener, whereas an angle of 180° is located directly behind. The elevation angle ranges from –90° (directly below the listener) to +90° (directly above the listener). In determining the direction of a sound source, the audible cues that a listener uses are based on dif-

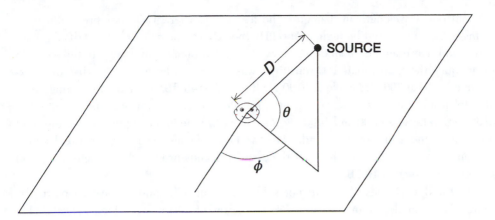

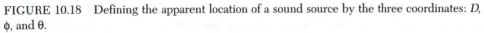

FIGURE 10.18   Defining the apparent location of a sound source by the three coordinates: D, ϕ, and θ.

ferences in time and intensity received stereophonically and also differences in the spectrum of a sound imparted by the directionally dependent filtering of the pinnae.

Any delay that a listener perceives between the time that a sound reaches one ear and the time that it reaches the other is called the *interaural time difference* (ITD). The listener can use ITD cues to determine the angular direction of a sound source.[17] If the sound source is centered behind or in front of the listener, the ITD is 0. As the angle is changed so that the ITD exceeds about 20 μs, a difference in direction can be perceived up to a maximum ITD of 0.6 ms. Resolution by ITD cues becomes less precise as the sound source moves toward a position that is lateral to the listener, because the change in the ITD per degree change in location becomes much smaller. A typical listener can resolve the location of a sound in front to about 2° and a lateral sound to about 10°.[18]

The *interaural intensity difference* (IID) provides another cue for determining direction. When the sound source is not centered, the listener's head partially screens the ear opposite to the source, casting a "shadow" that diminishes the sound received by that ear, particularly at higher frequencies. In addition, the pinna performs filtering that varies with the direction from which the sound reaches the listener, particularly at higher frequencies.[19] This filtering helps the listener determine whether a sound comes from above, below, in front, or behind.

The usefulness of the cues depends on the frequency content of the sound. Both ITD and IID cues are practically ineffective when the spectral energy of the sound resides below about 270 Hz; hence, the direction of such sounds cannot be determined. ITD cues are most effective in the frequency range of 270 to 500 Hz but contribute little above 1400 Hz, although differences in the arrival time of the attack portion of the envelope of a high-frequency sound can be used for localization. The closer a source is to a lateral position, the less serviceable are high-frequency ITD cues. A spectral component below 500 Hz produces very small IID cues, although such cues can be detected down to about 200 Hz.[20] The amount of intensity difference increases with frequency, so that above 1400 Hz IID cues predominate. This frequency arises because at 1400 Hz a typical adult head is about one wavelength in diameter; the frequency where IID cues predominate in younger listeners would be higher. At 6 kHz the IID can be as much as 20 dB for a lateral sound. For example, in an experiment using microphones implanted in the ears of a mannequin, the approximate IID sensitivity was a nearly undiscernible 0.1 dB/° to a maximum of 3 dB at 400 Hz, while at 6400 Hz it rose to 0.45 dB/° over the azimuthal range of ±45° from center.[21] The sensitivity at more lateral positions was less. In the intermediate region between 500 and 1400 Hz, the cues combine in a complicated manner that depends on the nature of the sound.[22] The two types of cues received from a real source ordinarily correlate. This is often not the case for sounds produced by electronic sound systems. (See section 10.2B.)

IID and ITD cues alone are not sufficient to unambiguously locate a particular source. For example, a source located directly in front of a listener produces IID and ITD values of 0, but so does a source directly behind the listener because it is also equidistant from both ears. As a matter of fact, a source centered above the listener is also equidistant, and so is a source in front of a listener at any elevation angle. Thus, subjects presented with a set of IID and ITD cues in a listening test often report a "front-to-rear reversal" of the acoustical image. Even in daily life, listeners can sometimes be confused about the apparent location of a sound, but when the sound has sufficient high-frequency content, the pinnae filter the incoming sound with a frequency response that depends on the direction from which the sound impinges on the ear. In addition, reflection of the sound off the torso, especially the shoulders, helps identify source locations above the listener. When a sound is of sufficient duration, listeners uncertain about its location commonly turn their heads so that one ear is closer to the source. This natural behavior makes simulation of directional cues more difficult.

Of these many factors, the pinnae are the most significant contributors to localization. Their filtering action is most pronounced above 4 kHz; hence, when listeners mistake the location of sound, it is most often at low frequencies. To increase the fidelity of localization, researchers have measured *head-related transfer functions* (HRTFs) over a wide range of incidence angles.[23] These functions express the frequency response imparted to the sound by the pinnae for a particular angle. Making matters more complicated, HRTFs also depend on the distance between the source and the listener. Because little variation is observed for source locations more than 2m away, HRTF sets are most often determined at this distance.

Three principal cues help a listener judge the distance of a sound source: the intensity of the sound, the ratio of reverberated to direct sound (R/D ratio), and the amount of high-frequency energy in the sound. The relative importance of the first cue depends on the familiarity of the listener with the sound. When hearing a sound for the first time, intensity tends to be a more influential cue than when an already established sound is moving around the listening environment. The amplitude received from a source producing a constant level diminishes inversely with the distance ($1/D$); for example, moving a source from 3m to 6m away reduces the received amplitude by one-half. Some researchers have found a reduction based on a loudness scale corresponding to $1/D^{3/2}$ produces better results on certain types of sounds.[24]

Except in an anechoic room, sound reaching a listener is comprised of both direct and reflected sound. The relative intensities of the direct and reflected sounds are often the dominant cues used to estimate the distance at which the sound source is located. When the sound source is close to the listener, the R/D ratio is low. As the distance between them becomes greater, the amount of direct energy decreases more rapidly than the reflected energy, so the ratio becomes larger. The *critical distance* is defined by an R/D ratio of 1; that is, the direct and reverberant sound have the same energy. At very large distances, little of the sound is received directly, and eventually an *audio horizon* is reached beyond which the source distance cannot be discerned. The relatively large amount of reverberation at large distances makes the sound more diffuse and the discrimination of source direction less accurate.

An additional, but less significant, cue at large distances is the relative absence of high-frequency components in the sound. This phenomenon exists because the attenuation imparted to a sound wave propagating through the atmosphere is greater at high frequencies.

Using reverberation as the basis for determining distance makes impulsive sounds easiest to locate. Long tones are the most difficult because listeners estimate distance almost entirely during the attack portion of the sounds[25] where the ITDs are most effective.

The preceding discussion has tacitly used the model of sound emanating from a single point with the listener attempting to identify that point. Some sounds may appear to be distributed over a region, as listeners to a symphony orchestra can attest. In a concert hall, the many sources of sound are blended in the reverberant environment into a sound image. The position of a soloist may be distinguished, but the mass of sound tends to be distributed across the stage. Thus, another perceptual parameter in aural localization is the *apparent source width* of a sound.

10.2B   Simulation of Directional Cues

To convince an audience of an imagined location, the appropriate directional and distance cues must be provided. This can be done either by placing a large number of loudspeakers around the performance space or by using a few speakers and creating the illusion of direction and distance by careful allocation of the signal among them.

The listener to a multichannel electronic sound system generally receives conflicting interaural (IID and ITD) directional cues. To best understand how the listener resolves these conflicts, it is necessary to consider separately the simulation of these cues in a laboratory situation.

Simulated ITD cues can be accurate only under extremely restricted conditions. Either a single listener must be placed in an accurately chosen position (the distance from the speakers known within 10 cm with the head fixed so that it cannot rotate more than a few degrees off center) or the listener must wear headphones. This is a consequence of the *precedence effect:* A listener receiving the same sound from multiple sources locates it at the closest source, not at a point between them, unless the separation in time is less than about a millisecond. For example, consider the configuration in figure 10.19 where the listener is equidistant from two loudspeakers, *L* and *R*, which are fed identical signals. In this case, the listener receives equal signals in each ear and believes that the source is centered at position I1. Suppose that loudspeaker R is moved a few centimeters farther to the right. This is equivalent to leaving loudspeaker R in its original position and slightly delaying the signal applied to it. The sound will now reach the left ear before the right one, so that the imagined source location shifts toward the left to position I2. If loudspeaker R is more than about 35 cm farther from the listener than loudspeaker L, the sound traveling from L will reach both ears before any sound from R arrives. Thus, the listener receives the same initial cues that would be provided by a single source located at L. The sound from loudspeaker R serves merely to reinforce the original sound and does not alter the listener's first impression that the sound emanates solely from L.

The sound that reaches an ear from the opposite loudspeaker is called *cross-talk*. It effectively limits the placement of auditory images to the area between the speakers. It is possible with special filters to compensate for the effect of cross-talk[26] and create images outside the loudspeakers. However, the filter's response must be calculated on the basis of some exact physical relationship between the listener and the speakers, and so this method is used only in laboratories and by audiophiles who are willing to position themselves with great accuracy. Finally, with or without filters, if loudspeaker R is moved a long distance away (> 10 m) so that its sound arrives more than 35 to 50 ms after the sound from L, an echo will be heard.

The direction of a sound source may also be simulated by providing the listener with cues of interaural intensity difference (IID). Return to figure 10.19. The two sound sources, L and R, are emitting exactly the same sound with equal amplitude. Again, the listener is situated equidistant from the loudspeakers (ITD = 0), and so the resulting image is centrally located at I1. When the amplitude of the left signal is increased, the image is displaced toward L at an angle that is determined by the ratio of the intensities of the signals delivered to the two loudspeakers. Specific examples of signal allocation formulas will be given in section 10.2F, but when one loudspeaker delivers a signal to the listener that is more than about 20 dB stronger than the signal from the other, the second loudspeaker will be perceived as not making a contribution to the sound.[27] IID

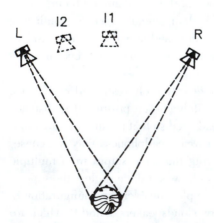

FIGURE 10.19   Listener positioned equidistant from two loudspeakers.

cues are less sensitive than ITD cues to the position of the listener. A listener moving off center will retain some of the intended sense of location. However, if the sound emitted by the two speakers is identical, the precedence effect can intervene and assign the location to the nearest speaker, depending on the spectral composition of the sound.

As stated above, IID cues are most effective for sounds at higher frequencies. Because the listener relies almost entirely on IID cues above 1400 Hz, the precedence effect will not be a factor. As a result, systems using only IID cues to localize the sound are most successful on signals with high frequencies or wide bandwidths.

The application of HRTFs to the signal can improve listeners' responses to localization cues and minimize the likelihood of front-to-back reversals. Figure 10.20 shows a system that can localize three distinct sources independently, but the arrangement can be modified for any number of sources.[28] A monophonic signal from each source is fed into a filter that is programmed to produce the desired azimuthal (ϕ) and elevation (θ) angles for that source. Each filter block contains a filter for each ear, which includes the appropriate HRTF, the frequency response of the transducers, and compensation for the spectral change incurred as the signal propagates from the transducers to the ear. The filtered signals are combined to produce a binaural output, which drives the transducers. To save computing resources, the right-ear HRTF is often taken as the mirror image of the left-ear HRTF, which assumes perfect lateral symmetry in the listener.

This system has certain limitations. HRTFs are generally measured using mannequins or microphonic probes positioned near a human subject's eardrum. But the size, shape, and orientation of pinnae vary among listeners—each person has an individual set of HRTFs. In addition, the filter responses are computed for the head of a single listener in a predetermined location; other listeners will perceive the cues differently. The most successful use of this approach is in virtual-reality systems, in which a single individual wears headphones as well as a device for monitoring the head position so that the HRTFs can be appropriately modified when the head is turned.

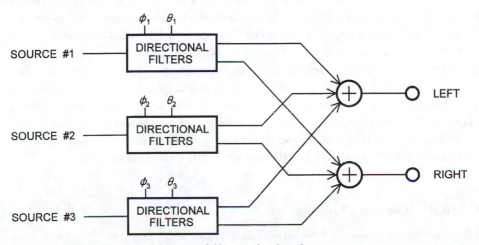

FIGURE 10.20   The use of directional filters to localize three sources.

10.2C Simulation of Distance Cues

To simulate distance cues, the intensity of the sound can be attenuated with distance as $1/D$. In addition, reverberated sound is added to the direct sound in a proportion dictated by the distance between the listener and the desired image. As the distance increases, so does the ratio of reverberated to direct sound. At the same time, the overall amplitude of the sound decreases, with the direct sound dropping faster than the reverberated.

It is useful to separate the reverberation into two components—global and local.[29] *Global reverberation* returns equally from all directions around the listener. *Local reverberation* comes from the same direction as the direct signal and derives from reflectors relatively nearby the source. When the sound is located close to the listener, most of the reverberation is global. This arrangement models an imaginary environment in which the listener is located in the center of a space with equal reflection in all directions. When the sound source is distant, most of the reverberation is local and comes from the same direction as the source because, in the imaginary environment, the source is closer to reflectors in that direction.

Because the reverberant characteristics vary from one environment to another, there is no absolute ratio of direct to reverberated sound that corresponds to a specific distance. Depending on the characteristics of the space to be simulated (such as its liveliness), the musician selects, at some reference distance, the ratio of reverberated to direct sound. One choice is to specify the critical distance, which defines the surface where the R/D ratio is 1.

The actual space for performance of the electronic composition must be considered when calculating distance cues, because a room adds reverberation of its own. In an anechoic room, the apparent sound source location has great latitude. As the reverberant qualities of a room increase, it becomes less feasible to simulate sources near the center of the listening space, because the percentage of reverberated sound cannot be brought below the level provided by the room. If computer music is to be performed in a room with substantial reverberation, such as a concert hall, it might be difficult to move the apparent source close to the listeners. The source location can be moved farther out by adding artificial reverberation, but it is hard to move it convincingly inside the perimeter because the reverberation of the room cannot be subtracted from what the listener hears.

Any room has so many different kinds of reflectors that the reverberation arriving at the listener is different from each direction. In fact, tests have shown that a low *interaural coherence*—a measurement that indicates there is little similarity between the reverberation received by each of the two ears—results in a more pleasing sound and a greater feeling of "immersion."[30] When loudspeakers emit signals containing identical reverberation, the interaural coherence is high, producing a sound that seems artificial to the listener. Therefore, each channel should have its own reverberator with slightly different parameters.

10.2D Creating a Listening Space

To simulate localization cues for a sound located at an imaginary point, the loudspeakers must be placed in such a way as to create a listening space within which the cues of localization can be delivered to one or more listeners. Distribution of the signals applied to each channel is calculated on the basis of some physical relationship among the loud-speakers and the listeners. The region in which the listeners receive the cues necessary to perceive the illusory location may be thought of as the *focal area* of the configuration. To avoid confusing the listeners with visual cues that conflict with aural ones (the *ventriloquism effect*), the loudspeakers should not be a dominant feature in the landscape of the performance space. Reducing the ambient light level can also increase the prominence of the aural information.

The musician must choose the dimensionality of localization and the number and position of the loudspeakers to realize a focal area large enough for the intended audience. The relatively expensive hardware to implement each channel compels the musician to minimize their number. Unless special filters are used with a specially positioned listener, two sources can localize the sound in only a portion of a two-dimensional space. A typical use of this configuration is to move the sound laterally in front of the listener(s) at a fixed distance, essentially a one-dimensional situation. Theoretically, a listener situated in the center of a triangle formed by three loudspeakers could be presented with the cues of a source located anywhere in a two-dimensional plane. However, a system of this nature produces cues that are valid only in an extremely small area. A more practical minimum configuration for creating a full two-dimensional plane uses four loudspeakers that mark the corners of a rectangle in which the listeners are centered. Similarly, four speakers forming a tetrahedron can minimally realize a three-dimensional listening space, but more are required for a listening area of any reasonable size. A configuration with eight speakers marking the corners of a rectangular prism is practical.

Audio material that includes HRTF information gives, in theory, accurate cues for only one listener because the choice of HRTF is calculated on the basis of the angular relationships between a particular listener and the loudspeakers. This is not to say that any other listeners present will feel neglected; listeners off the focal point who are not too close to a loudspeaker may still appreciate the motion by the sound sources, but the perceived paths will not be the exact ones that the composer intended.

The focal area can be enlarged by surrounding the listeners with a substantial number of speakers. In this way, the direction of the source can be simulated more accurately in a larger area because actual sources are available in a large number of directions. The actual number of speakers used depends on the angular resolution desired. Sixteen speakers placed in a circle gives a resolution of 22.5°, which allows a reasonable amount of location capability. More can be added with the corresponding increase in resolution.

Such large numbers of high-quality speakers can be extremely expensive. It is possible to alleviate this problem by splitting the sound on the basis of frequency, because loudspeakers that are obligated to produce only mid- and high-frequency sound can be much smaller and hence less expensive than those that must produce low-frequency sound as well. The less-directional low-frequency sound can be supplied by a single high-quality loudspeaker, while the mid- and high-frequency sounds are distributed to a number of smaller loudspeakers located on the periphery of the listening space. Because a listener assigns the location of a sound, in most cases, on the basis of mid- and high-frequency information, this arrangement makes more feasible the simulation of a sound source location through IID cues. A crossover frequency of 200 Hz has proven effective for systems of this kind.[31]

10.2E   Motion of Sound Sources

The preceding discussion has been concerned with the creation of an illusory location
for a stationary source. When the source location is moved about rapidly, another
acoustical phenomenon comes into play. The *Doppler effect* describes the change in
pitch that results when the source and the listener are moving relative to each other.
When a sound source and a listener are moving closer together, the wavefronts of the
sound will reach the listener more frequently, causing the perceived pitch to be raised
from its stationary value. Conversely, if the source and the listener are moving apart, the
pitch will appear lower.

The simulation of a "natural" situation that includes a Doppler shift of frequency
can be problematic, because it alters pitch succession, which is often employed as one
of the principal means of affecting musical continuity. The most successful applications
of Doppler shift in music are those in which the shift of frequency is an integral part of
the musical continuity and not simply a "special effect" that can be expected to wear thin
rather quickly. John Chowning's *Turenas* is a good example of the incorporation of
Doppler shift into a musical structure. (See section 10.3B.)

If the listener is stationary, the Doppler shift may be stated mathematically as:

$$f' = f \frac{c}{c - v}$$

where f is the stationary frequency, f' is the perceived frequency, c is the speed of sound
(approximately 345 m/s), and v is the speed of the source relative to the listener. If the
source and listener are moving closer together, v is positive. Notice that the Doppler
effect shifts all the frequencies in the sound by the same interval, preserving the harmonic relationships in the sound. For example, a sound moving at 19.36 m/s toward the
listener is raised by one half step (5.946%). After passing the listener, a sound receding
at that rate ($v = -19.36$ m/s) would be lowered by a little less than one half step (5.313%).

The Doppler shift derives from the relative speed of the listener and the source; that
is, the change in distance between them per unit of time. Thus, a sound moving in a circle centered on the listener will not change in frequency. A source that is moving directly
toward or directly away from the listener will exhibit the maximum shift for its speed.
When the source moves obliquely, it is more difficult to calculate the speed of the source
relative to the listener. Calculus can be used to transform a given source trajectory into
an expression for velocity. More often, the computer is enlisted to do the calculation by
breaking down the desired trajectory into short segments. The distance between the
source and the listener is calculated at the beginning and end of each segment. The
change in distance (Δd) over the length of the segment is divided by the time (Δt) that it
takes to traverse that segment. The quotient ($\Delta d/\Delta t$) is the average velocity (v) and is used
in the equation above to calculate the Doppler shift that occurs during the traversal of
that segment. Because v is an absolute velocity, the calculation of Δd requires that the
computer be given the actual physical dimensions of the listening space: the distance
from the listener to the loudspeakers.

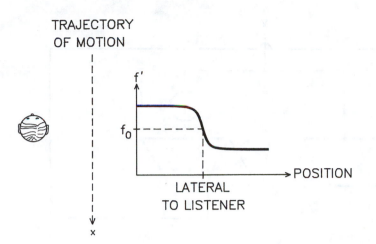

FIGURE 10.21   Doppler shift exhibited by a sound moving past a listener.

The Doppler effect can be used as a compositional element, dramatizing sounds that move past the listener. For example, consider the motion of a source in a straight line as shown in figure 10.21. When the source passes by the listener, the direction of the velocity changes from advancing to receding. This causes a marked pitch change because the pitch goes from being maximally raised to maximally lowered in a short amount of time. The closer the source comes to the listener, the more quickly the change takes place.

10.2F   Designs for Sound Localization

Figure 10.22 shows a design for locating the apparent source of a sound at any point on the line between two loudspeakers. This instrument simulates IID cues only, and so it works best on sounds with significant high-frequency energy. The incoming signal is applied equally to each branch of the design and then attenuated by the appropriate amount in each channel to "locate" the sound between them. The location is specified by the parameter x, which has a value between 0 and 1. When x is 0, all the sound emanates from the right loudspeaker.

In placing the apparent sound source between the loudspeakers, the power in the signal is allocated according to the value of x. That is, the power in the left speaker is given by x and the power in the right speaker is given by $1 - x$. The design apportions the power by operating on the amplitude of each signal, and so the square root of each control function is taken before multiplying it by the amplitude of a channel. To improve computational efficiency, the square-root function is stored in a lookup table. In practice, the value of x would be scaled to reflect the dimensions of the table.

By applying the appropriate function of time to x, the position of the incoming signal can be made to appear to move. If the change of x is linear, the sound will appear to move at a constant rate. A nonlinear change of x will cause the image of the source to accelerate and/or decelerate.

Figure 10.23 shows a quadraphonic listening space formed by four loudspeakers mark-

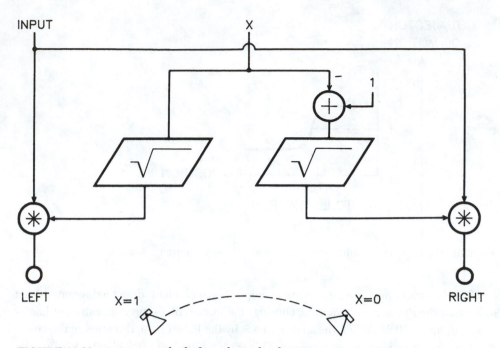

FIGURE 10.22   A stereo method of simulating localization cues.

ing the corners of a square. Through proper allocation of sound among the four loudspeak-ers, the illusion of source location can be created in the plane containing the listener and the loudspeakers. For computational convenience, the angular direction is measured on a scale from 0 to 512 (as shown in the figure). The conventional measure, degrees, is also shown.

The space is divided into four quadrants. To locate the sound in a particular quadrant, the two loudspeakers marking the boundaries of the quadrant contribute. The allocation of the sound to the loudspeakers depends on the angle (θ) between the intended location (I) and the line bisecting the quadrant. Thus, in any quadrant, the range of θ is $\pm 45°$.

If a sound is located in the quadrant in front of the listener (in between speakers LF and RF), the amplitudes of the signals at the loudspeakers (S_{LF}) and S_{RF}) will be apportioned by

$$S_{LF} \propto \frac{1}{2}\left(1 + \frac{\tan\theta}{\tan\theta_{max}}\right)$$

$$S_{RF} \propto \frac{1}{2}\left(1 - \frac{\tan\theta}{\tan\theta_{max}}\right)$$

The symbol $\propto$ designates proportionality. In this case, θ_{max} is $45°$ so that $\tan\theta_{max} = 1$. To save computation time, these angular allocation functions are often stored in lookup tables that are 512 places in length. The 512 positions correspond to the full $360°$ angle that encircles the listener in figure 10.23.

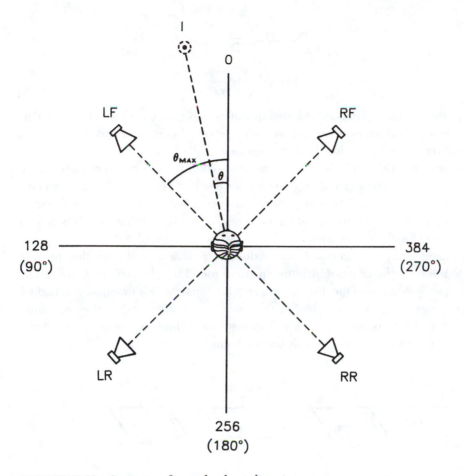

FIGURE 10.23   Geometry of a quadraphonic listening space.

The most important cue a listener uses to judge the distance (D) of a sound source is the ratio of the amplitudes of the reverberated to the unreverberated part of the sound. Figure 10.24 shows a signal-allocation design for placing sounds at the desired locations in a quadraphonic space. The design, based on the model of John Chowning[32] employs reverberators to simulate the effect of distance cues in sound localization. The energy of the direct sound is attenuated by $1/D$, whereas the reverberant energy is attenuated as $1/\sqrt{D}$. In this way, the reverberant energy decreases less than the direct sound as the distance increases. Sounds that are close to the listener have a higher proportion of direct energy. For reasons of convenience, $D = 1$ ordinarily represents the distance between loudspeakers and the listener.

The reverberated energy is divided between local and global reverberation. Because the proportion of local reverberation becomes more significant than global reverberation at large distances, the allocation of the two depends on distance as

$$\text{GLOBAL} \propto \frac{1}{D}$$

$$\text{LOCAL} \propto 1 - \frac{1}{D}$$

Four different reverberators with slightly different parameters should be used. This arrangement simulates a natural situation where the reverberant characteristics differ in the four directions surrounding the listening space.

The instrument shown in figure 10.24 has three controlling parameters: the distance (D); the angular direction (ANG), expressed as a value between 0 and 512; and the percentage of reverberation (PRV). The latter parameter sets the amount of reverberation present when the sound is located at the same distance as the loudspeaker. It is chosen on the basis of the desired characteristics of the space to be simulated.

By changing the angular direction and distance as functions of time, the apparent sound location may be changed. Arbitrary paths of sound travel can be programmed by designing a combination of the distance and angular functions. For example, function F1 shown in figure 10.25, applied to both the distance and the angular direction, will cause a spiral-shaped path of sound travel. AMAX represents the final angle for the sound, including each revolution, and DMAX the maximum distance.

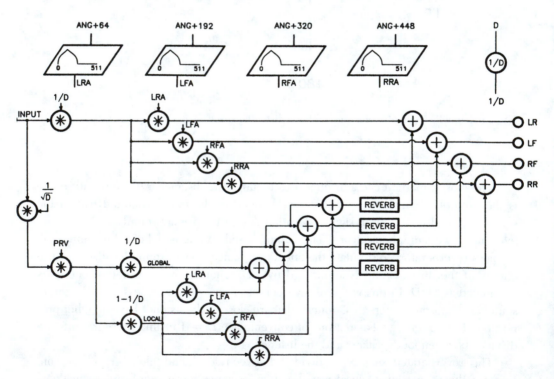

FIGURE 10.24   Quadraphonic "mover" instrument. The loudspeakers are arranged as in figure 10.23.

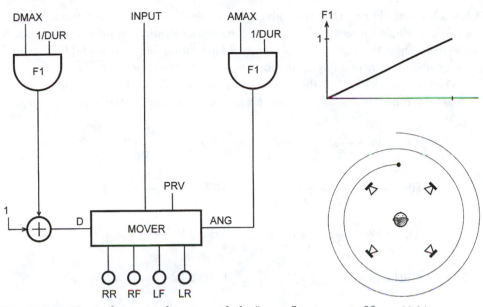

FIGURE 10.25   Realizing spiral motion with the "mover" instrument of figure 10.24.

John Chowning's implementation of a sound localization and movement program utilized computer graphics, so that he could display the sound travel path on the screen of a graphics terminal. Chowning included Doppler shift as an indication of sound travel velocity.

Some systems for sound localization in large spaces are based on the *ambisonic* method pioneered in the early 1970s by Michael Gerzon,[33] among others. Essentially a method of producing IID cues, it has been implemented in both two and three dimensions. Although larger numbers of loudspeakers can be used, a minimal three-dimensional system uses eight loudspeakers marking the corners of a cube and attempts to locate the sound at points on the surface of the sphere passing through the corners of the cube. To simplify the production and recording of the signals, four channels are produced containing the localization information in what is termed the "B-format." The four channels are designated by X, Y, Z, and W, and are subsequently decoded to provide the drive for the eight loudspeakers. As before, let ϕ represent the azimuthal angle and θ the elevation angle. Defining S as the input signal to be localized gives the following set of encoding equations:

$$X = S \cos\phi \cos\theta$$

$$Y = S \sin\phi \cos\theta$$

$$Z = S \sin\theta$$

$$W = \frac{1}{\sqrt{2}} S$$

A key advantage of this format is the ability to mix signals containing ambisonic location cues from multiple sources while retaining the original localization information for each individual source. In addition, transforms exist for rotating the entire sound field around a designated axis[34] by multiplying the four channels by the appropriate factors.

The loudspeaker signals in the cubic configuration are allocated (using the notation L/R for left/right, F/B for front/back, and U/D for up/down) according to the decoding scheme

$$LFU = W + \frac{1}{\sqrt{2}}(X + Y + Z) \qquad LFD = W + \frac{1}{\sqrt{2}}(X + Y - Z)$$

$$RFU = W + \frac{1}{\sqrt{2}}(X - Y + Z) \qquad RFD = W + \frac{1}{\sqrt{2}}(X - Y - Z)$$

$$LBU = W + \frac{1}{\sqrt{2}}(-X + Y + Z) \qquad LBD = W + \frac{1}{\sqrt{2}}(-X + Y - Z)$$

$$RBU = W + \frac{1}{\sqrt{2}}(-X - Y + Z) \qquad RBD = W + \frac{1}{\sqrt{2}}(-X - Y - Z)$$

Because these systems are designed for use with a large number of listeners, HRTF information included in the audio material does not evoke the intended spatial impression, because each listener occupies a unique position with respect to the loudspeakers.

10.3 MODIFICATION OF SAMPLED SOUND

In recent years, composers of computer music have turned more and more to the modification of natural sound for inclusion in their compositions. The modification of an LPC analysis of speech (section 7.1I) and the manipulation of phase vocoder data (section 7.3C) are two examples of this approach that have already been discussed. This section will examine other methods that can be used to manipulate files of sampled sound, followed by some descriptive compositional examples.

10.3A *Musique Concrète*

Musique concrète is the term used by its inventor, the French composer Pierre Schaeffer, to distinguish the new genre from traditional, notated "abstract" music. Musique concrète is made from recordings of sounds from the "real world." The recordings are subjected to various manipulations in order to adapt them for inclusion into musical contexts. The early works of *musique concrète* were made from sound sources far removed from the concert hall. For example, Schaeffer composed his first work using recordings of the sounds associated with trains, and one of the compositions by Schaeffer's colleague, Pierre Henry, is *Variations on a Door and a Sigh.*[35]

The early experiments in *musique concrète* were made on phonograph records, but the new genre turned to the medium of the tape recorder in the early 1950s. A number of standard tape-manipulation techniques developed and became part of the repertoire of techniques for composing *musique concrète*—or, as it was called in the United States, tape music.

The principal techniques for making *musique concrète* were developed around the natural possibilities for sound processing with the analog tape recorder. They were: cutting and splicing tape, tape loops, change of tape speed, change of direction of tape, tape delay, and combinations of the above into successions of sounds known as *montages,* or into simultaneous combinations called *mixages.* Today, these operations are performed on sounds that have been stored in digital form on the hard disk of a computer system equipped with the appropriate software. All the techniques developed for analog technology are still in use on computer systems. In addition, digital signal-processing techniques greatly expand the repertoire and nuance for the manipulations of recorded sound.

In computer music, these methods of manipulating recorded sounds are commonly grouped under the term *sampling.* In the basic technique of sampling, a natural sound is digitally recorded for a predetermined length and stored in a sound file on a disk or in a wave table in computer memory. Once it is sampled and stored, the sound can be modified. In fact, it is rare that a sound file is used without some editing; at the very least, samples at the beginning and end of the record are trimmed so that the sound starts and stops at the expected times, but many other modifications are possible. For example, the sound can be passed through an envelope generator (see section 4.5) that is triggered by external events.

Cutting and splicing serve as means for reordering recorded sound. This technique can also serve to extract fragments from a larger context. The classic example of this is the work that Japanese composer Joji Yuasa made in the 1960s out of the nonverbal "uhs" and "ahs" uttered in interviews by public figures in response to difficult questions. Cutting and splicing are done with the use of a sound editor. A sound editor provides many of the same functions for the musician as a word processing program does for the writer. A typical sound editor includes the visual display of the sound in time-versus-amplitude form (often at different degrees of resolution simultaneously) and provides a repertoire of operations for editing the sound. Figure 10.26 shows the display of a sound segment with Sound Designer II, by Digidesign. The musician cuts and splices sounds by the familiar "cut and paste" operations of computer editors. The sound editor provides the facility to listen to segments of sound chosen by highlighting with the mouse. One of the traditional problems of cutting and splicing—audible clicks at edit points—is addressed in most sound editors through provision for applying envelopes of arbitrary shape and length to the segment of sound chosen.

To increase the timbral similarities between tones played at different pitches, a fixed formant can be imparted by passing the sampled sound through a band-pass filter (see section 6.3). Filtering delivers the best results when the original sampled sound is recorded at a dynamic level that has a rich spectrum. In other words, an audible formant cannot be created when there is little energy present to filter in that region of the spectrum.

Sound editors have greatly facilitated the work for composers making music from fragments of recorded sound. For example, Luciano Berios's *Thema* (1958) was made by extensive cutting, splicing, and mixing of fragments of a reading and vocal rendition of

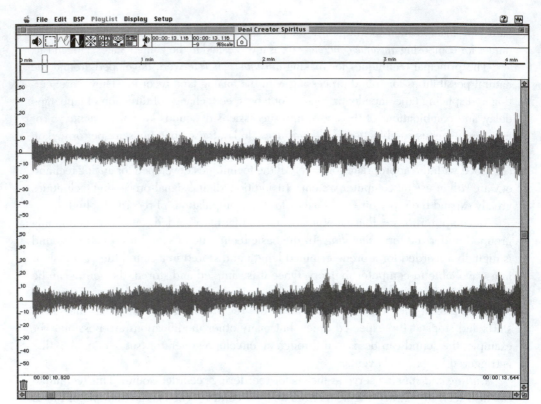

FIGURE 10.26   Display of a sound segment by the Sound Designer II sound-editing software.

part of James Joyce's *Ulysses*. In 1981, Berio commented, "It's surprising now to think that I spent several months of my life cutting tape while today I could achieve many of the same results in much less time by using a computer."[36]

A *loop* is made by joining sounds end to end in such a way that the recorded passage will repeat continuously on playback. A loop can be made out of a single sound, such as a gong tone; or cutting and splicing can order a diverse group of sounds for use as a loop. Looping avoids the "tape recorder" effect because the duration of the tone can be lengthened without affecting its pitch. A common use of a sound loop is as a background in front of which other, more finely detailed sounds are heard. Steve Reich and Charles Amirkhanian have made entire compositions out of loops repeating limited groups of sounds—often fragments of speech. Many sound editor programs enable one to listen to a selected sound file or sound segment in loop form—beginning playback again as soon as it is finished. Sound editors, too, typically enable one to insert pointers to indicate loop points within a sound file.

The success of this technique depends heavily on the specification of the end points of the waveform to be looped. Because it is repeated, the beginning and end of this waveform must have the same amplitude to avoid audible transients at the transition. A widely used technique is to mark the beginning and end of the waveform at points where it crosses 0 with the same slope. For instance, specifying the beginning of the segment at a zero crossing with a rising slope would require that the end point of the sig-

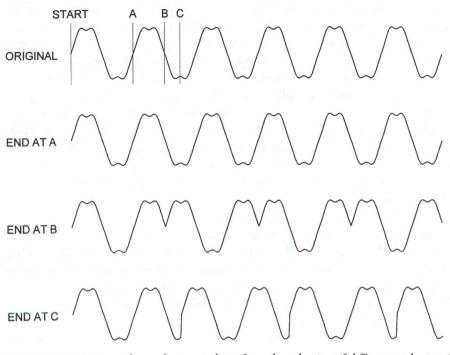

FIGURE 10.27   Looped waveforms resulting from the selection of different endpoints for the segment to be repeated.

nal also cross 0 with a rising slope. As an example, figure 10.27 shows the consequences of selecting various end points on the original sampled waveform. Terminating at point A results in a smooth transition when the waveform segment is repeated. The repetitive waveforms produced by ending the segment at either point B or C are dissimilar to the original and would have audible discontinuities, creating an abundance of harmonics that could potentially cause aliasing.

Another feature of sound editors that provides the possibility of great musical variety is *transposition.* In tape music, transposition was accomplished by changing the tape speed. American composer Vladimir Ussachevsky used speed change of tape loops extensively in his work, often on sounds of percussion instruments such as cymbals and piano.

The simplest sampling equipment accomplishes this by sending samples from the wave table to a D/A converter at a sampling rate according to the desired interval of transposition. On the computer, changing the sampling rate has an effect similar to tape speed change. For example, all the frequency components of a sound recorded at 44.1 kHz will sound an octave lower when played back at 22.05 kHz and take twice as long to play. This variable-playback sampling-rate (VPSR) method is relatively easy to implement in hardware. However, it only works properly on systems equipped with a low-pass filter with a variable cutoff frequency that tracks the sampling rate, because the filter is needed to smooth the output and suppress any components above the Nyquist frequency. The VPSR technique also makes it more difficult to digitally process the samples with other unit generators such as digital filters. Thus, it is preferable to maintain a sampling rate that does not vary with the rate at which the sampled sound is being scanned.

Decimation and *interpolation* are the digital techniques for raising and lowering, respectively, the frequency of recorded sounds without changing the sampling rate. One can raise the frequency of a sound one octave by eliminating every other of its samples. However, aliasing can result, especially if the original sound has significant energy in the upper portion of its spectrum. For example, at a sampling rate of 44.1 kHz, if the original sound has a fundamental frequency of 1500 Hz, the sound can contain up to 29 harmonics without aliasing. If, before eliminating every other sample, the 1500-Hz tone is filtered to contain a maximum of 14 harmonics, every other sample can be eliminated to create a 3-kHz tone with no aliasing. This is most easily accomplished using a special digital filter called a *decimating low-pass filter*, which not only eliminates the requisite number of samples but also properly filters the sound.

Intuitively, one might think that the interpolation of new sample values between pairs of original samples to lower a sound an octave would create no problems with aliasing. Unfortunately, this is not the case. Simple linear interpolation creates aliased components that can be especially prominent on bright sounds. Some interpolation schemes take into account several samples on either side of the new sample when calculating its value. These methods of higher-order interpolation have been shown to be improvements but are still audibly imperfect. The best approach uses an *interpolating low-pass filter*,[37] which not only interpolates but also alters the frequency content to minimize aliasing.

For speed changes other than integers, interpolating and decimating low-pass filters can be combined into a single filter algorithm. Figure 10.28 shows a block diagram of such a system. The first block, the interpolator, fills in $m - 1$ samples between every pair of samples in the original. The third block, the decimator, eliminates $n - 1$ samples between every pair of the interpolated samples. The low-pass filter, inserted between the interpolator and the decimator, has a cutoff frequency that depends on the choice of m and n. The filter smooths the interpolated waveform to eliminate any aliasing that would result from the interpolation or decimation process. The frequency of the signal coming out of the system, f_{out}, is given by the relationship:

$$f_{out} = f_{in}\,\frac{n}{m}$$

where f_{in} is the input frequency. Thus, the choice of the integers, m and n, determines the change in frequency. For example, to lower the frequency of a sound by a perfect fourth (a

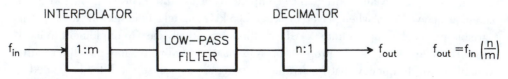

FIGURE 10.28 Block diagram of an interpolation/decimation algorithm that enables a sound to be transposed.

change in frequency by the factor 3/4), one would set $m = 4$ and $n = 3$. Because the interpolation process creates many additional samples, additional memory in the filter algorithms is required to accommodate them. The actual amount depends on the accuracy desired.

Playing back a sound in the *reverse order* of its samples provides a further means of varying the recorded sound. Playing a sound backwards reverses its characteristic envelope and spectral evolution. Reverse piano tones, for example, entail a crescendo in which the spectrum becomes increasingly rich. Reversed recordings of piano and cymbal sounds are often used to lead into other sonic events.

Tape delay is a reverberation-like effect that was easily obtained on a tape recorder by simultaneously playing back a sound while rerecording it. On an analog tape recorder this effect was possible because the magnetic record head and the read head were separated by enough distance to produce a noticeable delay. It is implemented on a computer with delay lines of the sort described in section 10.1B.

In addition to the implementation of the musique concrète techniques with origins in analog tape manipulation, the computer has fostered a variety of purely digital ones as well. These are implemented in many different forms of software. Some are found as features in general-purpose synthesis and processing languages such as Csound or Cmusic. Others exist as standalone programs in which a number of digital signal-processing algorithms are implemented. One of the latter is Soundhack,[38] a body of programs for sound manipulation written by Tom Erbe for the Macintosh and Powerbook lines of computers.[39] Soundhack's contribution to the field was acknowledged in 1996 when it was awarded first prize in the first international computer music software competition sponsored by the Groupe de Musique Experimentale de Bourges (France).

Soundhack offers the musician a wide variety of operations to perform on recorded sound including a binaural filter, convolution, phase vocoder, spectral mutation, varispeed, and spectral dynamics, among others. The *binaural filter* imposes an HRTF (head-related transfer function) to enable the musician to control the apparent location of a sound (see section 10.2A). Figure 10.29 shows the screen through which a dialog is established to specify the desired position or trajectory for the sound for sound placement. This general form is followed for the other Soundhack operations as well.

Convolution is becoming a favorite operation for transforming two separate sound files into a file that incorporates some of the characteristics of each. Convolution in Soundhack entails treating one file as an impulse response and the other as the input to that impulse. It is a method very closely related to cross-synthesis (see section 7.1G), in which two sounds are combined to produce a digital signal whose spectrum is related to the spectra of the individual sounds.

A useful way to interpret convolution is as a dynamic filtering operation. The operation of convolution performed on two signals in the time domain is equivalent to the multiplication of their spectra in the frequency domain. Suppose digital signals $x(n)$ and $w(n)$ with discrete Fourier transforms $X(k)$ and $W(k)$, respectively, are convolved to produce the digital sequence $y(n)$ with a corresponding spectrum $Y(k)$. The frequency-domain expression for the convolution operation can then be written as

$$Y(k) = X(k)W(k)$$

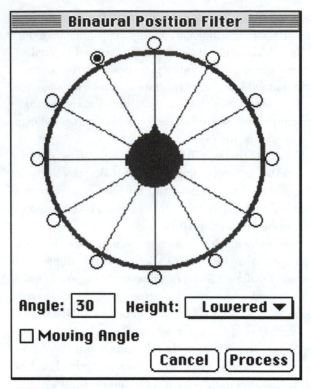

FIGURE 10.29   Screen used on Soundhack to specify the location of a sound.

When spectrum $X(k)$ has a peak at 2 kHz, for example, the spectrum of the output, $Y(k)$, will also have a maximum. Thus, one way to conceptualize convolution is as a filtering process in which one signal is passed through a filter whose frequency response is the spectrum of the other signal. Because multiplication is commutative, it is not possible to state which input is the one being filtered and which determines the parameters of the filter; they essentially filter each other. However, passing a sound through a filter that varies dynamically in sympathy with the spectrum of another sound has the potential to yield some musically interesting results.

The phase vocoder described in section 7.3 gives the user the possibility of time stretching a sound file without changing its frequency content. It has other applications as well. The *phase vocoder* implemented in Soundhack gives the user a myriad of options to obtain the right combination of parameters for accomplishing the desired effect.

Spectral mutation[40] provides a facility for making timbral *cross-fades*. This feature of Soundhack was realized with a great deal of involvement and encouragement by composer Larry Polansky. Spectral mutation takes two sound files, the *source* and the *target*, to produce a new sound file, the *mutant*. The source and target files are broken into time frames and the spectrum is calculated in bands for each frame. In the simplest operation, the mutant file is created by interpolating amplitude/phase information from the spectrum of each source. An interpolation parameter provided to the musician allocates the proportion of each source. The resulting spectral description of the mutant file is then retransformed into samples. The spectral mutation feature implements several other methods of combining the sources such as interpolating only certain frequency bands. The spectral mutation function provides a great variety of interpolation trajectory types for effecting the mutation from one timbre to another.

The *varispeed* function, based on the analog technique of changing tape speed, implements a 10-octave varispeed control. One of its features is the ability to change speed according to an arbitrary function of time. One can also control the number of points used by the necessary smoothing filters in the interpolation/decimation process.

The *spectral dynamics* functions perform the conventional dynamic processes of gating, ducking, expansion, and compression. The algorithm separates the sound into uniformly spaced frequency bands. A threshold level can be declared either for each individual band or for the bands as a whole. In compression mode, when the level of a particular band exceeds the threshold, the amplitude of that band is reduced by a specified amount. In the converse operation of expansion, the sound is expanded when the amplitude of the bands exceeding the threshold is increased. One application of expansion is to reduce the perception of ambient noise (such as hiss) by not increasing the amplitude of those bands where there is no signal. Because an audio signal constantly varies, the rate at which these processes activate influences their success. Soundhack allows the response speed to be optimized for the contents of a particular sound file by the specification of a time constant.

10.3B   Compositional Examples

John Chowning's composition *Turenas* (1972)[41] demonstrates two important and original techniques: computer simulation of instrument-like tones with FM synthesis and sound travel in a quadraphonic space. The compositional concern in *Turenas* with "naturalness" is expressed in the title which is an anagram of "Natures." *Turenas*, a 10-minute work in three parts, invites the listener to experience a new and very special world of sound.

The most dramatic element of the first and third parts of the work is the travel of the sounds. For the traveling sounds, Chowning designed a computer orchestra of predominantly percussive sounds. In doing so, he took advantage of our ability to perceive most easily the location of short, impulsive sounds. Even the more sustained sounds, for example, the electronic "insects" or "bats," have an impulsive aspect such as buzzing or clicking.

For the sound movement in *Turenas*, Chowning wrote a "front-end" for the Stanford Music 10 language, which enabled him to display graphically the path of travel for a sound around the listening space. He wrote software that caused calculated patterns to be displayed on a CRT screen. From the sound travel pattern and information regarding the distance between the loudspeakers and the speed of sound travel, Chowning's programs generated the control statements necessary to create the desired paths of travel. Figure 10.30 shows an example of a sound travel path heard near the beginning of *Turenas* together with the controls for the Music 10 orchestra.

The middle part of *Turenas*, while not as active from the standpoint of sound travel,

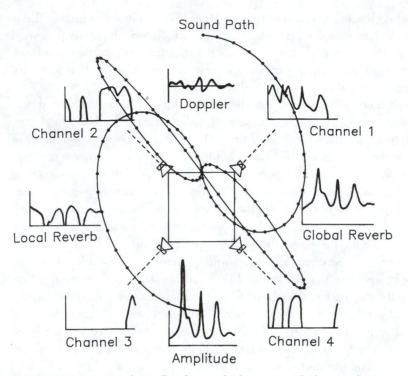

FIGURE 10.30   Sound travel path near the beginning of Chowning's *Turenas*. *(Reprinted with permission of John Chowning.)*

contains some very realistic brass, string, and wind instrument tones made with FM synthesis. This part of the work employs reverberation to create a sense of spaciousness.

Charles Dodge's *Earth's Magnetic Field*[42] makes extensive use of reverberation and location techniques. Both were used as ways of enhancing a rather simple timbre created by subtractive synthesis. There are two principal features of the computer application in *Earth's Magnetic Field:* temporal and timbral. The composition is a musical setting of the succession of values that are produced by an index of the effect of the sun's radiation on the magnetic field that surrounds the earth. Each value of the index represents an average of the readings for a 3-hour period, at 12 monitoring stations throughout the world. Because there are eight 3-hour periods in a 24-hour day, the year's activity is represented by 2920 readings. The form of the original index resembles music notation and is called a *Bartels musical diagram* after its inventor, Julius Bartels. In a Bartels musical diagram, a reading can assume one of 28 possible values. For the composition, the 28 values of the index were mapped into four octaves of diatonic C. Meantone temperament was used in playing the notes of the piece.

In the year chosen for the composition, 1961, the data exhibit 21 "sudden commencements": points where sudden increases in the values of the index occur. These breakpoints were chosen as the sectional divisions of the work. The 21 sections delimited by sudden commencements (S.C.) were grouped into five parts:

PART	S.C. SECTION
I	1–3
II	4–6
III	7–10
IV	11–15
V	16–21

The graph in figure 10.31 was employed to control several aspects of the composition. It shows the value of the highest reading within an S.C. section versus the length of the section. For example, the changing tempo of the first part of the piece is based on an application of the graphical pattern to speed. Between 30 and 1600 articulations per minute were made with the tempo feature of Music 4BF. The continuous change of tempo is heard in parts I, III, and IV of the work.

A second variety of temporal control is heard in parts II and V. Here, a fixed tempo of one beat per second is used. A compositional subroutine was used to group the readings into notes in the following way: a succession of two identical readings was played as a single note lasting for one second. The whole group of intervening readings before the next pair of identical readings was also played in one second. The actual number of different, equally timed tones during the second beat depends on the number of readings that occur between double readings. In the data upon which this piece was constructed, the number of these varies from 2 to 25.

The instrument designs for *Earth's Magnetic Field* use different sorts of filters to create "radiant effects," which reflect in some metaphorical sense the nature of the solar radiation itself. The instrument designs also contribute to the gradual transformation that takes place in the sound of the work. The composition begins with tones that focus on the fundamental frequency with simple timbre. These are gradually replaced with

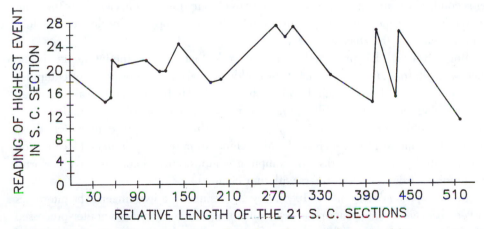

FIGURE 10.31 "Sudden commencement" graph used to control aspects of the composition in Dodge's *Earth's Magnetic Field.*

diffuse textures with secondary pitches around the fundamental. It is primarily as a result of the instrument designs that the pitches of the individual readings are subsumed into reverberating textures in which certain pitches are favored over others and in which the "aura" sounded around the pitches are equally prominent with, or even more prominent than, the notes themselves.

The first part of the work is sounded with the configuration shown in figure 10.32. The sound is plain and straightforward. Its most prominent feature is the continual acceleration and deceleration that outlines the pattern of the sudden-commencement graph.

The second part of the composition employs the fixed tempo of one beat per second. The sound of part II results from feeding the output of the instrument from part I (the "basic instrument") into three reverberation unit generators, with reverberation times of 2.5, 5, and 10 seconds. The effect of spaciousness is achieved by positioning the output of each reverberator in a different initial location between the two loudspeakers and moving it slowly between them. The sound in part II is quite bright, owing to the reverberation that prolongs the high harmonics created by the nonstandard use of a balance unit generator as described in section 6.9.

The third part of the piece again includes continuous fluctuations in tempo. The basic instrument is fed into a single comb filter with a reverberation time of 2.5 seconds and a loop time of 30 ms. This causes the loudness of certain tones to be greatly changed. Pitches with periods close to multiples of the loop time of the comb are emphasized, even exaggerated, while tones with frequencies that fall between the peaks of the filter are relatively attenuated. As described above, the comb filter also adds frequencies of its own, due to ringing.

Part IV, using continuous time, feeds the output of the basic instrument into a single all-pass network with the same loop time as the comb filter of the previous section. In this section, not only does the tempo fluctuate in a variation on the pattern of figure 10.31, but so do the amplitude of the tones and their apparent location between the two loudspeakers.

The final part of *Earth's Magnetic Field* uses six comb filters and two all-pass networks to create "super-reverberated" effects. Once again, the tempo is fixed at one beat per second. There are a great many secondary pitches in this section, caused by the combined effect of several combs and all-passes with different loop times prolonging the harmonics created by the "balance effect."

Roger Reynolds has produced a series of works that "explore the interaction of the voice with illusory auditory spaces."[43] Reynolds has taken full advantage of computer techniques for reverberation and localization of sound. He has been especially involved in developing means for controlling the apparent movement of voices in quadraphonic space. Reynolds' computer music compositions exhibit a structure in which those aspects of the musical texture created with techniques of reverberation and localization form a central part of the works. His computer compositions all combine live performers and/or recordings of performers with four-channel tape.

In *Voicespace IV: The Palace* (1980), Reynolds contrasts a live singer (who alternates between bass and countertenor registers) with a recording containing computer-processed sound of the singer's voice. The recording for the processed voice consists of a reading of the poem, "The Palace," by Jorge Luis Borges and includes certain "extended vocal techniques." The reader, Philip Larsen, a singer highly experienced in experimental vocal

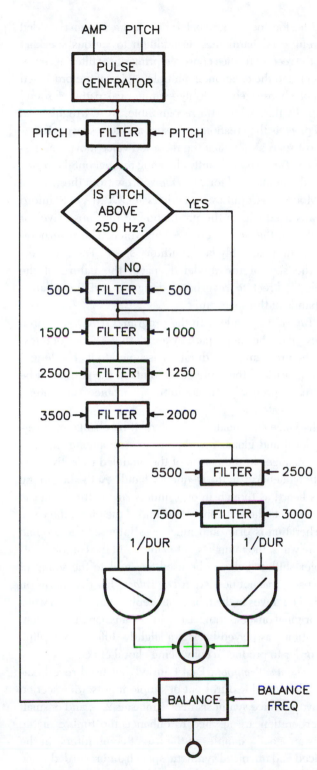

FIGURE 10.32   Basic design for sound of Dodge's *Earth's Magnetic Field.*

music, has an extraordinary voice with a four-octave range. For *The Palace,* Larsen recorded Tibetan Chant drone tones with reinforced harmonics, in addition to various speaking voices. The computer processing of the recorded voice consisted primarily of filtering, exaggerated reverberation, spatial location, and the creation of multiple copies of the processed voice in choruses. Reynolds did not choose geometrically symmetrical paths of sound travel, but rather chose to create paths that, while still recognizable, were irregular. An extremely important feature of this piece is the creation of illusory auditory space. He has designed not just one, but many "host spaces" in which the recorded voice moves on designated paths. The illusory space of *The Palace* is constantly changing throughout the piece.

The programming system that Reynolds used for *The Palace* drew from the work of Loren Rush, John Grey, James A. Moorer, Gareth Loy, and others at CCRMA of Stanford University. One way this system was used was in the production of the "obsessive" or extremely dense reverberated quality of the processed speaking voice. The reverberation time was 50 seconds—that of an unimaginably large auditory space. The reverberation controls were, effectively, the size of the modeled space, the nature of the reflective surfaces, the proportion of direct to reverberated signal, and the relative weighting of sound in frequency bands of the spectrum.

The sound movement in *The Palace* was made with the program QUAD, by Loren Rush. In this program, the user describes the sound path by answering a series of questions. A sound path is drawn with the program and a duration assigned to it. The length of the function describing the sound path and the number of points in the path must be specified in order to define the path precisely. In addition, a distance (in meters) between the loudspeakers must be indicated.

The computer processing of the voice continually "relocated" it by change of reverberation time (and distribution of local and global reverberant energy among the four loudspeakers). Also employed were changes in the nature of the modeled reflective surfaces, and thus changes of distribution of energy in the frequency bands. At the beginning of the piece, the recorded voice is heard as though in a gigantic space with an intense reverberant quality. It is placed off center to the left front. At the end of the piece, the voice has been relocated, and the reverberation is drier and much less intense. The looping sound near the end of the piece ("the walls, the ramparts," etc.) moves in the complex pattern shown in figure 10.33. Doppler shift, which can be used to simulate the sound of rapidly moving physical bodies in space, was not needed in *The Palace.* For the chorus on the words, "The date which the chisel engraves in the tablet," six replications of each word were clustered in time around the original on a random basis with a Gaussian distribution. (See section 11.1B(5).) Each replication was played back at a slightly different sampling rate and retuned to the original in order to produce a convincing choral effect.

In *Six Fantasies on a Poem by Thomas Campion,* Paul Lansky[44] has used reverberation techniques to create complex, elaborated textures out of simple inputs. (See section 7.1I for aspects of the work that involve voice synthesis.) For Fantasies 2, 4, and 6, small amounts of natural-sounding reverberation are applied to enhance the timbre of the voice. The third and fifth Fantasies are good examples of the use of comb filters. In the third Fantasy, "Her reflection," voiced and unvoiced synthetic speech and recorded voice were fed into large banks of comb filters. Often, as many as 18 comb filters were used at

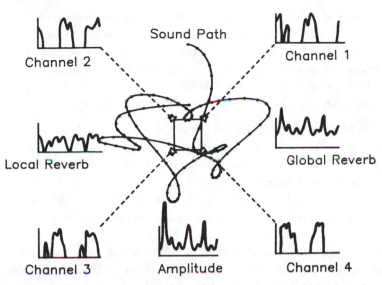

FIGURE 10.33   Sound path and travel function for Reynolds's *The Palace. (Reprinted with the permission of Roger Reynolds.)*

once. Each was a double comb filter in which the output was fed back into the input. This technique has the effect of sharpening the peaks of the emphasized frequencies and increasing the attenuation of those between. The loop times of the combs were related to each other by one of two methods: equal differences and equal ratios in time.

The result of the process is only occasionally intelligible, and then as highly reverberated speech. More often, only an impression of the voice input is present in the pitched and noisy textures created by the combs.

For the fifth Fantasy, banks of comb filters were applied to a whispered reading of the poem, rendering it largely indistinct. Attention is drawn to the percussion sounds made from small portions of the speech. To do this, Lansky designed special filters (like comb filters, but with a unity gain factor) to prevent decay of an input signal. He applied a signal to one of the filters, changed the rate at which the signal was sampled, and thus produced foldover, which created the desired musical effect. This is equivalent to creating a wave table out of digitized sound and then sampling it as an oscillator would using various sampling increments. (See section 4.3.)

Gerald Bennett's composition *Rainstick* is an excellent example of a work that combines computer sound synthesis and sound modification. The source for the sound to be modified by the computer came from recordings of a Native American instrument whose original purpose was for use in conjuring rain. The composer describes the instrument he used:

It is a 78 cm. long piece of bamboo with a diameter of 7 cm. and is closed at each end by a membrane made of hide. More than 100 fine pieces of wood, about the size of toothpicks, have been set into holes drilled across the bamboo tube and glued into place. The tube is filled with small pebbles. When the tube is quickly turned into a vertical position, the pebbles fall to the lower end, striking the traversal pieces of wood on their way down. Because the pieces of wood are fixed to the tube, the walls of the tube amplify the sound of the wood, and the result sounds very much like rain. When the pebbles hit the hide at the end, the sound is like that of drops of water falling into a puddle. If one moves the rainstick slowly into a vertical position, the pebbles run down the side of the tube, making a quite different sound, perhaps more like flowing water.[45]

Indeed, the range of water-related sounds that occur in the work—all taken from the sounds of the rainstick itself—is very wide. Bennett was "fascinated that the rainstick could make both continuous and discontinuous sound and could modulate between them." The sorts of modification of the recorded sound found in *Rainstick* include various sorts of direct sound-file manipulation such as playing the sound backwards, all-pass filtering to make the discontinuous sounds more continuous, and changing the speed of the sound file (and thus its frequency content).

An analysis of the sound of the rainstick is used in an important way in the piece. Bennett derived a series of proportions from the timing of salient events in one of the rainstick recordings. This numerical series

0.0   0.2137   0.4188   0.553   0.6525   0.718   0.7609   0.8715   1

is used in a variety of ways to impart a sense of great unity about the work. The proportions of the series are used to determine timing of events at all levels of the work—sometimes the rhythm of a phrase reflects the pattern, sometimes it is heard in other ways—in a different order, for example. The series determines the lengths of the eight sections of the work, as well. The way in which the intervals between members of the series decrease until 0.7609 and then increase again to the end can be readily heard in the timing of some places in the work. The series is used for frequency relationships as well as timing. Bennett writes, "All transpositions, but also all center frequencies for band-pass filtering, all choices of discrete pitches for the (synthesized) singing voices were determined by turning this set of proportions into the vertical plane and then using it to determine frequencies."

Bennett's specific way of making discrete frequencies from the series is as follows. He first decided to map the proportions into the frequency space between middle C (261.6 Hz) and the C two octaves higher (1046.5 Hz). The resulting list of frequencies was computed by first noting that $\log_{10}(1046.5) = 3.0197$, $\log_{10}(261.63) = 2.4177$, and their difference is 0.6020. From these values, the frequencies were calculated from

$$
\begin{aligned}
\text{antilog}(2.4177) &= 261.63 \\
\text{antilog}(2.4177 + (0.2137 * 0.602)) &= 351.84 \\
\text{antilog}(2.4177 + (0.4188 * 0.602)) &= 467.54 \\
\text{antilog}(2.4177 + (0.553 * 0.602)) &= 563.13 \\
\text{antilog}(2.4177 + (0.6525 * 0.602)) &= 646.41 \\
\text{antilog}(2.4177 + (0.718 * 0.602)) &= 707.84 \\
\text{antilog}(2.4177 + (0.7609 * 0.602)) &= 751.21 \\
\text{antilog}(2.4177 + (0.8715 * 0.602)) &= 875.66 \\
\text{antilog}(2.4177 + (1.0 * 0.602)) &= 1046.50
\end{aligned}
$$

The antilog function is equivalent to 10^α where α is the argument of the function. These frequencies are heard at prominent places in the work. In fact, a chord formed by playing the tones all at once is prominently sounded at the end of the work.

The most prominent use of recognizable pitches is with the synthesized singing vocal tones. Bennett synthesizes both the female and the male singing voice using the FOF method of synthesis.[46]

In *Nekyia,* composer Gareth Loy has made a composition that is like a nonverbal drama in which the movement of synthetic and concrete material intermingles. The effect is often that of recorded sounds; at other times, it is like that of synthetic variants of recorded sounds. The quadraphonic *Nekyia* extensively employs reverberation and localization of sound as well as techniques of musique concrète. Reverberation and localization are central to the composition, as can be seen in one of Loy's statements about the piece: "One intent with which the piece was shaped included a desire to form images of dense space, where the sound materials could be thought of as sonic actors or dancers, moving in two dimensions."[47] Loy continues, "I wanted the sound-space to surround the listener, to bring the listener into the same plane of motion as the sound-actors." The movement of sound in *Nekyia* goes beyond its more usual uses. In *Nekyia,* the patterns of circular and spiral movement of sound are used to demarcate the formal structure of the composition.

Concrete sounds play a major role in *Nekyia.* The vocabulary of sounds captured from the "real world" ranges from the sound of shattering glass, through choruses of crickets, to rolling cymbal sounds. A good example of this can be heard near the end of the work where a "chorus" of rolling cymbal sounds is transposed up by a semitone six successive times. Loy writes, "The method utilized to compose the piece achieves the integration of synthetic and concrete techniques into one control structure." (See section 11.2C for aspects of *Nekyia* involving computer manipulation of musical motives.)

Hothouse, an electroacoustic composition by Paul Koonce, is an excellent example of the power the computer can bring to musique concrète. In this piece, the source material comes from recordings of a wide variety of musical instrument tones, vocal tones, bird calls, and other sounds of the sort that are usually thought of as "environmental" rather than "musical." The central metaphor of the work is that of the hothouse—a place where living things can grow, outside their native habitat in juxtaposition to other living things similarly taken from their expected environmental context. In the composition, we hear a range of sounds that could never have "lived" in the same place at the same time, yet which inform and enrich each other through their abutments.

There are few works in the literature of musique concrète that succeed as vividly as *Hothouse* in realizing the ideal of the *objet sonore* in the sense that the recognizable sounds become important to us, not for the recognition of their acoustical origin, but for their place in the piece of music they help form. One of the ways that the *objets sonores* are understood as "music" and not as "recorded sound" is through the very careful shading of the sounds through filtering of all sorts and sound localization. Placing the sounds in a completely new context where the sonic characteristics are imposed by the composer—a new sonic environment—succeeds very well in convincing us on a visceral level that what we are hearing is not the willful agglomeration of sonic elements, but rather a glimpse at a new universe of sonic relationships.

Jean-Claude Risset's *Sud* (1985), commissioned by the Groupe de Recherches Musicales (GRM) in Paris, is a work of musique concrète in four movements. It is symptomatic of the evolution of the field of electroacoustic music that, by the time of this composition, the GRM (noted for its invention and fostering of musique concrète) should have commissioned a work from the composer who is best known for his early original contributions to synthesis technique. In accepting the commission from GRM, Risset honored the group by making a piece that includes prominent use of concrete materials, yet treated in a highly original way that draws extensively on his background as a synthesist. The work is based on environmental recordings made in the south *(sud)* of France by the composer. While the work might be considered a kind of musical portrait of that countryside, it is remarkable for the way that it combines, contrasts, juxtaposes, and blends both natural, recorded sounds and purely synthesized sounds.

The fourth movement, for example, has as its recorded source material the sound of waves at the shore of the Mediterranean. This sound is subjected to what Risset has called "subtractive cross-synthesis"; that is, the sound is played through a set of filters tuned to pitches of a major-minor scale (G, B, E, F♯, G♯, B, E, F♮, G♮, B, E, F♯, G♯, etc.). Risset observes, "I used resonant filters tuned to these pitches to filter natural sounds. If the filters are sharply tuned and thus resonant, one gets the feeling of a harp tuned to those pitches and set into vibration by the sounds, which only leave the trace of their energy flux."[48]

In the third movement of *Sud*, we hear a similar scheme employed to produce what the composer calls a "bird's raga"—sharply tuned filters excited by bird song in such a way that we hear only the resulting scale of tuned filter tones "with rhythms and with quantized frequency contours originating from the bird's song."[49]

NOTES

1. Dempster, Stuart. "Standing Waves—1976." 1750 Arch Records (S-1775), 1979.

2. Sabine, W. C. "Reverberation." In R. B. Lindsay (ed.), *Acoustics: Historical and Philosophical Development.* Stroudsburg, Pa.: Dowden, Hutchinson, and Ross, 1972.

3. Harris, C. M. "Absorbtion of Sound in Air in the Audio Frequency Range." *Journal of the Acoustical Society of America*, 35(11), 1963, 14.

4. Blesser, B., and Kates, J. "Digital Processing in Audio Signals." In A. Oppenheim (ed.), *Applications of Digital Signal Processing.* Englewood Cliffs, N.J.: Prentice-Hall, 1978.

5. Schroeder, M. R. *Music Perception in Concert Halls* (Publication No. 26). Stockholm: Royal Swedish Academy of Music, 1979.

6. Schroeder, M. R., and Logan, B. F. "Colorless Artificial Reverberation." *Journal of the Audio Engineering Society*, 9(3), 1961, 192. Schroeder, M. R. "Natural Sounding Artificial Reverberation." *Journal of the Audio Engineering Society*, 10(3), 1962, 219–223.

7. Moorer, J. A. "About This Reverberation Business." *Computer Music Journal*, 3(2), 1979, 13–28.

8. Schroeder, M. R. "Digital Simulation of Sound Transmission in Reverberant Spaces" (Part 1). *Journal of the Acoustical Society of America*, 47(2), 1970, 424–431.

9. Bartlett, Bruce. "A Scientific Explanation of Phasing (Flanging)." *Journal of the Audio Engineering Society*, 18(6), 1970, 674–675.

10. Blesser, B. In A. Oppenheim (ed.), *Applications of Digital Signal Processing.* Englewood Cliffs, N.J.: Prentice-Hall, 1978.

11. Karplus, K., and Strong, A. "Digital Synthesis of Plucked-String and Drum Timbres." *Computer Music Journal,* 7(2), 1983, 43–55.

12. Jaffe, D. A., and Smith, J. O. "Extensions of the Karplus-Strong, Plucked-String Algorithm." *Computer Music Journal,* 7(2), 1983, 56–69.

13. Ibid.

14. Sullivan, C. "Extending the Karplus-Strong Algorithm to Synthesize Electric Guitar Timbres with Distortion and Feedback." *Computer Music Journal,* 14(3), 1990, 26–37.

15. Jaffe and Smith, "Extensions of the Karplus-Strong Plucked-String Algorithm."

16. Jaffe, D. A. "Ensemble Timing in Computer Music." *Computer Music Journal,* 9(4), 1985, 38–48.

17. Kuhn, George F. "Model for the Interaural Time Differences in the Azimuthal Plane." *Journal of the Acoustical Society of America,* 62(1), 1977, 157–166.

18. Kendall, G. "A 3-D Sound Primer: Directional Hearing and Stereo Reproduction." *Computer Music Journal,* 19(4), 1995, 23–46.

19. Hebrank, J., and Wright, D. "Spectral Cues Used in the Localization of Sound Sources on the Median Plane." *Journal of the Acoustical Society of America,* 56, 1974, 1829–1834.

20. Blauert, J. *Spatial Hearing: The Psychophysics of Human Sound Localization.* Cambridge: MIT Press, 1983.

21. MacPherson, E. A. "A Computer Model of Binaural Localization for Stereo Imaging Measurement." *Journal of the Audio Engineering Society,* 39(9), 1991, 604–621.

22. Gilliom, J. D., and Sorkin, R. D. "Discrimination of Interaural Time and Intensity." *Journal of the Acoustical Society of America,* 52, 1972, 1635–1644.

23. Shaw, E. A. G., and Vaillancourt, M. M. "Transformation of Sound-Pressure Level from the Free Field to the Eardrum in the Horizontal Plane." *Journal of the Acoustical Society of America,* 78, 1985, 1120–1122.

24. Begault, D. R. *3-D Sound for Virtual Reality and Multimedia.* Cambridge: AP Professional, 1994.

25. Von Bekesy, G. *Experiments in Hearing.* New York: McGraw-Hill, 1960.

26. Schroeder, M. R. "Computer Models for Concert Hall Acoustics." *American Journal of Physics,* 41(4), 1973, 461–471.

27. Barron, M., "The Subjective Effects of First Reflections in Concert Halls—The Need for Lateral Reflections." *Journal of Sound and Vibration,* 15, 1971, 475–494.

28. Begault, D. R. *Sound for Virtual Reality and Multimedia.*

29. Chowning, John. "The Simulation of Moving Sound Sources." *Computer Music Journal,* 1(3), 1977, 48–52. (Reprinted in the *Journal of the Audio Engineering Society,* 19, 1971, 2–6.)

30. Schroeder, M. R. *Music Perception in Concert Halls.*

31. Fedorkow, G., Buxton, W., and Smith, K. C. "A Computer-Controlled Sound Distribution System for the Performance of Electroacoustic Music." *Computer Music Journal,* 2(3), 1978, 33–41.

32. Chowning. "The Simulation of Moving Sound Sources."

33. Gerzon, Michael, "Periphony: Width-Height Sound Reproduction." *Journal of the Audio Engineering Society,* 21(2), 1972, 2–10.

34. Malham, D., and Myatt, A. "3-D Sound Spacialization Using Ambiosonic Techniques." *Computer Music Journal,* 19(4), 1995, 58–70.

35. Henry, Pierre. "Variations on a Door and a Sigh." Philips (DSY 836–898).

36. Schrader, Barry. *Introduction to Electro-Acoustic Music.* Englewood Cliffs, N.J.: Prentice-Hall, 1982, 181.

37. Schafer, R. W., and Rabiner, L. R. "A Digital Signal Processing Approach to Interpolation." *Proceedings of the Institute of Electrical and Electronics Engineers,* 61(6), 1973, 692–702.

38. Erbe, T. *Soundhack Manual.* Lebanon, N.H.: Frog Peak Music, 1994.

39. Macintosh and Powerbook are trademarks of Apple Computer.

40. Polansky, L., and Erbe, T. "Spectral Mutation in Soundhack." *Computer Music Journal,* 20(1), 1996, 92–101.

41. Chowning, John, "Turenas." *John Chowning,* Wergo, (WER 2012–50), 1988.

42. Dodge, Charles. "Earth's Magnetic Field." Nonesuch Records (H-71250), 1970.

43. Reynolds, Roger. "The Palace." New York: C. F. Peters, 1980. (Recorded on Vital Records, "Lovely Music" (VR 1801–2), 1982.)

44. Lansky, Paul. "Six Fantasies on a Poem by Thomas Campion." *Fantasies and Tableaux,* CRI Records (CD 683), 1994.

45. Bennett, Gerald. *Some Notes on the Composition and Analysis of Rainstick.* Bourges, France: Academie Internationale de la Musique Electroacoustique de Bourges, 1997.

46. Rodet, X. "Time-Domain Formant-Wave-Function Synthesis." In J. G. Simon (ed.), *Spoken Language Generation and Understanding.* Dodrecht: Reidel. Reprinted in *Computer Music Journal,* 8(3), 1984, 9–14.

47. Loy, Gareth. "Nekyia." Doctoral dissertation, Stanford Unversity, 1979. Recorded on *Computer Music Currents 5,* Wergo (WER 2025–2), 1990.

48. Risset, Jean-Claude. "Sud." Wergo (WER 2013–50), 1988.

49. Ibid.

11

COMPOSITION WITH COMPUTERS

Composers have been using the computer as an aid to writing music since the mid-1950s. In fact, composition with the computer predates the use of the computer as a medium to synthesize sound. The use of the computer has resulted in a great and healthy diversity of musical styles and ideas.

Although there are a number of different approaches to the matter of composing with a computer, most of the activities fall into two broad categories—aleatoric or "stochastic" music, in which events are generated according to the statistical characterization of a random process; and music in which the computer is used to calculate permutations of a set of predetermined compositional elements. In this chapter, we will examine the techniques of using the computer for both random and deterministic operations. Illustrations of the use of these techniques in actual compositions will be given to help the reader develop a sense of the compositional possibilities of computer-aided composition.

Other approaches to computer-aided composition, not covered here, do exist. For example, some believe that computers provide an ideal medium for testing the ideas of music theory in that the computer can be used to construct an instance of music that demonstrates a given theory.[1] The extent to which the computer-generated music coheres can be indicative of the completeness of the theory. For example, notions of hierarchical musical structure such as those of Heinrich Schenker could be tested by inventing a computer-programming system to realize a piece of music. Work in the area of generative grammars in linguistics has been influential on this and other approaches to computer-aided composition.[2]

11.1 ALEATORIC COMPOSITION WITH COMPUTERS

11.1A Random Processes

There are two general classes of random processes that have been used to generate material for music composition: random processes with independent observations, and processes in which previous results influence the current outcome in some way. When independent observations are taken of a random process, a given result does not depend on any previous results. The values of the results are distributed in a set or range with a pattern characteristic of a particular process. For example, tossing a coin represents a process where the set of possible results has two members (heads and tails), and the distribution pattern gives an equal chance to the two possible outcomes.

341

One way of expressing the influence of past outcomes of a random process on the current one is through the explicit use of *conditional probabilities*. In this case, the likelihood of the occurrence of a particular event is based on the results of one or more previous events. The probabilities are often chosen to model something from the "real world," such as a musical style or a natural language. Experiments using conditional probabilities have been made with the goal of modeling English on the basis of the probabilities of the occurrence of certain successions of letters.[3] In such a system, for example, if the first selection were the letter *b*, there could be a wide variety of choices for the second letter (*a, e, i, l, o, r, u, y*, and so on). Some of the choices would be more likely than others; for instance, there is a greater chance of an *e* following a *b* than a *y*. However, if the first choice were *q*, then the situation would be very different. In this case, the probability of choosing the letter *u* would be virtually certain.

The correlation of past events with the current one can also be characterized by a spectral description of the process. This can be conceptualized as the spectrum of the signal that would be generated if the random process were used to calculate the samples of a digital signal. These processes have been used to model a wide variety of natural processes, such as the profiles of mountain ranges, the "natural unevenness of human-produced vocal and instrumental tones,"[4] and so on. Several composers have determined parameters of musical scores by using a process with a particular spectrum. (See section 11.1H and 11.1J.)

When a random process is used compositionally, it is rare that the raw output from the process is translated into music directly. Certain examples of that approach can be found in the literature, but more often than not the output of the process is tested to examine its suitability for inclusion in the music. The tests can cover a wide range of possibilities, and the output of the same random process can be made into very different kinds of music, depending on the nature of the tests applied.

One should note that the success of music based on random processes resides not so much in the processes themselves as in the conditions under which the randomly generated elements are admitted into the composition. The first half of this chapter examines the outlines of several systems that have been used in the composition of music based on random processes.

11.1B   Probability and Random Processes

The concepts of randomness and probability were introduced in section 4.9 as they related to the generation of noise. This section will expand the discussion of these concepts and present some of the random processes that have been found useful for composition.

The likelihood that a particular event will occur can be expressed as a *probability*— as the ratio of the number of occurrences of that event to the total number of results of the random process. As an example, let the variable X be assigned to the random process of rolling a six-sided die. X can take on six possible values, which can be written as the set $\{1, 2, 3, 4, 5, 6\}$. If the die is properly balanced, there is an equal chance that any of the numbers will be rolled. Therefore, the probability of rolling a 2, for example, is 1/6. Mathematically, this probability, P, is written as

$$P\{X = 2\} = \tfrac{1}{6}$$

X is known as a *random variable* because its value is not explicitly calculated; instead, it is assigned a value on the basis of a random process. A random variable is normally characterized by the probability of its taking on a specific value or by the probability that its value will fall within a specified range of values.

Four of the properties of probabilities are:

1. The numerical value of a probability is always between 0 and 1. These two values, respectively, indicate the extreme cases in which the event never occurs or the event is certain.

2. The probability that an event will not occur can be found by subtracting the probability that it will occur from 1. In the above example of the die toss, the probability that a 2 will not be rolled is

$$P\{X \neq 2\} = 1 - P\{X = 2\} = \tfrac{5}{6}$$

3. The probability that any of several events will occur is equal to the sum of the probability of the individual events. For example, the probability of rolling an even number on a die is given by

$$P\{X = \text{even}\} = P\{X = 2\} + P\{X = 4\} + P\{X = 6\} = \tfrac{1}{6} + \tfrac{1}{6} + \tfrac{1}{6} = \tfrac{1}{2}$$

4. The sum of the probabilities of all possible events of a process must be equal to 1. This mathematically restates the obvious: an event must be found in the set of possible events.

The collection of the probabilities of all possible outcomes of a process is often expressed as a graph, such as that shown in figure 11.1: a plot of the probabilities for the various values that can be assigned to *X* as the result of rolling a die. In this case, *X* is known as a *discrete random variable* because the outcomes of the random process can take on only specific values. (That is, there is no chance of rolling, for example, a 3.51.)

Many random phenomena produce results that cannot be categorized into a discrete set of values. For example, the duration of a particular note in an instrumental performance has a certain amount of randomness because each time the piece is performed, the dura-

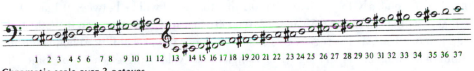

1 2 3 4 5 6   7 8   9 10 11 12   13   14 15 16 17 18 19 20 21 22 23 24 25 26 27 28 29 30 31 32 33 34   35 36 37

Chromatic scale over 3 octaves

FIGURE 11.1   Probabilities for the result of the random process of rolling a six-sided die.

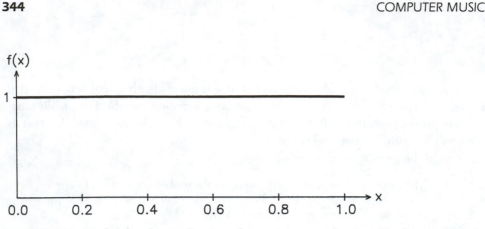

FIGURE 11.2   Probability density function of a continuous random variable that is uniformly distributed.

tion of that note will not be precisely the same. It might be possible to ascribe a range to the duration such as from 0.95 to 1.05 seconds, but there is actually an infinite number of values within the range: 0.998176 . . . , 0.998213 . . . , 1.023176 . . . , or any value within the range. The number of possible values is limited only by the precision with which the phenomenon is measured. The results of this kind of process are said to be continuous. Thus, a random variable used to describe this process is known as a *continuous random variable*.

The probabilities of a continuous random phenomenon are normally expressed by a *probability density function*, $f(x)$. An example of a continuous density function is shown in figure 11.2. This particular function is expressed algebraically as $f(x) = 1$ for $0 < x < 1$, denoting that all outcomes will fall in the range between 0 and 1. The flatness of the density curve indicates that there is an equal chance of this continuous random variable having a value anywhere in the range. A probability cannot be read directly from the vertical scale of the density graph. Instead, the density function is used to calculate the probability that an outcome will fall within a range of values by finding the area under the density curve in that range; that is, the area bounded on the top by the curve, on the bottom by the horizontal axis, on the left by the lowest number in the range, and on the right by the highest number in the range.

For example, using the density function of figure 11.2, what is the probability that the result will fall between 0 and 0.2? The area under the curve in this region is a rectangle with a height of 1 and a length of 0.2. Therefore, the probability is $1 \times 0.2 = 0.2$, or a 20% chance. Similarly, the probability is 0.1 that the result will be between 0.1 and 0.2; 0.01 that it will fall between 0.19 and 0.2; 0.00001 that it will be between 0.19999 and 0.2; and so on. Thus, as the region gets smaller, so does the probability. When taken to the limit of an infinitely small range (i.e., a single, exact value), there is a 0 probability of drawing that specific number. This may seem strange, but in a continuous process, there is an infinite number of possible outcomes. Because a probability compares the number of ways that an outcome can occur and the number of possible outcomes, there is a 0 probability that any specific number will be drawn. Thus, the measurement of probability in the continuous case can only predict the likelihood that a result will fall within a region of possible outcomes.

Both continuous and discrete random variables have been found to be useful in computer music. In the remainder of this section, we will present descriptions of some commonly used random processes along with algorithms to realize them. Each of the algorithms makes independent observations of a random process; the results generated do not depend on any previous result. There are two principal parameters that characterize any random variable: the range of values that it can assume and its mean. The *mean* denotes the midpoint of the probabilities. There is an equal chance that the outcome of a random process will fall above or below the mean.

11.1B(1)   UNIFORM DISTRIBUTION   The most commonly encountered type of random variable has a uniform probability distribution. The discrete random variable assigned to the process of rolling a die, for example, is uniformly distributed because there is an equal chance of obtaining any of the results. Similarly, a continuous random variable is uniformly distributed if there is an equal chance of the result occurring within any two sections of the range which are of equal length. The flat probability density function shown in figure 11.2 is characteristic of a uniformly distributed random process. The algorithms for generating random numbers found on most computer systems produce numbers that are very nearly uniformly distributed, but the actual range of values may differ among different implementations. For mathematical convenience, we will assume that a uniformly distributed random variable has a range between 0 and 1. In this case, the mean is 0.5. Section 11.1B(11) will demonstrate the scaling of random variables to fall within a desired range.

In the algorithms that follow, the floating-point random-number generating function, *fran,* will be used to generate various random variables with other than uniform distributions. The function *fran,* as defined here, generates values in the continuous range from 0 to 1. The reader is cautioned to make certain that the range of values produced by the random-number generator on the system used is the same. If the range of values is different, the output must be scaled appropriately before using it in the algorithms. Otherwise, many of the algorithms will not work as described.

11.1B(2)   LINEAR DISTRIBUTION   Figure 11.3 shows the density function of a linearly distributed, continuous random variable. In the case shown, it is most likely to obtain a low-valued result. The density function is given by:

$$f(x) = \begin{cases} 2(1-x) & 0 \le x \le 1 \\ 0 & \text{elsewhere} \end{cases}$$

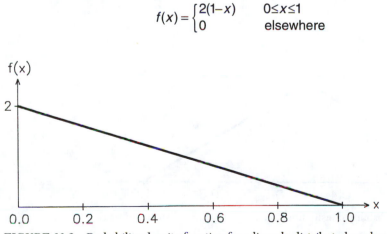

FIGURE 11.3   Probability density function for a linearly distributed random variable.

The algorithm for obtaining this distribution is a simple one: generate two uniformly distributed random numbers, u1 and u2, and then choose the smaller one for the result.

```
float xlnear()
{   // generates a linearly distributed random variable
float fran();
    float u1=fran();
    float u2=fran();
    if(u2 < u1)
        u1=u2;
    return u1;
}
```

The range of the random variable will be the same as the range of the *fran* function, 0 to 1. With this range, the mean of the distribution is 0.2929. If a discrete random-number generator is used instead of a continuous one, this distribution will also be discrete.

A linear distribution that is the reverse of the one above—that is, where the results closest to 1 are most likely—is obtained when the algorithm chooses the larger of two uniformly distributed random numbers.

11.1B(3) TRIANGULAR DISTRIBUTION Figure 11.4 illustrates the probability density of a triangularly distributed random variable, where a middle-valued result is most likely. This distribution can be obtained by generating two uniformly distributed random numbers and taking their average.

```
float triang()
{   // produces a triangularly distributed random variable
float fran();
    float u1=fran();
    float u2=fran();
    return 0.5*(u1+u2);
}
```

The range of the generated random variable is the same as the range of the *fran* function, 0 to 1. The mean is the average of the upper and lower limits of the range, in this case 0.5.

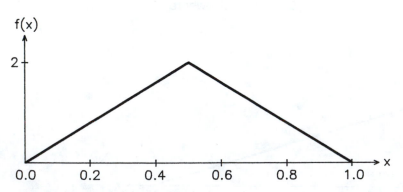

FIGURE 11.4   Probability density function of a triangularly distributed random variable.

11.1B(4) Exponential Distribution   An exponentially distributed random variable has a greater probability of assuming values closer to 0. Its density function (figure 11.5) is given by

$$f(x) = \lambda^{-\lambda x} \qquad x > 0$$

It is characterized by a parameter λ, which controls the amount of horizontal spread of the function. Choosing a large value for λ greatly increases the probability of generating a small number. The mean of the distribution is $0.69315 / \lambda$. The random variable takes on only values greater than 0, and there is, theoretically, no upper limit on the size of the number that can be generated. However, the chance of a very large result is quite low. For example, if $\lambda = 1$, the mean will be 0.69315 and 99.9% of all results will fall below 6.9078. In the general case, there is only a 1-in-1000 chance of generating a random number greater than $6.9078 / \lambda$.

The sizes of many natural phenomena are distributed exponentially. A good example is the magnitude of earthquakes, in which small tremors are much more common than catastrophic shocks.

The algorithm for generating an exponential distribution involves drawing a uniformly distributed random number with a value between 0 and 1 and taking its natural logarithm.

```
float expone(float lambda)
{  // computes an exponentially distributed random variable
   // with a spread determined by lambda
float fran();
float u;
   do
     u=fran();
   while (u == 0);
   return -log(u)/lambda;
}
```

This algorithm checks that the *fran* function has not produced a value of exactly 0, in order to prevent an error in the *log* function. The random-number functions found on many systems cannot generate precisely 0, in which case the *do* and *while* statements could be omitted.

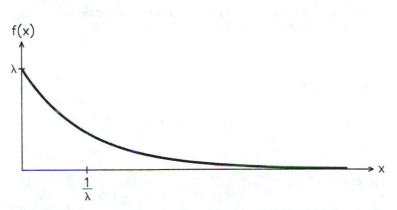

FIGURE 11.5   Probability density function of an exponentially distributed random variable.

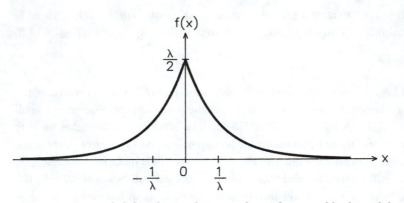

FIGURE 11.6   Probability density function of a random variable that exhibits a bilateral exponential distribution.

Certain applications require an exponentially distributed random variable that assumes both positive and negative values. The bilateral exponential distribution has this characteristic and a density function (figure 11.6) given by

$$f(x) = \frac{1}{2}\lambda e^{-\lambda |x|}$$

(In some places in the literature, this distribution is referred to as the first law of Laplace.) As before, the parameter λ controls the horizontal scale of the density function, and increasing λ causes the distribution to become more compact. The mean of the distribution is 0 and its range is unbounded both above and below the mean; 50% of the results fall between $\pm 1 / \lambda$.

The following algorithm generates random numbers with a bilateral exponential distribution.

```
float bilex(float lambda)
{  // computes a bilinear exponentially distributed random variable
   // with a spread governed by lambda
float fran();
float u,s;
   do
     u=2*fran();
   while (u == 0 | u == 2);
   if(u > 1)
   {
     u=2-u;
     s=-1;
   }
   else
     s=1;
   return s*log(u)/lambda;
}
```

To prevent errors in the *log* function, the algorithm includes a check to eliminate cases where the *fran* function has produced a value of either exactly 0 or exactly 1. As described above, on many systems these checks can be omitted.

11.1B(5) GAUSSIAN DISTRIBUTION   One of the most well-known distributions is the Gaussian or normal distribution. Its density function

$$f(x) = \frac{1}{\sqrt{2\pi}\sigma} \exp\left[-\frac{(x-\mu)^2}{2\sigma^2}\right]$$

(see figure 11.7) has the shape of a bell curve and is characterized by two parameters, μ and σ. The center of the density function, μ, is the mean value of the random variable. The spread of the density function is measured by a parameter called the *standard deviation*, or σ. 68.26% of all results will occur in the interval with a width of $\pm\sigma$, centered about the mean; the random variable is unbounded, both above and below the mean. 99.74% of all results fall within $\pm3\sigma$.

A Gaussian distribution can be approximated through the summation of uniformly distributed random numbers. The values produced by adding together an infinite quantity of uniformly distributed random numbers are distributed in a Gaussian pattern. In actual practice, a reasonably good approximation can be obtained by adding together a fairly small number. The following algorithm uses 12 and allows the standard deviation and mean to be set independently.

```
float gauss(float sigma, float mu)
{  // generates a Gaussian distributed random variable
   // with mean mu and standard deviation sigma
float fran();
   int k;
   int const N=12;
   float const halfN=6;
   float const scale=1; //scale varies with N as scale=1/sqrt (N/12).
   float sum=0;
   for(k=1; k <= N; k++)
     sum+=fran();
   return sigma*scale*(sum-halfN)+mu;
}
```

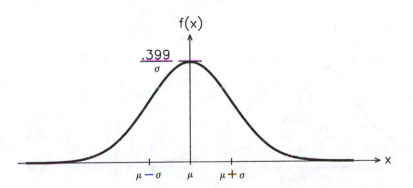

FIGURE 11.7   Gaussian (or normal) probability density function.

In contrast to a true Gaussian distribution, the random variable generated by this algorithm is bounded. It falls between $\mu \pm 6\sigma$. For most purposes, this is acceptable because only two results in a billion occurrences of a true Gaussian random process fall outside this range.

11.1B(6)   CAUCHY DISTRIBUTION   The density function (figure 11.8) of a Cauchy-distributed random variable is symmetric, with a mean of 0. The Cauchy density function is given by

$$f(x) = \frac{\alpha}{\pi(\alpha^2 + x^2)}$$

Like a Gaussian density function, it is unbounded both above and below the mean. At its extremes, $f(x)$ approaches 0 much more slowly than in the Gaussian case. Thus, values far removed from the mean are more common in a Cauchy process. The density is scaled by the parameter α, with a large α yielding a more widely dispersed curve. Half the results fall within the interval marked by $\pm \alpha$. 99.9% of all results occur between $\pm 318.3\alpha$.

A Cauchy-distributed random variable can be generated by taking the tangent of a properly scaled, uniformly distributed random variable.

```
float cauchy(float alpha)
{  // computes a Cauchy-distributed random variable with
   // a spread governed by the parameter alpha
   float fran(),u;
   float const pi=3.1415927;
   do
      u=fran();
   while(u == 0.5);
   u=u*pi;
   return alpha*tan(u);
}
```

To guard against errors in the *tangent* function, the algorithm eliminates cases where the *fran* function has generated a value of exactly 0.5.

Certain applications require a Cauchy-distributed random variable that can assume only positive values. For instance, this might be the case when note durations are cho-

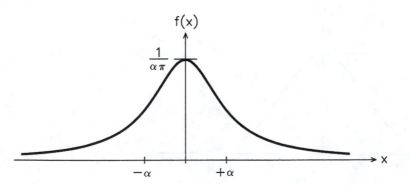

FIGURE 11.8   Probability density function of a Cauchy-distributed random variable.

sen according to this distribution. The negative half of the density function can be "folded" onto the positive half to obtain a function that is shaped like the right half of figure 11.8, but which has twice the probability density. The random variable produced has a minimum value of 0 and no upper bound. Its mean is α. To obtain this case, modify the routine above by setting the constant equal to 1.570796 (π / 2) instead of π. In addition, the *while* statement should be changed to check for u = 1 instead of u = 0.5.

11.1B(7) BETA DISTRIBUTION   The density function of a beta-distributed random variable can have several shapes as dictated by its defining parameters a and b. Its density function is given by

$$f(x) = \frac{1}{B(a,b)} x^{a-1}(1-x)^{b-1}$$

where $B(a, b)$ is Euler's beta function.[5] For this discussion, it is sufficient to point out that $B(a, b)$ does not affect the shape of the function. $B(a, b)$ is only a scaling function that gives an area of 1 under the density curve in the range of x between 0 and 1.

When a and b are both greater than 1, the beta density is reminiscent of a bell-shaped Gaussian density. When $a = b = 1$, it degenerates into the special case of the uniform distribution. Of greatest interest is the case of $a < 1$ and $b < 1$, which characterizes a distribution that has the greatest probability near both 0 and 1—a shape not found in any of the previously discussed distributions. Figure 11.9 shows the density function for $a = 0.4$ and $b = 0.6$. Some of the general relationships between the parameters and the shape of the density function are:

1. Parameter a controls the probability of values closest to 0; parameter b regulates those closest to 1.

2. The smaller a parameter value is, the greater is the probability at the extreme that it governs, and the less likelihood there is of a result near 0.5.

3. When $a = b$, the density is symmetric about 0.5.

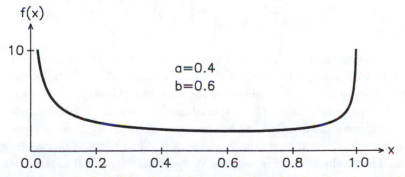

FIGURE 11.9   Probability density function of a beta-distributed random variable characterized by the parameters shown.

4. When $a \neq b$, the density is tilted so that it is more likely to generate results near the extreme controlled by the smaller parameter.

5. The mean is $a / (a + b)$.

The following algorithm[6] generates a beta-distributed random variable in the range 0 to 1.

```
float beta(float a, float b)
{   // computes a beta distributed random variable
    // controlled by parameters a and b
float fran();
float u1,u2,y1,y2,sum,ainv,binv;
  ainv=1/a;
  binv=1/b;
  do
  {
    do
      u1=fran();
    while (u1 == 0);
    do
      u2=fran();
    while (u2 == 0);
    y1=pow(u1,ainv); // function pow(x,y) is the exponentiation
                     // operation x^y
    y2=pow(u2,binv);
    sum=y1+y2;
  }
  while (sum > 1);
  return y1/sum;
}
```

This algorithm excludes values of the *fran* function that are precisely 0. As noted above, on many systems this check is unnecessary. However, specifying a value for either a or b that is extremely close to 0 creates the potential of an underflow error during exponentiation.

11.1B(8) WEIBULL DISTRIBUTION   A Weibull-distributed random variable takes on values that are greater than 0 with no upper limit. Its probability density can assume several different shapes and is controlled by two parameters, s and t. The density function is given by

$$f(x) = \frac{tx^{t-1}}{s^t} \exp-\left(\frac{x}{s}\right)^t$$

Parameter s serves only to scale the horizontal spread of the probability density, but parameter t has a great influence on the shape of the density. Figure 11.10 illustrates the dependence of the shape of the density function on the value of t. When t is less than 1, the density function favors small values. In the special case of $t = 1$, the Weibull distribution becomes the exponential distribution. As t increases above 1, the density function begins to exhibit a single maximum near the value of s. When $t = 3.2$, the density is nearly Gaussian. Large values of t accentuate the sharpness of the peak, thus increasing the chances of generating values close to s. There is a 99.9% probability that an outcome will fall below $6.9^{1/t}s$. Thus, it can be seen that choosing a small value for t greatly increases the likelihood of generating a large number.

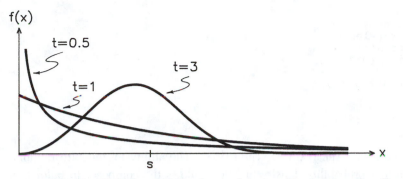

FIGURE 11.10   Weibull probability density function. Observe the great effect that the parameter *t* has on the shape of the function.

The following algorithm generates Weibull-distributed random numbers.[7]

```
float weibull(float s, float t)
{  // computes a Wiebull distributed random variable controlled
   // by parameters s and t, both of which must be greater than zero
float fran();
float u,a,tinv;
   tinv=1/t;
   do
     u=fran();
   while (u == 0 | u == 1);
   a=1/(1-u);
   return s*pow(log(a),tinv); // function pow is exponentiation
}
```

This algorithm eliminates values of the *fran* function that are exactly 0 or exactly 1. However, specifying a value for *t* that is extremely close to 0 runs the risk of computation errors during the exponentiation operation.

11.1B(9)   POISSON DISTRIBUTION   A Poisson-distributed, discrete random variable assumes integer values greater than or equal to 0. Its range has no upper bound and the distribution of probabilities is controlled by the parameter λ. The probability of drawing the integer *j* is given by

$$P\{X = j\} = \exp^{-\lambda} \frac{\lambda^j}{j!}$$

The mean of the distribution is λ. The result with maximum probability occurs at $j = \mathrm{int}(\lambda)$. However, if λ is an integer, the probability that $j = \lambda - 1$ will be as great as that of $j = \lambda$. Figure 11.11 shows a Poisson distribution for $\lambda = 2.2$.

The following algorithm[8] can be used to generate a Poisson-distributed random variable.

```
int poisson(float lambda)
{  // computes a Poisson distributed random variable
   // controlled by parameter lambda
   {
float fran();
```

```
      float u,v;
         int n=0;
         v=exp(-lambda);
         u=fran();
         while (u >= v)
         {
            u=u*fran();
            n++;
         }
         return n;
   }
```

11.1B(10) OBTAINING AN ARBITRARY DISTRIBUTION The ability to generate random variables with custom probability density functions allows the composer to tailor the random process to the compositional plan. The algorithm presented here enables the user to specify a desired probability density function (pdf) as a series of line segments.

The inputs to the random function *arbran* are the arrays x and p, which contain the locations of end points of each line segment as coordinate pairs. The entries in x and p hold the horizontal and vertical positions of the points, respectively. For instance, the example four-segment pdf shown in figure 11.12 would be stipulated by the arrays x = {1, 2, 3, 4, 5} and p = {0, 0.6, 0.2, 0.2, 0}. Because each end point of the line must be given, the number of points in each array is one larger than the number of line segments.

```
float arbran(float x[], float p[])
{  // generates a random variable that conforms to the piecewise
   // probability density function specified in arrays x and p
float fran();
float a,u,a0,slope,b,d,r;
   int k=0;
   a=0;
   u=fran();
   while (u > a)
   {
      a0=(x[k+1]-x[k])*(p[k+1]+p[k])/2;
      a+=a0;
      k++;
   }
   k--;
   slope=(p[k+1]-p[k])/(x[k+1]-x[k]);
   if (slope == 0)
```

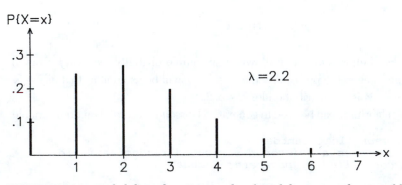

FIGURE 11.11   Probabilities for a Poisson-distributed discrete random variable.

```
      r=(u-a+a0)/p[k]+x[k];
   else
   {
      b=p[k]/slope-x[k];
      d=b*b+x[k]*x[k]+2*b*x[k]+2*(u-a+a0)/slope;
      if (slope > 0)
         r=-b+sqrt(d);
      else
         r=-b-sqrt(d);
   }
   return r;
}
```

In accordance with the properties of a pdf, proper operation of the algorithm requires that the area under the specified curve be 1. Hence, the pdf specified with line segments must be bounded; that is, there must be only a finite region in which the pdf is nonzero. Smooth curves can be approximated by connecting straight line segments between a number of representative points along the curve.

To relieve the musician from checking that a set of points specifies a pdf with an area of 1, the following routine can be used to properly scale the values. It takes in the arrays x and p and multiplies the values in p by the appropriate factor. The argument npts specifies the length of each array.

```
void pdfscale(float x[], float p[], int npts)
//   scales probability density function stored in arrays x and p
//   so that the area under the function is unity
{
   float a=0;
   for(int k=1; k<npts; k++)
      a+=(x[k]-x[k-1])*(p[k]+p[k-1])/2;
   for(k=0; k<npts; k++)
      p[k]=p[k]/a;
}
```

The function *pdfscale* would be run once prior to drawing any random numbers. After that, random numbers can be drawn by arbran as often as needed.

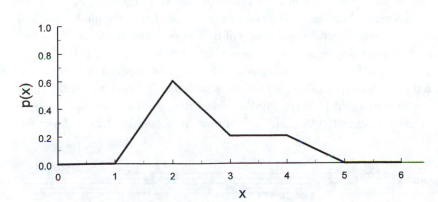

FIGURE 11.12 Example of an arbitrary probability density function specified as a series of straight line segments.

11.1B(11) MAPPING   Quite often, a particular application requires the transformation of the range of a generated random variable. This practice is called *mapping*. Let the range of the generated random variable, x, lie between a and b. After mapping, the transformed random variable, y, is to fall between c and d. The value of y is calculated from x by using the following relationship:

$$y = \frac{(d-c)}{(b-a)}(x-a) + c$$

If x is continuous, then y will be continuous. Likewise, a discrete x yields a discrete y.

As an example, suppose that a particular application required a beta-distributed random variable, y, in the range from 1 to 16. The function given above, *beta*, produces numbers in the range from 0 to 1. The output of the generator, x, would be scaled according to

$$y = 15x + 1$$

When a continuous distribution is used to choose parameters that have discrete values, the continuous random variable must be changed into a discrete one. This is accomplished by generating the continuous random variable, mapping it into the appropriate range, and then using the integer function (*int*) to obtain discrete results. Because the integer function truncates the fractional part of its argument, the upper limit of the mapped range, d, should be set to one more than the largest integer actually desired. The probabilities of the discrete random variable will have the same envelope as the probability density function of the continuous random variable used.

11.1C   Examples of the Use of Random Variables

The most obvious musical use of random processes is to use them to choose some or all of the elements in a musical score. As an example, we will apply the distributions shown in section 11.1B to the selection of pitch. First, let us simply create eight different successions of pitches, each one based on a different distribution. In doing so, however, we must make several musical decisions. For example, we must choose the pitch collection into which our randomly generated patterns will be mapped, and the span of musical register over which the mapping will be performed.

For the purposes of the demonstration, let us use 12 equal-tempered divisions of the octave over a three-octave span. Thus, we will work with the 37-tone range of the chromatic scale shown in example 11.1. For a further restriction, we will limit each example to the first 20 pitches generated by each random process. Example 11.2a–h shows the

EXAMPLE 11.1   Numerical representation of a chromatic scale over three octaves.

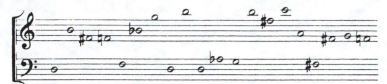

a)   Uniform random distribution

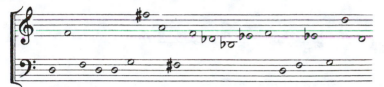

b)   Linear distribution

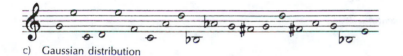

c)   Gaussian distribution

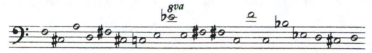

d)   Exponential distribution

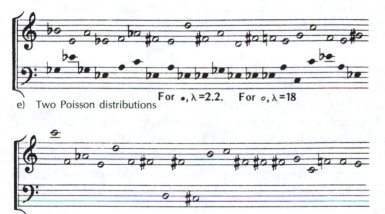

For •, λ =2.2.   For ○, λ =18

e)   Two Poisson distributions

f)   Cauchy distribution

EXAMPLE 11.2   Pitches chosen by various random processes.

successions of pitches that result from several of the random processes. The parameter values used to control each process are shown below each example.

In each case, the output of the generating algorithm used was mapped into the discrete range 1 to 37, corresponding to the pitches within the 37-tone registral span. For example, the uniform distribution (example 11.2a) was generated with the *fran* function

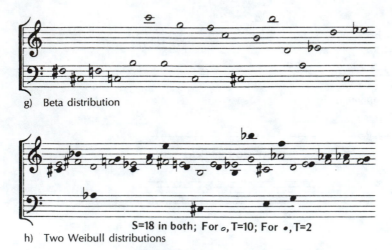

g)   Beta distribution

S=18 in both; For $\circ$, T=10; For $\bullet$, T=2

h)   Two Weibull distributions

EXAMPLE 11.2   *(continued)*

and mapped to produce a discrete random variable in the desired range using the following algorithm.

```
int randmap()
{   // returns a random integer between 1 and 37
float fran();
float u=37*fran()+1; // u is mapped such that 1<u<38
  int r=u; // takes the integer portion of u
  return r;
}
```

This algorithm assumes that the *fran* function does not produce a value of exactly 1.

In the cases of the Gaussian and Cauchy distributions, the mean of the distribution was set equal to 19 in order to center the distribution within the range. When the random variable was unbounded, as in the case of the Cauchy distrubution, the boundaries were taken to be the points at which there is a 1/1000 chance of generating a result beyond that limit. These boundaries were used in the mapping equation. The choice of 1/1000 is arbitrary and can be set depending on the dispersion of values desired. In certain situations, the mapping algorithm used should include tests to exclude generated values outside the range.

Certain observations can be made. The uniform distribution has a more-or-less even distribution of pitches throughout the register. By contrast, the linear distribution places the preponderance of its occurrences in the lower half of the register. The exponential distribution is relegated largely to the lowest octave. Both the Gaussian and the Cauchy distributions place pitches toward the midrange. However, in the Cauchy distribution, the dispersion of tones outside the midrange is greater than that of the Gaussian distribution. The majority of the Poisson-distributed pitches are near the value of λ. The beta distribution emphasizes pitches in the highest and lowest registers. For the Weibull distribution, choosing a large value of t concentrates the pitches in a rather narrow range.

Because the subject at hand is composition (and not, for example, real-time generation of music), we should feel no obligation to present the pitches in the order in which they were generated. The collection of pitches generated can be reordered for other musical purposes. This does not violate the principle by which they were generated, because taking independent observations of a random process prescribes only the distribution of elements and not their order. Example 11.3 shows the same pitch material as example 11.2a, but with the pitches in a new order that results from reversing the order position of the notes within pairs of the original. Example 11.4 shows another use of the same material. The pitches are ordered by taking every other pitch of the original and going through the original ordering twice. Of course, other orderings could easily be made by taking every third pitch of the original, or by any other rule that the composer might wish to impose.

In the previous examples, we chose to restrict our field of choice to pitches derived from 12 semitonal divisions of the octave. The choice of a pitch vocabulary is crucial for determining the kind of music that results from the random selection. Very different results would be obtained by using a completely diatonic collection, a whole-tone collection, a pentatonic collection, or an octatonic collection. Of course, with computer synthesis, there is no need to restrict the vocabulary to equal temperament or, for that matter, to standard divisions of the octave.

Random processes can also be used to structure the rhythm of a passage. One way to do this is to number the succession of attack points as shown in example 11.5, and then to assign an order that depends on the randomly distributed attack times. For convenience, we use the

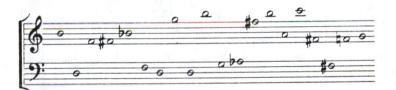

EXAMPLE 11.3   A reordering of the notes of Example 11.2a by reversing the order of the notes within pairs of the original.

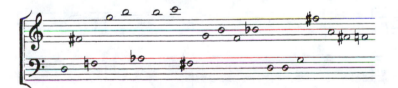

EXAMPLE 11.4   New ordering achieved by taking every other note of the sequence.

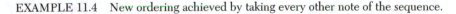

EXAMPLE 11.5   Numerical representation of a succession of attack points.

same mapping for attack points that we used earlier for pitch—the discrete range 1–37. The 37 attack points are arbitrarily shown in five measures of 2/4 time. Notice that the attack pattern reflects the distribution of the random process used to generate it. For instance, the attacks of the uniform distribution (example 11.6a) show a rather even distribution throughout the range of the 37 attack points. The Gaussian distribution (example 11.6b) clusters its attacks near the middle of the passage. The exponential distribution (example 11.6c) causes the attacks to be clustered at the beginning of the passage, and so on.

Another way to treat random distribution of rhythm is to calculate the duration separately from the attack time. In example 11.6, each note was given the same duration. Example 11.7 shows what happens when the duration of notes is calculated separately from the attack time. The method used here was one in which the random value in the

EXAMPLE 11.6   Attack points chosen by uniform distribution (a), Gaussian distribution (b), and exponential distribution (c).

EXAMPLE 11.7   Exponential distribution of attack point and duration.

range 1–37 represents the duration of the tone in sixteenths. Notice that the result, in most cases, is to create a complex musical texture in which the notes overlap. Naturally, the same scheme can be used to affect the dynamics of the tones as well as their orchestration and other attributes, such as timbre and playing style.

The musical possibilities for the use of random distributions in music composition are limitless. The approach requires that the composer assign to the computer most of the specific, note-by-note control over the evolution of the piece. In return, the composer obtains, at the very least, a means by which the music can exhibit patterns and successions that otherwise might not have come to mind. With this method, the composer plans the overall shape of the piece, and the computer fills in the detail using algorithms supplied by the composer. In our later discussions of the music of Lejaren Hiller, Iannis Xenakis, and others, we will show elaborate compositional uses of random-distribution patterns.

In contrast to using a random process to select musical elements directly, random variables are commonly used in a technique known as the "generate and test" method. This technique has been used successfully in a great deal of computer music including the first three movements of the *Illiac Suite* by Hiller and Isaacson.[9] In the generate and test method, as described earlier, a random number is generated, and then subjected to one or another of any number of tests to determine its suitability for the musical situation. For example, when using a range of the 88 tones of the piano keyboard, if the composer desires to have a passage of random music in which all pitches will be members of the diatonic scale of C, the test will exclude all other notes.

11.1D   Conditional Probabilities

Thus far, the random processes discussed have made independent observations; that is, the probability of obtaining a particular result is not influenced by any results that have occurred in the past. There is, however, an important class of random variables that exhibit conditional probabilities. In this case, the probability density of the next result depends on one or more past results. Thus, a sequence generated by a process of this type has an amount of relatedness between members of the sequence; that is, the random process prescribes not only the distribution of the members of the sequence, but also their order. There are several algorithmic methods for generating random variables influenced by past events. We will discuss three fundamental techniques: the explicit use of conditional probability tables, random walks, and processes that are specified in terms of their spectra.

A conditional probability is written mathematically in the discrete case as

$$P\{X_n = i \,|\, X_{n-1} = j\} = p_{ij}$$

This is interpreted as: the probability that $X = i$, given that the last value of X was j, is p_{ij}. Here, p_{ij} assumes values between 0 and 1 and is called a first-order probability because only one previous result is considered. For ease of understanding, the collection of conditional probabilities for a particular process is often presented in the form of a matrix called a *transition table*.

LAST PITCH

		C	D	E	G
	C	0.0	0.3	0.0	0.0
NEXT	D	1.0	0.3	0.3	0.0
PITCH	E	0.0	0.4	0.6	0.5
	G	0.0	0.0	0.1	0.5

TABLE 11.1   A transition table for generating a simple melody from four pitches.

As an example, consider the transition table (table 11.1). The random process that it describes is the generation of a simple melody composed from four pitches: C, D, E, and G. The columns represent the possible values of the last pitch, and the rows correspond to the possible values of the next pitch.

In this process, if the last pitch was G, for example, there is an equal probability of the next pitch being either E or G. However, there is no chance of selecting either C or D. Similarly, if the last pitch was C, it is certain that the next pitch will be D. The probability of repeating pitch E is 0.6. When using a transition table such as this, the initial pitch in a sequence can either be determined by some random means or be specified directly by the user of the algorithm. From then on, new values are generated using the transition table.

The entries in a transition table can either come from analyses of existing work or be the result of a compositional design. In the latter case, two rules should be followed: the sum of any column of conditional probabilities must be 1, so that the table encompasses all possible results. Second, the table designer should avoid choices of probabilities that lead to "dead ends." For instance, if in the example above, the probability that the pitch C follows the pitch C is 1, then once a C is selected, the algorithm will subsequently generate nothing but Cs.

The transition table above explicitly expresses the dependence of the current outcome on the previous one. However, the current outcome also depends, to a lesser extent, on earlier values. For example, using the transition table above, what is the probability of generating the sequence DEG if the current pitch is D? The probability of E given D is 0.4 and the probability of G given E is 0.1. The probability of both events happening is given by the product of the individual probabilities, and so the probability of DEG is 0.04 or a 4% chance. How likely is the sequence CDG if the current pitch is C? The sequence CD is certain ($p = 1$), but a G never follows a D ($p = 0$). Therefore, the sequence CDG is not obtainable using this transition table. Further examination of the table reveals that the sequences CCG, CEG, and CGG are also impossible, because only a D can follow a C. Thus, it can be said that if the current pitch is C, there is no chance that the pitch after next will be G. From this example, it can be seen that even though the transition table includes only first-order probabilities, the current outcome is influenced by results earlier than the previous one. The more distant the result, the less effect it has on the generation of a new value.

The random process above is characterized by the following relationship:

$$p_{ijk} = p_{ij}p_{jk}$$

That is, the probability of the sequence ijk is the same as the product of the probability that j will follow i and the probability that k will follow j. The variable p_{ijk} is known as a second-order probability because it expresses the dependence of the current outcome on the previous two. A process for which the relationship above holds is called a *Markov process;* it generates a sequence of results known as a Markov chain. A first-order transition table such as the one above is sufficient to describe a Markov process completely because all higher-order probabilities can be calculated by multiplying lower-order probabilities together. In a Markov process, the high-order probabilities tend to be rather small. This indicates that outcomes more than a few removed from the current one have very little influence on the process. There are other methods, in addition to first-order transition tables, that generate Markov chains. A common Markov process, the random walk, will be discussed in section 11.1F.

The following subroutine is an example of programming a process described by a first-order transition table. It assumes that the values of the conditional probabilities, p_{ij}, have been previously entered into the transition matrix p as a global variable.

```
int itt(int last)
{   // computes the next state in a random sequence determined
    // from the last state using the transition table stored in
    // the global array p
    float fran();
    float u,threshold;
    u=fran();
    threshold=0;
    int j=0;
    while(u > threshold)
    {
       threshold=threshold+p[j][last-1];
       j++;
    }
    return j; // the states are numbered beginning with 1
}
```

This algorithm generates outcomes represented by numerical codes beginning with 1.

Many random processes are not Markovian; the higher-order conditional probabilities are not directly related to the first-order ones as above. For instance, the choice of a particular pitch in a traditionally composed musical score is influenced by previous pitches more strongly than in a Markov process. Non-Markov processes are often approximated by a transition table of a higher order. If an event is directly influenced by the two previous events, for example, a second-order table would be used. The entries in the matrix would be second-order probabilities of the form p_{ijk}. The matrix would be three-dimensional and could be visualized as the next event (i) on the first axis, the last event (j) on the second axis, and the second-to-last event (k) on the third axis.

A table of any order is theoretically possible, depending on how closely linked the random process is with the past. Of course, the complexity of the program to utilize it, the difficulty of conceptualizing it, and the amount of data required to describe it all grow quickly with the order of the table. Letting the number of possible states be S and the order of the table be N, the number of entries in the table is then S^{N+1}. If the conditional probabilities are stored in a standard floating-point format, 4 bytes of memory will be needed for each entry. Thus, a sixth-order table describing the transitions among 12 pitches would require over 143 megabytes of memory. Certain efficiencies are possible when a large number of the entries are 0,[10] but high-order tables are still difficult to implement.

11.1E   Uses of Transition Tables

A good example of the results of an elementary statistical analysis of music was made in the 1950s by Harry F. Olson, the inventor of the RCA Sound Synthesizer.[11] In analyzing the successions of melodic tones in 11 songs by the 19th-century American composer Stephen Foster, Olson found the relative frequency of scale-step occurrences shown in table 11.2. The scale indicated is that of D major with one chromatic tone, G♯. Olson also tabulated the occurrence of particular rhythmic values in the same group of songs. Table 11.3 correlates the various ways of filling measures in 4/4 time. Tables 11.2 and 11.3 are known as zeroth-order transition tables because they do not take into account the influence of any previous values. Using these probabilities (but eliminating the possibility of a measure's rest), we generated the melodies in example 11.8. The melodies seem to exhibit little of the musical style on which the transition tables were based.

Table 11.4 tabulates the probabilities for the occurrence of a tone, given the previous tone as analyzed by Olson from the same body of music. Table 11.4 represents a first-order transition table. Example 11.9 shows two different melodic lines made from the transition table. The probability of every note after the first (which we set arbitrarily to D4) was determined from the probabilities in the table. Here, the examples appear to be somewhat closer to the melodic style of Stephen Foster's songs.

Table 11.5 shows a second-order transition table describing the probability of various three-tone successions. Example 11.10 shows two melodic lines made from the transition

PITCH	PROBABILITY
B3	.0047
C♯4	.0490
D4	.1578
E4	.0708
F♯4	.1035
G4	.0626
G♯4	.0463
A4	.1824
B4	.1143
C♯5	.0789
D5	.0816
E5	.0481

TABLE 11.2   Relative probability of scale-step occurence in 11 songs of Stephen Foster as analyzed by Olsen. *(Published with the permission of Dover Publications.)*

PATTERN	PROBABILITY
𝅝	.125
𝅗𝅥 𝅗𝅥	.250
♩ ♩ ♩ ♩	.125
𝅗𝅥 ♩ ♩	.125
♩ ♩ 𝅗𝅥	.125
♩ 𝅗𝅥 ♩	.125
𝄼	.125

TABLE 11.3   Relative probability of various rhythmic patterns in 11 songs of Stephen Foster. *(Reprinted by permission of Dover Publications.)*

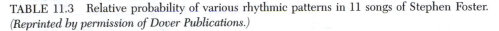

EXAMPLE 11.8   Two eight-measure melodies generated with the zeroth-order probabilities of Table 11.1 and Table 11.2.

table relating the probabilities of three-tone successions in the music of Stephen Foster. These melodies approach the style more closely than those of the previous examples.

From these musically elementary examples, it should be clear that transitional tables afford some possibilities in modeling a randomly generated music on previously composed music. Of course, as previously stated, transition tables can also be the result of compositional thought. The use of transition tables is not favored by all advocates of aleatoric choice of musical elements. Martin Gardner, who favors the generation of music by one-over-f noise (section 11.1G), asserts that music based on transitional tables, however closely related to the model in the small, is still random in the large.[12]

11.1F   Random Walks

A classic example of a Markov process is the controlled *random walk.* Consider a man on a stepladder that has three steps. At specified intervals, he tosses a coin, and if it comes up heads, he climbs up one step. If it comes up tails, he descends one step. The process is bounded, however, because on the top step the only way to go down; at the bottom, the only way is up. Thus, there are four possible levels that the man can occupy. Level 1 represents the ground level at the bottom of the ladder, and levels 2, 3, and 4 represent the three steps of the ladder in ascending order. Assume that the man is on

PREVIOUS PAIR OF PITCHES		B3	C#4	D4	E4	F#4	G4	G#4	A4	B4	C#5	D5	E5
B3	D4	0	0	1	0	0	0	0	0	0	0	0	0
C#4	D4	0	0	.3125	.3750	0	0	0	.3125	0	0	0	0
D4	B3	0	0	1	0	0	0	0	0	0	0	0	0
D4	C#4	0	0	1	0	0	0	0	0	0	0	0	0
D4	D4	0	.1250	.1250	.5625	.1250	.0625	0	0	0	0	0	0
D4	E4	0	0	.1875	.2500	.5000	0	0	.0625	0	0	0	0
D4	F#4	0	0	0	.4375	.1875	.1250	0	.2500	0	0	0	0
D4	G4	0	0	0	0	.6875	0	0	0	.3125	0	0	0
D4	A4	0	0	0	0	.2500	0	0	.7500	0	0	0	0
D4	C#5	0	0	0	0	0	0	0	0	0	0	1	0
D4	D5	0	0	0	0	0	0	0	.1250	.6875	.1875	0	0
E4	C#4	0	0	1	0	0	0	0	0	0	0	0	0
E4	D4	.0625	0	.0625	.2500	.3125	0	0	.0625	0	.0625	.1875	0
E4	E4	0	.0625	.7500	.0625	.1250	0	0	0	0	0	0	0
E4	F#4	0	0	.0625	.1875	.3750	.2500	0	.0625	.0625	0	0	0
E4	A4	0	0	0	0	0	0	0	.8125	.1875	0	0	0
E4	D5	0	0	0	0	0	0	0	0	0	1	0	0
F#4	D4	0	0	0	.7500	.1875	.0625	0	0	0	0	0	0
F#4	E4	0	.1250	.4375	.1875	.1250	0	0	.0625	0	0	.0625	0
F#4	F#4	0	0	.1875	.2500	.3750	.1250	0	.0625	0	0	0	0
F#4	G4	0	0	0	0	.2500	.1875	0	.3750	.1875	0	0	0
F#4	A4	0	0	0	0	.1250	0	0	.6250	.1875	0	.0625	0
F#4	B5	0	0	0	0	0	0	0	1	0	0	0	0
G4	F#4	0	0	0	.5000	0	.5000	0	0	0	0	0	0
G4	G4	0	0	0	0	0	.5000	0	.5000	0	0	0	0
G4	A4	0	0	.1250	0	0	0	0	.6250	0	0	.2500	0
G4	B4	0	0	0	0	0	0	0	1	0	0	0	0
G#4	A4	0	0	0	0	0	0	0	0	1	0	0	0
A4	D4	0	0	0	.6875	.3125	0	0	0	0	0	0	0
A4	F#4	0	0	.3125	.2500	.1875	.0625	0	.1250	.0625	0	0	0
A4	G4	0	0	0	0	1	0	0	0	0	0	0	0
A4	G#4	0	0	0	0	0	0	0	1	0	0	0	0
A4	A4	0	0	0	0	.2500	.0625	.0625	.3125	.3125	0	0	0
A4	B4	0	0	.0625	0	.0625	0	0	.7500	.0625	0	.0625	0
A4	D5	0	0	0	0	0	0	0	.3750	.3125	.1875	.1250	0
B4	D4	0	0	1	0	0	0	0	0	0	0	0	0
B4	F#4	0	0	0	.6875	.3125	0	0	0	0	0	0	0
B4	G4	0	0	0	0	0	0	0	0	1	0	0	0
B4	A4	0	0	.0625	0	.5625	.0625	0	.1250	.0625	0	.1250	0
B4	B4	0	0	0	0	.1250	0	0	.7500	0	0	.1250	0
B4	D5	0	0	0	0	0	0	0	.5625	.1250	.3125	0	0
C#5	B4	0	0	0	0	0	0	0	1	0	0	0	0
C#5	D5	0	0	0	0	0	0	0	0	.3750	0	0	.6250
D5	A4	0	0	0	0	.8750	0	0	.1250	0	0	0	0
D5	B5	0	0	0	0	0	.0625	0	.3125	.3750	0	.2500	0
D5	C#5	0	0	0	0	0	0	0	0	.7500	0	.2500	0
D5	D5	0	0	0	0	0	0	0	0	1	0	0	0
D5	E5	0	0	0	0	0	0	0	.3125	0	.6875	0	0
E5	A4	0	0	0	0	0	0	0	1	0	0	0	0
E5	C#5	0	0	0	0	0	0	0	0	0	0	1	0

TABLE 11.4 Relative probability of occurrence of three-tone sequences in Stephen Foster songs. (*Published by permission of Dover Publications.*)

EXAMPLE 11.9   Two melodies generated using the zeroth-order rhythmic probabilities of Table 11.3 and the first-order transition table (Table 11.4) for pitch.

LAST PITCH

	B3	C#4	D4	E4	F#4	G4	G#4	A4	B4	C#5	D5	E5
B3	0	0	.0625	0	0	0	0	0	0	0	0	0
C#4	0	0	.0625	.0625	0	0	0	0	0	0	0	0
D4	1	1	.1250	.3750	.1250	0	0	.0625	.0625	0	0	0
E4	0	0	.3125	.1875	.2500	0	0	0	0	0	0	0
F#4	0	0	.1875	.2500	.3125	.2500	0	.3125	.0625	0	0	0
G4	0	0	.0625	0	.1250	.1875	0	.0625	.0625	0	0	0
G#4	0	0	0	0	0	0	0	.0625	0	0	0	0
A4	0	0	.0625	.0625	.1250	.3750	1	.2500	.5625	0	.2500	.3750
B4	0	0	0	0	.0625	.1875	0	.1875	.1250	.5000	.4375	0
C#5	0	0	.0625	0	0	0	0	0	0	0	.1875	.6250
D5	0	0	.0625	.0625	0	0	0	.0625	.1250	.5000	.0625	0
E5	0	0	0	0	0	0	0	0	0	0	0	0

(left margin label: NEXT PITCH)

TABLE 11.5   Relative probability of occurrence of a pair of tones in Stephen Foster songs. (*Published by permission of Dover Publications.*)

EXAMPLE 11.10   Two melodies generated using the second-order probabilities of Table 11.4 for pitch choice.

level 3. The probability that he will next go to level 1, p_{13}, is 0, because he can only move one step at a time. The probability of staying on level 3, p_{33}, is also 0, because he changes levels on every toss. The probability of going to either level 4, p_{43}, or level 2, p_{23}, is 0.5.

The following algorithm simulates the controlled random walk described above.

```
int iwalk(int last)
{   // computes the next step of a random walk with reflecting
    // boundaries the argument last is the current position
    // of the walker
```

```
int const imin=1, imax=4; //sets the boundaries
float fran();
float u;
int j=last;
   u=fran();
   if (u > 0.5)
     j++;
   else
     j--;
   if (j>imax) // test upper boundary
     j=imax-1;
   if (j<imin) // test lower boundary
     j=imin+1;
   return j;
}
```

The boundaries of the walk can be changed by altering the constants imin and imax.

The controlled random walk above is described as having *reflecting boundaries*, because every time a boundary is reached, the walker is sent in the opposite direction. Another form of random walk uses *elastic boundaries;* the probability of moving toward a boundary decreases as the walker approaches it. In either case, the presence of the boundaries has the effect of increasing the probability that the walker will be found in a state near the middle. A third type of boundary, the *absorbing boundary,* causes the walk to cease when the boundary is encountered.

Another variation on the random walk determines by aleatoric means not only the direction but also the distance of the next position from the current one. As an example, consider a continuous random variable whose next value is generated by adding to the current value a Gaussian-distributed random variable with a mean of 0. In this case, called *Brownian motion,* there is an equal chance of the new value being either above or below the current one. Owing to the shape of the Gaussian distribution, small changes in value are more likely than large ones.

Composers such as Tracy Petersen[13] have used controlled random walks on musical parameters such as pitch contour where the boundaries were changed with time.

11.1G   Fractional Noises

Another way to characterize a random process is in terms of its spectrum. For example, the random processes introduced in section 4.9 for generating "noise sounds" were described in terms of the distribution of spectral energy versus frequency. Composers have also applied random processes characterized by their spectra to the choice of compositional parameters such as pitch. Section 4.9 describes the use of random processes to generate sequences of sample values that, when applied to a D/A converter, produce a "noise sound." The form of the distributed spectrum characteristic of such a signal depends on the process used to generate it. Thus, another way to characterize a random process is by its *power spectral density*—the variation of the energy in the sequence produced by the process versus frequency. (The spectral characterization applies only to the sequence of values of the random variable used to determine a particular parameter; it says nothing about the acoustical spectra of the actual sounds used in the music. As expected, these spectra will have the characteristics of the instruments that are used to play them.)

White noise has, by definition, a flat spectrum, and so varies with frequency as $1/f^0$. A random walk without boundaries has a spectrum that rolls off as the square of the frequency. Therefore, noise produced by this process is sometimes called $1/f^2$ noise, or *Brownian noise*. Both white noise and Brownian noise are members of a class of processes called *fractional noises* whose spectrum diminishes as $1/f^\gamma$, where $0 \le \gamma \le 2$. A particularly interesting case is $\gamma = 1$, or $1/f$ (one-over-f) noise, which has been observed in the patterns of many naturally occurring phenomena such as noise in electronic devices, annual amounts of rainfall, traffic flow, and economic data, to name just a few.[14] In fact, Clarke and Voss[15] analyzed several examples of music in various styles and found the loudness and pitch of all of them to be distributed as nearly $1/f$.

Values in a sequence generated by $1/f$ noise correlate logarithmically with the past. Thus, for example, the averaged activity of the last 10 values has as much influence on the current value as the last 100, as the last 1000, and so on. This remarkable property means that the process has a relatively long-term memory. In fact, $1/f$ noise has the best memory of any noise. White noise has no memory at all; $1/f^2$ noise places such a heavy weight on the previous event that events prior to the previous few have virtually no influence on the current outcome. Other fractional noises such as $1/f^{0.5}$ and $1/f^{1.5}$ have somewhat longer memory than Brownian noise, but do not approach the characteristics of $1/f$ noise.

As one might expect, a segment of a sequence generated by white noise has no similarity to any other segment. A segment of $1/f^2$ noise has some similarity to segments nearby, but virtually no similarity to those far removed or to the structure of the overall sequence. However, $1/f$ noise produces patterns said to be *self-similar*. Self-similarity is characteristic of much traditional music composition where the local detail mirrors the overall structure of the piece. As a result, some composers have chosen to use $1/f$ noise for compositional purposes.

The following algorithm of R. F. Voss[16] can be used to generate a $1/f$ sequence with a length set by the argument npts.

```
void oneoverf(int npts, float seqout[])
{   // generates a sequence of length npts with a 1/f spectrum
    // the result appears in array seqout
{
  float fran();
  float sum,rg[16];
  int k,kg,ng,threshold,np,nbits;
  nbits=1;
  np=1;
  float nr=npts;
  nr=nr/2;
  while(nr > 1)
  {
    nbits++;
    np=2*np;
    nr=nr/2;
  }
  for(kg=0; kg<nbits; kg++)
    rg[kg]=fran();
  for(k=0; k<npts; k++)
  {
    threshold=np;
    ng=nbits;
    while(k%threshold !=0)
    {
```

```
        ng--;
        threshold=threshold/2;
    }
    sum=0;
    for(kg=0; kg<nbits; kg++)
    {
        if(kg < ng)
            rg[kg]=fran();
        sum+=rg[kg];
    }
    seqout[k]=sum/nbits;
    }
}
```

The output is scaled to fall in the range of 0 to 1.

11.1H   Examples of the Use of Fractional Noises

Example 11.11 was made by selecting pitches and rhythms at random using white noise. The range of pitches was the two chromatic octaves above middle C. The range of rhythmic values was ♪.,♪,♩,♩. Most observers will agree that the passage exhibits little internal relatedness.

Example 11.12 is of brown or $1/f^2$ music. Here, the same ranges of pitch and rhythmic values were used for projecting a melody. The close correlation between adjacent choices results in a music that has been described by Gardner as a wandering "up and down like a drunk weaving through an alley."[17]

One-over-f ($1/f$) noise is generally agreed to produce the most aesthetically pleasing quality of the three types of noise. Example 11.13 shows a melody with the same ranges as the previous examples, and with $1/f$ correlation between successive pitches and rhythms. $1/f$ noise produces what are known as self-similar patterns. This appears

EXAMPLE 11.11   "White noise" music.

EXAMPLE 11.12   "Brown" music generated with $1/f^2$ noise.

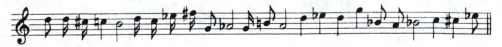

EXAMPLE 11.13   "$1/f$" music.

to be the reason for its greater aesthetic appeal. Its use guarantees that the resulting music will exhibit similar patterns in its large and small dimensions.

Charles Dodge's composition for tape alone, *Profile,* is an algorithmic composition in which the choice of all the elements of pitch, timing, and amplitude were made by the systematic application of 1/*f* fractional noise.[18] Dodge thinks of the work as a "musical fractal" in that the structure of the work exhibits multiple levels of scale and self-similarity. An example of a structure with multiple levels of scale is the von Koch snowflake pictured in figure 11.13. The figure is made by adding to each side of an equilateral triangle another equilateral triangle of smaller scale. The process is repeated at the next smaller level of scale to produce a more and more finely detailed figure. The von Koch snowflake is also a self-similar figure in that it projects the same shape on different scales.

Profile is a three-voice work created with an algorithm using 1/*f* noise to generate the musical detail—the pitch, timing, and amplitude. Each of the three lines exhibits statistical self-similarity. *Profile* is recursively time-filling in the same way the von Koch snowflake is recursively space-filling.

The algorithm to generate the work first creates the line that will serve as the slowest moving of the three voices. The composer sets a limit to the pitch-class (pc) diversity of the line (i.e., the number of different pitch classes, not including repetitions in the same or other octaves). A pitch-class diversity of 3 was chosen for the first of the three lines of *Profile.* Figure 11.14 shows the entire first line of *Profile* generated by the compositional algorithm.

After generating the first line, the algorithm goes back and creates a second line by the same method as the first. For each note of the first line, the algorithm creates a sec-

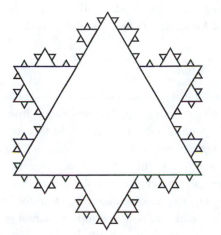

FIGURE 11.13   Von Koch snowflake.

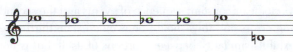

FIGURE 11.14   The first line of Dodge's *Profile.*

FIGURE 11.15   The relationship between the first pitch of line 1 of *Profile* and the first seven pitches of line 2.

ond line with a specified pitch-class diversity (in the case of the second line of *Profile*, a pc diversity of 5). Figure 11.15 shows the relationship between the first pitch of line 1 (E♭5) of *Profile* and the first seven pitches of *Profile*'s second line.

The third line stands in the same relation to the second as does the second to the first—for every pitch of the second line a new group of pitches is generated for the third line (in this case with a pc diversity of 4).

At this stage, the pitches of the work are stored in arrays as ordered successions. What remains is to assign durations to the pitches. This is done in a now familiar way: for every note of the third line the algorithm proceeds as if to generate a fourth line with a certain diversity of pc content. However, instead of actually choosing pitches, the algorithm simply keeps track of how many line 4 pitches would have been created for each pitch of line 3. This number is then multiplied by a time constant (0.025 s in the case of *Profile*), and the resulting number is assigned as the duration for the particular line 3 note. After all line three notes are assigned durations in this way, the durations of the line 2 notes are assigned by adding up the durations of the line 3 notes occupying the same time span as the line 2 notes, and so on for the durations of line 1 as well. Figure 11.16 shows all three of the lines for the first note of line 1 with their durations portrayed proportionally on the page.

Thus, *Profile* is an algorithmic composition composed of three musical lines that are statistically self-similar and of increasingly smaller scale. The reader is directed to the composer's article in the *Computer Music Journal* for further details about the work.[19]

11.1I   Use of Chaotic Responses in Composition

The use of the iterated response of a nonlinear dynamical system in computer music has been explored by a number of researchers in recent years. Applications range from direct sound synthesis[20] to the generation of the aspects of a musical score.[21] In this section, the mapping of the responses into pitch sequences will be discussed because their presentation on a musical staff provides graphic insight into the nature of the response.

A nonlinear system modeled by a set of difference equations can exhibit one of three types of responses starting from an initial condition. The response may converge to a steady state; the response may grow in amplitude until the limits on numerical representation in the system are reached; or the response may oscillate within defined limits, but no steady-state, periodic waveform can be identified. The latter type of response is termed *chaotic*. When the solution of a system of nonlinear equations is used for compositional purposes, the first type of response exhibits a periodic or constant sequence of events and the second type will probably cause computation errors and thus should be avoided. The third type results in a chaotic sequence that exhibits similarity between portions of itself, but is not

FIGURE 11.16   All three of the lines for the first note.

repetitive. Although it never converges to a stable result, this type of response stays within finite boundaries in a region called a *strange attractor.*

Researchers have engaged in a significant amount of investigation into chaotic responses in the past two decades. Such systems operate in multiple dimensions. To illustrate the basic approach, a simple two-dimensional system that can be rapidly calculated will be demonstrated.[22] Consider the system of equations

$$x_{n+1} = 1 + y_n - ax_n^2$$

$$y_{n+1} = bx_n$$

where *a* and *b* are positive constants. The state of this system at any sample *n* is given by the pair of values (x_n, y_n) with the next pair of values (x_{n+1}, y_{n+1}) calculated from the previous by the pair of equations above. The computation of this two-dimensional sequence begins with the composer's choice of initial conditions (x_1, y_1). The range of output values depends on the parameters *a* and *b*. With the parameters $a = 1.4$ and $b = 0.3$, a chaotic response is obtained where *x* falls within ± 1.4 and *y* in the interval bounded by approximately ± 0.4.

The numerical results can be applied to a composition by mapping the sequence of either *x* or *y* into a desired range of a compositional variable. The two example pitch sequences illustrated in example 11.14 were made by starting with the initial condition (0,0) and mapping the sequence of *x* values into a diatonic pitch collection beginning with C4 and ending at A6, represented by the integers 1 through 13.

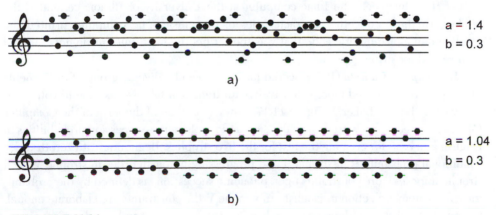

a)

$a = 1.4$
$b = 0.3$

b)

$a = 1.04$
$b = 0.3$

EXAMPLE 11.14

The values specified for a and b determine the nature of the response. When a is unity or less, the sequence becomes periodic. Example 11.14a shows the output for $a = 1.4$ and $b = 0.3$, which, after a initial transient, causes a chaotic response as shown in example 11.14b. Regions of similar pitch progressions can be identified, but duplicate sequences do not exist. Values of a above approximately $\sqrt{2}$ result in a response that grows beyond the numerical limits. To further prevent overflow, the parameter b should not exceed 0.3. Values of a close to, but not less than, unity cause the pitches to separate into high and low regions in a pattern that repeats itself after an initial transient. See example 11.14b with $a = 1.04$ and $b = 0.3$.

The response of a potentially unstable system such as this is fairly sensitive to the choice of initial conditions. With $a = 1.4$ and $b = 0.3$, choosing x_1 and y_1 both less than 0.5 results in a chaotic, bounded response. Increasing either of the initial values raises the risk of a runaway response. For example, the initial condition (1, 10) with $a = 1.4$ and $b = 0.3$ causes the values of x and y to overflow the numerical capability of the machine. This type of algorithm is also sensitive to roundoff errors in the computer calculations, and therefore should be implemented in double-precision arithmetic.

Numerous other types of nonlinear dynamical systems with higher dimensions are available and can be applied to aspects of a composition in a variety of ways. The reader is referred to the literature for other examples.[23]

11.1J   Compositional Uses of Randomness

Lejaren Hiller was the first composer to have extensively investigated computer-aided composition. Hiller's computer music tends to fall into two categories: dramatic, often satirical, theater pieces; and more didactic pieces that demonstrate particular compositional techniques. Examples of the former include *An Avalanche for Pitchman, Prima Donna, Player Piano, Percussionist,* and *Prerecorded Playback* (1968) and *HPSCHD* (with John Cage, 1969). Examples of the latter category are *Illiac Suite* (1957), *Computer Cantata* (1963), *Algorithms I* (1968), and *Algorithms II* (1972).

The programs for the *Illiac Suite* were developed by Hiller and Isaacson in the mid-1950s.[24] For this piece, the Illiac computer at the University of Illinois generated the pitches, rhythms, and other characteristics of the music. The computer printed the results in an alphanumeric code that was transcribed by hand into music notation and then scored for string quartet.

In *Computer Cantata* (1963), scored for soprano and a diverse group of instruments plus tape, Hiller worked more extensively with transition tables (this time in collaboration with Robert A. Baker).[25] Figure 11.17 shows an outline of the form of the *Computer Cantata.* The composers used an analysis of random phoneme-succession probabilities in English as a basis for creating the text for the five strophes. Beginning with zeroth-order conditional probabilities in strophe I and progressing to fourth order in strophe V, each strophe imposes more constraints upon phoneme succession, as defined by the probabilities of phoneme selection in English. In strophe V, the constraints are elaborate enough to provide English-sounding words such as "perpus" (purpose) and "sayd" (said).

A plan of progressive similarity was worked out for elements in the music of the

I.   Prolog to Strophe I   (Rhythm Study for Percussion)
        Strophe I   (Zeroth—order Stochastic Approximation)

II.   Prolog to Strophe II   (Totally Organized Instrumental Music)
        Strophe II   (First—order Stochastic Approximation)

III.   Prolog to Strophe III   (Polytempered Computer Sounds)
        Strophe III   (Second—order Stochastic Approximation)
        Epilog to Strophe III   (Polytempered Computer Sounds)

IV.   Strophe IV   (Third—order Stochastic Approximation)
        Epilog to Strophe IV   (Totally Organized Instrumental Music)

V.   Strophe V   (Fourth—order Stochastic Approximation)
        Epilog to Strophe V   (Rhythm Study for Percussion)

FIGURE 11.17   Outline of the form of Hiller and Baker's *Computer Cantata*. (*Published with permission of* Perspectives of New Music.)

strophes as well. The following progression of transition-table order was used for the five strophes: zeroth-, first-, second-, first-, zeroth-order. As a basis for the selection of musical elements, Hiller and Baker analyzed an excerpt from the second movement of Charles Ives's *Three Places in New England* for occurrence of pitches, durations, rests, dynamics, and playing style. The results were used in designing the transition tables. In addition, each of the five strophes contains a "prolog" and/or an "epilog" for which the material was often generated without reference to a stylistic model. For example, figure 11.18a[26] diagrams the patterns of density of attack points (initiations of notes and rests), the density of actual attacks, and dynamics for the prolog to strophe I; figure 11.18b diagrams these parameters for the epilog to strophe V. The density of attacks is around 2 per second at the beginning of the prolog; it progresses to around 128 at the end. The epilog reverses the process; the density is around 16 at its beginning and falls off to around 1 at the end. The figure also shows the inverse relationship between dynamic level and the density of attacks in these sections of the piece. This section of the *Computer Cantata* is particularly clear in the way the computer is used to realize a musical intention. Here, the composers specified a general shape for the texture and dynamics and left the filling in of the details to the computer.

Other parts of *Computer Cantata* are organized according to serial principles (similar to those found in *Structures* by Pierre Boulez) or other more theoretical considerations (e.g., calculation and control of "harmonic dissonance").

Iannis Xenakis refers to his computer-generated instrumental compositions *ST/10–1,080262*, *ST/48–1,240162*, *Atrees*, and *Morsima-Amorsima* as *stochastic music*. By this term, Xenakis refers to a "world of sound masses, vast groups of sound-events, clouds, and galaxies governed by new characteristics such as density, degree of order,

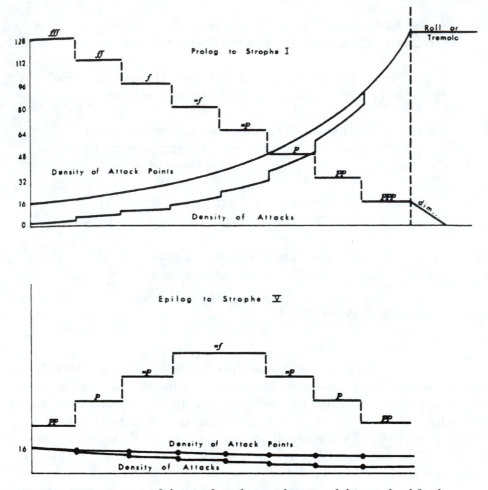

FIGURE 11.18   Patterns of change of attack point density and dynamic level for the two sections of *Computer Cantata*. (*Reprinted with permission of* Perspectives of New Music.)

and rate of change, which required definitions and realizations using probability theory."[27] The Stochastic Music Program (SMP), which Xenakis developed for his computer-aided compositions, relies on probabilistic descriptions of the music. In using SMP, the patterns of distribution of notes take precedence over the selection of the individual notes. Xenakis describes this process by means of an analogy to the way in which clouds or rain are perceived—as a statistical distribution of particles. The shape, density, degree of order, and rate of change among a large number of elements are more apparent than are the characteristics of any single element.

Figure 11.19 shows an overview of the SMP.[28] The following descriptions will help clarify the figure:

"Compute Length of Section"—Here, the computer is instructed to choose a section length according to an exponential distribution of values. The composer specifies an average value for the section length. Because the exponential dis-

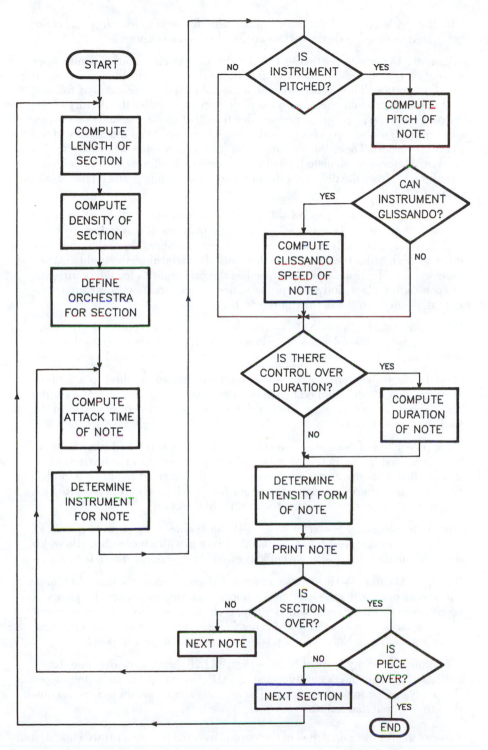

FIGURE 11.19 Overview of the SMP program of I. Xenakis. (*Published with permission of John Myhill.*)

tribution has no upper limit, a maximum value for section length is set. If the generated value exceeds the maximum, another value is chosen.

"Compute Density of Section"—The density, or average number of notes per second of a given section after the first, depends in part on the density of the previous section. The process by which the value is determined is as follows: first, a binary random choice is made to determine whether the density of the current section will be greater or smaller than that of the previous one. Next, two random numbers are chosen in the range between 0 and the density of the previous section. Then, the absolute value of the difference between the two random numbers is calculated. Finally, the calculated difference is either added or subtracted from the density of the previous section, depending on the results of the first step.

"Define Orchestra for Section"—First, the instruments of the orchestra are divided into timbre classes in which a single instrument can belong to more than one class and each class has more than one member. Then, the composer gives a zeroth-order transition table that is used to determine the timbre classes for a section. The transition table specifies the probabilities for the occurrence of each timbre class, and these probabilities are changed by linear interpolation, depending on the density of the section.

"Computer Attack Time of Note"—Time between attacks is chosen by the same method used for the selection of section length. It is a deviation from the average, calculated by taking the average number of notes per second for a section.

"Determine Instrument for Note"—A random number, applied to a timbre-class transition table supplied by the composer, selects the timbre class for the note. Then, a second random number determines which instrument within the timbre class is chosen.

"Compute Pitch of Note"—If the chosen instrument is pitched, the choice of pitch is limited by the range, designated by the composer, of the instrument. If it is the first note, the choice is random within the range. If the instrument has played before, there is a dependence on the previous choice similar to that described above for determining the density of a section.

"Compute Glissando Speed of Note"—If the timbre class permits glissando, choice of glissando speed is by Gaussian distribution with a mean glissando width of 0. This implies that a slow glissando is more likely to occur than a fast one.

"Compute Duration"—The duration of a note is determined on the basis of a Gaussian random process that is scaled by a number of factors, such as the frequency of occurrence of an instrument within a timbre class. For example, if an instrument plays few notes, then its notes would generally be longer. Another factor is the maximum length an instrument can play, which is specified by the composer.

"Determine Intensity Form of Note"—Figure 11.20 shows some dynamic shapes available for notes in compositions using SMP. The composer indicates shapes that apply to a particular instrument. The intensity shapes are then chosen at random from within that range.

Upon completion of the calculation of the steps above, the program prints a line describing all the attributes of the note just generated. The program repeats its steps until all notes of all sections have been generated.

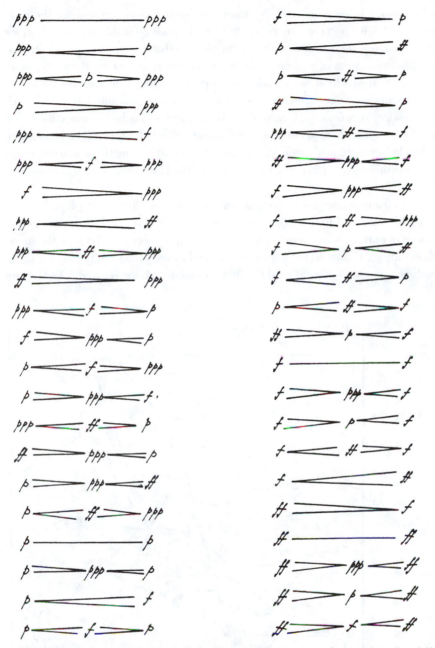

FIGURE 11.20 The 44 intensity forms from mean intensity values: *ppp, p, f,* and *ff. (Reprinted with permission of Indiana University Press.)*

More recently, Xenakis, through his Center for Mathematics and Music (CeMaMu) just outside Paris, has been experimenting with the production of computer music through direct digital synthesis of sound.

Larry Austin is the composer of numerous works of vocal, instrumental, and electronic music. He has been a leading figure in the American musical avant-garde since the early 1960s. Austin has been using computers—both as a compositional aid and a medium for sound synthesis—since the late 1960s. One of the themes that recurs in Austin's output is that of basing some aspects of a piece of music on natural phenomena. For example, in *Maroon Bells* (1976) the melodic lines of a live voice part and a tape "derive from the actual contours" of a mountain range.[29] *Canadian Coastlines* (1981), was commissioned for broadcast by the Canadian Broadcasting Corporation. It is a piece of stochastic music for which Austin used the computer to generate much of the musical detail. The limits within which the stochastic choices were made were determined by a chart tracing the actual coastlines of a number of bodies of water in and around Canada. The chart used for the composition is shown in figure 11.21.

Canadian Coastlines comprises an eight-voice canon, with four parts played live on instruments and voice and four parts prerecorded on tape using a digital synthesizer. The succession of entrances and tempo courses of the eight voices, each given the name of a Canadian city, are shown on the figure. The voice labeled Hamilton begins the piece and proceeds at a tempo of ♩ = 60 until the first 200 seconds have elapsed. The Coburg

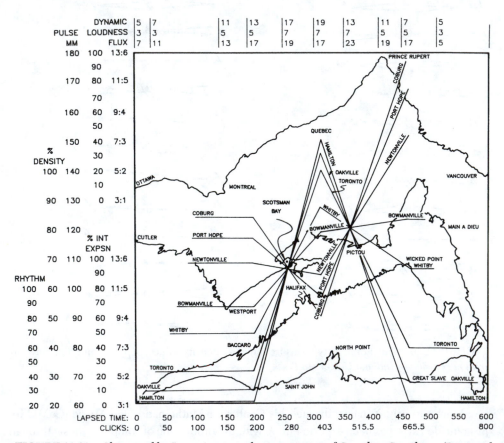

FIGURE 11.21   Chart used by Larry Austin in the composition of *Canadian Coastlines*. (*Reprinted with permission of Larry Austin.*)

voice enters after 100 seconds rest and plays its canonic voice at ♩ = 120 so that it catches up to Hamilton at the elapsed time of 200 seconds. The other six voices, by appropriate choice of their tempi between the rates of Hamilton and Coburg, reach the same point in the canon at the same point in time. The composer has chosen tempo relationships throughout the piece to ensure that there are, during the course of the piece, five of the junctures where the voices all come briefly together.

The relationships in tempo can be heard most clearly during the first 200 seconds of the work. Figure 11.22 shows the assignment of instruments to the canonic voices for the version recorded on Folkways FTS 37475. Observe that each line of the canon is assigned a pair of instruments (the human voice is treated as an instrument in the piece) with one instrument playing a "melodic" version of the line and the other a "rhythmic" version. The pair of instruments on a line plays the canon part in unison with the "rhythmic" instrument making many repeated, shorter notes out of the longer notes in the melody.

Other aspects of the music were determined by the stochastic decisions applied to various parameters of the music for every 5 seconds of its 10-minute duration. The algorithms for dynamic flux, textural density, melodic interval expansion, and rhythm make their choices within the limits determined by the four coastlines shown in figure 11.21. Actually, the four coastlines in the figure are made up of seven coastline fragments taken from geographic maps and freely concatenated by the composer to obtain the pattern of change desired for the elements of the music. For example, the uppermost coastline in the figure controls the *dynamic flux;* not the dynamic level as such, but rather the rate of dynamic change at a particular point in the piece. The application of the coastline to the dynamic flux ensures that the piece will begin and end with relatively little dynamic fluctuation. At the high point, however, there will be a great deal of change of dynamic level.

The coastline labeled Cutler affects the *textural density* of a particular canonic line. In other words, it controls the proportion of playing time versus rest for a line. Thus, at the beginning of the piece there will be a 70% probability of a line having a note as opposed to a rest. That probability changes throughout the piece in response to the curvature of the coastline.

The third coastline from the top controls the general intervallic vocabulary for a partic-

	INSTRUMENT	
VOICE	**MELODIC**	**RHYTHMIC**
Hamilton	Viola	Harp
Oakville	Flute	Contrabass
Toronto	Voice	Marimba
Whitby	Euphonium	Marimba
Bowmanville	Synclavier	Synclavier
Newtonville	Synclavier	Synclavier
Port Hope	Synclavier	Synclavier
Coburg	Synclavier	Synclavier

FIGURE 11.22   Assignment of instruments to the canonic voices of *Canadian Coastlines.*

ular moment of the piece. At the bottom of the *interval expansion* scale, the interval vocabulary is restricted to a predomination of seconds with a few thirds. As the coastline rises to the northeast, the number of allowed intervals increases from seconds through sevenths and falls back down near the end. The choice for this parameter was based on a variation of $1/f$ noise inspired by Benoit Mandelbrot's concepts.[30] The actual pitches chosen are arrived at indirectly by the succession of intervals. The process shapes the contour of the canon theme by weighting the choice of interval by the direction of the coastline, up or down.

The coastline at the bottom of the figure controls the probabilities for rules that affect rhythm.

In addition to the use of the digital synthesizer for some of the sound in *Canadian Coastlines,* Austin took advantage of another aspect of the possibilities of digital synthesis as well. In order to make it possible for the eight canonic lines to be accurately coordinated during live performance, the composer used New England Digital Corporation's Synclavier synthesizer to prepare a separate *click track* for each of the lines. During performance, the players wear small plug-style earphones and follow the changing tempi of their parts from the clicks they hear.

The click tracks make it possible to coordinate a performance of this rather complex work without a conductor. In fact, for the first performance of *Canadian Coastlines* the musicians coordinated their live performance from broadcast studios in three different cities—Halifax, Toronto, and Winnipeg. The sound of the full "computer band" was mixed at CBC studios in Toronto and broadcast throughout Canada from there.

11.2   DETERMINISTIC COMPOSITION WITH COMPUTERS

11.2A   Introduction

Computers are particularly well suited to aid in the composition of music where, at some level of the composition, there is an amount of repetition or recurrence of musical material. In contrast to the random generation of new musical patterns for compositional use, the computer can be used to manipulate input data that serve as the basic material of the composition. This compositional method is often implemented by first devising a shorthand or code by which the compositional operations and relationships are entered into the computer. The composition is then built through a sequence of commands that invoke programs for the performance of specific permutations and variations on designated parts of the input data. There are two principal types of music to which deterministic techniques are most commonly applied: motivic music and serial music. Canonic textures, which may or may not be either motivic or serial, also lend themselves to this sort of treatment. In this part of the chapter we will examine the use of the computer in all these types of music.

11.2B   Motivic Music with Computers

A musical *motive* is the smallest melodic/rhythmic fragment of a musical theme—often only two or three notes—that can be independently varied and manipulated. Willi Apel writes that in the music of Bach and Beethoven, "motives are the very building blocks or germinating cells of the musical composition."[31] One needs only to recall the motive of Beethoven's Fifth Symphony to realize how pervasive the motive elements of a musical composition can be.

In the 20th century, motivic variation has been used by a number of composers for the unification of the elements of composition. Certain composers have constructed entire compositions out of single, simple motives.

To ensure sufficient variety in music built on a motive, the motive is typically subjected to an assortment of variation techniques. Some common variations of motives include repetition, transposition, and alteration of melodic contour and rhythmic features.

Example 11.15a shows a melodic/rhythmic motive. Examples 11.15b and c show the separate pitch and rhythmic components of the motive, respectively. Example 11.16 shows the effect of transposition of the pitches of the motive, first by one semitone (example 11.16a) and then by six semitones (example 11.16b).

The following subroutine transposes a sequence of pitches by a specified number of semitones. For simplicity, the pitches are represented by numerical codes in the range of 1 to 88, corresponding to the keys on a piano. In this system, for example, middle C is denoted by 40, and the C above that by 52. Many other notational schemes are in use, and the reader may have to adapt the algorithms that follow to the particular system used.

```
void transpose(int npitch, int pitchin[], int pitchout[], int nsteps)
// transposes pitch sequence of length npitch in array pitchin
// by nsteps and deposits the result in array pitchout
{
  int j;
  int const minpitch=1, maxpitch=88;
  for(j=0; j<npitch; j++)
  {
    pitchout[j]=pitchin[j]+nsteps;
    if(pitchout[j] < minpitch)
      pitchout[j]=minpitch;
    if(pitchout[j] > maxpitch)
      pitchout[j]=maxpitch;
  }
}
```

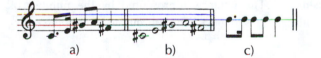

a)　　　　　b)　　　　　c)

EXAMPLE 11.15　A musical motive (a), its constituent pitch succession (b), and its rhythm (c).

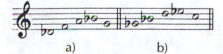

a)　　　　　b)

EXAMPLE 11.16　Transposition of the motivic pitch succession up a half step (a) and up a tritone (b).

The argument npitch specifies the number of notes contained in the motive. The array pitchin holds the list of pitches to be transposed. The array pitchout designates the storage for the result of the transposition. The argument nsteps specifies the number of semitones encompassed in the transposition. It can be either positive or negative, depending on the direction of transposition. The algorithm limits transposed pitches to the range of 1 to 88. For many applications, the reader may wish to reduce the range.

The following example program illustrates the use of the subroutine. It transposes the motive of example 11.15 up two semitones. The array pin holds the original sequence of pitches. The transposed list is deposited in the array pout.

```
#include <iostream.h>
void transpose(int npitch, int array[], int pitchout[], int n);

void main()
// example calling program for subroutine transpose
{
   int const npitch=5; // number of pitches
   int pin[npitch]={40,44,48,49,46};
   int pout[npitch], index;
   int nsteps=2; // number of steps to transpose
   cout << "pitches before calling transpose\n";
   for(index=0; index<npitch; index++)
      cout<< " " << pin[index];
   transpose(npitch,pin,pout,nsteps);
   cout<<"\n\ pitches after calling transpose\n";
   for(index=0; index<npitch; index++)
      cout<< " " << pout[index];
}
```

Notice that in transposition the melodic contour of the original motive is preserved. A common technique for the compositional variation of a motive is that of displacement of its pitches to other octaves. Example 11.17 shows instances of *registral displacement* of the motive in example 11.15a. In example 11.17a, the final two pitches are placed one octave below their original. Example 11.17b shows the motive in ascending intervals, and example 11.17c scatters the pitches over a three and a half octave range. Of course, it is common to apply registral displacement to transpositions of motives as well.

For the following registral displacement subroutine, the musician supplies a succession of pitches and displacements. The latter is represented by the number of octaves, up or down, that a particular pitch is to move. The subroutine returns the registrally transformed motive.

```
void regdsp(int npitch, int pitchin[], int pitchout[], int reg[])
// displaces motive of length npitch stored in array pitchin by
// the number octaves stored in array reg and deposits result in
// array pitchout
{
   int j;
   int const minpitch=1, maxpitch=88;
   for(j=0; j<npitch; j++)
   {
      pitchout[j]=pitchin[j]+12*reg[j];
      if(pitchout[j] < minpitch) // check lower pitch boundary
         pitchout[j]=minpitch;
```

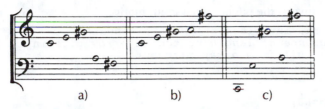

EXAMPLE 11.17 Three displacements of the registers of the motivic pitch succession.

```
    if(pitchout[j] > maxpitch) // check upper pitch boundary
        pitchout[j]=maxpitch;
   }
}
```

As above, the argument npitch specifies the number of pitches in the motive, and pitchin and pitchout designate the input and output arrays of the pitches, respectively. The array reg holds the registral displacements. There are always as many elements in the array reg as there are in each of the pitch arrays.

As an example, the following program uses the subroutine above to displace the pitches of the motive in example 11.15a (stored in array pin) by the amounts specified in the array reg. The resulting list of pitches is stored in the array pout and for the indicated data takes the form of example 11.17c.

```
#include <iostream.h>
void regdsp(int npitch, int ain[], int aout[], int reg[]);

void main()
// example calling program for subroutine regdsp
{
  int const npitch=5;
  int pin[npitch]={40,44,48,49,46};
  int reg[npitch]={-2,-1,0,-1,1};
  int pout[npitch], index;
  cout <<"pitches before calling regdsp\n";
  for(index=0; index<npitch; index++)
    cout<< " " << pin[index];
  regdsp(npitch, pin,pout,reg);
  cout<<"\n\ pitches after calling regdsp\n";
  for(index=0; index<npitch; index++)
    cout<< " " <<pout[index];
}
```

Another often encountered operation on the pitches of a motive is that of *inversion*. Example 11.18 shows an inversion of the motive. Notice that the inversion operation is the reversal of the direction of the intervals, exactly in semitones, and not simply a changing of the melodic contour of the motive. Naturally, transposition of the inversion is also possible.

EXAMPLE 11.18 Inversion of the motive's pitch succession.

The following subroutine inverts the pitches of an input motive.

```
void invert(int npitch, int pitchin[], int pitchout[])
// inverts pitch sequence of length npitch in array pitchin
// and returns the result into array pitchout
{
  int j;
  int const minpitch=1;
  int const maxpitch=88;
  pitchout[0]=pitchin[0]; // the first pitch remains the same
  for(j=1; j<npitch; j++)
  {
    pitchout[j]=pitchout[j-1]-(pitchin[j]-pitchin[j-1]);
    if(pitchout[j] < minpitch) // check for pitch below limit
      pitchout[j]=minpitch;
    if(pitchout[j] > maxpitch) // check for pitch above limit
      pitchout[j]=maxpitch;
  }
}
```

The arguments have the same meaning as in the transpose subroutine above.

Example 11.19 shows the *retrograde* of the motive. Retrograde is the reversal of the order of the pitches of a motive. The retrograde subroutine produces an exact reversal of the order of the input motive.

```
void retro(int npitch, int pitchin[], int pitchout[])
// reverses pitch sequence of length npitch stored in array
// pitchin and puts result in array pitchout
{
  int j,k;
  for(j=0; j<npitch; j++)
  {
    k=npitch-1-j;
    pitchout[k]=pitchin[j];
  }
}
```

Once again, the same arguments are used. One can also combine the previous routines in order to make an inversion of the retrograde of a motive.

Example 11.20 shows two less standard operations on motives. In example 11.20a, the intervals of the motive have been expanded by one semitone so that it contains only the perfect fourth, major second, and major third, and no minor seconds or minor thirds. A contraction of the intervals is shown in example 11.20b. Here, all intervals except minor

EXAMPLE 11.19   Retrograde of the motive's pitch succession.

a)   b)

EXAMPLE 11.20   Expansion (a) and contraction (b) of the motive's interval succession.

seconds are reduced by a semitone each. The minor second is arbitrarily exempted from the contraction in this example to avoid repeating tones.

The following subroutine implements both expansion and contraction. The number of semitones is specified by the argument nsteps. A positive value of nsteps indicates expansion; a negative one indicates contraction. The algorithm does not permit an interval to be contracted to less than a minor second. Further, if the original motive contains repeated notes, the algorithm retains the repetitions.

```
void expand(int npitch, int pitchin[], int pitchout[], int nsteps)
// expands motive of length npitch in array pitchin by nsteps and
// stores result in array pitchout
{
  int j,interval;
  int const minpitch=1;
  int const maxpitch=88;
  pitchout[0]=pitchin[0]; // first pitch remains the same
  for(j=1; j<npitch; j++)
  {
    if(pitchin[j] == pitchin [j-1])
      pitchout[j]=pitchout[j-1]; // do not expand repeated notes
    else
    {
      interval=abs(pitchin[j]ñpitchin[j-1])+nsteps;
      if(interval < 1)
        interval=1; // no interval less than a minor second
      if(pitchin[j] > pitchin[j-1])
        pitchout[j]=pitchout[j-1]+interval; // ascending interval
      else
        pitchout[j]=pitchout[j-1]-interval; // descending interval
    if(pitchout[j] < minpitch) // check lower pitch limit
        pitchout[j]=minpitch;
    if(pitchout[j] > maxpitch) // check upper pitch limit
        pitchout[j]=maxpitch;
    }
  }
}
```

The arguments pitchin, pitchout, and npitch have the same meaning as above.

There are numerous examples in the music literature of operations on the rhythm of motives. Example 11.21 shows three transformations of the motivic rhythm of Example 11.15c. Example 11.21a is an augmentation of the motivic rhythm, and example 11.21b is a diminution. The operations are represented here in common music notation. They represent a change in duration in each case by a factor of 2. More complicated relationships, some of which could be very difficult to notate for instrumental performance, can be implemented with ease for computer synthesis.

Example 11.21c shows the retrograde of the rhythm of the motive of example 11.15c. The computer can be programmed to transform rhythmic motives through algo-

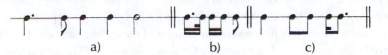

a)   b)   c)

EXAMPLE 11.21   Augmentation (a), diminution (b), and retrograde (c) of the motive's rhythm.

rithms similar to those presented above for pitch. It is necessary to represent the rhythmic values in some kind of numerical code. Naturally, it is assumed that the composer would combine separate operations on the pitch and rhythm of a motive in order to build a composition of this sort.

11.2C Compositional Uses of Computers with Motivic Music

Computers have proven to be helpful in the composition of music where the clear interrelationships of motivic material are manipulated to form the surface of the composition. Example 11.22 shows the first three phrases of "Cadenza," the fourth of Dexter Morrill's *Studies for Trumpet and Tape* (1975).[32] Here, each phrase of the trumpet part has the same shape, ending on a sustained D5. The tape part is similar in all three phrases, consisting of a line rising in the bass and followed by the answer of "distant trumpets" in the treble register. The "distant trumpets" consist of computer trumpets playing variations on the opening line of the live instrument. The basic "rising line" was put into the computer and then varied by using the "motive" feature of Leland Smith's Score program.[33] The second and third phrases were produced as programmed variations on the first phrase, thus eliminating the necessity to re-enter into the computer all of the notes of the subsequent phrases.

Another example of motivic manipulation with the computer in Morrill's composition comes in measures 14, 15, and 16 of the same movement (see example 11.23). Here, the computer echoes the trumpet motive in measure 14 and then presents the same motive in rhythmic augmentation and at different transpositions in a descending pattern through measures 15 and 16.

Gareth Loy, whose techniques of *musique concrète* with computers were discussed in chapter 10, has employed motivic manipulations extensively in his composition *Nekyia*.[34] In addition to the standard motivic techniques of transposition, inversion, retrogression, augmentation, and diminution, Loy employs techniques that can only be realized on the computer. These include "progressive, linear, and nonlinear scaling of melodic contours where the scaling itself is subjected to mutation. A simple example would be a gradual pitch expansion or contraction through time of small repeated melodic phrases." One of the motivic techniques that Loy applies to the time dimension of the work is involved in the transformation of a rhythmic motive consisting of "a grace note followed by a sixteenth, followed by a dotted eighth tied to a rest. . . . This fragment is repeated over and over, each time becoming less and less like the original rhythmic statement of the fragment and more and more like its rhythmic inversion. [This is accomplished by] an interpolation of the duration of the notes in the phrase by millisecond amounts from its rhythmic rectus to its inversion."[35]

11.2D Canonic Imitation with Computers

The computer can greatly facilitate the composition of works that include canonic imitation of one voice by another. The imitation can be applied systemically by computer programs, even when there are subtle differences in speed between parts of the canon. Example 11.24 shows the opening of *Study No. 36 for Player Piano* by Conlon Nancarrow.[36] The four voices of the strict canon proceed through the melody in the tempo proportions of 17:18:19:20.

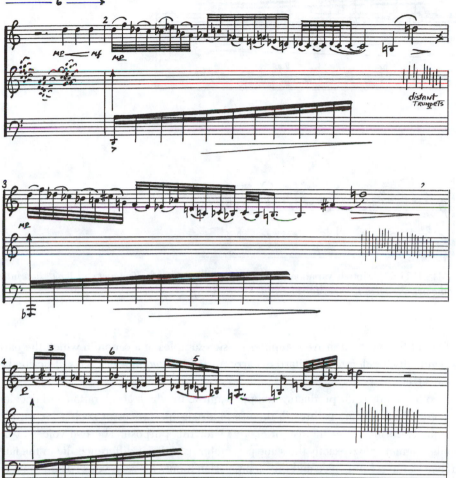

EXAMPLE 11.22   The first three phrases of "Cadenza" from Dexter Morrill's *Studies for Trumpet and Tape. (Reprinted with the permission of Dexter Morrill.)*

Thus, all voices have the same number of measures, but all proceed at different tempi. The plan of the piece is for successively faster tempi (85, 90, 95, 100 for the four lines) so that the voices all come to the same place in the canon for a brief moment in the middle of the work. After that point, they diverge, but now with the slowest voice trailing the others by more and more until it is left to finish the work as it had begun, alone.

In the Nancarrow example, all lines proceed at a fixed, constant tempo. With computer software, it is relatively straightforward to create canonic lines that entail continuous change of tempi as well. Realization of the lines by means of digital synthesis, as with player pianos, presents no problems that need to be solved by human performers. The limits are simply those of human perception.

EXAMPLE 11.23   Motivic variation in Dexter Morrill's *Studies for Trumpet and Tape.* (Reprinted *with the permission of Dexter Morrill.)*

One of the most extensive computer music examples of a canon in which the parts independently accelerate and ritard is Larry Austin's *Canadian Coastlines,* described in section 11.1J.

Another method for producing computer music in which acceleration and deceleration of the parts occurs is through the use of a score preprocessor such as Score 11.[37] Example 11.25 illustrates the use of Score 11 for this purpose. The two voices of the canonic fragment have exactly the same parameter lists. Their differences lie in the later entrance of the second voice and the "tempo" statements for each voice. The tempo for the first voice accelerates over the first 12 beats from beat = 60 to beat = 120. It then ritards over the next 12 beats back to the original tempo. The pattern of tempo of the second voice is quite different. The voice enters 6 beats after the first, and then accelerates for 18 beats from beat = 60 to beat = 120. Example 11.26 shows the music notation for the canonic fragment.

Observe that it would be difficult to create a canon of this sort where the two voices begin with successive entrances and then follow different rates and shapes of acceleration and ritard such that the lines reach their ending points simultaneously. Even though Score 11 supplies a variety of "shapes" from which to choose for the tempo change, it would still be difficult. John Rogers has proposed and implemented a general solution to the problem.[38] Through careful definition of the meanings of acceleration and ritard, Rogers has written software that enables one to map accelerating and ritarding lines into a user-specified span of time. The program then calculates the steepness of the tempo change curve in order to fit the desired span of time. John Melby has employed Rogers's software extensively to create canonic tex-

EXAMPLE 11.24   The opening of *Study No. 36 for Player Piano* by Conlon Nancarrow. (*Published with permission of Soundings Press.*)

tures in which he varies the acceleration and ritard at different rates within the same time span.

11.2E   Serial Music with Computers

Computers have also been enlisted to aid in the composition of music based on 12-tone rows. In some ways, 12-tone composition can be viewed as a more systematic approach to motivic composition, because in 12-tone music, all the pitch material is derived from

EXAMPLE 11.24   *(continued)*

```
i1 0 24;
tempo 12 60 120/ 12 120 60;
p3 rh 8./16/8*2/4*2;
p4 no c4/e/gs/a/fs;
p5 nu 20000;
end;
i2 6 18;
tempo 18 60 120;
p3 rh 8./16/8*2/4*2;
p4 no c4/e/gs/a/fs;
p5 nu 20000;
end;
```

EXAMPLE 11.25   Computer score for a canonic fragment in which the two parts have different patterns of change of tempo.

a single ordering of all 12 tones of the chromatic collection. The major difference between the methods is that a 12-tone row does not imply a registral disposition or a rhythmic pattern. In "classical" 12-tone technique, the operations of transposition, inversion, retrogression, and retrograde inversion are applied to a 12-tone row to produce other orderings of the chromatic collection.[39] Example 11.27 shows the four basic forms of a 12-tone row.

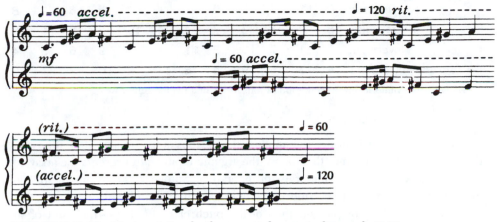

EXAMPLE 11.26 Music notation for the canonic fragment of Example 11.25

EXAMPLE 11.27 The original (O) twelve-tone row and its inversion (I), its retrograde (R), and its retrograde-inversion (RI).

Because the 12-tone series implies nothing about the musical use in terms of register, the notation shows only the pitch classes without any octave placement.

When making 12-tone music with the computer, each pitch class is assigned a numerical code in the range of 0 to 11. Table 11.6 shows the same 12-tone row as in example 11.27 expressed numerically with 0 = C, 1 = C♯, and so on. This notation enables an operation on a row, or set, to be described mathematically. Subroutines for the operations of classical 12-tone music are given below. The subroutine sertran indicates that transposition is the addition of a constant to the pitch class number, modulo 12. For example, the transposition of pitch class 7 by eight semitones is 3; that is, 7 + 8 = 15, which is relocated to a number less than 12 by the operation 15 − 12 = 3.

```
void sertran(int pitchin[], int pitchout[], int nsteps)
// transposes 12-tone row in array pitchin by nsteps and
// places the result in array pitchout
{
   int const npitch=12;
   int j;
   for(j=0; j<npitch; j++)
     pitchout[j]=(pitchin[j]+nsteps)%npitch;
}
```

Original:	0	11	5	2	10	1	4	7	3	6	9	8
Retrograde:	8	9	6	3	7	4	1	10	2	5	11	0
Inversion:	0	1	7	10	2	11	8	5	9	6	3	4
Retrograde–Inversion:	4	3	6	9	5	8	11	2	10	7	1	0

TABLE 11.6   Numerical representation of four forms of a twelve-tone row.

The argument nsteps indicates the number of half steps of the transposition interval. In this subroutine and the ones that follow, the argument pitchin represents the array containing the row that is to undergo the operation. Similarly, the argument pitchout denotes the array where the results of the operation are to be placed.

Inversion is the complementation of the pitch class number—the result of subtracting the pitch class number from 12.

```
void serinvert(int pitchin[], int pitchout[])
// inverts 12-tone row in array pitchin and places the result
// in array pitchout
{
  int const npitch=12;
  int j;
  for(j=0; j<npitch; j++)
    pitchout[j]=(12-pitchin[j])%npitch;
}
```

Retrogression is the reversal of the order of pitch classes.

```
void seretro(int pitchin[], int pitchout[])
// computes the retrograde of the 12-tone row contained in
// array pitchin and deposits the result in array pitchout
{
  int const npitch=12;
  int j;
  for(j=0; j<npitch; j++)
    pitchout[npitch-1-j]=pitchin[j];
}
```

Retrograde inversion is the simultaneous reversal of the order and complementation and can be realized by the successive application of the seretro and serinvert subroutines.

As an example, the following program demonstrates the use of the seretro subroutine. The row to be reversed is stored in the array rowa. The result of the retrograde operation is deposited in the array rowb.

```
#include <iostream.h>
void seretro(int row1[], int row2[]);

main()
// example calling program that displays pitch rows
{
  int const npitch=12;
  int rowa[npitch]={1,3,5,7,9,11,0,2,4,6,8,10};
  int rowb[npitch];
  int index;
  cout << "pitches before calling seretro.\n";
  for(index=0; index<npitch; index++)
    cout<< " " << rowa[index];
```

```
        seretro(rowa,rowb);
        cout<<"\n\ values after calling seretro.\n";
        for(index=0; index<npitch; index++)
          cout<< index << " " rowb[index] << " \n";
        return(0);
    }
```

In addition to the classical 12-tone operations, contemporary composers commonly perform the M5 and M7 operations on the row used. The M5 operation is the reordering of the pitch classes by multiplying each member of the row by 5, modulo 12. M7 renders a similar permutation through multiplying by 7, modulo 12. The subroutines M5 and M7, given below, use the same arguments as the routines above.

```
void M5(int pitchin[], int pitchout[])
// performs the M5 operation on the 12-tone row contained in
// array pitchin and places the result in array pitchout
{
  int const npitch=12;
  int j;
  for(j=0; j<npitch; j++)
    pitchout[j]=(5*pitchin[j])%npitch;
}

void M7(int pitchin[], int pitchout[])
// performs the M7 operation on the 12-tone row contained in
// array pitchin and puts the result in array pitchout
{
  int const npitch=12;
  int j;
  for(j=0; j<npitch; j++)
    pitchout[j]=(7*pitchin[j])%npitch;
}
```

Since World War II, composers have applied principles of serialization to additional dimensions of the music. Serial ordering of a number of parameters, including rhythm, dynamics, register, timbre, and articulation, has been implemented in some cases. The following discussion shows three different methods that have been employed for serializing rhythm.

The first method, and perhaps the simplest, is to create a series of durations analogous to the series of pitch classes. Once a durational row is established, it can be subjected to the same permutations as the pitch row. Example 11.28a shows 12 duration classes and their ordering into a series. Example 11.28b illustrates the same row series used in example 11.27 and then its inversion, retrogression, and retrograde inversion. Many European composers, including Olivier Messiaen, Pierre Boulez, and Luigi Nono, have employed serialization of rhythm in their works using methods similar to the one demonstrated above.[40] In actual practice, there is no restriction against using a different row for each separate musical parameter; nor, for that matter, against using a durational series with 7 members, for example, rather than 12.

A second common practice is to employ the same series for both pitch and rhythm. American composers Milton Babbitt, Charles Wuorinen, and others have used this technique, known as the *time-point system*.[41] The time-point system equates the modulus of the octave in pitch to the modulus of the measure in time. The implementation of the time-point system, then, is in measures with 12 attack points each, such as 3/4 (12 ♪ 's), 4/4 (12 ♪ 's), 12/8 (12 ♪ 's), and so on.

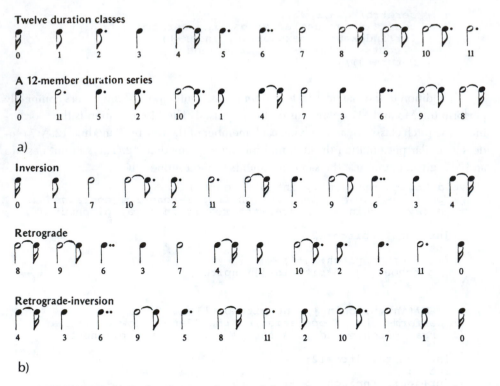

EXAMPLE 11.28   (a) Twelve duration classes and their ordering into a twelve-member duration series. (b) Inversion., retrograde, and retrograde-inversion of duration series shown in Figure 11.28a.

The "time pointing" of a 12-tone row involves the assignment of the pitch-class numbers to the corresponding rhythmic division of the measure. To maintain the correct order of the row, the time points are placed in ascending order within a measure; lower pitch-class numbers are assigned to the proper place in the measure following. Consider the row of example 11.27 (0, 11, 5, 2, 10, 1, 4, 7, 3, 6, 9, 8), which translates into the following succession of time points:

The other 12-tone operations—transposition, retrogression, inversion, and retrograde inversion—are made simply by "time-pointing" the form of the set derived by that operation.

Wuorinen has pointed out that there can be a wide variety of applications for the time-point system.[42] For example, using the same basic set, there is no requirement for a one-to-one conformance of pitch and time-point set. Thus, the succession of time-point sets may be completely different from the succession of pitch sets. He has also shown how the modulus for the time points may be altered in length for every measure

EXAMPLE 11.29   An example from Wuorinen in which the time-point modulus (the measure) varies. *(Reprinted with the permission of Longman, Inc.)*

while still characteristically relating the time points to each other. Example 11.29 shows such a situation. Other examples from his book show situations in which the time-point set determines changes in dynamics.

Serialization of successions of rhythmic proportions has been employed in composition by Henry Weinberg,[43] John Melby, and others. Melby carried this approach into computer-aided composition by building the entire surface of the composition with compositional subroutines. The rhythmic system employed by Melby begins with the composition of a series of proportions, which yields the 12 attack points. The series of proportions, not the attack points themselves, are then subjected to transformations by operations. For example, the proportions 1:5, 5:1, 3:2, 2:1, and 1:3 yield the following succession of 12 attack points:

(The ratios mean "one in the time of five beats," "five in the time of one beat," and so on.) The inversion of the series is 5:1, 1:5, 2:3, 1:2, 3:1 with the musical notation

The retrogression of the series is 1:3, 2:1, 3:2, 5:1, and 1:5, or

Finally, the inversion of the retrograde in Melby's system would be 3:1, 1:2, 2:3, 1:5, and 5:1, or

Unlike the time-point system, there is no provision for permuting the order of the attack points by the operation of transposition. Instead, Melby uses musical tempo as the temporal analogy to transposition in pitch. For example, playing a passage at a rate of 3:2 faster than the original tempo would be analogous to a transposition in frequency by a perfect fifth.

11.2F Compositional Example of Serial Music

Barry Vercoe's *Synapse for Viola and Computer-Synthesized Tape*[44] is a 12-tone work in which the combinatorial relationships[45] between viola and tape are carefully controlled. The overall shape of the work involves a progression from relative clarity of texture and rhythmic homophony in the first few measures (example 11.30), through a middle section of great contrapuntal subtlety, to a very diverse and dense polyphony before the climax, and a return to relative simplicity near the end of the work. Example 11.31 shows the performance score for the point in the work where the texture is at its thickest. Here, where the viola and tape each play six-note groups, the tape part was composed with the aid of a computer program that disposed the six-note groups according to the set form designated by the composer. Vercoe specified only the set form and the general dynamic and envelope characteristics of the music for the passage; the computer supplied the sound on the basis of the composer's general directions.

Vercoe composed *Synapse* during a very short period of intense activity in the fall of 1976. He employed two useful methods when working on the composition. First, he would compose a passage at his desk at home, and then, later that same day, program the computer to play the passage at MIT's Experimental Music Studio. This gave him a nearly immediate aural feedback on his musical ideas.

Because the first performance was to take place shortly after the completion of the composition, Vercoe took advantage of another feature of computer synthesis for making

EXAMPLE 11.30 Opening of Barry Vercoe's *Synapse*. (*Published with the permission of Barry Vercoe.*)

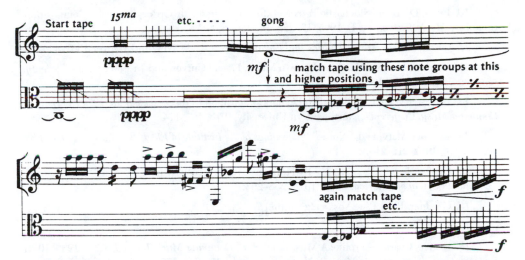

EXAMPLE 11.31   Section from the middle of *Synapse*. *(Published with the permission of Barry Vercoe.)*

the task of learning the viola part easier. He prepared a tape for the violist with the synthesized accompaniment in one audio channel and computer realization of the viola part in the other. Using this tape, the violist could practice the part either with the accompaniment alone or with a "correct" performance of his own part with which to play along. The method helped Marcus Thompson learn to play the difficult part in a very short time.

NOTES

1. Howe, H. S., Jr., and Kassler, Michael. "Computers and Music." In Stanley Sadie (ed.), *The New Grove Dictionary of Music and Musicians.* Washington, D.C.: Grove Dictionaries of Music, Inc., 1980, 603–615.

2. Roads, C. *Composing Grammars* (2nd ed.). San Francisco: Computer Music Association, 1978.

3. Pierce, J. R. *Symbols, Signals, and Noise.* New York: Harper and Row, 1961.

4. McNabb, Michael. "Dreamsong: The Composition." *Computer Music Journal,* 5(4), 1981, 36–54.

5. Kreysig, Erwin. *Advanced Engineering Mathematics* (2nd ed.). New York: Wiley, 1967, 714.

6. Knuth, Donald. *The Art of Computer Programming,* vol. 2, *Semi-Numerical Algorithms* (2nd ed.). Reading, Mass.: Addison-Wesley, 1973, 115.

7. Ruckdeschel, F. R. *BASIC Scientific Subroutines* (vol. 1). Peterborough, N.H.: Byte McGraw-Hill, 1981, 157.

8. Knuth, 117.

9. Hiller, L., and Isaacson, L. *Experimental Music.* New York: McGraw-Hill, 1959.

10. Lyon, D. "Using Stochastic Petri Nets for Real-Time Nth-Order Stochastic Composition." *Computer Music Journal,* 19(4), 1995, 13–22.

11. Olson, Harry F. *Music, Physics, and Engineering* (2nd ed.). New York: Dover, 1967, 430–434.

12. Gardner, Martin. "White and Brown Music, Fractal Curves, and 1/f Fluctuations." *Scientific American,* 238(4), 1978, 16–31.

13. Petersen, Tracy L. "Interactive Digital Composition." *Proceedings of the 1978 International Computer Music Conference,* Northwestern University, 1978, 167–174.

14. Keshner, Marvin. "1/f Noise." *Proceedings of the Institute of Electrical and Electronics Engineers,* 70(3), 1982, 212–218.

15. Clarke, J., and Voss, R. F. "1/f Noise in Music: Music from 1/f Noise." *Journal of the Acoustical Society of America,* 63(1), 1978, 258–263.

16. Gardner, 1978. (See Voss's algorithm.)

17. Ibid.

18. Dodge, Charles. "Profile: A Musical Fractal." *Computer Music Journal,* 12(3), 1988, 10–14. Recorded on *Electroacoustic Music 1,* Neuman Records (450–73), 1990.

19. Ibid.

20. Truax, B. "Chaotic Nonlinear Systems and Digital Synthesis: An Exploratory Study." *Proceedings of the 1990 International Computer Music Conference.* San Francisco: Computer Music Association, 100–103.

21. Pressing, J. "Nonlinear Maps as Generators of Musical Design." *Computer Music Journal,* 12(2), 1988, 35–46.

22. Henon, M. "A Two-Dimensional Mapping with a Strange Attractor." *Communications in Mathematical Physics,* 50, 1976, 69–77.

23. Bidlack. "Chaotic Systems as Simple (but Complex) Compositional Algorithms." *Computer Music Journal,* 16(3), 1992, 33–47.

24. Hiller and Isaacson. *Experimental Music.*

25. Hiller, Lejaren A., Jr., and Baker, Robert A. "Computer Cantata: A Study in Compositional Method." *Perspectives of New Music,* 3(1), 1964, 69–90.

26. Ibid.

27. Xenakis, Iannis. *Formalized Music.* Bloomington: Indiana University Press, 1971, 182.

28. Myhill, John. "Stochastic Music Program." *Proceedings of the Third International Computer Music Conference,* Northwestern University, 1978, 272–317.

29. Austin, Larry. "Hybrid Musics: Four Compositions." Irida Records (022), 1980. (See especially the album notes.)

30. Mandelbrot, Benoit B. *Fractals: Form, Chance, and Dimension.* San Francisco: Freeman, 1977.

31. Apel, Willi. *Harvard Dictionary of Music* (17th printing). Cambridge: Harvard University Press, 1966, 462.

32. Morrill, Dexter. "Studies for Trumpet and Computer." Chenago Valley Music Press, 1975. (Recorded on Golden Crest Records (RE-7068), 1976.)

33. Smith, Leland. "Score: A Musician's Approach to Computer Music." *Journal of the Audio Engineering Society,* 20(1), 1972, 7–14.

34. Loy, Gareth. "Nekyia." Doctoral dissertation, Stanford University, 1979. Recorded on *Computer Music Corrents 5,* Wergo (WER 2025–2), 1990.

35. Ibid.

36. Nancarrow, Conlon. "Study No. 36 for Player Piano, Selected Studies for Player Piano." In Peter Garland (ed.), *Soundings* (Book 4). Berkeley: Soundings Press, 1977, 220–272. Recorded on *Conlan Nancarrow* vol. 4, Wergo (WER 60167–50), 1988.

37. Brinkman, Alexander. "Data Structures for a Music-11 Preprocessor" (Score 11). *Proceedings of the International Computer Music Conference,* North Texas State University, Denton, Texas, 1981.

38. Rogers, John, and Rockstroh, John. "Score Time and Real-Time." *Proceedings of the 1978 International Computer Music Conference*, Northwestern University, 1978, 332–353.

39. Babbitt, Milton. "Some Aspects of Twelve-Tone Composition." *The Score and I.M.A. Magazine,* 1955, 53–61. (Reprinted in *Twentieth Century View of Music History.* New York: Scribner's, 1972, 364–371.)

40. Smith-Brindle, Reginald. *Serial Composition.* London: Oxford University Press, 1966, 163–167.

41. Babbitt, Milton. "Twelve-Tone Rhythmic Structure and the Electronic Medium." *Perspectives of New Music,* 1(1), 1962, 49–79. (Reprinted in *Perspectives on Contemporary Music Theory,* Benjamin Boretz and Edward T. Cone (eds.). New York: Norton, 1972, 148–179.)

42. Wuorinen, Charles. *Simple Composition.* New York: Longman, 1979.

43. Weinberg, Henry. "A Method of Transferring the Pitch Organization of a Twelve-Tone Set through All Layers of a Composition." Doctoral dissertation, Princeton University, 1966.

44. Vercoe, Barry. "Synapse." Composer's Recording, Inc. (CRI SD393), 1978.

45. Babbitt, 1962.

12

REAL-TIME PERFORMANCE OF COMPUTER MUSIC

The relatively slow computation speed and high cost of early computers caused the initial research and realization of computer music to be performed at institutions that had extensive computing resources available. In most instances, the digital samples of the musical signal were computed at a rate considerably slower than the sampling rate so that composers generally realized their pieces a small portion at a time using magnetic tape to store the sections. Naturally this arduous approach severely limited the performance possibilities for computer music.

With the advent of the microprocessor in the mid 1970s, it became possible to put computers on stage to calculate sample values in real time as well as to control sound-production algorithms in increasingly sophisticated ways. This new ability for a performer to interact in real time with a computer precipitated an enormous outpouring of commercial digital instruments as well as software to control them. The vast majority of commercial offerings use the traditional paradigm of a single performer controlling a single instrument where the primary purpose of the performer is to trigger a succession of musical events while controlling the sound within the range of the instrument. The widespread availability and relatively low cost of commercial instruments has tended to steer the live performance of a large portion of modern computer music along these lines. However, this is far from the only possible approach to the performance of computer music.

This chapter will present various modes of computer-music performance and some of the wide range of devices that can be used to change the actions of a performer into musical information. Methods of transmitting information between pieces of computer-music equipment will be discussed as well as the use of a computer to respond musically to the sound from a live performer. The work of a number of individuals involved in the live performance of computer music will be given as examples.

12.1 MODES OF REAL-TIME COMPUTER MUSIC

There are a number of ways of making music in real time with a computer. Certain constraints are imposed by both hardware configurations and software design. The object, as always, is to match the right computer configuration with the planned task.

Probably the most straightforward use of a computer to make music in real time is in what is called *electronic-organ mode*. Here, the computer is attached to a controller (most commonly a keyboard, but some of the other possible controllers are described in section 12.2). With the appropriate software, the musician plays the keyboard in much the same manner as performing on an electronic organ, but with the advantage of certain freedoms offered by the computer-based synthesizer such as flexibility of tuning. The number and complexity of preselected computer "instruments" and/or sampled sounds (when playing on a sampling synthesizer) varies from one synthesizer to another. Generally, the breadth and quality of sounds available is determined by the synthesizer manufacturer. The performer often has the option of using "canned" sound designs, prerecorded samples, sounds designed for a specific composition, sounds sampled for a specific composition, or some combination of the above.

There are a number of positive features of making computer music in "electronic-organ" mode. One is the potentially wide range of sound and timbre to be found at the performer's fingertips. Another is that some systems enable the performer to "tune" the timbre in real time with controls on the computer console. The musical success of this way of making computer music depends very heavily on the traditional musical skills of the performer.

Another way of using the computer in real-time music making has been dubbed the *music-minus-one mode.* Here, the live performer adds a part to a preprogrammed musical texture, often by means of a keyboard. The prerecorded music consists of all score and sound materials not to be performed live. These are prepared in advance and stored on disk. During performance, the live part is played simultaneously with the preset musical materials as they are retrieved from memory.

The live computer-music performance system often functions in this mode as a multi-track recording facility. The performer can make one pass at a part of a musical texture and then replay that track while recording the next layer, and so on. The individual layers are stored as computer instructions and data, and so can be edited easily and directly. The music-minus-one mode has a greater flexibility and facility of performance than the electronic-organ mode, because only part of the music score is performed live. Thus, the textures generally can be denser than is otherwise possible with a single performer. One of the earliest implementations of this mode was designed for the GROOVE system—a digital/analog hybrid system at Bell Laboratories. (See section 1.5B.)

Player-piano mode stands at an opposite extreme to electronic-organ mode. Here, the score and orchestra information are prepared in advance of the performance, and the live performance system runs on its own during the performance. In many cases, this might result in a situation little different from playing a recording at the concert. In others, however, it could offer significant differences. For example, unlike a recording, the score could easily be changed from one performance to the next, either by determinate or random means.

A closely related mode of live computer music is made with a real-time mixing program. Here, the sound files are prepared in advance and the performance involves combining and sequencing them and possibly modifying them by filtering or other means. As with the player-piano mode, this mode can be as rigid at one extreme as the unvarying playback of a recording or as flexible as the situation described above where the musician changes the mix from one performance to another, or even changes aspects of the mix "on the fly" by manual intervention as in the next mode described, conductor mode.

Because a computer can generate a large number of simultaneous musical lines, it is feasible to have the performer function more like the conductor of an orchestra than as the player of an individual instrument. *Conductor mode*, where a pre-established score is "interpreted" during playback, is related to the player-piano mode. However, here the performer intervenes to influence the evolution of a performance. The degree of intervention and interaction can range from control of nuance in the sound of a pre-determined score to control over processes that create an entirely new score. One of the ways conductor mode is used is to initiate the performance of predefined subscores at desired times.

Synthetic-performer mode is the term coined by Barry Vercoe to describe a computer program that drives a synthesizer in response to the gestures of a live performer interpreting a piece of music.[1] The computer emulates the musical decisions of an accompanist who will vary his or her interpretation—changes in tempo, articulation, dynamics, and the like—according to the audible cues of the other live performer.

Synthetic performer mode is very closely related to musical situations emulated in programs written by Roger Dannenberg and Robert Rowe, both of whom have created music for live and synthetic performers where at least some of the musical material itself is improvised by the computer in real time. Section 12.4 will elaborate on this mode.

12.2   PERFORMANCE DEVICES

Musical instruments are devices designed to transform the actions of performers into acoustical energy. Each instrument gives the musician a limited set of physical parameters that can be manipulated to produce a particular sound. For instance, the sound produced by a piano depends on the location, velocity, and acceleration of the performer's fingers and, if the pedals are used, feet. Other instruments use other physical quantities, such as air pressure, as a principal control mechanism. In computer music a wide variety of devices has been created to convert performance gestures into signals to control parameters of a sound-production process. These controllers range from the sensing of involuntary responses such as a human heartbeat,[2] to instruments with interfaces that resemble the controls on traditional instruments, to inventions that sense the actions of performers in entirely new ways.

An instrument provides one or more dimensions of control, although these dimensions are often not completely independent. For instance, a simplistic way to view a clarinet is as a two-dimensional controller with pitch determined by the pattern of covered holes on the tube and amplitude corresponding to blowing pressure. In reality, these controls are not completely independent—e.g., the register can be changed and the pitch can be "bent" by certain actions by the player at the mouthpiece. Yet, if one was to build a digital clarinet interface that sensed pressure and finger position, two independent streams of data would emerge, and it would be incumbent on the sound-generating algorithm to effect the appropriate combination of the data to realize the desired gestural control of aspects of the sound.

A parameter can be either discrete or continuous as is, for example, pitch in a xylophone or a trombone, respectively. By definition, the control signal produced by a digital instrument is discrete, and so the issue becomes one of resolution. A controller designed to select one of the equal-tempered pitches available on a standard piano would need a minimum resolution of 1 part in 88. The minimum resolution required for a perceived continuity of pitch is much greater and depends on the size of the "just noticeable difference" (JND) in pitch which has been determined by psychoacousticians (see chapter 2).

A performance device is also characterized by the number of simultaneous events it can produce. For example, a trumpet produces single musical events in succession, while the six strings of a typical guitar can sound all at once.

Control latency measures the time between the action of a performer and the production of the acoustical response. Unless it is excessive, performers quickly measure this parameter while playing their instruments and adjust their timing accordingly. The latency of an instrument should be constant. When the transmission rate of a digital system connecting computer instruments is insufficient or marginal (see section 12.3), the latency will vary with activity level—an unpredictable situation that performers find highly annoying.

A control device can produce either instantaneous or continuous values. For example, a momentary contact, push-button switch makes electrical connection only during the time that it is depressed, and as such is used to trigger events. A value may be associated with the trigger, such as the travel time of the switch during its transition (a measure of depression velocity) and can be used to control an aspect of the synthesis process. By contrast, the adjustment of a knob or slider on an electronic device sets a parameter to a value that it retains until the next time the performer touches it. Other devices continuously sense the position of some physical feature of the performer. The time-varying signal produced can be applied as an envelope in sound production algorithms.[3]

Just as an audio signal is represented in sampled form, signals from continuous transducers must also be sampled on a regular basis to produce a digital stream of numbers that can be used to control a sound-production process. The sampling rate required depends on the expected rate of variation of the signal as well as the time resolution required for controlling events. The minimum rate needed is sometimes determined by making an analogy with video signals that use 30 frames per second and are capable of properly representing most motions for the eye, but such a system often lacks sufficient responsiveness. Additional time resolution is often needed, and rates as high as 1000 times per second are used for some purposes.[4]

As computer-music systems have become more available, a wide diversity of devices for real-time performance has emerged. What follows is not presented as an exhaustive description of available devices—a task that is best left to the journals. Instead, it highlights several representative examples chosen to demonstrate particular principles of control.

The piano-style keyboard or *clavier* is one of the most popular musical controllers, primarily because it can produce multiple events over a wide frequency range, and there is a large base of musicians already trained in its use. The simplest claviers act as a group of momentary switches that transmit pitch and timing information. In computer synthesis, the pitches need not be restricted to equal temperament—other tuning systems can be programmed (see section 2.3). Dynamic expression is enabled by sensing the key velocity and/or pressure. Both the attack and release velocity can be encoded by measuring the travel time of the key from one position to another. The most common use of attack velocity is to control the amplitude of the tone, but many synthesis algorithms also link velocity with timbre so that striking a key more forcefully produces a richer spectrum. Key velocity has also been used for *cross switching,* where one of two timbres is chosen based on the relationship of the velocity to a specified threshold value.[5] The related *cross-fade mode* mixes two timbres with their relative proportions computed from the key velocity.

Some of the more sophisticated claviers offer the musician a further method of expression not available on traditional keyboard instruments by enabling the steady-state portion of the tone to be influenced while the key is held down. Sensing applied pressure is a common technique for realizing this feature. Robert Moog[6] invented a way to provide additional degrees of freedom by sensing in two dimensions the position of the performer's finger on a key.

Another parameter in the design of a keyboard controller is the number of concurrent events it can support. Simple claviers may respond to a maximum of four depressed keys at once, although many devices set the maximum at ten—one for each finger—which serves most musical purposes.

The use of a clavier as a controller limits the musical gestures that can be made by the performer. In an attempt to extend the range of expression, a few keyboard controllers include a breath controller attachment. This device senses the pressure applied by the performer to a mouthpiece. As with any musical instrument, training and practice is required of the player to obtain satisfactory results. Many other types of controllers are commercially marketed today. Most of them communicate with the computer via the MIDI interface bus—a standard interconnection scheme that will be described in section 12.3. A MIDI drum comprises a rubber pad that can sense the velocity of the drumstick when it is hit. Other MIDI instruments available resemble wind instruments such as saxophones and trumpets, and produce signals based on the breath pressure or velocity at the mouthpiece and the position of the keys. MIDI guitars typically send out six signals—one for each string. Four-string bass guitars are also available. With so many channels to transmit concurrently, the response may feel a little slow at times.

Max Mathews has investigated the relationship of a conductor to an orchestra in order to determine an effective controller for the conductor mode of computer music.[7] He concluded that a conductor has two important duties: to control the tempo of the piece at a fairly microscopic level, and to control the amplitude and balance of the ensemble. On the other hand, a conductor does not have control over the sequence of pitches played by the performer. The first result of this research was the *sequential drum*—a pad covering both a grid of wires and microphone.[8] When a performer strikes the pad with a drumstick, four parameters are generated—the time of the event, which can be used as a trigger; the position of the strike in two dimensions (x,y); and the intensity of the strike (z). A typical use of the sequential drum was to sequence through a score stored in computer memory. In this way, the performer could beat the tempo of the music, control its loudness by the force of the drumming, and set the balance or other timbral qualities by the strike position on the drum head. Conducting a stored score with a sequential drum gives the performer the degrees of freedom necessary to impart considerable nuance into the music, yet it does not grant the freedom to play a wrong pitch.

The *radio drum* is a successor to the sequential drum.[9] The drumsticks used in this instrument contain miniature radio transmitters, and the drum pad houses an array of small antennas. The apparatus determines the three-dimensional position (x, y, z) of each drumstick on a continuous basis, not just when the drum is struck. This capability enables the measurement of the velocity of the sticks in three dimensions. An imaginary surface above the drum pad is declared so that passing a drumstick through it is considered a "beat." Because the position of the sticks is observed at all times, not just when they strike the pad, the radio drum became known as the radio baton. A compositional example made by Jon Appleton will be presented in section 12.5.

Some composers have been interested in using the movements of dancers to control the performance of a computer-music composition. A range of techniques, from embedding an array of small mercury switches in a dance costume to using ultrasound to sense the position of the performer, has been investigated. An ultrasonic distance finder (sonar) is used in many cameras to determine the focal length. These devices can be adapted to measure the distance between a performer a single fixed point on stage.[10] Uncertainties in the distance measurement cause slight fluctuations in the value—thus, the most reliable applications compare the distance measure to a series of threshold values, then initiate a new action when the performer crosses into a new zone.

Multiple ultrasonic transducers can be used to capture the position of a dancer in multiple dimensions. In the GAMS system developed by Will Bauer and Bruce Foss,[11] the performer carries an ultrasonic microphone that receives pulse-encoded signals from four ultrasonic loudspeakers located at the corners of the performance space. The position of the microphone can be determined to a precision as good as ±5 mm if it is sampled frequently enough. The system not only produces the three-dimensional location (x, y, z)—it measures the velocity of motion, as well as the acceleration in the three dimensions. The propagation time of the ultrasound and the processing time give the unit a latency of about 30 ms.

12.3 STANDARD INTERFACES FOR MUSICAL DEVICES

A wide variety of computer-music devices has been developed to perform a broad range of tasks. To realize a desired musical facility, an assortment of devices can be connected together to form a system. But in order to do so, the signals between the devices must be compatible. In other words, there must be an appropriate definition of the communications protocol between elements of the system. The definition of a digital data signal is considerably more complex than an analog one because, in addition to specifying the connection hardware and the voltage levels, one must also specify the data rate, the data format, and method of encoding information. Originally, computer-music systems used custom interfaces, but manufacturers soon realized that a universal interface that allowed equipment from a variety of sources to be interconnected would greatly stimulate interest in the field.

Of necessity, any communications protocol imposes limitations that restrict the range of ideas it can support. This section discusses two commercially available standards for musical information transmission: the widely available MIDI protocol[12] and the more recent, higher-performance ZIPI protocol.[13] In both cases, this text is not intended to be exhaustive, but it will serve to introduce the basic concepts behind each protocol.

In 1981 a standard for information transmission between pieces of commercial electronic music equipment was proposed by Dave Smith of Sequential Circuits. Originally named the universal synthesizer interface (USI), its inception is generally marked by a meeting between Smith and representatives of other manufacturers at the National Association of Music Merchants (NAMM) Summer Exposition in 1981. At that time, several manufacturers were developing unique interface protocols, but Smith's proposal gained wide and rapid acceptance by virtue of its relatively low cost and detailed definition. By 1982 it enjoyed the support of a major group of manufacturers, and the renamed Musical Instrument Digital Interface (MIDI) flourished. Originally envisioned as a method of controlling synthesizers, MIDI has subsequently been applied to a large variety of sound-processing equipment, such as reverberators and sound mixers. The precision and repeatability of control afforded by MIDI has resulted in its widespread use both in the studio and in live performance situations. However, the speed and method used for data transfer, chosen for its relatively low cost, limit its usefulness for certain types of music and performance methods, although considerable effort has been expended in the past few years to develop hardware and software techniques to work around some of these limitations.

The hardware portion of the MIDI standard specifies the interconnection between pieces of equipment as a path for serial data running asynchronously at a rate of 31.25 kilobaud. The serial method of transmission sends the data one bit a time. This technique is not nearly as fast as its parallel counterpart, but it reduces the implementation cost considerably because only one hardware circuit is required. Employing an asynchronous method of transmission also saves cost because the data clocks in the equipment involved in the interchange need not run in perfect unison. To make the timing of the data unambiguous to the receiver, an 8-bit byte of data is framed by a start bit and a stop bit.

Thus, the transmission of each data byte actually requires 10 bits to travel down the circuit, one after the other. The unit of baud is a measure of the rate of data transmission; on a relatively simple system such as MIDI, a single baud corresponds to 1 bit per second. Given 10 bits transmitted per byte, a rate of 31.25 kilobaud means that at most 3125 bytes can be relayed from one MIDI device to another each second. As another cost-saving measure, the MIDI communications bus is essentially unidirectional, so that it does not promote two-way conversations between devices.

The MIDI standard enables the interconnection of a myriad of electronic-music devices. There are three types of connectors that can be placed on a particular device. As its name implies, a connector labeled OUT is a port from which MIDI signals emerge to drive other devices. In a similar fashion, a connector labeled IN is the entry point through which data is received. A third type of connector found on receivers is labeled THRU—it is an output that echoes the data received at the IN connector of the device. The MIDI cables used to interconnect these ports are terminated at each end by a 5-pin DIN[14] connector, chosen for its low cost and widespread availability. Only three of the five pins (#2, 4, and 5) are used in the current MIDI standard.

The THRU connector enables multiple pieces of MIDI equipment to be connected in a series or daisy-chain fashion as shown figure 12.1. The signal from the controller is passed through each of the devices so that each has access to the data. Each MIDI com-

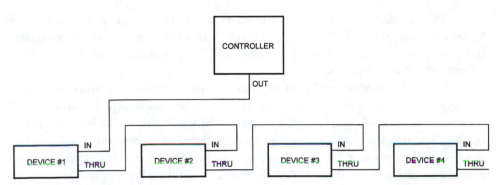

FIGURE 12.1   Series connection of MIDI devices.

mand sent down the chain embeds a numerical address in its code so that a particular device recognizes and responds only to signals addressed to it.

In the daisy-chain method of interconnection, a delay is incurred as the MIDI signal is relayed between the IN and THRU ports. As a result, devices farther down the chain might be noticeably late in responding to their commands. In assembling large systems, a device known as a *MIDI through box* can be used to enable the parallel (or star) connection of devices (see figure 12.2). The through box distributes the MIDI input signal to each of its outputs so that all connected devices receive the MIDI data simultaneously.

MIDI was defined with 16 channels corresponding, in principle, to the number of devices that can be controlled. However, a particular piece of equipment capable of performing multiple functions may use multiple addresses to distinguish them. In the days when only synthesizers were MIDI controlled, 16 channels seemed generously sufficient, but the expanded use of MIDI to control a wide variety of sound-processing

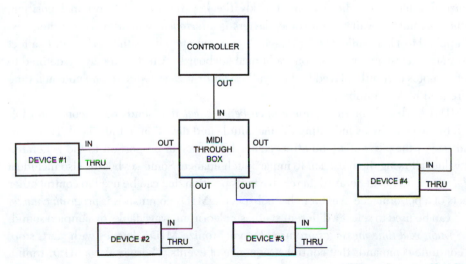

FIGURE 12.2   Parallel connection of MIDI devices requires an additional piece of hardware.

equipment has necessitated special equipment to increase the number of available MIDI channels. These devices take in a single MIDI line from the system controller and divide the data among several separate MIDI output circuits such that each distributes 16 unique addresses.

A personal computer usually serves as the master controller in a MIDI system. To enable this function, an interface card that plugs into the computer and provides MIDI connectors is required. In addition, appropriate software to drive the interface and to assist in creating the data stream that encodes the desired musical result must be installed on the computer. These applications most often take the form of sequencer programs; their attributes are described in Section 1.5B. Inputs to the program can be made using the computer keyboard or a mouse. This approach is often not suitable for live performance, but it can be used to implement complex musical gestures that sometimes cannot be achieved any other way.

Commercially available MIDI input devices provide a more traditional interface between the musician and the digital system. The most common device is the clavier, which can be an electronic keyboard attached to a synthesizer or a *MIDI controller keyboard*, which has no sound-generating capability and only initiates and controls MIDI events. The commands sent over the MIDI bus were defined with a clavier in mind, so they will be summarized below in that context. However, all types of MIDI controllers, including those described in section 12.2, use the same command set to transmit their control parameters.

Striking a key on a clavier produces a three-byte MIDI data sequence: a *Note On* command, followed by the *note (key) number* to indicate pitch (middle C is designated 60), and then a numerical value that is a measurement of the *key velocity* imparted by the performer. When multiple keys are struck to play a chord, the commands are sent in the order the keys are depressed. Releasing a key also initiates a three-byte sequence: a *Note Off* command, followed by the number of the note that has been turned off, and a numerical value that indicates how quickly the key returns to its original position. Another parameter available on some claviers is *aftertouch*, which measures the pressure applied to a key while it is depressed. This parameter allows the performer to affect the sound in a way not available on traditional keyboards. Aftertouch may be defined to affect all notes currently played by the synthesizer or it can modulate one note at a time (referenced by key number).

MIDI keyboards often include a *pitch-bend wheel* that sends out a command followed by two data bytes indicating the magnitude and direction of the wheel. This command moves the pitch of a tone off its center frequency in proportion to the generated data value, allowing the musician to impart pitch nuance. Some keyboards also include a *modulation wheel* to generate data relative to its position that can be used to control other aspects of a performance. Another channel-specific MIDI commands is *program change*, which can be used to select a different synthesis algorithm, wave table, or sampled sound.

System real-time messages are used to synchronize MIDI devices with start, stop, and continue commands that control a sequence of events. There is also a MIDI timing clock that transmits a pulse 24 times per quarter note at the current tempo.

System-common messages include *song select* and *song position pointer*. The *song select* command chooses between multiple sequences stored in memory. The *song position pointer* designates a particular place in a sequence from which playback begins after the receipt of a continue command.

System-exclusive messages provide the vehicle to transfer blocks of information into and out of particular instruments. A unique identification number is assigned to a manufacturer of MIDI equipment for use in designating their system-exclusive messages. Beyond that, manufacturers are free to define messages to transmit as much information as necessary in any format desired. This command type is often used to implement functions not supported in the original MIDI definition. For example, sampled sounds can be transferred between instruments with appropriate system-exclusive messages.

As MIDI became accepted for use in the studio production of music, the need arose for a means of synchronizing the MIDI stream of commands with other media, such as previously recorded tapes, video, and film. The MIDI standard provides a definition of MIDI Time Code (MTC) which can be used to synchronize MIDI-compatible devices. MTC contains an *absolute* description of the time in hours, minutes, seconds, and fractions of a second. This format stands in contrast to the 24 pulses per quarter note provided by system real-time messages, which is a *relative* measure of time because the tempo is not fixed.

In recent years, devices have been produced to synchronize MIDI devices with SMPTE[15] time code—an accurate, reliable format that is standard throughout most of the entertainment industry. This form of time code is based on the standard used for color video, in which there are 29.97 frames per second. Europeans use a similar time code called EBU,[16] which runs at 25 frames per second. A SMPTE translating device reads the time code from the external process and produces MTC for transmission to the MIDI devices. Although such time codes were originally developed to control television and motion pictures, they may also be used for projects that comprise strictly audio. A typical use of this method entails recording one track of SMPTE time code on a tape, then recording the desired audio on other tracks. The tape can then be played back to trigger the appropriate MIDI events at the frame numbers programmed into the MIDI controller.

MIDI was created as an inexpensive way to control commercial synthesizers and is oriented toward the initiation of sequences of events (notes). In such applications it has been very successful. Its low data rate places a greater burden on the devices that are being controlled. In other words, MIDI can initiate a complex timbral evolution, but generally it will not be able to control the fine details of the sound—in terms of its command set and transmission speed, it has only a limited ability to vary the synthesis model and its parameters during the course of a sound.[17] That task is primarily left to the algorithms used in the sound synthesis devices. MIDI does provide parameters such as pitch bend, which can be varied by the performer, but again its usefulness is somewhat restricted by the low data rate.

When many events are initiated simultaneously, or when many control parameters are to be transmitted, the capacity of the MIDI bus will be exceeded.[18] There are several methods, each with its own liabilities, for handling this situation:

1. The excess data can be ignored with the corresponding loss of information.

2. The data can be serviced as fast as possible in the exact order it was received. This technique can result in a "smearing" of a transmitted musical chord, for example.

3. Through the use of more sophisticated algorithms, the data for several events intended to sound simultaneously can be held and then triggered all together after the receipt of all data.

One of the principal problems in a system such as this with insufficient transmission bandwidth is a non-uniform latency, so that the time elapsed between the action by a performer and the sonic event varies.

Another limitation of MIDI compared to a general purpose synthesis system is temporal resolution. Because it is primarily directed at music that is specified with traditional notation, MIDI breaks time into coarser segments, stipulating a number of ticks per quarter note at the current tempo.

To address the limitations of MIDI, another standard for musical data interchange called ZIPI has been developed through the cooperative efforts of Zeta Music and the Center for New Music and Audio Technologies (CNMAT) at the University of California, Berkeley.[19] The hardware specification mandates a *minimum* data rate of 250 kilobaud (8 times faster than MIDI) and sets no upper limit on the bandwidth that may be obtained as computer hardware speed continues to increase. ZIPI devices are connected in a ring around a ZIPI *hub*, a piece of hardware that sequentially passes a *software token* around the ring. When a device has the token, it can transit data to any other device in the ring. In this way, the ZIPI bus provides for full two-way communication between devices. Up to 253 devices can be connected in the ring.

The software portion of ZIPI is the Musical Parameter Description Language (MPDL), which provides for efficient and detailed control of the musical devices.[20] MPDL provides a large set of commands and parameters, many of which greatly facilitate the control of sound on a nearly continuous basis. Data types are designated for such standard parameters as loudness and pitch, but also for controlling many other aspects of the sound such as articulation, inharmonicity and the pitched/unpitched balance in the spectrum, as well as the apparent location of the sound. ZIPI implements commands by notes, by instrument, or by families of instruments so that the alteration of groups of notes can be done more efficiently. By contrast, to change an aspect of a sound in MIDI, the command must be either addressed to a specific note that is sounding or to the entire channel.

12.4   INTERACTIVE PERFORMANCE

Computer music compositions written for live performance often include performers playing traditional acoustic instruments. In the early days, the only viable method was to have the performer play along with a previously recorded tape of an electronically realized part. As computers became faster, some performers began to play with parts synthesized in real time. Either approach represents a one-way interaction in which the performers' actions are influenced by what they hear from the electronic source. As a logical extension, more recent hardware and software advances have enabled dialogues between performers and the computer based on the acoustic signals produced.

12.4A   Extracting Parameters from Musical Sound

To obtain musical signals suitable for interpretation by a computer, microphones are used to convert sounds produced by the performers into electrical signals that are subject to real-time analysis. The results of the analysis are used to control aspects of the computer-generated score. Three attributes of a musical tone are commonly extracted for use as control signals: the onset time, determined by a threshold detector; the amplitude envelope, captured by an envelope follower; and the frequency, discriminated by a pitch detector. Of the three processes, pitch detection is the most difficult and least reliable.

The *onset time* is determined as the point at which the peak amplitude of a signal exceeds a particular threshold value. This information can be used to trigger events in the computer and is a key component in the *score following mode* of interactive performance.[21] In the simplest form, the computer plays along with the performer, and the succession of onset times is used to establish the tempo for the computer. Approaches to score following will be discussed in section 12.4B.

The output of an *envelope follower* has many applications. For instance, the extracted time-varying envelope can be imposed on another sound by means of multiplication. Envelopes can also be used to control a parameter of a unit generator such as the cutoff frequency of a filter. Many unusual effects can be derived by performing mathematical operations on the envelope before using it as a control signal. For example, subtracting the envelope from a constant that is larger than the maximum value of the envelope yields a signal that has the reverse characteristics of the original; e.g., when the original is at its peak, the processed envelope is at its minimum.

Pitch information is obtained either by analyzing the signal from an acoustic instrument with a *pitch detector* or, when the performer is playing an instrument that generates MIDI signals, by reading the note number and possibly the pitch-bend information from the MIDI data stream. The acquired sequence of pitches can be used to identify the current location in a score that the computer is trying to follow. The sequence of pitches may also be played after a delay to create a canon, or they may be transformed in some way (e.g., transposed) before they are played back. More sophisticated performance programs can even invoke compositional algorithms based on the received sequence, performing motivic manipulation (section 11.2) or generating stochastic events (section 11.1).

Reliable pitch detection can be troublesome when the acoustic waveform has a complex spectrum. Because they are trying to estimate the fundamental frequency, pitch detection devices include a low-pass filter near the input to reduce the harmonic energy. The effect of this processing in the time domain is to smooth the waveform to increase the likelihood of an accurate pitch measurement. The measurement of pitch is considerably more difficult when energy from more than one source is found in the input. As a result, signals applied to pitch detectors generally come from microphones placed very near the instrument to be pitch-tracked.

For real-time applications, the latency in the pitch detection process must be short. However, there is a basic limitation on the speed pitch detection which slows its responsiveness: in general, at least one cycle must be received by the pitch detector in order to evaluate its frequency. In other words, at least one period of the waveform must elapse before the pitch detector can report a value. Because frequency and period are inversely related, this latency is considerably more noticeable on low pitches.

Several approaches exist for pitch detection ranging from the rudimentary to some that are too intensive to be implemented in real time. Merely taking the Fast Fourier Transform (FFT) of the input signal does not give sufficient resolution for the measurement (see section 7.2). The simplest approach to real-time detection measures the period of the waveform as the time between "zero crossings"—points on the waveform at which the amplitude crosses 0 with similar slopes. This method works best on the smooth waveform characteristic of a signal with little harmonic energy. As an example, consider the waveforms shown in figure 12.3. The unfiltered waveform contains a formant that causes considerable ringing during the course of a cycle. An algorithm programmed to detect zero crossings where the waveform is increasing could report several possible points of crossing on each cycle of the unfiltered waveform. Passing the waveform through a simple low-pass filter before pitch detection secures the correct, unambiguous result.

The more reliable *autocorrelation technique* compares the input signal with delayed

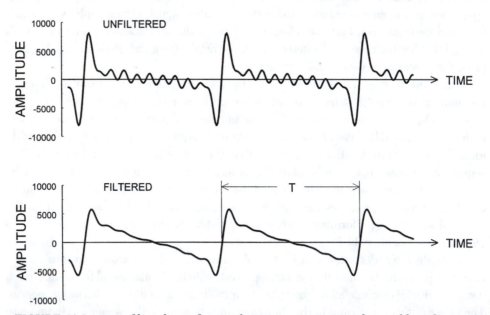

FIGURE 12.3   An unfiltered waveform with many zero crossings that could confuse a pitch detector. Passing the waveform through a low-pass filter ensures the proper measurement of the period (*T*).

images of itself. The highest output is obtained when the amount of delay is exactly one period. Because autocorrelation requires a very large number of computations, high-speed approximations to the algorithm are generally implemented in pitch detectors. Some of the other approaches to pitch detection that have been implemented involve frequency-agile digital filters with center frequencies that are varied to determine the frequency of the waveform passing through them by looking for either a maximum or minimum response.[22]

12.4B   Approaches to Interactive Performance

In the *score following mode* of interactive performance, the computer becomes an accompanist that responds to the sounds created by a live performer. The computer generally plays a precomposed score stored in its memory, and the challenge becomes the temporal alignment of this score with the score being played by the performer. Pattern-matching algorithms are used to determine the current position in the performance score. These algorithms examine the sequence of onset times, the detected sequence of pitches, or both. The pattern matching algorithm compares the musical information from the performer with its record of the performer's score. A match generates the appropriate musical event from the computer. Although it is easiest to analyze a succession of monophonic pitches, methods for handling polyphony have also been devised.[23] Here, one of the challenges is the small but random variation in the sequence of attacks of the notes in a chord.

Systems that match only pitch information allow the performer a full range of rubato but have difficulty following large vibratos and trills.[24] They can also suffer from the sometimes unreliable data produced by pitch detectors measuring complex sounds. As a result, many systems work primarily with the pattern of onsets (rhythm) and use pitch as an alternate means when a temporal pattern match is not found or when it is uncertain.

Score following is not as simple as one might think initially, because the software must align events temporally in the computer part with the next *expected* beat from the performer.[25] Some systems can receive a *count in* from the performer, if desired, as a method of promoting synchronization from the beginning of the piece.[26] The success of score following can be significantly improved, especially for music containing rubato passages, by incorporating information gained from rehearsals.[27] Performers who frequently play with a particular system also gain a sense of its "personality" and adjust their playing for the best response.[28]

The computer part synthesized on systems that derive temporal information by examining one note at a time from the performer tends to change speed abruptly. A smoother temporal contour is made by storing the tempi over a period of time and computing the current value as a weighted sum of the previous tempi. The most recent value receives the most weight in the summation and the importance of previous values is generally tapered off in a geometric sequence (e.g., 1, 1/2, 1/4, . . .). As a further measure, a small amount of randomness is sometimes added to the onset times of the computer events to make the interaction between the performer and machine sound less mechanical.

One of the problems that should be considered in the development of interactive performance is how to direct the response of the computer when an error is made, either by the performer or by a pitch detector. A recovery plan should be implemented so that the computer's performance does not become completely lost under a fault condition.

Robert Rowe has developed one of the most notable systems for interactive performance, known as Cypher.[29] The system can serve three related functions: listening, composing, and playing. In the first function, Cypher obtains musical data from a live performer by reading the stream of MIDI data that is generated. The program analyzes these data for such categories as density, loudness, tempo, register, and harmony. It sorts the lines into phrases and then analyzes the phrases to deliver a high level of information to the other system functions.

The response to the musical input can be formulated in one of three ways. The input can be used to trigger the playing of a stored musical line which, if desired, can be synchronized to the temporal pattern of the input. A more common response is to transform the input in some way. For example, the input line can be transposed, a chord can be dissected and arpeggiated, or a portion of an input line might be "looped"—that is, repeated a specific number of times. The phrase also might be modified using a motivic transformation such as those described in section 11.2. A third type of response is to activate a compositional algorithm with parameters taken from the analysis of the input. Often this takes the form of a constrained random process (see section 11.1) that generates a score that is then synthesized into sound.

Another approach to interactive performance is to use the computer as a sound processor. In this mode the audio received from the performer is modified in some way. A simple example would be filtering the sound, but more frequently, complex operations such as the convolution (see section 10.3) of input signal with a stored sound file are performed.[30] The received sound may also be used to influence the parameters of a sound-synthesis process.

12.5   COMPOSITIONAL EXAMPLES

There have been numerous approaches to the composition of computer music for live performance. Of necessity, these were influenced by the technical capabilities of the equipment available to the composer at the time of composition. In fact, one of the impediments to writing enduring computer music is the relatively short lifetime of most electronic and computer instruments. This section will detail several different approaches to the composition of computer music intended for live performance.

Composer Jon Appleton was one of the inventors of the first digital synthesizer, the Synclavier, in the early 1970s. The Synclavier was a portable, real-time computer-music performance instrument comprising a computer, fast for its day, together with special-purpose synthesis hardware and a piano-style keyboard mounted in a console along with a variety of knobs, buttons, pedals, and a "mod" wheel for the real-time control of the synthesizer. The Synclavier demonstrated in a forward-looking way the great potential of digital synthesis for real-time performance. It predated the inexpensive, portable digital synthesizers that became the standard in the 1980s. The later models of the Synclavier became more oriented to the recording studio and were less portable for live performance. Appleton continued to use the Synclavier to make such tape pieces as *Homenaje a Milanes* (1986) and *Dima Dobralsa Domoy*[31] (1993) but he also followed a strong compositional interest in creating music for live computer performance. For this side of his compositional activity he uses a portable computer music instrument well suited for concert use. That instrument is the Radio Baton, invented by computer music pioneer Max Mathews. The Radio Baton is a performance instrument that is played like a drum and transmits MIDI information to a computer with an attached synthesizer, sampler, or other MIDI-driven device. Specifically, the Radio Baton consists of a box containing five radio receivers, which resembles a rectangular drum head. The drum is activated by a gesture from one of its two attached batons, each containing a radio frequency transmitter, which resemble soft, felt-headed percussion mallets. The Radio Baton transmits three data streams in response to a stroke: the x-position of the stroke, its y-position, and its magnitude.

A typical use of the Radio Baton is for the program executed on the host computer to "play" a preloaded score using the MIDI code it receives from a nuanced live performance. Since the score is already in the computer, the musician's drum strokes advance the program through the score, eliminating one of the more vexing problems of live performance—playing wrong notes. Yet, even with the guarantee of a "note-perfect" performance, there is plenty for the musician to concentrate on, because the exact placement and strength of the baton strokes can have very important musical consequences.

Example 12.1 shows measures 49–53 from the score to Appleton's *Pacific Rimbombo.*[32] In each measure the arrows indicate baton strokes. For example, in measure 49, the drum is struck four times at the tempo of the performer's choice. Each stroke initi-

*Length of sustain, this instrument has a very short attack and decay.
**From quite dry to a medium reverberation.

Notes: In measure 53 one beat starts this series of notes which follow at a tempo, envelope, loudness and reverberation level to be determined by the performer.

Margin numbers 8, 9, 11, 12 refer to instrument definitions.

Arrows refer to baton beats.

EXAMPLE 12.1   Excerpt from Jon Appleton's *Pacific Rimbombo.* (Reprinted with permission of the composer.)

ates a sixteenth note figure from the synthesizer. Notice the separation of staves with the designations of 8 and 9 in the left margin. The numbers refer to "instruments" on the synthesizer used to make the sound for the piece, with the notes in the upper staff sounding on instrument 8 and with the notes on the lower staff on instrument 9. It might appear from measures 49, 50, and 51 that the performer needs to trigger the drum on each and every beat. This is not the case, as illustrated in measure 52 where the drum strokes are in a quarter, half, quarter pattern.

At measure 53 a very different sort of performance is suddenly required of the musician. Here, after an initial stroke to signal arrival at the measure (a MIDI program change), both batons are pressed to the surface of the drum. The left/right position (x) of the left baton determines the tempo at which the succession of notated pitches is played. Its up/down position (y) affects the length of the sustain portion of each note. The position of the right baton similarly performs two functions: x determines the loudness while y controls the amount of reverberation, from quite dry to a medium amount.

Pacific Rimbombo illustrates how Appleton has adjusted his own real-time performance technique from that of a keyboard player in his Synclavier days to the more recent use of percussion-style mallets for the activation of MIDI-based hardware. In all of his composition for real-time systems, Appleton has made music that is traditionally expressive while showing the way to the future of live performance in computer music.

SoundColors, created by Mara Helmuth, is an excellent example of the sort of "sound installation" that can be made to run in real time on a computer. Helmuth writes, "*Sound-Colors* creates a sound environment of shifting colors."[33] It offers the listener a choice of up to seven sound files composed for the piece to be mixed together using the no longer commercially available NeXT computer. *SoundColors* is played by the listener in real time by first selecting which of the sound files to mix and then assigning attributes to them that govern their role in the mix. The interface facility for the mixing is a program named Collage!, which mixes the specified sound files stochastically within the guidelines set by the listener. As shown in figure 12.4, the listener has, for each sound file, control by means of sliders over the general amplitude level and its variability; the general range of durations and its variability; and the silence between plays and the variability of that attribute of the mix.

Helmuth designed the seven sound files listed in figure 12.5 for *SoundColors.* The sound file "cymbals" was made by phase vocoding a recorded cymbal sound and then transposing the sound on resynthesis. "Bells" was made by transposing the sound of a recorded metal bell as well as filtering it with a program to simulate room ambiance. "Beads" is an almost unprocessed recording of the agitation of a string of bamboo beads. "Brakedrums" is processed between analysis and synthesis by transposition only. These four sound files together are designated "Au concrète" and can be invoked together using a "Mode" function implemented in Collage!. The fifth sound file, "mellipse," is the most heavily processed of the sounds. It consists of smoothly changing events, based on a recording of a spoon striking a pot lid, and is made through a variety of modification techniques including windowed time-stretching, elliptical filtering, processing to impart room ambiance, and transposition of the recording. The last two sound files, "evolviolin" and

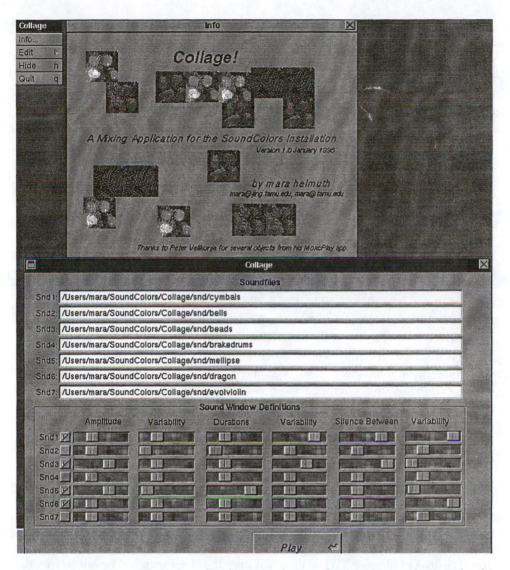

FIGURE 12.4 User interface for the Collage! program. *(Reprinted with permission of Mara Helmuth.)*

"dragonesque," are both made from granular sound techniques. Evolviolin was made by the granular sampling of a recorded violin and dragonesque is a pure, unmodified granular synthesis. The latter two sound files are described by the composer as "widely varying, sometimes fierce, granular synthesis sounds."

SoundColors is not intended for concert performance. The composer states, "The intent is to create a relaxed environment in which to contemplate the sound. The best location is a room or hallway where people can either move around or sit down and focus on the music. It may be placed in front of large windows, where people may look out while manipulating the sounds."

Category	Source	Processing
beads	bamboo beads	minimal
bells	metal bell	transposition, rooms
brakedrums	brakedrum	transposition
cymbals	cymbal	transposition
melliptical	pot lid	windowed time-stretching, elliptical filtering, rooms, transposition
evolviolin	violin	granular sampling
dragonesque	granular synthesis	none

FIGURE 12.5   Sound files designed by Mara Helmuth for *SoundColors*. *(Reprinted with permission of Mara Helmuth.)*

Larry Polansky and David Rosenboom began writing the computer-music language HMSL[34] in the early 1980s, and Phil Burk added object-oriented programming features in the mid-1980s. HMSL has continued to evolve in response to different musical needs expressed by its users. One of the motivations for the creation of HMSL was to devise a language in which experiments in musical form could be made in real time. Larry Polansky's composition *B'rey'sheet (In the beginning ...) (Cantillation Study #1)*,[35] an interactive work for live singer and computer, is an especially clear example of the use of computer software to do this. It was written in 1984 and is one of the earliest pieces made using HMSL.

B'rey'sheet is the first in a series of Polansky's "Cantillation Studies." The vocal line is based on "Masoretic cantillation melody for the singing of Torah" (from the 11th or 12th century). The voice in *B'rey'sheet* intones the chant for the first 17 verse-sections of the Torah. The music that the computer plays at a given moment is dependent on a number of things, including the material the voice is singing at that time. In a very real sense, the computer part can be regarded as a real-time harmonization of the vocal line.

The text of *B'rey'sheet* describes the creation of the world and the "gradual imposition of cosmological order." While the voice sings the chant without embellishment, the computer part dramatizes the meaning of the text: at the beginning of the work the computer part is a chaotic, rapidly changing succession of gestures bearing what seems to be a remote relation to the voice. By the end of the work, the computer plays the melody of the chant in unison with the voice as it pitch-tracks the voice in real time. The change during the course of the work in the relation between the computer part and the voice articulates its overall form very clearly.

One of Polansky's ongoing concerns in composition has been experimental intonation. In *B'rey'sheet* the pitches of the vocal line are sung in the just-tuned scale shown in figure 12.6. The voice is heard throughout the work in characteristic chant style as shown in figure 12.7. The tuning of the computer part is what Polansky has called "paratactical." It refers to a situation in which the precise tones of the computer are deter-

FIGURE 12.6   Just-tuned scale used by Larry Polansky for *B'rey'sheet*. *(From L. Polansky, Computer Music Journal, 18(2), 1994, 59–77. Reprinted with permission of Larry Polansky.)*

mined not by reference to a scale, but rather by their intervallic relationship to the tracked pitch of the voice at the moment.

With each of the successive 17 verses of the trope, the tuning of the computer part uses a progressively lower limit on the ratios of the just intervals between the voice and the computer. Thus, at the beginning of the work a 17-limit tuning vocabulary is employed. That is, all of the frequency ratios use 17 in the numerator (e.g., 17:16, 17:15, 17:14, etc.) along with intervals from all the lower limit tunings as well (16-, 15-, 14-limit, etc.). At the second verse, the upper limit is changed to 16, and so on down to the 3-limit of the final three verses. At the end of the work the harmonic ratios are all perfect just fifths with the harmonic ratio 3:2 *(Pythagorean tuning)*. Randomness plays a role in determining which particular frequency ratio, within the governing limit, to invoke at a given time. The frequency ratio to use is determined stochastically, and that ratio is then applied to the pitch of the voice, as analyzed by the pitch tracker.

Not only is the tuning of the intervals between voice and computer simplified in the work with time, but other aspects of the computer part are similarly made more congruent to the voice as well. Throughout the work the computer "listens" (through a pitch-to-MIDI converter) to the voice. At the beginning of the work the computer creates many tones of its own to each of those of the tracked pitch of the voice. But as the work evolves, the computer creates new tones less and less frequently.

B'rey'sheet was intended to be performed with an inexpensive, portable hardware configuration. The work was originally performed on the Amiga computer. It took advantage of the Amiga's four channels of sound output with direct memory access (DMA), enabling Polansky to operate on the sound output in real time from HMSL without interrupting the sound. Polansky chose to use four sine-wave outputs and to alter the sound through real-time waveshaping techniques. In keeping with similar global changes in

FIGURE 12.7   Characteristic vocal line from *B'rey'sheet. (Reprinted with permission.)*

randomness and harmonic ratios, at the beginning of the work a new random value for waveshaping the sine tones is chosen very frequently (in the audio range). At the end, new values are chosen at a subaudio rate.

B'rey'sheet is but one of a number of works that Larry Polansky has made using HMSL. These range from live, interactive compositions such as the one just discussed to others that involve the superimposition of complex, canonically related voices made from sampled sound.

Tod Machover began using computers in his music in the 1970s. His first works employed direct digital synthesis to make tapes either to be played alone or to be played in conjunction with live instruments.[36] Since the early 1980s his work has concentrated on the live performance of computer music, often in theatrical contexts. Machover's first opera *Valis*[37] has been performed internationally. Based on writings of Philip K. Dick, this work was Machover's first to develop what has become a hallmark of his musical style—the blending and juxtaposition of popular music idioms with styles associated with concert music.

His live computer music is known for using something he calls *hyper instruments*. Hyper instruments are instruments that use digital sound synthesis (with the control usually conveyed with MIDI in Machover's work to date) to respond to the performance gestures associated with acoustic instruments. A particularly striking example of the use of hyper instruments can be heard in *Bug Mudra*,[38] a work for live acoustic and digital instruments. Here the virtuoistic performances of the live instruments are manipulated to a certain degree with the EXOS Dextrous Hand Master, worn on one of the conductor's hands. This device responds to intricate hand movements and is used to send signals to control aspects of the sound of the live instruments.

Brain Opera (1996) is the title of a more recent work in which some of the sound used as raw material in each performance is manipulated live from recordings made of audience members just prior to the performance.

Curtis Bahn is a composer of live and electroacoustic music with an extensive background in improvisatory performance. Recently he has begun to combine his playing with his computer music in a successful effort to synthesize the diverse character of his musical experience. To that end he has founded and plays bass in an improvisation ensemble that combines improvisatory new music with world music (the percussionist is a Japanese folk drummer who plays festival drums with the group) and with computer music.

The ensemble integrates the use of the computer as a means of coordinating the "free" improvisation through graphic representation of the scores from which the improvisations emanate, as well as a source of sound (through playback from disk) and sound processing (through outboard MIDI devices). The sounds stored on computer disk for real-time access come from a wide range of sources including sound synthesis, *musique concrète*, and material drawn from recordings of Bahn's earlier electroacoustic music. The computer also operates the outboard sound processing through MIDI messaging.

Figure 12.8 diagrams the two types of computer usage by the improvisatory ensemble—score selection and electroacoustic sound production (either recorded or MIDI). The main performance display of figure 12.9 shows what a player would see on the com-

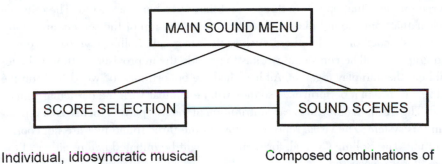

Individual, idiosyncratic musical scores combining traditional musical notation and computer-aided composition/performance coordination.

Composed combinations of sounds and MIDI control settings for improvisational performance.

FIGURE 12.8   Arrangement of the software system used by Curtis Bahn for live performance. *(Reprinted with permission of Curtis Bahn.)*

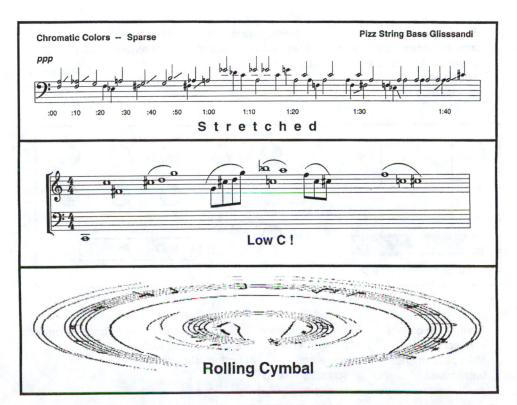

FIGURE 12.9   Main performance display when three files are being accessed. *(Reprinted with permission of Curtis Bahn.)*

puter screen in the situation where three sound files were being accessed. The example makes clear that some sound files, such as the one at the top of the screen, are represented in music notation while others, such as the recorded "Rolling Cymbal," are represented graphically. The concept at work is to provide the improvisers with visual cues that will help them to play together. All have had the opportunity to "woodshed" on the material in advance of a performance, so they will be familiar with the particular sounds displayed. The freedom of the musical contribution of the live players themselves is paramount in this system. The visual representations of the three sound files are not coordinated in time. The Rolling Cymbal, for example, might be initiated before either of the other two files was accessed.

Another aspect of the system is one that addresses an important problem of combining live players with computer playback of prerecorded sound—how to provide for the possibility that the prerecorded sound will seem to follow the improvisation of the live players. With Bahn's system, it is not necessary for the sound of a displayed score to be audible at all times. This approach allows, for example, the players to see a score and begin to play (around) it before the listeners actually hear the recorded sound. It is a strategy that can be used as a way of anticipating the recorded sound by the live musicians.

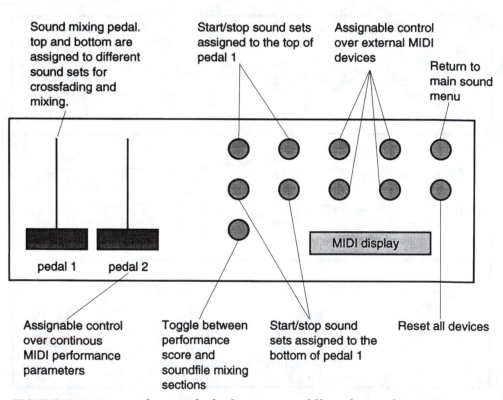

FIGURE 12.10   Main performance display for mixing sound files and manipulating MIDI parameters. *(Reprinted with permission of Curtis Bahn.)*

Figure 12.10 shows the main performance control screen. Here the player controlling the computer determines the course of the improvisation through cross-fading and mixing of sound files on the disk with pedal 1 and manipulating the MIDI performance parameters with pedal 2. The selection of files and their start and stop times, as well as the particulars of the states of the MIDI-controlled gear, are manipulated through the use of the other controls on the screen.

The composer Cort Lippe is most active in realizing works that take advantage of the computer to create sound in real time. In a series of works, Lippe has used very high-speed digital signal processors to create works for live instruments in which the computer part is made out of the sound of the live instrument in real time. His work for solo clarinet and ISPW (IRCAM Sound Processing Workstation)[39] is a good example of what an imaginative composer can do with real-time interaction between a live performer whose instrument is digitally tracked and sampled, and the computer, which can either output sampled sound to add to the live sound or can synthesize sound in real time.

Roger Dannenberg and Barry Vercoe are credited with independently solving the problem of real-time score following in the early 1980s.[40] It is known as score following because the computer has access to the output of the live performer's performance through MIDI data, and a copy of the live performer's score. By matching the two, the computer can keep track of where it is in the piece of music. The problem is to write software that will enable a computer to participate in a live performance and to coordinate its part with a live performer whose tempo may fluctuate for expressive or other purposes. The desired effect is for a computer instrument to slow down or speed up by just the right amount to keep in sync with the live performer and to do so without moving too quickly in one direction or the other.

Dannenberg has demonstrated his solution to this problem on a number of occasions at conferences and on compact disc.[41] He plays a trumpet, and his software follows the nuanced performance. It tracks his rendition of *Greensleeves* with the changes in note speed necessary to keep pace with the trumpet, while sounding that its decisions of when to play and at what speed are musically appropriate.

Dannenberg has published a further development along these lines. Here, the computer follows the lead of a live performer not only to coordinate with it, but also to compose its own "improvised" musical contribution. In Dannenberg's *Jimmy Durante Boulevard*,[42] a rather elaborate composition/improvisation situation was created that took input from players, coordinated their lines, and added a computer part to them.

Robert Rowe was one of the first composers to advocate and practice live, interactive computer music composition. His *Flood Gate*[43] is a work for violin, piano, and computer system. In *Flood Gate*, the violin and piano play music that is fully notated in some places and partially or completely improvisatory in others. The computer follows the instruments through a technique that Rowe has called *score orientation*.[44] With score orientation, the computer program looks for a succession of high-level cues (there are 61 such cues in the 10-minute *Flood Gate*) and recognizes the cues through pattern matching. The cues are embedded in the fully notated sections of the instrumental music that will vary only slightly from one performance to another.

The computer adds electroacoustic sound in two ways. First, following the considerations programmed by the composer, the computer "listens" to the acoustic instruments (through pitch-to-MIDI converters) and contributes music on the basis of the speed, density, harmony, rhythm, among other traits that it encounters. In the fully notated sections, the computer's contribution varies only slightly (through tightly constrained randomness) from one performance to another. In the improvisatory sections the computer contributes in much the same way—its output is a transformation of the instrumental music; but in every performance the computer music for these sections will differ from previous performances. At different places in the piece, one can hear where the computer imitates quite closely the characteristics of the acoustic instruments with which it is playing—when the piano plays fast and high, for example.

The second sort of contribution is algorithmically composed music that the computer produces in real time either from preprogrammed compositional algorithms or on the basis of stored patterns from earlier in this or other performances. In the recording of *Flood Gate*, the passage approximately between 6:00 and 7:00 is one in which the computer is more prominent than either of the other instruments and is creating its music in real time.

NOTES

1. Vercoe, B. "The Synthetic Performer in the Context of Live Performance." *Proceedings of the 1984 International Computer Music Conference.* San Francisco: Computer Music Association, 1984, 199–200.

2. Knapp, R. B., and Lusted, H. "A Bioelectric Controller for Computer Music Applications." *Computer Music Journal,* 14(1), 1990, 42–47.

3. Rubine,D., and McAvinney, P. "Programmable Finger-Tracking Instrument Controllers." *Computer Music Journal,* 14(1), 1990, 26–41.

4. Ibid.

5. Pressing, J. "Cybernetic Issues in Interactive Performance Systems." *Computer Music Journal,* 14(1), 1990, 12–25.

6. Moog, R., and Rhea, T. "Evolution of the Keyboard Interface: The Bösendorfer 290SE Recording Piano and the Moog Multiply-Touch-Sensitive Keyboards." *Computer Music Journal,* 14(2), 1990, 52–60.

7. Boulanger, R. "Conducting the MIDI Orchestra, Part 1: Interviews with Max Mathews, Barry Vercoe, and Roger Dannenberg." *Computer Music Journal,* 14(2), 1990, 34–46.

8. Mathews, M. V. "The Sequential Drum." *Computer Music Journal,* 4(4), 1980, 45–60.

9. Mathews, M. V., Boie, R., and Schloss, A. "The Radio Drum as a Synthesizer Controller." *Proceedings of the 1989 International Computer Music Conference.* San Francisco: Computer Music Association, 1989.

10. Chabot, X. "Gesture Interface and a Software Toolkit for Performance with Electronics." *Computer Music Journal,* 14(2), 1990, 15–27.

11. Bauer, W., and Foss, B. "GAMS: An Integrated Media Controller System." *Computer Music Journal,* 16(1), 1992, 19–24.

12. Rothstein, Joseph. *MIDI: A Comprehensive Introduction,* 2nd ed. Madison, Wisc.: A-R Editions, 1995.

13. McMillen, K., Simon, D., and Wright, M. "A Summary of the ZIPI Network." *Computer Music Journal,* 18(4), 1994, 74–80.

14. Deutsch Industrie Norm (DIN) is a German standard for audio connectors, which has also been used widely in personal computers.

15. Society of Motion Picture and Television Engineers.

16. European Broadcasting Union.

17. Loy, G. "Musicians Make a Standard: The MIDI Phenomenon." *Computer Music Journal,* 9(4), 1985, 8–26.

18. Moore, F. R. "The Dysfunctions of MIDI." *Computer Music Journal,* 12(1), 1988, 19–28.

19. McMillen, K., Simon, D., and Wright, M. "A Summary of the ZIPI Network."

20. McMillen, K., Wessel, D. L., and Wright, M. "The ZIPI Music Parameter Description Language." *Computer Music Journal,* 18(4), 1994, 52–73.

21. Rowe, R. "Machine Listening and Composing with Cypher." *Computer Music Journal,* 16(1), 1992, 43–63.

22. Lane, J. "Pitch Detection Using a Tunable IIR Filter." *Computer Music Journal,* 14(3), 1990, 46–59.

23. Bloch, J. J., and Dannenberg, R. B. "Real-Time Computer Accompaniment of Keyboard Performance." *Proceedings of the 1985 International Computer Music Conference.* San Francisco: Computer Music Association, 1985, 279–289.

24. Puckette, M. and Lippe, C. "Score Following in Practice." *Proceedings of the 1992 International Computer Music Conference.* San Francisco: Computer Music Association, 1992, 182–185.

25. Allen, P. and Dannenberg, R. "Tracking Musical Beats in Real Time." *Proceedings of the 1990 International Computer Music Conference.* San Francisco: Computer Music Association, 1990, 140–143.

26. Vantomme, J. D. "Score Following by Temporal Pattern." *Computer Music Journal,* 19(3), 1995, 80–59.

27. Vercoe, B. and M. Puckette. "Synthetic Rehearsal: Training the Synthetic Performer." *Proceedings of the 1985 International Computer Music Conference.* San Francisco: Computer Music Association, 1985, 275–278.

28. Kimura, M. "Performance Practice in Computer Music." *Computer Music Journal,* 19(1), 1995, 64–75.

29. Rowe, R. *Interactive Music Systems: Machine Listening and Composing.* Cambridge: MIT Press, 1993.

30. Pressing, J. "Cybernetic Issues in Interactive Performance Systems."

31. Appleton, Jon. "Dima Dobralsa Domoy." Jon Appleton: Contes de la mémoire. Emprientes DIGITALes (IMED 9635), 1996.

32. Appleton, Jon. "Pacific Rimbombo." *CDCM Computer Music Series,* 15, (CRC2180), 1992.

33. Helmuth, Mara. Personal Communication, 1996.

34. Polansky, L. "Live Interactive Music in HMSL." *Computer Music Journal,* 18(2), 1994, 59–77.

35. Polansky, Larry. "B'rey'sheet." *Theory of Impossible Melody,* Artifact (CD 1004), 1991.

36. Machover, Tod. "Soft morning, city!" CRI Records, 1984.

37. Machover, Tod. *Valis,* Bridge Records, (BCD 9007).

38. Machover, Tod. "Bug Mudra." *Flora,* Bridge Records, (BCD 9020), 1990.

39. Lippe, Cort. "Music for Clarinet and ISPW." *The Composer in the Computer Age VII,* Centaur (CEI30), 1996.

40. Puckette, M. "Something Digital." *Computer Music Journal,* 15(4), 1991, 66.

41. Dannenberg, Roger. "An Accompaniment Demonstration." Recorded on CD accompanying Mathews, M. V., and Pierce, J. R. *Current Directions in Computer Music Research.* Cambridge: MIT Press, 1989.

42. Dannenberg, Roger. "A Composed Improvisation." Recorded on CD accompanying Mathews, M. V., and Pierce, J. R. *Current Directions in Computer Music Research.* Cambridge: MIT Press, 1989.

43. Rowe, Robert. "Floodgate." *Cultures Electroniques 5: Le Chant du Monde.* LDC 278051/52, 1988.

44. Rowe, R. "Machine Listening and Composing with Cypher," 60.

Glossary

Acoustics   The study of the physics of sound.

A/D converter   See data converters.

Additive synthesis   Production of sound by direct summation of component frequencies. Generally, each component is produced by a separate sinusoidal oscillator.

Address   A number that designates a particular location in a computer memory.

Aliasing   In a digital sound system, the reflection of frequencies higher than the Nyquist frequency to lower frequencies. An "aliased" frequency is one that, after reflection, is indistinguishable from a lower, unreflected frequency.

Algorithm   A step-by-step procedure for accomplishing a task. Each step must be defined unambiguously and there must be a definite path to the completion of the algorithm. Most algorithms can be translated into a programming language and executed on a computer.

All-pass network   A device that recirculates a signal through a delay line. It is used as an element in a reverberator. The steady-state amplitude response of an all-pass network is flat.

Amplify   To increase the amplitude of a signal. In computer music, amplification is generally accomplished by means of multiplication by a constant greater than one.

Amplitude   In acoustics, the peak amount of atmospheric displacement of a sound, measured in units of pressure (Newtons per square meter). In computer music, amplitude describes the value of the largest sample of a signal.

Amplitude response   In a filter, the ratio of the amplitude of the output signal to that of the input signal. The amplitude response most often varies with frequency.

Analog signal   An electronic signal that varies continuously—that is, it has a value at every point in time.

Argument   A value applied to a function that determines the output value of the function.

Array   A collection of values stored in the computer in tabular form. An array can have one or more dimensions.

ASCII   American Standard Code for Information Interchange. A standard convention for representing alphanumeric characters in binary form.

Assembly language   A low-level language that requires the programmer to express an algorithm as a sequence of specific machine instructions.

Asynchronous   (1) Characteristic of two or more processes that do not run at exactly the same rate. (2) Characteristic of a process in which the events are triggered randomly.

Attack   The segment of the envelope of a tone in which the amplitude increases from 0 to its peak. This segment is also called the rise.

Attack time   A term used to denote the starting time of a musical tone.

Attenuation   The reduction of the amplitude of a sound or a component of the sound.

Band-pass filter   A filter that passes frequencies in a specified region and attenuates frequencies both above and below that region. Its passband is characterized by a center frequency, a bandwidth, and a midband gain.

Band-reject filter   A filter that attenuates frequencies in a specified region and passes frequencies both above and below that region. Its stopband is characterized by a center frequency, a bandwidth, and the maximum amount of attenuation.

Bandwidth   (1) A measure in Hertz of the width of the passband or stopband of a filter. (2) A measure of the width of the frequency region occupied by the spectrum of a signal.

Beating   A noticeable and periodic reduction in the amplitude of a sound caused by the interference of closely tuned frequency components.

Binary number   A number whose digits can assume one of two states: 0 or 1. Each digit position has a value two times the value of the position to its right.

Bit   A single binary digit. It can assume one of two states: 0 or 1. It is the smallest unit of information recognized by a digital computer.

Byte   In most computer systems, a group of eight bits. A byte is capable of assuming 256 unique states. It is the most common measure of memory capacity.

Carrier wave   The wave to which the modulation is applied. The carrier wave is altered in sympathy with the modulating signal.

Cascade connection   The relationship between two devices in which the output of the first is applied to the input of the second.

Cent   A unit of measure used in tuning to compare the ratio of two frequencies. One cent corresponds to a frequency ratio of $1:2^{1200}$ or $1:1.0005778$. There are 1200 cents in an octave.

Center frequency   The frequency about which the passband of a filter is symmetrically disposed.

Chorus effect   The creation from a single voice of the percept of multiple voices in unison.

Clavier   A keyboard of the type found on a piano or organ.

Code   Text for an algorithm written in a programming language.

Coefficient   A constant used to multiply a signal. In a filter algorithm, a set of coefficients determines the characteristics of the filter. In the algebraic expression of a transfer function for a waveshaper, a set of coefficients determines the spectrum of the shaped waveform.

Comb filter   A device that recirculates a signal through a delay line. It is used as an element in a reverberator. The amplitude response of a comb filter exhibits peaks and valleys that are equally spaced in frequency.

Component   A single frequency element found in a spectrum.

Composing program   A program that generates a musical score using algorithms and parameters supplied by the composer.

Computer-aided composition   One of a number of approaches in which the mathematical and logical powers of the computer are enlisted to assist in the expression of the composer's musical ideas.

Constant   A numerical value that does not change during the course of a program.

Continuous (1) Characteristic of a signal in which every point on the waveform is smoothly connected to the rest of the waveform. (2) Characteristic of a random process in which the results can fall anywhere within a range of values.

Cosine wave A sinusoidal waveform whose phase relative to a sine wave is 90°.

CPU (central processing unit) Controls the operation of the computer by interpreting instructions and executing them.

Critical band A measure of the ability of the ear to discriminate adjacent tones. Critical band plays an important role in masking of tones, and in the perception of loudness and timbre. The width of a critical band varies with frequency.

CRT (cathode ray tube) A device most often found in a data terminal for the visual display of information.

Cutoff frequency The frequency that marks the transition from passband to stopband in a filter. It is normally defined by the frequency at which the signal is attenuated by 3 dB.

Cycle One repetition of a periodic waveform.

D/A converter See data converters.

Data A collection of information.

Data converters Devices that transform analog signals to digital form, and the reverse. They are known as A/D and D/A converters, respectively.

Decay In a simple three-segment envelope, that portion of the envelope of a tone in which the amplitude decreases from its sustained value to 0. In an ADSR envelope (see section 4.5) the decay is from the peak amplitude to the steady-state value.

Decibel (dB) A unit of relative measure used to compare the intensity of two signals on a logarithmic scale. Under certain conditions the decibel can be used to compare the amplitudes of two signals, as well.

Diatonic The collection of pitches in a major scale.

Digital Characteristic of a system or device that handles information in numerical quantities.

Discrete Discontinuous. For example, a digital signal is discrete in that it is comprised of values at specific points in time.

Discrete summation formula In sound synthesis, a mathematical relationship that expresses the sum of sinusoids in compact form.

Disk A peripheral device for storing large quantities of information. A disk consists of a rotating platter coated with magnetic material that stores information in the pattern of its magnetism.

Distortion index A control on the amount of distortion, and hence the spectral content, produced by a waveshaping instrument. The distortion index generally has a large effect on the amplitude of the signal as well.

Distortion synthesis A class of sound synthesis techniques, including frequency modulation, nonlinear waveshaping, and the explicit use of discrete summation formulas, in which a controlled amount of distortion is applied to a simple waveform. All distortion synthesis techniques have an index that controls spectral richness.

Doppler shift The perceived change in frequency observed when a sound source and a listener are moving relative to each other.

Dynamic range The range of amplitudes that can be represented in a system. Dynamic range is limited on the low end by the noise of the system, and on the high end by distortion.

Dynamics   The various indications in music notation for change of loudness level in a musical passage.

Editor   A computer program that enables the entry and modification of program text and data files in the computer.

Envelope   The shape of the amplitude variation during the course of a tone. A simple envelope consists of three segments: attack (rise), steady-state, and decay.

Envelope generator   A device for imparting an amplitude envelope on a tone.

Execution   The actual performance by a computer of a program instruction.

Exponential   Characteristic of a phenomenon that changes by the same ratio in a given time interval. For example, an exponential decay diminishes by a factor of two every time a fixed interval of time passes.

FFT (fast Fourier transform)   A numerical technique, optimized for rapid computer execution, for determining the frequency content of a digital signal.

File   A collection of information stored in the computer's external memory. A file may contain a program, data, or both.

Filter   A device that passes certain frequencies and attenuates others. The four principal types of filters are low-pass, high-pass, band-pass, and band-reject.

Flanging   The process of adding a signal to a delayed image of itself where the amount of delay is swept from a maximum amount to 0 over time.

Flowchart   A graphical representation of the logic in an algorithm or a program. In instrument design, a flowchart shows the interconnections among the unit generators.

Foldover   See aliasing.

Formant   A peaking in the spectral envelope of a tone. A formant is caused by resonances in the instrument or vocal tract. Formants make an important contribution to our perception of timbre.

FORTRAN (FORmula TRANslation)   An algebraically oriented programming language suited for tasks that require a great deal of numerical calculation.

Fourier analysis   The process of breaking down a waveform into its component frequencies.

Fourier transform   The mathematical technique for changing the time-domain representation of a signal (its waveform) into a frequency-domain representation (its spectrum).

Frequency   The rate of repetition of a periodic waveform. Frequency is measured in Hertz (Hz).

Frequency domain   A way of characterizing a signal in terms of its frequency components. The representation of a signal in the frequency domain is called its spectrum.

Frequency modulation (FM)   The alteration of the frequency of a carrier wave by another signal called the modulating wave.

FM synthesis   The alteration or distortion of the frequency of one oscillator by a signal coming from another. This process produces a waveform with many more spectral components than the presence of only two oscillators might imply.

Frequency response   In a filter, the ratio of the output signal to the input signal versus frequency. The frequency response consists of two parts: amplitude response and phase response.

Function   In mathematics, a way of expressing the dependence of the value of one quantity on the values of other quantities. In computer languages, a function is an algorithm that is passed parameters and returns a result based on the parameters.

Fundamental   Ordinarily the lowest frequency component in a harmonic spectrum. Under most conditions, the perceived pitch of a tone is at the frequency of the fundamental.

Fusion   The perception of a group of tones or spectral components as a single acoustic entity.

Gain   In a device, the ratio of output amplitude to input amplitude. When the gain is larger than one, amplification exists.

Glissando   A tone that exhibits a continuous change of frequency, either up or down.

Grain   A burst of acoustical energy that is not long enough for it, taken in isolation, to evoke the sensation of pitch.

Granular synthesis   The use of a large of number of grains to synthesize sound.

Hardware   The electronic equipment that forms a computer system.

Harmonic   A spectral component that is an exact integer multiple of the fundamental frequency.

Head-related transfer function (HRTF)   An expression that describes the filtering action of the pinnae as sound is received by the ear. HRTFs vary with the direction of sound travel and among listeners.

Hertz (Hz)   A unit of measure for frequency. It denotes the number of repetitions per second of a periodic waveform.

High-pass filter   A filter that passes frequencies above a specified cutoff frequency and significantly attenuates frequencies below that point.

Index of modulation   A measure of the amount of modulation, and thus the spectral richness, produced in a frequency modulation instrument.

Initialization   In a sound synthesis program, the setting of parameter values prior to the actual process of calculating sample values.

Impulse response   The waveform produced when a filter is excited by a single unit-amplitude input sample with all preceding and following samples set to 0.

Instruction   In a computer, a numerical code stored in memory that represents an operation for the computer to perform.

Instrument design   A synthesis algorithm for realizing a particular class of sounds.

Interactive   Characteristic of a situation in which the user and the computer program respond to each other's actions on an approximately real-time basis. Any live-performance situation is interactive by definition.

Interface   The boundary or means of connection between two or more elements in a computer system. An interface can be between hardware devices, pieces of software, or a user and a computer system.

Integrated circuit   A large number of interconnected electronic devices fabricated on a small piece of silicon.

Interpolation   The process of finding values intermediate to specified values. The two most common methods of interpolation are linear and exponential.

Interval   The musical name for the ratio in frequency between two tones. Pairs of tones separated by the same musical interval share a similar quality.

Inversion   The reversal of direction of a musical interval. For example, the inversion of the interval C/E♭ is C/A.

I/O (input/output)   (1) A class of devices that provide the means for communication between the computer and its users or other computer hardware. (2) The process of communication between the computer and its users or other computer hardware.

Just noticeable difference (JND)   In psychoacoustics, the smallest amount of change of a physical parameter such as amplitude that is discernible by a listener.

Karplus-Strong algorithm   An instrument design in which a signal is recirculated in a delay line through a low-pass filter. The algorithm is relatively efficient at simulating the sound of a plucked string.

Kilohertz (kHz)   1000 Hertz.

Language (computer)   A rigidly defined set of conventions for expressing algorithms. Once transmitted to the computer, a program translates the encoded algorithm into machine instructions.

Linear   (1) Characteristic of a phenomenon that changes by the same amount over a given interval of time. (2) Characteristic of a signal processor in which a change in amplitude of the input signal produces a similar change in the amplitude of the output signal.

Linear prediction   In a sampled data system, the process of determining the relationships that enable the value of the next output sample to be calculated as a weighted combination of previous output samples.

Localization   The process of synthesizing cues that create the auditory illusion of the placement in space of a sound source.

Logarithmic   Characteristic of a phenomenon in which changes are perceived on the basis of the ratio of the change.

Lookup table   An array, such as a wave table used by an oscillator, containing precomputed values of a mathematical function. Its use can save a great deal of computer time because a program can simply retrieve values from the table instead of performing extensive calculations.

Loudness   The subjective response to the amount of acoustical power received by the ear.

Low-pass filter   A filter that passes frequencies below a specified cutoff frequency and significantly attenuates frequencies above that frequency.

Machine language   The actual numerical codes for specific computer instructions.

Markov process   A conditional random process in which the higher-order probabilities can be calculated as the products of first-order probabilities.

Masking   The reduction in sensitivity to amplitude due to the fatigue of neurons on the basilar membrane. This phenomenon often causes softer tones to be "covered up" by louder ones.

Memory   The repository of both programs and data. It is divided into discrete locations that are distinguished by unique numerical addresses.

Microsecond (μs)   One-millionth of a second.

Mixer   A device for combining signals by adding them together.

Modulating wave   The signal that alters the carrier wave in some way.

Modulation   The alteration of the amplitude, frequency, or phase of a carrier wave in accordance with a modulating signal. The signal resulting from the modulation has a more complex spectrum than would be obtained by the simple addition of the carrier wave and the modulating wave.

Morphing   The transformation of one sound to another.

Motive   A characteristic melodic/rhythmic fragment in a piece of music, out of which larger units such as phrases are made.

Musique concrète   A form of tape or electronic music made from "concrete" (i.e., recorded) sounds. In most *musique concrète* the recorded sounds are modified electronically from their original form.

Music 4   An influential language for sound synthesis created by Max V. Mathews at the Bell Laboratories in the early 1960s and exported to other institutions.

Noise   Sound with a distributed spectrum. The most common form, white noise, sounds like hissing.

Nonlinear processor   A signal-processing device in which a change in the amplitude of the input does not produce a similar change in the amplitude of the output signal. This alters the waveform, and hence the spectrum, of a signal passing through it.

Nonlinear synthesis   See waveshaping.

Nyquist frequency   In a digital sound system, the frequency at one-half the sampling rate. It is the theoretical upper limit to the faithful representation of frequency components in the system.

One-over-f (1/f) noise   Noise with a spectrum that rolls off directly with frequency.

Onset   The time at which a tone begins.

Operating system (OS)   An organized collection of software that provides many useful services to the users of a computer. It also controls the flow of work in the system.

Orchestra   A collection of computer instrument designs.

Oscillator   A device for generating a periodic waveform. Its two principal controls are amplitude and frequency of repetition of the waveform.

Overflow   The condition that occurs when the result of a mathematical operation exceeds the capacity of the format used for number representation.

Parallel connection   The relationship among devices where the same signal is applied to the inputs of all devices simultaneously. The outputs of the devices are combined to form a single signal.

Parameter   A value input to an algorithm that is used in calculating the output. In computer music, a parameter in the score controls an attribute of the sound produced by a computer instrument.

Partial   A spectral component of a sound. It may or may not be harmonically related to the fundamental.

Passband   The frequency region in which a filter passes signals with little or no attenuation.

Period   The time occupied by one repetition of a periodic waveform.

Periodic wave   A signal comprised of repetitions of a waveform at a particular frequency.

Peripheral   A device connected to the CPU in a computer system. Peripherals usually provide for user communication or external memory.

Phase   A means of comparing the relative position in time of two waveforms or of marking a specific point on a waveform.

Physical model   A synthesis algorithm directly based on the mechanics of a natural sound production process. The control parameters of a physical model are couched in terms of the items used in the process.

Pitch   The subjective response to frequency.

Pitch Detector   A device that measures the period of a waveform in order to estimate the fundamental frequency of a sound.

Pole   A resonance. A filter that implements a pole causes a peak in the spectral envelope of a signal passing through the filter at the frequency of the pole.

Polynomial   An algebraic expression that takes the form of the sum of a series of terms where each term consists of a coefficient multiplying a variable raised to a power.

Precedence effect   In the presence of the same sound from several sources, the phenomenon by which a listener attributes the location of the source on the basis of the sound that arrives first. This occurs even when subsequent sounds have higher amplitudes.

Probability   The likelihood of obtaining a given outcome of a random process. It is expressed as the ratio of the number of occurrences of that outcome to the total number of results of the random process.

Probability density function   A mathematical expression that indicates the likelihood of a continuous random variable occurring within a range of values.

Program   A sequence of instructions to accomplish a specific task that can be executed by a computer.

Psychoacoustics   The study of the way humans perceive sound. It includes such subjective responses to sound as pitch, loudness, duration, timbre, and apparent location.

Pulse   A waveform with significant amplitude only during a relatively brief portion of its period. A pulse has a very rich spectrum.

Q   A measure of the selectivity of a filter. A filter with a high Q has a very narrow bandwidth.

Random   Characteristic of a process that, under repeated observations with the same conditions, does not always produce the same results.

Random variable   A variable that takes on a value as a result of a random process. A random variable is discrete when it can take on only specific values; it is continuous when it can assume any value within a range.

Real time   Characteristic of a process in which data is processed at the same rate as it is taken in or used. For example, a digital synthesizer is said to operate in real time when its calculation rate equals the sampling rate.

Recursive filter   A digital filter that determines the value of its current output sample on the basis of past input and output samples.

Resolution   The fineness to which a quantity can be represented in a digital system.

Resonance   A spectral peak, such as a formant.

Reverberation   The multiple reflections of sound in a room causing sound to be heard after all sources have ceased.

Ring modulation   The process of combining two signals by multiplication. Ring modulation produces sidebands but suppresses both the carrier and modulating frequencies.

Rise time   The duration of the attack segment of the envelope of a tone.

Rolloff   (1) The rate at which a spectral envelope of a tone decreases with frequency. (2) The rate at which the attenuation of a filter increases in the stopband. Both are expressed in units of dB/octave.

Sampling   The process of representing a waveform by measuring its value at discrete points in time.

Sampling increment   In a digital oscillator, the amount added to the current phase to determine which location in the wave table to use next. The sampling increment is directly proportional to frequency.

Sampling rate   The frequency at which samples are generated or taken in a digital sound system.

Score   A list of musical events. Each event has attributes, or parameters, to describe it. Common parameters include designation of instruments to play, starting time, duration, frequency, and amplitude.

Score editor   A computer program that enables entry and modification of scores.

Score preprocessor   A computer program that enables the encoding of scores in a syntax that is easy to read and bears a strong, intuitive relation to the encoded music. The score preprocessor translates the code into the parameter list score format required by the music-synthesis language.

Serialism A kind of music based on an ordered set of elements, such as a twelve-tone row. It often includes serialization of other elements, such as rhythm, as well.

Series connection See cascade connection.

Sideband A product of modulation whose frequency depends on the frequencies of both the carrier and modulating waves.

Signal A temporal phenomenon, whether electrical or digital, that carries information.

Signal processor A device that modifies a signal passing through it.

Signal-to-noise ratio (SNR) A numerical comparison of the signal level to the noise level in a system.

Signal-to-quantization noise ratio (SQNR) A numerical comparison of the signal level to the level of the noise resulting from the necessity to represent a digital signal with finite resolution.

Sine wave A sinusoidal waveform whose phase is taken to be 0.

Sinusoid A smooth waveform whose spectrum contains only one component frequency.

Software Programs that can be executed by a computer.

Spectral envelope The outline showing the distribution of acoustical energy with frequency. A spectral envelope can exhibit formant peaks.

Spectrum The representation of a signal in terms of its frequency components.

Steady state The portion of the envelope of a tone in which the amplitude remains relatively constant.

Steady-state analysis The characterization of the response of a device, such as a filter, to a sinusoid that has been applied to the device long enough for the output of the device to settle to a constant response.

Steady-state response The response of a filter to a constant periodic input signal.

Stochastic process See random process.

Stopband The frequency region in which a filter provides the greatest amount of attenuation.

Subscore A part of a score, such as a group of proximate notes. Some score editors enable operations on subscores.

Subroutine A subprogram invoked from the main program or from another subprogram.

Subtractive synthesis A technique that uses filters to alter the spectral content of a sound.

Synthesis The realization of electronically-generated acoustical elements.

Synthesizer A device that implements synthesis algorithms, most often in real time.

Timbre The characteristic tone quality of a particular class of sounds.

Time domain A way of characterizing a signal in terms of its amplitude fluctuations versus time. The representation of a signal in the time domain is called its waveform.

Transducer A device that converts mechanical energy, such as a sound wave or the action of a performer, into electrical signals. All manual input devices, including claviers, computer keyboards, sliders, etc. are transducers.

Transfer function In a nonlinear processor, an expression that determines output values on the basis of input values.

Transposition The raising or lowering, by a specified musical interval, of the frequency of musical tones.

Tuning   Any one of a number of systems for distributing, or mapping, musical intervals into frequency.

Twelve-tone music   Music based on a twelve-tone row; that is, on an ordering of all twelve tones and permutations of that ordering (see serialism).

Underflow   The condition that occurs when the result of a mathematical operation is too small to be accurately represented in the data format that is used. This phenomenon can occur, for example, when two nearly equal numbers are subtracted from each other.

Unit generator   An algorithm that performs a particular function of sound generation, modification, or combination. It is controlled by parameters obtained from a score or transducer.

Variable   In a computer program, a reference to a memory location whose value can change during the course of the program.

Vibrato   A perceptibly slow quasi-periodic excursion both above and below the fundamental frequency of a tone.

Waveform   In acoustics, the pattern of pressure variation versus time in a sound. The shape of the waveform can have a great effect on the perceived timbre.

Wavelets   A group of mathematical functions used to analyze the frequency content of time-varying signals.

Waveshaper   See nonlinear processor.

Waveshaping   A technique of distortion synthesis that creates complex spectra from simple tones by explicitly altering the shape of the waveform.

Wave table   An array in which sequential values represent the successive points in a single cycle of a wave.

White noise   Noise with a uniformly distributed spectrum. White noise has a "hissing" sound.

Window   The interval from which a group of successive samples are taken for analysis.

Zero   An antiresonance. A filter that implements a zero causes a dip in the spectral envelope of a signal passing through it at the frequency of the zero.

Index

A

Absorbing boundary, 369
Acoustical quanta, 19, 262
Acoustic phonetics, 222–225
Acoustics, 25–27
   of a room, 289–292
A/D, *see* analog-to-digital converter
Additive synthesis, 49, 73, 87–90
   data requirements, 89
Address, 2
Adjustable filters, 183–184
ADSR envelope, 84
Affricate, 225
AFM, *see* asymmetrical FM synthesis
Aftertouch, 411
Aleatoric composition, 341–382
Algorithm, 7
Algorithms I (Hiller), 374
Algorithms II (Hiller), 374
Aliasing, 65–66
All-pass network, 297
   fractional delay, 306, 307
   use in a plucked-string algorithm,
     304–308
   use in a reverberator, 298–300
All-pole filter, 174, 200, 211–212, 233–234
All-zero filter, 200, 204–205
Ambisonics, 321–322
Amirkhanian, Charles, 324
Amplification, 75
Amplitude, 20, 26
   oscillator, 75
   perception, 42–44
Amplitude envelope, 46
   ADSR, 84
   of partials, 55
     approximation with line segments, 56
   parameters, 81

segment shapes, 82
   unit generator, 80
Amplitude functions
   in additive synthesis, 88
   interpolation, 89
Amplitude modulation, 90–92
Amplitude response, 172
Amplitude scaling, 151–152, 164, 166
Analog signal, 12, 62
Analog-to-digital (A/D) converter, 12, 13, 14,
    62
   quantization noise, 67
   resolution, 67
Analysis by synthesis, 54
Apel, Willi, 383
Apparent source width, 311
Appleton, Jon, 41, 407, 416
   Dima Dobralsa Domoy, 417
   Homenaje a Milanes, 417
   Pacific Rimbombo, 417–418
Arbitrary probability distribution, 354–355
Arras (Truax), 274–275
Artificial language, 7
ASCII (American Standard Code for Infor-
    mation Interchange), 4, 12
Assembly language, 8
Asymmetrical FM (AFM) synthesis, 164–167
Asynchronous granular synthesis, 269–270
Atrees (Xenakis), 377
Attack, 46, 80
   effect on timbre, 82
   time, 81
Attenuation, 75
Audio horizon, 311
Auditory localization, 308–322
Auditory Scene Analysis (Bregman), 59
Auditory streams, 59
Augmentation of a motive's rhythm, 388
Aural harmonics, 43–44

The Authors

Charles Dodge gained recognition early in his career as a composer of orchestral and chamber music. He went on to become one of the early composers to realize the vast potential of the computer for broadening the composer's palette. His *Speech Songs*, completed in 1972, startled the new music world with its charming and humorous use of synthetic speech and has become a classic of early computer music. He has also composed a series of works combining acoustic instruments with computer sound, including his widely-performed *Any Resemblance Is Purely Coincidental* which sets together a computer-synthesized Caruso voice with a live piano accompaniment.

Dodge has been honored with an achievement award from the American Academy/Institute of Arts and Letters, several Composer Fellowships from the National Endowment for the Arts, a Woodrow Wilson National Fellowship and two Guggenheim Fellowships. His recent commissions include those from the Bourges Festival of Electro-Acoustic Music in France, the Los Angeles Philharmonic's New Music Group, the American Guild of Organists, and the Bicentennial Celebration of the Medical School at Dartmouth College.

Dodge's compositions have been released on compact disc by the MIT Experimental Music Studio, Perspectives of New Music, and on the Centaur, Crystal, Neuma, New Albion, and Wergo labels. Dr. Dodge is Visiting Professor of Music at Dartmouth College.

Thomas A. Jerse has worked extensively in the development of hardware and software for musical applications. He is a former Assistant Professor of Music and was the first Technical Director of the Center for Computer Music at Brooklyn College of the City University of New York. His teaching experience also includes positions as a Lecturer at the University of California Davis and as an Assistant Professor at The Citadel. Dr. Jerse has an extensive background in the electronics industry, serving as a Research and Development Project Manager in the Signal Analysis Division of the Hewlett-Packard Company for over a decade. Born in Michigan, Dr. Jerse received a BSEE from the University of New Mexico, a MSEE degree from Stanford University, and a PhD from the University of Kentucky. He currently holds the position of Principal Engineer with the Boeing Defense and Space Group.